Antique Trader.

AMERICA'S #1 SELLING PRICE GUIDE

Antiques & Collectibles

2018 PRICE GUIDE 34TH EDITION

Eric Bradley

Published by

Krause Publications, a division of F+W Media, Inc.
700 East State Street • Iola, WI 54990-0001
715-445-2214 • 888-457-2873
www.krausebooks.com

To order books or other products call toll-free 1-800-258-0929
or visit us online at www.krausebooks.com

ISSN 1536-2884
ISBN-13: 9781440248405
ISBN-10: 1440248400

Cover Design by Rebecca Vogel & Nicole MacMartin
Designed by Rebecca Vogel, Nicole MacMartin & Sandi Carpenter
Edited by Eric Bradley
Printed in the United States of America

10 9 8 7 6 5 4 3 2 1

FRONT COVER:

Hans Wegner Papa Bear chair on teak frame, circa 1950, upholstered in plum-colored fabric, 39" x 35-1/2" x 28". $6,738 (Rago Arts and Auction Center, www.ragoarts.com)

Tiffany Studios leaded glass peony border bronze floor lamp, circa 1910, 74-1/2" tall, 24" diameter. $131,000. (Courtesy of Heritage Auctions, ha.com)

Chanel multicolor gripoix glass cuff bracelet. Classic example of Chanel's exquisite taste in costume jewelry, 2" w x 6" l., $2,125 (Courtesy of Heritage Auctions, ha.com)

BACK COVER:

Iridescent glass floriform cabinet vace, circa 1900, marked Quezal, 5-1/8" tall. $813 (Courtesy of Heritage Auctions, ha.com)

Casablanca (Warner Brothers, 1942), half sheet movie poster, 22" x 28", Humphrey Bogart and Ingrid Bergman. $23,000. (Courtesy of Heritage Auctions, ha.com)

CONTENTS

LISTINGS

INTRODUCTION

WELCOME TO THE most complete visual reference to the world of fine art and collectibles available on the market today: Welcome to the *Antique Trader Antiques & Collectibles Price Guide*. With this 100 percent visual guide, you never have to second guess what you're looking at or looking for. That's what's makes this book the No. 1 selling reference book on the wide world of fine art and collectible – each entry is illustrated with a full-color photograph to make it easier than ever to compare and contrast it with the antiques you find every day.

    This year's edition looks at the world of live auctions, online sales, dealer's booths and group shops to show you what's selling and what collectors

This medium green 8-inch tall applied-top soda bottle, circa 1853, from Eagle Soda Works (Sacramento, Calif.), is a classic California Gold Rush example. ....**$200-$400**

Courtesy Holabird Americana, holabirdamericana.com

Nebraska-born Regionalist artist Dale Nichols (1904-1995) created *Mid-Nation Winter*, a striking 30" x 40" painting that sold at auction for **$120,000**.

Courtesy Shannon's Fine Art Auctioneers, shannons.com

Fine examples of "Smalls", Chinese carved group of nine spinach jade items, largest: 4-1/2" t... **$7,767**

are pursuing in today's market. It also shows you the values of some of the most commonly found antiques to help you estimate the value of your own collection. Some items will be very familiar – in fact, you may already own them – but there are others that are extraordinary and unique in their own right. Both examples are useful to help you understand where your collectible ranks in terms of condition, rarity, value and eye appeal. Good, Better, Best, we say and nothing helps you better than an actual image of the antique you're seeking.

Here are our annual picks of some of the hottest areas in the hobby:

American/Americana Art – As you'll read later in the book, American Regionalism is experiencing an impressive resurgence. Americana art is hotly pursued by institutions and collectors alike. Second only to Contemporary Art (which is the fastest-growing segment of the art world), Americana art auction records are seemingly being broken year after year. Look for New England snow scenes, Southern art and studies.

Smalls – Objects not bigger than a breadbox, these items are coveted by Millennials, the newest generation to hit the hobby. These shoppers are seeking for unique items that do not dominate a space but rather accent their unique taste and serve as objet d'art, or art object. These objects are not paintings but small, three-dimensional decorative arts.

Bottles – "The world of antique bottle collecting has taken a full turn from collecting pretty old purple and blue bottles in the desert to investment-quality pieces envious of any art museum," said Fred Holabird of Holabird Western Americana Collections, LLC. "With key rarities often trading in tens of thousands of dollars, a new breed of collector has emerged, seeking beauty and rarity." Bottles remain one of the top collectibles with values still climbing for rare and early examples.

Toys – An old standby, toys also are seeing an uptick in interest as both collections take flight and by people seeking a unique item for display. Examples in top condition are commanding previously unimaginable prices, but nice examples from the late 1930s through the 1950s may be found at very reasonable prices. These prices are enticing new collectors to enter the hobby.

Maps – Both graphical and informative, the market for high-end maps has shown a serious increase in the previous years, especially for regional maps of North America. Collectors are keen on displaying their "stomping grounds" and examples from vintage to antique maps and charts are doing very well at both the low and high ends of the market.

Illustration Art – Original drawings, paintings and sketches from old magazines, books, periodicals and the like are high on collector's wish list. The art often combines both stunning graphics and typography, which blend to create a

A fine example of illustration art comes courtesy of George Timothy Tobin (1864-1956). An illustrator/realist active in Vermont, Tobin did this ink, pencil and watercolor for Harper's Bazaar, in 1907. ....**$4,000**

Courtesy Bruneau & Co. Auctioneers, bruneauandco.com.

A vibrant multi-colored map of California and Nevada, with a Virginia City insert, published by A.L. Bancroft & Co., San Francisco, 1882, in near-mint condition, 52" x 64" t.............**$2,783**

Courtesy Holabird Americana, holabirdamericana.com

Toys, such as this 1950s "B-341 Express Cruiser" (Bandai, Japan), are fun, colorful and easy to display......................**$13**

Courtesy Serious Toyz, serioustoyz.com

> "...there is one key task to keep in mind before you start buying or selling:
>
> # Research. Research. Research."

Pinbacks, circa mid-1960s, tin litho and celluloid, depicting The Beatles, The Rolling Stones, The Monkeys and They Byrds, measuring 1-3/8" w. to 3-1/5" w. ....$130 set

wonderful piece suitable for home or office. The more famous the artists the more valuable the work has become.

Pop Culture – American pop culture is being snapped up by Chinese, Japanese and American collectors. There are even stories of Brazilian collectors beginning to appreciate the uniquely American innovations that accentuate 20th century culture. Although The Beatles and the like from the British Invasion were born in England, American fans gave rise to the groups and its flood of merchandise that changed world culture forever. These vintage items are hot commodities that appeal to a growing segment of the international market. You'll find more about collecting The Beatles in the book.

TRENDS

- Brick and mortar antiques shops in high-traffic, tourist areas are still doing brisk business; however, last year marked an uptick in the online sales of fine art and collectibles – a 7 percent increase – from 2017.
- Vintage American crafts such as wood turning, jewelry and wall art are just now beginning to show up at auction to better than expected prices.
- Fine art, classic cars and comics buffs are all lifting the low end of the market as nostalgia meets collectors' money years.
- The market for 20th century antique and vintage mass-produced furniture is still soft, but period furniture from the 19th century is doing very well. The trick for market leading values is for the piece to be both an identifiable design and in desirable condition. The only values being found for 20th century furniture is in the area of studio furniture (items made in limited quantities by notable artists).
- Attendees dwindling at live auctions. If the auction offers internet bidding then you can expect higher prices. Country auctions are still the domain of pickers and show dealers, but collectors are finding great items through online auction sites.
- Single-owner collections with interesting provenance or back-story are performing exceptionally well at all price points.

If any of the categories in this book pique your interest, there is one key task to keep in mind before you start buying or selling: Research. Research. Research.

And that's where this visual reference guide comes in. In this edition we've expanded and updated the most popular sections and added new ones, too. You'll notice special attention is drawn to the very best items pursued by collectors as Top Lots. Special features show why some categories are irresistible to collectors. We've also been on the road - like many of you - meeting dealers, auctioneers, collectors, and show managers who gave us the scoop on what's really happening in the hobby. You'll see their smiling faces along with their top tips, opinions, and collecting advice in various chapters across this new edition under the header "Inside Intel." We hope this helps you get to know the people behind the prices.

Antique Trader.

ABOUT ANTIQUETRADER.COM

We think you'll be impressed with the layout, sections, and information in this year's annual book. Because the antiques world (like everything else) is constantly changing, I invite you to visit AntiqueTrader.com and make it your main portal into the world of antiques.

Like our magazine, AntiqueTrader.com's team of collectors, dealers, and bloggers share information daily on events, auctions, new discoveries, and tips on how to buy more for less. Here's what you'll find at AntiqueTrader.com:

Free eNewsletters: Get a recap of the world of antiques sent to your inbox every week.

Expert Q&A columns: Learn how to value and sell your collections online and for the best prices.

The Internet's largest free antiques library: Dig into thousands of articles on research, prices, show reports, auction results, and more.

Blogs: Get vital how-to information about topics that include selling online, buying more for less, restoring pieces, spotting fakes and reproductions, displaying your collections, and finding hidden gems in your town!

Show guides: Check out the Internet's most visited antiques events calendar for links to more than 1,000 auctions, flea markets, conventions, and antiques shows worldwide.

A book of this size and scope is a team project and special thanks are owed to Editorial Director Paul Kennedy; editors Antoinette Rahn, Editor and Online Editor and Content Manager of Antique Trader magazine; Karen Knapstein, Print Editor of Antique Trader magazine; Editor Kris Manty; Goldmine magazine Editor Pat Prince; Sports Collector's Digest Editor Bert Lehman; and designer Rebecca Vogel whose herculean task is to make visual sense out of thousands of images and hundreds of thousands of written words spanning a vast array of collecting categories; and several specialists, dealers and shops. Ever the professionals, they work year round to make this book a best seller. We also thank the numerous auction houses and their staffs for generously providing images. Their hard work and great ideas are always focused on one goal: selecting the topics, images and features our readers will find the most fascinating. We hope you enjoy the results.

Eric Bradley is the author of *Harry Potter: The Unofficial Guide to the Collectibles of Our Favorite Wizard; Mantiques: A Manly Guide to Cool Stuff; Picker's Pocket Guide: SIGNS;* and *Picker's Pocket Guide – Toys.* He is a seven-time editor of *Antique Trader Antiques & Collectibles Price Guide,* America's No. 1 selling price guide. A former editor and an award-winning investigative journalist with a degree in economics, he has appeared in The Wall Street Journal, GQ, Four Seasons Magazine, Bottom Line/Personal and The Detroit News, among others. He is the Public Relations Director at Heritage Auctions, HA.com, the world's largest collectibles auctioneer, and lives near Dallas with his wife and three children.

CONSIGNING AT AUCTION

THE AUCTION BUSINESS has changed significantly over the last 30 years due in part to societal changes and to technological advancements. Buying and selling estate goods and collections has never been more accessible. With the advent of the Internet, location is no longer an impediment to selling items that may not be wanted locally, but are in high demand elsewhere. In addition to auction firms' own websites with their online bidding capabilities, LiveAuctioneers, BidSquare, Invaluable, AuctionZip, Proxibid, iGavel and other online auction platforms are allowing auctioneers to bring buyers and sellers together.

Whether you want to sell a single item or an entire third-generation collection, there are thousands of auction specialists across the country who are dedicated to helping sellers achieve the highest prices possible. During any given week, there are specialists hard at work aiding collectors, heirs and executors in finding new homes for everything from fine art to quirky collections. Without consignments, there would be no auction houses. As Cindy Stephenson of Stephenson's, in Southampton, Pennsylvania, says, "We are working for the consignor; they're our main customer."

Auction firms are tasked with getting top dollar for the consignors' property. To do that, the auction house invests time in researching, cataloging and advertising before the auction opens. Consignors with quality antiques and collectibles should be drawn to auction houses willing to dedicate those resources to achieve the maximum bid. The percentage the auctioneers charge the consignors (and the premium collected from buyers) is to cover their investment and overhead in selling the consignments. Selling keeps auctioneers in business; a consignment without a sale is wasted effort for everyone.

Stephenson's holds auctions every Friday and has been in business since 1962. The firm, which sells coins, silver and gold, antique and fine decorative arts, and firearms, pulls in consignments from New Jersey, Delaware and Pennsylvania on a regular basis, but have picked up consignments for their specialty auctions from as far away as Florida, Connecticut and California. Cindy Stephenson says her firm only takes items they believe will sell, which is why Stephenson's has a 100 percent sell-through rate. She explains, "If I can't sell it, I'm spinning my wheels and taking up space with that."

LOCATION IS NOT A CONSIGNMENT FACTOR

Many auction houses use online resources not only as bidding platforms, but also to gather information and consignments. In addition to their Signature auctions, Heritage Auctions, based in Dallas, holds weekly online specialty auctions selling books and autographs, comic books, movie posters, sports, luxury accessories, wine, timepieces and jewelry, and various numismatic categories. The firm's online consignment portal puts potential consignors directly in touch with the appropriate category experts.

Becky Dirting, vice president of Collectibles at Heritage Auctions, explains, "In addition to eight offices around the world, Heritage Auctions regularly hosts appraisal events across the United States where collectors can meet with more than a dozen category specialists in one place for free auction evaluations of their treasures. Heritage experts also support various collecting communities around the world with booths and appearances at conventions, trade shows, expos, as well as on radio and television. For large collections and estates, consignment directors are also willing to meet a collector in his or her home or other location for an onsite visit. Our Free Auction Evaluation tool on HA.com makes it easy for clients to request a free estimation of auction value and even allows for the submission of digital photos to aid in the evaluation process."

Deirdre Magarelli, of Pook & Pook Inc., Downingtown, Pennsylvania, points out, "The internet in general has eliminated location as a barrier for both consignors and buyers. Consignors can email digital photographs to us from anywhere in the world."

Representatives from some auction firms periodically attend antiques shows, sports shows and firearms shows across the country where they meet with potential consignors. Dan Morphy Auctions, Denver, Pennsylvania, holds 40 to 50 auctions per year. Dan Morphy reports his firm logs the most miles when it comes to show attendance. "We attend about 150 shows a year. No other auction house comes close to the number of shows we attend each year."

Tony Greist, department head of James D. Julia Inc.'s Fine Arts, Antiques & Asian Division, reports they have agents throughout the United States and overseas, as necessary. Regarding location as a factor in the consignment process, "Many consignments may be dealt with through the process of telephone, mail and email."

Alex Winter, president of Hake's Americana & Collectibles, says, "We do whatever it takes to get a collection. This includes traveling for it and/or making accommodations to have it delivered."

Jeffrey S. Evans of Jeffrey S. Evans & Associates explains, "The consignment process doesn't take very long. We ask that potential consignors send photos or a list of the items they are interested in selling."

He continues, "The sale date would be determined by the types of materials. We have specialized sales, so we would put the items in the sale deemed most appropriate by our specialists."

COMMUNICATION IS KEY

All the auction houses we spoke with had one belief in common: Clear communication is the key to ensuring that consignors are satisfied with their experience. Before his passing in January 2017, Don Presley, of Don Presley Auctions in Santa Ana, California, said he didn't go anywhere without his iPad so he could educate potential consignors on what items like theirs are fetching at auction. Presley, whose firm deals primarily in antiques, art and higher-end collectibles, told us, "Most consignors are more concerned with how much items will bring." He met with potential consignors and not only educated them by visiting other auctioneers' results on LiveAuctioneers. com, but also showed them how they could research how much money various items are earning at auction.

Cindy Stephenson echoes the belief: "We try to keep them informed from the very beginning. If they have an idea of what the pieces will bring at auction, that's the most important thing. If there's an unrealistic expectation, that's where problems begin."

Greist explains, "We go out of our way to cover all of the details of the process in advance of signing a contract, he said. "In addition, we feel it is very important to be realistic, conservative and absolutely truthful about the estimates that we publish for each item we offer."

Evans says, "We provide a pre-auction estimate in the catalog for every lot, but if a consignor would like an estimate before sending items they would need to ask."

Deirdre Magarelli advises, "Every consignor should have a contract going into any commitment. Read the contract. Make sure you, as the consignor, understand what the commission rates mean. For example, the commission is taken out of the hammer price, not the realized price. Make sure you understand what these terms mean so you are not surprised when you receive payment."

ESTABLISHING MINIMUM BIDS AND RESERVES

Auction houses research past auction results, not only from their own sales but results from other auction houses as well, to establish realistic presale estimates. Many, including Don Presley Auctions and Jeffrey S. Evans & Associates, set their minimum bids at 25 percent of the low estimate.

When it comes to auction reserves, Evans says, "We only accept reserves on items of significant value; otherwise the minimum bid is started at a quarter of the low estimate." He continues, "Only items with reserves will not sell; if they don't sell there would be a buy-in fee."

Magarelli explains, "If an item does not meet a reserve set by the consignor, the consignor must pay the auction house a fee to cover their expenses (i.e. 5 percent of the reserve amount)."

RECEIVING PAYMENT

Magarelli says, "Make sure you understand when your items are going to be sold and when you will be paid for them. Some auction houses, like ours, pay out within 30 days, but others pay out after several months."

Dirting explains, "At Heritage, 45 days after the auction closes, a settlement check is mailed. Heritage takes great pride in the fact that every consignor has been paid in full and on time since 1976."

Alex Winter says Hake's begins "paying consignors as soon as one week after the close of the auction and typically have all payments issued within 45 days from the close."

Jeffrey Evans explains, "The payout is 30 days after the auction, which allows time for the items to be paid for and any returns to be completed. Dan Morphy also says payment is usually completed within 30 days after close of auction, and that,

"From the day someone consigns to the day payment is issued, it's usually a six-month time period."

Don Presley Auctions has an even quicker payout. The firm closes the auction 10 days after the auction is over and issue checks immediately after the consigned item is paid for, usually around two weeks, on average.

IF IT DOESN'T SELL

Items that are put up for auction without reserve will usually sell. If the item is passed, some auction houses will simply return it. Others, like Heritage Auctions, Don Presley Auctions and James D. Julia Auctioneers, will list the item as a post-auction buy or will work with the consignor to try to negotiate a private sale or will re-list in a future auction. Deirdre Magarelli explains Pook & Pook's process: "If an item does not sell at auction, the auction house contacts the consignor and gives them two options: The item can be retrieved by the consignor or it can be re-offered in another auction at a lower estimate."

Hake's offers "a post-auction sale of any unsold item. These are posted on our website for as long as the consignor likes, up until the next auction goes live." After all, no sale means no payment for anyone.

EVERYTHING ELSE

Run-of-the-mill household and decorator items are best suited for general estate or merchandise auctions, of which there are hundreds across the United States. James D. Julia Auctioneers is generally not interested in single items with potential values of less than $1,500. Countless other auction houses, such as Don Presley Auctions, Hake's Americana and Jeffrey S. Evans & Associates, are open to consignments with single-item values of a few hundred dollars or even less. Pook & Pook, Don Presley and Hake's even work with other local auction houses in arranging sale of items that are inappropriate for their own firms.

One thing to keep in mind is the lower the item value, the higher the percentage of the auctioneer's fee to cover their costs. For example, Don Presley's commission depends on the value of the item and ranges from 10 to 35 percent, with the average running 25 percent. Presley explained, "I can't sell a $100 or $200 item for 10 percent."

The general estate auction business is booming. When asked how his auction business is doing, one local auctioneer jokes, "People are dying to have auctions with me."

A visit to AuctionZip.com's auctioneer directory (www.auctionzip.com/Auctioneer-Directory/) shows a seemingly endless list, which includes location and contact information. [By registering on the website and logging in, which is free, you can avoid the annoying pop-ups.] South Coast Auctions (www.southcoastauction.net) of Santa Ana, California, reportedly holds the largest weekly merchandise auctions in Southern California, selling everything from bric-a-brac to vehicles and industrial equipment.

Members of younger generations are no longer finding value in estate goods. As a result, demand has waned for many vintage, antique and collectible items. Rather than taking their time to search out a quality-made vintage piece for their new home, a young couple may visit their local Pier 1 Imports, Home Goods or Ikea store and purchase a new item that may or may not survive a relocation in the future.

Decades ago, families were larger and inheritances were a windfall to the heirs, no matter how meager. Surviving family members were often happy to receive items from an estate. A set of special-occasion china inherited from grandparents held both sentimental and practical value; the inheritance meant you had something to remind you of them, and it also meant you didn't have to go out and purchase a "good" set of china yourself. Don Presley said "Limoges dinner sets are now tough to sell for more than a few hundred dollars because they can't go in the dishwasher."

NON-AUCTION OPTIONS

Dirting says, "If Heritage Auctions determines that particular items are not suitable for auction, we try to point collectors to more appropriate resources in their local area and/or online. If a consignor is not convinced the auction method is right for a particular piece or collection, Heritage offers a comprehensive Private Treaty service for those rare and unique objects of value."

Sterling Associates of Closter, New Jersey, also offers estate sale and tag sale services. The firm's Stephen D'Atri explains that the only items they're not interested in selling at their auctions are industrial equipment and non-decorative items. He says although they're not interested in your refrigerator or farm tractor, unlike many other auction houses, they're fine with selling contemporary décor, because "They have to find a home also." D'Atri says they offer local "tag sales and cleanouts as another option for the items that aren't worth transporting if there are enough of those items." Although Sterling Associates won't coordinate donations, they do offer a cleanout service: they organize and empty out the house into a dumpster.

If there is simply no market demand for collectibles, auction consignors may not be happy with the results no matter which auction house they choose. For example, large lots of collector plates and Beanie Babies may bring $1 or $2 apiece. So what should you do if you are told your items are not suitable as auction consignments?

The auctioneers we spoke with had several suggestions, some of which include:
- Try listing on craigslist.org. D'Atri says "It's hard work, but it's a viable option if you want to make a few dollars."
- Outsourcing to a local auction.
- Donating to a thrift store, veterans' group, church or other non-profit organization. (Speak with your tax adviser or accountant to see how you can maximize the benefit of donating.)
- Selling outright to a dealer.
- Consigning at a local resale store. Some items are better suited to auction

houses that have a successful history selling specialty items, but there is always a place to turn for more information.

When considering selling a specialty item, such as fine art, fine antiques, folk art or any number of other eagerly sought after collectibles, it's in the consignor's best interest to hire an auction house that has the attention of dedicated collectors who actively pursue those items. Consignors need to do their research by contacting consignment specialists themselves so they can make informed decisions.

It's wise to get more than one estimate when considering auction consignment as an option. Weigh the pros and cons when comparing services, rates, references and results.

Communication is key. Before signing a consignment contract, make sure you understand all the details and leave no question unanswered. It's in both the consignor's and auction house's best interest that transactions run as smooth as possible. Content consignors and happy bidders keep auction houses in business and that keeps the collecting market afloat.

— Karen Knapstein

AUCTION **CONSIGNMENT DIRECTORY**

Heritage Auctions
478 Jackson St.
San Francisco, CA 94111
800-872-6467
www.ha.com
www.ha.com/consign
9 a.m. - 5 p.m.; Sat By appt. PDT
bid@ha.com
Free pre-consignment evaluation

I.M. CHAIT Gallery
9330 Civic Center Drive
Beverly Hills, CA 90201
310-285-0182 Fax: 310-285-9740
www.chait.com
www.chait.com/consign.asp
Established 1969
11 a.m. - 5 p.m. PDT
Jake Chait
chait@chait.com
310-285-0182
Asian art, antiques, fine art, jewelry, and natural history.
Free pre-consignment evaluation
References Upon Request
Family run and operated since 1969. Strong buyer pool of over 50,000, and one of the first auction houses in America with auctions exclusively dedicated to Asian art.

Julien's Auctions
9665 Wilshire Blvd., Suite 150
Beverly Hills, CA 90210
310-836-1818
Fax: 310-742-0155
www.juliensauctions.com
Established 2003
9 a.m. - 5 p.m. PDT
Michael Doyle
info@juliensauctions.com
310-836-1818
Entertainment memorabilia (Hollywood, sports and rock 'n' roll).
Free pre-consignment evaluation
References Upon Request
Julien's Auctions is the auction house to the stars, and we get top prices.

Los Angeles Modern Auctions (LAMA)
16145 Hart St.
Van Nuys, CA 91406
323-904-1950 Fax: 323-904-1954
www.lamodern.com
Established 1992
9 a.m. - 5 p.m. PDT
Peter Loughrey
peter@lamodern.com
323-904-1950

20th and 21st century modern and contemporary fine art and design
Free pre-consignment evaluation
Simply put, we get the best prices for modern art and design.

COLORADO

Artemis Gallery Ancient Art/ Artemis Gallery LIVE
Online
Boulder County, CO 80027
720-890-7700
www.artemisgallerylive.com
Established 1993
24 Hrs - Online
Teresa Dodge
Teresa@artemisgallery.com
720-890-7700, ext. 1103
Antiquities, ancient and ethnographic art
Free pre-consignment evaluation
References Upon Request

Leslie Hindman Auctioneers
960 Cherokee St.
Denver, CO 80204
303-825-1855 Fax: 303-825-0450
www.lesliehindman.com
9 a.m. - 5 p.m. MDT
www.lesliehindman.com/about/appraisals-events
Annie McLagan
anniemclagan@lesliehindman.com
Free pre-consignment evaluation
References Upon Request

CONNECTICUT

Schwenke Auctioneers/ Woodbury Auction
710 Main St. South
Woodbury, CT 06798
203-266-0323 Fax: 203-266-0707
www.woodburyauction.com
Established 2009
9 a.m. - 5 p.m. EDT (Summer hours)
M-Thu 9 a.m. - 1 p.m. EDT
Thomas Schwenke
consign@woodburyauction.com
203-266-0323
American, French, Asian mid-century modern and contemporary decorative arts
Free pre-consignment evaluation
References Upon Request
We provide the ultimate in personalized auction services for both buyers and sellers, with primary effort given to maximize property values through careful research, and aggressive marketing.

FLORIDA

Burchard Galleries
2528 30th Ave. N.
St. Petersburg, FL 33713
727-821-1167
Fax: 727-821-1814
www.burchardgalleries.com
Established 1979
9 a.m. - 5 p.m. CDT
Jeffrey Burchard
mail@burchardgalleries.com
Antiques, fine art, jewelry, and military.
Free pre-consignment evaluation
References Upon Request
Auction firm internationally recognized for consistently bringing quality estate antiques and fine art to the marketplace. Thirty years of personal experience in full-service estate liquidation, computerized marketing and online bidding, and extensive pre-sale evaluation process.

Freedom Auction Company
1601 Desoto Rd.
Sarasota, FL 34234
941-725-2166
www.freedomauctions.com
Established 2008
By appt.
Brian P. Hollifield
brianphollifield@aol.com
Antiques, mid-century, modern, coins, and jewelry
Free pre-consignment evaluation
References Upon Request
High volume auctions at your place or ours.

Leslie Hindman Auctioneers
324 Royal Palm Way, Suite 102
Palm Beach, FL 33480
561-833-8053 Fax: 561-833-8052
www.lesliehindman.com
www.lesliehindman.com/about/appraisals-events
9 a.m. - 5 p.m. EDT
Free pre-consignment evaluation
References Upon Request

Leslie Hindman Auctioneers
850 6th Ave. S.
Naples, FL 34102
239-643-4448 Fax: 239-643-1432
www.lesliehindman.com
www.lesliehindman.com/about/appraisals-events
9 a.m. - 5 p.m. EDT
Kristin A. Vaughn
kristinvaughn@lesliehindman.com

Free pre-consignment evaluation
References Upon Request

Louis J. Dianni, LLC
11110 W. Oakland Park Blvd., Suite 314
Sunrise. FL 33351
914-595-7013
www.louisjdianni.com
9 a.m. - 5:30 p.m. EDT
Louis J. Dianni
info@louisjdianni.com
Antiques, arms and art
Free pre-consignment evaluation
References Upon Request
Operates out of Florida location from
Oct. 20-April 15.

Palm Beach Modern Auctions
417 Bunker Rd.
West Palm Beach, FL 33405
561-586-5500
Fax: 561-586-5540
www.modernauctions.com
www.modernauctions.com/selling.asp
Established 2011
10 a.m. - 5 p.m. CDT
Rico Baca
info@modernauctions.com
561-586-5500
Mid-century modern art, furniture,
luxury goods, and decorative art
Free pre-consignment evaluation
References Upon Request
*We are a full service boutique auction house
specializing in modern, with an established
in-house client base from Palm Beach,
Florida, America's wealthiest zip code.*

GEORGIA

Atlanta Auction Company
133 S. Clayton St.
Lawrenceville, GA 30046
www.atlantaauctionco.com
10 a.m. - 4 p.m.; Sat & Sun By appt.,
CDT
Lori Karlson
lkarlson2@aol.com
404-213-9429
Antiques, art, cars, and business and
estate liquidation
Free pre-consignment evaluation
References Upon Request

ILLINOIS

Leslie Hindman Auctioneers
1338 West Lake Street
Chicago, IL 60607
312-280-1212 Fax: 312-280-1211

www.lesliehindman.com
www.lesliehindman.com/about/
appraisals-events
Established 1982
9 a.m. - 5 p.m. CDT
Mary Kohnke
marykohnke@lesliehindman.com
312-334-4236
Full service
Free pre-consignment evaluation
References Upon Request
*Leslie Hindman Auctioneers is one of the
largest full service auction houses in the
nation and an industry leader for more
than 30 years. View a list of experts: Arts
of the American West: Maron Hindman,
maron@lesliehindman.com; Asian Works
of Art: Benjamin Fisher, benjaminfisher@
lesliehindman.com; Fine Art: Zachary
Wirsum, zachary@lesliehindman.com; Fine
Books and Manuscripts: Kathryn Coldiron,
kathryncoldiron@lesliehindman.com; Fine
Furniture and Decorative Arts: Corbin Horn,
corbinhorn@lesliehindman.com; Fine
Jewelry and Timepieces: Alexander Eblen,
alexandereblen@lesliehindman.com; Luxury
Accessories and Vintage Fashion: Anne For-
man, anneforman@lesliehindman.com*

Rock Island Auction Company
7819 42nd St. W.
Rock Island, IL 61201
800-238-8022 Fax: 309-797-1655
www.rockislandauction.com
Established 1993
8 a.m. - 5 p.m. CDT
Jessica Tanghe and Kevin Hogan
jtanghe@rockislandauction.com/
khogan@rockislandauction.com
800-238-8022
Firearms, edged weapons and
military artifacts
*The #1 firearms auction house in the world
for 11 consecutive years.*

Susanin's Auctioneers & Appraisers
900 South Clinton St., Chicago, IL 60607
312-832-9800 Fax: 312-832-9311
www.susanins.com
Established 1994
info@susanins.com
Free pre-consignment evaluation

IOWA

**Jackson's International Auctioneers
& Appraisers of Fine Art and Antiques**
2229 Lincoln St.
Cedar Falls, IA 50613
800-665-6743 Fax: 319-277-1252
www.jacksonsauction.com
www.jacksonsauction.com/consignments/

Established 1969
8 a.m. - 5 p.m. CDT
Jessica Brogan
consignments@jacksonsauction.com
319-277-2256
All fine art and antiques
Free pre-consignment evaluation
References Upon Request
*Jackson's International is one of the coun-
try's premiere service providers for the sale
and appraisal of fine art and antiques. For
over 40 years, Jackson's has assisted clients
coast-to-coast successfully appraising and
bringing to market hundreds of millions of
dollars worth of fine art and antiques.*

LOUISIANA

Crescent City Auction Gallery
1330 St. Charles Ave.
New Orleans, LA 70130
504-529-5057 Fax: 504-529-6057
www.crescentcityauctiongallery.com
www.crescentcityauctiongallery.com/
selling.aspx
Established 2008
10 a.m. - 5 p.m. CDT
Adam Lambert
info@crescentcityauctiongallery.com
504-529-5057
Local estates, fine art (particularly
Southern or Louisiana interest), bric-a-
brac, pottery, silver, jewelry, art glass,
American, English and Continental
furniture, lighting, and oriental carpets.
Free pre-consignment evaluation
References Upon Request
*Crescent City Auction Gallery is a privately
owned auction company and one of New
Orleans' premier auctioneers of fine art
and antiques. CCAG is proud of their
participation in the rich history and tradition
of the New Orleans auction culture. With the
combined experience of 60+ years, CCAG's
auctioneers and staff, we pride ourselves in
providing the best services to both sellers
and buyers.*

MAINE

Barridoff Galleries
401 Cumberland Ave.
Portland, ME 04101
207-772-5011 Fax: 207-772-5049
www.barridoff.com
www.barridoff.com/consignments/
form.php
Established 1977
By appt.
Robert Elowitch
fineart@barridoff.com
Fine art of all periods. From Old Master

to contemporary, including American, European, Japanese and Chinese works of art.
Free pre-consignment evaluation
References Upon Request
Barridoff Galleries was the first auction house in Maine to specialize in the auction of fine art. It is the only auction house in Maine to offer only works of art at two auctions a year which are held in April and October. The Galleries boasts many world auction records and consistently strong prices in all categories. Barridoff Galleries responds to potential consignors and auction buyers within 24 hours with accurate condition reports.

Thomaston Place Auction Galleries
51 Atlantic Hwy.
Thomaston, ME 04861
207-354-8141 Fax: 207-354-9523
www.thomastonauction.com
Established 1995
8:30 - 5 p.m. EDT
Kaja Veilleux and John D. Bottero
appraisal@kajav.com
207-354-8141
Art, antiques, coins, jewelry, silver, Asian, weapons, vehicles, and real estate
Free pre-consignment evaluation
References Upon Request
Extensive appraisal and auction experience, meticulous research, strategic worldwide marketing, state-of-the-art auction technology, and discreet and caring consignor service.

MARYLAND

Crocker Farm, Inc.
15900 York Rd.
Sparks, MD 21152
410-472-2016 Fax: 877-815-6954
www.crockerfarm.com
www.crockerfarm.com/contact
Established 2004
By appt.
Anthony Zipp
info@crockerfarm.com
410-472-2016
American stoneware and redware pottery
Free pre-consignment evaluation
References Upon Request
The world's leading auction of antique American stoneware and redware.

Mosby & Co. Auctions
5714-A Industry Lane
Frederick, MD 21704
240-629-8139 Fax: 888-815-7740
www.mosbyauctions.com
10.m. - 5 p.m. EDT
Keith Spurgeon
keith@mosbyauctions.com
240-629-8139
Toys, advertising, and circus memorabilia.
Free pre-consignment evaluation
References Upon Request

MASSACHUSETTS

Eldred's
1483 Route 6A
East Dennis, MA 02641
508-385-3116 Fax: 508-385-7201
www.eldreds.com
www.eldreds.com/customerservice/consignment.php
Established 1950
9 a.m. - 4:30 p.m. EDT
Annie Lajoie
annie@eldreds.com
508-385-3116 x114
Americana, paintings, Asian art, Marine, and sporting
Free pre-consignment evaluation
Competitive rates, New England's oldest auction house, prompt payment, and more than 65 years in business.

MICHIGAN

American Glass Gallery
P.O. Box 227
New Hudson, MI 48165
248-486-0530 Fax: 248-486-0538
www.americanglassgallery.com
Established 2008
John Pastor
jpastor@americanglassgallery.com
248-486-0530
Antiques bottles, flasks, blown glass
Free pre-consignment evaluation
References Upon Request

MISSOURI

Leslie Hindman Auctioneers
32 North Brentwood Blvd.
Clayton, MO 63105
314-833-0833 Fax: 314-833-5393
www.lesliehindman.com
www.lesliehindman.com/about/appraisals-events
Bridget Melloy
bridgetmelloy@lesliehindman.com

Free pre-consignment evaluation
References Upon Request

NEVADA

Morphy Auctions, Las Vegas
4520 Arville St., #1
Las Vegas, NV 89103
702-382-2466 Fax: 702-382-6513
www.morphyauctions.com/lasvegas
9 a.m. - 3p.m. PDT
info@morphyauctions.com
Free pre-consignment evaluation
References Upon Request
More than 40 years experience. Unquestioned integrity and quality of items. Leader in coin-operated devices sold at auction.

NEW JERSEY

21st Century Antiques
210 Ivy Rd.
Beverly, NJ 08010
609-877-6843 Fax: 609-877-6843
www.allthingsold.com
Established 1998
9 a.m. - 5 p.m EDT. and by appt.
Chris Doerner
dolltoy@hotmail.com
609-877-6843
General antiques collectibles, dolls and toys, and on-site estate auctions
Free pre-consignment evaluation
References Upon Request
We understand that consignor antiques and collectibles are often far more than just "merchandise"; they are fond memories, and deserve to be treated with care and respect, regardless of their value. It is our sensitivity to that and our core value as a support to the customers that make us worth looking into.

Bertoia Auctions
2141 DeMarco Dr.
Vineland, NJ 08360
856-692-1881 Fax: 856-692-TOYS (8697)
www.bertoiaauctions.com
Established 1986
9 a.m. - 5 p.m. EDT
Michael Bertoia
toys@BertoiaAuctions.com
856-692-1881
Antique toys, banks, trains, and dolls
Free pre-consignment evaluation
References Upon Request
Leader worldwide in antique toy auctions for over 30 years.

RSL Auction Company
295 US Highway 22 East, Suite 204 W
Whitehouse Station, NJ 08889
412-343-8733 Fax: 412-344-5273
www.rslauctions.com
Established 2004
M-F 9 a.m. - 5 p.m. EDT
Ray Haradin
raystoys@aol.com
412-343-8733
Antique toys and folk art
Free pre-consignment evaluation
References Upon Request
We are the best at selling early toys and banks.

Sterling Associates Inc.
70 Herbert Ave.
Closter, NJ 07624
201-768-1140 Fax: 201-768-3100
www.antiquenj.com
Established 1987
10 a.m. - 4 p.m. EDT
Stephen D'Atri
sterlingauction@gmail.com
201-768-1140
Estates and antiques
Free pre-consignment evaluation
References Upon Request
Experience, integrity and personalized service.

NEW YORK

Cottone Auctions
120 Court St.
Geneseo, NY 14454
585-243-1000 Fax: 585-243-6290
www.cottoneauctions.com
www.cottoneauctions.com/fine-art-and-antique-consignments
Established 1980
9 a.m. - 4 p.m. EDT
Matt Cottone
matt@cottoneauctions.com
585-243-1000
Fine art and antiques.
Free pre-consignment evaluation
References Upon Request
Have a highly successful track record of realizing maximum price results and delivering prompt payments.

Grey Flannel Auctions
13 Buttercup Lane
Westhampton, NY 11977
631-288-7800 Fax: 631-288-7820
www.greyflannelauctions.com
Established 1989
9 a.m. - 5 p.m. EDT
Michael Russek

michael@greyflannelauctions.com
631-288-7800 ext. 230
Premium-quality, game used
sports memorabilia
Free pre-consignment evaluation
References Upon Request
We are the world's foremost authenticators and auctioneers of high-profile sports memorabilia, trusted by countless Hall of Famers, sports museums and institutions.

Heritage Auctions
445 Park Ave. Near 57th St.
New York, NY 10022
212-486-3500 Fax: 212-486-3527
www.ha.com
www.ha.com/consign
10 a.m. - 6 p.m. EDT
bid@ha.com
Free pre-consignment evaluation

Louis J Dianni, LLC
982 Main St., Suite 175
Fishkill, NY 12524
914-474-7710 Fax: 888-371-4620
www.louisjdianni.com
Established 1980
Louis J. Dianni
Antiques, arms and art
Free pre-consignment evaluation
References Upon Request
Typical auction has 1,000 to 2,000 lots, 6,000 registered bidders from 70 countries. (In New York from May 1-Oct. 15.)

Swann Auction Galleries
104 East 25th St.
New York, NY 10010
212-254-4710
www.swanngalleries.com
Established 1941
10 a.m. - 6 p.m. EDT
swann@swanngalleries.com
212-254-4710
Fine art, rare and antiquarian books, posters, photography and illustration art. For a complete list of departments, visit our website.
Free pre-consignment evaluation
References Upon Request
Swann has a 75 year legacy as a family-run business. We pride ourselves on our expertise, authenticity and long-standing client relationships.

OHIO

Humler & Nolan
225 East 6th Street
Cincinnati, OH 45202

513-381-2041
www.humlernolan.com
Established 1991
9 a.m. - 4 p.m. EDT
Riley Humler
rhumler@humlernolan.com
American and European art pottery, art glass and paintings. With a special emphasis on Rookwood Pottery.
Free pre-consignment evaluation
References Upon Request
We have been selling Rookwood and other American and European art pottery, art glass and paintings since 1991 and have a stellar reputation for honesty, scholarship and customer service.

Rachel Davis Fine Art
1301 West 79th St.
Cleveland, OH 44102
216-939-1190 Fax: 216-939-1191
www.racheldavisfinearts.com
Established 1987
Tue - Sat 10 a.m. - 5 p.m. EDT
Rachel Davis
rdavis@racheldavisfinearts.com
216-939-1190
Paintings, prints and sculpture
Free pre-consignment evaluation
References Upon Request
Cleveland's oldest auction house specializing in the sale of fine art. We give honest, realistic expectations.

Top Hat Auctions, Appraisals & Sales
3775 Old Columbus Rd. NW,
Suites 103 & 102
Columbus, OH 43213
614-419-9161
Established 2007
Wed - Sun 10 a.m. - 5 p.m. EDT
Michael G. Kraft
tophatsells@yahoo.com
614-419-9161
Pottery, art glass, small antiques and estates
Free pre-consignment evaluation
Top Hat Auctions provides top quality professional auction services.

PENNSYLVANIA

Bullock's Bid 'N Buy
4635 Scrubgrass Road
Grove City, PA 16127
814-786-7129
www.paauctioneerbullock.com
Established 2007
7:30 a.m. - 10 p.m. EDT
Darlene Bullock

dbullock1515@verizon.net
724-372-1066
Antiques and collectibles
Free pre-consignment evaluation
References Upon Request
*Because we recognize our number one
responsibility is integrity and trust. We are
dedicated to accomplishing, educating,
and building a rapport with our buyers
and sellers, and performing to the highest
professional standards.*

Cordier Auctions & Appraisals
1500 Paxton St.
Camp Hill, PA 17104
717-731-8662 Fax: 717-731-9830
www.cordierauction.com
Established 1980
9 a.m. - 5 p.m. EDT
info@cordierauction.com
717-731-8662
Antiques, fine art, real estate, firearms,
jewelry, coins, sterling, and single
consignments and estates.
Free pre-consignment evaluation
References Upon Request
*Decades of experience, a full-time profes-
sional staff, secure 12,000-square foot auction facility, and many satisfied customers.*

Hake's Americana & Collectibles
3679 Concord Rd.
York, PA 17402
866-404-9800 Fax: 717-434-1690
www.hakes.com
Established 1967
9 a.m. - 5:30 p.m. EDT
Kelly McClain
mkelly@hakes.com
866-404-9800 ext. 1636
Pop culture collectibles and Americana
Free pre-consignment evaluation
References Upon Request
*Hake's is America's first and most
diversified collectibles auction house.
Commission rates as low as 10% and no
additional fees. We set records in hundreds
of collecting categories.*

Lark Mountain Auction Co.
369 Johnson St.
Wilkes-Barre Township, PA 18702
570-822-8855
www.auctionzip.com/PA-
Auctioneers/339903.html
Established 2013
By appt.
Barbara Conover
bft1317@aol.com
570-301-3107

Antiques and household collectibles
References Upon Request
*Ethical, friendly staff, quick payment, and
good advertising.*

Material Culture
4700 Wissahickon Ave., Suite 101
Philadelphia, PA 19144
215-438-4700 Fax: 215-438-4710
www.materialculture.com
Established 20+ years ago
9 a.m. - 5 p.m. EDT
George Jevremovic
expert@materialculture.com
215-438-4700
Fine carpets and textiles, Asian arts, fine
folk and outsider art, ethnographic arts,
antiques, modern design, fine books,
jewelry and timepieces, and silver and
objects de vertu
Free pre-consignment evaluation
References Upon Request
*We conduct auctions throughout the year,
covering a vast and eclectic array of diverse
material, periods, styles and price ranges.
Whether you are an individual or a business,
seeking to consign a single object, a collection, or an estate; or a museum of university
seeking to de-accession items, our specialists and experienced staff will provide you
with individualized attention and service
through the entire auction process.*

Morphy Auctions
2000 N. Reading Rd.
Denver, PA 17517
877-968-8880 Fax: 717-336-7115
www.morphyauctions.com
Established 1997
M-Sun 9 a.m. - 4 p.m. EDT
Dan Morphy
dan@morphyauctions.com
717-335-4569
Fresh to market collections
Free pre-consignment evaluation
References Upon Request
*Record-setting prices realized, strategic mar-
keting campaigns, and unrivaled experts.*

Noel Barrett Antiques & Auctions Ltd.
PO Box 300
Carversville, PA 18913
215-297-5109 Fax: 215-297-0457
www.noelbarrett.com
Established 1987
9 a.m. - 5 p.m. EDT
Noel Barrett
toys@noelbarrett.com
Antique toys and advertising
Free pre-consignment evaluation

References Upon Request
*Outstanding reputation for honest and
fair dealing.*

Old Toy Soldier Auctions USA
1039 Lakemont Dr.
Pittsburgh, PA 15243
412-343-8733 Fax: 412-344-5273
www.oldtoysoldierauctions.com
Established 2005
9 a.m. - 5 p.m. EDT
Ray Haradin
raytoys@aol.com
412-343-8733
Toy soldiers
Free pre-consignment evaluation
References Upon Request
*We are the only auction house in the world
that exclusively specializes in toy soldiers.*

Pook & Pook, Inc.
Attn: Consignment Dept.
463 E Lancaster Ave.
Downingtown, PA 19335
610-269-4040 Fax: 610-269-9274
info@pookandpook.com
www.pookandpook.com
Established 1984
Free pre-consignment evaluation
References Upon Request
*If you have any questions regarding the
consignment process, feel free to call at
any time.*

Stephenson's Auctioneers
& Appraisers
1005 Industrial Blvd.
Southampton, PA 18966
215-322-6182 Fax: 215-364-0883
www.stephensonsauction.com
Established 1962
9 a.m. - 5 p.m.; F 2 p.m. - 9 p.m.;
Sat 9 a.m. - noon EDT
Cindy Stephenson
info@stephensonsauction.com
215-322-6182
Antiques, jewelry, coins, and firearms
Free pre-consignment evaluation
References Upon Request
*Full service auction house running weekly
auctions year round.*

SOUTH CAROLINA

Manifest Auctions
361 Woodruff Rd.
Greenville, SC 29607
864-520-2208 Fax: 864-520-2210
www.manifestauctions.com
www.manifestauctions.com/auction-

steps/
Established 2014
9 a.m. - 6 p.m. EST
Manning Garrett
info@manifestauctions.com
864-520-2208
Coins, currency, art glass, pottery,
advertising, antiques, and railroadiana
Free pre-consignment evaluation
References Upon Request
Our low rates get consignors more money.

TENNESSEE

Case Antiques Inc. Auctions & Appraisals
2240 Sutherland Ave., #101
Knoxville, TN 37919
865-558-3033
www.caseantiques.com
Established 2005
By appt.
Sarah Drury
sarah@caseantiques.com
615-812-6096
Fine Art and sculpture, southern regional
art and antiques, silver, pottery, and
historic documents, maps and weapons.
Free pre-consignment evaluation
References Upon Request
*Top-notch customer service, multiple
auction records, reasonable commission
rates and terms, worldwide marketing,
professional photography and cataloging,
three accredited appraisers on staff.*

Case Antiques Inc.
Auctions & Appraisals
116 Wilson Pike Circle, #102
Brentwood, TN 37027
615-812-6096
www.caseantiques.com
By appt.
Sarah Drury
sarah@caseantiques.com
615-812-6096

John W. Coker Ltd.
1511 W. 11-E
New Market, TN 37820
865-475-5163 Fax: 865-475-5055
www.antiquesonline.com
Established 1971
By appt.
John Coker
john@antiquesonline.com
865-475-5163
Pre 1900 antiques and fine art
References Upon Request

*More than 40 years experience. Let a knowl-
edgeable dealer deal with it, serving greater
Knoxville area.*

TEXAS

Heritage Auctions
3500 Maple Avenue
17th Fl.
Dallas, TX 75219
800-872-6467 Fax: 214-409-1425
www.ha.com
www.ha.com/consign
9 a.m. - 5 p.m.; Sat 9 a.m. - 1 p.m. CDT
Holly Culbreath (Inquiries coordinator,
Fine & Decorative Arts) 877-437-4824
x1444; Joe Bumpas (Projec coordinator,
Charity Auctions) 877-437-4824 x1953;
David Mayfield (Coins and VP, Heritage
Auctions) 800-872-6467 x1277; Dustin
Johnston (Director of Currency Auctions)
877-437-4824 x1302; Tom Slater
(Director of Americana Auctions) 877-
437-4824 x1441; Jill Burgum (Senior
Director of Fine Jewelry) 877-437-4824
x1697; Grey Smith (Director of Vintage
Movie Poster Auctions) 877-437-4824
x1367; Nate Schar (Director of Luxury
Real Estate) 855-261-0573; Chris Ivy
(Director of Sports Auctions) 877-437-
4824 x1319; Mark Prendergast (Director
of Trusts & Estates) 877-437-4824
x1632; James Gannon (Director of Rare
Books) 877-437-4824 x1609; Lon
Allen (Managing Director of Comics
& Comic Art) 877-437-4824 x1261;
Aron Meystedt (Founder and Director of
Intellectual Property) 877-437-4824
x1362; Margaret Barrett (Director of
Entertainment & Music Memorabilia)
877-437-4824 x1912; Ed Jaster (Senior
VP, Heritage Auctions, Illustration Art
& Photography) 877-437-4824 x1288;
Barbara Conn (Consignment Director of
Luxury Accessories, NY) 877-437-4824
x1336; Craig Kissick (Consignment
Director of Fine Minerals) 877-437-4824
x1995; Jim Wolf (Director of Watches &
Fine Timepieces) 877-437-4824 x1659;
Frank Martell (Director of Fine & Rare
Wine) 877-437-4824 x 1753
bid@ha.com
With more than 40 categories, it's easy
to secure a free estimation of value
from Heritage Auctions Visit Heritage
Auctions' easy to use Free Auction
Evaluation to select your category,
submit a brief description, or even
upload snapshots of your rare coins,

fine art and collectibles. The most
appropriate Heritage specialist will
contact you promptly. Learn more at
ha.com/consign.
Free pre-consignment evaluation
*Founded in 1976, Heritage Auctions is the
world's third largest auction house and the
world's largest collectibles auctioneer with
annual sales of more than $900 million.
Heritage clients enjoy unprecedented access
to more than 900,000+ online bidder members and unparalleled standards of honesty
and transparency as well as the latest
advancements in technology via HA.com.
Heritage Auctions offers consignors an
unmatched depth of expertise with access to
3.4+ million prices realized and a network
of 500+ specialist employees around the
world. We are always looking to acquire
interesting items, whether through consignment or by outright purchase, and we spend
or disburse millions of dollars every business day, on average, keeping our clients'
demands satisfied.*

Kasper Auction Co.
8714B Clearbrook Trail
Austin, TX 78729
512-673-9958
www.kasperauctionco.com
Established 2015
8 a.m. - 8 p.m. CDT
Robin Kasper
robin@kasperauctionco.com
Multifaceted estates and consignments.
Free pre-consignment evaluation
References Upon Request
*We are a small auction company and can
offer our clients personalized services to
meet their needs.*

LL Auctions
PO Box 1371
Dickinson, TX 77539
713-248-6186
www.TexasAuctions.biz
Established 2002
8:30 a.m. - 5:30 p.m. CDT
Lisa Gay or John Gay
lisa@texasauctions.biz
713-248-6186
Estates
Free pre-consignment evaluation
References Upon Request
*We do online auctions (licensed by the
state of Texas) and reach a large group of
bidders. We are also a full service company. We can pick up and pack up, offering
turn-key service.*

Simpson Galleries
6116 Skyline Drive, Suite 1
Houston, TX 77057
713-524-6751 Fax: 713-524-6752
www.simpsongalleries.com
Established 1962
M-Thu 10 a.m. - 4 p.m.; F 10 a.m. -
noon CDT
Ray Simpson Jr.
ray@simpsongalleries.com
713-524-6751
Fine art, antiques, and
mid-century modern
Free pre-consignment evaluation
References Upon Request
*We are a third generation auction house
having more than 50 years experience in
the marketing and selling of fine art
and antiques.*

VIRGINIA

Bremo Auctions
320 Pantops Center
Charlottesville, VA 22911
434-293-1267 Fax: 434-293-0898
www.bremoauctions.com
Established 2013
9 a.m. - 5 p.m. EDT
Cecily Reynolds
info@bremoauctions.com
High-end art, period furniture
and accessories
Free pre-consignment evaluation
References Upon Request
*Our personalized service is unparalleled and
our customer loyalty speaks volumes.*

Jeffrey S. Evans & Associates
2177 Green Valley Lane
Mt. Crawford, VA 22841-2430
540-434-3939
www.jeffreysevans.com
info@jeffreysevans.com
Established 2009
9 a.m. - 5 p.m. EDT

Quinn & Farmer Auctions
2109 India Rd.
Charlottesville, VA 22901
434-293-2904 Fax: 888-728-6102
www.quinnfarmer.com
Established 2012
10 a.m. - 4 p.m.; Sat noon - 4 p.m. EDT
Skip Usry
information@quinnfarmer.com
434-293-2904
Fine and decorative art, mid-century
modern furniture, coins, and southern

material items
Free pre-consignment evaluation
References Upon Request

Quinn's Auction Galleries
360 S. Washington St.
Falls Church, VA 22046
703-532-5632 Fax: 703-552-1996
www.quinnsauction.com
M-Th. 10 a.m. - 4 p.m.; Fri 10 a.m. - 5
p.m.; Sat 10 a.m. - 2 p.m. EDT
David Quinn
info@quinnsauction.com
703-532-5632
Fine and decorative art, mid-century
modern furniture, Netsuke, and
Asian items
Free pre-consignment evaluation
References Upon Request

**Waverly Rare Books at Quinn's
Auction Galleries**
360 S. Washington St.
Falls Church, VA 22032
703-532-5632 Fax: 703-552-1996
www.quinnsauction.com
Established 1977
Monika Schiavo
monika.schiavo@quinnsauction.com
703-532-5632 x 300
Rare books, maps, autographs,
and photos
Free pre-consignment evaluation
References Upon Request

WISCONSIN

Leslie Hindman Auctioneers
525 East Chicago St.
Milwaukee, WI 53202
414-220-9200 Fax: 414-220-9220
www.lesliehindman.com
www.lesliehindman.com/about/
appraisals-events
9 a.m. - 5 p.m. CDT
Sara Mulloy
saramulloy@lesliehindman.com
414-220-9200
Free pre-consignment evaluation
References Upon Request

Paul Auction Co. Inc.
N131 County Rd. S
Kewaskum, WI 53040
262-338-3030 Fax: 262-626-2430
www.paulauction.com
Established 1969
Mike Paul
mike@paulauction.com

262-338-3030
Antiques
Free pre-consignment evaluation
References Upon Request
*Sterling reputation for honesty. Broad depth
of knowledge in Wisconsin antiques.*

CANADA

A.H. Wilkens Auctions & Appraisers
299 Queen St. East
Toronto, ON M5A 1S7 Canada
416-360-7600 Fax: 416-360-8900
www.ahwilkens.com
Established 2009
9 a.m. - 5 p.m. EDT
Asian, silver, decorative arts
Free pre-consignment evaluation
*Leading Canadian auction house, with a
good online presence*

GERMANY

Auction Team Breker
P. O. Box 50 11 19
50971 Koeln, Germany
Otto-Hahn-Str. 10
50997 Koeln (Godorf)/Cologne, Germany
Tel. +49/2236/38 43 40
Fax +49/2236/38 43 430
Tues - Fri 9 am - 5 pm
www.Breker.com
Auction@Breker.com
U.S. representative: Andrew Truman
207-485-8343
AndrewAuctionTeamBreker@gmail.com
Technical Antiques & Fine Toys

Hermann Historica
Linprunstr 16
D-80335, Munich, Germany
49-89-54726490 Fax: 49-89-
547264999
www.hermann-historica.com
Established 1982
10 a.m. - noon/2:30 p.m. - 6 p.m. CEST
Thomas Rief
contact@hermann-historica.com
49-89-54726490
Antique arms and armor, antiquities,
orders, militaria, and
historical collectibles.
Free pre-consignment evaluation
www.roseberys.co.uk
M-F 9:30 a.m. - 5:30 p.m. BST
Peter Greenway
valuations@roseberys.co.uk
44 (0) 2087612522
Fine art, antiques, and Islamic and
Indian arts
Free pre-consignment evaluation

ADVERTISING

TODAY'S MARKET FOR antique advertising items is white hot. Items of a particularly strong interest are porcelain signs, rare tins, advertising trays, pocket mirrors, antique displays, and pinbacks. Strong collecting bases exist for advertising material from the oil and gas, country store, tobacco, and breweriana fields.

Advertising has been called the every man's art. That art has now rivaled the prices paid for Picasso sketches and Renoir studies.

"It really was the closest people came in those days to real art," said Wayne Yoder, a Wisconsin auctioneer who has watched collector's tastes evolve from glassware to high-end signs. "They were everywhere at the time and they had true art that people still want to own today."

To understand the passion behind collecting advertising it helps to understand the art and the ad campaigns that created them. Both were not created by chance. These are the end result of market study, product study, consumer sentiment, and return on investment. Advertising items are punchy, beautiful, visually arresting, and designed to capture your attention in a 10th of a second. Even the plainest ad items collected today have some aspect of graphic design that catches a collector's eye, even if the value isn't terribly high.

Advertising items are the wellspring of a consumer-driven economy. The diversity we enjoy today shows just how lucrative that consumer class can be. A robust middle class America was the chief driver of this advertising boom. As such, most ads are for consumer products marketed to this consumption class, such as gasoline, soft drinks, beer, alcohol, food stuffs, and various other consumables. Consumables like these required a steady stream of advertising to maintain sales against competitors. These remain the most popular and most valuable items among collectors.

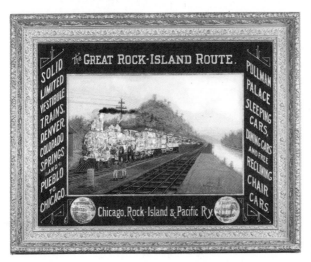

The current world record for the most valuable advertising sign is $165,000 in 2011 for a Rock Island Railroad reverse glass sign measuring 54" wide by 43" tall. The sign was made in 1890 by an employee of the firm and is believed to be the first sign made for the railway company. It eventually found its way into Rock Island's Los Angeles, Calif., offices for a time before it ended up in private collection and passed down through three generations over 85 years.

When it came to auction, bidding was fierce and quickly blew its $50,000 pre-auction estimate out of the water.

Objects made to promote goods that are not customarily produced or distributed for sale to consumers are also sought by collectors, but on the whole they generally do not enjoy the same level of collectability as signs promoting non-consumer goods. For instance, a 27-inch sign for Armour's Animal and Poultry Feeds, which was marketed exclusively to livestock farmers, may currently be found at auction for roughly $800. A 27-inch sign advertising Coca-Cola may be had for roughly $1,900. Both signs may have avid collecting bases but Coke enjoys more household brand awareness than Armour's animal feeds, despite its catchy tagline promising greater profits.

When all of these elements – the talent, the typography, the characters, the slogans, and the calls to action – come together it's easy to see why advertising items stir such strong passion among collectors.

That passion often translates into big dollars.

▶ Tapper, Mr. Peanut tapper used as window display to capture attention of passersby, rare, 28" t., ...**$23,000**

Showtime Auction Services, showtimeauctions.com

Standee, 1922, cardboard countertop standee, easel back chessboard design, J. Allen St. John image from cover of the 1922 novel, the fifth in Edgar Rice Burroughs' Barsoom series, first published in "Argosy All-Story Weekly" in 1922, standee advertises the publication as a complete novel by A. C. McClurg in Nov. 1922. 9-1/4"w. x 12-7/8" t.,... **$713**

Hake's Americana & Collectibles, hakes.com

Thermometer, 1940s silk-screened heavy tin thermometer for Wichita Falls, TX garage "Geo. W. Blandin Auto Parts & Body Works, 9" dia......... **$118**

Hake's Americana & Collectibles, hakes.com

Sign, 1960s, Quaker State Oil Refining Corp., painted formed steel sign has large "Ask For Quaker State Motor Oil" advertising text in Quaker State's colors, 24» dia., ... **$273**

Hake's Americana & Collectibles, hakes.com

Sign, Ford Parts, circa 1960, oval, double-sided porcelain, original mounting grommets, 24" w., ... **$525**

Hake's Americana & Collectibles, hakes.com

Sign, from a set of five advertisements for Peek Frean English biscuits, including examples from Carr, Macfarlane, Huntley & Palmers biscuit makers, 24-1/4: h. x 19-5/8" w. **$1,625**

Heritage Auctions, HA.com

Corner sign, 1910s, convex oval reverse painted glass sign, Kamm and Schellinger Brewing Co's Beer, original tin frame, rare, 16-1/2 x 28"., ...**$10,980**

Showtime Auction Services, showtimeauctions.com

Sign, 1910s, Lansing Farm Wagon, Lansing Wagon Works Co., Lansing, Michigan, manufacturers of farm lumber and freight wagon, log trucks and brown's patent loose jointed bob sleds. Sold by W.A. Rawley, Worchester, N.Y. Lithographer, Gies and Co. Litho, Buffalo, N.Y., rare, 30-1/2 w. x 24-1/2" t., ...**$27,450**

Showtime Auction Services, showtimeauctions.com

Store display, 1940, Friskies Dog Food Mechanical Store Display, dog tails would wag back and forth, rare, 39-3/4" x 27-1/2" x 9-1/2"., ... **$3,355**

Showtime Auction Services, showtimeauctions.com

Flange sign, 1920s, Mennen's Borated Talcum Die Cut Tin Flange Tray Sign, 22-1/2" x 14-1/2". **$3,355**

Showtime Auction Services, showtimeauctions.com

Tray, 1920s, Ekhardt & Becker's Detroit, 13" dia., ... **$976**

Showtime Auction Services, showtimeauctions.com

Sign, reverse glass painted, Schlitz Brewing Co. Milwaukee, framed in period gesso, 20" x 27"., ... **$3,416**

Showtime Auction Services, showtimeauctions.com

Clock, 1960s, Pam Clock Co., metal body clock with dome glass cover over tin litho clock face, clock face has "Prestolite Batteries" name and logo, 15-1/4" w. x 15-1/4" l., ... **$171**

Hake's Americana & Collectibles, hakes.com

Poster, circa 1920, Klaus - Caramel Mou Á La Creme candy advertisement, 39"w. x 55" t., ... **$604.87**

Hake's Americana & Collectibles, hakes.com

▲ Sign, circa 1910, cardboard, Piedmont Cigarettes Oversized Tri-Fold, one of two known, 61" w. x 40" h., ...**$36,000**

Heritage Auctions, HA.com

Sign, 1920s, cardboard, Tiger Chewing Tobacco Die Cut, 8" w. x 26" t., ... **$2,440**

Showtime Auction Services, showtimeauctions.com

▶ Sign, circa 1910, milk glass, framed French Art Nouveau, painted, E. Laroque & ses Fils, 34-1/4 h. x 57" w., ...**$250**

Heritage Auctions, HA.com

Sign, circa 1900, metal, Stetson Hats, brass-plated sheet metal with embossed border and painted letters, wood frame, original suspension chain, 29-1/2" w. x 8" t., ... **$625**

Heritage Auctions, HA.com

Pocket mirror, Hobo/Kidney & Bladder Remedy Rare Medical Product, text "Clear Up Your Complexion With/(product package)/Eliminate The Poisons From The System", 2-3/4 t., ...**$118**

Hake's Americana & Collectibles, hakes.com

◀ Sign, circa 1890, tin, William F. "Buffalo Bill" Cody, lithographed tin sign depicting the great showman and Indian scout, signed in the plate "Sincerely Yours W. F. Cody 'Buffalo Bill'", 14" w. x 20" t., ... **$2,500**

Heritage Auctions, HA.com

AUTOGRAPHS

THE MARKET FOR historical and seldom seen autographs remains particularly robust, however, prices are also on the rise for those from celebrities, sports figures and famous authors. Presidential autographs prior to 1940 remain highly-sought after among collectors and institutions alike.

The market for celebrity scientists, modern Presidents and current heads of industry are not commanding high prices in today's market. This makes the opportunity to collect these types of autographs a low-cost hobby before prices increase in the future.

Take for instance the autograph of Steve Jobs. In 1992, Jobs signed a rare poster promoting the inaugural NeXTWORLD Expo held in San Francisco. Little did he know his signature would be one of the most coveted among collectors

– particularly because Jobs did not sign very many documents during his lifetime. The autographed poster sold in early 2017 for $16,000.

Like most autographs, the story associated with the signature contributes greatly to the value. In the case of the Jobs poster, Apple purchased NeXT in 1997 for $429 million and 1.5 million shares of Apple stock, with Jobs, as part of the agreement, returning to the company he had co-founded in 1976, said Bob Eaton, CEO of RR Auctions, who offered the poster at auction.

For the last few years, autograph collectors have been forced to "branch out" away from traditional clipped signatures so often seen in established collections. Why? Blame the digital age. More digital correspondence means even fewer signatures. Therefore, collectors are pursuing older items such as autographed magazines, period photographs as well as passports and even driver's licenses. A passport from the private collection of Whitney Houston sold in 2015 for a surprising $15,000.

It may be hard to believe that signatures of Steve Jobs and Whitney Houston can command three or four times as much as a signature by Abraham Lincoln or Thomas Jefferson. With autographs it all comes down to context, clarity, condition and rarity. Eye appeal helps a great deal, too. A signed cut autograph, so named because the signature is cut from perhaps a check, autograph book or some other piece of paper, to a signed photo makes a world of difference to collectors.

MOST DANGEROUS AUTOGRAPHS TO COLLECT

Not all autographs are safe or easy to get and some are downright dangerous to a collector's checkbook. The Beatles remain at the top of the list of the most often copied and faked historical and entertainment autographs. They are the most heavily forged band in the world. The following list of the most dangerous historical and entertainment autographs to collect is compiled annually by Professional Sports Authenticator (PSA), the largest and most trusted third-party grading and authentication company in the world.

1. The Beatles – ($5,000 for a signed cut signature to $15,000 or more for a signed photo.)
2. Elvis Presley – ($1,500 for a signed cut signature to $35,000 or more for a signed contract or letter.)
3. Neil Armstrong – ($1,500 for a signed cut signature to $4,000 or more for a signed photo.)
4. John F. Kennedy – ($1,750 for a signed cut signature to $25,000 or more for a presidential letter/document.)
5. Michael Jackson – ($350 for a signed cut signature to $1,000 or more for a signed photo.)
6. Marilyn Monroe – ($2,500 for a signed cut signature to $15,000 or more for a signed photo.)
7. Led Zeppelin – ($1,200 for a signed cut signature to $4,500 or more for a signed photo.)
8. Jimi Hendrix – ($2,500 for a signed cut signature to $7,500 or more for a signed photo.)
9. The Rolling Stones – ($1,200 and up for a signed photo and $3,500 and up for a signed guitar.)
10. *Star Wars: The Force Awakens* Cast – ($500 and up for a cast-signed photo and $50-$250 for individual key cast members.)

George Washington, "Go: Washington," one page, both sides, May 12, 1799, signed seven months before his death, Washington writes from Mount Vernon to John Marshall, Edward Carrington, and William Heth regarding the structure of a national army to be raised for a possible war with France, 8" x 9- ½" **$25,000**

RR Auction

James Monroe, as president and John Quincy Adams, as secretary of state, one page, 20.75 x 16.5, September 20, 1824, white paper seals remain affixed to left side, documents signed by both Monroe and Adams remain scarce and highly sought-after.. **$2,000**

RR Auction

Che Guevara, one page, signed in Spanish, signed "Che," January 22, 1960, a provisional certificate for a $300,000 bank bond from the Cuban National Bank, registering the terms and conditions of the "Issuance of 'Bonds of the National Institute of Savings and Housing, 1959–1979.'" Guevara was at the very top of Castro's government when this document was signed. Diminutively signed solely as "Che," symbolically showing the Cuban financial sector his distaste for money and the class distinctions it brought about. In fine condition, 14" x 11" **$1,700**

RR Auction

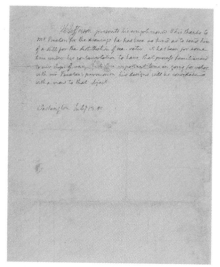

George Washington and Thomas Jefferson, highly desirable partly printed double sided, signed "G:o Washington" as president and "Th: Jefferson" as secretary of state, one page, June 11, 1794, three-language ship's papers issued to "Samuel Rolfe, master or commander of the Brig called the Edmund…lying at present in Newburyport bound for Cape Nicolas Mole." Signed in the center by President Washington and countersigned by Secretary of State Jefferson. 12-3/4" x 15-3/4 ....**$19,000**

RR Auction

Thomas Jefferson, as president, one page, July 13, 1805. In full: "Th: Jefferson presents his compliments & his thanks to Mr. Buxton for the drawings he has been so kind as to send him of a still for the distillation of sea–water. It has been for some time under his contemplation to have that process familiarized to our ships of war, which lose important time in going for water." 7-3/4" x 9-1/5 .... **$8,500**

RR Auction

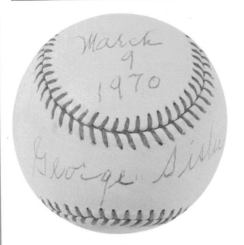

George Sisler, Spalding Tri-County League baseball signed in blue ballpoint on the sweet spot, "George Sisler," with the date on the north panel, "March 9, 1970." In fine condition, with spots of soiling to the lower panel, Sisler is considered rare in single-signed baseballs, fine with letter of authenticity from PSA/DNA.
.... **$2,000**

RR Auction

Sigmund Freud, signed "Freud," one page, on personal letterhead, July 3, 1929. Letter to "Dr. Clark," in full: "I can't see how you come to offer me a check for your reception in Vienna. I received you as a distinguished colleague, gave you no consultation." double-matted and framed with a portrait to an overall size of 10" x 16"
.... **$2,700**

RR Auction

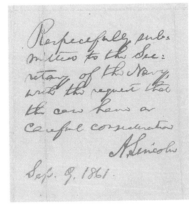

Queen Elizabeth II and Prince Philip, matte-finish, full-length portrait, original mount, signed on the mount in fountain pen, "Elizabeth 1961" and in black ink, "Philip." The reverse of frame bears collector's notations indicating that the signatures were obtained during the Royal Tour of Italy in 1961, framed, 7" x 8-1/2". **$800**

RR Auction

Abraham Lincoln, Civil War–dated handwritten endorsement, signed as president, "A. Lincoln," dated September 9, 1861, on the reverse of the second integral page of a letter originally written to Gideon Welles by University of Maryland founder Congressman Charles B. Calvert, one page, 6.5" x 8", September 5, 1861, Lincoln's autograph endorsement, in full: "Respectfully submitted to the Secretary of the Navy, with the request that this can have a careful consideration."...................... **$5,500**

RR Auction

Albert Einstein, on matte-finish photo, signed in fountain pen, "A. Einstein, 1942." 4-3/4" x 3-1/5"... **$4,000**

RR Auction

Frank Sinatra, James J. Kriegsmann publicity photo of a young Sinatra, signed and inscribed in fountain pen, "To Mary Claire—Sincerely, Frank Sinatra." Fine, 8" x 10-1/4"........................ **$1,400**

RR Auction

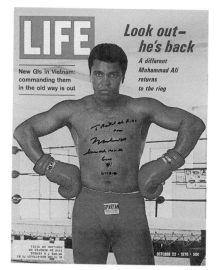

Muhammad Ali, signed issue of Life magazine from October 23, 1970, inscribed, "To Butch the King from Muhammad Ali, Serve God, He is the goal, 6-18-90," adding a small sketch of a heart, fine. **$350**

RR Auction

Winsor McCay, illustrated autograph, "Will See You in Slumberland", created this intricately detailed miniature for Howard Norris, a devoted collector of personalized inscriptions. 4.25" x 7"
.... **$13,145**

Heritage Auctions, HA.com

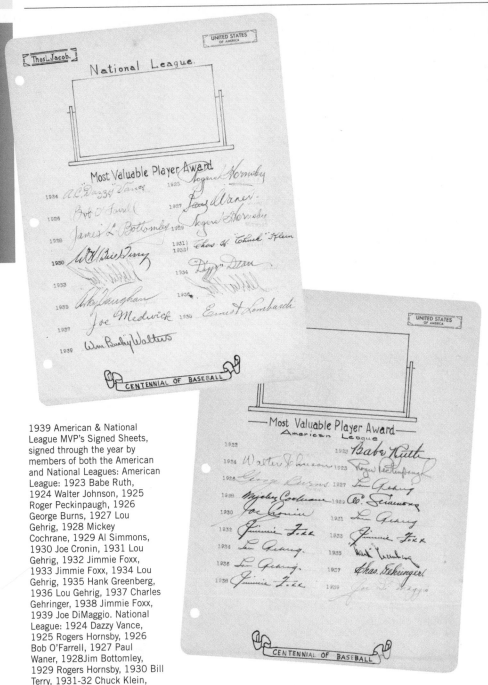

1939 American & National League MVP's Signed Sheets, signed through the year by members of both the American and National Leagues: American League: 1923 Babe Ruth, 1924 Walter Johnson, 1925 Roger Peckinpaugh, 1926 George Burns, 1927 Lou Gehrig, 1928 Mickey Cochrane, 1929 Al Simmons, 1930 Joe Cronin, 1931 Lou Gehrig, 1932 Jimmie Foxx, 1933 Jimmie Foxx, 1934 Lou Gehrig, 1935 Hank Greenberg, 1936 Lou Gehrig, 1937 Charles Gehringer, 1938 Jimmie Foxx, 1939 Joe DiMaggio. National League: 1924 Dazzy Vance, 1925 Rogers Hornsby, 1926 Bob O'Farrell, 1927 Paul Waner, 1928 Jim Bottomley, 1929 Rogers Hornsby, 1930 Bill Terry, 1931-32 Chuck Klein, 1933 Carl Hubbell, 1934 Dizzy Dean (secretarial), 1935 Arky Vaughan, 1936 Carl Hubbell, 1937 Joe Medwick (secretarial), 1938 Ernie Lombardi, 1939 Bucky Walters **$78,000**

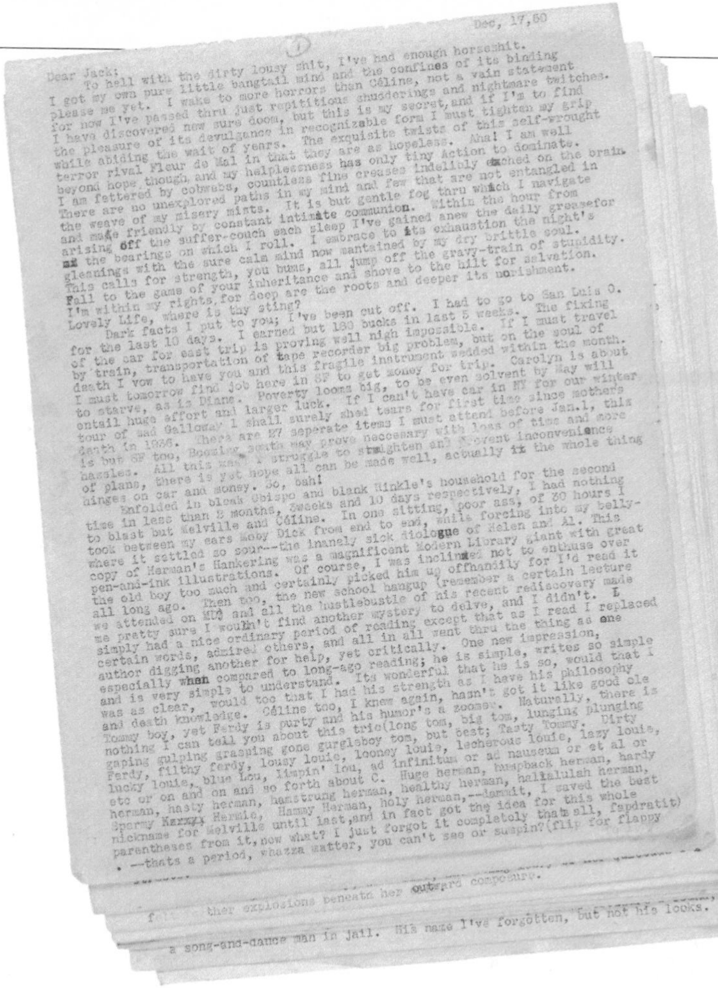

Neal Cassady, Dec. 17, 1950, written while high on speed, the "Joan Anderson Letter" had an immediate impact on author Jack Kerouac, who transformed its verve into a lasting influence on literature (Kerouac mentions the letter in Part Five of his best-selling On the Road—not to mention capturing the tone, drive and music of Cassady's prose in that novel). **$206,250**

Heritage Auctions, HA.com

Whitney Houston, final United States passport, issued on May 9, 2007, valid until May 8, 2017; signed "Whitney E. Houston" in blue ink, and includes a watermarked photo of Houston, from the Estate of Whitney E. Houston, 3.5" x 5". **$15,000**

Heritage Auctions, HA.com

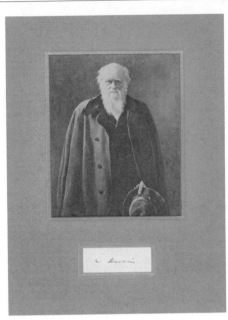

Sir Isaac Newton, from a group of three framed autographs including Sir Humphrey Davy, and Charles Darwin, 19" x 10-1/4". **$4,750**

Heritage Auctions, HA.com

BANKS

MOST COLLECTIBLE BANKS were designed for one purpose: to encourage children to save money. How well the bank accomplished this task makes all the difference in making it collectible by later generations.

Manufactured from the late 1800s to the mid-1900s, mechanical, still, and register banks (which indicate the value of the coins deposited) are marvels of ingenuity made of tin, lead, or cast iron. Although banks come in all makes and functions, the most desirable banks employ a novelty or mechanical action when a coin is placed inside. Banks are sought after because they so efficiently represent the popular culture at the time they were made. This is evident in the wartime register banks sporting tin lithographic decorations of superheroes or animation characters or the cast iron figures that propagated racial stereotypes common from 1880 to 1930. Many early cast iron bank models have been reproduced during the years, especially in the 1950s and 1960s. A key indicator of a reproduction is fresh, glossy paint or dull details in the casting.

According to 10 years of sales data on LiveAuctioneers.com, most mechanical banks sell at auction for between $500 and $1,000. Morphy Auctions is the world leader in selling mechanical banks.

"There are a dozen or so collections that I know of that would bring over $1 million," said Dan Morphy, owner and founder of Morphy Auctions. "There are dozens of other bank collections that would fall in the six figure ranges."

Morphy says condition – like all other categories of collecting – is king. "Banks in top condition seem to be the trend these days," he said.

So, on the basis of affordability, now is the time to start a collection. "I always tell new collectors that they should buy what they like," Morphy said. "Even if you pay a little more than you should for a bank, the value in the enjoyment of owning it will more than offset the high price one may pay."

A top on Morphy's list to offer at auction is a Darkey & the Watermelon mechanical bank. Otherwise known as the Football Bank, it was designed and patented by Charles A. Bailey on June 26, 1888. Known as the leader in mechanical bank design, Bailey's Darkey & the Watermelon bank incorporated all of his imagination and design talents: When the right leg of a figure is pulled back into position, a coin is then placed in a small football; a lever in the figure's coattails is pressed and the football with coin is kicked over into a large watermelon. Only four of these banks are known to exist.

"That would be my dream bank," Morphy said, "in that I would also want to buy it!"

Like their predecessors crafted nearly 150 years ago, contemporary banks blur the line between tool and toy. Some modern banks that may make

Arcade flat-top Yellow Cab Bank with nickel-plated driver, the front doors inscribed Yellow Cab Court 5700, 8" l. **$1,100**

Courtesy Pook & Pook, www.pookandpook.com

interesting collectibles in the future include digital register banks that tabulate coin and paper money deposits or those licensed by famous designers. But beware – antique banks are still being reproduced and can be found very cheaply at lesser-quality flea markets or sold online.

For more information on banks, see *The Official Price Guide to Mechanical Banks* by Dan Morphy (morphyauction.com).

J. & E. Stevens cast iron Professor Pug Frogs Great Bicycle Feat mechanical bank, good condition. $2,600

Courtesy Pook & Pook, www.pookandpook.com

Shepard Hardware Co. cast iron Uncle Sam mechanical bank, some paint loss, excellent condition. **$1,600**

Courtesy Pook & Pook, www.pookandpook.com

Cast Iron Safe Deposit Bank, still bank, No 10A Grey-Iron Casting Co. Mount Joy, PA., most original paint remains intact, 4-1/2" x 5 x 3-1/2". **$700**

Courtesy Showtime Auction Services, showtimeauctions.com

Cast iron man with arms, still bank and pen rest, excellent condition, 3 1/2" h. **$475**

Courtesy Pook & Pook, www.pookandpook.com

▼ Cast Iron Washer Bank and Maytag Building Bank, fair to good condition.....................$100

Courtesy King's Galleries, kinggalleries.com

J. & E. Stevens cast iron Clown on Globe mechanical bank, good condition.....................$700

Courtesy Pook & Pook , www.pookandpook.com

Mechanical coin-op bank with birds, patent date Jan 23 1883, 6-1/2" h x 8-1/2" w. $225

Courtesy Pook & Pook, www.pookandpook.com

Painted cast iron Mr. Peanut bank, 8" h x 3-1/2" w. $150

Courtesy King's Galleries, kinggalleries.com

Vintage J. & E. Stevens Jolly Mechanical Bank, 7" h. $250

Courtesy EstateOfMind Auctions, estateofmind.biz

Campbell Soup Boy and Girl Coin Bank, 3-1/2" h x 4-1/2" w. $25

Courtesy King Galleries, kinggalleries.com

John Harper cast iron Transvaal Money Box, still
bank, replaced pipe and baseplate, very good
condition. **$500**

Courtesy Pook & Pook, www.pookandpook.com

J. & E. Stevens cast iron Magician Mechanical
Bank, areas of restoration and repaint, including
head and left arm. **$1,200**

Courtesy Pook & Pook, www.pookandpook.com

Cast iron U.S. Mail Still Bank
with an eagle finial, 9-1/2" h.
.... **$600**

Courtesy Pook & Pook, www.pookandpook.com

Painted cast iron Businessman
Bank, 8" h x 4" w.................**$25**

Courtesy King Galleries, kinggalleries.com

J. & E. Stevens cast iron Tammany Mechanical
Bank, very good condition................................ **$325**

Courtesy Pook & Pook, www.pookandpook.com

THE BEATLES

THE FIRST WAVE of Beatlemania broke over the U.S. in 1964 when The Beatles appeared on *The Ed Sullivan Show*. More than 50 years after that historic evening, that storm has swelled into a tsunami as a new era of Beatlemania has hit the collecting world hard.

"The Beatles rule the world of music and entertainment memorabilia like few others," says Noah Fleisher, author of *The Beatles: Fab Finds of the Fab Four*. "I might even venture to say, having watched the market for the best Beatles material explode in the last five years, that they may well be the only sure-fire bet in music memorabilia that a collector could have right now."

Recent auction results support Fleisher's contention. At auction, John Lennon's lost Gibson J-160E guitar sold for $2.4 million; the drum head on Ringo Starr's drum kit from that *Ed Sullivan Show* sold for more than $2 million; and a Beatles-signed "Sgt. Pepper's Lonely Hearts Club Band" album gatefold sold for nearly $300,000.

Everything from autographs to photos, albums, clothing, licensed plastic Beatles guitars and especially the real things are hotly pursued.

"The music was the doorway and the merchandising was the fix," Fleisher says. "We're all so fascinated by how they did what they did that we got personally involved with their stories and their images. How do you feel close to your idols? To people that you love with all your heart and soul but to whom you have almost no chance of ever meeting? You buy the stuff."

When it comes to selling Beatles memorabilia there are few, if any, who can match Darren Julien, the CEO and president of Julien's Auctions in Los Angeles.

"The Beatles are so popular because their music is still relevant and their fan base is not only global but it transcends all age groups," Julien said. "Their fan base only continues to increase and, for many, buying an item from their life or career is like buying a memory from their past.

"Beatles memorabilia is the blue chip of the collectibles market. Items from their career tend to go up gradually and consistently, unlike some celebrities who spike high and sometimes end low."

As a matter of debate, there may be no better investment in the memorabilia market today than a Beatles item.

"The items that bring the most and are the most sought-after are items that were used/worn on stage," Julien says. "The market for these items has dramatically increased. For

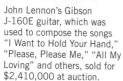

John Lennon's Gibson J-160E guitar, which was used to compose the songs "I Want to Hold Your Hand," "Please, Please Me," "All My Loving" and others, sold for $2,410,000 at auction.

Image courtesy of Julien's Auctions

The Beatles line-up photograph signed on back by George Harrison, Paul McCartney and Pete Best. Albert Marion, a local wedding photographer, took the photograph on Dec. 17, 1961, during The Beatles' first professional photography session **$4,800**

Image courtesy of Julien's Auctions

Early pre-Beatles photograph, (from left) George Harrison, John Lennon and Paul McCartney, 1958. Photo taken by Mike McCartney, Paul's brother, at a wedding reception. Harrison was a mere 15 in the photo. ... **$1,000**

Image courtesy of Julien's Auctions

instance, guitars that Christie's sold for around $100,000 in recent years, we now sell for more than $500,000. Beatles garments have also dramatically increased in recent years as museums and investors now look for iconic items that can be on display or that will increase in value."

"The Beatles are not going anywhere. I think their legendary status and collectability will only continue to increase. Items that we see selling for $500,000 now, I believe, will someday soon be worth $2 million to $3 million."

The value of the memorabilia mirrors the band's career to a tee, Fleisher says.

"The early part of their fame can be documented by massive amounts of material that was released with their names and images on it, much of which they didn't control" Fleisher notes. "The middle period, when they stopped touring, and the end, saw a good bit less of the trinket type pop culture material. Their image was more mature and the market in memorabilia matured the same way, focusing on autographs, records and more personal material. The end of the band saw very little material, and you can see in the book it's much more scarce from the final period of the band's time together and more valuable for that scarcity."

Items closely tied to The Beatles demand top dollar. Band-used gear – guitars, drums, even cases that carried equipment – are the ultimate prize for the biggest players in the Beatles memorabilia field.

"With this band it all comes back to the music," Fleisher says. "They are working now on their fifth successive generation and the music sounds as fresh, innovative and inspiring as it ever has. As long as the tunes these men wrote and recorded together continue to sound so damn good, I cannot imagine that the attendant memorabilia won't continue to bring a premium. The $2.4 million paid for John's Gibson J-160E is going to look like a bargain in 20 years."

Beatles publicity photograph, 1962, by Peter Kaye, Liverpool. The leather jackets are gone, replaced by the suits that would come to define their early rise to fame. **$2,240**

Image courtesy of Julien's Auctions

◀ Beatles signed tour program, 1965, depicting the band as Saturday morning cartoon. **$19,200**

Image courtesy of Julien's Auctions

▼ The Beatles at the Cavern Club photo, 1961, 8" x 10" photo of The Beatles, with Pete Best on drums, taken at Liverpool club that first brought them attention....................**$750**

Photo taken by Gloria Stavers.

◀ Cavern Club stage-used microphone, late 1950s/early 1960s, from the famous Liverpool, England, club where The Beatles performed nearly 300 times early in their career.
.... **$10,625**

Image courtesy of Heritage Auctions, HA.com

top lot

Beatles Gear Drums Up Stunning Results

This Ludwig bass drum head, with the iconic "drop-T" logo, was on Ringo Starr's drum kit during The Beatles' debut on *The Ed Sullivan Show*, February 9, 1964. The show officially launched the British Invasion, changing rock history forever. The Remo Weather King head is prominently painted with The Beatles "drop-T" logo and "Ludwig." The drum kit became a visual trademark for the band, as important to The Beatles' stage show as their hair, suits, boots, guitars and amplifiers. In short, it is one of the most iconic musical symbols on the planet.

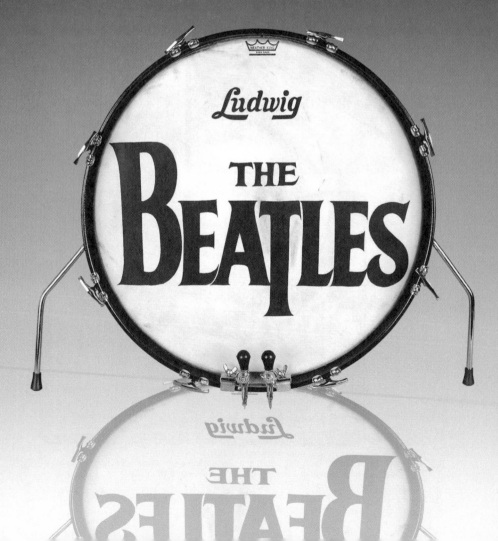

Jim Irsay, owner of the Indianapolis Colts football team and a rock memorabilia enthusiast, paid **$2,050,000** for the drum head during a sale at Julien's Auctions, Los Angeles. Irsay has a collection of about 175 historically significant guitars. Christopher McKinney, who curates the Irsay collection, said in many ways the drum head was more significant to people than a Beatles guitar. "If you showed the guitar to 20 people, one might recognize what it is," McKinney said. "If you show the drum head to 20 people, most will be able to identify with it."

One-sheet movie poster from The Beatles' movie *Help!*, 1965, highly coveted. **$1,920**

Image courtesy of Julien's Auctions

Sgt. Pepper's Lonely Hearts Club Band Gold Record from the Record Industry Association of America, commemorating more than $1 million worth of sales for The Beatles' 1967 release, *Sgt. Pepper's Lonely Hearts Club Band*, an album that spent 175 weeks on the American charts. **$8,125**

Image courtesy of Julien's Auctions

Abbey Road Gold Record from the Record Industry Association of America, commemorating more than $1 million worth of sales for The Beatles' 1969 release, *Abbey Road*, an album that spent 129 weeks on the American charts. **$5,937**

Image courtesy of Julien's Auctions

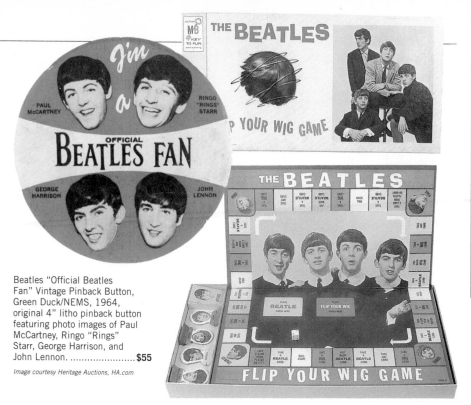

Beatles "Official Beatles Fan" Vintage Pinback Button, Green Duck/NEMS, 1964, original 4" litho pinback button featuring photo images of Paul McCartney, Ringo "Rings" Starr, George Harrison, and John Lennon. **$55**

Image courtesy Heritage Auctions, HA.com

▲ The Beatles Flip Your Wig Game, 1964, Milton Bradley, includes game board, cardboard cutouts for each member of The Beatles, numbered die and two decks of cards. **$140**

Image courtesy Heritage Auctions, HA.com

▲ ▶ Beatles Record Player, NEMS, 1964, four-speed portable record player with carrying case. With only about 5,000 produced, the record player is considered by most collectors to be one of the ultimate pieces to own of all commercial Beatles memorabilia.

.... **$2,750**

Image courtesy Heritage Auctions, HA.com

◄ ▼ Beatles Bobb'n Head Figures, Car Mascots, Inc., 1964, with original box and cardboard insert that keeps the heads from "bobb'n."
....$1,075

Image courtesy Heritage Auctions, HA.com

Beatles Wristwatch, Bradley Time, 1964, dial bears the group's individual portraits placed at the 12:00, 3:00, 6:00, and 9:00 positions with the text: "The Beatles", "Shockproof". $600

Image courtesy Heritage Auctions, HA.com

▲ Beatles blue lunchbox with original matching Thermos, Aladdin, 1965. The first Aladdin lunchbox dedicated to a rock group. $750

Image courtesy Heritage Auctions, HA.com

Beatles School Bag, Burnel Ltd. of Canada, 1964, 12" x 9", gusseted tan vinyl school bag with handle and shoulder strap with Beatle images in brown below the flap and on either side of the latch with facsimile signatures between the images. $1,750

Image courtesy Heritage Auctions, HA.com

BOOKS

WITH AN EXCESS of 100 million books in existence, there are plenty of opportunities and avenues for bibliophiles to feed their enthusiasm and build a satisfying collection of noteworthy tomes without taking out a second mortgage or sacrificing their children's college funds. With so many to choose from, the true challenge is limiting a collection to a manageable size and scale, adding only volumes that meet the requirements of bringing the collector pleasure and holding their values.

What collectors are really searching for when they refer to "first editions" are the first printings of first editions. Every book has a first edition, each of which is special in its own right. As Matthew Budman points out in *Collecting Books* (House of Collectibles, 2004), "A first represents the launching of a work into the world, with or without fanfare, to have a great impact, or no impact, immediately or decades later. ... Holding a first edition puts you directly in contact with that moment of impact."

Devon Gray, director of Fine Books and Manuscripts at Skinner, Inc., www.skinnerinc.com, explains the fascination with collectible books: "Collectors are always interested in landmarks of human thought and culture, and important moments in the history of printing."

What makes a first edition special enough to be considered collectible is rarity and demand; the number of people who want a book has to be greater than the number of books available. So, even if there are relatively few in existence, there has to be a demand for any particular first edition to be monetarily valuable.

Learning how to recognize first editions is a key to protecting yourself as a collector; you can't take it for granted that the person you are buying from (especially if he or she is not a professional bookseller) has identified the book properly. Entire volumes have been written on identifying first editions; different publishing houses use different means of identification, many utilizing differing methods and codes. However, Richard Russell, who has been collecting and selling books since 1973, offers these clues in his book, *Antique Trader Book Collector's Price Guide*:

• The date on the title page matches the copyright date with no other printings listed on the copyright page (verso).

• "First Edition," "First Printing," "First Issue" or something similar is listed on the copyright page.

• A publisher's seal or logo (colophon) is printed on the title page, copyright page, or at the end of the text block.

• The printer's code on the copyright page shows a "1" or an "A" at one end or the other (example: "9 8 7 6 5 4 3 2 1" indicates first edition; "9 8 7 6 5 4 3 2" indicates second edition).

As is the case with so many collectibles, condition is paramount. If a book was published with a dust jacket, it must be present and in great condition to attain the book's maximum value. Gray uses an example to illustrate the importance of condition.

"A book with a very large value basically has further to fall before it loses it all," she says. "A great example is the first edition of the printed account of the Lewis and Clarke expedition. In bad condition its value is in the four-figure range; in better condition, it gets up to five figures; and in excellent condition, six figures."

A signature enhances a book's value because it often places the book in the author's

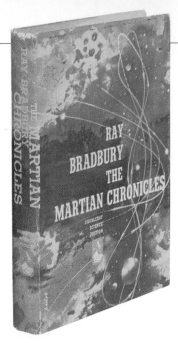

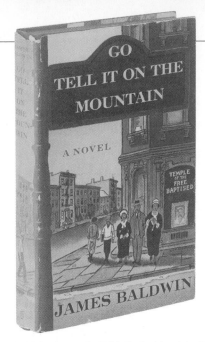

Bradbury, Ray, The Martian Chronicles, Garden City, NY: Doubleday, 1950. 8vo, publisher's gray-green cloth lettered in red, spine slightly faded, mottling to boards, dust jacket, spine panel slightly tanned, tape ghosts to free endpapers, inscribed first edition in unrestored jacket..... **$2,500**

Courtesy of Swann Galleries, www.swanngalleries.com

Baldwin, James, Go Tell It On the Mountain, New York: Knopf, 1953. 8vo, publisher's russet cloth; dust jacket, closed tear along front flap, spine panel faded with light chipping to tips; contents clean; slipcase. First edition of the author's first book... **$594**

Courtesy of Swann Galleries, www.swanngalleries.com

hands. Cut signatures add slightly to a book's value because the author didn't actually sign the book – he or she may have never even held the book with the added cut signature. When the book itself is signed, even if with a brief inscription, it holds a slightly higher value. If the author is known for making regular appearances and accommodating all signature requests, the signature adds little to the value of the book because the supply for signed examples is plentiful.

"Real value potential comes into play with association material," Gray explains. "For example, a famous novelist's Nobel-winning story is based on a tumultuous affair he had with a famous starlet under his heiress-wife's nose, and you have the copy he presented to his wife, with her 'notes.'"

Even a title that has been labeled as "great," "important," or "essential" doesn't mean a particular edition – even a first edition – is collectible or monetarily valuable. After all, if a much-anticipated book is released with an initial print run of 350,000, chances are there will be hundreds of thousands of "firsts" to choose from – even decades after publication. Supply far outweighs demand, diminishing value.

The overly abundant supply of book club editions (which can be reprinted indefinitely) is just one of the reasons they're not valued by collectors. Some vintage book club editions were also made from inferior materials, such as high-acid paper using lower quality manufacturing processes.

Determining if a book is a book club edition is easier than determining if it is a first edition. Some of the giveaways that Matthew Budman lists in *Collecting Books* include:

• No price on dust jacket
• Blind stamp on back cover (small impression on the back board under the dust jacket); can be as small as a pinprick hole

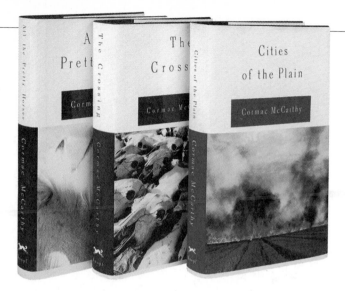

McCarthy, Cormac, [The Border Trilogy.] All the Pretty Horses; The Crossing; Cities of the Plain. New York: Knopf, 1992; 94; 98. Together, 3 volumes. 8vo, publisher's 1/4 cloth, uniformly lettered in silver; dust jackets; bright copies. First editions. **$875**

Courtesy of Swann Galleries, www.swanngalleries.com

- "Book Club Edition" (or similar notation) on dust jacket
- Books published by the Literary Guild after World War II are smaller format, thinner and printed on cheap paper.

Fledgling book collectors should also be aware of companies that built a burgeoning business of publishing a copious number of "classic" and best-seller reprints; just a few of the long list are Grosset & Dunlap, Reader's Digest, Modern Library, A.L. Burt, Collier, Tower and Triangle. Many of these companies' editions are valued only as reading copies, not as collectibles worthy of investment.

Proper care should be implemented early on when building a collection to assure the books retain their condition and value. Books should be stored upright on shelves in a climate-controlled environment out of direct (or even bright indirect) sunlight. Too much humidity will warp covers; high temperatures will break down glues. Arrange them so similar-sized books are side-by-side for maximum support, and use bookends so the books don't lean, which will eventually cause the spines to shift and cause permanent damage.

A bookplate usually will reduce a book's value, so keep that in mind when you're thinking of adding a book with a bookplate to your collection, and avoid adding bookplates to your own volumes. Also, don't pack your volumes with high-acid paper such as newspaper clippings, and always be careful when placing or removing them from the shelf so you don't tear the spine.

Building a book collection – or any collection, for that matter – on a budget involves knowing more about the subject than the seller. Learning everything possible about proper identification of coveted books and significant authors involves diligence and dedication, but the reward is maximum enjoyment of collecting at any level.

– Karen Knapstein

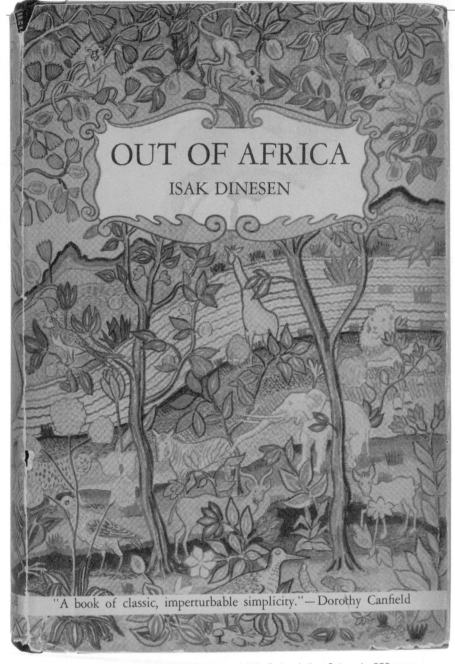

OUT OF AFRICA

ISAK DINESEN

"A book of classic, imperturbable simplicity." — Dorothy Canfield

Dinesen, Isak, Out of Africa. New York: Random House, 1938. Early printing. Octavo. ix, 389 pages. Publisher's original black cloth spine lettered in gilt and rust cloth boards. Dust jacket. Modest wear to the edges of the boards; minor toning to contents; former owner's bookplate on the front free endpaper; jacket with scattered soiling and chipping to the edges. $94

Courtesy of Heritage Auctions, www.ha.com

Brönte, Charlotte, Shirley, A Tale. By Currer Bell. 3 volumes. London: Smith, Elder and Co., 1849. 8vo, contemporary 1/2 leather over marbled boards, spines gilt-titled, front cover of vol. 1 detached, boards scuffed, occasional staining to contents, terminal blank of vol. 3 with early owner's manuscript notes on verso, housed in full morocco clamshell case with gilt inscription..... **$423**

Courtesy of Swann Galleries, www.swanngalleries.com

Bukowski, Charles, Septuagenarian Stew: Stories & Poems. Santa Rosa: Black Sparrow Press, 1990. First edition. This edition limited to 251 numbered and lettered hardcover copies, with original silkscreen print, colophon and original silkscreen print signed by the author. Publisher's quarter-cloth bindings in a clear acetate jacket. Near fine.. **$250**

Courtesy of Heritage Auctions, www.ha.com

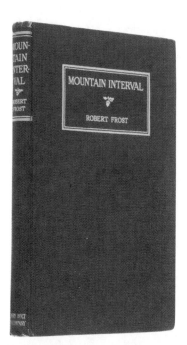

Frost, Robert, Mountain Interval. New York: Henry Holt and Company, 1916. First edition, second state. Octavo. Publisher's binding. Minor rubbing to extremities. Bookplate. Near fine.................. **$94**

Courtesy of Heritage Auctions, ha.com

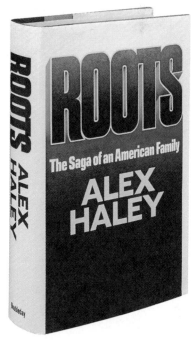

Haley, Alex, Roots. New York: Doubleday, 1976. 8vo, publisher's 1/4 cloth-backed boards; dust jacket, slight discolorations along spine panel folds only visible on verso. **$618**

Courtesy of Swann Galleries, swanngalleries.com

top lot

Kerouac's *Dharma Bums* Manuscript

Beat writer Jack Kerouac's original typescript manuscript for his third book, *The Dharma Bums* (1958), typed by Kerouac from his original scroll manuscript, sold at auction for *$137,500*. Much like his first book, *On the Road*, Kerouac originally wrote *The Dharma Bums* on a single scroll over the course of 11 days – fuelled by copious quantities of booze and narcotics.

Few writers represent the Beat Generation more than Kerouac (1922-1969). The Beat Generation sprang from the late 1940s, an underground, anti-conformist youth movement with aspects that morphed into the counterculture of the 1960s.

"Certainly, Allen Ginsberg, William S. Burroughs and Kerouac are the literary giants of Beat Generation literature," says James Gannon, Heritage Auction's director of rare books. "Kerouac's spontaneous prose and autobiographical material solidified his position among America's postwar writers." Kerouac's 1957 novel, *On the Road*, about two friends on a cross-country quest for meaning and true experience, earned glowing reviews. *The New York Times* proclaimed Kerouac the voice of his generation and a surge of fame and success ensued. *The Dharma Bums* followed, a tale of friends exploring nature and Buddhism in search of truth and enlightenment.

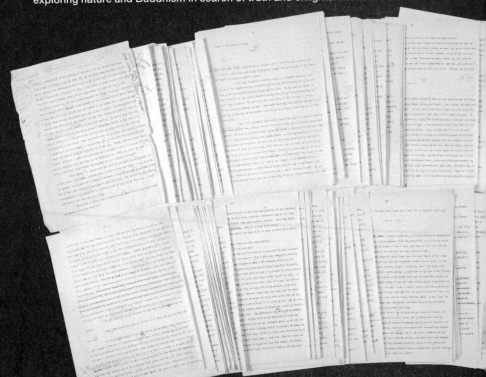

After Kerouac typed the original *Dharma Bums* manuscript he sent it to his publisher, Viking Press. However, Viking sent back the text with numerous changes, including removal of some of the more sexually explicit sections. Kerouac viewed the Viking edits as an insult.

On the cover of *The Dharma Bums* manuscript Kerouac emphatically wrote in red ink: "Dharma Bums Ms. (with Viking Press Changes that I rejected)."

In a letter to girlfriend and fellow writer, Joyce Glassman, Kerouac explained: "I had to go to NY the other day mad as a hatter to contest Viking's (expletive) idea of making as much as 4,000 corrections on Dharma Bums. They said copy-editing hadnt hurt ROAD but that was a short-sentence style that couldnt be hurt. They agreed first to start all over again…if they are trying to sneak over their ersatz version of DB on me they've lost a writer…"

Despite Kerouac's reaction, a number of the changes appear in the final text.

The typescript was passed along to Kerouac's mother after his death. The non-profit, Kerouac Project (www.kerouacproject.org) later purchased the typescript. They auctioned the piece via Heritage Auctions to raise funds for their mission to help the careers of writers and artists inspired by the legacy of Kerouac.

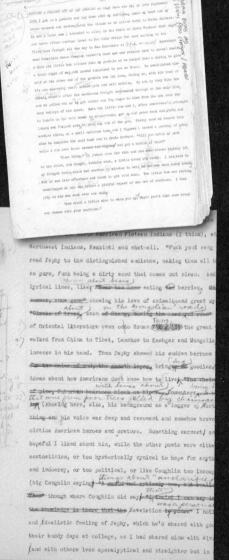

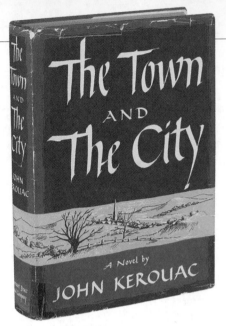

Hemingway, Ernest, *Winner Take Nothing*.
New York: Charles Scribner's Sons, 1933. 8vo,
publisher's black cloth with gilt paper labels,
extremities rubbed, spine creased; first state
dust jacket with Stalling's review of Death in the
Afternoon on rear panel, few small professional
edge restorations, unclipped; internally unmarked.
.... **$715**

Courtesy of Swann Galleries, swanngalleries.com

Kerouac, Jack [as John.], *The Town and the City*.
New York: Harcourt, Brace, and Company, 1950.
8vo, publisher's red cloth, minor rubbing to spine
tips and corners; dust jacket, spine panel faded,
few wrinkles and scratches, cellotape repair
mending short closed tear to lower spine panel
corner on recto; front hinge split, contents clean.
First edition of Kerouac's first book, signed by him
as John Kerouac on front flyleaf.
.... **$3,750**

Courtesy of Swann Galleries, swanngalleries.com

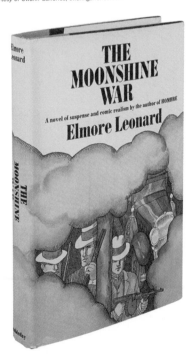

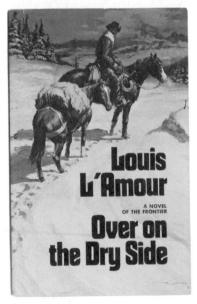

Leonard, Elmore, The Moonshine War. New York:
Doubleday, 1969. 8vo, publisher's green and
black cloth; unclipped dust jacket, light age-
toning; contents clean. First edition. The basis for
the 1970 film directed by Richard Quine. **$344**

L'Amour, Louis, Over on the Dry Side. Saturday
Review/Dutton, 1975. First edition, first printing.
Signed and inscribed by the author. Rubbing and
toning. Tape to verso of dj. Very good. **$100**

Courtesy of Swann Galleries, swanngalleries.com

Courtesy of Heritage Auctions, ha.com

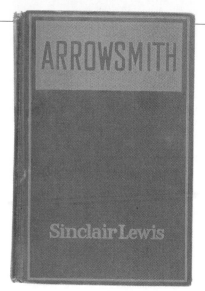

Lewis, Sinclair, Arrowsmith. New York: Harcourt, Brace and Company, 1925. Inscribed by the author. Publisher's cloth. Rubbing, soiling, staining, and wear to covers and spine. Spine and corners bumped with some loss at head. Toning and thumb soiling along text block and throughout. Front hinge separating.................. **$275**

Courtesy of Heritage Auctions, ha.com

Nabokov, Vladimir, Lolita. Putnam's Sons, 1958. 8vo; price-clipped dust jacket, minimal shelf-wear, one short closed tear. First American edition in the first issue dust jacket preceded by the first edition published in Paris by the Olympia Press in 1955. New York: G.P.................................... **$688**

Courtesy of Swann Galleries, www.swanngalleries.com

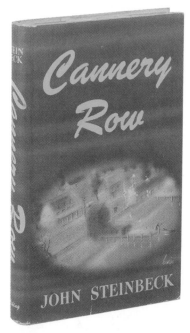

Rand, Ayn, The Fountainhead. Indianapolis: Bobbs-Merrill, 1943. 8vo, publisher's gilt-lettered red cloth, mottling to covers; dust jacket, edge wear with some loss to spine panel head not affecting lettering, few creases and short closed tears... **$7,250**

Courtesy of Swann Galleries, swanngalleries.com

Steinbeck, John, Cannery Row. New York: Viking, 1945. 8vo, publisher's blue-lettered buff cloth, areas of light discoloration to joints as usual; dust jacket, light dust-soiling; cloth slipcase. **$750**

Courtesy of Swann Galleries, www.swanngalleries.com

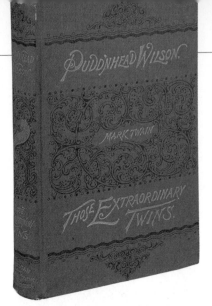

Thomas, Dylan, *A Child's Christmas in Wales.* New York: James Laughlin, 1954. 32 pages, bound in beige paper with red and black lettering, 12mo (5-1/4" x 7-1/2"), dust jacket (in protective sleeve). This famous children's book was published posthumously following the untimely November 9, 1953, death of the Welsh poet, playwright and short-story writer. The front endpaper includes the handwritten name of a previous owner... **$239**

Courtesy of Heritage Auctions, ha.com

Twain, Mark, The Tragedy of Pudd'nhead Wilson. Illustrated with author portrait frontispiece; marginal drawings throughout. Hartford: American Publishing Co., 1894. 8vo, publisher's russet cloth gilt, spine tips lightly rubbed; ex-collection Frederick Norton Finney, signed by him in pencil on front flyleaf and with his bookplates to front pastedown and early blank. First edition, first issue. **$293**

Courtesy of Swann Galleries, www.swanngalleries.com

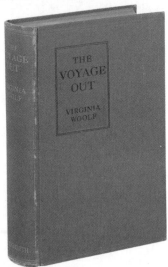

Woolf, Virginia, The Voyage Out. Kirkpatrick A1. London: Duckworth, 1915. 8vo, original green cloth stamped in black on cover, gilt on spine, joints, tips, and spine ends with modest rubbing; small bookplate on front pastedown. With 6 pages of advertisements and 16-page catalogue at end. One of 2,000 copies. First edition of Woolf's first book... **$1,000**

Wilder, Thornton, The Bridge of San Luis Rey. Illustrated by Amy Drevenstedt, New York: Albert & Charles Boni, 1927. 8vo, pictorial cloth, spine ends and tips rubbed and lower tips bumped; unclipped dust jacket, clean tear to front panel, scattered creasing and light soiling, two images of Wilder mounted to front matter; cloth chemise and 1/4 morocco slipcase. First American trade edition signed by Wilder. **$488**

Courtesy of Swann Galleries, www.swanngalleries.com

Courtesy of Swann Galleries, swanngalleries.com

BOTTLES

INTEREST IN BOTTLE COLLECTING continues to grow, and more collectors are spending their free time digging through old dumps and foraging through ghost towns, digging out old outhouses, exploring abandoned mine shafts, and searching for their favorite bottles at antiques shows, swap meets, flea markets, and garage sales. In addition, the internet has greatly expanded, offering collectors numerous opportunities and resources to buy and sell bottles with many new auction websites, without even leaving the house.

Most collectors, however, still look beyond the type and value of a bottle to its origin and history. Researching the history of a bottle is almost as interesting as finding the bottle itself.

In addition to numerous bottle auctions, along with 15 to 20 antique bottle shows held each month by bottle clubs across the United States, England, Australia, and Europe, there have been major archeological finds, shipwreck discoveries in the Gulf of Mexico and the Baltic Sea, bottles found in attics, and of course many great bottle digs across the country.

All of this good news demonstrates that the hobby is not only strong, but continues to gain popularity while bringing an overall greater awareness to a wider spectrum of antiques collectors. While attending shows and talking with collectors and dealers from across the country, the consensus is that the hobby is doing well and growing stronger, and some recent auctions continue to excite collectors.

At the end of 2016/early 2017, Norm Heckler Auctions, Woodstock Valley, Connecticut, conducted a few auctions that produced astonishing results: One of the most rare and desirable flasks it has ever sold, a Double Eagle historical flask, early Pittsburgh district, Pittsburgh, Pennsylvania, 1820-1840, bright yellow green, GII-5, sold for $57,330; another flask, a "Baltimore" and Monument-"Corn For The World" and partially husked ear of corn, Baltimore Glass Works, Baltimore, Maryland, 1860-1870, brilliant peacock blue, quart, GVI-4, sold for $24,570; and a "Triton Spouting Spring / T / Saratoga N.Y." - "Triton Water" mineral water bottle, America, 1860-1870, bluish aquamarine, pint, T #S-55B, rare and in fine condition, sold for $4,680.

In late 2016 and early 2017, Jim Hagenbuch and his crew at Glass Works Auction, East Greenville, Pennsylvania, also saw some excellent results with auctioning the Bob Ferraro collection of early American bitters and whiskey bottles. Ferraro's iconic 45-year collection included only 141 lots, but many of the bottles are extremely rare and one-of-a-kind pieces, and the three-part auction racked up more than $482,000. The top three lots were bitters bottles: A People's Favorite Bitters barrel with diagonal rings and thought to be the best of three or four known, closed at $30,000; a Crow's Celebrated Tonic Bitters bottle, thought to be the only known example, sold for $20,000; and a sapphire blue Wolf Pittsburg barrel, one of two known examples, also sold for $20,000.

Fine Old Gin label under glass, circa 1890, extremely rare, 11-1/2" h.
....................................**$20,000**

Courtesy of Dan Morphy Auctions, www.morphyauctions.com

Pair of Victorian barber bottles, hand-blown Bristol blue satin semi-opaque glass, original bloom-shaped top stoppers, satin finish, all hand-painted floral and bird decoration, gilt trim, bell-shaped form, one is marked on both the stopper and underside of the body with number 175, the other is with a gold number 24, circa late 1800s/early 1900s), approx. 10" h with stoppers, 7-1/2" without stoppers, 3-3/4" base diameter. **$130**

Courtesy of Antiques and Art by IMEON, www.liveauctioneers.com/antiques-and-art-by-imeon

Barber bottle, Loetz art glass, green iridescent, 9" h. **$225**

Courtesy of Rich Penn Auctions, richpennauctions.com

always find any bottles, but you can still help someone unexpectly: According to an October 2016 press release by the Battle Creek Michigan Police Department, police got a call from a woman who saw a man digging in a hole in a vacant lot behind her block. She said he had a blue tarp and looked like he put something in the waist-deep hole the day before. Police investigated and after finding clear markings of a hole that has recently been filled in, and some paper that had not been in the ground long, forensic lab technicians were called in and began hand-digging in the area. No specific information led police to believe this was related to a crime, but because there are cold cases that still have missing evidence, they decided to excavate the hole. Digging down, lab specialists found some paper remnants, a cigarette butt, an energy bar wrapper, a large rock, and an empty brandy bottle. After a local news station aired the story, a man called into the station and said he had been given permission by the property owner to dig in the lot for antique bottles. Despite spending several hours searching for evidence that was nonexistent, police said it turned out to be beneficial real-life training for their forensic lab technicians since hand digging for evidence is not a skill that is easily practiced and it provided invaluable experience, should they ever encounter a similar crime scene.

For more information on bottles, see *Antique Trader Bottles Identification & Price Guide*, 8th edition, and *Picker's Pocket Guide: Bottles*, both by Michael Polak.

Two barber bottles, hand-blown amethyst glass with hand-painted Verederma and windmill scenes, 8" h. **$200**

Courtesy of Rich Penn Auctions, richpennauctions.com

Victorian barber's bottle, striped cranberry glass, 6-3/4 h x 3-3/4" w. **$80**

Courtesy of Hudson Valley Auctions, www.hudsonvalleyauctions.com

Lot of three Seitz Beer bottles, each 9-1/2" h.......................**$25**

Courtesy of Dan Morphy Auctions, www.morphyauctions.com

▶ Lot of five Kuebler's embossed beer bottles, largest 9-1/4" h.. **$50**

Courtesy of Dan Morphy Auctions, www.morphyauctions.com

▲ Conrad & Co., rare and hard to find, 11-1/2" h.............. **$125**

Courtesy of Dan Morphy Auctions, www.morphyauctions.com

▶ Original and rare pre-prohibition Gallatin Lager Beer bottle from Bozeman, Montana, dated 1906, label reads "Julius Lehrkind Bozeman, Mont. / The Famous Gallatin Lager Beer," 3" diameter, 11-1/2" h............. **$150**

Courtesy of North American Auction Company, www.northamericanauctioncompany.com

Group of three early blown glass flasks or bottles: a mid-19th century, American, GIX-11 scroll flask, aquamarine, pint size, sheared mouth, eight-point upper and lower star, the base with rough pontil mark; second quarter 19th century cornucopia-urn pictorial flask, olive green, GIII-4, pint, sheared mouth and rough pontil mark, possibly Coventry Glass Works (Coventry, CT); blue-green mold-blown moon-shaped flask, embossed to one side with a leaping deer and chasing dog, the other a hunting trophy; scroll flask 7" h, cornucopia flask 5-1/4" h, hunt flask 5-3/4" h..**$100**

Courtesy of Ahlers & Ogletree Auction Gallery, www.aandoauctions.com

William Henry Harrison: Tippecanoe clear glass ink bottle, in the shape of the Harrison log cabin, cider barrel appears on both sides which are inscribed "Harrison" and "Tippecanoe," 4" h.......... **$3,600**

Courtesy of Heritage Auctions, ha.com

St. Drakes Plantation Bitters figural bottle, honey amber, 17 logs on two sides, with six logs on the remaining sides, six small raised dots under the base arranged in a circle, circa 1862, 10" h, 2-7/8" square. **$375**

Courtesy of Jeffrey S. Evans & Associates, www.jeffreyevans.com

"Doctor Fisch's Bitters" glass figural bottle, medium amber, circa 1866-1880, molded as a fish, applied collared mouth and smooth base, embossed "W. H. Ware, Patented 1866" at one side, "Doctor Fisch's Bitters" on the other, 11-3/4" h....................................... **$300**

Courtesy of Schmidt's Antiques Inc., www.schmidtsantiques.com

▶ Glass milk bottle, Los Angeles, c. 1900, embossed with Magen David and "OUR OWN DAIRIES, INC.," 5-1/4" h. **$50**

Courtesy of J. Greenstein & Co., Inc., www.jgreenstein.com

▲ Paulus Dairy-Butztown, PA milk bottle, react-text: 186, 9-1/2" h. **$70**

Courtesy of Hartzell's Auction Gallery, Inc., hartzellsauction.com

Bokale 5¢ soda fountain syrup bottle, glass label, 12" h. **$100**

Courtesy of Dan Morphy Auctions, www.morphyauctions.com

Early Coca-Cola soda fountain syrup bottle, decal on the front most likely a copy, has a rubber surface instead of a glass covering on the label, 10-1/2" h. **$225**

Courtesy of Dan Morphy Auctions, www.morphyauctions.com

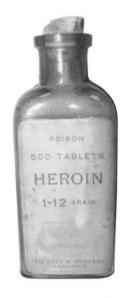

500 tablet brown glass heroin poison bottle, Eli lily and Co. original front paper label, 1-12 grain, cork stopper. **$110**

Courtesy of Lemar Auctions and Estate, lemarauctions.com

Three Goody Soda bottles with toppers, 10 and 12 ounce, two root beer and one orange, two of the toppers feature the Goody logo and one a pilot with planes in the background. **$90**

Courtesy of Paige Auction, www.paigeauction.com

Golden Drops Whiskey bottle, circa 1890s, paper label, 11" h.................................. **$1,800**

Courtesy of Dan Morphy Auctions, www.morphyauctions.com

Two blown glass gin bottles, circa 1800, the taller a clear olive green, the shorter a browner olive green, both square tapered form with rough pontils, react-text react-text: 190, 10" and 9-1/4". **$170**

Courtesy of Leland Little Auctions, www.lelandlittle.com

Bourbon back bar bottle, circa 1900, enameled lettering, horse head stopper, 13-1/2" h.......**$225**

Courtesy of Dan Morphy Auctions, www.morphyauctions.com

BRASS COLLECTIBLES

BRASS IS A yellow alloy mainly of copper and zinc but it can include other metals. Generally used for decorative articles, brass' durability makes it ideal for inlays, wall insets and tools. The inexpensive, yet strong metal makes it ubiquitous across many cultures and objects for thousands of years. In modern times, brass was particularly favored during the Art Deco Movement of the 1930s and the modernist movement of the 1960s and 70s, the complete opposite of the darkly patinated copper and bronze used during the Arts and Crafts and Art Nouveau Movements. It was also a favored metal to use for accenting firearms and swords. The metal's ability to withstand strong pressure and heat made it ideal for lanterns and locomotive pressure gauges.

Among the most heavily collected items today include chandeliers, figurines and statues, nautical items, clocks and pocket watches, and even microscopes. All of these items can be readily found at your local thrift store and flea markets. In fact, there are sellers on Etsy.com who specialize in bringing unique brass items to market.

The market for brass has been remarkably steady, but is showing signs of an upswing. Younger buyers who are attracted to simple forms and uses, particularly bookends, affordable jewelry, designer candlesticks and even furniture, favor the color. Generally, vintage examples of mass-produced bookends can be found between $5 and $50, depending on the venue. Brass figurines make attractive décor items and many brass items were produced with a practical use in mind, so many of the antiques can still be used for their intended purpose.

Solid examples of bookends are commanding higher prices these days, particularly figural examples of animals and people. High-quality castings are back in style. Low-quality castings are also holding their values (even if those values are not particularly high to begin with).

With brass, the older the object, the more value it offers to the decorator or collector. Home items from the late 1700 and early 1800s are collected based on their use. Several artists who worked in brass continue to see their values climb. Artists such as Franz and Karl Hagenauer, Josef Hoffman, Wiener Werkstatte, Peter Muller-Munk and Harry Bertoia all used brass as a medium due to its versatility. Most all of Bertoia's musical sculptures employ brass.

Unlike other decorative mediums such as silver, gold or bronze, brass can tarnish and pit heavily if left in salt water or when exposed to some household cleaning solutions

Yacht's Bell, circa late 19th/early 20th century, clapper with sailor-made rope-work pull. 9-1/2" h., 10" d. **$200**

Eldred's Auctioneers & Appraisers, www.eldreds.com

VISIT WWW.ANTIQUETRADER.COM

WWW.FACEBOOK.COM/ANTIQUETRADER

such as ammonia. Interestingly, many people are introducing artificial patinas to common, low-value brass objects for decorative effects. This can be achieved by applying vinegar, salt, some window cleaners and even hardboiled eggs. The brass object is placed into an airtight container for several hours to acquire the desired coloration, such as a ruddy, rust or green or even bronze look. Collectors should be aware of these artificial patinas if they are on the lookout for authentic pieces.

Since it is easy to make a new piece look old, it's not surprising to learn Chinese and Japanese brass objects are being heavily reproduced. Both cultures were adept at using the metal in objects and tools, but many items were made for religious ceremonies. Again, the learned collector should study commonly used designs and castings before investing a lot of resources here. Sloppy or blurry castings are a sure sign the piece is new and is only worth décor value. The market for Indian brass has plummeted due to the mass amounts of imports flooding into the country. Brass from India should only be purchased from a reputable dealer or auction house.

The key to collecting quality brass items is based on careful observation. First, a quality brass item should not have any machining or mold marks or any other evidence that modern machinery was used in the making of the piece. Second, try to find out as much as possible about the time period in which apiece was made. This will help you understand the composition of the item and where is likely came from. The best quality brass items often have maker's marks, which gives collectors much interesting stories and a source where the item was made. Unlike silver, these makers' marks are most often found on the bottom of the piece or even hidden behind felt padding on the bottom.

Candle set, three pieces including five holders with hanging crystal prisms, intricate bodies mounted to stone bases, maker unknown. $150

Heritage Auctions, www.HA.com

Door knocker, Federal Period (first half of 19th century) Connecticut, eagle-form, original hand-turned posts, 6-1/4" h. x 6-1/4" w. **$110**

Eldred's Auctioneers & Appraisers, www.eldreds.com

Wall plaques, gilt brass, first half 20th century. 10-1/4" h. x 12-1/2" w. x ¼" d. **$175**

Heritage Auctions, www.HA.com

Firescreen, partial, silvered, Art Deco, first half 20th century, 27" h. x 30-3/4" w. x 8" d. **$1,500**

Heritage Auctions, www.HA.com

Foghorn, circa first half of 20th century, marked "Siebe Gorman & Co. London", horn, walnut-mounted leather bellows and iron foot pump, height 24-1/2" h.. 22" w., 11-1/2 d. **$200**

Eldred's Auctioneers & Appraisers, www.eldreds.com

Polished brass cat paperweight, after Hagenauer, 20th century, 4-5/8" h. **$220**

Heritage Auctions, www.HA.com

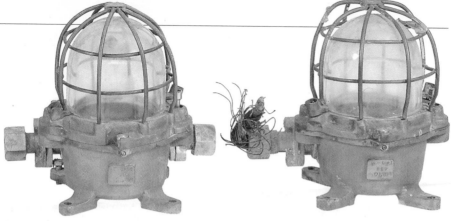

Lamps, pair, bulkheads, 20th century, 11" h. $120

Eldred's Auctioneers & Appraisers, www.eldreds.com

Badge, U.S. Army quartermaster's sergeant-cap badge, circa 1903-1910, brass and silver, unmarked. $29

Heritage Auctions, ww.HA.com

Lamps, pair, onion lamps, circa late 19th century, red glass globes, 15-1/5" h. $110

Eldred's Auctioneers & Appraisers, www.eldreds.com

Bookends, matching pair, depicting a seated child, signed Old English, undated, 2" l x 3" d x 6" w. $15

Heritage Auctions, www.HA.com

Vase, Gorham, with pair of art deco brass drama wall masks, Marks to vase: GORHAM CO, (anchor), V4444, 10-1/2" h. $310

Heritage Auctions, www.HA.com

Necklace, double-pendant, gilt on alloy necklace, commemorating a visit from the French King Louis Philippe to Queen Victoria, 1844, 17" l. **$15**

Heritage Auctions, www.HA.com

Pocket pen knife, 3" l.
.................................**$21**

Heritage Auctions, www.HA.com

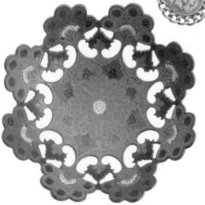

Dish, enameled Anglo-Indian, circa 1980, demi-spherical brass body with pierced wall, shaped rim and polychrome enamel decoration, underside retaining original paper label MADE IN INDIA, 9-1/2". **$24**

Heritage Auctions, www.HA.com

Candlesticks, group including prickets, circa 19-20th centuries, tallest 21-3/4" h. **$400**

Heritage Auctions, www.HA.com

Candlesticks, group of 14, Georgian style, circa early 19th century, tallest 4-1/2" h.............................**$175**

Heritage Auctions, www.HA.com

CERAMICS

belleek

THE NAME BELLEEK refers to an industrious village in County Fermanagh, Northern Ireland, on the banks of the River Erne, and to the lustrous porcelain wares produced there.

In 1849, John Caldwell Bloomfield inherited a large estate near Belleek. Interested in ceramics and having discovered rich deposits of feldspar and kaolin (china clay) on his lands, he soon envisioned a pottery that would make use of these materials, local craftspeople, and waterpower of the River Erne. He was also anxious to enhance Ireland's prestige with superior porcelain products.

Bloomfield had a chance meeting with Robert Williams Armstrong, who had established a substantial architectural business building potteries. Keenly interested in the manufacturing process, he agreed to design, build and manage the new factory for Bloomfield. The factory was to be located on Rose Isle on a bend in the River Erne.

Bloomfield and Armstrong then approached David McBirney, a highly successful merchant and director of railway companies, and enticed him to provide financing. Impressed by the plans, he agreed to raise funds for the enterprise. As agreed, the factory was named McBirney and Armstrong, then later D. McBirney and Co.

Although 1857 is given as the founding date of the pottery, it is recorded that the pottery's foundation stone was laid by Mrs. J. C. Bloomfield on Nov. 18, 1858. Although not completed until 1860, the pottery was producing earthenware from its inception.

With the arrival of ceramic experts from the (William Henry) Goss Pottery in England, principally William Bromley, Sr. and William Wood Gallimore, Parian ware was perfected and, by 1863, the wares we associate with Belleek today were in production.

With Belleek Pottery workers and others emigrating to the United States in the late 1800s and early 1900s, Belleek-style china manufacture, known as American Belleek, commenced at several American firms, including Ceramic Art Co., Colombian Art Pottery, Lenox, Inc., Ott & Brewer, and Willets Manufacturing Co.

Throughout its Parian production, Belleek Pottery marked its items with an Irish harp and wolfhound and the Devenish Tower. Its second period began with the advent of the McKinley Tariff Act of 1891 and the (revised) British Merchandise Act as Belleek added the ribbon "Co. FERMANAGH IRELAND"

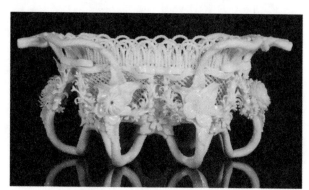

Rathmore four-strand lattice basket with coral handles and feet, circa 1920, applied porcelain ribbons and flowers, pearl glaze, signed with applied tag with impressed marks reading "Belleek (Co. Fermanagh.) Ireland," firing separation on one leaf under one handle, 5-1/4" x 11-3/4" x 6-1/2". $1,700

Courtesy of Soulis Auctions, Lone Jack, Missouri, www.dirksoulisauctions.com

beneath its mark in 1891. Both the first and second period marks were black, although they occasionally appeared in burnt orange, green, blue, or brown, especially on earthenware items. Its third period begin in 1926, when it added a Celtic emblem under the second period mark as well as the government trademark "Reg No 0857," which was granted in 1884. The Celtic emblem was registered by the Irish Industrial Development Association in 1906 and reads "Deanta in Eirinn," and means "Made in Ireland." The pottery is now utilizing its 13th mark, following a succession of three black marks, three green marks, one gold mark, two blue marks, and three green marks. The final green mark was used only a single year, in 2007, to commemorate its 150th anniversary. In 2008, Belleek changed its mark to brown. Early earthenware was often marked in the same color as the majority of its surface decoration. Early basketware has Parian strips applied to its base with the impressed verbiage "BELLEEK" and later on, additionally "Co FERMANAGH" with or without "IRELAND." Current basketware carries the same mark as its Parian counterpart.

Tridacna tea set, each item except waste bowl with first period black mark, circa 1867-1890, waste bowl marked with green 6th mark, 1965-1980, chip to cover of sugar bowl; tray 15-1/2" x 14", teapot 3-1/2" x 7-1/2", waste bowl 3" x 3-1/2", creamer 2-1/2" x 5", cups 2" x 4-1/4", saucers 5-1/4" dia........................ **$1,050**

Courtesy of Soulis Auctions, Lone Jack, Missouri, www.dirksoulisauctions.com

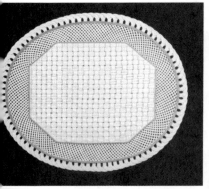

Hexagonal four-strand lattice tray with gold porcelain braid, circa 1920s, pearl glaze, signed under base with impressed porcelain tag, professionally repaired, inner rope twist rim different color of gold, restoration residue, 1-1/4" x 16-1/4" x 20-1/4". **$450**

Courtesy of Soulis Auctions, Lone Jack, Missouri, www.dirksoulisauctions.com

Three-strand lattice basket, covered, handle and flowers on lid, pearl glaze, signed under base with impressed porcelain tag, handles broken and repaired, firing separations on some floral stems on lid, 5-1/2" x 10-1/2" x 8-1/2".. **$250**

Courtesy of Soulis Auctions, Lone Jack, Missouri, www.dirksoulisauctions.com

Round four-strand covered basket, applied florals on lid, pearl glaze, signed under base with impressed porcelain tag, two hairline cracks to strands on rim, 6" x 8". **$625**

Courtesy of Soulis Auctions, Lone Jack, Missouri, www.dirksoulisauctions.com

Prince of Wales covered ice pail, vessel on stand with figural cover on cylindrical body with figures in relief raised on mermaid figural support, gold 7th mark (1980-1992) inside base, purchased in Dublin in 1983, 18-1/2" h. **$1,000**

Courtesy of Soulis Auctions, Lone Jack, Missouri, www.dirksoulisauctions.com

DeJeuner tea set plus tea kettle, all signed with second period black mark (1891-1926), standard DeJeuner arrangement of teapot, creamer, sugar, two cup and saucer sets, and tray, with matching tea kettle, teapot 7" x 7-1/2", tray 17-1/2" x 14".........................**$1,100**

Courtesy of Soulis Auctions, Lone Jack, Missouri, www.dirksoulisauctions.com

Round covered basket, four-strand lattice, two coral handles, applied flowers and clover, pearl and polychrome glaze, signed under base with impressed porcelain tags, one chipped spline on rim under one handle, 5" x 8-1/4". **$600**

Courtesy of Soulis Auctions, Lone Jack, Missouri, www.dirksoulisauctions.com

Oval four-strand porcelain basket, applied roses and clover, pearl glaze, signed under base with impressed porcelain tag, 4" x 12-1/4" x 9-1/2". **$400**

Courtesy of Soulis Auctions, Lone Jack, Missouri, www.dirksoulisauctions.com

Henshall woven four-strand porcelain basket, applied flowers and clover, overhead handle, pearl and polychrome glaze, signed under base with blue Belleek ink stamp, signed by Richard K. DengenHardt (1924-2000), founder of Belleek Collectors' International Society, hand-numbered 344-95 S, 4" x 8-3/4" x 6-3/4"...................... **$225**

Courtesy of Soulis Auctions, Lone Jack, Missouri, www.dirksoulisauctions.com

Rathmore four-strand lattice basket with coral handles and feet, applied porcelain ribbons and flowers surrounding outer basket, pearl and polychrome glaze, commissioned from Belleek factory, signed under base with impressed porcelain tags, 4-3/4" x 10" x 6" with Salem, Massachusetts Evening News article from Feb. 9, 1987, regarding commissioned piece. **$1,150**

Courtesy of Soulis Auctions, Lone Jack, Missouri, www.dirksoulisauctions.com

Two four-strand baskets: Henshall porcelain basket with two handles and applied flowers along rim, pearl and polychrome glaze, signed with impressed porcelain tags under base, 2-1/2" x 6-1/2" x 8", and Shamrock basket with applied flowers on rim, pearl and polychrome glaze, signed with impressed porcelain tags under base, 2-1/4" x 5-1/2"... **$375**

Courtesy of Soulis Auctions, Lone Jack, Missouri, www.dirksoulisauctions.com

Melvin woven four-strand square basket, applied forget-me-nots, pearl and polychrome glaze, signed under base with impressed porcelain tags, 3" x 8" x 8"...**$350**

Courtesy of Soulis Auctions, Lone Jack, Missouri, www.dirksoulisauctions.com

Henshall four-strand lattice basket, single raised handle and applied flowers, pearl and polychrome glaze, signed under base with impressed porcelain tags, 5" x 10-3/4". **$375**

Courtesy of Soulis Auctions, Lone Jack, Missouri, www.dirksoulisauctions.com

Tridacna pattern snack sets and plates, eight Tridacna snack sets with 6th green mark, eight Tridacna plates with 4th green mark, eight similar plates with 5th green mark, largest plates 10-1/4" dia. **$160**

Courtesy of Soulis Auctions, Lone Jack, Missouri, www.dirksoulisauctions.com

Contemporary Belleek articles, two objects with fifth mark, 1955-1965 period, and third with sixth green mark, 5-1/4" to 7-1/4". **$375**

Courtesy of Soulis Auctions, Lone Jack, Missouri, www.dirksoulisauctions.com

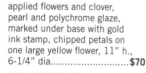

Coral and shell open salts, set of 12, each stamped with third period black mark, 1" x 3" x 1-3/4". **$140**

Courtesy of Soulis Auctions, Lone Jack, Missouri, www.dirksoulisauctions.com

◄ Tall flowered vase with applied flowers and clover, pearl and polychrome glaze, marked under base with gold ink stamp, chipped petals on one large yellow flower, 11" h., 6-1/4" dia. **$70**

Courtesy of Soulis Auctions, Lone Jack, Missouri, www.dirksoulisauctions.com

► Echinus footed bowl, covered, on raised foot with three mermaids, pearl and polychrome glaze, gold ink stamp, 8-1/4" x 4-1/2". **$275**

Courtesy of Soulis Auctions, Lone Jack, Mo.; www.dirksoulisauctions.com

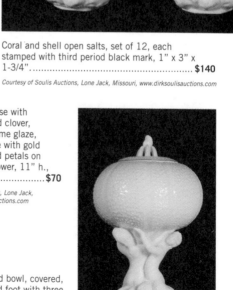

CERAMICS

buffalo pottery

INCORPORATED IN 1901 as a wholly owned subsidiary of the Larkin Soap Co., founded by John D. Larkin of Buffalo, New York, in 1875, Buffalo Pottery was a manufactory built to produce premium wares to be included with purchases of Larkin's chief product: soap.

In October 1903, the first kiln was fired and Buffalo Pottery became the only pottery in the world run entirely by electricity. In 1904, Larkin offered its first premium produced by the pottery. This concept of using premiums caused sales to skyrocket and, in 1905, the first Blue Willow pattern pottery made in the United States was introduced as a premium.

The Buffalo Pottery administrative building, built in 1904 to house 1,800 clerical workers, was the creation of a 32-year-old architect named Frank Lloyd Wright. The building was demolished in 1953.

By 1910, annual soap production peaked and the number of premiums offered in the catalogs exceeded 600. By 1915, this number had grown to 1,500. The first catalog of premiums was issued in 1893 and continued to appear through the late 1930s.

John D. Larkin died in 1926, and during the Great Depression, the firm suffered severe losses, going into bankruptcy in 1940. After World War II, the pottery resumed production under new management, but its vitreous wares were generally limited to mass-produced china for the institutional market.

Among the pottery lines produced during Buffalo's heyday were Blue Willow (1905-1916), Gaudy Willow (1905-1916), Deldare Ware (1908-1909, 1923-1925), Abino Ware (1911-1913), historical and commemorative plates, and unique hand-painted jugs and pitchers. In the 1920s and 1930s, the firm concentrated on personalized wares for commercial clients including hotels, clubs, railroads, and restaurants.

For more information on Buffalo Pottery, see *Antique Trader Pottery & Porcelain Ceramics Price Guide*, 7th edition.

— Phillip M. Sullivan

Two Deldare plates, circa 1911, "MISFORTUNE AT TULIP HALL" and "DR SYNTAX SOLILOQUISING," artist signatures, each marked "1911 / BUFFALO / POTTERY / EMERALD / DELDARE / WARE / UNDERGLAZE," Buffalo, New York, some crazing and wear, 7-3/8" dia., 8-3/8" dia. **$222**

Courtesy of Jeffrey S. Evans & Associates, www.jeffreysevans.com

Deldare garden seat/ jardinière stand, circa 1908, "The Great Controversy," "All you have to do [is] teach the Dutchman / English," "Ye Lion Inn" on top, signed "W. FORRESTER," black printed mark on base, Buffalo over sign: "MADE AT / ye / BUFFALO / POTTERY / DELDARE WARE / UNDERGLAZE / 1908," Buffalo, New York, some crazing, 13-7/16" h. **$702**

Courtesy of Jeffrey S. Evans & Associates, www.jeffreysevans.com

Deldare calendar plate, circa 1910, whimsical polychrome designs of fairies, insects, and birds on the rim and interior and 1910 calendar dates, "W.FOSTER" artist signature, black printed mark on base, Buffalo over sign: "MADE AT / ye / BUFFALO / POTTERY / DELDARE WARE / UNDERGLAZE," 1910 date mark, Buffalo, New York, 9-3/8" dia... **$164**

Courtesy of Jeffrey S. Evans & Associates, www.jeffreysevans.com

Deldare jardinière, circa 1909, "Ye Lion Inn," signed "W. FOSTER," black printed mark on base with Buffalo over sign: "MADE AT / ye / BUFFALO / POTTERY / DELDARE WARE / UNDERGLAZE / 1909," Buffalo, New York, some crazing, 9-1/8" h x 12" dia. (opening). **$1,053**

Courtesy of Jeffrey S. Evans & Associates, www.jeffreysevans.com

Deldare tall tankard pitcher, circa 1909, straight-sided, polychrome design "The Fallowfield Hunt / The Hunt Supper," artist signed by "P.HALL," black printed mark on base with Buffalo over sign: "MADE AT / ye / BUFFALO / POTTERY / DELDARE WARE / UNDERGLAZE / 1909," Buffalo, New York, 12-1/8" h. **$152**

Courtesy of Jeffrey S. Evans & Associates, www.jeffreysevans.com

CERAMICS

Deldare tankard pitcher, circa 1909, octagonal, paneled body with high spout and molded handle, polychrome design "Ye Lion / INN / Ye Old English Village," artist signed by "J. NEKOLA," black printed mark on base with Buffalo over sign: "MADE AT / ye / BUFFALO / POTTERY / DELDARE WARE / UNDERGLAZE / 1909," Buffalo, New York, 9-3/4" h. .**$82**

Deldare Waldorf Lunch anniversary platter, circa 1915, "Waldorf / Lunch" at top center, "REOPENING OF WALDORF LUNCH No. ONE," made for the 11th anniversary, "Dancing ye Minuet" design, signed "J. GERHARDT," black printed mark on base with Buffalo over sign: "MADE AT / ye / BUFFALO / POTTERY / DELDARE WARE / UNDERGLAZE," 1909 date mark, Buffalo, New York, 12-1/8" x 9-1/8"...**$468**

Two Deldare Dr. Syntax plates, circa 1910, "SYNTAX STAR GAZING" and "emerald" Deldare design for ground and edge, artist signature, marked "1911 / BUFFALO / POTTERY / EMERALD / DELDARE / WARE / UNDERGLAZE"; one blue transfer plate, "Doctor Syntax / disputing his / Bill with the / Landlady," marked on base "BUFFALO POTTERY / SEMI-VITREOUS / 1909," Buffalo, New York, minor wear, crazing, 9-3/8" dia. **$322**

Deldare Heirlooms platter/ tray, circa 1908, polychrome "Heirlooms" design, three women in colonial dress around a table, houses with fencing and landscapes as the border, artist's signature "W. FOSTER" [William Foster] in lower left corner, black printed mark on back with Buffalo over sign: "MADE AT / ye / BUFFALO / POTTERY / DELDARE WARE / UNDERGLAZE / 1908," Buffalo, New York, minor crazing and wear, 13-3/4" x 10-1/2".. **$117**

Courtesy of Jeffrey S. Evans & Associates, www.jeffreysevans.com

Deldare humidor, circa 1910, "YE LION INN" design on sides and cover, intertwining artists' initials, black printed mark on base with Buffalo over sign: "MADE AT / ye / BUFFALO / POTTERY / DELDARE WARE / UNDERGLAZE," Buffalo, New York, 6-7/8" h. **$263**

Courtesy of Jeffrey S. Evans & Associates, www.jeffreysevans.com

Deldare emerald Art Nouveau plate, circa 1911, floral geometric medallion in the center, "emerald" design on edge with artist signature "B. WILLON [or WILLOW]," marked "1911 / BUFFALO / POTTERY / EMERALD / DELDARE / WARE / UNDERGLAZE," Buffalo, New York, 8-3/8" dia. **$222**

Courtesy of Jeffrey S. Evans & Associates, www.jeffreysevans.com

Deldare shield back candle holder, circa 1909, men in colonial dress on back of interior, houses on candle holder and interior base, black printed mark on base with Buffalo over sign: "MADE AT / ye / BUFFALO / POTTERY / DELDARE WARE / UNDERGLAZE," 1909 date mark, Buffalo, New York, small glaze flake, 6-7/8" h. **$293**

Courtesy of Jeffrey S. Evans & Associates, www.jeffreysevans.com

CERAMICS

Native American tall ceramic pitcher, first quarter 20th c., green ground, polychrome images of two Native American chiefs, marked below designs "CHIEF HOLLOW HORN BEAR / (SIOUX)" and "CHIEF WOLF ROBE / (CHEYENNE)," embossed floral decoration at base, marked with small purple transfer "BUFFALO / POTTERY" on base, Buffalo, New York, minor wear, crazing, 14" h. **$129**

Courtesy of Jeffrey S. Evans & Associates, www.jeffreysevans.com

Albino Ware Ralph Stuart plate, circa 1912, neutral tone design of windmill and several boats with artist signature "R. STUART," likely for Ralph Stuart, hand-painted "BUFFALO / POTTERY / 1912 / ABINO WARE / No 231" on base, Buffalo, New York, some crazing, 6-5/16" dia. **$176**

Courtesy of Jeffrey S. Evans & Associates, www.jeffreysevans.com

Four Fallowfield Hunt articles, circa 1935: one cup, 2-1/8" h, one dish, 5-1/4" dia., one dish, 7-3/4" dia., one plate, 7-3/16" dia., with "Ye Olde / Ivory" ground, all with variations of the "Fallowfield Hunt" design, marked "Ye Olde / Ivory / Buffalo China" on base and additional "DBF," Buffalo, New York. **$94**

Courtesy of Jeffrey S. Evans & Associates, www.jeffreysevans.com

Jasperware John D. Larkin medallion, 1925, profile of John D. Larkin, the founder of Larkin Soap and Buffalo Pottery, in a white clay over a rich dark blue ground, inscribed on back: "John D. Larkin / Oct 5 1925 / made at / Buffalo Pottery / Wood," Buffalo, New York, minor scuffs, 5-3/4" x 7-1/8".
.... **$263**

Courtesy of Jeffrey S. Evans & Associates, www.jeffreysevans.com

Rip Van Winkle ceramic pitcher, circa 1906, brown transfer designs of young and old Rip Van W inkle on opposite sides and polychrome overpaint, marked in brown transfer "BUFFALO / POTTERY / 1906 / UNDERGLAZE / WARRANTED," Buffalo, New York, crazing, minor staining, 5-7/8" h.. **$94**

Courtesy of Jeffrey S. Evans & Associates, www.jeffreysevans.com

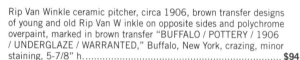

Blue Willow ceramic wash set, circa 1910, lot of eight: pitcher, 11-1/2" h; basin, 16-3/4" dia.; pitcher, 7-3/4" h; covered soap dish with draining disc; toothbrush mug; vase, 4-7/8" h; chamber pot with cover, 7-1/2" h; slop jar, 9-1/8" h, all having blue chinoiserie transfer design in the "Blue Willow" pattern, all marked "SEMI-VITREOUS / BUFFALO POTTERY," with date marks ranging from 1910-1911, three pieces with additional "NYMPH" below mark, Buffalo, New York, five pieces undamaged, others with light hairlines, small flakes, glaze crazing and staining. **$222**

Courtesy of Jeffrey S. Evans & Associates, www.jeffreysevans.com

CERAMICS

Tom and Jerry footed punch bowl and 12 cups, circa 1930, yellow clay and black transfer lettering reading "Tom and Jerry," all marked "Colorido Ware / Buffalo China / MADE IN U.S.A.," Buffalo, New York, two minor manufacturing flaws, cups 3-7/8" h, punch bowl 6-5/8" h x 11-1/4" dia. **$59**

Courtesy of Jeffrey S. Evans & Associates, www.jeffreysevans.com

Fourteen American historical plates, first quarter 20th c., all with dark green rims, monochrome and polychrome designs of each view of Independence Hall, the US Capitol, Faneuil Hall, the White House, Niagara Falls, Mount Vernon; one plate with Martha Washington, one plate with George Washington, both in green, marked "BUFFALO / POTTERY," some with "SEMI-VITREOUS," some with eagle emblem on base, several with painted 1906, 1907, and 1908 dates, Buffalo, New York, one 1/2" bruise on rim, two hairlines, 7-1/2" dia. to 7-11/16" dia..**$82**

Courtesy of Jeffrey S. Evans & Associates, www.jeffreysevans.com

top lot!

Roosevelt Bears ceramic pitcher, circa 1907, paneled, with four sides, having "ROOSEVELT / BEARS" on front of the spout, brown and polychrome transfer designs with images of the bears and text from the stories, brown transfer mark on base with "BUFFALO / POTTER / 1907 / COPYRIGHT EDWARD STERN & C / UNDERGLAZE / WARRANTED," Buffalo, New York, 8" h.
"The Roosevelt Bears, Their Travels and Adventures," written by Seymour Eaton and illustrated by V. Floyd Campbell, first appeared in 1905 as a newspaper series and follows Teddy-B and Teddy-G through their adventurous trip to the eastern United States.
.... $702

Three Gaudy Willow saucers, 1905, scalloped rims with brown transfer "Willow" design and "Gaudy" polychrome enamel coloring with gilding, all marked "FIRST OLD WILLOW WARE / MANUFACTURED IN / AMERICA / BUFFALO POTTERY / 1905," some additional codes and painters' numbers and marks, Buffalo, New York, 6" dia. **$82**

Courtesy of Jeffrey S. Evans & Associates, www.jeffreysevans.com

top lot

Fred Harvey Thunderbird plate, circa 1930, "Thunderbird" logo design used by the Harvey enterprise for advertising with Art Deco geometric designs above and below bird and scalloped polychrome lines on edge, interlocking "FH" on edge, possibly made as a prototype, marked on base "COLORIDO / WARE / BUFFALO / CHINA / PATENT APPLIED FOR," small brown painted line near foot rim, minor wear on front surface, 9-3/4" dia. $1,989

Fred Harvey created one of the first chain restaurants through the Atchison, Topeka & Santa Fe Railway (AT&SF) with restaurants along the rail line. Known as Harvey Houses with the waitresses referred to as "Harvey Girls," the restaurant model developed into hotels lines and tourism including the "Indian Detours" tours with automobiles called "Harvey Cars." Special thanks to the Restaurant Ware Collectors Network (www.restaurantwarecollectors.com) for their help identifying this pattern.

Three Blue Willow graduated pitchers, 1906-1907, all having an ovoid form with molded spout, dark cobalt blue handles, and gilding, all with a blue chinoiserie transfer design in the "Blue Willow" pattern, marked "Buffalo Pottery" on base, 1906 and 1907 date marks, Buffalo, New York, one short manufacturing hairline, some wear to gilding, glaze crazing, some staining, 5-1/2" h to 7" h. **$105**

Courtesy of Jeffrey S. Evans & Associates, www.jeffreysevans.com

Five Blue Willow graduated platters, 1908-1916, all with blue chinoiserie transfer design in the "Blue Willow" pattern, all marked "SEMI-VITREOUS / BUFFALO POTTERY," with date marks ranging from 1908-1916, Buffalo, New York, some glaze crazing and staining, sizes from 10-3/4" x 8-3/4" to 14-1/4" x 18-1/8". **$199**

Courtesy of Jeffrey S. Evans & Associates, www.jeffreysevans.com

CERAMICS

chinese export porcelain

LARGE QUANTITIES OF porcelain have been made in China for export to America from the 1780s, much of it shipped from the ports of Canton and Nanking. A major source of this porcelain was Ching-te-Chen in Kiangsi province, but wares were also made elsewhere. The largest quantities were blue and white. Prices fluctuate considerably, depending on age, condition, decoration and other variables.

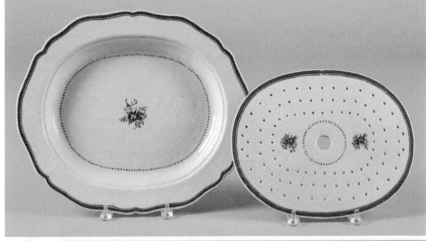

Two blue and white platters, 19th c., both with strainer inserts, 13-1/4" l x 16" w, 15" l x 18" w. **$720**

Courtesy of Pook & Pook, Inc., www.pookandpook.com

VISIT WWW.ANTIQUETRADER.COM

WWW.FACEBOOK.COM/ANTIQUETRADER

Five-piece garniture: two covered jars, three flared vases, 19th c., underglaze blue with gilt decoration, polychromed reserves of birds and flowers, both covers restored, one jar with rim chips, tallest 9-1/2" h. **$3,250**

Courtesy of Leslie Hindman Auctioneers, www.lesliehindman.com

Eight Canton plates, 19th c., three plates with small hairline, one with rim chip, 8-1/2" dia. **$225**

Courtesy of Pook & Pook, Inc., www.pookandpook.com

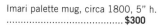

Imari palette mug, circa 1800, 5" h. **$300**

Courtesy of Pook & Pook, Inc., www.pookandpook.com

CERAMICS

Pseudo tobacco leaf platter, 19th c., 11" l x 14-3/8" w. **$1,599**

Courtesy of Pook & Pook, Inc., www.pookandpook.com

Pair of Canton candlesticks, 19th c., 7" h. **$660**

Courtesy of Pook & Pook, Inc., www.pookandpook.com

Teapot, 19th c., small rim flake, 5-1/2" h. **$88**

Courtesy of Pook & Pook, Inc., www.pookandpook.com

▲ ▼ Pink lotus bowl and tea caddy, bowl 3-1/4" h x 7" dia., caddy 5-1/8" h. **$270**

Courtesy of Pook & Pook, Inc., www.pookandpook.com

Two chargers, circa 1800, depicting immortals in combat, nobleman and consort, 11" dia. **$1,968**

Courtesy of Pook & Pook, Inc., www.pookandpook.com

Five pieces of Chinese Export blue and white porcelain, 19th c.: water bottle, 8-3/4" h, pitcher, sauce tureen, teapot, and covered bowl. **$720**

Courtesy of Pook & Pook, Inc., www.pookandpook.com

Famille Rose porcelain candlesticks, 19th c., modeled as foo dogs, 7" l. **$2,750**

Courtesy of Leslie Hindman Auctioneers, www.lesliehindman.com

▲ ▶ Punch bowl, circa 1800, pink floral decoration, 4-3/4" h x 11-1/4" dia.................. **$308**

Courtesy of Pook & Pook, Inc., www.pookandpook.com

▲ ▶ Bowl, circa 1800, figural decoration, 4-1/2" h x 10-1/4" dia. **$431**

Courtesy of Pook & Pook, Inc., www.pookandpook.com

Pair Famille Rose porcelain garden seats, 19th c., minor chips to glazing and paint, 19-1/2" h. **$688**

Courtesy of Leslie Hindman Auctioneers, www.lesliehindman.com

Canton tureen and undertray, 19th c., 9" h x 13" w. **$480**

Courtesy of Pook & Pook, Inc., www.pookandpook.com

▶ ▼ Canton reticulated basket and undertray, 19th c., 4-3/4" h x 11" w. $277

Courtesy of Pook & Pook, Inc., www.pookandpook.com

▶ Covered vase, 19th c., sepia reserves on pale orange ground with gilt and purple grapevine decoration, foo dog finial, 12" h. $225

Courtesy of Leslie Hindman Auctioneers, www.lesliehindman.com

◀ Pair Famille Rose vases, 19th c., raised trailing vine decoration with cartouches of figures in garden settings, mounted as lamps, one wooden leg broken, vase 12-1/4" h.**$2,750**

Courtesy of Leslie Hindman Auctioneers, www.lesliehindman.com

C

Pair vases, Rose Medallion, two pair of Foo Dogs and four dragon figures, subdivided with panels: two panels depicting an aristocratic family enjoying the out of doors and two display colorful flower garden w/ butterflies and exotic birds, both with red Chinese lettering in circle, 15" h........ **$100**

Courtesy of Mark Mussio, Humler & Nolan, www.humlernolan.com

Charger, flowering branches within alternating panels enclosing birds and plants, small rim chip, minor pitting, 14-1/2" dia. **$50**

Courtesy of Leslie Hindman Auctioneers, www.lesliehindman.com

Platter, 19th c., orange floral decoration, 14-1/2" l x 17" w. **$277**

Courtesy of Pook & Pook, Inc., www.pookandpook.com

Pair Rose Famille Verte vases with covers, foo dog finials, minor gilt loss, 13-1/2" h. **$238**

Courtesy of Leslie Hindman Auctioneers, www.lesliehindman.com

◀ Two Rose Medallion candlesticks, 19th c., 7-3/4" h. **$200**

Courtesy of Pook & Pook, Inc., www.pookandpook.com

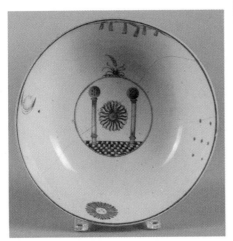

Arms of New York porcelain plate, late 18th/early 19th c., small gilt stars painted over a dark blue ground on rim with central polychrome design of the Arms of New York depicting Liberty and Justice as well as acorns, unmarked, gilt overpaint on minute rim flake, 7-7/8" dia. **$497**

Courtesy of Jeffrey S. Evans & Associates, www.jeffreysevans.com

Masonic bowl, circa 1800, broken in half and reglued, two 4" hairlines, 4-3/4" h. x 11-3/8" dia. **$450**

Courtesy of Pook & Pook, Inc., www.pookandpook.com

Rose Canton deep bowl, 19th c., minor gilt loss, 15-3/4" dia. **$750**

Courtesy of Leslie Hindman Auctioneers, www.lesliehindman.com

Urn, late 19th/early 20th c., having underglaze blue floral, bird, and insect designs, unmarked, 12-5/8" h. **$761**

Courtesy of Jeffrey S. Evans & Associates, www.jeffreysevans.com

Pair Canton trays, 19th c., elongated octagonal form, river landscape, crazing, discoloration, grime deposits, pitting, minor edge chip, 9-5/8" w. **$688**

Courtesy of Leslie Hindman Auctioneers, www.lesliehindman.com

CERAMICS

coalport porcelain

COALPORT PORCELAIN WORKS (John Rose & Co.) operated at Coalport, Shropshire, England, from about 1795 to 1926. In 1926, production was moved to Staffordshire. Since 1951 the firm has operated as Coalport China, Ltd., producing bone china.

Coalbrookdale dresser tray with receptacles for two covered jars, 20th century, each piece signed "Coalbrookdale by Coalport" in blue, tray 12-1/2" x 10". **$775**

Courtesy of Soulis Auctions, Lone Jack, Missouri, www.dirksoulisauctions.com

Coalbrookdale basket, cartouche-form, with applied porcelain florals on asymmetrical form with embossed scrolls at border trimmed in gold, interior with hand-painted florals and insects, 4-1/2" x 12" x 9-1/4". **$350**

Courtesy of Soulis Auctions, Lone Jack, Missouri, www.dirksoulisauctions.com

Three Coalbrookdale covered pieces, vase with two smaller covered containers, each piece signed in blue, chipped flowers on lid of one small jar, largest 8-1/2" x 5". **$160**

Courtesy of Soulis Auctions, Lone Jack, Missouri, www.dirksoulisauctions.com

Coalbrookdale teapot and sugar, both signed "Coalbrookdale by Coalport" on base, teapot 7" x 6-3/4". **$500**

Courtesy of Soulis Auctions, Lone Jack, Missouri, www.dirksoulisauctions.com

Coalbrookdale tazza with applied porcelain florals in high relief, centered by hand-painted lakeside view, 3-1/4" x 9-1/2" x 7-1/4"........................ **$150**

Courtesy of Soulis Auctions, Lone Jack, Missouri, www.dirksoulisauctions.com

Eight bone china service plates with classical motifs for Tiffany, late 19th century, each plate with different profile head of classical god or goddess in one of six pink medallions, pale orange borders and white husk swags, green-printed Coalport mark and gilt mark for retailer Tiffany & Co., 10-1/4" dia... **$320**

Courtesy of Brunk Auctions, www.brunkauctions.com

Pair of painted porcelain portrait vases, circa 1915, Lavinia & Dorothy, Shropshire, England, marked "COALPORT, ENGLAND, (crown), as. 1750, V5299," light rubbing to gilt decoration, 13-1/2" h... **$1,500**

Courtesy of Heritage Auctions, www.ha.com

Partial coffee service in Japanese Grove design, circa 1890, Aesthetic Movement, underglaze blue, gilt ground.. **$638**

Courtesy of Strawser Auctions, www.strawserauctions.com

Ten gilt decorated cabinet plates, retailed by Pitkin and Brooks, Chicago, each with raised gilt scalloped border on cream ground, 10" dia.
.... **$1,008**

Courtesy of Clars Auction Gallery, www.clars.com

Indian Tree china service, 74 pieces, 16 dinner plates, 10-3/4" dia.; 11 dessert plates; 12 bread plates, 6" dia.; 17 teacups; 17 saucers; and creamer, two broken plates. **$445**

Courtesy of Michaan's Auctions, www.michaans.com

CERAMICS

contemporary

THE PROLIFIC TREND of contemporary ceramics appearing in museum exhibits, auctions and at shows the last few years has not gone unnoticed. In many cases, American ceramic art is gaining respect and preference as the medium of choice of many of today's most popular artists. The versatile and inexpensive material is easy to manipulate. The artist may express fine details of figurative sculptures or ugly mugs, such as popular face jugs, which were first made as early as the 14th century.

"We are just now adopting the perception of ceramics as fine art," said Katie Nartonis, director of 20th & 21st Century Art at Heritage Auctions in Dallas. "California gave rise to an active American ceramic art scene since the 1950s, and studio ceramics are getting a second glance from collectors as well."

It is always easy to find modern ceramics at garage sales and thrift stores, but it's not always easy to recognize the artist or an object's potential value upon first inspection. That fact almost cost the Caddo Indian Nation a rare piece of pottery that turned up in a Goodwill thrift store donation box. Goodwill placed the pear-form, 7-1/2-inch piece of pottery, decorated with two rows of symmetrical raised spikes, up for bids on shopgoodwill.com, the charity's online auction website. Buyers placed bids before a few astute historians alerted Goodwill of its potential historical value. Sure enough, tucked deep inside was a note that stated the item was "found in a burial mound near Spiro, Oklahoma, in 1970."

Historians think the simple ceramic pot originated from Oklahoma's Spiro Mounds archaeological site and could be thousands of years old. Members of the Caddo Indian Nation maintained a permanent settlement from approximately 800 to 1450, but they have inhabited the general area for 8,000 years. Goodwill returned the piece to the tribe.

Several 20th century modern and contemporary artists known more for their watercolors or oils expanded into ceramics. Collectors avidly pursue Wassily Kandinsky's glazed porcelain cups and saucers, which he produced in 1923. A pair recently sold for $1,250, an affordable sum compared to the artist's famed geometric and abstract paintings, which have sold for $1.6 million.

Bowl, Vivika & Otto Heino, incised and modeled decoration, browns, cream and blue glazes, incised Vivika + Otto, 4-3/4" h x 8-3/4" at widest point **$200**

Courtesy of Mark Mussio, Humler & Nolan, www.humlernolan.com

Lidded box, William Wyman (studied under Charles Abbott at the Massachusetts College of Art), incised Wyman '56, 3-1/4" h x 4-7/8" dia. **$80**

Courtesy of Mark Mussio, Humler & Nolan, www.humlernolan.com

VISIT WWW.ANTIQUETRADER.COM

WWW.FACEBOOK.COM/ANTIQUETRADER

Tall vase, Polia Pillin, signed Pillin in black slip, fine overall crazing, 12" h. **$850**

Courtesy of Mark Mussio, Humler & Nolan, www.humlernolan.com

Feelie, Rose Cabat, white with blue glaze, inscribed "Cabat, A," fine overall crazing, 3-5/8" h. **$375**

Courtesy of Mark Mussio, Humler & Nolan, www.humlernolan.com

Vase, Polia Pillin, three women, each netting small fish, Pillin in black slip, fine overall crazing, single tiny glaze nick, 9" h. **$500**

Courtesy of Mark Mussio, Humler & Nolan, www.humlernolan.com

Vase, Paul Katrich, luster glaze, dark blue ground with lighter blue, gold and red clouds, Katrich wafer seal and original #1544 tag, 6-3/8" h. **$400**

Courtesy of Mark Mussio, Humler & Nolan, www.humlernolan.com

Vase, Bizarre by Clarice Cliff, orange and maroon rings on the bottom half and a floral decoration above, marks: Gloria in orange slip, "hand painted Bizarre by Clarice Cliff Newport Pottery England" in black, 7-7/8" h. **$170**

Courtesy of Mark Mussio, Humler & Nolan, www.humlernolan.com

Vase, Paul Katrich Studio, luster ware, hypnotizing coiled design raised on front, back in gold and copper luster with cobalt blue and silvery white, Paul Katrich raised Grecian Sphinx trademark, 6-1/2" h.. **$500**

Courtesy of Mark Mussio, Humler & Nolan, www.humlernolan.com

Porcelain vase, carved and painted by Stephanie Young, signed and dated on the bottom along with "Toiler # 2" notation. Toilers are pieces made by the artist to be used as fund-raisers for appropriate causes. In this case, the recipient was The Soaring Hawks Foundation to benefit students at Ethel M. Taylor Academy, a pre-kindergarten through sixth grade Cincinnati Public School located in the Millvale area of Western Cincinnati, 13-7/8" h. **$2,100**

Courtesy of Mark Mussio, Humler & Nolan, www.humlernolan.com

Dodie Thayer Lettuce Ware tureen, cover, undertray, 20th c., tureen incised Dodie Thayer Jupiter '90 under foot, tray incised Dodie Thayer, minor craquelure, 7-1/2" h x 13-1/4" dia. **$4,375**

Courtesy of Leslie Hindman Auctioneers, www.lesliehindman.com

Bottle vase, William and Polia Pillin, luster glaze, incised W + P Pillin, 6-5/8" h......................... **$275**

Courtesy of Mark Mussio, Humler & Nolan, www.humlernolan.com

Bowl, Vivika & Otto Heino, incised and modeled decoration, coppery brown crystalline glaze, light blue and yellow highlights, incised Vivika + Otto, 4-1/4" h x 9" at widest point. **$3,325**

Courtesy of Mark Mussio, Humler & Nolan, www.humlernolan.com

Charger, Aaron Bohrod for Century House, incised with trio of smiling fish among coiled designs and covered in a jet black high glaze, incised "Century House, Aaron Bohrod, 1951," 11-3/4" dia. **$400**

Courtesy of Mark Mussio, Humler & Nolan, www.humlernolan.com

Low bowl, hand thrown, Ed and Mary Scheier, painted faces inside bowl, incised Scheier on underside, edge nick, 1" h x 6-7/8" dia. **$180**

Courtesy of Mark Mussio, Humler & Nolan, www.humlernolan.com

▶ Two Marvin Blackmore, Blackmore Studios rainbow vases, circa 2000, intricately carved, slip-covered and etched earthenware, with hummingbirds, eagle, and bear, Dolores, Colo., with studio certificates of authenticity, 7" x 8", 6" x 9" **$3,500**

Courtesy of Rago Arts, www.ragoarts.com

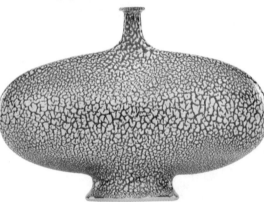

Zoomorphic glazed stoneware bottle, 1950s, stoppered, incised circles, by Leza McVey (1907-1984), Cleveland, Ohio, glazed stoneware, incised Leza, 6-1/2" x 3-1/2". **$2,625**

Courtesy of Rago Arts, www.ragoarts.com

Elongated vase, by Brother Thomas Bezanson (1929-2007), blue kairagi glaze, Weston, Vt., glazed porcelain, no visible markings, 8" x 11-1/2" x 3-1/2". **$2,500**

Courtesy of Rago Arts, www.ragoarts.com

Bowl, Gertrud and Otto Natzler, 1963, Los Angeles, Calif., signed NATZLER, original paper label M595, 2-1/2" T-line from rim, 4" x 10". **$1,188**

Courtesy of Rago Arts, www.ragoarts.com

Acoma Pottery olla vase, polychrome, signed "OPHELIA.S.LEON," 9" x 11". **$150**

Courtesy of Soulis Auctions, Lone Jack, Mo.; www.dirksoulisauctions.com

CERAMICS

CERAMICS

cowan

R. GUY COWAN opened his first pottery studio in 1912 in Lakewood, Ohio. The pottery operated almost continuously, with the exception of a break during World War I, at various locations in the Cleveland area until it was forced to close in 1931 due to financial difficulties.

Many of the 20th century's finest artists began with Cowan and its associate, the Cleveland School of Art. This fine art pottery, particularly the designer pieces, is highly sought after by collectors.

Many people are unaware that it was due to R. Guy Cowan's perseverance and tireless work that art pottery is today considered an art form and found in many art museums.

For more information on Cowan pottery, see *Antique Trader Pottery & Porcelain Ceramics Price Guide*, 7th edition.

Vase, Larkspur Blue Luster glaze with iridescence or oilspot effect, marked "Cowan" in ink on base and "635," 9-5/8" h. x 3-3/8" w. top, 3-5/8" w. base. **$78**

Courtesy of Fusco Auctions, www.fuscoauctions.com

◄ Candlestick in shape of groundhog holding candleholder with open book with inscription "Light Seeking Light Doth Light of Light Beguile," 1925, green mottled matte glaze, designed by Frank Nelson Wilcox (Cleveland School, 1887-1964) and produced from 1912-1931, made for Rowfant Club of Cleveland, Ohio, signed underneath by R. C. Cowan, number 98 of 156, repair to base, 9-1/4" h., 5-1/8" base. **$510**

Courtesy of Fusco Auctions, www. fuscoauctions.com

▲ Ivory seahorse candleholders, bottoms marked with Cowan logo, 4-1/4" h. x 4-1/4" w. **$40**

Courtesy of Just Art Pottery, www.justartpottery.com

top lot

Schreckengost made this important early piece after his return from Vienna while working for Cowan Pottery in Cleveland. It was included in the first one-man show of his career in Akron, Ohio in 1931. Provenance includes these exhibitions: Akron Art Institute, Akron, Ohio, "One Man Show," 1931; W. & J. Sloane, New York, 1931; Syracuse Museum of Fine Arts, Syracuse, New York, "2nd Ceramics National Exhibition," 1933; Fort Wayne Museum, Fort Wayne, Indiana, "One Man Show," 1936; Halle Brothers, Cleveland, Ohio, "Contemporary Designers Show," 1937; and Reinberger Gallery, Cleveland Institute of Art, Cleveland, Ohio, "Viktor Schreckengost: Retrospective Exhibition," March 14-April 3, 1976.

Charger, "Early Greek" by Viktor Schreckengost (American, 1906-2008), 1931, hand-thrown glazed earthenware, signed in underglaze "VIKTOR SCHRECKENGOST / COWAN POTTERY," 14-3/4" dia..**$5,250**

▶ Charger, Viktor Schreckengost "Danse Moderne" (Jazz Plate), 1931, impressed circular Cowan logo and "Cowan" in block letters, front coated with clear acrylic, 11-1/4" dia. **$5,000**
Courtesy of Mark Mussio, Humler & Nolan, www.humlernolan.com

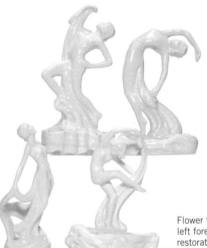

Flower frogs, four nudes: Pavlova with tight line in left forearm, Heavenward, Repose, and Grace with restoration to right arm, all with impressed Cowan logos, all with crazing, tallest 7-7/8" h. **$600**

Courtesy of Mark Mussio, Humler & Nolan, www.humlernolan.com

CERAMICS

dedham

DEDHAM POTTERY WAS originally organized in 1866 by Alexander W. Robertson in Chelsea, Massachusetts, and became A.W. & H. Roberson in 1868. In 1872, the name was changed to Chelsea Keramic Art Works and in 1891 to Chelsea Pottery, U.S.A. About 1895, the pottery was moved to Dedham, Massachusetts, and was renamed Dedham Pottery. Production ceased in 1943. High-fired colored wares and crackleware were specialties. The rabbit is said to have been the most popular decoration in blue on crackleware.

Morning/night pitcher with raised rooster and smiling sun on one side and raised owl and moon on opposite, 5" h.; magnolia pattern plate, 6" dia.; eggcup, rabbit, 2-1/4" h.; and two double eggcups, rabbit, 3" h. **$406**

Courtesy of Willis Henry Auctions, Inc., www.willishenryauctions.com

CERAMICS

Salad bowl with two-ear rabbit, 3-1/2" h., 8-3/4" dia., and charger with two-ear rabbit, two incised rabbit tails on bottom, 12-1/4" dia..................**$438**

Courtesy of Willis Henry Auctions, Inc., www.willishenryauctions.com

Rare hexagonal cheese dish with 10 two-ear rabbits, blue decal on back, 7" w.; rare hexagonal cheese dish with horse chestnut design, blue decal, 7" w.; and rare lotus-edged serving bowl with 12-rabbit border, blue decal on bottom, 1-1/2" h., 9-1/4" dia. **$469**

Courtesy of Willis Henry Auctions, Inc., www.willishenryauctions.com

Three iris pattern plates, 8-1/2" dia., first in dark cobalt with impressed rabbit tail and rectangular blue decal on bottom; second with lighter blue decoration, blue decal, rim chip; and third with small circle signature in one iris, impressed rabbit tail and decal on bottom, rim chip; with plate with seven irises on blue leaf background, tight crackle, two impressed rabbit tails and blue decal on bottom, 9-3/4" dia. **$250**

Courtesy of Willis Henry Auctions, Inc., www.willishenryauctions.com

Two horse chestnut pattern plates, both with rabbit decals on back, 8-1/2" dia.; two grape pattern plates in deep cobalt blue, both with decals on reverse, 8-1/2" dia.; and snow tree pattern plate, blue decal on reverse, small rim chip, 8-1/2" dia. **$250**

Courtesy of Willis Henry Auctions, Inc., www.willishenryauctions.com

Seven rabbit plates, various Dedham and Chelsea artists, three rare plates stamped "E E" with Chelsea Pottery marks (1881-1895), some with impressed rabbit tails, some with blue decals, 8-1/4" to 8-1/2" dia. **$375**

Courtesy of Willis Henry Auctions, Inc., www.willishenryauctions.com

Rare duck pattern charger, 10 swimming ducks with water lilies, blue rabbit decal on bottom, 12" dia.; plate with eight ducks, two impressed rabbit tails and blue decal on bottom, chipping on foot, hairline at rim, slightly raised surface, 10" dia.; and plate with raised tufted duck, medium dark blue, impressed rabbit tail on back, 8-1/2" dia..**$250**

Courtesy of Willis Henry Auctions, Inc., www.willishenryauctions.com

Lotus pattern edged serving bowl, blue decal on bottom, 2" h., 9" dia.; two plates with rabbit decals, one with minor rim chips, other with rim chip and crack, 8-1/2" dia.; and two azalea pattern chargers, both with blue rabbit decals on bottom, 11-3/4" and 12" dia..............**$531**

Courtesy of Willis Henry Auctions, Inc., www.willishenryauctions.com

Four plates, each with blue ink stamp on base, three 6" dia., one 8-3/8" dia. **$218**

Courtesy of Conestoga Auction Co., www.conestogaauction.com

Three plates, each with two-ear rabbit border and blue ink stamp on base, 6" dia., 8-1/2" dia., and 10" dia. **$61**

Courtesy of Conestoga Auction Co., www.conestogaauction.com

CERAMICS

Coffeepot with rabbit band at bottom of handle, separate dome lid with age line, two decals on bottom, 8" h.; large cup and saucer with dark blue rabbit design, blue decals on bottom of both, cup 4" h., saucer 6-1/2" dia.; cup and saucer in grape pattern, rare "Dedham Tercentenary 1582-1882" stamp on saucer bottom, rabbit decals, 6" dia. **$375**

Courtesy of Willis Henry Auctions, Inc., www.willishenryauctions.com

Three items, each with two-ear rabbit border and blue ink stamp on base: plate 6-3/8" dia., plate 8-3/4" dia., and bowl 4-1/2" dia. **$121**

Courtesy of Conestoga Auction Co., www.conestogaauction.com

Plate with duck border and blue ink stamp on base, 10-1/4" dia. **$121**

Courtesy of Conestoga Auction Co., www.conestogaauction.com

Creamer and sugar with two-ear rabbit border, blue ink stamp on base, glaze flaw on rim of sugar, creamer 3-3/4" h.
.... **$61**

Courtesy of Conestoga Auction Co., www.conestogaauction.com

CERAMICS

delft

IN THE EARLY 17TH CENTURY, Italian potters settled in Holland and began producing tin-glazed earthenwares, often decorated with pseudo-Oriental designs based on Chinese porcelain wares. The city of Delft became the center of this pottery production, and several firms produced the wares throughout the 17th and early 18th century. A majority of the pieces featured blue-on-white designs, but polychrome wares were also made. The Dutch Delftwares were also shipped to England, where eventually the English copied them at potteries in such cities as Bristol, Lambeth, and Liverpool. Although still produced today, Delft peaked in popularity by the mid-18th century.

For more information on Delft pottery, see *Antique Trader Porcelain & Pottery Ceramics Price Guide, 7th edition.*

Two Delft blue and white wall pockets, 18th c., 6-7/8" h, 7-5/8" h.
.... **$677**

Courtesy of Pook & Pook, Inc., www.pookandpook.com

Delft polychrome bowl, 18th c., 5" h x 10-1/4"
dia. **$840**

Courtesy of Pook & Pook, Inc., www.pookandpook.com

Delft polychrome charger, mid-18th c., 13-3/8"
dia. **$1,046**

Courtesy of Pook & Pook, Inc., www.pookandpook.com

Two Delft blue and white druggist jars, 18th c.,
inscribed "S. Albus" and "No 7," 7" h, 11-1/2"
h. **$660**

Courtesy of Pook & Pook, Inc., www.pookandpook.com

Delft polychrome charger, mid-18th c., 13-1/4"
dia. **$450**

Courtesy of Pook & Pook, Inc., www.pookandpook.com

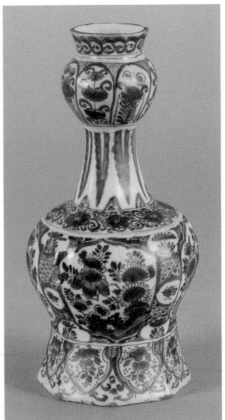

Delft blue and white bulb vase, 18th c., 10-1/2"
h. **$123**

Courtesy of Pook & Pook, Inc., www.pookandpook.com

Tin-glazed Van Eenhoorn earthenware tazza, Dutch, late 17th/early 18th c., raised pedestal foot and raised, molded gadrooning on rim, intricate floral and geometric design on interior and on foot, joined "VE" on base, Lambertus Van Eenhoorn, at De Metaale Pot, Delft, Holland, professional restoration, minor glaze flakes, 3-1/4" h x 10-1/8" dia. **$2,808**

Courtesy of Jeffrey S. Evans & Associates, www.jeffreysevans.com

Pair of plates, scattered edge chips, areas of loss to glaze, pitting, firing imperfections, shelf wear to foot rim, 10-3/8" dia. **$438**

Courtesy of Leslie Hindman Auctioneers, www.lesliehindman.com

Pair of Delft polychrome sporting fish plates, 18th c., 8-3/4" dia. **$1,560**

Courtesy of Pook & Pook, Inc., www.pookandpook.com

CERAMICS

Tin-glazed earthenware cruet set, Dutch, 18th c., two handled bottles with covers and handled doubled stand on raised feet, geometric and floral blue painted designs, intertwining "AK" mark on all three pieces, likely Adrianus Kocx, De Grieksche A (The Greek A), Delft, Holland, one 1/2" flake on rim of base, minor glaze flakes, crazing, 6-1/2" h. **$995**

Courtesy of Jeffrey S. Evans & Associates, www.jeffreysevans.com

Tin-glazed earthenware butter tub/ dish, Dutch, circa 1760, two raised, pierced handles opposite one another on sides, delicate flat cover with floral-molded finial, intricate blue floral designs on cover and sides, overlapping "AP" in blue on base, likely Anthony/Antonius Pennis, Delft, Holland, professional restorations, 3-1/4" h x 4-5/8" dia. **$351**

Courtesy of Jeffrey S. Evans & Associates, www.jeffreysevans.com

Tin-glazed earthenware vase, Dutch, second half 18th c., molded panels with relief decoration of cartouche and flowers, large painted bird, initials and numerals marked on base, surface hairlines, 3/8" flake, shallow chips, roughness on edges, 10-1/2" h. **$263**

Courtesy of Jeffrey S. Evans & Associates, www.jeffreysevans.com

Tin-glazed earthenware charger, Dutch, late 17th/ early 18th c., lobed and pointed rim, with painted panels on interior and floral designs within, central heron or stork bird design surrounded by intricate painted foliage, antique metal hanger on back and sides, marked on base with claw design in blue and "490" below, De Porcelayne Claeuw (The Porcelain Claw), Delft, Holland, 1-1/4" flake on foot rim, 1" flake underside of rim, minor shallow chips and roughness on rim and foot, 13-7/8" dia. **$351**

Courtesy of Jeffrey S. Evans & Associates, www.jeffreysevans.com

Pair of tin-glazed earthenware wall pockets, English, 18th c., relief-molded flowers, shells, and central birds, painted in blue on overall cornucopia shapes, "2" painted on back of both, otherwise unmarked, possibly Liverpool, England, minor glaze flakes, 8-1/8" l.. **$2,340**

Courtesy of Jeffrey S. Evans & Associates, www.jeffreysevans.com

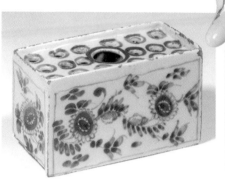

Tin-glazed earthenware flower brick, 18th c., vine and floral designs on sides, blue surrounding the piercing on the top, raised foot on base and raised rim, unmarked, London / Bristol / Liverpool, England, and other areas, chips, flake, roughness, 4-1/2" x 2-5/8" x 2-3/16". **$497**

Courtesy of Jeffrey S. Evans & Associates, www.jeffreysevans.com

Two tin-glazed earthenware plates, English, circa 1760, elaborately scalloped rims, slightly raised foot rim, floral sprays on rim and floral arrangement on interior, unmarked, likely Bristol, England, shallow chips and roughness on rim and foot, 8-7/8" dia. **$497**

Courtesy of Jeffrey S. Evans & Associates, www.jeffreysevans.com

Pair of tin-glazed earthenware plates, Dutch, 17th/early 18th c., courting figures and dog in landscape with intricate floral and geometric design on rim, unmarked, professional restoration, minor shallow chips and roughness on rim, 10-1/4" dia. **$263**

Courtesy of Jeffrey S. Evans & Associates, www.jeffreysevans.com

Tin-glazed earthenware near pair of garniture vases, Dutch, late 17th/early 18th c., octagonal paneled shape, relief-molded cartouches on front with figures walking near a pier with a ship and landscape surrounded by intricate geometric and floral designs, both marked with painted blue axe design, one having an additional "114," De Porceleyne Byl (The Porcelain Axe), Delft, Holland, shallow chips and roughness on rims and feet, 7-1/2" h. $117

Courtesy of Jeffrey S. Evans & Associates, www.jeffreysevans.com

Tin-glazed earthenware colander/ cress dish, 18th c., raised foot rim, dark blue floral and geometric designs on sides and interior, pierced inner bowl and larger central hole, rectangular cut-out on side, unmarked, likely Bristol, England, 3/4" flake, area of restoration, shallow chips and roughness on rim and foot, 3-1/4" h x 8-7/8" dia. $644

Courtesy of Jeffrey S. Evans & Associates, www.jeffreysevans.com

Tin-glazed earthenware teapot, 18th c., diminutive, having a short high spout, angled C-shape handle, paneled and fluted sides and cover, and intricately painted blue floral designs on sides and cover, marked with what appears to be an overlapping "JD," likely Jan Dextra, Delft, Holland, minor glaze flakes, 4-3/4" h. $1,112

Courtesy of Jeffrey S. Evans & Associates, www.jeffreysevans.com

CERAMICS

doulton and royal doulton

DOULTON & COMPANY, LTD., was founded in Lambeth, London, in about 1858. It operated there until 1956 and often incorporated the words "Doulton" and "Lambeth" in its marks. Pinder, Bourne & Co. Burslem was purchased by the Doultons in 1878 and in 1882 became Doulton & Co., Ltd. It added porcelain to its earthenware production in 1884. The "Royal Doulton" mark has been used since 1902 by this factory, which is still in operation.

John Doulton, the founder, was born in 1793. He became an apprentice at the age of 12 to a potter in south London. Five years later he was employed in another small pottery near Lambeth. His two sons, John and Henry, subsequently joined their father in 1830 in a partnership he had formed with the name of Doulton & Watts. Watts retired in 1864 and the partnership was dissolved. Henry formed a new company that traded as Doulton and Co.

In the early 1870s the proprietor of the Pinder Bourne Co., located in Burslem, Staffordshire, offered Henry a partnership. The Pinder Bourne Co. was purchased by Henry in 1878 and became part of Doulton & Co. in 1882.

With the passage of time, the demand for the Lambeth industrial and decorative stoneware declined whereas demand for the Burslem manufactured and decorated bone china wares increased.

Doulton & Co. was incorporated as a limited liability company in 1899. In 1901 the company was allowed to use the word "Royal" on its trademarks by Royal Charter. The well-known "lion on crown" logo came into use in 1902. In 2000 the logo was changed on the company's advertising literature to one showing a more stylized lion's head in profile.

Today Royal Doulton is one of the world's leading manufacturers and distributors of premium grade ceramic tabletop wares and collectibles.

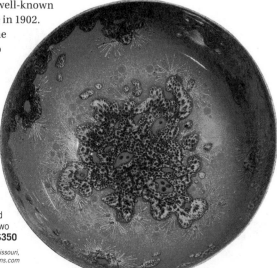

Flambé Sung bowl with Royal Doulton logo, Flambé, signed "SUNG," 3-1/4" x 7". The Flambé Sung glaze technique was developed by Charles Noke and Fred Moore in the 1920s, resulting in no two pieces achieving the same effect..........**$350**

Courtesy of Soulis Auctions, Lone Jack, Missouri, www.dirksoulisauctions.com

VISIT WWW.ANTIQUETRADER.COM

WWW.FACEBOOK.COM/ANTIQUETRADER

The Doulton Group comprises Minton, Royal Albert, Caithness Glass, Holland Studio Craft, and Royal Doulton. Royal Crown Derby was part of the group from 1971 until 2000, when it became an independent company. These companies market collectibles using their own brand names.

Flambé Sung vase, inscriptions on base include NOKE for artist Charles Noke and "FM" for artist Fred Moore, Royal Doulton logo, "SUNG," and "Flambé," 5-3/4" h. **$300**

Courtesy of Soulis Auctions, Lone Jack, Missouri, www.dirksoulisauctions.com

Two Flambé vases, smaller one signed with initials of Fred Moore, Royal Doulton logo and "SUNG" on bottom, larger one marked with Royal Doulton logo, "Flambé," "Veined," and "1605" on bottom, larger vase 6" h. **$300**

Courtesy of Soulis Auctions, Lone Jack, Missouri, www.dirksoulisauctions.com

Flambé bowl, likely Sung, mottled blue-red exterior with hand-painted red or gold flowers inside with outlining in black, Royal Doulton flambé ink stamp logo, acquisition numbers 37-1971 in white paint on bottom indicating loan to Chicago Art Institute in early 1970s, 3-1/8" h., 9" dia **$600**

Courtesy of Mark Mussio, Humler & Nolan, www.humlernolan.com

C

Two figurines, "The Orange Lady" and "The Pied Piper," 8-1/4" h. and 9" h. $100/pair

Courtesy of Pook & Pook, Inc., www.pookandpook.com

Flambé vase, Royal Doulton logo over "Flambé" over "Veined" over "1S18" under base, scratch on bulbous side of vase, 9-3/4" x 6-1/2". $160

Courtesy of Soulis Auctions, Lone Jack, Missouri, www.dirksoulisauctions.com

Pair of vases with hand-carved cartouche reserves of pastoral cattle in panels on each vase and flanked by hand-painted birds, circa 1880s, artists' initials "BHB" for Hannah B. Barlow and "FEB" for Florence E. Barlow and impressed factory marks under base, each 16" h. Hannah and Florence Barlow were sisters who worked together at the Doulton factory in Lambeth, London, England for more than 40 years. Florence specialized in painting flowers and birds, while Hannah depicted horses and other animals. .. $1,200

Vase with hand-carved scene of sheep with figural griffon heads at shoulder, 1883, artist's initials "BHB" for Hannah B. Barlow and another artist's initials along with impressed factory and date marks under base, 11-1/4" x 8-3/4". $825

Courtesy of Soulis Auctions, Lone Jack, Missouri, www.dirksoulisauctions.com

Courtesy of Soulis Auctions, Lone Jack, Missouri, www.dirksoulisauctions.com

Pair of vases with hand-carved hunting dogs and deer surrounding body, 1882, artist's initials "BHB" for Hannah B. Barlow plus three more artists, "EB" and "HH" and "FEL" for Francis E. Lee, impressed factory and date marks under base, each 15" h., 6-3/4" dia. flared rims..... **$1,300**

Courtesy of Soulis Auctions, Lone Jack, Missouri, www.dirksoulisauctions.com

Art Nouveau mosaic vase with artist's initials "EP" for Emily J. Partington, impressed factory marks under base, other artist initials "EDL" for Edith D. Lupton, "hh" for Alic G. Hellis, "PP" and "ELF", 9-1/4" x 6-3/4".. **$1,800**

Courtesy of Soulis Auctions, Lone Jack, Missouri, www.dirksoulisauctions.com

Vase, 1884, Ernest Jarrett for Doulton Lambeth, signed under base with artist's initials "JE" and "MA" with impressed factory and date marks, chip to rim, 14-1/2" h., 7-1/4" dia. **$150**

Courtesy of Soulis Auctions, Lone Jack, Missouri, www.dirksoulisauctions.com

Pair of vases, stamped "Doulton Lambeth England" and number 9383, scratched "LB" monogram, each 16-1/2" h. **$550**

Courtesy of Soulis Auctions, Lone Jack, Missouri, www.dirksoulisauctions.com

Pair of square jardinières, 1877, artist signed, factory marking inside dated 1877, two chips on each, 6-1/2" x 8" x 8". **$675**

Courtesy of Soulis Auctions, Lone Jack, Missouri, www.dirksoulisauctions.com

Blue Children/Babes in Woods tapering vase with waisted neck and flaring rim, marked "Royal Doulton" in black ink with blue artist initials, 9-3/4" h. **$190**

Courtesy of Soulis Auctions, Lone Jack, Missouri, www.dirksoulisauctions.com

Jardiniere, 1881, artist's initials "GTH" for George Hugo Tabor and "HEH" for Harriet E. Hibbut, impressed factory marks under base, small flake on inner rim, 5-1/4" x 10-1/4". **$110**

Courtesy of Soulis Auctions, Lone Jack, Missouri, www.dirksoulisauctions.com

Loving cup with hand-carved hunting dogs and stag, 1880, artist's initials "BHB" for Hannah B. Barlow and "FEB" for Florence E. Barlow, sterling rim and impressed factory and date marks under base, 6-3/4" x 7". **$425**

Courtesy of Soulis Auctions, Lone Jack, Missouri, www.dirksoulisauctions.com

◄ Putto figure candlestick, 1880, signed "EB(?)" under base, hand-scribed date mark and impressed factory mark, 10-1/2" x 4-1/2". **$850**

Courtesy of Soulis Auctions, Lone Jack, Missouri, www.dirksoulisauctions.com

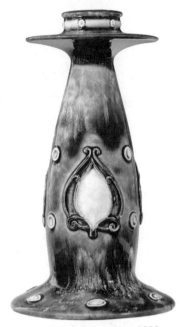

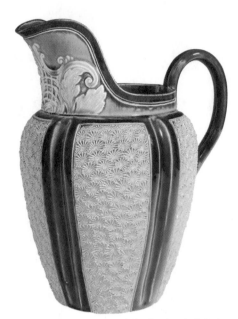

Art Nouveau candlestick, circa 1900, factory marks and artist initials "MW" and "hd" under base, 7" x 4"...... **$150**

Courtesy of Soulis Auctions, Lone Jack, Missouri, www.dirksoulisauctions.com

Pitcher, 1902, hand-decorated, Doulton Lambeth factory marks, artist's initial "H" and impressed date stamp under base, 11" h. x 8-1/4". **$170**

Courtesy of Soulis Auctions, Lone Jack, Missouri, www.dirksoulisauctions.com

Tankard, 1878, artist's initials "HEH" for Harriet E. Hibbut, impressed factory and date marks under base, glazed firing line near bottom of applied strap handle, 8-1/2" x 5". ... **$180**

Courtesy of Soulis Auctions, Lone Jack, Missouri, www.dirksoulisauctions.com

Jug with hand-carved scene of donkeys, 1875, artist's initials "BHB" for Hannah B. Barlow with impressed factory and date marks under base, 9-3/4" x 6".......................**$575**

Courtesy of Soulis Auctions, Lone Jack, Missouri, www.dirksoulisauctions.com

Vase, 1876, artist's initials "EM" for Emma Martin with impressed factory and date marks under base, 10-3/4" x 5-1/2".................................**$180**

Courtesy of Soulis Auctions, Lone Jack, Missouri, www.dirksoulisauctions.com

CERAMICS

fiesta

THE HOMER LAUGHLIN China Co. originated with a two-kiln pottery on the banks of the Ohio River in East Liverpool, Ohio. Built in 1873-'74 by Homer Laughlin and his brother, Shakespeare, the firm was first known as the Ohio Valley Pottery, and later Laughlin Bros. Pottery. It was one of the first white-ware plants in the country.

After a tentative beginning, the company was awarded a prize for having the best white-ware at the 1876 Centennial Exposition in Philadelphia.

Three years later, Shakespeare sold his interest in the business to Homer, who continued on until 1897. At that time, Homer sold his interest in the newly incorporated firm to a group of investors, including Charles, Louis, and Marcus Aaron and the company bookkeeper, William E. Wells.

Under new ownership in 1907, the headquarters and a new 30-kiln plant were built across the Ohio River in Newell, West Virginia, the present manufacturing and headquarters location.

In the 1920s, two additions to the Homer Laughlin staff set the stage for the company's greatest success: the Fiesta line. Dr. Albert V. Bleininger was hired in 1920. A scientist, author, and educator, he oversaw the conversion from bottle kilns to the more efficient tunnel kilns.

In 1927, the company hired designer Frederick Hurten Rhead, a member of a distinguished family of English ceramists. Having previously worked at Weller Pottery and Roseville Pottery, Rhead began to develop the artistic quality of the company's wares, and to experiment with shapes and glazes. In 1935, this work culminated in his designs for the Fiesta line.

Fiesta was produced until 1973, when waning popularity and declining sales forced the company to discontinue the line. But renewed appreciation of Art Deco design, coupled with collectors scrambling to buy the discontinued Fiesta on the secondary market, prompted the company to reintroduce the line on Fiesta's 50th anniversary in 1986, spawning a whole new generation of collectors.

Bowls, cream soup, original six colors, 6-5/8" w. across handles x 5-1/16", 2-1/4" h.............................**$145**
Courtesy of Strawser Auctions, www.strawserauctions.com

CERAMICS

For more information on Fiesta, see *Warman's Fiesta Identification and Price Guide* by Glen Victorey.

FIESTA COLORS

From 1936 to 1972, Fiesta was produced in 14 colors (other than special promotions). These colors are usually divided into the "original colors" of cobalt blue, light green, ivory, red, turquoise, and yellow; the "1950s colors" of chartreuse, forest green, gray, and rose (introduced in 1951); medium green (introduced in 1959); plus the later additions of Casuals, Amberstone, Fiesta Ironstone, and Casualstone ("Coventry") in antique gold, mango red, and turf green; and the striped, decal, and Lustre pieces. The colors that make up the "original" and "1950s" groups are sometimes referred to as "the standard 11." In many pieces, medium green is the hardest to find and the most expensive Fiesta color.

FIESTA COLORS AND YEARS OF PRODUCTION TO 1972

Antique Gold 1969-1972	Ivory 1936-1951
Chartreuse 1951-1959	Mango Red (same as original red) 1970-1972
Cobalt Blue 1936-1951	Medium Green.............................. 1959-1969
Forest Green................................ 1951-1959	Red .... 1936-1944 and 1959-1972
Gray 1951-1959	Rose.. 1951-1959
Green 1936-1951	Turf Green 1969-1972
(often called light green when comparing it to other green glazes; also called "original" green)	Turquoise 1937-1969
	Yellow 1936-1969

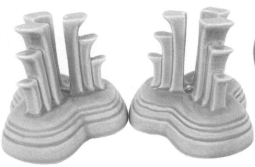

Pair of tripod candleholders, green, 3-1/2" x 4-1/2" **$182**

Courtesy of Strawser Auctions, www.strawserauctions.com

Pair of bulb candleholders, cobalt, 3-3/4" h. x 2-1/2" w. **$36**

Courtesy of Strawser Auctions, www.strawserauctions.com

Nappy bowl, rare, ivory with red stripes, 8-1/2" dia. **$2,420**

Courtesy of Strawser Auctions, www.strawserauctions.com

Sweets comport, green, marked HLC, 3-1/2" h., 5-1/8" dia... **$91**

Courtesy of Strawser Auctions, www.strawserauctions.com

"Chamberstick" employee-imagined experimental piece made with demitasse saucer, stem from sweets comport and cup ring handle, possibly only one known to exist, featured on page 192 of *Collector's Encyclopedia of Fiesta*, 10th edition, by Bob and Sharon Huxford. ... $5,566

COURTESY OF STRAWSER AUCTIONS, WWW.STRAWSERAUCTIONS.COM

Kitchen Kraft pie server, cobalt. $97

Courtesy of Strawser Auctions, www.strawserauctions.com

Eggcup, chartreuse, 3-3/8" x 3-1/8"...............................$103

Courtesy of Strawser Auctions, www.strawserauctions.com

Marmalade, cobalt, 4-7/16" h. with lid, 3-1/8" dia.............$218

Courtesy of Strawser Auctions, www.strawserauctions.com

Mustard, ivory with red stripe, rare, minor rim nick to lid, minor hairline to base, 3-1/16" h. with lid, 2-1/2" dia. $3,872

Courtesy of Strawser Auctions, www.strawserauctions.com

CERAMICS

BOTTOM MARKS

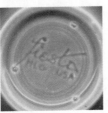 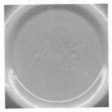

Bottom of No. 1 mixing bowl in green, showing sagger pin marks, the "Fiesta/HLCo. USA" impressed mark, and the faint "1" size indicator. The impressed size mark on the bottom of the No. 2 mixing bowl in yellow is too faint to be seen in this image.

Two different impressed marks on the bottoms of relish tray inserts.

An ink stamp on the bottom of a piece of Fiesta.

Notice the different bottoms of two ashtrays. The top one has a set of rings with no room for a logo. The bottom ashtray has rings along the outer edge, opposite of the ring pattern on the ashtray above. The red example is an older example. The yellow ashtray with the logo can be dated to after 1940.

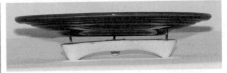

A 9" cobalt blue plate rests on a stilt with sagger pins to show the basic idea of how it worked. Please note that this stilt is not the exact one that would have been used by Homer Laughlin China Co., but rather an updated style in use today by many ceramic studios.

Bottom of a teacup saucer in turquoise, showing sagger pin marks and the "Genuine Fiesta" stamp.

Bottom of 6" bread plate in turquoise, showing "Genuine Fiesta" stamp.

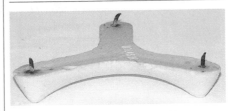

Fiesta pieces were glazed on the underside, so before being fired, each piece was placed on a stilt to keep it off the floor of the kiln. The stilt was made up of three sagger pins positioned an equal distance from each other to form three points of a triangle. If you inspect the underside of any piece of Fiesta, which has a completely glazed bottom, you will notice three small blemishes in a triangular pattern. Later in Fiesta's production run, the undersides of pieces were glazed and then wiped, creating a dry foot, before going into the kiln to be fired.

Examples of impressed Fiesta bottom marks.

Plate group, all 11 colors, 6" dia. **$42**
Courtesy of Strawser Auctions, www.strawserauctions.com

Plate group, 10 colors (missing rose), 10" dia. **$182**
Courtesy of Strawser Auctions, www.strawserauctions.com

Kitchen Kraft spoon, red. **$61**
*Courtesy of Strawser Auctions,
www.strawserauctions.com*

Plate, ivory with red stripe,
minor wear, 9" dia. **$333**
*Courtesy of Strawser Auctions,
www.strawserauctions.com*

Deep plate set, all 11 colors, 1-1/2" d., 8-1/2" dia..$103

Courtesy of Strawser Auctions, www.strawserauctions.com

Sectioned/grill plates, six colors, 10-1/2" dia. $103

Courtesy of Strawser Auctions, www.strawserauctions.com

Kitchen Kraft large canister, red. $91

Courtesy of Strawser Auctions, www.strawserauctions.com

Kitchen Kraft small canister, green....................................$97

Courtesy of Strawser Auctions, www.strawserauctions.com

Kitchen Kraft small canister, cobalt, with paper label.......$375

Courtesy of Strawser Auctions, www.strawserauctions.com

Four individual Kitchen Kraft casseroles, red, cobalt, yellow, and green, two with paper labels.
.... **$250**

Kitchen Kraft four-piece stack set, red, 5-1/4" dia., 2-1/4" h.
.... **$157**

Courtesy of Strawser Auctions, www.strawserauctions.com

Syrup pitcher with "DripCut" top, green, 1938-1940, 5-3/4" h., 3-5/8" dia. without handle.
.... **$133**

Courtesy of Strawser Auctions, www.strawserauctions.com

Sauce boat, medium green, 4-7/8" x 8" x 4-1/2"........................ **$97**

Courtesy of Strawser Auctions, www.strawserauctions.com

CERAMICS

CERAMICS

frankoma

JOHN FRANK STARTED his pottery company in 1933 in Norman, Oklahoma, but when he moved the business to Sapulpa, Oklahoma, in 1938, he felt he was home. Still, he could not know the horrendous storms and trials that would follow him. Just after his move, on Nov. 11, 1938, a fire destroyed the entire operation, which included the pot and leopard mark he had created in 1935. Then in 1942, the war effort needed men and materials, so Frankoma could not survive. In 1943, John and Grace Lee Frank bought the plant as junk salvage and began again.

ORIGINAL CREATION by FRANKOMA

The time in Norman had produced some of the finest art ware that John would ever create and most of the items were marked either "Frank Potteries," "Frank Pottery," or to a lesser degree, the "pot and leopard" mark. Today these marks are avidly and enthusiastically sought by collectors. Another elusive mark wanted by collectors shows "Firsts Kiln Sapulpa 6-7-38." The mark was used for one day only and denotes the first firing in Sapulpa. It has been estimated that perhaps 50 to 75 pieces were fired on that day.

The clay Frankoma used is helpful to collectors in determining when an item was made. Creamy beige clay known as "Ada" clay was in use until 1953. Then a red brick shale was found in Sapulpa and used until about 1985 when, with the addition of an additive, the clay became a reddish pink.

Rutile glazes were used early in Frankoma's history. Glazes with rutile have caused more confusion among collectors than any other glazes. For example, a Prairie Green piece shows a lot of green but it also has some brown. The same is true for the Desert Gold glaze; the piece shows a sandy-beige glaze with some brown. Generally speaking, Prairie Green, Desert Gold, White Sand, and Woodland Moss are the most puzzling to collectors.

In 1970 the government closed the rutile mines in America, and Frankoma had to buy it from Australia. It was not the same, so the results were different. Values are higher for the glazes with rutile. Also, the pre-Australian Woodland Moss glaze is more desirable than that created after 1970.

After John Frank died in 1973, his daughter Joniece Frank, a ceramic designer at the pottery, became president of the company. In 1983 another fire destroyed everything Frankoma had worked so hard to create. They rebuilt, but in 1990, after the IRS shut the doors for nonpayment, Joniece, true to the Frank legacy, filed for Chapter 11 (instead of bankruptcy) so she could reopen and continue the work she loved.

Ringed Art Deco vase, No. 500, brownish maple, 1940s, bottom marked FRANKOMA and 500, 2-3/4" h. x 3" w. **$145**

Courtesy of Just Art Pottery, www.justartpottery.com

In 1991 Richard Bernstein purchased the pottery, and the name was changed to Frankoma Industries. The company was sold again in 2005 to Det and Crystal Merryman. Yet another owner, Joe Ragosta, purchased the pottery in 2008.

Frankoma Pottery was closed for good in 2010 with a factory closeout auction in Oklahoma in 2011.

Ada clay salt and pepper shakers, snail form, No. 558H, Desert Gold glaze, 1940s, 2" h. x 2" w. .. **$45**

Courtesy of Just Art Pottery, www.justartpottery.com

Ada clay bookends, bronco form, No. 423, Prairie Green glaze, 1940s, 5-1/2" h. x 5-1/4" w. **$325**

Courtesy of Just Art Pottery, www.justartpottery.com

Puma on Rock ivory bookends, No. 422, rare, by Joseph Taylor, Norman, Oklahoma, era, 1934-1938, bottom marked with "cat mark" used between 1934-1938, one bookend incised TAYLOR on back, 7-1/4" h. x 6" w. **$1,295**

Courtesy of Just Art Pottery, www.justartpottery.com

Mayan-Aztec pitcher, No. 551, Red Bud glaze, 1940s, bottom marked FRANKOMA and 551, 3-1/2" h. x 3" w. **$45**

Courtesy of Just Art Pottery, www.justartpottery.com

"Weeping Lady" bookends (in 1942 the name was changed to "The Dreamer Girl"), No. 427, Prairie Green glaze, possibly early Norman, Oklahoma, era, as-made condition, one bookend with glazed-over factory flaw to base edge, 5-1/2" h. x 5-1/2" w. **$425**

Courtesy of Just Art Pottery, www.justartpottery.com

Swan figurine, No. 168, Prairie Green glaze, 1940s, 3" h. x 3" w...**$90**

Courtesy of Just Art Pottery, www.justartpottery.com

Wagon wheel salt and pepper shakers, No. 94H, Desert Gold glaze, 1940s, 2-1/2" h. x 2-1/2" w. **$45**

Courtesy of Just Art Pottery, www.justartpottery.com

Tall English Setter figurine, No. 141, White Sand glaze, 1940s, bottom marked FRANKOMA, 5-1/4" h. x 8" l. from tip of tail to nose.
....**$350**

Courtesy of Just Art Pottery, www.justartpottery.com

Art Deco creamer, No. 93A, Prairie Green glaze, 1942, factory glaze skip to rim, bottom marked 93A, 3" h. x 3-1/4" w. **$50**

Courtesy of Just Art Pottery, www.justartpottery.com

"Gardener Girl" figurine, No. 701, Royal Blue glaze, 1940s, bottom marked 701, 6" h. x 2-3/4" w.
....**$125**

Courtesy of Just Art Pottery, www.justartpottery.com

CERAMICS

fulper pottery

FROM THE "GERM-PROOF Filter" to enduring Arts & Crafts acclaim – that's the unlikely journey of Fulper Pottery, maker of the early 20th century uniquely glazed artware that's become a favorite with today's collectors.

Fulper began life in 1814 as the Samuel Hill Pottery, named after its founder, a New Jersey potter. In its early years, the pottery specialized in useful items such as storage crocks and drainpipes fashioned from the area's red clay. Abraham Fulper, a worker at the pottery, eventually became Hill's partner, purchasing the company in 1860. Renamed after its new owner, Fulper Pottery continued to produce a variety of utilitarian tile and crockery. By the turn of the 20th century, the firm, now led by Abraham's sons, introduced a line of fire-proof cookware and the hugely successful "Germ-Proof Filter." An ancestor of today's water cooler, the filter provided sanitary drinking water in less-than-sanitary public places, such as offices and railway stations.

In the early 1900s, Fulper's master potter, John Kunsman, began creating various solid-glaze vessels, such as jugs and vases, which were offered for sale outside the pottery. On a whim, William H. Fulper II (Abraham's grandson, who'd become the company's secretary/treasurer) took an assortment of these items to exhibit at the 1904 Louisiana Purchase Exposition – along with, of course, the Germ-Proof Filter. Kunsman's artware took home an honorable mention.

Since Chinese art pottery was then attracting national attention, Fulper saw an opening to produce similarly styled modern ware.

Vase, seven-sided, shape 509, Chinese blue over mahogany over ivory flambé glazes, incised die stamp Fulper logo, tiny open glaze bubbles, single grinding nick, 9-7/8" h. **$150**

Courtesy of Mark Mussio, Humler & Nolan, www.humlernolan.com

Dr. Cullen Parmelee, who headed the ceramics department at Rutgers, was recruited to create a contemporary series of glazes patterned after those of ancient China. The Fulper Vasekraft line of art pottery incorporating these glazes made its debut in 1909. Unfortunately, Parmelee's glazes did not lend themselves well to mass production because they did not result in reliable coloration. Even more to their detriment, they were expensive to produce.

In 1910, most of Parmelee's glazes disappeared from the line. A new ceramic engineer, Martin Stangl, was given the assignment of revitalizing Vasekraft. His most notable innovation: steering designs and glazes away from reinterpretations of ornate Chinese classics and toward the simplicity of the burgeoning Arts & Crafts movement. Among his many Vasekraft successes: candleholders, bookends, perfume lamps, desk accessories, tobacco jars, and even Vasekraft lamps. Here, both the lamp base and shade were of pottery; stained glass inserts in the shades allowed light to shine through.

Always attuned to the mood of the times, William Fulper realized that by World War I the heavy Vasekraft stylings were fading in popularity. A new and lighter line of Fulper Pottery Artware, featuring Spanish Revival and English themes, was introduced. Among the most admired Fulper releases following the war were Fulper Porcelaines: dresser boxes, powder jars, ashtrays, lamps, and other accessories designed to complement the fashionable boudoir.

Fayence, a popular line of solid-color, open-stock dinnerware eventually known as Stangl Pottery, was introduced in the 1920s. In 1928, following William Fulper's death, Martin Stangl was named company president. The artware that continued into the 1930s embraced Art Deco as well as Classical and Primitive stylistic themes. From 1935 onward, Stangl Pottery became the sole Fulper output. In 1978, the Stangl assets came under the ownership of Pfaltzgraff.

Unlike wheel-thrown pottery, Fulper was made in molds; the true artistry came in the use of exceptionally rich, color-blended glazes. Each Fulper piece is one-of-a-kind. Because of glaze divergence, two Fulper objects from the same mold can show a great variance. While once a drawback for retailers seeking consistency, that uniqueness is now a boon to collectors: Each Fulper piece possesses its own singular visual appeal.

Oriental temple jar, shape 566, Chinese blue flambé over Mirror Black glazes, Fulper raised vertical oval mark, areas of fine crazing, 11-5/8" h.. **$325**

Courtesy of Mark Mussio, Humler & Nolan, www.humlernolan.com

Three-handled bulbous vase, early 20th century, purple matte glaze, raised vertical racetrack mark, burst glaze bubbles throughout, 6-1/4", 8-1/2" dia. **$313**

Courtesy of Rago Arts and Auctions, www.ragoarts.com

Twin-handled vase, Blue Snowflake crystals, raised mark obscured by glaze, 11-3/4" h. **$200**

Courtesy of Mark Mussio, Humler & Nolan, www.humlernolan.com

Squat twin-handled vase, shape 656, blue crystalline glaze, Fulper racetrack ink stamp, glaze skips and grinding nick, 6-1/4" h., 8-1/4" dia. **$150**

Courtesy of Mark Mussio, Humler & Nolan, www.humlernolan.com

Octagonal vase, shape 511, green crystalline glaze over soft yellow high glaze, incised Fulper mark, open glaze bubbles, 7-1/2" h. **$160**

Courtesy of Mark Mussio, Humler & Nolan, www.humlernolan.com

◀ Early square-handled vase, shape 452, Cucumber crystalline glaze, Fulper large rectangular ink stamp, open glaze bubbles, 4-3/4" h.......................... **$150**

Courtesy of Mark Mussio, Humler & Nolan, www.humlernolan.com

Pair of penguin flower frogs, blue, gray, and ivory matte glazes, rectangular vertical ink stamp, one with reglued base, one with repaired beak, 7", 4-1/2" dia. **$250**

Courtesy of Rago Arts and Auctions, www.ragoarts.com

Twin-handled vase, shape 659, Cucumber crystalline glaze, die-stamped "incised" Fulper logo, open glaze bubbles, 8-3/4" h. **$150**

Courtesy of Mark Mussio, Humler & Nolan, www.humlernolan.com

Flat-sided, two-handled vase, Leopard Skin crystals, small oval Fulper ink stamp logo, grinding chips, 8-1/8" h. **$170**

Courtesy of Mark Mussio, Humler & Nolan, www.humlernolan.com

Vase, green crystalline matte glaze, Fulper racetrack ink stamp, grinding roughness, 6" h. **$110**

Courtesy of Mark Mussio, Humler & Nolan, www.humlernolan.com

Vase, shape 536, caramel flambé over dark mahogany glazes, incised Fulper mark, 13-1/8" h. **$250**

Courtesy of Mark Mussio, Humler & Nolan, www.humlernolan.com

CERAMICS

grueby

FINE ART POTTERY was produced by the Grueby Faience and Tile Co. established in Boston in 1891. Choice pieces were created with molded designs on a semi-porcelain body. The ware is marked and often bears the initials of the decorators. The pottery closed in 1907.

GRUEBY

Rare seven-handled vase by George Kendrick, circa 1900, leathery glaze, circular pottery stamp /35, professional restoration to part of two handles, touch-ups to two high points, 10-1/4" x 8-1/2".
......................................**$31,250**

Courtesy of Rago Arts and Auctions, www.ragoarts.com

Tall vase with leaves and buds, circa 1905, circular faience stamp /23/N, opposing hairlines from rim, bruise, glaze scaling and lifting, small chips, 11-1/4" x 5-1/2"................**$625**

Courtesy of Rago Arts and Auctions, www.ragoarts.com

Vase with overlapping leaves, circa 1898-1910, ochre glaze, circular faience stamp, touch-up to rim, two touch-ups to shoulder, flecks to high points, peppering around shoulder, 9-1/4" x 5"........**$7,500**

Courtesy of Rago Arts and Auctions, www.ragoarts.com

top lot

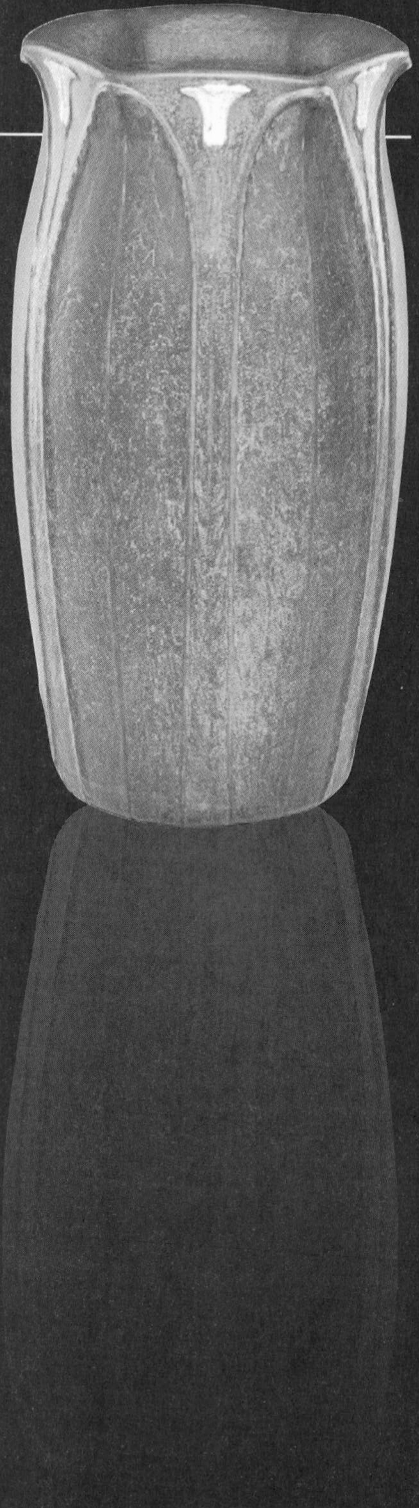

Massive two-color floor vase with leaves and flowers by Ruth Erickson, circa 1900-1909, russet and cream glazes, incised RE 9/28, touch-ups to chips on high points, hairline to base going up body, 21-1/2" x 11".. $40,625

Vase with leaves by Wilhelmina Post, , circa 1905, circular pottery stamp, incised WP, professional restoration to rim chip, glaze miss to body, 5-1/2" x 6-1/2". **$1,125**

Courtesy of Rago Arts and Auctions, www.ragoarts.com

Large vase, circa 1905, controlled blue drip glaze, circular pottery stamp, flecks to high points, grinding chips, 11" x 7-3/4"..................**$10,000**

Courtesy of Rago Arts and Auctions, www.ragoarts.com

Rare vase with leaves and fiddlehead fern handles by Wilhelmina Post, circa 1905, circular pottery stamp, incised WP, flecks to high points, 8-3/4" x 5". This model was first illustrated in a Grueby advertisement that ran in the December 1901 issue of House and Garden. Additional examples of this model are in the Metropolitan Museum of Art and the Museum of Fine Arts, Boston. **$11,250**

Courtesy of Rago Arts and Auctions, www.ragoarts.com

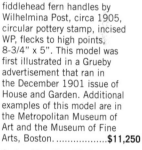

Vase with leaves, 1902, circular pottery stamp, incised DS 1902 with unknown artist cipher, flecks to high points, 9" x 6-1/2". **$3,500**

Courtesy of Rago Arts and Auctions, www.ragoarts.com

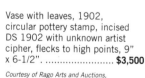

Vase with three-lobed leaves and buds, 1898-1902, matte green glaze, impressed round mark "GRUEBY FAIENCE Co/BOSTON.U.S.A" with lotus and incised artist's initials partially obscured by glaze, 7-7/8" h. **$1,408**

Courtesy of Brunk Auctions, www.brunkauctions.com

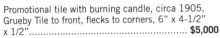

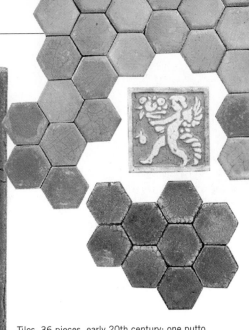

Tiles, 36 pieces, early 20th century: one putto tile, 26 hexagonal tiles in brown glaze, and nine tiles in green glaze, unmarked, some tiles with burst glaze bubbles, putto 1" x 6" sq., hexagonal 4" dia.. **$375**

Courtesy of Rago Arts and Auctions, www.ragoarts.com

Promotional tile with burning candle, circa 1905, Grueby Tile to front, flecks to corners, 6" x 4-1/2" x 1/2"... **$5,000**

Courtesy of Rago Arts and Auctions, www.ragoarts.com

Water lily three-color tile, impressed "[lily] Gruby Tile Boston," 6" x 6-1/4". **$492**

Courtesy of Saco River Auction Co., www.sacoriverauction.com

CERAMICS

hampshire pottery

HAMPSHIRE POTTERY WAS made in Keene, New Hampshire, where several potteries operated as far back as the late 18th century. The pottery now known as Hampshire Pottery was established by J. S. Taft shortly after 1870. Various types of wares, including art pottery, were produced through the years. Taft's brother-in-law,

Cadmon Robertson, joined the firm in 1904 and was responsible for developing more than 900 glaze formulas while in charge of all manufacturing. His death in 1914 created problems for the firm, and Taft sold out to George Morton in 1916. Closed during part of World War I, the pottery was later reopened by Morton for a short time and manufactured white hotel china. From 1919 to 1921, mosaic floor tiles became the main production. All production ceased in 1923.

Vase in molded leaf design, brown over blue matte glazes, Hampshire mark with shape number 93 and Emoretta mark, small professional restoration on side, 7-7/8" h..**$250**

Courtesy of Mark Mussio, Humler & Nolan, www.humlernolan.com

Two vases in molded design of flowers and leaves, both in green matte glazes, impressed Hampshire Pottery and Emoretta symbol, raised number 33, lighter green vase with glaze skips and open bubbles, 6-3/4" h.. **$325**

Courtesy of Mark Mussio, Humler & Nolan, www.humlernolan.com

Vase in molded flowers and leaves design, blue matte glaze, white highlights, impressed Hampshire Pottery and Emoretta symbol, raised number 33, professional rim repair, 6-3/4" h. .. **$120**

Courtesy of Mark Mussio, Humler & Nolan, www.humlernolan.com

Pitcher and bowl, pitcher in green crystalline matte glaze, marked Hampshire in block letters, small grinding chip, 5-1/2" h., and leaf-form bowl in blue and green matte glazes, Hampshire Pottery mark, shape 24, Emoretta mark, glaze roughness at base, 2" h., 4-1/2" dia. **$100**

Courtesy of Mark Mussio, Humler & Nolan, www.humlernolan.com

Pair of matching pitchers, green matte glazes, each impressed with Hampshire Pottery and raised number 512, both with minor stilt pulls, one slightly coming up side of base, 6-1/2" h... **$100**

Courtesy of Mark Mussio, Humler & Nolan, www.humlernolan.com

Vase, green matte glaze, four embossed leaves in crystalline glaze, Hampshire mark, illegible shape number, MO impressed, 3-1/2" h. **$160**

Courtesy of Mark Mussio, Humler & Nolan, www.humlernolan.com

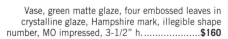

Vase, matte green glaze, incised Hampshire Pottery 54/1, 4-3/4" h..$100

Courtesy of Turner Auctions + Appraisals, www.turnerauctionsonline.com

◀ Three-handled vase, matte green glaze, impressed HAMPSHIRE, 4-3/4" h...................$100

Courtesy of Turner Auctions + Appraisals, www.turnerauctionsonline.com

Bowl, green matte glaze with charcoaling, Hampshire Pottery mark, Emoretta mark, 2-1/4" h., 5-3/4" dia..$110

Courtesy of Mark Mussio, Humler & Nolan, www.humlernolan.com

Arts & Crafts vase, brown glaze, bottom marked Hampshire Pottery, 33 and circled M, 7" h., 4" dia. $395

Courtesy of Just Art Pottery, www.justartpottery.com

139

CERAMICS

ironstone

DURABILITY. WHEN INTRODUCED IN THE EARLY 1800S, that was ironstone china's major selling point. Durability also accounts for the availability of vintage ironstone china, literally centuries after it first captivated consumers. Unlike its fragile porcelain contemporaries, this utilitarian earthenware was intended to withstand the ravages of time – and it has.

Ironstone owes its innate sturdiness to a formula incorporating iron slag with the clay. Cobalt, added to the mix, eliminated the yellowish tinge that plagued earlier attempts at white china. The earliest form of this opaque dinnerware made its debut in 1800 England, patented by potters William and John Turner. However, by 1806 the Turner firm was bankrupt.

Ironstone achieved its first real popularity in 1813, when Charles Mason first offered for sale his "Patent Ironstone China." Mason's white ironstone was an immediate hit, offering vessels for a wide variety of household uses, from teapots and tureens to washbowls and pitchers.

Although the inexpensive simplicity of white ironstone proved popular with frugal householders, by the 1830s in-mold and transfer patterns were providing a dose of visual variety. Among the decorative favorites: Oriental motifs and homey images such as grains, fruits, and flowers.

Mason's patented formula for white ironstone lasted 14 years. Upon its expiration, numerous other potteries jumped into the fray. By the 1840s, white ironstone found its way across the ocean, enjoying the same success in the United States and Canada as it had in England. By the 1880s, however, the appeal of white ware began to fade. Its successor, soon overtaking the original, was ironstone's most enduring incarnation, Tea Leaf, which was popular into the early 1900s.

Jardiniere, early 20th century, 10" h.
....$100

Courtesy of Leslie Hindman Auctioneers,
www.lesliehindman.com

Mason's pitcher commemorating jubilee of Queen Victoria, 6-3/8" h. **$37**

Courtesy of Pook & Pook, Inc., www.pookandpook.com

Twelve serving/table items, 19th century, England, including one monumental platter, 20-1/8" x 15-1/2", with impressed "T&R BOOTE" and "30" and three plates ranging from 9-5/8" to 10-5/8" dia., all impressed on base "J.EDWARDS / PRESIDENT SHAPE"; other marks include Goodfellow, Wedgwood, and Davenport; nine pieces undamaged, flakes, chips, wear on remainder. **$47**

Courtesy of Jeffrey S. Evans & Associates, www.jeffreysevans.com

Mason's Brocade pattern dinner service designed for Carl Forslund, 20th century, England, 239 transferware items including two large covered tureens, five platters of various sizes, 46 dinner plates, 12 shallow bowls, 12 double-handle bowls, 15 salad plates, 17 bread plates, 11 pitchers of various sizes, 12 kidney dishes, one punch bowl with ladle, and two lamps, printed mark, match holder restored, lamp 30", 8-1/2" dia. $438

Seven embossed items, 19th/early 20th century, England, including two-handled covered sugar dish with flared, scalloped foot, marked "JOHNSON & CO," 6" h.; shell-shaped dish with embossed face on one end and scalloped rim impressed "JAMES EDWARDS / DALEHALL," 8-1/2" x 5"; and platter with scalloped rim and embossed edge, impressed on base "JOHN ALCOCK / HEBE SHAPE," 18" x 14-1/2"; other marks include "POWELL BISHOP" and "E&C CHALLINOR".. ....$47

Courtesy of Jeffrey S. Evans & Associates, www.jeffreysevans.com

Six pieces of Wheat and Cable pattern by Elsmore & Forster, good condition with minor damage, platter 14-1/2" w. $190

Courtesy of Conestoga Auction Co., www.conestogaauction.com

CERAMICS

kpm

KPM PLAQUES ARE highly glazed, enamel paintings on porcelain bases that were produced by Konigliche Porzellan Manufaktur (KPM), the King's Porcelain Factory, Berlin, Germany, between 1880 and 1901.

Their secret, according to Afshine Emrani, dealer and appraiser at www.some-of-my-favorite-things.com, is KPM's highly superior, smooth, hard paste porcelain, which could be fired at very high temperatures.

"The magic of a KPM plaque is that it will look as crisp and beautiful 100 years from now as it does today," he said. Even when they were introduced, these plaques proved highly collectible, with art lovers, collectors, tourists, and the wealthy acquiring them for extravagant sums.

KPM rarely marketed painted porcelain plaques itself, however. Instead, it usually supplied white, undecorated ones to independent artists who specialized in this genre. Not all artists signed their KPM paintings, however.

While most KPM plaques were copies of famous paintings, some, commissioned by wealthy Americans and Europeans in the 1920s, bear images of actual people in contemporary clothing. These least collectible of KPM plaques command between $500 and $1,500 each, depending on the attractiveness of their subjects.

Gilded, hand-painted plaques featuring Middle Eastern or female Gypsy subjects and bearing round red "Made in Germany" stamps were produced just before and after World War I for export. They command between $500 and $2,000 each. Plaques portraying religious subjects, such as the Virgin Mary or the Flight into Egypt, command higher prices but are less popular.

Popular scenes of hunters, merrymakers, musicians, etc., generally fetch less than $10,000 apiece because they have been reproduced time and again. Rarer, more elaborate scenes, however, like "The Dance Lesson" and "Turkish Card Players" may be worth many times more.

Vase with oval scene of World War I-era German military biplane, oval surrounded by flower garlands, two sprays of flowers on back, fired-on gold, KPM scepter mark, red Orb and Cross, black Iron Cross (also on plane's wings and tail), painted numbers 148/145, other impressed marks, 13-5/8" h. **$750**

Courtesy of Mark Mussio, Humler & Nolan, www.humlernolan.com

Highly stylized portraits copied from famous paintings – especially those of attractive children or décolleté women – allowed art lovers to own their own "masterpieces." These are currently worth between $2,000 and $20,000 each. Romanticized portrayals of cupids and women in the nude, the most desirable KPMs subjects of all, currently sell for up to $40,000 each. Portraits of men, it must be noted, are not only less popular, but also less expensive.

Size also matters. A 4" x 6" inch plaque whose subject has

Plaque of European family outside home, three traveling cavaliers on horseback, man serving spirits, impressed "KPM," scepter mark and letter "H", plaque approximately 7-1/2" x 9-3/4", frame with maroon velvet mat 13" x 15-1/2".. **$1,600**

Courtesy of Mark Mussio, Humler & Nolan, www.humlernolan.com

been repeatedly reproduced may sell for a few thousand dollars. Larger ones that portray the same subject will fetch proportionately more. A "Sistine Madonna" plaque, fashioned after the original work by Rafael and measuring 10" x 7-1/2", might cost $4,200. One featuring the identical subject but measuring 15" x 11" might cost $7,800. A larger plaque, measuring 22" x 16", might command twice that price.

The largest KPM plaques, measuring 22" x 26", for example, often burst during production. Although no formula exists for determining prices of those that have survived, Afshine Emrani said that each may sell for as much as $250,000. Rare plaques like these are often found in museums.

The condition of a KPM plaque also affects its price. Most, since they were highly glazed and customarily hung instead of handled, have survived in perfect condition. Thus, those that have sustained even minor damage, like scratches, cracks, or chips, fetch considerably lower prices. Those suffering major damage are worthless.

KPM painted plaques arouse so much interest and command such high prices that, over the last couple of years, unscrupulous dealers have entered the market. According to dealer Balazs Benedek, KPM plaques are "the mother of all fakes. About 90 percent of KPM plaques are mid-to-late-20th century reproductions. And about 70 percent are not hand painted."

Collectors should be aware that genuine KPM paintings always boast rich, shiny, glazes that preserve their colors, and though subject matter may vary, they typically feature nude scenes, indoor portraits of women, or group gatherings in lush settings. Anything wildly different should raise suspicion.

Genuine KPMs, on their backs or edges, feature small icons of scepters deeply set in the porcelain, over the letters KPM. These marks are sometimes accompanied by an "H" or some other letter, which may indicate their production date or size. Some are imprinted with the size of the plaque as well, which facilitated sorting or shipping. Shallow or crooked imprints may reveal a fake.

– Melody Amsel-Arieli

CERAMICS

Plaque of cavalier, circa 1900, impressed mark, light surface abrasions, milkiness to glaze, plaque 10" x 7-1/2".. **$625**

Courtesy of Rago Arts and Auctions, www.ragoarts.com

Plaque of Napoleon in three-quarter length portrait, 19th century, in gilt metal easel-back frame, minor areas of abrasion from frame's edge, 6" h. x 4" w. **$750**

Courtesy of Leslie Hindman Auctioneers, www.lesliehindman.com

Plaque of maiden surrounded by cherubs, circa 1900, impressed mark, signed "Walther," light surface abrasions and wear, plaque 10" x 7-1/2". **$2,500**

Courtesy of Rago Arts and Auctions, www.ragoarts.com

Plaque of maiden feeding doves, circa 1900, impressed marks, light surface abrasions and wear, plaque 9-1/2" x 6-1/4"....................... **$1,875**

Courtesy of Rago Arts and Auctions, www.ragoarts.com

"Solitude" plaque of painted nude portrait of woman, 19th century, impressed marks, frame losses, scratches and losses at frame edge, light surface abrasions and wear, plaque 9-3/4" x 6-1/2".. **$2,625**

Courtesy of Rago Arts and Auctions, www.ragoarts.com

Plaque with scene of Madonna and child, 19th century, impressed mark on reverse, light abrasions, remnants of gold paint where plaque meets frame, plaque 7" x 5-1/4". **$563**

Courtesy of Rago Arts and Auctions, www.ragoarts.com

Oval plaque of young woman in green and white dress, late 19th century, marked, frame worn, 6-3/4" x 5"... **$219**

Courtesy of Rago Arts and Auctions, www.ragoarts.com

Plaque with scene from Lohengrin, late 19th century, partial paper label and impressed marks, light surface abrasions, plaque 10-1/4" x 12-3/4"... **$3,250**

Courtesy of Rago Arts and Auctions, www.ragoarts.com

CERAMICS

Plaque of military men on horseback greeted by family at doorstep, pencil notation on back "welcome home," marked KPM, mounted in gilt wooden frame, 7-1/2" x 10", frame 13" x 15". **$1,652**

Courtesy of Woody Auction, www.woodyauction.co

Oval plaque of brunette-haired woman seated on bench, elbow on knee, chin on hand, late 19th century, plaque mounted on red velvet board inset in gilt gessoed frame, verso with impressed scepter, "KPM" mark, losses to corner of frame, plaque 9" x 6-3/4", frame 15-1/2" x 13-1/2".. **$445**

Courtesy of Michaan's Auctions, www.michaans.com

Plaque of girl with bird, 19th century, impressed KPM marks, scepter mark, museum exhibition label verso, plaque 9-3/4" h. x 7-1/2" w., frame 19-1/2" h. x 17" w. **$1,400**

Courtesy of Kaminski Auctions, www.kaminskiauctions.com

Plaque of Kate Goddard Bailey, late 19th century, back reads "Kate Goddard Bailey, nee Weaver, September 1, 1882, on 25th Anniversary of marriage to Joseph J. Bailey Jr."; signed F. Wagner Wien, plaque 16" x 13-1/2", frame 26" x 22-1/4". **$381**

Courtesy of Michaan's Auctions, www.michaans.com

Figure of Aphrodite, 19th century, partial gilt porcelain, scepter mark in blue underglaze, chip to underside of interior rim, light chipping at shoulder to ribbons, vine to lap repainted, leaf to apple re-adhered, adhesive residue to foot, flaking and chipping to drapery on shoulder, scattered flea bites, 8-5/8" h. x 7-1/4" w. **$438**

Courtesy of Heritage Auctions, www.ha.com

CERAMICS

limoges

"LIMOGES" HAS BECOME the generic identifier for porcelain produced in Limoges, France, and the surrounding vicinity. More than 40 manufacturers in the area have, at some point, used the term to describe their work, and there are at least 400 different Limoges identification marks. The common denominator is the product itself: fine hard-paste porcelain created from the necessary components found in abundance in the Limoges region: kaolin and feldspar.

Until the 1700s, porcelain was exclusively a product of China, introduced to the Western world by Marco Polo and imported at great expense. In 1765, the discovery of kaolin in St. Yrieixin, a small town near Limoges, made French production of porcelain possible. (The chemist's wife credited with the kaolin discovery thought at first that it would prove useful in making soap.)

Limoges entrepreneurs quickly capitalized on the find. Adding to the area's allure: expansive forests, providing fuel for wood-burning kilns; the nearby Vienne River, with water for working clay; and a workforce eager to trade farming for a (hopefully) more lucrative pursuit. Additionally, as the companies would be operating outside metropolitan Paris, labor and production costs would be significantly less.

By the early 1770s, numerous porcelain manufacturers were at work in Limoges and its environs. Demand for the porcelain was high because it was both useful and decorative. To meet that demand, firms employed trained as well as untrained artisans for the detailed hand painting required. (Although nearly every type of Limoges has its fans, the most sought-after – and valuable – are

Plate with portrait of maiden, flow blue border, china white windows with hand applied raised gold flowers and gold trim surrounds, signed by well-known Limoges portrait painter E. (Etienne) Furlaud, stamped in green "G.D.(Demartine) & Cie, Limoges, France," 8-1/2" dia. **$80**

Courtesy of Mark Mussio, Humler & Nolan, www.humlernolan.com

those pieces decorated by a company's professional artists.) At its industrial peak in 1900, Limoges factories employed over 8,000 workers in some aspect of porcelain production.

Myriad products classified as Limoges flooded the marketplace from the late 1700s onward. Among them were tableware pieces, such as tea and punch sets, trays, pitchers, compotes, bowls, and plates. Also popular were vases and flower baskets, dresser sets, trinket boxes, ash receivers, figural busts, and decorative plaques.

Although produced in France, Limoges porcelain was soon destined for export overseas; eventually over 80 percent of Limoges porcelain was exported. The United States proved a particularly reliable customer. Notable among the importers was the Haviland China Co.; until the 1940s, its superior, exquisitely decorated china was produced in Limoges and then distributed in the United States.

By the early 20th century, many exporters in the United States were purchasing porcelain blanks from the Limoges factories for decoration stateside. The base product was authentically made in France, but production costs were significantly lower: Thousands of untrained porcelain painters put their skills to work for a minimal wage. Domestic decoration of the blanks also meant that importers could select designs suited to the specific tastes of target audiences.

Because Limoges was a regional designation, rather than the identifier of a specific manufacturer, imported pieces were often marked with the name of the exporting firm, followed by the word "Limoges." Beginning in 1891, "France" was added. Some confusion has arisen from products marked "Limoges China Co." (aka "American Limoges"). This Ohio-based firm, in business from 1902-1955, has absolutely no connection to the porcelain produced in France.

The heyday of quality French Limoges lasted roughly into the 1930s. Production continues today, but after WWII, designs and painting techniques became much more standardized.

Porcelain dinner service, A. Vignaud: 14 each dinner plates, dessert plates, butter plates, soup bowls, soup saucers, cups, and saucers, six demi cups, and six demi saucers, one cup with edge chip, dinner plates 10-1/2" dia. **$438**

Courtesy of Leslie Hindman Auctioneers, www.lesliehindman.com

Vintage Limoges is highly sought-after by today's collectors. They're drawn to the delicacy of the porcelain as well as the colors and skill of decoration; viewing a well-conceived Limoges piece is like seeing a painting in a new form. Valuation is based on age, decorative execution and, as with any collectible, individual visual appeal.

For more information on Limoges, see *Antique Trader Pottery and Porcelain Ceramics Price Guide*, 7th edition.

Center bowl, polychrome and gilt, 13-1/8" w. $88

Courtesy of Leslie Hindman Auctioneers, www.lesliehindman.com

Two sets of plates, circa 1900, 9-3/4" dia. and 7-1/2" dia. $400

Courtesy of Soulis Auctions, Lone Jack, Missouri, www.dirksoulisauctions.com

Le Tallec porcelain tableware for Tiffany & Co., 16 pieces, early 20th century: two small covered tureens with underplates and 14 plates with Asian motif and gilt accents, France, marked with Le Tallec's cypher, initials "AM" and "TIFFANY & CO PRIVATE STOCK HAND-PAINTED IN FRANCE," some plates with light scratches/wear, small chip to one tureen, plates 10-5/8" dia.....................................**$4,063**

Courtesy of Rago Arts and Auctions, www.ragoarts.com

Bolted urn, baluster form body with tapering neck, oval painted image of maiden with halo and open book in reserve against gilt ground with blue jeweled beading and raised gold floral enamels, underglaze signature for William Geurin beneath foot, one factory glaze miss on top of foot, 21-1/2" h.
.... **$675**

Courtesy of Soulis Auctions, Lone Jack, Missouri, www.dirksoulisauctions.com

Round chargers, hand-painted, brave in headdress, maiden in headdress, marked "T & V Limoges," both signed "Gilmer," 18" h..................**$590**

Courtesy of Woody Auction, www.woodyauction.com

CERAMICS

Haviland plate, cobalt blue border, hand-painted woman in statue garden, artist signed "S. Athrand," marked, 9-1/4" dia. **$148**

Courtesy of Woody Auction, www.woodyauction.com

Ball-shaped vase, green tones, floral décor, gold trim, Limoges (J.P.L.) mark, 7" x 8". **$118**

Courtesy of Woody Auction, www.woodyauction.com

Three-piece Haviland Limoges tea set, teapot with underplate, matching creamer and sugar, brown tones with pink and yellow rose décor, heavy gold trim, teapot 9" h. **$266**

Courtesy of Woody Auction, www.woodyauction.com

Tankard, hand-painted blackberry décor, gold trim, artist signed "A. Kohler," Limoges (J.P.L.) mark, 11-3/4" h. **$118**

Courtesy of Woody Auction, www.woodyauction.com

Two Coronet hand-painted plates, cavalier scenic décors, artist signed, 10-1/4" dia. **$59**

Courtesy of Woody Auction, www.woodyauction.com

Seven-piece chocolate set, H&H Limoges, chocolate pot with six matching cups and saucers, hand-painted rose décor, gold trim, artist signed, 11-1/2" h. **$1,062**

Courtesy of Woody Auction, www.woodyauction.com

Picture frame wall plaque, lake scene with girl and dog near shore, artist signed "PAL," maroon and gold border, 10-3/4" x 13-3/4"................. **$708**

Courtesy of Woody Auction, www.woodyauction.com

Tankard with figural green and blue tones with large pink rose décor, Limoges (JPL) mark, artist signed "Leana," 14-1/2" h. **$1,416**

Courtesy of Woody Auction, www.woodyauction.com

CERAMICS

Assembled nine-piece bowl and sherbet set, hand-painted rose décor with gold trim highlights , bowl with T&V Limoges mark, not exact pattern match, bowl 4-1/4" x 9-1/2", sherbets 3" h..................... **$2,124**

Courtesy of Woody Auction, www.woodyauction.com

Picture frame plaque, hand-painted rose décor with gold "frame," 11-1/4" x 14-1/2". **$207**

Courtesy of Woody Auction, www.woodyauction.com

Two-handled vase, hand-painted in green and blue tones with pink and yellow rose décor, 13-1/2" h. **$266**

Courtesy of Woody Auction, www.woodyauction.com

Scenic wall plaque of woman standing on marble terrace looking at her reflection, set in modern 18" x 14-1/2" frame, Limoges (D&C) mark, plaque 12" x 8-3/4". **$354**

Courtesy of Woody Auction, www.woodyauction.com

Chocolate pot, hand-painted in blue tones with pink rose décor, gold trim, marked "Limoges B&H" and "W.J. Alexander, Troy, New York," 9" h. **$708**

Courtesy of Woody Auction, www.woodyauction.com

CERAMICS

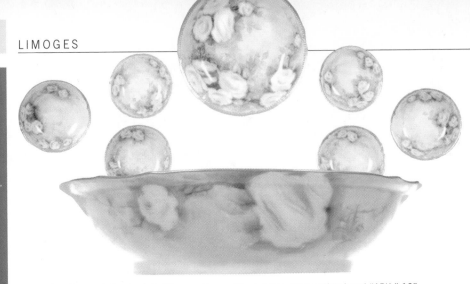

Seven-piece berry set, hand-painted in green tones with pink rose décor, artist signed "APK," 10" master bowl with six matching 5-1/4" berry dishes. $236

Courtesy of Woody Auction, www.woodyauction.com

"Incrustation Double Dorure Polie a L'agate" partial dinner service for 12 plus extras, 63 pieces, 1882-1900: 12 dinner plates, 10"; nine salad plates, 9-1/4"; 12 bread plates, 6-1/4"; 12 dessert plates, 7-1/2"; two teacups; 13 saucers, 5-1/2"; serving platter; and casserole, all ink-stamped "CH FIELD HAVILAND LIMOGES," numbered 26, with original wood shipping crates. $875

Courtesy of Rago Arts and Auctions, www.ragoarts.com

Oval pillow-shape vase with two handles, hand-painted night scene of village with lions watching from rocks, figural gold dragon handles, JPL mark, artist signed "A. Heidrich," "E.W. Donach" mark with original "Donach $1000 Reward" label, 10" x 9-1/2". $826

Courtesy of Woody Auction, www.woodyauction.com

CERAMICS

majolica

IN 1851, AN ENGLISH POTTER was hoping that his new interpretation of a centuries-old style of ceramics would be well received at the "Great Exhibition of the Industries of All Nations" set to open May 1 in London's Hyde Park.

Potter Herbert Minton had high hopes for his display. His father, Thomas Minton, founded a pottery works in the mid-1790s in Stoke-on-Trent, Staffordshire. Herbert Minton had designed a "new" line of pottery, and his chemist, Leon Arnoux, had developed a process that resulted in vibrant, colorful glazes that came to be called "majolica."

Trained as an engineer, Arnoux also studied the making of encaustic tiles, and had been appointed art director at Minton's works in 1848. His job was to introduce and promote new products. Victorian fascination with the natural world prompted Arnoux to reintroduce the work of Bernard Palissy, whose naturalistic, bright-colored "maiolica" wares had been created in the 16th century. But Arnoux used a thicker body to make pieces sturdier. This body was given a coating of opaque white glaze, which provided a surface for decoration.

Pieces were modeled in high relief, featuring butterflies and other insects, flowers and leaves, fruit, shells, animals, and fish. Queen Victoria's endorsement of the new pottery prompted its acceptance by the general public.

When Minton introduced his wares at Philadelphia's 1876 Centennial Exhibition, American potters also began to produce majolica.

For more information on majolica, see *Warman's Majolica Identification and Price Guide* by Mark F. Moran.

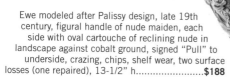

Ewe modeled after Palissy design, late 19th century, figural handle of nude maiden, each side with oval cartouche of reclining nude in landscape against cobalt ground, signed "Pull" to underside, crazing, chips, shelf wear, two surface losses (one repaired), 13-1/2" h.......................**$188**

Courtesy of Leslie Hindman Auctioneers, www.lesliehindman.com

Minton butter dish, circa 1860, circular body and underplate decorated as brown planked fence with leaves and purple berries, twin handles formed as head of cow, 8"dia. **$308**

Courtesy of Strawser Auctions/Nicolaus Boston, www.strawserauctions.com

William Brownfield and Sons advertising cookie jar, circa 1875, turquoise glazed sack tied with orange ribbon gnawed by white mouse, second white mouse disappearing into hole on other side, lid modeled as pile of Peak Frean biscuits (Peak Freen was a brand of popular Victorian biscuits), 8" h... **$584**

Courtesy of Strawser Auctions/Nicolaus Boston, www.strawserauctions.com

William Brownfield and Sons "Swirling Fish" pitcher, circa 1880, body formed as two entwined fish supported on waves, brown glazed handle terminating in green seaweed, design registered in January 1879, 11-1/2" h. **$1,968**

Courtesy of Strawser Auctions/Nicolaus Boston, www.strawserauctions.com

Jardinière and pedestal with mask decoration, late 19th century, jardinière crazed on underside, jardinière base repaired, 54-1/4" h. **$688**

Courtesy of Leslie Hindman Auctioneers, www.lesliehindman.com

Minton "Vintager with Basket" grape holder, circa 1865, designed by H. Protat (Minton's art director), man in medieval costume holding basket with woven pannier on his back, design taken from "The Grape Gatherers," 16" h............... **$738**

Courtesy of Strawser Auctions/Nicolaus Boston, www.strawserauctions.com

Three Minton articles, 19th century: tower jug with jester finial, pewter lid slightly warped; commemorative Shakespeare jug; and charger with profile medallion; each with impressed numbers and date cipher, each with crazing and light shelf wear, Shakespeare jug with minor glaze skips, charger with minor edge frets, tallest 12-3/4" h... **$1,125**

Courtesy of Leslie Hindman Auctioneers, www.lesliehindman.com

George Jones "Ribbon and Wheat" bread tray, pattern 1871, circa 1875, oval body, mottled green and brown center with wide border of lavender ribbon tied in bow at each end among wheat, berries, leaves, and blossoms, 13"........ **$400**

Courtesy of Strawser Auctions/Nicolaus Boston, www.strawserauctions.com

Jardinière with fixed lion mask ring handles and lion's paw feet, late 19th century, hairline crack to circular ring, hairline crack to vertical band, repaired break to paw foot, other minor losses and discolorations, 17-3/4" h. **$375**

Courtesy of Leslie Hindman Auctioneers, www.lesliehindman.com

George Jones game pie dish and cover, pattern 347, circa 1875, oval form with double branch handles, body decorated with rabbits in field, cobalt ground, registered design on Dec. 27, 1873, 13" dia. **$2,337**

Courtesy of Strawser Auctions/Nicolaus Boston, www.strawserauctions.com

Rare pair of saker falcon figurines by Hugo Lonitz, Neuhaldensleben, Germany, circa 1880, only known examples, life-size male and female perched on rocky ground, 20" h. and 18-1/2" h. The saker falcon is the national bird of Hungary and known as "Turul" in Hungarian mythology. Originally from Eastern Europe, Russia and the Balkans, the saker, known for its beauty, strength and speed, has been used for falconry for thousands of years. In the Middle East, where falconry is a national sport, the saker is the most celebrated bird. Like other birds of prey, the female is larger than the male.
.... $73,800

Rare pair of George Jones "Weaver Bird" vases, circa 1875, one vase modeled as bird's nest with large weaver bird swooping down to catch beetle, other to catch moth, held by bunch of cattails and blossoms, on ground domed base, each 9-1/2" **$10,455**

Courtesy of Strawser Auctions/Nicolaus Boston, www.strawserauctions.com

Pair of Minton lobed quatrefoil sky blue-glazed vases, circa 1870, each with lily leaves and white blossoms, handles formed as two winged putti, shaped cushioned base with lily leaves and white blossoms, 13-1/2" h. **$2,768**

Courtesy of Strawser Auctions/Nicolaus Boston, www.strawserauctions.com

Minton Gothic Revival eight-lobed plate designed by A.W.N. Putin, circa 1860, rim with raised ochre quatrefoils on cobalt blue ground, center with raised green-glazed vine leaves and ochre grapes against maroon ground, central white Tudor rose surrounded by band of ochre trefoil shapes against cobalt blue ground, 9-1/2" dia. A porcelain example of this plate can be seen in the collection at the Victoria and Albert Museum, London. **$1,230**

Courtesy of Strawser Auctions/Nicolaus Boston, www.strawserauctions.com

Minton Neo-Classical "Reader Vase" designed by Albert Carrier Belleuse, circa 1870, inscribed "A' Carrier," maiden in brown gown with open book, resting on gray lion mask-adorned pedestal, helmet-shaped bowl flowerholder with garlands of roses and female figurehead to front, green oval pedestal base, 19-1/2" h. x 18" w. **$2,460**

Courtesy of Strawser Auctions/Nicolaus Boston, www.strawserauctions.com

Minton game tureen and cover, circa 1878, base modeled as oval
pâté mold in yellow, ochre, and blue on fixed basketwork tray or
stand with rope handles, cover with heads of two hares and two
mallards on cobalt-glazed dome with yellow florets, impressed
"MINTONS" with date cipher and "Shape no 1990," 19" l. **$27,060**

Courtesy of Strawser Auctions/Nicolaus Boston, www.strawserauctions.com

George Jones Neo-Classical
cobalt blue-glazed amphora
vase, circa 1875, three
acanthus-and-berry-decorated
square section supports, legs
and rams' head-decorated
high handles, trefoil mottled
pedestal base, 15-1/4" h. ... **$861**

*Courtesy of Strawser Auctions/Nicolaus Boston,
www.strawserauctions.com*

Minton "Mushroom" tureen, circa 1875, oval fern and ivy tree trunk with green ground, fixed undertray,
fox at either end watching two mallards, lid modeled as top of tree trunk with ivy and mushroom
handle, 7-1/2" h. x 16" w. **$9,840**

Courtesy of Strawser Auctions/Nicolaus Boston, www.strawserauctions.com

CERAMICS

marblehead

MARBLEHEAD POTTERY WAS organized in 1904 by Dr. Herbert J. Hall as a therapeutic aid to patients in a sanitarium he ran in Marblehead, Massachusetts. It was later separated from the sanitarium and directed by Arthur E. Baggs, a fine artist and designer, who bought out the factory in 1916 and operated it until its closing in 1936. Most wares were hand-thrown and decorated and carry the company mark of a stylized sailing vessel flanked by the letters "M" and "P."

Vase with stylized flowers by Arthur Hennessey and Sarah Tutt, early 20th century, stamped ship mark MP, signed HT, 5-1/4" x 3-1/4"......... **$1,625**

Courtesy of Rago Arts and Auctions, www.ragoarts.com

Tile of blue and black vase with pink and purple flowers, no artist signature, partial Marblehead Pottery label on back, 6" sq., framed 9-7/8" sq.. **$400**

Courtesy of Mark Mussio, Humler & Nolan, www.humlernolan.com

Vase with repeating leaves and berries, impressed Marblehead ship logo, original Marblehead Pottery label, 3-1/4" h. **$1,000**

Courtesy of Mark Mussio, Humler & Nolan, www.humlernolan.com

Vase with dark blue speckled mat glaze, impressed Marblehead logo, 9-5/8" h. **$350**

Courtesy of Mark Mussio, Humler & Nolan, www.humlernolan.com

Vase with dark blue mat glaze, impressed Marblehead ship logo, overall crazing, 8-7/8" h. **$200**

Courtesy of Mark Mussio, Humler & Nolan, www.humlernolan.com

Vase with blue mat glaze, impressed Marblehead logo, 3-1/2" h. **$225**

Courtesy of Mark Mussio, Humler & Nolan, www.humlernolan.com

Vase with green mat glaze with dripped purple mat glaze, impressed Marblehead ship logo, overall crazing, open glaze bubbles, 8-7/8" h. **$275**

Courtesy of Mark Mussio, Humler & Nolan, www.humlernolan.com

top lot !

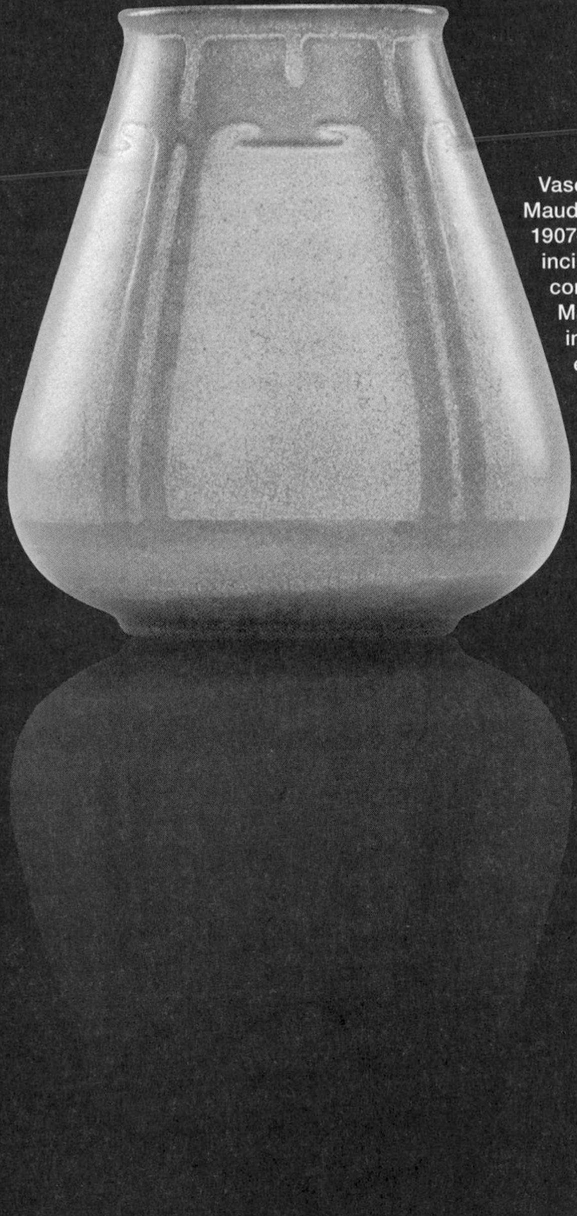

Vase with geometric design by Maude Milner and Sarah Tutt, circa 1907-1910, stamped ship mark MP, incised MT, 5-3/4" x 5". Milner contributed few designs to Marblehead's repertoire, and only in the first years of the pottery's existence. $10,000

CERAMICS

Vase with geometric design by Arthur Hennessey and Sarah Tutt, 1910s, stamped ship mark MP, incised HT, 3-3/4" x 4-1/4"........................ **$7,500**

Courtesy of Rago Arts and Auctions, www.ragoarts.com

Vase with light purple mat glaze, impressed Marblehead ship logo, 3" h. **$100**

Courtesy of Mark Mussio, Humler & Nolan, www.humlernolan.com

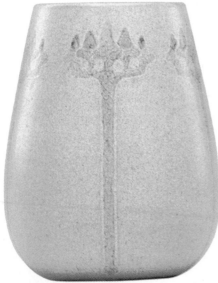

Ovoid vase with stylized trees by Arthur Hennessey and Sarah Tutt, circa 1910s, glazed terracotta, impressed ship mark, MP, signed H.T., 7", 4" dia. **$938**

Courtesy of Rago Arts and Auctions, www.ragoarts.co

Vase with stylized plants by Arthur Hennessey and Sarah Tutt, early 20th century, stamped ship mark MP, incised HT, 4-1/2" x 3-1/2". **$3,250**

Courtesy of Rago Arts and Auctions, www.ragoarts.com

CERAMICS

martin brothers

MARTINWARE, THE TERM used for this pottery, dates from 1873 and is the product of the Martin brothers – Robert, Wallace, Edwin, Walter, and Charles – and is often considered the first British studio pottery. From first to final stages, the hand-thrown pottery was completely the work of the team. The early wares may be simple and conventional, but the Martin brothers built their reputation by producing ornately engraved, incised, or carved designs as well as rather bizarre figural wares. The amusing face jugs are considered some of their finest work. After 1910, the work of the pottery declined and can be considered finished by 1915, though some attempts were made to fire pottery as late as the 1920s.

Glazed stoneware bird jar and cover, circa 1898, signed along base and head Martin Bros. London + Southall, 9-1898, 13-1/4" h. **$42,500**

Courtesy Heritage Auctions, www.ha.com

Glazed stoneware leering hatter bird jar and cover, circa 1888, signed along base and lid R.W. Martin & Brothers, London & Southall, 12.1888, 11-3/4" h. **$30,000**

Courtesy Heritage Auctions, www.ha.com

Glazed stoneware bird jar and cover, circa 1901, signed along base and lid Martin Bros. London + Southall, 1-1901, 7-5/8" h. **$8,000**

Courtesy Heritage Auctions, www.ha.com

▶ Glazed stoneware bird-form spoon warmer, circa 1900-1910, signed along base and interior Martin Bros, London + Southall. Warmer was originally accompanied by a lower half, now absent, 4" h x 5-1/4" dia. **$1,125**

Courtesy Heritage Auctions, www.ha.com

▶ Small glazed stoneware bird, circa 1913, signed along base RW Martin + Bro, London + Southall, 18-6-1913, 3-1/2" h........ **$6,000**

Courtesy Heritage Auctions, www.ha.com

Glazed stoneware quizzical bird jar and cover, circa 1904, signed along base and lid R.W. Martin + Bros. London + Southall, 25. 5. 1904, 6-1/2" h. **$10,000**

Courtesy Heritage Auctions, www.ha.com

Glazed stoneware grotesque and long beaked bird jar and cover, circa 1884, engraved to base, cover, and flange R.W. Martin & Brothers, Southall + London, 6.1884, observed under blacklight, appears to have a stabilized hairline crack and firing cracks to the interior of the body, 14" h. **$81,250**

Courtesy Heritage Auctions, www.ha.com

Glazed stoneware grotesque bird jar and cover, circa 1893, signed along base and lid Martin Bros 1893, London + Southall, 10-3/8" h. **$27,500**

Courtesy Heritage Auctions, www.ha.com

Glazed stoneware grotesque double-sided face jug, circa 1911, signed to underside R. W. Martin & Bros, London & Southall, 11-3-1911, 6" h. **$4,250**

Courtesy Heritage Auctions, www.ha.com

Glazed stoneware triple Wally Bird jar and cover, circa 1906, signed along base and lids R.W. Martin Bros. London + Southall, 27.2.1906, 7-3/4" h x 8-1/8" w. **$40,000**

Courtesy Heritage Auctions, www.ha.com

CERAMICS

Pitcher with dragon handle, 1878, by Robert W.
Martin, England, glazed stoneware, incised R.W.
Martin Southall 2-78/65, professional restoration
to handle, 7-3/4" x 5-1/2". **$938**

Courtesy of Rago Arts, www.ragoarts.com

Large stoneware vase with
snake handles, 1900, England,
incised 11-1900 Martin Bros.
London + Southall, chip to one
handle, 11-1/2" x 6". **$13,750**

Courtesy of Rago Arts, www.ragoarts.com

Vase with dragon, lizards, and beetle, 1889, Robert W. Martin,
England, glazed stoneware, incised 3-1889 R.W. Martin + Bros
London + Southall, crack around top of shoulder/ bottom of neck
(possibly reglued break), 9-1/2" x 6-1/2". **$1,875**

Courtesy of Rago Arts, www.ragoarts.com

CERAMICS

mccoy

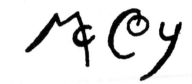

THE FIRST MCCOY with clay under his fingernails was W. Nelson McCoy. With his uncle, W. F. McCoy, he founded a pottery works in Putnam, Ohio, in 1848, making stoneware crocks and jugs.

That same year, W. Nelson's son, James W., was born in Zanesville, Ohio. James established the J. W. McCoy Pottery Co. in Roseville, Ohio, in the fall of 1899. The J. W. McCoy plant was destroyed by fire in 1903 and was rebuilt two years later.

It was at this time that the first examples of Loy-Nel-Art wares were produced. The line's distinctive title came from the names of James McCoy's three sons, Lloyd, Nelson, and Arthur. Like other "standard" glazed pieces produced at this time by several Ohio potteries, Loy-Nel-Art has a glossy finish on a dark brown-black body, but Loy-Nel-Art featured a splash of green color on the front and a burnt-orange splash on the back.

George Brush became general manager of J. W. McCoy Pottery Co. in 1909. The company became Brush-McCoy Pottery Co. in 1911, and in 1925 the name was shortened to Brush Pottery Co. This firm remained in business until 1982.

Separately, in 1910, Nelson McCoy, Sr. founded the Nelson McCoy Sanitary and Stoneware Co., also in Roseville. By the early 1930s, production had shifted from utilitarian wares to art pottery, and the company name was changed to Nelson McCoy Pottery.

Designer Sydney Cope was hired in 1934, and was joined by his son, Leslie, in 1936. The Copes' influence on McCoy wares continued until Sydney's death in 1966. That same year, Leslie opened a gallery devoted to his family's design heritage and featuring his own original art.

Nelson McCoy, Sr. died in 1945, and was succeeded as company president by his nephew, Nelson McCoy Melick.

A fire destroyed the plant in 1950, but company officials – including Nelson McCoy, Jr., then 29 – decided to rebuild, and the new Nelson McCoy Pottery Co. was up and running in just six months.

Nelson Melick died in 1954. Nelson, Jr. became company president and oversaw the company's continued growth. In 1967, the operation was sold to entrepreneur David Chase. At this time, the words "Mt. Clemens Pottery" were added to the company marks. In 1974, Chase sold the company to Lancaster Colony Corp., and the company marks included a stylized "LCC" logo. Nelson, Jr. and his wife, Billie, who had served as a products supervisor, left the company in 1981.

In 1985, the company was sold again, this time to Designer Accents. The McCoy pottery factory closed in 1990.

For more information on McCoy pottery, see *Warman's McCoy Pottery*, 2nd edition, by Mark F. Moran.

Loy-Nel-Art three-handled loving cup, green and brown with wheat décor, unmarked, minor base chip, 6" x 6"... $36

Courtesy of Woody Auction, www.woodyauction.com

Brush-McCoy Jewel pattern candlesticks, marked with shape number 030, one broken and reglued, 7" h. $140

Courtesy of Mark Mussio, Humler & Nolan, www.humlernolan.com

Brush-McCoy Greek Key pattern matte green jardinière with white enameling, impressed 222 below, overall crazing with surface scuffs and scratches, 8-1/2" x 10-1/4". $70

Courtesy of Mark Mussio, Humler & Nolan, www.humlernolan.com

Loy-Nel-Art vase with tulip, dark brown ground, impressed Loy-Nel-Art / McCoy mark, 3-3/4" h., 4-3/4" dia.. $36

Courtesy of Martin Auction Co., www.martinauctionco.com

Large Loy-Nel-Art vase, shape number stamp on bottom not fully legible, minor scuff marks, 10-1/4" h. x 6-1/4" w. **$90**

Courtesy of Just Art Pottery, www.justartpottery.com

Loy-Nel-Art vase with yellow iris and leaves, crazing, 11-1/4" h. x 5-1/2" w. **$165**

Courtesy of Just Art Pottery, www.justartpottery.com

Davy Crockett cookie jar, 1957, marked "USA" on base, approximately 10" h. **$156**

Courtesy of The Auction Gallery of Boca Raton, agobr.com

CERAMICS

meissen

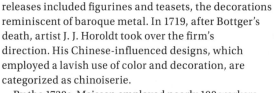

KNOWN FOR ITS finely detailed figurines and exceptional tableware, Meissen is recognized as the first European maker of fine porcelain.

The company owes its beginning to Johann Friedrich Bottger's 1708 discovery of the process necessary for the manufacture of porcelain. "Rediscovery" might be a better term, since the secret of producing hard paste porcelain had been known to the Chinese for centuries. However, Bottger, a goldsmith and alchemist, was the first to successfully replicate the formula in Europe. Soon after, The Royal Saxon Porcelain Works set up shop in Dresden. Because Bottger's formula was highly sought after by would-be competitors, in 1710 the firm moved its base of operations to Albrechtburg Castle in Meissen, Saxony. There, in fortress-like surroundings, prying eyes could be successfully deflected. And, because of that move, the company name eventually became one with its locale: Meissen.

The earliest Meissen pieces were red stoneware, reminiscent of Chinese work, and incised with Chinese characters. Porcelain became the Meissen focus in 1713; early releases included figurines and teasets, the decorations reminiscent of baroque metal. In 1719, after Bottger's death, artist J. J. Horoldt took over the firm's direction. His Chinese-influenced designs, which employed a lavish use of color and decoration, are categorized as chinoiserie.

By the 1730s, Meissen employed nearly 100 workers, among them renowned modelers J. G. Kirchner and J. J. Kandler. The firm became known for its porcelain sculptures; subjects included birds, animals, and familiar figures from commedia dell'arte. Meissen dinnerware also won acclaim; in earlier attempts, the company's white porcelain had only managed to achieve off-white.

Mythological group, the "Capture of Triton," Crossed Swords mark in blue under glaze, impressed 110 and hand inscribed G35 beneath, small repair to back tip of the pink garment, few fern fronds and plants missing, chip on Triton's hand, antenna missing, 13-1/2" h x 10" l...................................**$800**

Courtesy of Mark Mussio, Humler & Nolan,
www.humlernolan.com

Tea and coffee service, 11 pieces, tray 16" w. $125
Courtesy of Leslie Hindman Auctioneers, www.lesliehindman.com

Now, at last, there were dazzling white porcelain surfaces that proved ideal for the exquisite, richly colored decoration that became a Meissen trademark.

Following Horoldt's retirement in the mid-1700s, Victor Acier became Meissen's master modeler. Under Acier, the design focus relied heavily on mythological themes. By the early 1800s, however, Meissen's popularity began to wane. With production costs mounting and quality inconsistent, changes were instituted, especially technical improvements in production that allowed Meissen to operate more efficiently and profitably. More importantly, the Meissen designs, which had remained relatively stagnant for nearly a century, were refurbished. The goal: to connect with current popular culture. Meissen's artists (and its porcelain) proved perfectly capable of adapting to the prevailing tastes of the times. The range was wide: the ornate fussiness of the Rococo period; the more subdued Neoclassicism of the late 1700s; the nature-tinged voluptuousness of early 20th century Art Nouveau; and today's Meissen, which reinterprets, and builds on, all of these design eras.

Despite diligent efforts, Meissen eventually found its work widely copied. A crossed-swords trademark, applied to Meissen pieces from 1731 onward, is a good indicator of authenticity. However, even the markings had their imitators. Because Meissen originals, particularly those from the 18th and 19th centuries, are both rare and costly, the most reliable guarantee that a piece is authentic is to purchase from a reputable source.

Meissen porcelain is an acquired taste. Its gilded glory, lavish use of color, and almost overwhelmingly intricate detailing require just the right setting for effective display. Meissen is not background décor. These are three-dimensional artworks that demand full attention. Meissen pieces also often tell a story (although the plots may be long forgotten): a cherub and a woman in 18th century dress read a book, surrounded by a bevy of shepherdesses; the goddess Diana perches on a clock above a winged head of Father Time; the painted inset on a cobalt teacup depicts an ancient Dresden cathedral approached by devout churchgoers. Unforgettable images all, and all part of the miracle that is Meissen.

Pair of ornithological plates, 19th c., decorated with birds and insects, 9-1/2" dia. **$125**

Courtesy of Leslie Hindman Auctioneers, www.lesliehindman.com

Triangular dish, 20th c., 9" h. **$188**

Courtesy of Leslie Hindman Auctioneers, www.lesliehindman.com

Dessert service: 12 plates, teapot, creamer, covered sugar, two cups, two saucers, tazza, plates 8-1/2" dia. **$688**

Courtesy of Leslie Hindman Auctioneers, www.lesliehindman.com

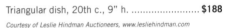

Meissen porcelain cabinet cup and saucer of American interest, circa 1876, with relief busts of George Washington, Benjamin Franklin, and an American Eagle, 5-1/4" h x 6 7/8" dia. **$1,342**

Courtesy of Pook & Pook, Inc., www.pookandpook.com

Inkstand, 20th c., four monkeys above an openwork back having rocaille and foliate scrolls, together with bell and inkwell, each bearing a crossed swords mark in underglaze blue, inkstand 8-5/8" w. **$1,000**

Courtesy of Leslie Hindman Auctioneers, www.lesliehindman.com

Pair of figural master salts, Blue Onion, 19th/20th c., modeled as reclining lady and gentleman, each bearing a crossed swords mark in underglaze blue, incised and impressed numbers to the underside, 6-3/4" w. **$313**

Courtesy of Leslie Hindman Auctioneers, www.lesliehindman.com

Assembled tea service, 19 items total, teapot 3-1/2" h. **$344**

Courtesy of Leslie Hindman Auctioneers, www.lesliehindman.com

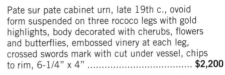

Porcelain terrier figure, late 19th c., painted black
and white, Germany, painted mark, chip to underside
of tail, 6" x 5" x 3-1/2" **$531**

Courtesy of Rago Arts, www.ragoarts.com

Pate sur pate cabinet urn, late 19th c., ovoid
form suspended on three rococo legs with gold
highlights, body decorated with cherubs, flowers
and butterflies, embossed vinery at each leg,
crossed swords mark with cut under vessel, chips
to rim, 6-1/4" x 4" **$2,200**

Courtesy of Soulis Auctions, Lone Jack, Mo.; www.dirksoulisauctions.com

Porcelain figure, 19th c.,
classical maiden resting upon a
tree along a stream, Germany,
cobalt crossed swords under
glaze, numbers "S 107" incised
and "137" impressed, black grit
in porcelain throughout, small
chips and losses throughout, 16-
3/4" x 7" x 7-3/4" **$1,625**

Porcelain stein, late 19th c., reserve of boar hunt scene on cobalt
ground, hinged lid with landscape scene on underside, all with gilt
scrollwork decoration, Germany, marked, restoration, few areas of
slight wear to gilt decoration, 8" h. **$938**

Courtesy of Rago Arts, www.ragoarts.com

CERAMICS

mettlach

CERAMICS WITH THE NAME METTLACH were produced by Villeroy & Boch and other potteries in the Mettlach area of Germany. Villery & Boch's finest years of production are thought to be from about 1890-1910.

▲ Four-liter master stein, 1903, pewter lid with detailed eagle thumb lift, military scene paint under glaze pays tribute to Germany's pre-World War I military, incised Mettlach Abbey trademark with numerals 2227, GESCHUTZT and date mark for 1903, 20-1/2" x 6-1/2".. **$950**

Courtesy of Soulis Auctions, Lone Jack, Missouri, www.dirksoulisauctions.com

▶ Master stein with bands of glazed engraved designs encircling top above textured ground with heraldic trophies in high relief and jeweled slip designs encircling full-length etched portrait of cavalier with weaponry, downturned halberd and lidded flagon, incised Mettlach Abbey trademark, numbered 1498 under base, 21" h.................. **$975**

Courtesy of Soulis Auctions, Lone Jack, Missouri, www.dirksoulisauctions.com

Villeroy & Boch scenic charger, marked V&B Mettlach logo, impressed "1044 FB No 1, 85," hand-marked "140Y, JB" on back, 17" dia **$100**

Courtesy of Mark Mussio, Humler & Nolan, www.humlernolan.com

Paint under glaze master stein/pitcher, 1929, 3.25L, printed under glaze with drinking gnomes, inlaid lid with gnome thumb rest, impressed mark on base "METTLACH / VB" below tower and "2183," printed "1031 / GESCHUTZT," 14" h. **$199**

Courtesy of Jeffrey S. Evans & Associates, www.jeffreysevans.com

Etched half-liter stein, number 1475, gnomes at work motif, pewter lid and thumb lift, impressed Abbey mark "VILLEROY & BOCH" and "METTLACH" surrounding "PATENT" and 1475, additional smaller impressed numbers "20" and "83" on base. **$350**

Courtesy of Soulis Auctions, Lone Jack, Missouri, www.dirksoulisauctions.com

Etched half-liter stein, number 1797, playing card motif, inscription on lid in German and date 1900, base with impressed Abbey mark "METTLACH" and "VB" initials, Gegen Nachbildung Geschützt, 1797 (form), smaller impressed numbers "34" and "90"...................**$390**

Courtesy of Soulis Auctions, Lone Jack, Missouri, www.dirksoulisauctions.com

Salt-glazed half-liter stein, number 1727, German motto in cartouche, impressed Abbey mark "METTLACH" and "VB" initials, 1727, smaller impressed numbers "20", "11" and "09" on base. **$80**

Courtesy of Soulis Auctions, Lone Jack, Missouri, www.dirksoulisauctions.com

1891 Villeroy & Boch Mettlach trade catalog, hardcover, date on illustrated cover September 1890, with multiple supplements referencing catalog, inserted but not bound in endpapers, including stoneware price guide, one for "old fashioned articles," and bound stoneware supplement, all dated September 1891, all elements with photographs of items, German text; normal toning and minor foxing to pages, tear along spine at front endpapers, wear to cover and illustration, rubbing and bumping of leather, loss to reverse board paper, 10-1/2" x 7-1/2". $600

Courtesy of Soulis Auctions, Lone Jack, Missouri, www.dirksoulisauctions.com

▼ Etched stein with inlaid lid and mosaic trim, circa 1892, signed "H. Schlitt" in etched design, impressed markings under base, Mettlach Abbey trademark, numerals 2065, GEGEN NACHBILDUNG GESCHUTZT, 14-3/4" h. $375

Courtesy of Soulis Auctions, Lone Jack, Missouri, www.dirksoulisauctions.com

CERAMICS

Black Whale of Ascalon three-liter stein, commemoration of old German story and drinking song, white relief scenes against blue ground, bands of glazed decoration and incised lettering, large alligator figural handle, inlaid lid with sea turtle, base marked with incised Abbey trademark and Mettlach 2194, large repaired chip at front edge of foot..... **$450**

Courtesy of Soulis Auctions, Lone Jack, Missouri, www.dirksoulisauctions.com

Jeweled three-liter stein with etched figure in front of barrel with background of hops, 1912, signed "C Wurth" for decorator Christian Wurth (1820-1902), incised Mettlach Abbey trademark, numbered 1940, "US Patent" and "Made in Germany" to base, 17" h. **$650**

Courtesy of Soulis Auctions, Lone Jack, Missouri, www.dirksoulisauctions.com

Monumental two-piece beer tap head, design of DeKannenburg castle scene, identical to image on stein 2580, signed "Heinr. Schlitt," image of knight at castle entrance, 30" h. **$1,900**

Courtesy of Soulis Auctions, Lone Jack, Missouri, www.dirksoulisauctions.com

Pair of paint-under-glaze plaques: first plaque with portrait of man with violin in embossed portico, columns at each side and frieze of cherubs in relief below, music and sword at one corner, markings on back: impressed 2274 11 and other faint numerals, DEC 5231 in brown under glaze; second plaque of matching coloration and mold with embossed grapes hanging from archway and differing musical allegory, portrait of man holding chalice and pipe or small baton, markings on back: impressed 2275 11 and two other faint numerals, DEC 5231 in brown under glaze; overall crazing to each, approximately 26" x 18".
.... **$2,000**

Courtesy of Soulis Auctions, Lone Jack, Missouri, www.dirksoulisauctions.com

CERAMICS

minton

THOMAS MINTON established the Minton factory in England in 1793. The factory made earthenware, especially the blue-printed variety, and Thomas Minton is sometimes credited with the invention of the blue "Willow" pattern. For a time, majolica and tiles were also important parts of production, but bone china soon became the principal ware.

For more information on Minton, see *Antique Trader Pottery & Porcelain Ceramics*, 7th edition.

Pair of covered urns, 19th century, handled baluster form, polychrome floral decoration against Bleu Celeste ground, circular foot ending in square plinth, one crazed on underside, light rubbing and surface scratches, 8-3/4" h..... **$594**

Courtesy of Leslie Hindman Auctioneers, www.lesliehindman.com

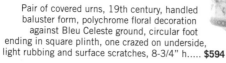

Dinner service: 11 dinner plates, 12 luncheon plates, 12 salad plates, 12 bread plates, 12 soups, 12 soup saucers, 12 small bowls, 12 teacups, 12 saucers, and serving platter, retailed by Tiffany & Co., one cup with broken handle, dinner plate 10-1/2" dia..**$438**

Courtesy of Leslie Hindman Auctioneers, www.lesliehindman.com

VISIT WWW.ANTIQUETRADER.COM

WWW.FACEBOOK.COM/ANTIQUETRADER

Pate-sur-pate plate with center decoration of dancing putto within gilt cracked ice ground and gilded foliate and key fret border, circa 1884, impressed and printed marks, mark for retailer Thomas Goode & Co., London, slight wear to gilding on edges, light surface scratches, 9-1/2" dia. **$1,188**

Courtesy of Rago Arts and Auctions, www.ragoarts.com

"Maiden Gathering Water" Parian figure, circa 1854, marks: (arrow-three dots), (backwards S), F, (logotype), 20" h....................................... **$750**

Courtesy of Heritage Auctions, www.ha.com

▲ Parian porcelain group, "Ariadne and the Panther," base professionally repaired, 14-1/2" h.
.... **$375**

Courtesy of Neadeau's Auction Gallery, www.nadeausauction.com

◄ Monumental majolica urn with stand, late 19th century, integrated stand of more recent vintage, in-painting to supporting putti, restoration throughout neck and one ram-form handle, 35" h., 36" dia... **$3,625**

Courtesy of Heritage Auctions, www.ha.com

◄ Pate-sur-pate olive green plaque by Louis Solon, circa 1890, painted and hand-tooled in white slip with couple fleeing fire as two putti use tools to undermine their escape, sky with gilt stars, signed "L. Solon," light surface abrasions, 7-1/2" x 6-1/2"..**$13,750**

Courtesy of Rago Arts and Auctions, www.ragoarts.com

▲ Pate-sur-pate blue-ground plaque by Louis Solon, circa 1873, painted and hand-tooled in white slip with bound maiden kneeling beside palm frond, attended by cupid raising coronet as arrows threaten and pierce her heart, signed "L. Solon," light surface abrasions, 6-1/2" x 7-1/2". **$15,000**

Courtesy of Rago Arts and Auctions, www.ragoarts.com

◄ Pate-sur-pate olive green plaque by Louis Solon, circa 1890, painted and hand-tooled in white slip with maiden swooning while bound to column, attended by cupid wielding bow and raining arrows at her heart, signed "L. Solon," partial paper label on verso, light surface abrasions and wear, 10-5/8" x 6-1/2"..........**$13,750**

Courtesy of Rago Arts and Auctions, www.ragoarts.com

Pate-sur-pate dark olive green plaque by Louis Solon, late 19th century, painted and hand-tooled in white slip with cupid orating from raised dais as six seated classical maidens scribe his lesson, signed "L. Solon," restoration to upper left corner, light surface abrasions and wear, 7" x 14-1/4"...**$15,000**

Courtesy of Rago Arts and Auctions, www.ragoarts.com

Pair of hand-painted moon vases with bird's nest, butterfly and foliage décor, signed Minton, neck and rim repaired, 14" h. **$1,230**

Courtesy of John McInnis Auctioneers, www.mcinnisauctions.com

Twenty-four Gothic Revival encaustic tiles inlaid in medieval style, five different designs by A.W.N. Pugin (Augustus Welby Northmore Pugin, 1812-1852), late 19th century, some stamped verso "Minton & Company/Stoke Upon Trent," "W. Goodwin," "Lou Dunne Hereford," many with chips and losses at corners, some glaze loss, most 6" x 6", five 4-1/2" x 4-1/2". **$384**

Courtesy of Brunk Auctions, www.brunkauctions.com

Pate-sur-pate flask vase, flattened moon vase form with bottle neck and side handles, pate-sur-pate oval panels of woman with cupid on front, lyre with roses and filigree on back, artist initials "H.H.," stamped Minton on bottom, 10-1/2" h. x 8" w. x 3-1/4".. **$1,845**

Courtesy of Fontaine's, www.fontainesauction.com

CERAMICS

mochaware

MOCHA DECORATION IS FOUND on basically utilitarian creamware or yellowware articles and is achieved by a simple chemical reaction. A color pigment of brown, blue, green, or black is given an acid nature by infusion of tobacco or hops. When this acid nature colorant is applied in blobs to an alkaline ground color, it reacts by spreading in feathery seaweed designs. This type of decoration is usually accompanied by horizontal bands of light color slip.

Produced in many Staffordshire potteries from the late 18th until the late 19th centuries, its name is derived from the similar markings found on mocha quartz. In addition to the seaweed decoration, mocha wares are also seen with earthworm and cat's-eye patterns or a marbleized effect.

▼ Two pitchers, 19th century, larger restored, smaller with light crow's foot to base, 6" h. and 7" h.....**$640**
Courtesy of Pook & Pook, Inc., www.pookandpook.com

Two pearlware pitchers, 19th century, first with rare double blue band centered with double twisted cable, 5-1/2" h.; second with single blue band above wide tan band with seaweed decoration, 6-1/2" h.; seaweed pitcher with likely original firing crack to rim, spout repair.
.... **$900**

Courtesy of Leland Little Auctions, www.lelandlittle.com

CERAMICS

Pitcher with seaweed and band décor, 19th century, spout chip, crack from rim at handle, 7-3/4" h. $270

Courtesy of Stanton Auctions, Hampden, Massachusetts

Mug with blue and blue-green bands and dark brown stripes on light mocha ground, 19th century, fine overall crazing, short hairline from rim, 6-1/4" h. $60

Courtesy of Kaminski Auctions, www.kaminskiauctions.com

Dipped ceramic bowl in "London shape" with cabled slip design in brown, white, black and blue over dark yellow or orange ground, circa 1830, unmarked, 3-1/4" h., 6-5/16" dia........................ $410

Courtesy of Jeffrey S. Evans & Associates, www.jeffreysevans.com

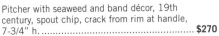

Pitcher with seaweed motif and orange bands, 18th century, overall crazing, base chips, 7" h. $584

Turned pitcher with Wedgwood blue bands and dark brown checkerboard bands, 18th century, small chips at base, 9-1/4" h. **$308**

Courtesy of Kaminski Auctions, www.kaminskiauctions.com

Bowl with banded seaweed design, circa 1790, 3-1/2" h., 7" dia. **$330**

Courtesy of Kaminski Auctions, www.kaminskiauctions.com

Milk pitcher with bands and earthworm pattern, 18th century, 5" h. **$615**

Courtesy of Kaminski Auctions, www.kaminskiauctions.com

Child's cup with marbleized glaze, 18th century, 4" h. **$369**

Courtesy of Kaminski Auctions, www.kaminskiauctions.com

CERAMICS

moorcroft

WILLIAM MOORCROFT WAS first employed as a potter by James Macintyre & Co., Ltd. of Burslem, Staffordshire, England, in 1897. He established the Moorcroft pottery in 1913. Walter Moorcroft, William's son, continued the business upon his father's death and made wares in the same style. The majority of the art pottery wares were hand thrown, resulting in a great variation among similarly styled pieces. Colors and marks are keys to determining age. The company initially used an impressed mark, "Moorcroft, Burslem"; a signature mark, "W. Moorcroft," followed. Modern pieces are marked simply "Moorcroft," with export pieces also marked "Made in England."

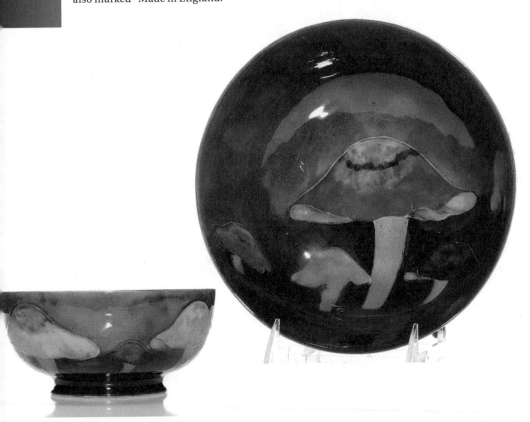

Bowl, Claremont, internal and external decoration, circa 1918, impressed "Moorcroft Burslem M 74," signed W. Moorcroft in green slip, rim chip restoration, entire surface oversprayed, 3-3/4" h x (widest point) 8-1/4" dia. $225

Courtesy of Mark Mussio, Humler & Nolan, www.humlernolan.com

Handled bowl, Macintyre Florian Ware, Macintyre Florian Ware ink stamp logo with registry mark, signed in green slip, W.M. des., W., M 1691 in red slip, minor staining inside, 3-1/8" h. **$400**

Courtesy of Mark Mussio, Humler & Nolan, www.humlernolan.com

Urn, two-handled Pomegranate, cobalt blue ground, impressed Cobridge factory mark, circa 1918-1929, painted signature in green, Made in England and shape number 333, 8-3/4" h.
.... **$500**

Courtesy of Mark Mussio, Humler & Nolan, www.humlernolan.com

Lidded teapot and tea tile, Moorcroft-Macintyre "Dura Ware," poppy design, both marked Macintyre Burslem England ink stamp logo, registry numbers. Tea tile marked "Made for Twiss Bros Ilfracombe," two obscure open bubbles. Teapot 5" h, tray 6-1/8" dia. **$200**

Courtesy of Mark Mussio, Humler & Nolan, www.humlernolan.com

Vase, Claremont, circa 1905, made for Shreve and Company in San Francisco and a survivor (per oral history) of the 1906 earthquake. At one time the vase had electroplated silver, a Shreve addition, but the silver is quite dull and does not want to polish. During the 1906 earthquake, the vase sustained damage resulting in three cracks running across the bottom and coming up the sides. Marked "W. Moorcroft des. Shreve San Francisco" in green slip, registry number 420081, 10" h x 10-1/2" dia.
.... **$600**

Courtesy of Mark Mussio, Humler & Nolan, www.humlernolan.com

Bowl, early Spanish design, incised W. Moorcroft and what appears to be Spaulding Shop Chicago, professional rim chip restoration, 2-7/8" h x 7" dia.
.... **$150**

Courtesy of Mark Mussio, Humler & Nolan, www.humlernolan.com

Vase, Cornflower, Powder Blue glaze, impressed factory mark, painted Walter Moorcroft initials, with original Moorcroft 4-page sales brochure, 5" h. **$300**

Courtesy of Mark Mussio, Humler & Nolan, www.humlernolan.com

Vase, Leaf & Berry, flambé glaze, impressed factory mark, facsimile signature, printed Royal Warrant label, 3-3/4" h. **$225**

Courtesy of Mark Mussio, Humler & Nolan, www.humlernolan.com

Vase, 2008, floral decoration, female nudes as bodies of trees, limited to 20 pieces, this is number 18, marked Moorcroft Made In Stoke on Trent England, date, edition, artist signature, decorator and designer cyphers, 13-3/4" h..**$450**

Courtesy of Mark Mussio, Humler & Nolan, www.humlernolan.com

Twin handled vase, Claremont, marked W. Moorcroft des. in green slip, "Made for Spaulding & Co. Rd No 420081," faint crazing, 7-1/2" h x 7-7/8" w. **$1,800**

Courtesy of Mark Mussio, Humler & Nolan, www.humlernolan.com

Pomegranate vase, circa 1913-1916, impressed Cobridge factory mark, painted signature in green, Moorcroft Burslem England and what appears to be shape 948, faint crazing, 7-7/8" h. **$300**

Courtesy of Mark Mussio, Humler & Nolan, www.humlernolan.com

▶ Lamp vase, Leaf & Berry, 1928-1949, unusual ochre, tan, blue and touches of purple glaze, impressed factory mark, painted facsimile signature, printed Royal Warrant label, factory cast holes in side and bottom for wiring, 13" h. **$400**

Courtesy of Mark Mussio, Humler & Nolan, www.humlernolan.com

Twin handled vase, cobalt ground, large pansy decoration, circa 1918-1929, impressed Cobridge factory mark, painted signature, Moorcroft Made in England, faint crazing, 7-3/4" h.
.... **$425**

Courtesy of Mark Mussio, Humler & Nolan, www.humlernolan.com

Pomegranate vase, early 1920s, blue ground, painted William Moorcroft signature, impressed "Moorcroft Burslem England," faint crazing, 10-5/8" h. **$250**

Courtesy of Mark Mussio, Humler & Nolan, www.humlernolan.com

Plate, pansy design, impressed Cobridge factory mark, Made in England, painted Walter Moorcroft initials in blue, faint crazing, 8-1/2" dia. **$150**

Courtesy of Mark Mussio, Humler & Nolan, www.humlernolan.com

Plate, Leaf & Berry design under rich flambé glaze, impressed Made in England factory mark, facsimile signature, painted Walter Moorcroft initials, faint crazing, 8-1/2" dia. **$225**

Courtesy of Mark Mussio, Humler & Nolan, www.humlernolan.com

Spanish bowl, internal and
external decoration, signed only
W. Moorcroft in green slip on
the bottom, minor scratches in
bottom, 5-1/4" h x 10-5/8" w.
.... **$1,100**

Courtesy of Mark Mussio, Humler & Nolan,
www.humlernolan.com

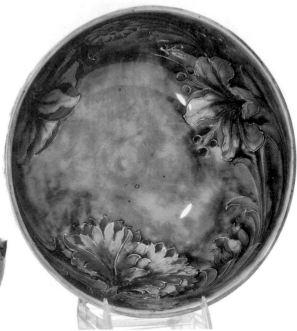

Bowl, flared rim, pomegranate
decoration on the interior,
impressed Cobridge factory
mark, painted William Moorcroft
signature in green, faint crazing,
3-1/4" h x 9-1/8" dia...........**$150**

Courtesy of Mark Mussio, Humler & Nolan,
www.humlernolan.com

CERAMICS

newcomb college

THIS POTTERY WAS established in the art department of Newcomb College in New Orleans in 1897. Each piece was hand-thrown and bore the potter's mark and decorator's monogram on the base. It was always studio business and never operated as factory. Newcomb College pieces are scarce, with the early wares eagerly sought. The pottery closed in 1940.

Vase with twilight scene in pink, green and blue by Sadie Irvine, 1919, mat glaze, Newcomb logo, date code (KQ55) for 1919, initials of potter Joseph Meyer, shape number 340, Irvine's incised monogram, three tight lines descending from rim, 3-1/2" h. **$1,000**

Courtesy of Mark Mussio, Humler & Nolan, www.humlernolan.com

Vase painted by Sadie Irvine, Newcomb College logo, date code TZ3, cipher for potter Kenneth Smith, conjoined monogram for Sadie Irvine, Newcomb College paper sticker, 3-1/4" h., 5" dia. **$475**

Courtesy of Mark Mussio, Humler & Nolan, www.humlernolan.com

CERAMICS

Vase by Henrietta Bailey, impressed Newcomb logo, incised artist's monogram, date code NS15, number 22, grinding chips, 3" h., 5" dia......... **$425**

Courtesy of Mark Mussio, Humler & Nolan, www.humlernolan.com

Vase with spiderwort by Sadie Irvine , 1923, marked NC/SI/NL85/25, original paper label, flecks to foot ring, 5" x 5-1/4"......................**$750**

Courtesy of Rago Arts and Auctions, www.ragoarts.com

Vase, shiny coated with blue over turquoise green glazes, impressed Newcomb College logo, number 1941, 3-1/4" h. **$200**

Courtesy of Mark Mussio, Humler & Nolan, www.humlernolan.com

Tyg with stylized iris by Katherine Kopman, 1901, blue flowers on green ground, high glaze, impressed Newcomb logo, Joseph Meyers monogram, U for type of buff clay, black slip painted artist's monogram, date code for 1901 (D 63), letter X, number 1 in triangle, faint crazing, chip off foot ring, 5-5/8" h. **$6,750**

Courtesy of Mark Mussio, Humler & Nolan, www.humlernolan.com

Tall vase with paperwhites by Henrietta Bailey, 1920, marked NC/KY98/83/HBH, dark scuffs to body, 10-1/4" x 4-1/4".
.... **$875**

Courtesy of Rago Arts and Auctions, www.ragoarts.com

Vase with wild roses by Sadie Irvine, 1923, marked NC/ SI/226/NP19, small burst glaze bubble near rim made during production, 6-3/4" x 4". .. **$1,250**

Courtesy of Rago Arts and Auctions, www.ragoarts.com

Early cabinet vase with pine trees by Gladys Bartlett, 1907, marked NC/GB/BT34/O, 4" x 3".
.... **$4,063**

Courtesy of Rago Arts and Auctions, www.ragoarts.com

Landscape vase with oak trees and Spanish moss by Sadie Irvine, 1932, bottom marked with logo, TX46, KS for potter Kenneth Smith and cipher for Irvine, tight hairline descending from rim, 3-1/4" h., 4-1/4" dia... **$1,650**

Courtesy of Just Art Pottery, www.justartpottery.com

CERAMICS

CERAMICS

nippon

THE JAPANESE NAME for Japan is Nippon and Nihon, but only one has become known as the collectible porcelain produced in a variety of styles. From teapots to humidors, Nippon porcelain was made in Japan from 1891 to 1921. This 30-year span is often called the Nippon Era. It saw countless porcelain makers and decorators produce items for the export market. The category is currently is seeing soft sales as tastes change, but this represents an ideal time for collectors to jump in and begin accumulating wonderfully-decorated articles for a fresh collection.

Nippon is actually a general term that was used following the 1891 McKinley Tariff Act, which required that all wares exported to the United States carry a mark indicating their country of origin. The Japanese decided to use the word Nippon. By 1921, import laws changed and the words "Made in" were required for all markings. The law also required the country to replace the word Nippon with the English name "Japan" on all wares sent to U.S. markets.

WORLD WAR I

The boon in Nippon porcelain can be credited to World War I. With European imports at a standstill Japan became the supplier to fill the void in the marketplace. The affordable china appealed to mid-market households seeking pretty objects for the home. Nippon should not be confused with higher-end Japanese porcelain such as Imari, which appealed to a more affluent collecting base, which were also produced during the Nippon era.

Many Japanese factories produced Nippon porcelain, much of it hand-painted or transfer ware floral

Vase, 12-1/4" t. x 7". **$140**

Manny's Oriental Rugs & Gallery, Inc., www.mannysrugs.com

Humidor, "Dancing Frogs", porcelain, 6-1/2' h.
.... **$1,300**

EstateofMind Auctions, www.estateofmind.biz

VISIT WWW.ANTIQUETRADER.COM

WWW.FACEBOOK.COM/ANTIQUETRADER

decorations. Heavy gold or gilded accents were used, as was applied slip-glaze beading (used most notably for moriage Nippon porcelain). As a result, most collectors of Nippon specialize in European-styled porcelains.

Like today, Nippon porcelain was produced almost exclusively to satisfy American tastes. At the time it was much less expensive than its European counterparts, which led to a boon in production and consumption overseas. This explains why today's thrift stores and antiques shops are awash in Nippon porcelain still at highly competitive prices. Knowledgeable collectors familiar with the various marks are able to discern the exact date period within the Nippon era, as some markings were used in the early years where as others were used in later years.

Although much of Nippon's decoration focused on standard florals, there were three distinct lines that appealed to those seeking exotic art from the East.

MORIAGE

Moriage is a special type of raised decoration used on some Japanese pottery, practically dripping with pastel ceramic accents. Sometimes pieces of clay were shaped by hand and applied to the item; sometimes the clay was squeezed from a tube in the way we apply cake frosting. The result is a beautiful mix of raised relief against a sold colored ground. The effect is quite beautiful and prices remain strong for elaborate examples. A 12-inch vase covered in pink and magenta roses and entwined with heavily ornate moriage detail is valued at $500 to $600 if it retains 95 percent of the original applied and slip-glaze decoration.

DRAGONWARE

Decorated in dark grays and blues, Nippon era Dragonware was marketed as an exotic, mid-market decorative item from the Orient. Dragons were applied in the moriage fashion and accented with slip-glazed decoration.

The style was used primarily on tea and coffee service sets, which are now available very affordably. Prices of Dragonware rise for unusual forms, rather than decoration. A bulging, covered container can bring more than $500. Light-colored variations of the Dragonware line from early in the period can bring $300 or more at a well-attended auction.

NORITAKE

Noritake wares produced during the Nippon era have been highly collectible for many decades. The Noritake Company was first registered in 1904. Until 1917 the word Nippon appeared on the back-stamp (this differs from Nippon as used in denoting the country of origin). From 1918, "Noritake" appeared on the back stamp. Highly collectible items were produced between 1921 and 1940, prior to the United States' involvement in World War II.

Unlike Dragonware, the chief value factor of Noritake is the extent the artist produced floral patterns on the pieces of porcelain. With Noritake, design is king. A stunning Nippon/old Noritake Coralene vase can sell for more than $2,000 in today's market.

TODAY'S PRICING

Nippon porcelain is far from its peak in the early 1980s; changing tastes have affected this market in a deep and substantial way. Only extraordinary and finely painted examples of exotic locations or subjects are commanding top dollar in today's market. Items that once sold for $175 to $225 can now be had for less than $50. In today's market, prices are based on the size of the piece, rather than the art painted on its surface. Objects smaller than 10 inches may be purchased for as little as $20, whereas prices for large vases larger than 12 inches can exceed $100.

New collectors are advised to be aware that a number of Nippon markings are being reproduced on new porcelain wares.

Hand-painted with a desert seascape, moriage rim, marked on the back with an ink stamp, measures 10 inches...**$25**

Dirk Soulis Auctions, www.dirksoulisauctions.com

A hand-painted scenic landscape with a moriage tree and moriage rim, marked on the back, 10 inches. Two missing 'cherry' beads on the moriage tree. **$110**

Dirk Soulis Auctions, www.dirksoulisauctions.com

Each painted with a scenic landscape, large tray measures 12-3/4" x 5-1/4", small trays 3-1/2" x 1-3/4".................. **$35**

Dirk Soulis Auctions, www.dirksoulisauctions.com

A berry bowl strainer with matching underplate, gold moriage, marked with blue inkstamps, bowl measures 3.5 x 7, plate measures 8 inches. And a covered cheese dish with gold moriage and hand-painted poppies, marked under the base, measures 4.5 x 7.75 x 6 inches. Very good condition. **$20**

Dirk Soulis Auctions, www.dirksoulisauctions.com

Three Nippon vases, all with green ink stamps under the bases, measure from 7-1/2" to 8-1/2". **$70**

Dirk Soulis Auctions, www.dirksoulisauctions.com

▶ Table lamp with moriage jeweled shoulders and hand-painted vineyard grapes, iron base, glass finial, measures 13-1/2" to the top of the base, 25 inches to the finial. **$20**

Dirk Soulis Auctions, www.dirksoulisauctions.com

Heavy gold moriage with jewels, set consists of a teapot, sugar, creamer, five teacups and six saucers, marked with blue ink stamps under the bases, teapot measures 6 x 9, sugar 5 x 7, creamer 3-1/2 x 5-1/2, teacups 2 x 4-1/2 and saucers 5-1/2 inches..**$450**

Dirk Soulis Auctions, www.dirksoulisauctions.com

CERAMICS

Hand-painted with a landscape with swans, marked on the back with an ink stamp, 10".......**$25**

Dirk Soulis Auctions, www.dirksoulisauctions.com

Plaque, hand-painted with molded in relief and painted decoration of two buffalo. Green M in wreath mark, 10-3/4". **$80**

Jacksons Auctions, www.jacksonsauction.com

With moriage jeweled gold rims and hand-painted game birds, marked with ink stamps verso, 9" each. One plate is broken in several pieces and poorly repaired, mostly visible from the back. One plate has one broken red jewel. Another has several broken gold jewels on the inner most rim. No other chips, cracks or repairs. **$350**

Dirk Soulis Auctions, www.dirksoulisauctions.com

Vase, lake reserves with swans, heavy gilt, spider crack to bolted base, small crack to bottom of lid, 17" h. **$250**

William Bunch Auctions & Appraisals, www.bunchauctions.com

Lidded powder jar with gold moriage, marked under the base, 4" x 7", vase with moriage and hand-painted flowers, marked under the base 9" x 5-1/2"...**$10**

Dirk Soulis Auctions, www.dirksoulisauctions.com

Hand-painted with flowers, a bird and a landscape, marked under the bases, measure from 5 to 7-1/2 inches. **$60**

Dirk Soulis Auctions, www.dirksoulisauctions.com

CERAMICS

george ohr

GEORGE OHR, THE eccentric potter of Biloxi, Mississippi, worked from about 1883 to 1906. Some think him to be one of the most expert throwers the craft will ever see. The majority of his works were hand-thrown, exceedingly thin-walled items, some of which have a crushed or folded appearance. He considered himself the foremost potter in the world and declined to sell much of his production, instead accumulating a great horde to leave as a legacy to his children. In 1972, this collection was purchased for resale by an antiques dealer.

GEO. E. OHR
BILOXI, MISS.

Bisque potato novelty bank, Biloxi, MS, 1888-92, stamped GEO. E. OHR, BILOXI, MISS, 3" x 4-1/2" x 3". **$1,500**

Courtesy of Rago Arts, www.ragoarts.com

Large vessel, gunmetal glaze, Biloxi, MS, 1898-1910, script signature, 3-1/4" x 5-3/4". . **$750**

Courtesy of Rago Arts, www.ragoarts.com

Low folded vessel, green and brown speckled glaze, Biloxi, MS, 1895-96, stamped GEO. E. OHR BILOXI, MISS, 2" x 6" x 3-1/2" **$2,125**

Vase, irregular rim, crusty, black mat body, brown highlights in the throat, incised "Biloxi," 2-3/4" h. **$1,000**

Courtesy of Mark Mussio, Humler & Nolan, www.humlernolan.com

Large bowl with folded rim, green and gunmetal glaze, Biloxi, MS, 1895-96, stamped G.E. OHR BILOXI, 2-1/2" x 6-1/2" **$1,188**

Courtesy of Rago Arts, www.ragoarts.com

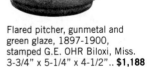

Flared pitcher, gunmetal and green glaze, 1897-1900, stamped G.E. OHR Biloxi, Miss. 3-3/4" x 5-1/4" x 4-1/2".. **$1,188**

Courtesy of Rago Arts, www.ragoarts.com

VISIT WWW.ANTIQUETRADER.COM

WWW.FACEBOOK.COM/ANTIQUETRADER

Baluster vase, green and gunmetal speckled glaze with melt fissures, Biloxi, MS, 1897-1900, stamped G.E. OHR Biloxi, Miss., touch-up to edge of foot ring, 5" x 2-1/2". **$1,875**

Courtesy of Rago Arts, www.ragoarts.com

Barrel-shaped novelty and tall vase, Biloxi, MS, circa 1900, both marked, restorations to each, hairline on tall vase, 8-1/2" x 4-1/4", 3" x 3". ... **$625**

Courtesy of Rago Arts, www.ragoarts.com

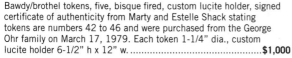

Bawdy/brothel tokens, five, bisque fired, custom lucite holder, signed certificate of authenticity from Marty and Estelle Shack stating tokens are numbers 42 to 46 and were purchased from the George Ohr family on March 17, 1979. Each token 1-1/4" dia., custom lucite holder 6-1/2" h x 12" w. **$1,000**

Courtesy of Mark Mussio, Humler & Nolan, www.humlernolan.com

Tall corseted vase, lobed rim, brown and ochre speckled glaze, Biloxi, MS, 1897-1900, stamped G.E. OHR Biloxi, Miss., extensive professional restoration, 7-1/4" x 3".... **$1,625**

Courtesy of Rago Arts, www.ragoarts.com

GEORGE OHR

Hat novelty, brown and celadon glaze, Biloxi, MS, 1897-1900, stamped G.E. OHR Biloxi, Miss., three stilt pulls, four chips, 2-1/2" x 5-1/4" x 5". **$625**

Courtesy of Rago Arts, www.ragoarts.com

Exceptional large vase with ribbon handles, 1900, in-body twist, ruffled rim, rare raspberry, purple, green and gunmetal pigeon-feather glaze, Biloxi, Miss., stamped G.E. OHR Biloxi, Miss., incised S Jeb-1900, minuscule glaze fleck to one handle, 11-3/4" x 6-1/2" **$87,500**

Courtesy of Rago Arts, www.ragoarts.com

Fine large vase with ribbon handles, 1897-1900, multicolor sponged-on glaze, Biloxi, Miss., stamped G.E. OHR Biloxi, Miss., 8-1/2" x 5-1/2". **$46,875**

Courtesy of Rago Arts, www.ragoarts.com

Vase with ribbon handles, 1897-1900, in-body twist, gunmetal glaze, Biloxi, Miss., stamped G.E. OHR Biloxi, Miss., 6-1/2" x 4-3/4" **$11,250**

Courtesy of Rago Arts, www.ragoarts.com

Two small vases, multicolor glazes, Biloxi, MS, 1895-1900, both marked, professional restorations to ruffled vase, tiny flecks on other, 3" x 3", 2-1/2" x 3-1/2". **$1,250**

Courtesy of Rago Arts, www.ragoarts.com

CERAMICS

overbeck

THE OVERBECK STUDIO POTTERY was founded by four sisters, Hannah, Mary Francis, Elizabeth and Harriet, in the Overbeck family home in Cambridge City, Indiana, in 1911. A fifth sister, Margaret, who worked as a decorator at Zanesville Art Pottery in 1910, was the catalyst for establishing the pottery, but died the same year.

Launching at the tail end of the Arts & Crafts movement and believing "borrowed art is bad art," the sister potters dedicated themselves to producing unique quality pieces with original design elements, which often were inspired by the natural world. Pieces can also be found in the Art Nouveau and Art Deco styles, as well as unique figurines and grotesques. The studio used several marks through the years, including an incised O and incised OBK, often accompanied by the artist's initials. The pottery ceased production in 1955.

Rare draft horse figurine by Mary Frances Overbeck, incised OBK, small flecks/chips to edges of feet, firing lines made during production, 6-1/2" x 6-1/2" x 2-1/2". **$1,063**

Courtesy of Rago Arts and Auctions, www.ragoarts.com

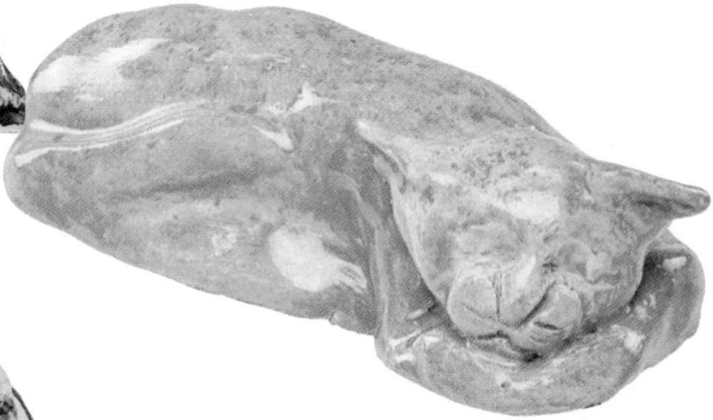

Rare sleeping cat figurine by Mary Frances Overbeck, unmarked, small rough spot to one ear, several firing lines, glaze misses made during production, 2" x 7" x 3-1/4". **$1,000**

Courtesy of Rago Arts and Auctions, www.ragoarts.com

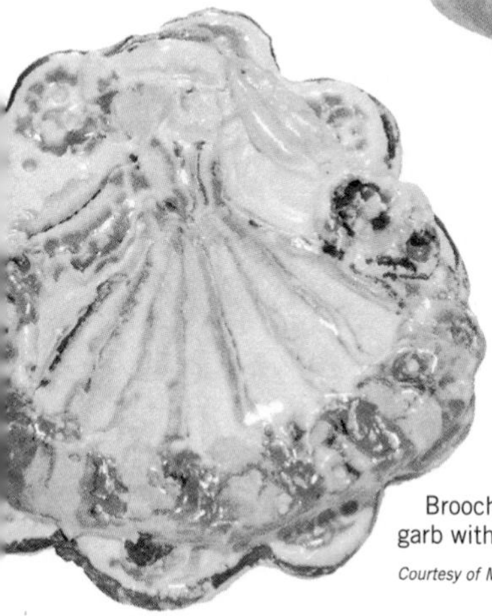

Brooch of blonde Southern belle in traditional garb with incised Overbeck logo, 2" h.............. **$110**

Courtesy of Mark Mussio, Humler & Nolan, www.humlernolan.com

VISIT WWW.ANTIQUETRADER.COM

WWW.FACEBOOK.COM/ANTIQUETRADER

Vase excised with squirrels by Mary Frances
Overbeck, incised OBK/MF, stilt pulls, 4" x 4".
.... **$2,500**

Courtesy of Rago Arts and Auctions, www.ragoarts.com

Large vase with Asian figures with lanterns by
Elizabeth and Mary Frances Overbeck, circa
1920, incised OBK/E/F, dark scuffs around base,
11-1/2" x 6"..**$10,000**

Courtesy of Rago Arts and Auctions, www.ragoarts.com

Vase with three similar panels of stylized cactus in
green against mauve ground, carved and painted
by Elizabeth and Hannah Overbeck, marked with
Overbeck logo, initials E and H, 6-1/8" h....... **$2,700**

Courtesy of Mark Mussio, Humler & Nolan, www.humlernolan.com

Vase with three panels of butterflies in green
against brown ground, carved and painted
by Elizabeth and Hannah Overbeck, marked
with Overbeck logo and initials E and H, line
descending from rim, with copy of Kathleen R.
Postle's The Chronicle of the Overbeck Pottery,
vase 5-3/8" h. **$3,000**

Courtesy of Mark Mussio, Humler & Nolan, www.humlernolan.com

Wall pocket of abstract bird and branch by Mary Frances Overbeck, incised OBK/F, 8" x 4-1/2" x 2-1/2".. **$2,250**

Courtesy of Rago Arts and Auctions, www.ragoarts.com

Vase excised with cardinals by Elizabeth and Hannah Overbeck, incised OBK/E/H, fleck or stilt pull to foot ring, minor scuffs to body, 4-1/2" x 3-3/4".. **$5,313**

Courtesy of Rago Arts and Auctions, www.ragoarts.com

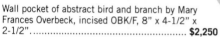

Vase excised with stylized birds by Elizabeth and Mary Frances Overbeck, incised OBK/E/H, 5-1/4" x 3-1/2". **$3,750**

Courtesy of Rago Arts and Auctions, www.ragoarts.com

Vase excised with figures walking in rain, glazed-over marks, stilt pulls, 5" x 3"...................... **$5,938**

Courtesy of Rago Arts and Auctions, www.ragoarts.com

CERAMICS

owens

OWENS POTTERY WAS the product of the J. B. Owens Pottery Co., which operated in Ohio from 1890 to 1929. In 1891 it was located in Zanesville and produced art pottery from 1896, introducing Utopian wares as its first art pottery. The company switched to tile after 1907. Efforts to rebuild after the factory burned in 1928 failed, and the company closed in 1929.

Jardinière in brown and blue by Henri Deux, 1900s, unmarked, 7-1/2" x 9". **$250**

Courtesy of Rago Arts and Auctions, www.ragoarts.com

Arts & Crafts vase in green mat glaze, carved by Hester Pillsbury, impressed Owens, number beneath, Pillsbury monogram incised on side, 6-3/4" h., 7" dia. **$325**

Courtesy of Mark Mussio, Humler & Nolan, www.humlernolan.com

Soudaneze vase with pair of violets, impressed Owens 202, fine crazing, light scratches, small glaze skips, 4" h. **$100**

Courtesy of Mark Mussio, Humler & Nolan, www.humlernolan.com

Lightweight vase of cyclamen by Charles Dibowski, incised JBO circular mark, artist's monogram, faint overall crazing, 6-1/2" h. **$200**

Courtesy of Mark Mussio, Humler & Nolan, www.humlernolan.com

Tile of stag running through pine woods next to lake with harvest moon on horizon, tile 17-7/8" x 12", frame 16-1/2" x 22-1/2". **$1,300**

Courtesy of Mark Mussio, Humler & Nolan, www.humlernolan.com

◄ Vase with sunburst and palm fronds in rust, yellow and green by Albert Haubrich, signed A. Haubrich, unmarked, surface scratches, 13-3/4" h............**$225**

Courtesy of Mark Mussio, Humler & Nolan, www.humlernolan.com

Jardinière and pedestal with nearly life-size three-dimensional storks and cattails in green mat glaze, glaze nick on pedestal rim, small nick on one bird, 43-1/2" h. combined.........................**$2,500**

Courtesy of Mark Mussio, Humler & Nolan, www.humlernolan.com

◄ Utopian floor vase with large stork by Albert Haubrich, artist signed in orange slip, unmarked, fine overall crazing, glaze scratches, 22-1/2" h............**$300**

Courtesy of Mark Mussio, Humler & Nolan, www.humlernolan.com

◄ Mission vase and oak stand, circa 1905, drip glaze, cold paint, red over dark green oil paint, red paint "305 Mission Pottery" mark on bottom, paper label on stand marked 305, minor nicks to paint, undisplaced piece in rim from converging cracks, vase 9-1/2" h., with stand 11-3/8" h. Owens Mission pottery was cold painted, most likely by August Hutaf. **$300**

Courtesy of Mark Mussio, Humler & Nolan, www.humlernolan.com

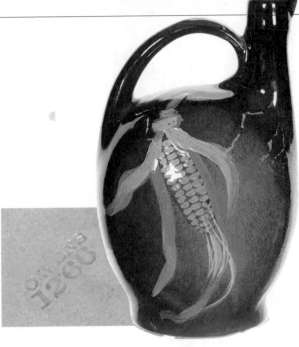

Vase with embossed grape decoration, shape 215, green mat glaze, impressed Owens 215, stilt pull, open glaze bubble, 15-3/8" h. **$1,400**

Courtesy of Mark Mussio, Humler & Nolan, www.humlernolan.com

Utopian whiskey jug with corn cob décor and brown glaze, 7-1/2" h. **$71**

Courtesy of Woody Auction, www.woodyauction.com

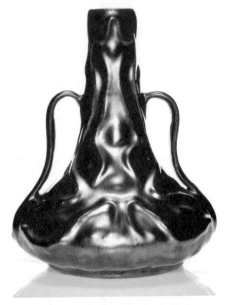

Lightweight cruet, unknown artist, incised artist's marks, shape number 839, 6-3/8" h. **$50**

Courtesy of Mark Mussio, Humler & Nolan, www.humlernolan.com

Feroza twin-handled vase with variegated brown metallic glaze, unmarked, drilled through bottom, 9-3/4" h. **$150**

Courtesy of Mark Mussio, Humler & Nolan, www.humlernolan.com

CERAMICS

paul revere pottery

PAUL REVERE POTTERY may appear sporadically in today's auction market, but there is no mistaking it once you get a glimpse.

The playful designs – sometimes with wisdom-infused illustrations, depictions of nature, and daily life of the early 20th century – and practical quality construction seem to be what defines this form of pottery, but there is much more to it.

Paul Revere Pottery is, in fact, a glorious extension of a greater educational effort that began with three women in late 19th century Boston. In the midst of tremendous social and cultural change and economic disparity among people, Edith Brown (1872-1932), Edith Guerrier (1870-1958), and Helen Storrow (1864-1944) came together to provide young immigrant women in the North End neighborhood of Boston with opportunities to experience various facets of life, and in turn gain new skills.

The Saturday Evening Girls (SEG) Club grew out of the Saturday Evening Girls Story Hour, which was established by Guerrier in 1899 as part of the North Bennet Street Industrial School (NBSIS). The school was established for the purpose of training newly arrived immigrants in the North End neighborhood (largely Italian and Jewish families) in skilled trades. Not only was the Boston Public Library branch of the NBSIS the place where the Saturday Evening Girls Club took shape, it was the first trade school in America, according to the book *Saturday Evening Girls* by Meg Chalmers and Judy Young (Schiffer Publications).

Guerrier (a librarian and writer) and Brown (an artist) met while attending the Museum School of Boston's Museum of Fine Arts. In the early 20th century, the two women, who were living together by this time, met Helen Osborne Storrow, a longtime philanthropist in Boston. With a shared focus of social and political reform, empowerment of women, and the importance of honing various skills and creative endeavors, the three formed a bond that would change the lives of many and eventually bring Paul Revere Pottery into existence.

In the early years the club incorporated lessons in practical business and trade skills, with creative programs such as storytelling and dance. Following a trip to Europe in 1906, Guerrier and Brown began researching the possibility of incorporating pottery-making classes into their club curriculum. Upon seeing some of the early pieces the group created, Storrow purchased a home in the North End of Boston, near the Old North Church. This provided space to designate individual rooms for the pottery-making process, an area to sell the pottery, and rooms for club meetings. On the upper floor were apartments, including one where Guerrier and Brown lived.

Given that this new "headquarters" was located near the Old North Church, the very same place Paul Revere had instructed his fellow Sons of Liberty to hang lanterns to signal movement of British troops ahead of the American Revolution, the brand would become Paul Revere Pottery.

While the SEG Club continued to offer its original programming for younger girls, the pottery was specifically the work of older teenage girls and young women. The SEG pottery-making curriculum was filled with valuable lessons, including day-to-day business practices, operation and maintenance of equipment, and the importance of mentoring and exposure to a variety of creative interests.

By 1915, Paul Revere Pottery by Saturday Evening Girls was attracting widespread interest,

CERAMICS

and expansion of the program and its operation was necessary. The group moved from its original Hull Street location to Brighton, Massachusetts, where the kiln, furnace, workrooms, and sales space were built according to the designs of Brown and Guerrier. Until this point, pottery production was handled by a group of more than 50 SEG members working part-time and a small number of decorators working full-time. With the incorporation of the Paul Revere Pottery Co. in 1916, it became a full-time business and remained as such until operations ceased in 1942.

The expansion of the business was a chance to put the things the young women were learning into a full-time career on a larger scale. And for directors Brown, Guerrier and Storrow, it created a platform to demonstrate the SEG's effectiveness in incorporating various reforms in the workplace and having an even longer-lasting impact on the lives of its participants.

One example of this can be seen in the life of Sara Galner Bloom, one of the most prolific of the SEG artists. She was a familiar face in NBSIS programs, having attended a variety of club offerings over the years, according to Nonie Gadsden, author of *Art and Reform: Sara Galner, the Saturday Evening Girls, and the Paul Revere Pottery.* (Gadsden is also the Katharine Lane Weems Senior Curator of American Decorative Arts and Sculpture at the Museum of Fine Arts, Boston, and is currently working on a book about a Tiffany window, circa 1890s, which was gifted to the museum.)

Upon completing her required schooling, which at the time lawfully concluded at the age of 14, some of Galner's teachers attempted to help her continue with her education. However, as was the case for many immigrant youths, her parents were depending on her to enter the workforce and add to the family's income, Gadsden explained. While working first as a department store clerk and then a dressmaker, Galner continued her work at the SEG pottery. Eventually she chose to enroll in evening high school classes (much to her father's dismay), but also remained an active SEG member. A few years into her pottery work, Galner was offered a full-time position at the pottery by Brown. An offer she turned down, due to the fact that the rate of pay ($4 per week) was less than what she earned as a dressmaker. A counter-offer by Brown and a negotiation by Galner resulted in a salary of $7 per week for herself and the rest of the SEG pottery artists, Gadsden said.

This was in addition to the already uniquely positive work conditions at the pottery for this time. In addition to receiving a wage that was greater than many other factory wages of the day, employees of the Paul Revere Pottery Co. worked eight-hour workdays instead of the usual 12-plus hours, Saturday was a half-day, and they received paid vacations, according to the book *Saturday Evening Girls.*

"It was a clean, healthy, and educational work environment for girls who didn't get much handed to them in life," Gadsden said. "Brown and Guerrier took these girls under their wings and exposed them to a variety of experiences and opportunities, but that's not to say

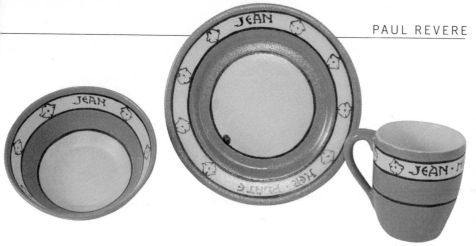

Breakfast set: plate, bowl and mug with rosettes and marked with name "Jean" (produced pieces could be personalized for an additional $8), all pieces marked on bottom with S.E.G., 12-22 and cipher for Fannie Levine, plate and bowl in mint condition, mug with hairline descending from rim, plate 1/2" h., 7-3/4" dia., bowl 2-1/4" h., 5-1/2" dia., mug 3-3/4" h. x 4-1/4" w. including handle...**$475**

Courtesy of Just Art Pottery, www.justartpottery.com

the girls didn't work for it."

Galner's work is some of the most acclaimed of the Paul Revere Pottery legacy. One of the most recognizable aspects of her work is the use of floral designs, as well as the very popular bread and milk children's sets. Not only was she an accomplished pottery artist, but later she went on to manage a Paul Revere Pottery shop established in Washington, D.C.

The simple and relatable designs developed by Brown and other SEG artists, and elevated by Galner, are part of the appeal this pottery enjoys today.

Interest in Paul Revere Pottery, as limited as its exposure may be, is represented in prices paid at auction. Having brought many examples to auction – including a record-setting glazed ceramic fireplace depicting a wooded landscape by Saturday Evening Girls artists Fannie Levine, Albina Mangini, and Brown that sold for $219,750 (with buyer's premium) in 2013 – David Rago, principal of Rago Arts and Auctions, explained some of what sets this style of pottery apart.

"Little material better describes the Arts & Crafts [movement] in America," Rago said. "Conceived by women, decorated by women, focusing on kitchen ware, centered on designs that are both sophisticated and simple, the intent of SEG was to better the lives of women who needed a boost by involving them in the arts."

In February 2015, during a sale by Rago, an SEG wall pocket with a poppies design measuring 6" x 4" sold for $2,750. In Chalmers & Young's book, samples of 1921 Paul Revere Pottery catalog pages show that a wall pocket of this size sold for between $2.50 and $4, depending on the design.

"The appeal of Saturday Evening Girls Paul Revere Pottery is tied in with the general interest in Arts & Crafts pottery because it is handmade, often hand-thrown and decorated by a known person," said Riley Humler, principal of Humler & Nolan. "The main appeal still has to do with the quality of the art and often, although simple in design, the better pieces are stunning in execution and composition, and most often done in soft, matt glazes."

Eventually Galner married Morris Bloom and had three children. The children didn't know much at all about their mother's time as an SEG, according to Gadsden, who met Galner's son and daughter-in-law during a lecture at the Museum of Fine Arts in Boston. It was clear from their first meeting that Galner's son, Dr. David L. Bloom, was a fan, although he knew less about it than one might expect. As Gadsden explained, at the time many people – especially those who immigrated to the United States – spoke less of the past and focused more on the future. It was by chance at an exhibition that Dr. Bloom saw a pot on display in the MFA exhibition "The Art That is Life" like the one his mother had. The pot had the familiar "S.E.G." signature and Galner's initials on the bottom. That sparked his fascination not only in the pottery, but its social history and his mother's role in it.

Mug with band of rabbits and bushes, bottom marked with Paul Revere Pottery logo, 3-1/2" h. x 4-1/2" w. **$325**

Courtesy of Just Art Pottery, www.justartpottery.com

"What initially shocked me was how little he knew about his mother's life and work with the SEGs," Gadsden said. "However, he had met his mother's fellow artists and spent time with them (at regular SEG reunions) and knew they were special to her, but not a lot about that connection. That intrigued me."

That led to a sharing of information between Dr. Bloom and Gadsdsen and deeper dialogue about SEG, which led Gadsden to request one or two examples of the Paul Revere Pottery that Bloom had acquired in the years following his mother's death, to display at the Museum of Fine Arts in Boston. Instead, Dr. Bloom donated part of the collection to the museum and the rest is a promised gift. In all, more than 130 items of Paul Revere Pottery came to be part of the museum collection in 2006.

Although Galner may not have regaled her children with stories of her years as an artist of Paul Revere Pottery, she passed on much of the practical sensibilities, work ethic, appreciation and engagement in a creative and culturally diverse community, and a progressive mindset to her children. For the retired Dr. Bloom, who became one of the nation's leading radiologists, he gives the credit for his success and the person he is to his mother, said Gadsden, whose telling of the events surrounding this family intrigued Frederic Sharf, a trustee of the Museum of Fine Arts so much so that he underwrote her book.

To sum up the lessons and influences the SEG Club and development of Paul Revere Pottery brought forth is a challenge, Gadsden said, when asked what valuable insights people today can take away from the program and product.

"There is talent and skill in all areas of society," she said. "It just needs to be given the opportunity to flourish. Every work of art has a personal story behind it, about the people who created it and the experiences they encountered. There is remarkable value in that."

Today the market for Paul Revere Pottery is thin as pieces are scarce, according to Rago and Humler. As the market for early 20th century decorative art has narrowed, it has pushed the cream to the top, Rago said. This is true of most of the pottery from the Arts & Crafts period, he added.

"That prices for the best, rarest work have risen so dramatically hasn't necessarily translated to more pieces coming to market," Rago said. "The people who own it, love it because it is truly fine and lovable ware, spiritually wrought and well designed, and they remain loathe to sell it."

The seldom-seen scenic pieces with no lettering are most sought-after or garner the most interest at auctions, Humler said.

"Lots of pieces were made for children's breakfast sets with bowl, pitcher, mug or plate, and often these have dates and children's names included with the design," he said. "The best pieces will be scenic or floral pieces that do not reference anyone. And as in most art pottery, if an item is of great quality, big is better than small."

During an auction presented by Humler & Nolan in early 2015, a three-piece SEG children's breakfast set (mug, bowl and plate) featuring an illustration of racing rabbits and the name "Joan Audrey Carlson" on each piece commanded $350. In the 1921 Paul Revere

Pottery catalog, a similar set purchased new would have cost $8.

One aspect of Paul Revere Pottery that lends itself to identification, and, in turn, avoiding reproductions is the signature and markings on each piece.

"Because the work is almost always signed, artist signed, and dated, this makes determining (the period of a) piece a fairly easy matter," Rago said.

Becoming as familiar as possible with the subject of Paul Revere Pottery, or any work for that matter, is a primary step before buying anything, advised Humler and Rago. In addition to being well-versed in the various types of signatures, gaining knowledge about the materials used in the development of the pottery and attributes of the different periods, along with seeking out reputable people to buy from, go a very long way to ensuring the opportunities one has to acquire historic SEG works are positive.

"I cannot emphasize enough the importance of scholarship when being a collector," Humler said. "Know your area better than the people from whom you buy, and you should be way ahead of the game."

Although it's been more than 105 years since the first Saturday Evening Girls pottery was created by the hands of young immigrant women of Boston's North End, as a result of the tireless commitment of Guerrier, Brown and Storrow, the influence and impact of this educational and empowering experience lives on in the pottery enjoyed by many, and through the descendants of the women artisans who transformed simple clay into something spectacular.

— Antoinette Rahn

Vase with dark blue mat glaze, Paul Revere ink stamp, 12-5/8" h. **$150**

Courtesy of Mark Mussio, Humler & Nolan, www.humlernolan.com

Assembled tea set with decorative border: teapot, creamer, sugar bowl, five teacups, six saucers, most with impressed Paul Revere stamp, teapot signed S.E.G., teapot 4-1/4", 8-1/2" dia. **$281**

Courtesy of Rago Arts and Auctions, www.ragoarts.com

Glossy green vase, bottom marked SEG, professional restoration to small chip at rim, 6" h., 4-3/4" dia. $265

Courtesy of Just Art Pottery, www.justartpottery.com

Vase with band of stylized tulips, mat finish, marked P.R.P. with obscure date, stray color runs and spots, 4-5/8" h....................$425

Courtesy of Mark Mussio, Humler & Nolan, www.humlernolan.com

Vase with band of white tulips and leaves, bottom marked with Paul Revere Pottery logo, dated 7-24, with artist cipher for Fannie Levine, mint condition, 6" h., 4-3/4" dia.......................$1,595

Courtesy of Just Art Pottery, www.justartpottery.com

Pitcher with scenic band of trees by artist with initials JMD, marks: date, 10-20, PRP, artist's initials in black slip, 7" h. $450

Courtesy of Mark Mussio, Humler & Nolan, www.humlernolan.com

Circular trivet with clipper ship on high seas in relief with turquoise, tan and blue glossy glazes, "P.R.P." in black slip painted on back, 4-1/2" dia. $100

Courtesy of Mark Mussio, Humler & Nolan, www.humlernolan.com

Tile of swan on water with trees in background by Albina Mangini, "AM" in black slip on back, small chips to three corners, 4-1/4"..........................$100

Courtesy of Mark Mussio, Humler & Nolan, www.humlernolan.com

Square inkwell with semi-gloss blue glaze, original "Paul Revere Pottery Boston Mass" paper label with $2.50 retail price, 2-1/8" h., 3-1/8" sq......$80

Courtesy of Mark Mussio, Humler & Nolan, www.humlernolan.com

CERAMICS

red wing pottery

VARIOUS POTTERIES OPERATED in Red Wing, Minnesota, starting in 1868, the most successful being the Red Wing Stoneware Co., organized in 1877. Merged with other local potteries through the years, it became known as Red Wing Union Stoneware Co. in 1906 and was one of the largest producers of utilitarian stoneware items in the United States.

After a decline in the popularity of stoneware products, an art pottery line was introduced to compensate for the loss. This was reflected in a new name for the company, Red Wing Potteries, Inc., in 1936. Stoneware production ceased entirely in 1947, but vases, planters, cookie jars, and dinnerware of art pottery quality continued in production until 1967, when the pottery ceased operation altogether.

For more information on Red Wing pottery, see *Warman's Red Wing Pottery Identification and Price Guide* by Mark F. Moran.

STONEWARE

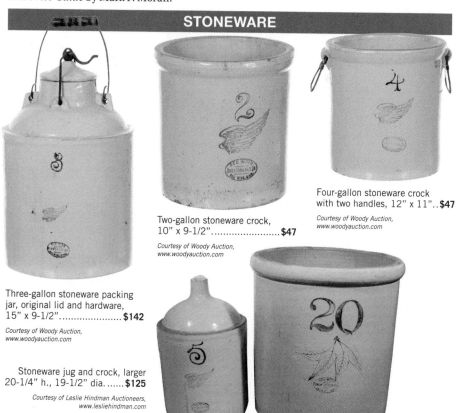

Two-gallon stoneware crock, 10" x 9-1/2".........................**$47**

Courtesy of Woody Auction, www.woodyauction.com

Four-gallon stoneware crock with two handles, 12" x 11"..**$47**

Courtesy of Woody Auction, www.woodyauction.com

Three-gallon stoneware packing jar, original lid and hardware, 15" x 9-1/2".......................**$142**

Courtesy of Woody Auction, www.woodyauction.com

Stoneware jug and crock, larger 20-1/4" h., 19-1/2" dia.......**$125**

Courtesy of Leslie Hindman Auctioneers, www.lesliehindman.com

VISIT WWW.ANTIQUETRADER.COM

WWW.FACEBOOK.COM/ANTIQUETRADER

Five-gallon stoneware handled jug with original Redlix wooden spigot, 18" x 12". **$47**

Courtesy of Woody Auction, www.woodyauction.com

Five-gallon packing jar, no lid or hardware, some chipping on edges, 15-1/2" x 11-1/2"......**$71**

Courtesy of Woody Auction, www.woodyauction.com

Ten-gallon stoneware crock, 16" x 15".........................**$100**

Courtesy of Woody Auction, www.woodyauction.com

Six-gallon crock, two handles, 14" x 12". **$71**

Courtesy of Woody Auction, www.woodyauction.com

Fifteen-gallon stoneware crock, line along one side, 18" x 17-1/2". **$94**

Courtesy of Woody Auction, www.woodyauction.com

Twenty-gallon stoneware crock, line along one side, 20" x 19". **$106**

Courtesy of Woody Auction, www.woodyauction.com

ART POTTERY & MISCELLANEOUS

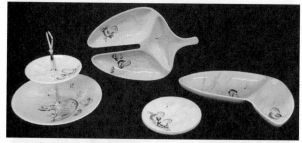

Bob White pattern dinnerware by Red Wing, 110-plus pieces: two-gallon water cooler with lid, beverage server with cover and stand, 20" platter with two-warmer stand, two two-quart covered casseroles, divided vegetable bowl, gravy boat with cover, nut bowl, cookie jar, relish dish, two butter dishes, large and small water pitchers, six tumblers, creamer, covered sugar, bread tray, 13 11" plates, figural hors d'oeuvre quail, teapot with cover and metal stand, salad plates, cups and saucers, mug, salt and pepper shakers, etc., some pieces with minor chips....... **$885**

Courtesy of Woody Auction,
www.woodyauction.com

Twin-handled vase with variegated Nokomis glaze, blue Red Wing Art Pottery ink stamp, 10-1/8" h.
.... **$150**

Courtesy of Mark Mussio, Humler & Nolan,
www.humlernolan.com

CERAMICS

redware

RED EARTHENWARE POTTERY was made in the American colonies from the late 1600s. Bowls, crocks, and all types of utilitarian wares were turned out in great abundance to supplement pewter and hand-made treenware. The ready availability of the clay, the same used in making bricks and roof tiles, accounted for the vast production. The lead-glazed redware retained its reddish color, although a variety of colors could be obtained by adding various metals to the glaze. Interesting effects occurred accidentally through unsuspected impurities in the clay or uneven temperatures in the firing kiln, which sometimes resulted in streaks or mottled splotches. Redware pottery was seldom marked by the maker.

Philadelphia redware spaniel, dated 1870, signed Geo. Diehl Philadelphia, Pa, heavy flaking to nose, scattered small flakes, 7-3/4" h. **$519**

Courtesy of Pook & Pook, Inc., www.pookandpook.com

Eight redware shallow bowls, 19th c., expected wear, 6" to 8-1/4" dia. **$225**

Courtesy of Pook & Pook, Inc., www.pookandpook.com

VISIT WWW.ANTIQUETRADER.COM

WWW.FACEBOOK.COM/ANTIQUETRADER

Redware reclining lamb, 19th c., with mottled orange and yellow glaze, flaking to ears, nose, and around base, 11-3/4" l............................... **$1,188**

Courtesy of Pook & Pook, Inc., www.pookandpook.com

Large redware bowl, 19th c., yellow and brown slip splashes, glaze losses, 7" h x 12-1/4" dia. **$4,148**

Courtesy of Pook & Pook, Inc., www.pookandpook.com

Redware charger, 19th c., with yellow slip decoration, wear and chips to rim, 11-1/2" dia...**$175**

Courtesy of Pook & Pook, Inc., www.pookandpook.com

Redware crock, 19th c., impressed John Bell Waynesboro, light wear, 6-3/4" h. **$150**

Courtesy of Pook & Pook, Inc., www.pookandpook.com

Redware plate, 19th c., yellow and green slip decoration, few chips/losses/wear to center, 9-1/2" dia.. **$163**

Courtesy of Pook & Pook, Inc., www.pookandpook.com

Pennsylvania redware crock, 19th c., impressed John W Bell Waynesboro PA, general light wear, 4-3/4" h. **$275**

Courtesy of Pook & Pook, Inc., www.pookandpook.com

Greg Schooner (contemporary) sgrafitto redware
charger, 12" dia. **$288**

Courtesy of Pook & Pook, Inc., www.pookandpook.com

Pennsylvania redware bird whistle, 19th c., signed
on underside M. M. Bergy, 2-1/2" h. **$1,125**

Courtesy of Pook & Pook, Inc., www.pookandpook.com

Charger, Shenandoah Valley redware, dated
1829, possibly Peter Bell, Winchester, Virginia, or
Hagerstown, Maryland, loss to decoration, several
old rim chips, 11-1/4" dia. **$1,708**

Courtesy of Pook & Pook, Inc., www.pookandpook.com

Redware quintal vase, 19th c., one opening
restored, some roughness to rims, 7" h. **$3,690**

Courtesy of Pook & Pook, Inc., www.pookandpook.com

Charger, Montgomery County, Pennsylvania sgrafitto redware, circa 1815, attributed to John Neis, with green tulip tree decoration on yellow ground, 1" rim repair, bottom left third of plate broken off and reattached, some flaking to glaze, 12-1/4" dia.. **$2,750**

Courtesy of Pook & Pook, Inc., www.pookandpook.com

Solomon Bell redware pitcher 19th c., impressed S. Bell & Son Strasburg VA, 9-3/4" h. **$500**

Courtesy of Pook & Pook, Inc., www.pookandpook.com

Pitcher with lid, possibly Jugtown, light wear to body, 7-3/4" h. **$221**

Courtesy of Pook & Pook, Inc., www.pookandpook.com

Pitcher, Alamance County, North Carolina redware, circa 1800, yellow and brown slip decoration, loss to decoration, heavy below spout, several old rim chips, 9 3/4" h. **$5,250**

Courtesy of Pook & Pook, Inc., www.pookandpook.com

top lot

Barry Cohen (American, 1934-1990) was an artist with an affinity for early American folk art. In 1975, The Abby Aldrich Rockefeller Folk Art Center in Williamsburg, Virginia, hosted an exhibition of 50 platters and vessels from the artist's collection. At Cohen's death, his well-documented folk art collection was comprised of 248 objects, including 36 stoneware and redware examples, of which this is one: Octagonal redware plate, 19th c., yellow slip dot in diamond decoration, green splashes, 6-1/8" dia. $9,000

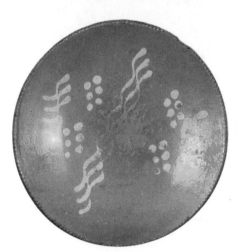

Plate, Pennsylvania redware, 19th c., with yellow slip decoration, wear, few glaze flakes, 10-1/2" dia. **$172**

Pennsylvania redware pie plate, 19th c., green and brown wavy slip lines, 6-3/4" dia. **$600**

Redware kneeling woman, 19th c., probably
Pennsylvania, few small flakes, 4" h. **$366**

Courtesy of Pook & Pook, Inc., www.pookandpook.com

Figural bottle/flask, Shenandoah Valley redware,
19th c., attributed to Solomon Bell, Strasburg,
Virginia, chips to spout, couple glaze flakes.
Illustrated in Rice & Stoudt, "The Shenandoah
Pottery," fig. 17, 7-7/8" h. **$6,710**

Courtesy of Pook & Pook, Inc., www.pookandpook.com

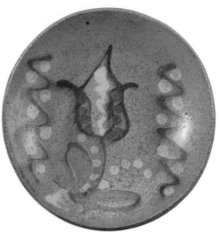

Pennsylvania redware pie plate, 19th c.,
attributed to Diehl pottery, yellow, green, and
brown slip tulip decoration, 7-3/4" dia. **$14,400**

Courtesy of Pook & Pook, Inc., www.pookandpook.com

Redware fat lamp, Jacob Medinger (Montgomery
County, Pennsylvania 1856-1932), 6-3/4" h.... **$793**

Courtesy of Pook & Pook, Inc., www.pookandpook.com

CERAMICS

rockingham

THE MARQUIS OF Rockingham first established an earthenware pottery in the Yorkshire district of England around 1745, and it was occupied afterwards by various potters. The well-known mottled brown Rockingham glaze was introduced about 1788 by the Brameld Brothers and became immediately popular. It was during the 1820s that the production of true porcelain began at the factory, and it continued to be made until the firm closed in 1842.

Since that time the so-called Rockingham glaze has been used by various potters in England and the United States, including some famous wares produced in Bennington, Vermont (see Bennington Pottery). Very similar glazes were also used by potteries in other areas of the United States including Ohio and Indiana, but only wares specifically attributed to Bennington should use that name. The following listings include mainly wares featuring the dark brown mottled glaze produced at various sites here and abroad.

Pitcher in Pond Lily pattern, chocolate over brown glaze, embossed United States Pottery Co. type F ribbon mark under base, Lyman, Fenton & Co., Bennington, Vermont, 1852-1858, glued break, shallow loss, small chip, 10-1/4" h., 5" dia. rim. **$439**

Courtesy of Jeffrey S. Evans & Associates, www.jeffreysevans.com

Spaniel figure, circa 1900, unsigned, glaze loss on back of head, 9-1/2" x 6-3/4". **$70**

Courtesy of Soulis Auctions, Lone Jack, Missouri, www.dirksoulisauctions.com

Flint glaze teapot and pitcher, 19th century, crack near spout of pitcher and opposite toward handle, crow's foot to base, teapot with hairlines to lid flange, pitcher 9-1/4" h. **$50**

Courtesy of Soulis Auctions, Lone Jack, Missouri, www.dirksoulisauctions.com

Teapot, 19th century, small flaw on foot, 9" x 10-1/2" x 7-3/4"..**$75**
Courtesy of Soulis Auctions, Lone Jack, Missouri, www.dirksoulisauctions.com

Mermaid flask, 19th century, 8" x 4". **$75**

Courtesy of Soulis Auctions, Lone Jack, Missouri, www.dirksoulisauctions.com

CERAMICS

rookwood

MARIA LONGWORTH NICHOLS founded Rookwood Pottery in 1880. The name, she later reported, paid homage to the many crows (rooks) on her father's estate and was also designed to remind customers of Wedgwood. Production began on Thanksgiving Day 1880 when the first kiln was drawn.

Rookwood's earliest productions demonstrated a continued reliance on European precedents and the Japanese aesthetic. Although the firm offered a variety of wares (Dull Glaze, Cameo, and Limoges for example), it lacked a clearly defined artistic identity. With the introduction of what became known as its "standard glaze" in 1884, Rookwood inaugurated a period in which the company won consistent recognition for its artistic merit and technical innovation.

Rookwood's first decade ended on a high note when the company was awarded two gold medals: one at the Exhibition of American Art Industry in Philadelphia and another later in the year at the Exposition Universelle in Paris.

Significant, too, was Maria Longworth Nichols' decision to transfer her interest in the company to William W. Taylor, who had been the firm's manager since 1883. In May 1890, the board of a newly reorganized Rookwood Pottery Co. purchased "the real estate, personal property, goodwill, patents, trade-marks ... now the sole property of William W. Taylor" for $40,000.

Under Taylor's leadership, Rookwood was transformed from a fledgling startup to successful business that expanded throughout the following decades to meet rising demand.

Throughout the 1890s, Rookwood continued to attract critical notice as it kept the tradition of innovation alive. Taylor rolled out three new glaze lines – Iris, Sea Green, and Aerial Blue – from late 1894 into early 1895.

At the Paris Exposition in 1900, Rookwood cemented its reputation by winning the Grand Prix, a feat largely due to the favorable reception of the new Iris glaze and its variants.

Over the next several years, Rookwood's record of achievement at domestic and international exhibitions remained unmatched.

Throughout the 1910s, Rookwood continued in a similar vein and began to more thoroughly embrace the simplified aesthetic promoted by many Arts & Crafts figures. Production of the Iris line, which had been instrumental in the firm's success at the Paris Exposition in 1900, ceased around 1912. Not only did the company abandon its older, fussier underglaze wares, but the newer lines the pottery introduced also trended toward simplicity.

Iris glaze vase with pansy by Constance Baker, 1903, marks: Rookwood logo, date, shape 849 and artist's incised initials, fine overall crazing, 9-1/4" h.
.... **$1,100**

Courtesy of Mark Mussio, Humler & Nolan, www.humlernolan.com

Unfortunately, the collapse of the stock market in October 1929 and ensuing economic depression dealt Rookwood a blow from which it did not recover. The Great Depression took a toll on the company and eventually led to bankruptcy in April 1941.

Rookwood's history might have ended there were it not for the purchase of the firm by a group of investors led by automobile dealer Walter E. Schott and his wife, Margaret. Production started once again. In the years that followed, Rookwood changed hands a number of times before being moved to Starkville, Mississippi, in 1960. It finally closed its doors there in 1967.

Iris glaze vase with poppies by Laura Lindeman, 1904, marks: Rookwood logo, date, shape 909 C, incised W for white Iris glaze and artist's initials, fine overall crazing, 8-1/2" h...... **$750**

Courtesy of Mark Mussio, Humler & Nolan, www.humlernolan.com

Standard Glaze teapot with goldfinch preparing to dine on blackberries by Mary Nourse, 1894, marks: Rookwood logo, date, Special shape S 1150, impressed W for white clay and artist's incised initials, professional repair to lid and spout, 9" h. **$550**

Courtesy of Mark Mussio, Humler & Nolan, www.humlernolan.com

Standard Glaze vase with daffodils by Carrie Steinle, 1898, marks: Rookwood logo, date, shape 735 DD and artist's monogram, faint overall crazing, 7" h. **$200**

Courtesy of Mark Mussio, Humler & Nolan, www.humlernolan.com

Standard Glaze mug with portrait of Sioux Chief High Bear by Adelize Sehon, 1901, marks: Rookwood logo, date, shape 830 D, artist's incised initials and "High Bear Sioux," fine overall crazing, 6-1/4" h. **$2,300**

Courtesy of Mark Mussio, Humler & Nolan, www.humlernolan.com

Standard Glaze vase with spider chrysanthemums by Grace Young, 1895, marks: Rookwood logo, date, shape 796 and artist's monogram, fine overall crazing, burst glaze bubble near rim, 10" h. **$300**

Courtesy of Mark Mussio, Humler & Nolan, www.humlernolan.com

top lot

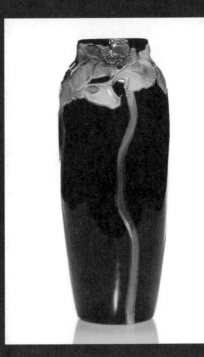

Black Iris vase with carved and reticulated red poppy decoration by John Dee Wareham, 1901, marks: Rookwood logo, date, shape 907 D and artist's incised initials, faint crazing and line at rim, 10-5/8" h. Wareham is the only Rookwood decorator to consistently place cut-outs in his designs. $15,000

ROOKWOOD MARKS

Rookwood employed a number of marks on the bottom of its vessels that denoted everything from the shape to the size, date, and color of the body, to the type of glaze to be used.

COMPANY MARKS

1880-1882

In this early period, a number of marks were used to identify the wares.

1. "ROOKWOOD" followed by the initials of the decorator, painted in gold. This is likely the earliest mark, and though the wares are not dated, it seems to have been discontinued by 1881-1882.
2. "ROOKWOOD / POTTERY. / [DATE] CIN. O." In Marks of American Potters (1904), Edwin AtLee Barber states, "The most common marks prior to 1882 were the name of the pottery and the date of manufacture, which were painted or incised on the base of each piece by the decorator."
3. "R. P. C. O. M. L. N." These initials stand for "Rookwood Pottery, Cincinnati, Ohio, Maria Longworth Nichols" and were either painted or incised on the base.
4. Kiln and crows stamp. Barber notes that in 1881 and 1882, the trademark designed by the artist Henry Farny was printed beneath the glaze.
5. Anchor stamp: Barber notes that this mark is "one of the rarest."
6. Oval stamp.
7. Ribbon or banner stamp: According to Barber, "In 1882 a special mark was used on a trade piece... the letters were impressed in a raised ribbon.
8. Ribbon or banner stamp II: A simpler variation of the above stamp, recorded by Herbert Peck.

1883-1886

1. Stamped name and date.
2. Impressed kiln: Appears only in 1883.

1886-1960

Virtually all of the pieces feature the conjoined RP monogram. Pieces fired in the anniversary kilns carry a special kiln-shaped mark with the number of the anniversary inside of it.

1955

A diamond-shaped mark that reads: "ROOKWOOD / 75th / ANNIVERSARY / POTTERY" was printed on wares.

1960-1967

Occasionally pieces are marked "ROOKWOOD POTTERY / STARKVILLE MISS"; from 1962 to 1967 a small "*" occasionally follows the monogram.

DATE MARKS

Unlike many of their contemporaries, Rookwood seems very early on to have adopted a method of marking its pottery that was accurate and easy to understand.

From 1882-1885, the company impressed the date, often with the company name, in block letters (see 1883-86, No. 1).

Although the date traditionally given for the conjoined RP mark is June 23, 1886, this marks the official introduction of the monogram rather than the first use.

Stanley Burt, in his record of Rookwood at the Cincinnati Museum, noted two pieces from 1883 (Nos. 2 and 3) that used the monogram. The monogram was likely designed by Alfred Brennan, since it first appears on his work.

From 1886 on, the date of the object was coded in the conjoined "RP" monogram.

1886: conjoined "RP" no additional flame marks.

1887-1900: conjoined "RP" with a flame added for each subsequent year. Thus, a monogram with seven flames would represent 1893.

1900-1967: conjoined "RP" with 14 flames and a Roman numeral below the mark to indicate the year after 1900. Thus, a monogram with 14 flames and the letters "XXXVI" below it signifies 1936.

CLAY-TYPE MARKS

From 1880 until around 1895, Rookwood used a number of different colored bodies for production and marked each color with a letter code. These letters were impressed and usually found grouped together with the shape number, sometimes following it, but more often below it.

The letter "S" is a particularly vexing designation since the same initial was used for two other unrelated designations. As a result, it is particularly important to take into account the relative position of the impressed letter.

R = Red

Y = Yellow

S = Sage

G = Ginger

W = White

O = Olive

P = From 1915 on, Rookwood used an impressed "P" (often found perpendicular to the orientation of the other marks) to denote the soft porcelain body.

SIZE AND SHAPE MARKS

Almost all Rookwood pieces have a shape code consisting of three or four numbers, followed by a size letter. "A" denotes the largest available size, "F" is the smallest. According to Herbert Peck, initial designs were given a "C" or "D" designation so that variations could be made. Not every shape model, however, features a variation in every size.

GLAZE MARKS

In addition to marking the size, shape and year of the piece, Rookwood's decorators also used a number of letters to designate the type of glaze to be used upon a piece. Generally speaking, these marks are either incised or impressed.

"S" = Standard Glaze to be used. (Incised.)

"L" = Decorators would often incise an "L" near their monogram to indicate that the light variation of the Standard Glaze was to be used. (Incised.)

"SG" = Sea Green Glaze to be used.

"Z" = from 1900-1904 designated any piece with a Mat Glaze. (Impressed)

"W" = Iris Glaze to be used.

"V" = Vellum Glaze to be used; variations include "GV" for Green Vellum and "YV" for Yellow Vellum.

OTHER MARKS

"S" = If found away from the shape number, this generally indicates a piece that was specially thrown at the pottery in the presence of visitors. (Impressed.)

"S" = If this precedes the shape number than it denotes a piece that was specifically thrown and decorated from a sketch with a corresponding number. Because of the size and quality of pieces this letter has been found on, this probably signifies a piece made specifically for an important exhibition.

"X" = Rookwood used a wheel ground "x" to indicate items that were not of first quality. There has been some suggestion that decorators and salespersons might have conspired to "x" certain pieces that they liked, since this designation would reduce the price. Since there are a number of items that appear to have been marked for no apparent reason, there may be some truth to this idea. Unfortunately, as this idea has gained credence, many pieces with obvious flaws have been listed as "marked x for no apparent reason," and collectors should be cautious.

Generally, the mark reduces the value and appeal of the piece. Peck describes a variation of the "x" that resembles an asterisk as indicating a piece that could be given away to employees.

"T" = An impressed T that precedes a shape number indicates a trial piece.

▶◆▲ = These shapes (crescents, diamonds, and triangles) are used to indicate a glaze trial.

"K1" and "K3" = circa 1922, used for matching teacups and saucers

"SC" = Cream and Sugar sets, circa 1946-1950

"2800" = Impressed on ship pattern tableware

SOME LINES OF NOTE

Aerial Blue: Commercially, this line was among the least successful. As a result, there are a limited number of pieces, and this scarcity has increased their values relative to other wares.

Black Iris: This line is among the most sought after by collectors, commanding significantly more than examples of similar size and design in virtually any other glaze. In fact, the current auction record for Rookwood – over $350,000 – was set in 2004 for a Black Iris vase decorated by Kitaro Shirayamadani in 1900.

Iris: Uncrazed examples are exceptionally rare, with large pieces featuring conventional designs commanding the highest prices. Smaller, naturalistically painted examples, though still desirable, are gradually becoming more affordable for the less advanced collector.

Production Ware: This commercial and mass-produced artware is significantly less expensive than pieces in most other lines.

Standard Glaze: These wares peaked in the 1970s-1980s, and the market has remained thin in recent years, but regardless of the state of the market, examples of superlative quality, including those with silver overlay, have found their places in the finest of collections.

Wax Mat: This is among the most affordable of the hand-decorated lines.

Rare carved black Standard Glaze vase with red-hot-poker flowers by John Dee Wareham (vase appears to be Black Iris but is Standard Glaze, per auction house), clay added to vase and then cut back for raised floral decoration, 1899, marks: Rookwood logo, date, shape 732 B and artist's monogram, wheel ground X due to glaze skips at base, fine overall crazing, scratches in glaze, 10-1/2" h. **$3,500**

Courtesy of Mark Mussio, Humler & Nolan, www.humlernolan.com

CERAMICS

Standard Glaze handled vase with yellow roses by Matt Daly, 1891, marks: Rookwood logo, date, shape 604 C and artist's monogram, scattered crazing and light glaze scratches, 9-1/8" h. **$300**

Courtesy of Mark Mussio, Humler & Nolan, www.humlernolan.com

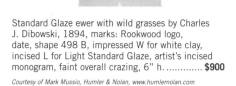

Standard Glaze ewer with wild grasses by Charles J. Dibowski, 1894, marks: Rookwood logo, date, shape 498 B, impressed W for white clay, incised L for Light Standard Glaze, artist's incised monogram, faint overall crazing, 6" h. **$900**

Courtesy of Mark Mussio, Humler & Nolan, www.humlernolan.com

Standard Glaze tyg with orange carnations by Constance Baker, 1897, tyg sent to Gorham Manufacturing Co. where silver overlay was added; marks: Rookwood logo, date, shape 330 E, triangle-shaped esoteric mark and Baker's monogram, fine overall crazing, 4-1/2" h. **$800**

Courtesy of Mark Mussio, Humler & Nolan, www.humlernolan.com

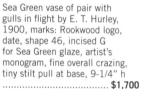

Scenic Vellum vase by Lenore Asbury, 1917, marks: Rookwood logo, date, shape 814 A, impressed V for Vellum, artist's incised initials, fine overall crazing, glaze nicks at base, 13-3/4" h. **$1,800**

Courtesy of Mark Mussio, Humler & Nolan, www.humlernolan.com

Sea Green vase of pair with gulls in flight by E. T. Hurley, 1900, marks: Rookwood logo, date, shape 46, incised G for Sea Green glaze, artist's monogram, fine overall crazing, tiny stilt pull at base, 9-1/4" h **$1,700**

Courtesy of Mark Mussio, Humler & Nolan, www.humlernolan.com

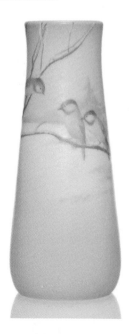

▲ Scenic Vellum vase with large trees and lake beneath pink sky by E. T. Hurley, 1938, marks: Rookwood logo, date, shape 892 C and artist's monogram, 10-5/8" h..**$2,500**

Courtesy of Mark Mussio, Humler & Nolan, www.humlernolan.com

◄ Vellum glaze vase with winter scene, trio of chickadees gathered on snow-covered branch, by Kataro Shirayamadani, 1907, marks: Rookwood logo, date, shape 950 D, impressed V for Vellum, artist's incised monogram, fine overall crazing, 9-1/8" h. **$3,600**

Courtesy of Mark Mussio, Humler & Nolan, www.humlernolan.com

Two-owl candle sconce in green over brown mat glazes, 1910, marks: Rookwood logo, date, shape 1688, wheel ground X likely due to open glaze bubbles, professional repair to rim nicks, 11-1/2" x 6-1/8" **$1,100**

Courtesy of Mark Mussio, Humler & Nolan, www.humlernolan.com

Design Crystal vase with floral decoration by Jens Jensen, 1943, marks: Rookwood logo, date, shape 6185 F and artist's monogram in brown slip, wheel ground line designating piece as second, possibly due to decoration being obscure near base, scattered crazing, 5-1/2" h. **$150**

Courtesy of Mark Mussio, Humler & Nolan, www.humlernolan.com

Porcelain pilgrim flask vase with floral motif by William Hentschel, 1923, marks: Rookwood logo, date, shape 2627, artist's monogram in green slip, portion of original Rookwood showroom label, 9-5/8" h. **$225**

Courtesy of Mark Mussio, Humler & Nolan, www.humlernolan.com

▶ ▼ Scenic vase by E. T. Hurley, 1945, marks: Rookwood logo, date, shape 6197 C, artist's monogram and 5053 in brown slip, 8-1/2" h. ... **$10,500**

Courtesy of Mark Mussio, Humler & Nolan, www.humlernolan.com

▲ Vellum vase with ring of flowers at shoulder by Lenore Asbury, 1927, marks: Rookwood logo, date, shape 494 B, incised V for Vellum glaze, artist's initials, 4-7/8" h. **$500**

Courtesy of Mark Mussio, Humler & Nolan, www.humlernolan.com

CERAMICS

roseville pottery

ROSEVILLE IS ONE OF THE MOST widely recognizable of potteries across the United States. Having been sold in flower shops and drug stores around the country, its art and production wares became a staple in American homes through the time Roseville closed in the 1950s.

The Roseville Pottery Co., located in Roseville, Ohio, was incorporated on Jan. 4, 1892, with George F. Young as general manager. The company had been producing stoneware since 1890, when it purchased the J. B. Owens Pottery, also of Roseville.

The popularity of Roseville Pottery's original lines of stoneware continued to grow. The company acquired new plants in 1892 and 1898, and production started to shift to Zanesville, just a few miles away. By about 1910, all of the work was centered in Zanesville, but the company name was unchanged.

Young hired Ross C. Purdy as artistic designer in 1900, and Purdy created Rozane – a contraction of the words "Roseville" and "Zanesville." The first Roseville artwork pieces were marked either Rozane or RPCO, both impressed or ink-stamped on the bottom.

In 1902, a line was developed called Azurean. Some pieces were marked Azurean, but often RPCO. In 1904 at the St. Louis Exposition, Roseville's Rozane Mongol, a high-gloss oxblood red line, captured first prize, gaining recognition for the firm and its creator, John Herold.

Many Roseville lines were a response to the innovations of Weller Pottery, another Zanesville pottery, and in 1904 Frederick Rhead was hired away from Weller as artistic director. He created the Olympic and Della Robbia lines for Roseville. His brother Harry took over as artistic director in 1908, and in 1915 he introduced the popular Donatello line.

By 1908, all handcrafting ended except for Rozane Royal. Roseville was the first pottery in Ohio to install a tunnel kiln, which increased its production capacity.

Frank Ferrell, who was a top decorator at the Weller Pottery by 1904, was Roseville's artistic director from 1917 until 1954. This Zanesville native created many of the most popular lines, including Pine Cone, which had scores of individual pieces.

Many collectors believe Roseville's circa 1925 glazes were the best of any Zanesville pottery. George Krause, who in 1915 became Roseville's technical supervisor responsible for glaze, remained with Roseville until the 1950s.

Company sales declined after World War II, especially in the early 1950s when cheap Japanese imports began to replace American wares, and a simpler, more modern style made many of Roseville's elaborate floral designs seem old-fashioned.

In the late 1940s, Roseville began to issue lines with glossy glazes. The company also tried to offset its flagging artware sales by launching a dinnerware line – Raymor – in 1953. The line was a commercial failure.

Roseville issued its last new designs in 1953. On Nov. 29, 1954, the facilities of Roseville were sold to the Mosaic Tile Co.

For more information on Roseville, see *Warman's Roseville Pottery*, 2nd edition, by Denise Rago.

BOTTOM MARKS

There is no consistency to Roseville bottom marks. Even within a single popular pattern like Pine Cone, the marks vary.

Several shape-numbering systems were implemented during the company's almost 70-year history, with some denoting a vessel style and some applied to separate lines. Though many pieces are unmarked, from 1900 until the late teens or early 1920s, Roseville used a variety of marks including "RPCo," "Roseville Pottery Company," and the word "Rozane," the last often with a line name, i.e., "Egypto."

The underglaze ink script "Rv" mark was used on lines introduced from the mid-to-late teens through the mid-1920s. Around 1926 or 1927, Roseville began to use a small, triangular black paper label on lines such as Futura and Imperial II. Silver or gold foil labels began to appear around 1930, continuing for several years on lines such as Blackberry and Tourmaline, and on some early Pine Cone.

From 1932 to 1937, an impressed script mark was added to the molds used on new lines, and around 1937 the raised script mark was added to the molds of new lines. The relief mark includes "U.S.A."

All of the following bottom mark images appear courtesy of Adamstown Antique Gallery, Adamstown, Pennsylvania.

Impressed mark on Azurean vase, 8" h.

Raised mark on Bushberry vase.

Ink stamp on Cherry Blossom pink vase, 10" h.

Wafer mark on Della Robbia vase, 10-1/2" h.

Gold foil label and grease pencil marks on Imperial II vase, 10" h.

Impressed mark on Iris vase.

Ink stamps on Wisteria bowl, 5" h.

Impressed marks on Rozane portrait vase, 13" h.

Blackberry pattern square basket, shape 334, unmarked, faint crazing, 6-5/8" h. **$275**

Courtesy of Mark Mussio, Humler & Nolan, www.humlernolan.com

Carnelian II pattern wall pocket in pink and green, shape 1246-7", shape mark in red crayon, retail sticker "The Maylo" on back, factory glaze grind to upper back corner, 8-1/4" h. **$90**

Courtesy of Mark Mussio, Humler & Nolan, www.humlernolan.com

Cherry Blossom pattern vase in pink, shape 617, unmarked, fine overall crazing, 4-1/8" h. **$200**

Courtesy of Mark Mussio, Humler & Nolan, www.humlernolan.com

Two Donatello pattern vases, unmarked, light stained crazing on each, 10" x 5-3/4", 9-1/2" x 5-1/4". **$150**

Courtesy of Soulis Auctions, Lone Jack, Missouri, www.dirksoulisauctions.com

Earlam pattern vase in tan and blue, shape 519-7" marked in orange crayon on bottom, 7-1/8" h. **$150**

Courtesy of Mark Mussio, Humler & Nolan, www.humlernolan.com

Ferella pattern vase in red, shape 510-9", unmarked, 9-1/8" h. **$375**

Courtesy of Mark Mussio, Humler & Nolan, www.humlernolan.com

Fuchsia pattern floor vase in blue, shape 905-18", faint Roseville 905-18" markings, fine crazing, 18-1/4" h........**$400**

Courtesy of Mark Mussio, Humler & Nolan, www.humlernolan.com

Fujiyama/Woodland pattern vase with incised stalk of hollyhocks, golden brown and green glaze over tan stippled backdrop, ink stamped "Fujiyama" beneath, chip below and at side of base, glaze wear to front base rim, surface stains, 10-3/4" h................**$400**

Courtesy of Mark Mussio, Humler & Nolan, www.humlernolan.com

Futura pattern "elephant leg" vase, shape 435-10", unmarked, two open glaze bubbles, small nick at base, 10" h. **$300**

Courtesy of Mark Mussio, Humler & Nolan, www.humlernolan.com

Futura pattern fan vase in mottled blue and tan, shape 82-6", unmarked, 6" h. **$225**

Courtesy of Mark Mussio, Humler & Nolan, www.humlernolan.com

Futura Blue Sunray pattern vase in trial glaze colors of dark green and pink instead of traditional blue on blue, shape 81-5-1-5, marked "Dark Green Matt Pink" in blue crayon, two tight lines at rim, 5-1/8" h. **$1,500**

Courtesy of Mark Mussio, Humler & Nolan, www.humlernolan.com

Rare Pauleo Arts & Crafts pattern vase with stalks of thistle blossoms and foliage hand-painted in fired-on gold over reflective black glaze, "Pauleo Pottery" wafer, incised 231, professionally repaired glaze nicks, 13-3/4" h. **$800**

Courtesy of Mark Mussio, Humler & Nolan, www.humlernolan.com

Pine Cone pattern basket in brown, shape 353-11", Roseville U.S.A. 353-11", 11-1/8" h. **$400**

Courtesy of Mark Mussio, Humler & Nolan, www.humlernolan.com

Pine Cone pattern urn in blue, shape 912-15", marked Roseville 912-15", professional rim repair, 15-1/4" h. **$325**

Courtesy of Mark Mussio, Humler & Nolan, www.humlernolan.com

Pine Cone pattern triple bud vase in green, shape 113-8", unmarked, 8-1/2" h. **$120**

Courtesy of Mark Mussio, Humler & Nolan, www.humlernolan.com

Rozane Woodland pattern vase with incised leafy stem of white flowers and buds, teal backdrop blending into tan, artist monogram, possibly GJ, incised on side of base, Rozane Ware Woodland seal, 14-1/4" h. .. **$1,700**

Courtesy of Mark Mussio, Humler & Nolan, www.humlernolan.com

Tuscany pattern vase in pink, shape 346-9", unmarked, 9-1/8" h. **$70**

Courtesy of Mark Mussio, Humler & Nolan, www.humlernolan.com

Experimental vase with deeply carved tulips by Frank Barks (modeler at Roseville), incised "Barks Trial" on bottom, professional restoration to glaze flake, fine overall crazing, 9-3/8" h. **$1,900**

Courtesy of Mark Mussio, Humler & Nolan, www.humlernolan.com

CERAMICS

r.s. prussia

ORNATELY DECORATED CHINA marked "R.S. Prussia" and "R.S. Germany" continues to grow in popularity. According to the Third Series of Mary Frank Gaston's *Encyclopedia of R.S. Prussia* (Collector Books, Paducah, Kentucky), these marks were used by the Reinhold Schlegelmilch porcelain factories located in Suhl in the Germanic regions known as "Prussia" prior to World War I, and in Tillowitz, Silesia, which became part of Poland after World War II. Other marks sought by collectors include "R.S. Suhl," "R.S." steeple or church marks, and "R.S. Poland."

The Suhl factory was founded by Reinhold Schlegelmilch in 1869 and closed in 1917. The Tillowitz factory was established in 1895 by Erhard Schlegelmilch, Reinhold's son. This china customarily bears the phrase "R.S. Germany" and "R.S. Tillowitz." The Tillowitz factory closed in 1945, but it was reopened for a few years under Polish administration.

Prices are high and collectors should beware of the forgeries that sometimes find their way onto the market. Mold names and numbers are taken from Mary Frank Gaston's books on R.S. Prussia.

The "Prussia" and "R.S. Suhl" marks have been reproduced, so buy with care. Later copies of these marks are well done, but the quality of porcelain is inferior to the production in the 1890-1920 era.

Collectors are also interested in the porcelain products made by the Erdmann Schlegelmilch factory. This factory was founded by three brothers in Suhl in 1861. They named the factory in honor of their father, Erdmann Schlegelmilch. A variety of marks incorporating the "E.S." initials were used. The factory closed circa 1935. The Erdmann Schlegelmilch factory was an earlier and entirely separate business from the Reinhold Schlegelmilch factory. The two were not related to each other.

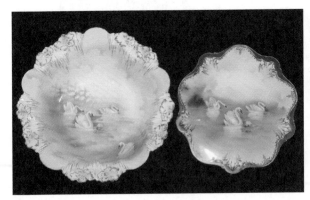

Icicle mold bowl and plate with "Four Swans on the Lake" décor, both with red mark, both with light glaze rubs, bowl 3" x 11", plate 9" dia.. **$190**

Courtesy of Soulis Auctions, Lone Jack, Missouri, www.dirksoulisauctions.com

Icicle mold biscuit jar with "Four Swans on the Lake" décor, signed with RS Prussia red mark on base, professionally repaired lid, some overspray, 5" x 9". **$150**

Courtesy of Soulis Auctions, Lone Jack, Missouri, www.dirksoulisauctions.com

Medallion mold dresser tray with cream center, rose garland, green border, medallion portraits of LeBrun I & II, Potacka, 11-3/4"..................... **$207**

Courtesy of Woody Auction, www.woodyauction.com

Ribbon and jewel mold two-handled cake plate with "Dice Throwers" décor, fading around border, 10-1/2" dia... **$118**

Courtesy of Woody Auction, www.woodyauction.com

Plate with pale green center and pink rose décor, cobalt blue border with gold trim highlights, 9-3/4" dia.. **$325**

Courtesy of Woody Auction, www.woodyauction.com

Swag and tassel mold bowl with peacock décor and unusual rose "sunset" coloring, 10-3/4" dia. **$413**

Courtesy of Woody Auction, www.woodyauction.com

Six-sided bowl with cream center and wildflower décor, black and cobalt blue border, gold trim highlights, unmarked, 10-3/4" dia. **$708**

Courtesy of Woody Auction, www.woodyauction.com

Acorn mold bowl in yellow and green with pink rose décor, 10-1/4" dia. **$35**

Courtesy of Woody Auction, www.woodyauction.com

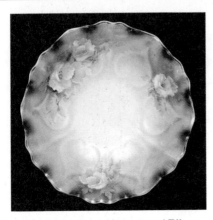

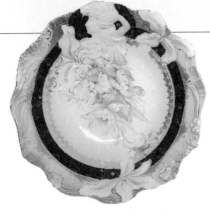

Impressed heart mold bowl in cream and Tiffany satin finish with poppy décor, 10" dia................. **$47**

Courtesy of Woody Auction, www.woodyauction.com

Hidden image bowl with cream center with wildflower décor, cobalt blue and lighter blue border with gold trim highlights, unmarked, 8-1/4" dia.. **$148**

Courtesy of Woody Auction, www.woodyauction.com

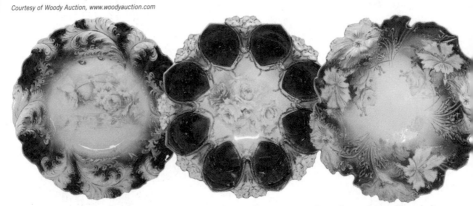

Plume mold bowl with reflecting flowers décor, cobalt blue, gold stencil highlights, 10-3/4" dia......................... **$649**

Courtesy of Woody Auction, www.woodyauction.com

Mold #90 bowl with cream center and pink rose décor, cobalt blue domes, gold highlights, 10-1/4" dia. **$266**

Courtesy of Woody Auction, www.woodyauction.com

Carnation mold bowl in cobalt blue with yellow and pink rose décor, light blue and cream highlights, 9-3/4" dia. **$472**

Courtesy of Woody Auction, www.woodyauction.com

Mold #90 bowl with cream center and poppy décor, rare four seasons medallion highlights, strong gold stencil, 10-1/4" dia. **$4,130**

Courtesy of Woody Auction, www.woodyauction.com

Early marked Prussia plate with reticulated border and scene of two women in garden with cherub, heavy gold border, 8-1/2" dia............................ **$71**

Courtesy of Woody Auction, www.woodyauction.com

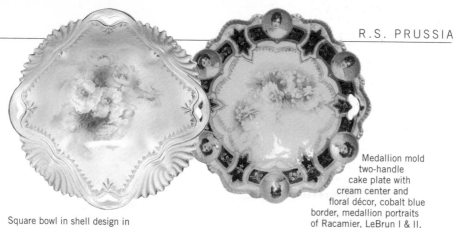

Square bowl in shell design in cream and lavender with poppy décor, 11". **$295**

Courtesy of Woody Auction, www.woodyauction.com

Medallion mold two-handle cake plate with cream center and floral décor, cobalt blue border, medallion portraits of Racamier, LeBrun I & II, gold tapestry background, unmarked, 11-1/4"............. **$531**

Courtesy of Woody Auction, www.woodyauction.com

Iris mold coffeepot with winter season portrait décor in white satin finish with lavender highlights, rim nick, 9-1/4" h. **$2,124**

Courtesy of Woody Auction, www.woodyauction.com

Mold #343 plate with winter season keyhole portrait and red border with scattered pink floral décor and gold trim, some gold worn, 9" dia.................... **$1,298**

Courtesy of Woody Auction, www.woodyauction.com

Fleur-de-lis mold pedestal creamer and sugar with summer season portrait décor in white and lavender satin finish........................... **$354**

Courtesy of Woody Auction, www.woodyauction.com

Carnation mold cake plate with six matching dessert plates in cobalt blue, cake plate with small section of discoloration on back glaze, 11" dia., dessert plates 7-1/2" dia..$1,652

Courtesy of Woody Auction, www.woodyauction.com

Ball vase with fall season portrait décor and purple lustre background, 5". **$472**

Courtesy of Woody Auction, www.woodyauction.com

CERAMICS

sèvres

SÈVRES PORCELAIN, THE GRANDEST of ultimate luxury, artistic ceramics, was favored by European royalty, the aristocracy of the 19th century, and 20th century great collectors. Its story begins in 1708, when, following frenzied experimentation, German alchemist Johann Bottger discovered the formula for strong, delicate, translucent hard-paste porcelain. Unlike imported white chinaware, Bottger's porcelain could also be painted and gilded. Soon potteries across Europe were producing decorative items with fashionable gilt and flowers.

French potters lacked an ample source of kaolin, a requisite for hard-paste porcelain, however. So from clay and powdered glass, they developed a soft-paste formula. Soft-paste, though more fragile, could be fired at a lower temperature than hard-paste. This allowed a wider variety of colors and glazes.

The Sèvres porcelain factory was originally founded at Chateau de Vincennes in 1738. Its soft-paste porcelain was prized for its characteristic whiteness and purity. By the time this workshop relocated to Sèvres in 1756, its craftsmen were creating small porcelain birds, figurals of children in white or delicate hues, and innovative pieces with characteristic rosy-hued backgrounds. They also produced detailed allegorical and thematic pieces like "Flute Lesson," "Jealousy," and "Justice and the Republic," which sparkle with transparent, colorless glazes.

The introduction of unglazed, natural-toned "biscuit" porcelain, a favorite of Madame de Pompadour, the mistress of Louis XV, followed. Many of these molded sculptures portray lifelike sentimental or Classical scenes. Biscuit porcelain is extremely fragile.

Madame de Pompadour also adored Sèvres' porcelain flowers, the most delicate item produced during these early years.

Vase with oxblood-style flambé glaze, 1892, striated shades of red, blue and black with white porcelain showing through with green spots, marked S92 in black on bottom, 10" h......... **$1,700**

Courtesy of Mark Mussio, Humler & Nolan, www.humlernolan.com

Legend has it that, to further the company's production, she once presented Louis XV with a profusion of Sèvres vases abloom with colorful porcelain pretties, petal upon tinted petal atop cunningly wired "stems."

When Louis XV assumed full control of Sèvres porcelain in 1759, he insisted on flawless, extravagant creations, many of which he commissioned for his personal collection. In his travels, he also spread the Sèvres reputation for opulent ornamentation, vivid colors, and fine glazes.

The renowned Sèvres mark, elaborate blue interlaced Ls, was born of his royal patronage and helps determine dates of production. Other marks, either painted or incised, indicate specific Sèvres painters, gilders, sculptors, and potters by name.

Louis XV's successor, Louis XVI, continued to support the royal Sèvres tradition. He not only set prices and arranged exhibitions, but also marketed pieces personally.

Although kaolin deposits were discovered near Limoges in 1768, Sèvres began producing hard-paste porcelain commercially only from 1773. During this period, they continued to produce soft-paste items as well.

After suffering financial ruin during the French Revolution, Sèvres, in addition to creating traditional pieces for the luxury market, began producing simpler, less expensive items. During this period, its craftsmen also abandoned their old-fashioned soft-paste formula for hard-paste porcelain.

Sèvres porcelain regained its former glory under Napoleon Bonaparte, who assumed power in 1804. He promoted elaborately ornamented pieces in the classical style. The Empire's richly decorated, themed dinner sets, for example, were enjoyed by distinguished guests, visiting rulers, and Napoleon himself. These pieces typically feature florals, landscapes, or cameo portraits framed by solid gold edging accented with stylized palm fronds, the ancient Greek symbol of victory.

Two vases with oxblood-style flambé glaze, 1892, striated shades of red, blue and black with white porcelain showing through, larger vase marked S92 in black on bottom, possibly experimental piece with BX 904 notation in black slip inside foot ring, 9" h., smaller vase marked BX 9-3CH on bottom, impressed Nd, 5" h. **$850**

Courtesy of Mark Mussio, Humler & Nolan, www.humlernolan.com

Pair of vases, Paul Milet Art Deco flambé, square bronze bases, each marked with MP Sèvres ink stamp logo, circular gold foil labels with "L.B. Paris Made in France," each base stamped "Made in France," 11" h. **$950**

Courtesy of Mark Mussio, Humler & Nolan, www.humlernolan.com

CERAMICS

Paul Millet oval red dresser box with hinged cover, ormolu mounts, signed under base, 4" x 7" x 5-1/2"..$575

Courtesy of Soulis Auctions, Lone Jack, Mo.; www.dirksoulisauctions.com

Along with dinner sets and coffee services, tea services were among Sèvres' most popular creations. During the early 1800s, when passion for that luxury potion peaked, Greek or Etruscan pottery inspired the design of many Sèvres teapots. These were valued not only for their beauty, but also because, as porcelain, they could withstand the heat.

Many Sèvres shapes, which range from simple cylindrical vases to elaborate perforated potpourri jars, were innovative for their times. Some, like a gondola-shaped vase designed to hold aromatic petals or another with elephant-head handles fitted as candle arms, serve a double purpose. Sèvres also created a wide selection of decorative utilitarian objects, including tobacco jars, lidded ewers and basins, painted plaques, punch bowls, sorbet coolers, and milk jugs.

The range of Sèvres creations is extensive, varying in shape, historical styles, motifs, and ornamentation. Vases typically feature double round, oval, or elliptical finely painted scenes edged in white against pastel backgrounds. One side portrays figures, while the other features flower bouquets. Their lavish gilding, a royal touch reserved especially for Sèvres creations, is often embellished with engraved detail, like flowers or geometric motifs. Many fine pieces like these, if rarely or never used, are still found in pristine condition.

Simple plates and tea wares can be found for a few hundred dollars. Because large numbers were made to accompany dessert services, quite a few Sèvres biscuit porcelains have also survived. These fragile pieces command between $3,000 to as much as $70,000 apiece.

According to Errol Manners, author, lecturer, and proprietor of London's H & E Manners: Ceramics and Works of Art, the Sèvres market has strengthened considerably in recent years. "Pieces linked directly to the Court and very early experimental wares, which appeal to more serious and academic collectors, command the highest prices of all," he said. "Major pieces can command a few hundred thousand dollars. A set of Sèvres vases can command over $1 million."

Manners recommends that would-be collectors visit museums and consult serious dealers and collectors before purchasing a Sèvres piece. "And read the books," he said. "There are really no shortcuts. It takes serious study."

Collecting Sèvres porcelain is, in his experience, "a minefield for the unwary, since many fakes and pastiches – showy, decorative 'Sèvres-style' imitations – abound. These were produced during the 19th century in the style of the 18th century, but not by Sèvres," he said.

"While Sèvres-style pieces are not authentic Sèvres, they may be authentic antiques," according to Edan Sassoon, representing the Artes Antiques and Fine Art Gallery in Beverly Hills, California. "If they faithfully imitate Sèvres pieces in quality, style, and opulence, they may not only have decorative value, but may also be quite expensive. In today's market, a piece of Sèvres-style porcelain, depending on its color, condition, size, and quality, may command hundreds of thousands of dollars."

— Melody Amsel-Arieli

Pate-sur-pate vase with nude, circa 1900, artist signed "JA," ram's-head handles, gold enameling, 15" h. x 7-1/2" w..$10,063

Porcelain vase, 20th century, 14-1/4" h. **$344**

Courtesy of Leslie Hindman Auctioneers, www.lesliehindman.com

Pair of covered pedestal urns with yellow background and hand-painted courting scene, each with scene on reverse, gilt metal trim, handles and base, marked, 17-1/2" h.............. **$649**

Courtesy of Woody Auction, www.woodyauction.com

Vase, Taxile Doate, four colors, four assorted head profiles, two men in helmets and two women within medallions, bands with jeweled badges, glossy glazed pale blue backdrop and white mat glazed body with glazed beading, green "T. Doat, Sèvres," impressed 1907, 8-3/8" h.............. **$3,000**

Courtesy of Mark Mussio, Humler & Nolan, www.humlernolan.com

Potpourri with cover, late 19th century, domed lid with oval reserves of airborne cherubs and bronze acanthus finial on cobalt ground, hand-painted, signed "Collot," base with ormolu handles, cobalt blue porcelain socle on bronze foot, Sèvres Chateau De Longpre mark, stamped FRANCE under base, artist signed on cover, decal mark of Chateau De Longpre Manufacture Francaise inside lid, hand-painted "France" in blue lettering, 9-3/4" x 8-1/4"... **$425**

Courtesy of Soulis Auctions, Lone Jack, Missouri, www.dirksoulisauctions.com

CERAMICS

spatterware

SPATTERWARE TAKES ITS NAME from the "spattered" decoration, in various colors, used to trim pieces hand-painted with rustic center designs of flowers, birds, houses, etc. Popular in the early 19th century, most was imported from England.

Related wares, called "stick spatter," had freehand designs applied with pieces of cut sponge attached to sticks, hence the name. Examples date from the 19th and early 20th century and were produced in England, Europe, and America.

Some early spatter-decorated wares were marked by the manufacturers, but not many. Twentieth century reproductions are also sometimes marked, including those produced by Boleslaw Cybis.

Blue spatter miniature tea service with fort pattern, teapot, covered sugar, creamer, and four cups and saucers, teapot 4-1/4" h. **$840**

Courtesy of Pook & Pook, Inc., www.pookandpook.com

Red spatter basin with peafowl pattern, 4-5/8" h, 14-3/4" dia. **$240**

Courtesy of Pook & Pook, Inc., www.pookandpook.com

CERAMICS

Blue spatter covered entrée dish with holly berry pattern, 7-1/2" l x 10-1/4" w..........................**$120**

Courtesy of Pook & Pook, Inc., www.pookandpook.com

Red, blue and green rainbow spatter covered sugar with drape pattern, 19th century, 5-1/4" h.
....**$390**

Courtesy of Pook & Pook, Inc., www.pookandpook.com

Red spatter toddy plate with peafowl pattern, 4-7/8" dia....................................**$431**

Courtesy of Pook & Pook, Inc., www.pookandpook.com

Unusual covered sugar with red and blue rainbow spatter on rim and peafowl pattern variant on body, 4-1/2" h... **$3,120**

Courtesy of Pook & Pook, Inc., www.pookandpook.com

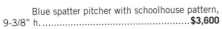

Blue spatter pitcher with schoolhouse pattern, 9-3/8" h. **$3,600**

Courtesy of Pook & Pook, Inc., www.pookandpook.com

Rainbow spatter miniature teapot, sugar and two cups with shed pattern; teapot with chips to lid, repairs to rim of pot and tip of spout; sugar with mismatched lid and rim repair; cup shattered and reglued, hairline. **$1,875**

Courtesy of Pook & Pook, Inc., www.pookandpook.com

Blue spatter plate with tulip, 19th century, light stain to center, 9-1/4" dia. **$197**

Courtesy of Pook & Pook, Inc., www.pookandpook.com

Blue spatter plate with tulip pattern, 19th century, glaze wear to blue, 9-1/4" dia. **$86**

Courtesy of Pook & Pook, Inc., www.pookandpook.com

Red spatter plate with tulip pattern, 19th century, green glaze bubbles, light staining, 9-1/4" dia.
....**$123**

Courtesy of Pook & Pook, Inc., www.pookandpook.com

Yellow spatter covered sugar with thistle pattern, 19th century, 7-3/4" h. **$600**

Courtesy of Pook & Pook, Inc., www.pookandpook.com

Yellow spatter pitcher with tulip pattern, 19th century, 7-3/4" h. **$1,140**

Courtesy of Pook & Pook, Inc., www.pookandpook.com

Brown spatter teapot with purple star, 6" h. **$120**

Courtesy of Pook & Pook, Inc., www.pookandpook.com

Purple and black rainbow spatter pitcher and basin, pitcher 11-1/4" h., basin 4-1/2" h, 13-1/8" dia. **$390**

Yellow and black rainbow spatter covered sugar, 19th century, hairline, extensive crazing, 4-1/4" h. **$180**

Courtesy of Pook & Pook, Inc., www.pookandpook.com

Courtesy of Pook & Pook, Inc., www.pookandpook.com

Five blue spatter plates with pomegranate, thistle, star, and peafowl patterns, 8-1/4" to 9-1/2" dia..........................**$840**

Courtesy of Pook & Pook, Inc., www.pookandpook.com

Four pieces of yellow spatter: plate with tulip pattern, 8-1/4" dia., saucer with transfer eagle, cup with blue cockscomb pattern, and cup with four-petal flower pattern..................**$2,160**

Courtesy of Pook & Pook, Inc., www.pookandpook.com

▼ Red, blue, and green rainbow spatter plate, cup and saucer, plate 9-3/8" dia. **$120**

Courtesy of Pook & Pook, Inc., www.pookandpook.com

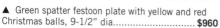

▲ Green spatter festoon plate with yellow and red Christmas balls, 9-1/2" dia............................**$960**

Courtesy of Pook & Pook, Inc., www.pookandpook.com

▶ Red spatter waste bowl with parrot, 3-1/8" h, 5-5/8" dia..**$540**

Courtesy of Pook & Pook, Inc., www.pookandpook.com

CERAMICS

spongeware

SPONGEWARE: THE NAME SAYS IT ALL. A sponge dipped in colored pigment is daubed onto a piece of earthenware pottery of a contrasting color, creating an overall mottled, "sponged" pattern. A clear glaze is applied, and the piece fired. The final product, with its seemingly random, somewhat smudged coloration, conveys an overall impression of handmade folk art.

Most spongeware, however, was factory-made from the mid-1800s well into the 1930s. Any folk art appeal was secondary, the result of design simplicity intended to facilitate maximum production at minimum cost. Although mass-manufacturing produced most spongeware, it did in fact originate in the work of independent potters. Glasgow, Scotland, circa

Three blue sponge pitchers, one with chip to base, one with reglued chip to rim, small rim hairlines, 9" h. **$125**

Courtesy of Pook & Pook, Inc., www.pookandpook.com

1835, is recognized as the birthplace of spongeware. The goal: the production of utilitarian everyday pottery with appeal to the budget-conscious. Sponged surface decorations were a means of adding visual interest both easily and inexpensively.

Since early spongeware was quickly made, usually by amateur artisans, the base pottery was often insubstantial and the sponging perfunctory. However, due to its general usefulness, and especially because of its low cost, spongeware quickly found an audience. Production spread across Great Britain and Europe, finally reaching the United States. Eventually, quality improved, as even frugal buyers demanded more for their money.

The terms "spongeware" and "spatterware" are often used interchangeably. Spatterware took its name from the initial means of application: A pipe was used to blow colored pigment onto a piece of pottery, creating a spattered coloration. Since the process was tedious, sponging soon became the preferred means of color application, although the "spatterware" designation remained in use. Specific patterns were achieved by means of sponge printing (aka "stick spatter"): A small piece of sponge was cut in the pattern shape desired, attached to a stick, then dipped in color. The stick served as a more precise means of application, giving the decorator more control, creating designs with greater border definition. Applied colors varied, with blue (on white) proving most popular. Other colors included red, black, green, pink, yellow, brown, tan, and purple.

Because of the overlap in style, there really is no "right or wrong" in classifying a

CERAMICS

particular object as "spongeware" or "spatterware"; often the manufacturer's advertising designation is the one used. Spatterware, however, has become more closely identified with pottery in which the mottled color pattern (whether spattered or sponged) surrounds a central image, either stamped or painted free-hand. Spongeware usually has no central image; the entire visual consists of the applied "splotching." Any break in that pattern comes in the form of contrasting bands, either in a solid color matching the mottling, or in a portion of the base earthenware kept free of applied color. Some spongeware pieces also carry stampings indicating the name of an advertiser, or the use intent of a specific object ("Butter," "Coffee," "1 Qt.").

Much of what is classified as spatterware has a certain delicacy of purpose: tea sets, cups and saucers, sugar bowls, and the like. Spongeware is more down-to-earth, both in intended usage and sturdiness. Among the many examples of no-nonsense spongeware: crocks, washbowl and pitcher sets, jugs, jars, canisters, soap dishes, shaving mugs, spittoons, umbrella stands, washboards, and even chamber pots. These are pottery pieces that mean business; their shapes, stylings, and simple decoration are devoid of fussiness.

Spongeware was usually a secondary operation for the many companies that produced it and was marketed as bargain-priced service ware; it's seldom marked. Today, spongeware is an ideal collectible for those whose taste in 19th century pottery veers away from the overly detailed and ornate. Spongeware's major appeal is due in large part to the minimalism it represents.

Two blue sponge pitchers, larger one with firing pop below handle, smaller one with rim flake, 8-3/4" h. and 10" h. **$100**

Courtesy of Pook & Pook, Inc., www.pookandpook.com

Two rainbow sponge pitchers, smaller one with faint glaze lines, 9" h. and 10-3/4" h... **$125**

Courtesy of Pook & Pook, Inc., www.pookandpook.com

Green sponge pitcher, 7-1/4" h., and lidded crock with flakes to lid, 6" h. **$50**

Courtesy of Pook & Pook, Inc., www.pookandpook.com

CERAMICS

staffordshire

STAFFORDSHIRE FIGURES AND GROUPS made of pottery were produced by the majority of the Staffordshire, England, potters of the 19th century and were used as mantle decorations or "chimney ornaments" as they were sometimes called. Pairs of dogs were favorites and were turned out by the carload, and 19th century pieces are still readily available. Well-painted reproductions also abound, and collectors are urged to exercise caution before purchasing.

The process of transfer-printing designs on earthenware developed in England in the late 18th century, and by the mid-19th century most common ceramic wares were decorated in this manner, most often with romantic European or Asian landscape scenes, animals or flowers. The earliest transferwares were printed in dark blue, but a little later light blue, pink, purple, red, black, green, and brown were used. A majority of these wares were produced at various English potteries right up until the turn of the 20th century, but French and other European firms also made similar pieces and all are quite collectible.

The best reference on this area is Petra Williams' *Staffordshire Romantic Transfer Patterns – Cup Plates and Early Victorian China* (Fountain House East, 1978).

Pair of cow creamers, each with professional repairs, 4-1/2" h x 6-3/4" w. **$1,313**

Courtesy of Pook & Pook, Inc., www.pookandpook.com

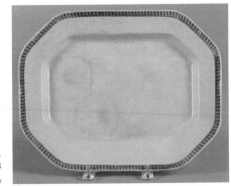

Red feather-edge platter, 19th century, staining, 11-1/4" l x 14-1/2" w. **$313**

Courtesy of Pook & Pook, Inc., www.pookandpook.com

Blue teapot with chinoiserie decoration, 19th century, 10-1/4" h.. **$100**

Courtesy of Pook & Pook, Inc., www.pookandpook.com

Pink lustre pitcher, 19th century, with transfer decoration of Queen Victoria and Prince Albert commemorating their marriage, "MARRIED — FEB 10th, 1840," marked "Davenport" on underside, light hairline, 8-3/4" h. **$388**

Courtesy of Pook & Pook, Inc., www.pookandpook.com

Purple coronation pitcher, 19th century, transfer decoration of Queen Victoria, 6-1/2" h............. **$363**

Courtesy of Pook & Pook, Inc., www.pookandpook.com

Coronation ABC plate, 19th century, transfer decoration of Queen Victoria, light staining, 6-1/8" dia... **$388**

Courtesy of Pook & Pook, Inc., www.pookandpook.com

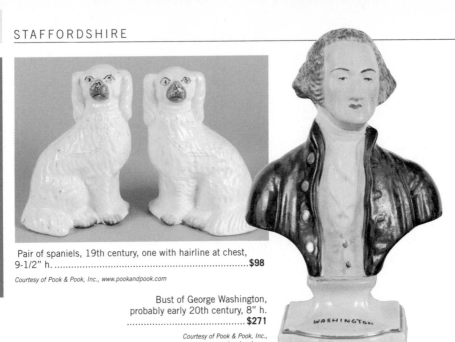

Pair of spaniels, 19th century, one with hairline at chest, 9-1/2" h. $98

Courtesy of Pook & Pook, Inc., www.pookandpook.com

Bust of George Washington, probably early 20th century, 8" h. $271

Courtesy of Pook & Pook, Inc., www.pookandpook.com

Two stirrup cups with hound and bull, 19th century, 4-1/2" h and 5-1/2" h. $1,080

Courtesy of Pook & Pook, Inc., www.pookandpook.com

Creamware teapot, probably by William Greatbatch, late 18th century, depicting "The Prodigal Son in Excess" and "The Prodigal Son in Misery," 5-1/8" h. $660

Courtesy of Pook & Pook, Inc., www.pookandpook.com

Watch hutch, Pratt-type, early 19th century,
8-1/2" h. $800

Courtesy of Pook & Pook, Inc., www.pookandpook.com

▲ Hawk figure on spiral-turned
base, circa 1800, overall green
and brown mottled glazing,
6-1/2" h. $1,046

*Courtesy of Pook & Pook, Inc.,
www.pookandpook.com*

Pair of recumbent Dalmatians, circa 1850, 4" h x
4-1/2" w. $138

Courtesy of Leslie Hindman Auctioneers, www.lesliehindman.com

Pair of spaniels, 19th/20th
century, each seated with
locket, with two cats and
porcelain creamer, spaniels
10" h. $100

*Courtesy of Leslie Hindman Auctioneers,
www.lesliehindman.com*

▶ Six English transfer-printed plates in dark blue, second quarter 19th century, marked "MOULIN SUR LA MARNE / A CHARENTON," impressed "E. WOOD & SONS BURSLEM / WARRANTED / SEMI CHINA," Enoch Wood & Sons, Burslem, Staffordshire, England, 9-3/8" dia. **$322**

Courtesy of Jeffrey S. Evans & Associates, www.jeffreysevans.com

English transfer-printed pitcher and basin in blue, circa 1860, Eon pattern with windmill, figures, and landscape on sides and interior, marked with registration mark and "G. WOOLISCROFT," George Wooliscroft, Tunstall, Staffordshire, England, flake on foot rim of basin, pitcher 11-1/2" h, basin 14-1/2" dia. .. **$152**

Courtesy of Jeffrey S. Evans & Associates, www.jeffreysevans.com

English transfer-printed ceramic pitcher and basin, second half 19th century, high molded handle and wide spout, architectural scenery and geometric patterning, both marked "ENGLAND / ABBEY / 1790 / GEO.JONES&SONS," George Jones & Sons, Staffordshire, England, pitcher 11-3/4" h, basin 4-7/8" h, 14-3/8" dia..............................**$82**

Courtesy of Jeffrey S. Evans & Associates, www.jeffreysevans.com

Three transfer-printed flow ceramic platters in mulberry, mid-19th century, marked "VINCENNES" and for John Alcock, John Alcock, Cobridge, Staffordshire, England, one with hairline crack, 17-1/2" x 13-7/8"... **$152**

Courtesy of Jeffrey S. Evans & Associates, www.jeffreysevans.com

Historical blue plate, 19th century, depicting Bank of the United States, Philadelphia, 10-1/8" dia........................ **$308**

Courtesy of Pook & Pook, Inc., www.pookandpook.com

Historical blue platter, 19th century, depicting Christiansburg Danish Settlement on Gold Coast of Africa, 14-1/2" l. x 18-1/2" w. **$1,476**

Courtesy of Pook & Pook, Inc., www.pookandpook.com

10 Things You Didn't Know About Margaret Tafoya

Margaret Tafoya
(1904-2001).

Photo courtesy "Margaret Tafoya: A Potter's Heritage and Legacy."

1 A black Santa Clara Pueblo storage jar, with a heavily incised kiva step pattern and Avanyu design, circa 1950, signed on the bottom by revered Pueblo pottery master Margaret Tafoya, sold for $9,680 during the 2016 Auction in Santa Fe. According to the provenance, the pot, which measures 11 1/4 inches by 12 inches, was purchased directly from Ms. Tafoya by Hilda and Harold Street between 1950 and 1952 and went on to be a cherished decorative piece in the lobby of the Taos Inn and in the Streets' home.

2 Margaret Tafoya (1904-2001) began making pottery at a young age, learning the pottery-making process and precise carving techniques from her mother, Sarafina. Although many may recognize Maria Martinez's name as a pioneer of this type of pottery, it was Margaret and her mother Sarafina who were the first to sell Indian pottery, reports Margaret's grandson, Jeff Roller (www.jeffroller.com). In fact, the two women were said to have taught Ms. Martinez how to make black pottery.

3 The Tafoya family's heritage of making pottery, as verified by several museums, dates back seven generations, Roller explained. Before her passing in 2001, Margaret Tafoya identified pottery pieces made by at least three generations of Tafoya artists that came before her.

4 With intricately carved geometric designs and a burnished red surface, a redware jar produced by Ms. Tafoya in the third quarter of the 20th century, sold for $19,680 at auction in April of 2014. The jar, with a large tapering base and slightly fluted neck and signed Margaret Tafoya on the base, also earned a first place blue ribbon during the 1972 Original American Indian & Western Relic Show, held in Los Angeles, California.

5 As is the case with many artifacts sought after by collectors today, the Santa Clara Pueblo pottery began as an invention of necessity. The family used to sell fruits, vegetables, pies, and bread they grew and made, to travelers who passed through the pueblo train station. In order to make transport of the goods to the station easier, Margaret and her mother carried the items in the pots. It was said that when the travelers spotted the pots and jars that contained the food, they became as interested in purchasing the vessels as the food they held. The women were quick to respond with a price of $5, for both large and small pieces.

6 Margaret Tafoya's work has been the subject of several books and museum exhibitions over the years. She was awarded the National Endowment for the Arts Award in 1984 and a National Heritage Fellowship.

7 Today about 20 members of Margaret Tafoya's family are active potters, including her children, such as daughter Toni Roller (www.toniroller.com), grandchildren and now great-grandchildren. They remain dedicated to creating pottery using the traditional methods and materials utilized by Margaret and Sarafina. Many of the practices used today are methods passed down through the generations and refined by the women when they began selling the pottery to the public. In an effort to provide the best pottery possible, they incorporated techniques including screening the clay and volcanic ash, and using sandpaper to smooth the surface before burnishing, Roller explained.

8 Margaret Tafoya was noted for creating some of the largest clay vessels of the time, making each by hand.

9 She is among the artists whose profiles are featured at the National Museum of Women in the Arts (www.nmwa.org).

10 Among the methods Margaret Tafoya adhered to in order to create the unmistakable black finish of the Santa Clara Pueblo pottery was using pine slabs and manure during the firing process.

– Compiled by Antoinette Rahn

Sources: Jeff Roller, grandson of Margaret Tofoya and a potter working at Santa Clara Pueblo Pottery; Auction in Santa Fe, LiveAuctioneers, www.nmwa.org; "Margaret Tafoya: A Potter's Heritage & Legacy," by Laurence & Mary Ellen Blair

CERAMICS

CERAMICS

teco pottery

TECO POTTERY WAS the line of art pottery introduced by the American Terra Cotta and Ceramic Co. of Terra Cotta (Crystal Lake), Illinois, in 1902. Founded by William D. Gates in 1881, American Terra Cotta originally produced only bricks and drain tile.

Because of superior facilities for experimentation, including a chemical laboratory, the company was able to develop an art pottery line, favoring a mat green glaze in the earlier years but eventually achieving a wide range of colors including a metallic luster glaze and a crystalline glaze. Although some hand-thrown pottery was made, Gates favored a molded ware because it was less expensive to produce. By 1923, Teco Pottery was no longer being made, and in 1930 American Terra Cotta and Ceramic Co. was sold.

For more information on Teco Pottery, see *Teco: Art Pottery of the Prairie School* by Sharon S. Darling (Erie Art Museum, 1990).

Vase in aventurine glaze with coppery crystals, impressed Teco logo, incised 3270, minor scratches, 4" h................... **$400**

Courtesy of Mark Mussio, Humler & Nolan, www.humlernolan.com

Vase with pretzel-twist handles, shape 257, stamped "Teco" once and incised "257," minor scuffs, restoration to small base chip, 11" h........................ **$700**

Courtesy of Mark Mussio, Humler & Nolan, www.humlernolan.com

Handled pitcher in mat green glaze, shape 294, charcoaling in glaze, designed by W. D. Gates, impressed Teco logo, 8-3/4" h. **$450**

Courtesy of Mark Mussio, Humler & Nolan, www.humlernolan.com

◀ Floor vase with four applied strap handles and mat green glaze, stamped "Teco," incised shape 100 A, professional restoration to glaze loss, 21-1/8" h. **$3,600**

Courtesy of Mark Mussio, Humler & Nolan, www.humlernolan.com

▶ Vase with pinched sides and rim in mat medium brown glaze, impressed "TECO" twice and "360," 4-1/4" h.................. **$450**

Courtesy of Mark Mussio, Humler & Nolan, www.humlernolan.com

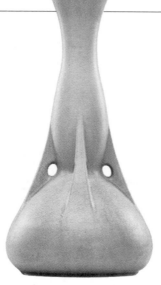

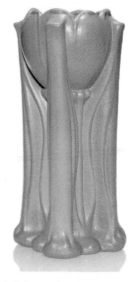

Art Deco vase attributed to Fritz Albert, professional restoration to rim, bottom marked "Teco" and "196," 13" h., 4-1/2" dia. **$1,325**

Courtesy of Just Art Pottery, www.justartpottery.com

Tall buttressed vase, circa 1910, stamped "TECO," minor scuffs and scratches, 13" x 7" **$5,625**

Courtesy of Rago Arts & Auctions, www.ragoarts.com

▲ Tulip vase in uncommon avocado mat green glaze, no marks visible due to heavy glaze, 11-1/2" h. **$1,900**

Courtesy of Mark Mussio, Humler & Nolan, www.humlernolan.com

◄ Spherical vessel, shape 339, circa 1910, William B. Mundie, stamped "TECO," 12" x 10". **$8,750**

Courtesy of Rago Arts & Auctions, www.ragoarts.com

► Tall cylindrical buttressed vase, shape 375, circa 1910, William D. Gates, stamped "TECO," hairline from rim, 11" x 3". **$2,625**

Courtesy of Rago Arts & Auctions, www.ragoarts.com

◄ Low bowl with cast leaf and berry design at shoulder, mat green glaze, light brown accents on berries, impressed "TECO" twice, 2-3/8" h., 9-1/4" dia..........................**$400**

Courtesy of Mark Mussio, Humler & Nolan, www.humlernolan.com

CERAMICS

CERAMICS

teplitz/amphora pottery

ANTIQUE DEALERS AND COLLECTORS
often refer to Art Nouveau-era art pottery
produced in the kaolin-rich Turn-Teplitz
region of Bohemia (today Teplice region,
Czech Republic) collectively as Teplitz. Over
the years, however, this area boasted many
different potteries. To add to the confusion,
they opened, closed, changed owners,
merged or shared common designers against
a background of changing political borders.

Although all produced pottery, their
techniques and products varied. Some ceramicists, like Josef Strnact and Julius Dressler,
produced brightly glazed faience and majolica earthenware items. According to Elizabeth
Dalton, Furniture and Decorative Arts Specialist at Michaan's Auctions, Alameda,

Portrait vase of woman in
crown surrounded by gold
corona, Reissner, Stellmacher
& Kessel, obverse with woods
and pink roses, furrowed
sides trimmed in mat gold,
impressed "Amphora," maroon
stamp "Turn Teplitz Bohemia,
RStK," artist conjoined initials
"WB" in gray slip, 5-3/4" h x
5" w. **$1,300**

*Courtesy of Mark Mussio, Humler & Nolan,
www.humlernolan.com*

California, a strong earthenware body rather than delicate,
brittle porcelain allowed more unusual manipulation of the
ceramic surface of their vases, flowerpots, and tobacco jars.

Alfred Stellmacher, who founded the Imperial and Royal
Porcelain Factory in 1859, produced fanciful, sculptural
creations noted for their fine design and quality. Many feature
applied natural motifs, Mucha and Klimt-like portraits, or
simulated jewels.

"The most collectible Teplitz pieces of all, however,
are those manufactured by the Riessner, Stellmacher
and Kessel Amphora Porcelain Works (RStK), which was
founded in 1892," said Stuart Slavid, vice president and
director of European Furniture, Decorative Arts and Fine
Ceramics at Skinner Auctions, Boston.

Archeology and history buffs may recognize amphoras
as ceramic vessels used for storage and transport in the
ancient world. Art collectors and dealers, however, know
amphoras as RStK pieces that incorporate undulating,
asymmetrical Art Nouveau interpretations of flora and
fauna – both natural and fanciful – in their designs. Many
RStK artists honed their skills at the Teplitz Imperial
Technical School for Ceramics and Associated Applied Arts.
Others drew on the fine ceramics manufacturing tradition
of nearby Dresden.

Producing Amphora was time-consuming and
prohibitively expensive. Each piece began with an artist's
drawing, which would typically include lifelike images of

snakes, sea creatures, dragons, maidens, flora, or fauna. Once approved, each drawing was assigned a style number, which would subsequently appear on the bottom of identically shaped pieces, along with the word "Amphora."

Using these drawings as their guides, craftsmen carved and fired clay models from which they created smooth plaster-of-Paris molds. These molds were then lined with thin layers of clay. Once the clay dried and the molds removed, the resulting Amphoras were fine-carved, hand-painted, and glazed. Finally they were refired, sometimes as many as 10 times. Since each was decorated in a unique way, no two Amphoras were exactly alike. Since their manufacture was so complex, reproducing one is nearly impossible.

RStK's innovative pieces earned international acclaim almost immediately. After winning prizes at both the Chicago and St. Louis World's Fairs, exclusive establishments, including Tiffany & Co., marketed them in the United States.

In addition to lavish Amphoras, Riessner, Stellmacher and Kessel also produced highly detailed, intricately crafted female busts, both large and small. Virgins, nymphs, and dancers, reflecting fashionable literary, religious, and mythological motifs and themes of the day, were popular choices. Larger busts, because they were so complex and so rarely made, were expensive from the start. Today these 100-year-old beauties, especially those who escaped the ravages of time, are extremely desirable.

In 1894, leading Viennese porcelain retailer Ernst Wahliss purchased the RStK Amphora. Paul Dachsel, a company designer and Stellmacher's son-in-law, soon left to open his own pottery. Dachsel was known for adorning fairly simple forms with unique, intricate, stylized Art Nouveau embellishments, as well as modern-looking applied handles and rims. These, along with his Secessionist works – those influenced by Austrian exploration of innovative artistic forms outside academic and historical traditions – are highly collectible today.

After Wahliss' death, the Amphora Porcelain Works – now known as the Alexandra Porcelain Works Ernst Wahliss – became known for Serapis-Wahliss, its fine white earthenware line that features intricate, colorful, stylized natural forms.

When Stellmacher established his own company in 1905, the firm continued operating as the Riessner and Kessel Amphora Works. After Kessel left five years later, Amphora Werke Riessner, as it became known, continued to produce Amphora pottery through the 1940s. In 1945, Amphora Werke Riessner was nationalized by the Czechoslovakian government.

Although many Amphoras retail for under $1,000, some are quite costly. Rare, larger pieces, probably commissioned or created expressly for exhibition, were far more prone to breakage in production and display, so they command far more.

Do Teplitz pieces make good investments? According to Stuart Slavid, "Considering their rarity, quality, and decorative appeal, there's still plenty of room for growth, especially at the higher end of the market. I personally think that higher-end Amphoras are exceptional. History says you can't go wrong buying the very best. There will always be collectors at that level."

— Melody Amsel-Arieli

Amphora vase with profile of woman bracketed by poppies, Riessner, Stellmacher & Kessel, white daisies in woman's hair, poppies and daisies with heavy slip highlights and outlined in white and gold, red "R.St.& K. Turn-Teplitz-Bohemia" logo, "Made in Austria," impressed numbers 465 and 12, 13" h. **$1,100**

Courtesy of Mark Mussio, Humler & Nolan, www.humlernolan.com

Amphora vase with poppy and clover highlighted and outlined in gold and white, Riessner, Stellmacher & Kessel, red "R.St.& K." Turn-Teplitz-Bohemia logo, "Made in Austria," impressed numbers 439 and 12, 9-1/4" h......... **$200**

Courtesy of Mark Mussio, Humler & Nolan, www.humlernolan.com

Amphora reticulated double-wall vase with life-size blackberries and leafed branches with gold accents, impressed "Amphora" and "Austria," each in ovals, with "3785 55" and stamped "K" in red, chips and filled separations, minor gold wear, 12" h, 6-1/4" dia. **$200**

Courtesy of Mark Mussio, Humler & Nolan, www.humlernolan.com

Amphora vase with reticulated rim with gold, Riessner, Stellmacher & Kessel, red stamp "Turn Teplitz Bohemia, RStK, Made in Austria," impressed crown and numbers under glaze, 6" h................ **$275**

Courtesy of Mark Mussio, Humler & Nolan, www.humlernolan.com

Amphora Works Florina double-sided pitcher with enameled flowers on Dachsel-like form, circa 1910, Imperial Amphora Turn logo and "Amphora Austria" in ovals, signed in black slip "Florina" with artist's initials, partial retailer's label, original red and green Amphora paper label, professional restoration to top handle, 20-1/8" h. **$200**

Courtesy of Mark Mussio, Humler & Nolan, www.humlernolan.com

Amphora vase, Reissner, Stellmacher & Kessel, with woman with flowers in her hair, "R.St.&K." red ink stamp logo, notation "Amphora Turn" in blue, impressed Amphora with number 572, 10-5/8" h... **$1,300**

Courtesy of Mark Mussio, Humler & Nolan, www.humlernolan.com

Amphora organic-form centerpiece with embossed circular cells or bubbles encircling top, waisted middle area with four elephant heads above organic tendrils, green glazes on base, impressed markings and remains of paper label, one ear chipped from underside, 11" x 9".................................. **$1,400**

Courtesy of Soulis Auctions, Lone Jack, Missouri, www.dirksoulisauctions.com

Amphora Gres-Bijou reticulated vase, Reissner, Stellmacher & Kessel, faux jewels and three-dimensional woman perched on shoulder, impressed crown and "Amphora Austria" on bottom, incised "Riessner" (sic) below woman, 6-1/4" h. **$1,000**

Courtesy of Mark Mussio, Humler & Nolan, www.humlernolan.com

Vase in iridescent blue with string of three-dimensional putti surrounding rim, Art Nouveau rectangular raised Amphora seal with woman's head at one end, 10" h. **$300**

Courtesy of Mark Mussio, Humler & Nolan, www.humlernolan.com

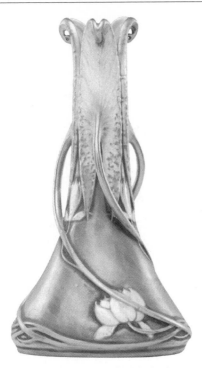

Amphora vase with flowers by Paul Dachsel, 1900, red "PD Turn-Teplitz MADE IN BOHEMIA" stamp, 9-1/2" x 5-1/4"................................ **$2,500**

Courtesy of Rago Arts and Auctions, www.ragoarts.com

Tall Amphora two-handled reticulated vase with birds, circa 1910, Riessner, Stellmacher & Kessel, glazed, gilt, and enameled earthenware, stamped "crown/ AMPHORA/AUSTRIA/12138/F," light wear to gilding, 15-3/4" x 6-3/4". **$563**

Courtesy of Rago Arts and Auctions, www.ragoarts.com

Amphora vase, Reissner, Stellmacher & Kessel, with young woman in Germanic dress and headdress in forest, slip trailing and heavy slip painting, red "R.St.&K." ink stamp logo, impressed 524 and 11, 8-3/8" h................ **$900**

Courtesy of Mark Mussio, Humler & Nolan, www.humlernolan.com

CERAMICS

van briggle pottery

THE VAN BRIGGLE Pottery was established by Artus Van Briggle, who formerly worked for Rookwood Pottery in Colorado Springs, Colorado at the turn of the 20th century. He died in 1904, but the pottery was carried on by his widow and others. From 1900 until 1920, the pieces were dated. It remains in production today, specializing in art pottery.

Bowl and flower frog, each in dark over light blue glazes, each with Van Briggle logo, bowl with incised 903 shape and 1915 date, both with fine crazing in light blue glaze, bowl 1-7/8" h, 8-1/8" dia., flower frog 2-1/2" h, 5-1/4" dia.............. **$100**

Courtesy of Mark Mussio, Humler & Nolan, www.humlernolan.com

Vase with band of flowers and green over brown mat glaze, 1903, incised AA Van Briggle logo, 1903 date, Roman numeral III, impressed shape number B 201, 3-1/4" h............................ **$1,100**

Courtesy of Mark Mussio, Humler & Nolan, www.humlernolan.com

Three pieces in mulberry glaze: vase with embossed floral decoration, dated 1920, 3-7/8" h; low vase with embossed designs, circa 1925, 2" h; and low bowl with flowers on shoulder, dated 1920, 1-1/2" h, 3-1/2" dia. **$225**

Courtesy of Mark Mussio, Humler & Nolan, www.humlernolan.com

Handled urn in mulberry glaze impressed with design of spear foliage on lengthy stems, 1917, cast hole at top of foot ring for conversion to lamp, incised Van Briggle logo, 1917 date and L5, 10-1/2" h...... **$450**

Courtesy of Mark Mussio, Humler & Nolan, www.humlernolan.com

CERAMICS

Vase in mulberry glaze, 12" h.
.... **$135**

Floral-form vase with Mountain Craig brown glaze, 1920s, incised company logo, "Van Briggle" and "Colo Spgs," 7-5/8" h. **$170**

"Poppy" vase with black-speckled green mat glaze, 1902, incised "AA Van Briggle 1902 III," impressed 2 D for shape number 2, restored kiln kiss on side, 7-3/4" h. **$1,100**

Low vase, shape 858, with green mat glaze and embossed leaves, incised AA mark and Van Briggle, faint crazing, 3-1/8" h, 6-1/2" dia. **$225**

Bowl in light blue mat glaze, 1905, incised company logo, Van Briggle, date and triangle-shaped esoteric mark, light crazing, 2-7/8" h, 5-1/4" dia.. **$190**

Three items in light blue mat glaze, each with Van Briggle logo, "Van Briggle, Colo Spgs," and shape number: mug with nick and stilt pull, 6-1/8" h.; bowl with grinding nick, 2" h., 3-1/8" dia.; and bowl, 1-7/8" h, 5" dia.
.... **$400**

Early Lorelei vase in pale blue mat glaze, 1902 (first year of production), faint outline of second figure near base, incised "AA VAN BRIGGLE 1902 III," light peppering around rim, bruise to one finger, 10" x 4"..$43,750

COURTESY OF RAGO ARTS AND AUCTIONS, WWW.RAGOARTS.COM

Early plate with hand-carved clutch of whirling stylized birds in relief and unusual blue/black glaze, circa 1907-1912, 6" dia. **$625**

Courtesy of Soulis Auctions, Lone Jack, Missouri, www.dirksoulisauctions.com

Original European metal vase that inspired Van Briggle, light peppering around rim, metal vase with wear and scratches throughout and misshapen rim, 7-3/4" x 4-1/2", with a Dos Cabezas vase in green glaze, 1906, incised "AA VAN BRIGGLE COLORADO SPRINGS 1906." **$7,500**

Courtesy of Rago Arts and Auctions, www.ragoarts.com

Vase with mulberry glaze and embossed flowers, incised Van Briggle logo and "Van Briggle, Colo. Spgs.," chips off base, 21-1/4" h. **$160**

Courtesy of Mark Mussio, Humler & Nolan, www.humlernolan.com

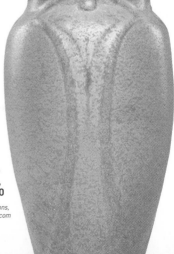

Early vase with stylized botanical design and mustard glaze, 1905, original paper label obscuring marks, deep crazing line near base, 6-1/4" x 4"...............**$2,000**

Courtesy of Rago Arts and Auctions, www.ragoarts.com

CERAMICS

wedgwood

IN 1754, JOSIAH Wedgwood and Thomas Whieldon of Fenton Vivian, Staffordshire, England, became partners in a pottery enterprise. Their products included marbled, agate, tortoiseshell, green glaze, and Egyptian black wares.

WEDGWOOD

In 1759, Wedgwood opened his own pottery at the Ivy House works, Burslem. In 1764, he moved to the Brick House (Bell Works) at Burslem. The pottery concentrated on utilitarian pieces.

Between 1766 and 1769, Wedgwood built the famous works at Etruria. Among the most-renowned products of this plant were the Empress Catherina of Russia dinner service (1774) and the Portland Vase (1790s). The firm also made caneware, unglazed earthenwares (drabwares), piecrust wares, variegated and marbled wares, black basalt (developed in 1768), Queen's or creamware, and Jasperware (perfected in 1774).

Bone china was produced under the direction of Josiah Wedgwood II between 1812 and 1822, and was revived in 1878. Moonlight Lustre was made from 1805 to 1815. Fairyland Lustre began in 1920. All Lustre production ended in 1932.

A museum was established at the Etruria pottery in 1906. When Wedgwood moved to its modern plant at Barlaston, North Staffordshire, the museum was expanded.

Fairyland Lustre Candlemas vase, circa 1925, designed by Daisy Makeig-Jones, marked with Wedgwood vase logo, England and Z5154, thin line of gold trim miss at rim, 10-1/2" h.............. **$1,650**

Courtesy of Soulis Auctions, Lone Jack, Missouri, www.dirksoulisauctions.com

"Argus Pheasant" Fairyland Lustre covered jar with birds and peonies in red against blue ground, marked with Coalport vase "Wedgwood Made in England" ink stamp logo, form number Z5486 and number 18 in red slip, minor wear on gold collar under lid, 9-1/2" h...**$2,500**

Courtesy of Mark Mussio, Humler & Nolan, www.humlernolan.com

Fairyland Lustre lidded dragon bowl, circa 1925, cover topped by model of Sybil, also known as widow of Zerepath, marked with Wedgwood vase logo, "Wedgwood," "Made in England" and Z4831 on base, underside of lid marked with Wedgwood vase logo, "Wedgwood" and "Made in England," 6" x 6-1/2". **$425**

Courtesy of Soulis Auctions, Lone Jack, Missouri, www.dirksoulisauctions.com

▶ Black basalt Triton candlestick, marked "WEDGWOOD" only inside bottom edge, interior firing line visible from inside, 11" h. **$550**

Courtesy of Soulis Auctions, Lone Jack, Missouri, www.dirksoulisauctions.com

Pair of black basalt covered urns, marked with "Wedgwood" and letter "J," 8-1/4" h. **$1,200**

Courtesy of Soulis Auctions, Lone Jack, Missouri, www.dirksoulisauctions.com

Black basalt dolphin candleholder, stamped "WEDGWOOD" only on base with solitary S stamped above it, 8-3/4" x 6" x 3-1/4". **$800**

Courtesy of Soulis Auctions, Lone Jack, Missouri, www.dirksoulisauctions.com

Black basalt vestal lamps, marked "Wedgwood" and "Made in England," amateur repair to each finial, 8-1/2" x 7-1/2" x 3-1/4"..**$950**

Courtesy of Soulis Auctions, Lone Jack, Missouri, www.dirksoulisauctions.com

Capri Ware black basalt covered jar with enamels in Asian style inspired by Chinese Famille Rose porcelain, marked WEDGWOOD only, 8-3/4" x 8-1/2".. **$450**

Courtesy of Soulis Auctions, Lone Jack, Missouri, www.dirksoulisauctions.com

Pair of Etruria bolted and double-handled lidded urns by Wedgwood & Bentley, circa 1780, 7-1/4" x 3-1/2".
.... **$775**

Courtesy of Soulis Auctions, Lone Jack, Missouri, www.dirksoulisauctions.com

Blue Jasper cheese dome with continuous band of classical figures, early 20th century, impressed mark, crazing, hairline crack to edge of underplate, 10-1/2", 10-1/2" dia.................... **$500**

Courtesy of Rago Arts and Auctions, www.ragoarts.com

Blue Jasper chandelier canopy, pre-1890, white sprigged classical vignettes on blue, metal fittings and chains, marked "WEDGWOOD" and letter date code, possibly "ZHD," toning and age wear, 11-1/4" dia.. **$250**

Courtesy of Soulis Auctions, Lone Jack, Missouri, www.dirksoulisauctions.com

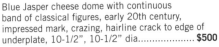

Blue Jasper cachepot, candlesticks, and potpourri bowl, early 20th century, impressed mark, chips to potpourri, surface scratches on cachepot, cachepot 8"... **$1,375**

Courtesy of Rago Arts and Auctions, www.ragoarts.com

Tricolor Jasper cabinet cup and saucer, 19th century, blue with white ribbons and garlands and small brown medallions with white vignettes, both marked "WEDGWOOD," small scattered firing separations on applied garlands, one larger separation on cup, cup 2-1/2" x 3-1/2", saucer 5-1/2" dia. **$400**

Courtesy of Soulis Auctions, Lone Jack, Missouri, www.dirksoulisauctions.com

Tricolor Jasper urn, black and white with yellow flower heads, two-piece bolted construction, stamped "WEDGWOOD" only, repaired finial, 11-1/2" h. **$1,300**

Courtesy of Soulis Auctions, Lone Jack, Missouri, www.dirksoulisauctions.com

Tin-glazed earthenware ewers after model by Flaxman, late 19th century, impressed mark, chips to bases, slightly worn surface with chips to tin glaze, old marks and scratches, some small firing cracks, 16-1/2". **$2,625**

Courtesy of Rago Arts and Auctions, www.ragoarts.com

Six plates, 19th century, two pairs, two other patterns, one plate with minor edge chips, one plate with glaze imperfection, 8-1/2" dia. **$438**

Courtesy of Leslie Hindman Auctioneers, www.lesliehindman.com

Three urns, 19th century, each in kantharous form with bands of cherubs, impressed marks, lacking inserts, worn surfaces, 9-1/2" x 13-1/2". **$938**

Courtesy of Rago Arts and Auctions, www.ragoarts.com

CERAMICS

CERAMICS

weller pottery

WELLER **WELLER**

WELLER POTTERY WAS made from 1872 to 1945 at a pottery established originally by Samuel A. Weller at Fultonham, Ohio and moved in 1882 to Zanesville, Ohio.

Weller's famous pottery slugged it out with several other important Zanesville potteries for decades. Cross-town rivals such as Roseville, Owens, La Moro, and McCoy were all serious fish in a fairly small and well-stocked lake. While Weller occasionally landed some solid body punches with many of his better art lines, the prevailing thought was that his later production ware just wasn't up to snuff.

Samuel Weller was a notorious copier and, it is said, a bit of a scallywag. He paid designers such as William Long to bring their famous discoveries to Zanesville. He then attempted to steal their secrets, and, when successful, renamed them and made them his own.

After World War I, when the cost of materials became less expensive than the cost of labor, many companies, including the famous Rookwood Pottery, increased their output of less expensive production ware. Weller Pottery followed along in the trend of production ware by introducing scores of interesting and unique lines, the likes of which have never been created anywhere else, before or since.

In addition to a number of noteworthy production lines, Weller continued in the creation of hand-painted ware long after Roseville abandoned them. Some of the more interesting Hudson pieces, for example, are post-World War I pieces. Even later lines, such as Bonito, were hand painted and often signed by important artists such as Hester Pillsbury. The closer you look at Weller's output after 1920, the more obvious the fact that it was the only Zanesville company still producing both quality art ware and quality production ware.

For more information on Weller pottery, see *Warman's Weller Pottery Identification and Price Guide* by Denise Rago and David Rago.

Three Coppertone pattern pieces, 1920s: bulbous vase embossed with leaves and perched frogs on side, console bowl with lily pads and perched frog, and frog figure; vase and bowl ink stamped, frog unmarked, two small chips to rim of vase, each vase 8", 9" dia. ... **$625**

Courtesy of Rago Arts and Auctions, www.ragoarts.com

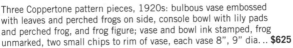

Delta pattern transitional vase with maroon flowers, impressed full-circle "Weller Louwelsa" with X9 and hand-incised "Matt," faint crazing, 8-7/8" h. **$425**

Courtesy of Mark Mussio, Humler & Nolan, www.humlernolan.com

VISIT WWW.ANTIQUETRADER.COM

WWW.FACEBOOK.COM/ANTIQUETRADER

Dickens Ware II pattern vase with portrait of Chief Hollow Horn Bear, incised by Gordon Mull, painted by Charles Upjohn, 1901, impressed "Dickens Ware Weller 302 11," signed "C.B. Upjohn 1901" and "G. Mull Sc" (for sculptor) side of portrait, incised name of subject, 11-1/8" h. **$1,000**

Courtesy of Mark Mussio, Humler & Nolan, www.humlernolan.com

Dickens Ware II pattern pitcher with jester by Charles Upjohn, impressed "Dickens Ware Weller" and 580, incised Upjohn monogram on body, spot near bottom that occurred during firing, 11-3/4" h....... **$150**

Courtesy of Mark Mussio, Humler & Nolan, www.humlernolan.com

Hudson pattern vase with floral décor and blue and cream background, signed "Timberlake," 10-3/4" h. **$590**

Courtesy of Woody Auction, www.woodyauction.com

Lamar pattern landscape vase with elk standing beneath tree with mountains in background, unmarked, overall crazing, light abrasions, 8-3/8" h.............**$275**

Courtesy of Mark Mussio, Humler & Nolan, www.humlernolan.com

Louwelsa pattern pillow vase with pair of rabbits painted by Hester Pillsbury, artist's signature in orange slip, impressed "Weller Louwelsa, K," and indecipherable shape number, overall crazing, grinding chip and scratches, 10" h. **$500**

Courtesy of Mark Mussio, Humler & Nolan, www.humlernolan.com

Red Louwelsa pattern vase with floral decoration, unmarked, open glaze bubbles, faint crazing, light glaze scratches, 8-1/2" h. **$300**

Courtesy of Mark Mussio, Humler & Nolan, www.humlernolan.com

CERAMICS

Pop Eye Dog in white, incised Weller Pottery mark, minor chipping at base, overall crazing, dark craze lines on back, 9-3/4" h. **$900**

Courtesy of Mark Mussio, Humler & Nolan, www.humlernolan.com

Rhead Faience or Weller Matt Ware (sometimes called Fru Russett) pattern covered humidor with American Indian incised design under curdled rust red glaze over dark graphite gray, signed "Rhead" on side, container incised X 511, "Rhead" under glaze, incised "Rhead" inside cover, 4-1/4" h., 6" dia. **$1,100**

Courtesy of Mark Mussio, Humler & Nolan, www.humlernolan.com

Marengo pattern six-sided vase in green with partial Weller Marengo Ware label, 9" h. **$160**

Courtesy of Mark Mussio, Humler & Nolan, www.humlernolan.com

Sicard pattern cylinder vase with calla lilies by Jacques Sicard, circa 1905, intentional drips from rim, several flowers carved or created with thick slip, signed "Weller Sicard," 23-1/2" h. **$2,500**

Courtesy of Mark Mussio, Humler & Nolan, www.humlernolan.com

Sicard pattern vase with poppies by Jacques Sicard, circa 1906, one side dark red with yellow flowers, opposite side with peach ground and yellow flowers, marked "Sicard Weller" on underside of twin handles, faint crazing, some crystalline effect to glaze, 5-1/8" h. **$700**

Courtesy of Mark Mussio, Humler & Nolan, www.humlernolan.com

Uncommon Woodcraft pattern planter with scenes of cows and ducks embossed on longer panels, ram's head on ends, impressed "Weller" in large block letters, 6-3/8" x 7" x 11-1/2". **$700**

Courtesy of Mark Mussio, Humler & Nolan, www.humlernolan.com

ZSOLNAY

ceramics

ZSOLNAY POTTERY WAS made in Pecs, Hungary, in a factory founded in 1862 by Vilmos Zsolnay. Utilitarian earthenware was originally produced with an increase in art pottery production from as early as 1870. The highest level of production employed more than 1,000 workers.

The Art Nouveau era produced the most collectible and valuable pieces in today's marketplace. Examples are displayed in major art museums worldwide. Zsolnay is always well marked and easy to identify. One specialty was the metallic eosin glaze.

With more than 10,000 different forms created over the years, and dozens of glaze variations for each form, there is always something new being discovered in Zsolnay. Today the original factory size has been significantly reduced with pieces being made in a new factory.

Three-lobed vase with stylized leaves around base and Labrador glaze, impressed "Zsolnay Pecs 6061," 2-1/2" h.......................................$250

Courtesy of Mark Mussio, Humler & Nolan, www.humlernolan.com

Modern vase with female figure clinging to side, referred to as "Escape" by collectors, newer Zsolnay ink stamp logo, minor scratches, 17-1/2" h...........$300

Courtesy of Mark Mussio, Humler & Nolan, www.humlernolan.com

Ribbed pitcher with handle, Labrador glaze, large gold "Zsolnay Pecs" ink stamp logo, smaller red "Made in Hungary" ink stamp logo, 6-1/2" h. $550

Courtesy of Mark Mussio, Humler & Nolan, www.humlernolan.com

Jardinière with iridescent scene of ducks flying over trees and hills, original "United States Customs" label, 11" x 15". $16,520

Two figures in iridescent green, both marked, deer at rest 4-1/2" x 4-1/2", child carrying basket 3" x 4-1/2". **$59**

Courtesy of Woody Auction, www.woodyauction.com

Fluted vase in eosin glaze, early 20th century, ink-stamped, 11-1/2", 7" dia. **$688**

Courtesy of Rago Arts and Auctions, www.ragoarts.com

Bison figure in iridescent green, marked, 6" x 9-1/4"................. **$207**

Courtesy of Woody Auction, www.woodyauction.com

Polychromed majolica planter, 20th century, impressed marks to underside: "(cathedral), ZSOLNAY, 1729-1," cracks to base, light glaze chipping and inpainting, restorations to relief, crazing, light firing lines, 17-7/8", 17" dia. **$813**

Courtesy of Heritage Auctions, www.ha.com

Two eosin glaze elephants, each with faint ink stamp logo, each 2-3/4" h. **$140**

Courtesy of Mark Mussio, Humler & Nolan, www.humlernolan.com

Red-speckled glazed pedestal bowl, 1873-1882, marks: "ZSOLNAY PECS, (five tower mark), 228, 7," crazing throughout, two repairs, missing flake to ruffled lip rim, 4-1/8" h., 6-1/8" dia. **$250**

Courtesy of Heritage Auctions, www.ha.com

Lustre marbled vase, circa 1900, marks: "(applied five tower mark), ZSOLNAY, PECS, 6014, M, 20," crazing, minor scuffing to one buttress, 7" h.. **$688**

Courtesy of Heritage Auctions, www.ha.com

▶ Faience floral vase, 1880s, five churches mark, "MADE IN AUSTRIA HUNGARIA," firing lines throughout, several small chips to flower petals, 20" x 10". **$1,500**

Courtesy of Rago Arts and Auctions, www.ragoarts.com

▼ Decorative box with red eosin glaze, circa 1914, raised five churches seal, stamped 8743, glazed-over firing lines to interior corners, light wear to top edges of base where lid meets edges, 5" x 7-1/4" x 4-1/2"...... **$938**

Courtesy of Rago Arts and Auctions, www.ragoarts.com

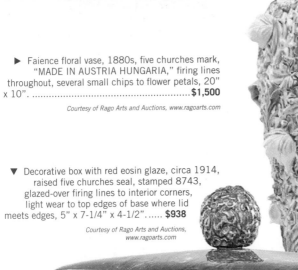

CHRISTMAS COLLECTIBLES

CHRISTMAS COLLECTIBLES INCLUDE ornaments, kugels, feather trees, candy containers, household décor, art and games, cards and a plethora of ephemera from every corner of the world. The market remains strong with demand strong for vintage ornaments and items of yesteryear. Currently, the Christmas market is still going strong for older items.

"It's all about supply and demand," said Craig McManus, chairman of The Golden Glow of Christmas Past [goldenglow.org], the main collecting club for fans of vintage holiday collectibles. "Years ago, you couldn't give away a box of Shiny Brites. Things like 1950s plastic Christmas items were usually discarded by collectors as 'junque.' Today, as younger collectors arrive on the scene, those items are now red-hot and collectible."

As newer collectors are exposed to and educated about older collectibles, they eventually trade up to things like figural glass, kugels and older Christmas items, McManus said. Kugels have set record prices at auction over the last couple years with a few rarer pieces fetching close to $20,000. Dresdens, Nodders and Belsnickle candy containers have also maintained their values. These items are still sought-after by longtime collectors.

McManus says people are increasingly collecting things from their childhoods. "Today, we see many newer Glow members interested in buying Shiny Brites (colorful ornaments), 50s plastics, blow molds, and other vintage Christmas lights, ornaments and decorations from the 1950s and 1960s, even into the 1970s. Seasoned collectors look for older, classic vintage and antique Christmas items like spun-cotton ornaments, figural glass ornaments,

German Belsnickle candy containers from the early 1900s.

Courtesy Craig McManus Christmas Collectibles

Dresdens, kugels, vintage Christmas lighting, holly china, Santas and ephemera."

New collectors to the holiday genre are advised to collect what they like. At Christmas collectible conventions (conventions are most often held during the summer) collectors new and old alike will find almost everything on their shopping list.

"[Collectors should] find those memorable treasures from your childhood and build from there," McManus says. "There are plenty of thins for newbies to collect including plastics, and many more common glass ornaments. Even kugel balls from the 1800s in more common colors can be purchased for $40-$50 a piece, or less. Start with more common collectibles, educate yourselves, and build up your collection from there.

Seasoned collectors are zeroing in on top condition.

"The best pieces would be in like-new or very good condition and could include: kugels in rarer colors like amethyst and orange or hard-to-find shapes like ribbed eggs and pears; clockwork nodders (Santa figures and animals like donkeys) that were originally used in store windows in the early 1900s to attract customers," McManus said.

Advanced collectors are paying a premium for 3D Dresden ornaments in uncommon designs; early Christmas figural light bulbs in rare molds and unique Christmas lighting in the original boxes; Belsnickles (originally sold as candy containers) in rare colors like pink, orange and purple; Christmas pull-toys and windups from the late 1800s or early 1900s, and large, three-dimensional ephemera Nativities.

More than 13,000 people now belong to The Golden Glow of Christmas Past's Facebook page. Discussions and photos are shared almost hourly and it is currently the best source to become a stronger Christmas collector.

"Facebook has been a tremendous outreach source for the Glow," McManus said. "While many of the people who like our public Facebook Group are not members, it is a great place for people to learn about the Glow, their Christmas collectibles and meet other collectors and Glow members. We typically have two or three people joining the Glow as paid members each day, who found us on Facebook.

"Social Media has changed the way organizations like the Glow can reach new members. Prior to us becoming active on Facebook, the Glow membership had been shrinking since our peak membership high in the mid-90s. Today we continue to break old membership records, thanks in a large part to Facebook."

A showcase of rare German clockwork nodders in animal form, many with German Santa dolls riding them.

Courtesy Craig McManus

Ornament, Germany, grape cluster Kugel Christmas ornament, brilliant dark blue, no scratches or chips, 5" l...**$175**

Morphy Auctions, www.morphyauctions.com

Nutcracker, American, circa 2004, Christopher Radko 'Snowy Sweets Swirl' Nutcracker, wood and glitter snowman nutcracker with a #917/2500 limited edition tag and original box, 13" t. **$45**

Leonard Auction, Inc., leonardauction.com

Postcards, group of 25 Christmas-themed post cards, circa 1908-1929, various publishers and dates, two unused..........................**$15**

Heritage Auctions, HA.com

Animation cel, *A Charlie Brown Christmas*, 1965, depicting characters Lucy, Charlie Brown and Snoopy production cel sequence and pan key master background setup, 45" l. x 8-1/5" h..........................**$59,750**

Heritage Auctions, HA.com

◄ Crackers, circa 20th century, original box of six Mead & Fields snowman snappers, cotton batting and crepe paper, never used condition and in original box which shows some wear, 17" l. **$125**

Bertoia Auctions, www.bertoiaauctions.com

► Marian Ebert Christmas card original art illustration (American Artist Group, 1950s), mixed media on illustration board, sleigh laden with gifts, background with Expressionistic blur of layered blue and white acrylic paint, artist's return-address stamp appears on reverse, excellent condition, 13-1/2" x 10-1/2". **$359**

Courtesy of Heritage Auctions, HA.com

Swedish Gevalia Santa Claus coffee tin, circa 1930, great lithographed image of Father Christmas holding lantern and walking stick, lettering on inside lid, elves pulling sleds on sides of can, excellent condition, 5" w x 9-1/2" h. **$1,050**

Courtesy of Bertoia Auctions, www.bertoiaauctions.com

Christmas lamp candy container, 98 percent red brick paper on base, original closure and wires, shade not original, 6-1/2" h............................**$400**

Courtesy of Morphy Auctions, morphyauctions.com

Santa figure in sleigh, a tin lithograph toy, Santa Claus in a tin plate toy with holly graphics around the Santa driver, sleigh shaped sides with swan head outline and graphics of Santa placing gifts under a tree beside the fireplace near a vignette of sleeping children, marked on the end 'Santee Claus Strauss Mechanical Toys' with their trademark world globe 'known the world over', 5-3/4" x 11" l. x 3" w... **$650**

Soulis Auctions, www.dirksoulisauctions.com

Candy container, circa 1800s, large German Santa Claus container with glass beard, composition figure wearing long brown robe flecked with mica, golden beads around his hood, holding lichen moss tree in arms, standing on mica flecked wood base, kind expression and deep blue eyes, 16" h.....**$22,500**

Bertoia Auctions, www.bertoiaauctions.com

Ornament, Germany, Dresden Christmas ornament, made of cardboard, 4-3/4" l.,.............**$95**

Jasper52 Auctions, www.jasper52.com

Figure, circa first half of 20th century, large papier-mache snowman with flocked body and top hat, red cloth scarf with white ball, standing on a snow dome, 17-1/5" x 8-1/4".......**$120**

Dirk Soulis Auctions, www.dirksoulisauctions.com

Hummel Christmas ornament in original box, 4-1/2" t.,...................**$5**

Martin Auction Co., www.martinauctionco.com

▲ Santa pulled by reindeer candy container, Germany, composition Santa, red felt robe, rabbit fur beard, holding feather tree sprig in loofah sleigh, ready to be loaded with Christmas gifts, pulled by splendid reindeer with glass eyes, lead antlers, full harness, his head removed for candy retrieval, 18" l. ...**$4,631**

Courtesy of Bertoia Auctions, www.bertoiaauctions.com

Santa with chenille legs ornament, Germany, retaining strong original paint, including matte face and hands, holding green Christmas tree, original composition black boots, 4 1/2" h. **$401**

Courtesy of Bertoia Auctions, www.bertoiaauctions.com

◀ Antique Christmas ornament, spun cotton boy on sled wearing turtle neck sweater and gray pants, hand-painted with full features, molded head, 4" l. **$225**

Courtesy of Stony Ridge Auction, www.stonyridgeauction.com

Rare Uncle Sam Santa squeaker postcard, seldom seen depiction of Uncle Sam as Santa Claus, basket of toys on his back, candle lit Christmas tree in hand, complete in his red, white and blue clothing, card squeaks when pressed, 3-1/2" x 5-1/2". **$803**

Courtesy of Bertoia Auctions, www.bertoiaauctions.com

Antique Christmas ornament, spun cotton Santa with paper apron, white suit and hood, carrying large axe, paper face, 4-1/4" h. **$90**

Courtesy of Stony Ridge Auction, www.stonyridgeauction.com

Antique Christmas ornament, Dresden, dwarf holding a money bag overhead, red shirt and blue pants, partial label on bag, 3-1/2" h. **$425**

Courtesy of Stony Ridge Auction, www.stonyridgeauction.com

Santa "Auto Show" box, complete, Santa driving an antique English automobile, holding box containing a silver tree with sixteen tiny ornaments and gold star for the top, unusual Christmas item, 10"...................................**$401**

Courtesy of Bertoia Auctions, www.bertoiaauctions.com

Coca-Cola cardboard Christmas bell, heavily embossed diecut from the late 1910s, colors strong and unfaded, this sign is extremely scarce and almost never shows up for sale, 12" l......................**$2,091**

Courtesy of Morphy Auctions, morphyauctions.com

Victorian feather Christmas tree, nice condition, paint on the base is slightly faded, 46-1/2" h. **$400**

Courtesy of Morphy Auctions, morphyauctions.com

Early St. Nicholas picture puzzle, ©1890 by McLoughlin Bros., this image of Santa Claus is the most copied illustration of Christmas ever, the puzzle is framed and comes with the original box, frame 22-1/2" x 15" overall; box 12" x 8". **$679**

Courtesy of Bertoia Auctions, www.bertoiaauctions.com

top lot

Rudolph the Red-Nosed Reindeer

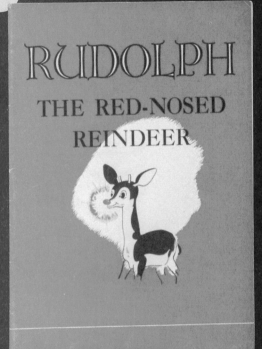

You know Dasher and Dancer and the rest of Santa's gang, but do you know who created the most famous reindeer of all?

That would be advertising copywriter Robert L. May, who in 1939, at the request of his employer, Montgomery Ward & Co., wrote the story of *Rudolph the Red-Nosed Reindeer.* Illustrated by Denver Gillen, more than 2.4 million copies of the book were distributed as a keepsake to the children customers of Montgomery Ward in its first year of publication. May drew on memories of his own painfully shy childhood when creating Rudolph. He decided on making a deer the central character of the book because his then 4-year-old daughter, Barbara, adored the deer in the Chicago zoo.

May considered Rodney, Rollo, Reginald and even Romeo before settling on Rudolph as the name of Santa's beloved reindeer. May donated his handwritten first draft and illustrated mock-up to his alma mater, Dartmouth College, before his death at age 71 in 1976, and his family later added to what has become a large collection of Rudolph-related documents and merchandise, including a life-sized papier-mâché reindeer that now stands among the stacks at the Rauner Special Collections Library.

In 1947, Montgomery Ward took the unusual step of giving the copyright to the book to May, who was struggling financially after the death of his first wife. "He then made several million dollars using that in various ways, through the movie, the song, merchandising and things like that," said Dartmouth College Archivist Peter Carini. "I think it's a great story because it shows how corporations used to think of themselves as part of civil society and how much that has changed."

In 1948, May's brother-in-law, Johnny Marks, wrote words and music to a Rudolph-based song. Though the song was turned down by such popular vocalists as Bing Crosby and Dinah Shore, it was eventually recorded by the singing cowboy Gene Autry. "Rudolph, the Red-Nosed Reindeer" was released in 1949 and became a huge hit, selling more records than any other Christmas song, with the exception of "White Christmas."

Rudolph's story was told anew in 1964 as a stop-action animation TV special on NBC. Narrated by Burl Ives, the TV Rudolph is now considered a classic holiday feature.

A first-issue, first edition of the book, "Rudolph the Red-Nosed Reindeer," with its original color illustrated wrappers, 10 1/4" x 7½", sold at auction for $425.

A first edition of "Rudolph, the Red-Nosed Reindeer", left, a photo of Robert May with his daughter, Barbara, right, and an original layout, top, are part of a special collection at Dartmouth College, Hanover, N.H. The items are from the estate of Robert May, a Dartmouth graduate who wrote the famous story in 1939 as part of a Montgomery Ward marketing campaign.

Plate, circa 1950s, by Viktor Schreckengost, chartreuse Christmas Eve cake plate, ranch-style by Salem China, inked backstamp with longhorn designed by Viktor Schreckengost, 12" w...................... **$125**

Heritage Auctions, www.HA.com

Sculpture, 20th century, Steuben Clear Glass and 18-karat gold, Christmas Tree, designed by James Houston, marks: 18 karat, STEUBEN, 12" h., ... **$1,187**

Heritage Auctions, HA.com

Ornaments, circa 1988-2000, set of 20, Lalique frosted-glass Christmas ornaments, marks: Lalique, France, 2-5/8" h. **$625**

Heritage Auctions, www.HA.com

Figurines, circa early 20th century, set of three snowmen embossed advertising for Kentucky tavern whiskey, largest at 12-1/5" t...............**$90**

Dirk Soulis Auctions, dirksoulisauctions.com

Ornament set, American but made in Poland, Germany, Italy, or Czech Republic, 2001 based on 1940s designs, Christopher Radko Shiny Brite, set of 12 Christmas ornaments, multi-colored bright ripple. **$10**

Advantage Auction Company, www.advantageauctionco.com

Windmill, made in Erzgebirge, Germany, Pyramid Windmill, 18" h., ... **$60**

Greenwich Auction, www.greenwichauction.net

▲ ▶ Charles Schulz inscribed Peanuts Christmas Book with Snoopy drawing and signature of the famous cartoonist........ **$1,100**
Courtesy of American Antique Auctions, www.americanantiqueauctions.net

◀ Noah's ark box and Santa Christmas book, German Noah's Ark lift-lid candy container, mid-19th century, lithographed paper on wood, 11" l; and fold-open, pop-up double-sided, honeycomb Christmas tree, Patent No. 1545750 Beistle, 11" h. **$200**

Courtesy of Stony Ridge Auction, www.stonyridgeauction.com

Antique Christmas ornament, glass snowman on sphere, holding broom, green hat, 6" h. **$150**

Courtesy of Stony Ridge Auction, www.stonyridgeauction.com

Ornament set, late 20th century, Hallmark Star Wars Ornaments, set of five, all mint-in-box. **$60**

Milestone Auctions, milestoneauctions.com

CLOCKS

WHEN I SPOTTED the dusty old mantle clock across the store, I wondered what stories it had to tell. Every mechanical mechanism keeps a record of its lifetime. Where was it made? What materials are inside? How was it constructed? Did previous owners care for the inner workings? Can it still be brought back to life?

The clock is one of mankind's oldest inventions. The word "clock" comes from the Latin word "clocca, meaning bell. The first mechanical clocks, driven by weights and gears, were invented by medieval Muslim engineers. The first geared mechanical clock was invented by an 11th century Arab engineer in Islamic Spain. The knowledge of weight-driven clocks was transferred to other parts of the Europe through Latin translations of Arabic and Spanish texts.

In the early 14th century, existing clock mechanisms that used water power were being adapted to take their driving power from falling weights. This movement was controlled by various forms of oscillating mechanisms. This controlled release of power – the escapement – marks the beginning of the true mechanical clock.

The mantle clock I discovered was a standard and common camelback Waterbury mantle clock made in Waterbury, Connecticut. It's neoclassical base and swooping wooden accents at either end of the dial made for an attractive find, despite being gray with years of dust and neglect. I could tell the original shellac finish was under there somewhere and the grime coating the clock's face easily smoothed away with a few rubs of clean thumb.

I hoped the inside was clean and the original pendulum was inside. The brass clockwork mechanism was still bright and inside was a lead pendulum still hanging from a suspension spring. For $15 it became my latest mechanical project.

I showed it to my friend Jim Wolf, the timepiece expert at Heritage Auctions, the world's largest collectibles auctioneer. A familiar smile appeared on his face like he had seen the exact same clock a thousand times before. And in fact, he had. "These are very common at clock shows all over the U.S.," he said. "Years ago you could buy these and almost any other mantle clock you see now in the Sears and Roebuck catalog for a few dollars."

TODAY'S MARKET

Unfortunately, the market for average and common clocks is severely depressed at the moment. Valued at $50 to $200, the

Mantle clock, American, United Clock Corp., figural form of Franklin D. Roosevelt's classic "Man of the Hour" clock, hollow pot metal with simulated bronze finish, ... **$100**

Heritage Auctions, www.HA.com

standard mantle clock can survive literally a century or more of use. Built to last with basic brass gears and a simple counterweight mechanism, clocks most commonly seen on today's market fall into this value bracket. This includes clocks made as late as 125 years ago. The reason is simple: demand is low and the clocks still work after years of use. Wear is minimal and although professional clock repair experts are getting harder to find, it doesn't take much time or money to get a vintage mantle clock calibrated to keep accurate time and chime when it's supposed to.

Novelty clocks produced from the 1950s on (think the iconic "Kit-Cat Clock" or the small-dial kitchen clocks of the 1960s) are also not commanding high prices these days. Many vintage styles are being reproduced with new quartz movements rather than the original electric ones. These reproductions have depressed the market for originals to the $20-$50 range for excellent, working examples.

The real value in today's clock market is seen in grandfather clocks made in New England (which are more often purchased as a form of early American woodworking or folk art) as well as high-end brand mantle clocks made by high-end makers or retailers of valuable wristwatches, such as Tiffany, Jager LeCoultre and the like. The movements some clock buyers seek have nothing to do with what's behind the face. Many clocks valued higher are often fashioned in very desirable forms such as Art Deco, Art Nouveau and Mid-Century Modern design movements. Clocks designed as part of these art movements can command prices of $1,000 or more.

The top end of the clock market can reach $1 million. In 2017, an English-made pagoda clock sold for $998,250, just shy of seven figures. That clock, however, was an elaborate automaton in which the clock function was second to the design and craftsman's talent.

My $15 investment clock is worth roughly $50 following a month of fun tinkering and tweaking, staining and resurfacing. Luckily for me a key was very affordable and the "labor of love" keeps decent time, with chimes on the half hour and hour. Nevertheless, our greatest value comes from the strong "tick-tock" heard across our home. Today's clock market may not be what it was, but there is no mistaking the classic appeal of a bygone day when the family clock had to be wound every seven days.

Mantle clock, silver with scallops, topped with bird and floral brocades, supported by a trio of cherubs on a four claw ornate silver base atop marble, 16" h. x 6-1/2" dia. **$530**

Heritage Auctions, HA.com

Robert Houdin Glass Dial Mystery Clock, 4-1/2" double plate glass dial, the fixed front plate has reverse painted black Roman hour numerals, gilt arrow pointer hand fixed to the rear glass plate which rotates, driven by gears on its outer edge contained in the brass bezel, 13.5" h x 5-1/4" w x 3". **$20,570**

Fontaine's Auction Gallery, www.fontainesauction.com

E. Howard & Co., Boston, Mass., floor standing regulator, signed and dated 1891, with gravity escapement by H. Conant, 90 in. high x 28 in. wide x 13.5 in. d **$24,200**

Fontaine's Auction Gallery, fontainesauction.com

Circa 1765 Japy Freres Chevron French Bronze and Marble Traveling Clock, depicts hand painted enamel scene on dial, bronze clock frame and feet, stamped chevron 8-Jour (day) to back, Swiss movement, serial number 16542, 7" h x 6-1/4" w. **$425**

Kodner, kodner.com

Early 20th century French gilt and patinated three-piece clock set by F. Pelissier, ...**$500**

Crescent City Auction Gallery, crescentcityauctiongallery.com

Magnificent rare 20th Century Sterling Silver Vermeil Gold Desk Clock with Breguet Movement, inlaid with emerald, ruby and stones, solid 18k gold latticework over Tri-color Guilloche enamel surface, London Hallmarks to doors, makers mark MM in a cartouche on underside with hallmarks London 1980, good condition, 6-3/4" h x 4-1/2" w. **$20,000**

Kodner, www.kodner.com

A Striking Pagoda Clock

This ornate and magnificent pagoda clock sold for nearly $1 million at auction. Built in England in the 18th century, the clock stands more than four-feet tall, weighs 100 pounds and has an engraved chessboard pattern brass top with five-inch painted metal dials on the front and both sides and Roman hour numerals. The time movement triggers the automaton mechanism once every two hours. The heavy bronze case has elegant color paste set jewels.

As beautiful as the clock is physically, it is equally enchanting musically. The clock plays two different tunes on a nest of eight bells, including the old Chinese folk song "Mo Li Hau," which has been popular in China and elsewhere since the 17th century. The pagoda animated every two hours, corresponding to the 12-hour Chinese time system, and the music played every two hours. The clock is a stunning achievement, reflected in the winning auction price $998,250

FONTAINE'S AUCTION, WWW.FONTAINESAUCTION.COM.

Bronze Animated European Locomotive Industrial Clock, bronze case on a black marble base with gilt rails, stick thermometer on funnel and compass in the top, 18" h x 18-1/2" w x 9"d.
.... **$22,990**

Fontaine's Auction Gallery, www.fontainesauction.com

Mantle clock, Ansonia Clock company, New York metal encased ornate mantel clock. Measures 13" (33cm) height by 15" (38cm) w.............. **$150-$200**

Antiques & Modern Auction Gallery, www.antiquesmodern.com

19th Century French Ormolu Dore Bronze Mantle Clock. Finely painted Sevres style porcelain panels, porcelain dial with painted courting scene. Some wear to gilt, 1 foot is loose otherwise good condition. Measures 16-1/2" H x 8-1/4" W.
.... **$550**

Kodner, kodner.com

Mantle clock, bronze figural white marble, features a mother (or goddess) with a cherub, or cupid... **$800**

Auction Life, www.auctionlifeflorida.com

Clock, American, maker unknown, circa 1935, art deco illuminated glass and gilt metal on wood base, side-lit, frosted nude figures, 11-7/8" h.
.... **$500**

Heritage Auctions, www.HA.com

Dwarf clock, Joshua Wilder (Hingham, Mass.), circa 1810, figured and banded mahogany case, 8-day time and strike, weight driven brass movement, 49" h. **$12,650**

Cotton Auctions, cottoneauctions.com

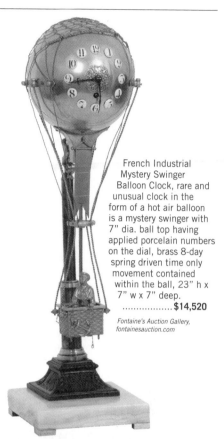

French Industrial Mystery Swinger Balloon Clock, rare and unusual clock in the form of a hot air balloon is a mystery swinger with 7" dia. ball top having applied porcelain numbers on the dial, brass 8-day spring driven time only movement contained within the ball, 23" h x 7" w x 7" deep.
.... **$14,520**

Fontaine's Auction Gallery, fontainesauction.com

French porcelain mantel clock, hand-painted putti figure painted to bottom panel and a applied porcelain cherub to the top, finished with a light blue and cream color with gold gilt accents throughout, marked France 3078, 12" h by 6" w.
.... **$200-$300**

Antiques & Modern Auction Gallery, antiquesmodern.com

Mid-Century LeCoultre Brass Zodiac Desk Clock, zodiac silhouette symbols with emerald green glass panel. 16 jewels unadjusted movement. Wear to paint, good condition. Measures 6" x 6".
.... **$600**

Kodner, kodner.com

Gruen Guild Cosmos Swiss Mantle Clock, mid-20th century, Marks: GRUEN GUILD, SWISS; COSMOS CORP, 9-7/8" h. **$687**

Heritage Auctions, HA.com

COCA-COLA

FOLLOWING THE NEAR complete liquidation of the Schmidt Collection of vintage and antique Coca-Cola collectibles and art in 2012, the market for vintage Coca-Cola items still remains soft, however, there appears to be growing interest in original art and exclusive items not available to the public.

Since 1886, Coca-Cola became known for its innovative slogans, designs and tendency to remain on the cutting edge of popular culture – whether it was 1938 or 2018. Far and away, Coca-Cola signs are the most heavily collected advertising signs in the entire hobby. It's easy to see why: the company's dedication to unusually high-quality images paired with the latest marketing mediums solidified the drink as America's brand and the passion collectors bring to Coke's signs is second to none.

Signs from Coca-Cola's earliest days remain among the most valuable, as seen in recent auction results.

Morphy Auctions of Denver Pennsylvania, sold off the Robert Newman collection of antique advertising for roughly $1.42 million, mainly on the back of scarce original Coca Cola art. The 1,300-lot sale showed Newman's reverence for Coca-Cola captured the eye of the brand's own archivists when his collection crossed the block in 2016. The collection was the talk of the hobby, especially considering the top lot was a piece no one had seen for decades. "The graphics and colors were exciting to me," Newman told the press at the auction preview the day before the sale. "They always used the best artists."

Newman did what all successful collectors should do when launching their journey: keep your discipline and focus on the rarest items in the best possible condition. Condition topped everything at the sale, with number grades assigned to catalog description to help bidders understand the varying levels of quality in the collection. This type of cataloging of a collection is unusual and was used to bolster bidder confidence in a market that has not made a lot of headlines in roughly five years.

The top lot of the sale was an amazing original oil painting featuring radio stars Edgar Bergen and Charlie

Rack, display rack for paper cartons of Coca-Cola, 48" h. **$526**

Manifest Auctions, www.manifestauctions.com

VISIT WWW.ANTIQUETRADER.COM

WWW.FACEBOOK.COM/ANTIQUETRADER

McCarthy peeking inside a cooler full of Coca-Cola. The original art from 1949 was acquired by Newman from a gentleman who received if directly from Bergen. The art was used in several advertisements, including the back cover of a 1951 edition of National Geographic.

The art was attributed to Haddon Hubbard "Sunny" Sundblom, Coca-Cola's primary artist during the company's 'golden years' of Coca-Cola's signage. Sundblom was also the artist who perfected Coke's depiction of Santa Claus in art spanning the 1930s and 1940s.

The artwork opened at $10,000 and fierce bidding pushed the lot ever higher in $1,000 increments. A total of 44 bids from the internet and the floor saw the value of the painting top out at a surprising $53,680 (including buyer's premium). The winning bidder? Coca-Cola itself. Bidders Ted Ryan and Justine Fletcher, who were in the gallery representing the famous Atlanta-headquartered company's archive department, cast the winning bid to add the piece to Coke's world-famous archive.

On her Coca-Cola collecting blog, Fletcher recounted the day and why she and Ryan focused on the Sundblom painting: "Ted and I walked the floor the morning of the auction, double-checking what we wanted to acquire for the Coke archives. We were able to win bids on other pieces of art, plus a clock, some white buttons, cardboard signs and posters. It was stiff competition as other Coca-Cola collectors were in attendance and bidding against us. This is serious business and not for the lighthearted; I was careful to keep my hands down and never nod towards the auctioneer!"

Fletcher added that the piece will be added to the firm's collection of collection of original art, which presently numbers more than 2,000 pieces.

Another piece in the auction that far exceeded expectations again stood out for being a one-of-a-kind item that floats at the top of the market. A 1930s sterling silver display bottle on a wood base with master craftsman level detailing sold for $35,380. Touted as "the greatest Coke display bottle made," the display stands 24-1/2" high and was crafted and given to a Coca Cola executive that over saw the building of the ocean-liner inspired Coca Cola bottling plant in downtown Los Angeles.

For more information on Coca-Cola collectibles, see *Petretti's Coca-Cola Collectibles Price Guide, 12th edition*, by Allan Petretti.

Window sign, 1937, trompe-l'oeil display, rare, 51" h. x 47" w.
......................$15,000-$20,000

Morphy Auctions, www.morphyauctions.com

Bicycle, circa 1960s, three wheels, red, female frame with soda cooler on two front wheels and Coca-Cola wire baskets flanking rear wheel, 62" l. **$2,200**

Mecum Auctions, www.Mecum.com

Tray, 1932 Coca-Cola Swimsuit Girl advertising tray, edge nicks and minor damage to the field, 10-1/2" x 13". **$150**

Manifest Auctions, www.manifestauctions.com

Poster, "Make Every Meal a Party", circa 1950s, unrestored, 29" x 42" **$167**

Heritage Auctions, www.ha.com

Sign, red Coca-Cola button form, circa 1940s, tin, 36" d. **$684**

SeriousToyz, serioustoyz.com

Sign, circa 1940s, enameled, tin, "Fountain Service Drink Coca-Cola", 63" x 48".............**$2,500**

Copake Auctions, Inc., www.copakeauction.com

Painting, oil on canvas, Haddon Sundblum, 1949, Edgar Bergen and Charlie McCarthy checking out a cooler full of Coca-Cola, artwork used in numerous company advertisements and also prominently featured on the back cover of an issue of National Geographic in 1951, 33"w. x 29" h..................................**$53,680**

Morphy Auctions, morphyauctions.com

Sign, 1920s, "Drink Coca-Cola Highballs (The Morning After), Whitehead & Hoag Co., Newark, N.J., celluloid, 11" l. ....**$10,455.**

Morphy Auctions, www.morphyauctions.com

Sign, figural form of a policeman crossing guard, 1950s complete with original interior "T" frame, post and cast iron base, 65-3/4" h. $2,280

Morphy Auctions, www.morphyauctions.com

Sign, 1940s, Kay Displays, Coca-Cola Cooler & Arrow, 31" h., ...$1,800

Morphy Auctions, morphyauctions.com

Drawing, Miss Coca-Cola, Erte, painted at the New York World's Fair in 1964, scarce, 14" h. x 11". ....$1,500-$3,000

Courtesy Auction Life, auctionlifeflorida.com

Display, circa 1930s, sterling silver Coca-Cola bottle, one-of-a-kind, made especially for a company executive who supervised the construction of the ocean liner-inspired Coca-Cola bottling plant in Los Angeles, 24" t......$35,380

Morphy Auctions, www.morphyauctions.com

Illustration, unknown American artist, original artwork served as basis for a large horizontal Coke poster, "A happy thought — refresh yourself," was used in 1927 magazine ads.............................$50,020

Morphy Auctions, morphyauctions.com

Sign, circa late 1940s, cardboard, "Have A Coke", original frame. $2,128

Barrett-Jackson, www.barrett-jackson.com

Toy truck, Sanyo, circa 1950s, "Route Truck", tin, original box, 12-1/2" l. **$453**

SeriousToyz

▶ Thermometer, Donaldson Art and Sign Company, 1950s, die-cut in the form of a bottle of Coca-Cola, 16" h. x 6" w. **$207**

Barrett-Jackson, www.barrett-jackson.com

Pinbacks, 1986, set of 60 as issued by Coca-Cola to commemorate 15th anniversary of Walt Disney World, 26" x 2.5" framed. **$200**

COIN-OPS

DID YOU KNOW coin-operated dispensers date back to ancient times when they were used in houses of worship to deliver holy water? You'd be hard-pressed to find one of those offered at auction today, but many other types of coin-operated gadget-like gizmos certainly come up for sale, and there are always eager buyers lining up to add them to collections.

Coin-ops, as they're often referenced by both marketers and aficionados, come in all shapes and sizes and fall into three main categories: gambling, including slot machines and trade stimulators; vending machines with service devices like scales and shoe shiners as a subcategory; and arcade machines. From simple post-World War II gumball and peanut machines that can usually be found for under $100, to rare antique arcade machines that bring to mind the fortune teller amusement working magic in the popular movie "Big" starring Tom Hanks, these are all considered collectible.

Today one of those talking fortune-teller machines can easily bring five figures at auction. Other interesting models without talking features can be purchased more reasonably, in the $1,000-$5,000 range, but none of them come cheap when they're in good working order.

Amusements such as these originated in penny arcades of the late 1800s. There were machines allowing patrons to demonstrate their skill at bowling, shooting or golf, among other pastimes, along with the familiar strength testers that sprang to life at a penny a pop. Some machines known as "shockers" were marketed as medical devices. In fact, one made by Mills, a huge manufacturer of coin-ops, was actually named Electricity is Life, and it would supposedly cure what ails you, according to Bill Petrochuk, an avid collector actively involved with the Coin Operated Collectors Association (http://coinopclub.org). Another lung tester, which operated by blowing into a mouthpiece attached to a hose causing water to rise in the device as a measurement tool, was eventually banned, ironically, due to the spread

Batmobile coin-operated ride, circa 1960s, heavy-duty Batmobile-replica ride, 25¢ for 30 seconds, black, yellow, aqua, and red painted car, 44" h. x 65" l. **$2,270**

Heritage Auctions

Zeno Chewing Gum coin-op, small crack in front below Zeno sign, coin entry chipped, no key to wind the mechanism, excellent condition, 16-1/2" h. .... $800-$1,000

of tuberculosis.

There are also those aforementioned trade stimulators, some of which skirted gambling laws, according to Larry DeBaugh, a frequent consultant for Morphy Auctions (www. morphyauctions.com), who knows his stuff when it comes to devices powered by pocket change. These machines stimulated the trade of businesses like tobacco stores and bars by offering patrons a chance to win products, many times by spinning reels or playing a game. Later machines dispensed gum on the side for each coin spent. Customers received something for their money, and presto, law enforcement couldn't technically deem it gambling.

The earliest trade stimulators were cigar machines with no gambling involved, however. They were truly cigar dispensers, and for a nickel a customer would get a cigar. What made it different from buying from the guy down the block is that you might get two or three for the same nickel using the machine. Petrochuk adds that these were used to free up some of the tobacco shop clerk's time as well. When taxes were imposed on cigars, requiring that they be sold from original boxes, these machines were no longer serviceable. They're now considered rare collectibles and sell for $10,000 and up in most instances, when you can find them.

There were also slot machines designed for use outside casinos that would vend a pack of mints, or do a bit of fortune telling, in the same way as later trade stimulators. These machines were fought by authorities for decades, according to DeBaugh. Finally, in the 1950s and 1960s, vending-style gambling machines of this sort were outlawed, and their makers concentrated their marketing efforts on Las Vegas going forward.

Traditional slot machines are quite popular today as well, and collectors like DeBaugh, who've studied, bought and sold these types of items for 35-40 years, have seen a bit of everything including those in pretty rough shape.

"An average machine, one that's seen a lot of play from the '40s or late '30s and is basically worn out, will run about $1,000. But they won't be worth anything unless they are restored. After they're running, you might have a $3,000 machine."

Petrochuk notes that collectors of coin-ops in general look for "nice, clean, original machines," but a very small percentage fall into that category. He likes to use the term "preservation" when referring to giving old coin-ops new life, as in keeping things as original as possible. He sees restoration as more of a redo that might require totally new paint or extensive replating. "These old machines took a real beating. A few battle scars are acceptable," he adds.

Preserving coin-ops means using as many original parts as possible to replace those that are worn, and fabricating new ones out of appropriate materials when needed. DeBaugh actually supplies Rick Dale of the History Channel's hit television series "American Restoration" with many parts salvaged from old slot machines that can't be repaired. He also notes that it's tough to find older slots from the early 1900s in anything but poor condition. The wood usually needs work, and sometimes the nickel or copper finishes will need to be replated as well.

Other unusual coin-ops beyond the familiar "one-armed bandits" include devices that sold match books, collar buttons, and sprays of perfume. Going even further into the unimaginable zone are machines that actually dispensed live lobsters via a game of sorts. Others even provided live bait for fishing excursions. Or, maybe a machine that dispensed gold bars in airports might pique your curiosity? These oddball items made the list of "10

Wrigley rotating gum dispenser, metal and glass, professionally restored, excellent condition, 14-1/2" h. ....**$400-$800**

Coin-operated Indian Motorcycle ride, 53" x 28" x 54"............**$7,500**

Heritage Auctions

Things You Didn't Know About Coin-Op Antiques" published in the 2014 edition of Antique Trader Antiques & Collectibles Price Guide.

Nut and gum dispensers are the most common vending models, but unusual brands in this category most definitely appeal to advertising collectors in addition to coin-op enthusiasts. In fact, many coin-ops are direct extensions of advertising collectibles since vending machines made in the 1920s and '30s, unlike those that dispense multiple types of snacks today, usually focused on a single brand. Hershey's machines dispensed chocolate bars. Wrigley's dispensers rotated to deliver packs of gum. There were even coin-operated dispensers for Dixie Cups. Add an unusual shape or size to the equation and advanced collectors will pay big bucks to own them.

Even those old-fashioned red, white, and blue stamp dispensers used in post offices 30-40 years ago appeal to collectors of newer machines, and those can be found for less than $100. If you want a slot machine for use in a "man cave" or game room, DeBaugh suggests looking at a Mills machine from the 1940s or '50s. Both high top and half top models can be found for around $1,000 in good working order. What's even better, they're dependable and reliable for home use for hours of coin-op fun.

— Pamela Y. Wiggins

Pinball machine, Williams Fairway, wooden rail, manufactured by Williams Manufacturing Co., Chicago, circa 1949, 24-1/2" w. x 64-1/2" h. x 53" d. Williams Fairway is purported to be one of the earliest golf-related upright pinball machines ever made.............................. **$1,434**

Heritage Auctions

Gumball machine, Leaf Play Ball, 1960, likely restored, 14" h. **$383**

Heritage Auctions

Master 1¢/5¢ vending machine, five turns for a nickel and one turn for a penny, original condition, box and keys present, excellent condition, 16" h. **$408**

Miniature Baseball World Champion coin-operated game, 1931, all original, accepts pennies and flips steel balls in spiral to obtain hits or outs, 16-1/2" x 10-1/4" x 8-1/2"... **$1,340**

Heritage Auctions

Advanced 1¢ Climax 10 vendor, circa 1915, with extended gooseneck coin entry, excellent condition, 20-1/2". .... **$1,000-$1,600**

Morphy Auctions

Glenn Ford's *Ocean's Eleven* slot machine, gift from Frank Sinatra, from fabled Sands Casino, Ocean's Eleven hotel-casino; one of several machines seen in the movie and later obtained by Sinatra, who gave them as gifts. **$6,572**

Heritage Auctions

Standard Gum Co. 1¢ aluminum gumball dispenser, original condition with marquee, working condition, padlock but no key, wall mounting bracket, very good condition, 17-1/2" h...........**$336**

Vintage coffee vending machine, 64" x 21-1/2" x 19-1/4."............................**$750**

Heritage Auctions

Baseball-themed gumball machine, 1958, fully functional, free standing, spring-operated "bat" hurls ball toward pockets representing hits and outs, 45" h. on heavy iron base............................**$650**

Heritage Auctions

Mutoscope Skyscraper traveling crane digger machine, 1920s, sold by Mills Sales Co. of Oakland, California, front compartment facades of Empire State Building, 42" h. x 23" w. x 20" d...........................**$1,093**

One-cent Pocket Lighter Fuel coin-op, missing piece of metal below cash door, otherwise good condition, 16"....**$400-$600**

Morphy Auctions

Pole Vault 1-cent skill game gum trade stimulator, as-found good condition, no key, not working, 14-1/2" h. ....**$300-$500**

Morphy Auctions

Chicago Club House 1¢ trade stimulator gum vendor in fair, as-found condition, 15-1/2" h. ....**$300-$500**

Morphy Auctions

Beatles pinball machine, Williams, 1966, reconditioned. **$4,182**

Heritage Auctions

Mills 5¢ Brownie slot machine, largest of countertop color wheels produced by Mills, earlier 20th century, approximately 21" w. x 29" h. x 11" d. **$9,775**

James D. Julia, Inc.

Gottlieb Frontiersman pinball machine, 5¢ play, one leg with vertical stress split, some replaced bumpers with celluloid bumper tops showing distress, lacking key but unlocked, 54" l. x 66" h. x 25" w.. **$374**

James D. Julia, Inc.

Caille Upright Slot Machine, 25¢ play, restored, antique copper finish, oak case, missing pay out pointer and cover for center of wheel, excellent condition, 69" h.
.....................$16,000-$24,000

Morphy Auctions

Jennings coin-drop trade stimulator, horse race theme on aluminum castings, very fine condition, 12-1/2" d. x 14" w. x 20" h. Depending upon where penny landed, player received 0 to 25 points, plus a gumball.
....$2,300

5¢ Real Moving Pictures arcade machine on original stand, excellent condition, 75" h.
.... $1,200-$1,400

Morphy Auctions

Rare 5¢ Blackhawk Brand Aspirin coin-operated dispenser, original excellent condition, 12" h.
...................................$500-$800

Morphy Auctions

Price 10¢ Collar Button Machine Co. vending machine full of collar buttons, excellent condition, 11-1/2" h.
.... $1,000-$1,200

Morphy Auctions

COINS

INTEREST IN COIN COLLECTING in the United States surged in the late 1850s when the smaller, copper-nickel Flying Eagle cent replaced the old large copper one-cent coin. Just two years later, the Indian Head cent replaced the Flying Eagle cent. People started putting aside the obsolete coins, and demand and prices for them rose. Professional coin dealers emerged to meet the demand, and by the 1870s, most major Eastern cities had coin clubs.

The next major development in coin collecting occurred in 1888 when Dr. George Heath of Monroe, Michigan – a physician by profession who moonlighted as a mail-order coin dealer – published the first issue of *The American Numismatist*. Like many other publications of the time, the magazine was a marketing tool for Heath's coin business. By 1891, Heath had shortened the serial's title to *The Numismatist*, and its readership formed the basis for the founding of the American Numismatic Association.

Coin collecting continued to grow in the early 20th century as exciting new designs made old coins obsolete. Ironically, the Great Depression brought another major development in coin collecting. In 1934, the Whitman Publishing Co. of Racine, Wisconsin, introduced the "penny board." It was essentially a big piece of cardboard with holes in it for each date and mint mark of Lincoln cents, starting in 1909. The boards sold for 25 cents each and were widely available in hardware stores, dime stores, shoeshine parlors, and gasoline stations.

The boards provided cheap entertainment during the economic struggles of the 1930s as people of all ages checked the one-cent coins in their pocket change for dates and mint marks that would fill an empty hole in the board. The boards developed into the modern-day coin folder, which many collectors use to store their holdings today.

Coin collecting enjoyed a boom period in the 1950s. War veterans and others had disposable income to devote to a hobby and could find coins of the late 1800s and early 1900s in circulation. What they couldn't find they could buy from the growing number of dealers who operated shops, set up at coin shows, or advertised in coin publications such as the newly founded *Numismatic News*.

Coin collecting is enjoying another renaissance thanks in part to U.S. Mint programs such as the America the Beautiful Quarters, which again provide a forum for collecting coins from circulation. Meanwhile, on the high end of the market, traditionally popular coins – such as Standing Liberty quarters, Walking Liberty half dollars, Morgan silver dollars, and gold coins – make hobby headlines when they sell at auction for eye-popping prices in top grades.

What makes a coin valuable? Precious-metal content provides the base value for any gold or silver coin. Prices for precious metals have surged in recent years, so the base values of gold and silver coins have surged with them.

Gold and silver coins with collectible or numismatic value sell for a premium above their precious-metal value. The extent of the premium depends on the coin's grade, its rarity, and the demand for the coin in the collector market. Premiums over precious-metal content can vary from a few percentage points for bullion coins to several hundred percent for high-quality or rare collectible coins. If the premium is high, the coin is not affected as much by fluctuating market prices for silver and gold bullion. If the premium is low, the coin's value is more likely to be affected by the ups and downs of the bullion markets.

Base-metal coins, such as one-cent and five-cent pieces, can also sell for well above their intrinsic value on the collector market because of their rarity, desirability, and condition.

Condition is stated in commonly used grading terms. Uncirculated coins, which show no signs of wear, are termed "mint state" or MS. A number usually follows to indicate varying degrees of condition within mint state (MS-67, MS-65, or MS-63, for example). Terms used to describe circulated coins, or coins showing wear, include "about uncirculated", "extremely fine", and "very fine", in descending order. (For more on grading, see *The Official American Numismatic Association Grading Standards for United States Coins.*

Most coins valuable enough to justify the fee have been graded by one of several professional coin grading services, a trend that started in the mid-1980s. Which service graded the coin is usually noted with the coin's grade when it is offered for sale.

The following examples of U.S. coins are quite rare and in Mint State. While you may never come accross such outstanding examples, these coins speak to the beauty and value to be enjoyed in the hobby of coin collecting.

ABBREVIATIONS

CAC – Certified Acceptance Corporation
ICCS – International Coin Certification Service
PCGS – Professional Coin Grading Service
PMG – Paper Money Guaranty

1793 Flowing Hair large cent, wreath reverse, vine and bars on edge, PCGS MS-66+ brown, one of two finest known. **$528,750**

Courtesy of Heritage Auctions, ha.com

1909-S Lincoln cent, "V.D.B." designer's initials (Victor David Brenner) on reverse at 6 o'clock position, PCGS MS-67 red..........................**$94,000**

Courtesy of Heritage Auctions, ha.com

1935 Buffalo nickel, PCGS MS-68..............**$57,500**
Courtesy of Heritage Auctions, ha.com

1916-D Winged Liberty (Mercury) dime, PCGS MS-66, fully struck bands around fasces on reverse...**$63,250**

Courtesy of Heritage Auctions, ha.com

1927-S Standing Liberty quarter, PCGS MS-65, Liberty's head on obverse fully struck. **$149,500**

Courtesy of Heritage Auctions, ha.com

1921-S Walking Liberty half dollar, PCGS MS-65, CAC verification.......................................**$117,500**

Courtesy of Heritage Auctions, ha.com

1893-S Morgan dollar, lowest mintage (100,000) among circulation strikes in series, NGC MS-65. ....**$329,000**

Courtesy of Heritage Auctions, ha.com

1895 Morgan dollar, only proofs of this issue are known to exist, NGC proof-66 cameo...........**$88,125**

Courtesy of Heritage Auctions, ha.com

1926-D Peace dollar, PCGS MS-67.............**$20,125**

Courtesy of Heritage Auctions, ha.com

1861 Liberty gold $5, PCGS MS-66, CAC verification...**$152,750**

Courtesy of Heritage Auctions, ha.com

1907 Saint-Gaudens gold $20, Roman numerals in date, high relief, flat rim, PCGS MS-68......**$316,250**

Courtesy of Heritage Auctions, ha.com

COMIC BOOKS

BACK IN 1993, Sotheby's auctioned a copy of *Fantastic Four #1* (1961) that was said to be the finest copy known to exist. It sold for $27,600, which at the time was considered an unheard-of price for a 1960s comic. A few years ago Heritage Auctions sold that same copy for $203,000 ... and it's not even the finest known copy anymore.

It used to be that only comics from the 1930s or 1940s could be worth thousands of dollars. Now, truly high-grade copies of comics from the Silver Age (1956-1969 by most people's reckoning) can sell for four, five, or even six figures. Note I said truly high-grade. Long gone are the days when a near mint condition copy was only worth triple the price of a good condition copy. Now near mint is more like 10-20 times good, and sometimes it's as much as a factor of 1,000.

A trend of the last couple of years has been that the "key" issues have separated even further from the pack, value-wise. Note that not every key is a "#1" issue – if you have

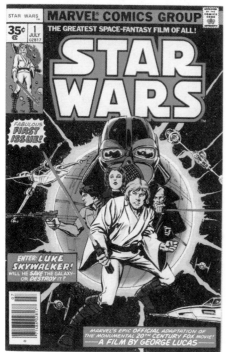

Star Wars #1 (Marvel, 1977), CGC VF/NM 9.0, extremely rare 35¢ variant edition, which was test marketed in a small, select area of the US, part 1 of the Star Wars movie adaption. Howard Chaykin cover and art.
.....................................$12,547

Courtesy Heritage Auctions, ha.com

Amazing Fantasy #15, Tales of Suspense #39, and *Journey into Mystery #83*, you've got the first appearances of Spider-Man, Iron Man, and Thor. (Beware of reprints and replica editions, however.)

The most expensive comics of all remain the Golden Age (1938-1949) first appearances, like Superman's 1938 debut in *Action Comics #1*, several copies of which have sold for $1 million or more. However, not every single comic from the old days is going up in value. Take western-themed comics. Values are actually going down in this genre as the generation that grew up watching westerns is at the age where they're looking to sell, and there are more sellers than potential buyers.

Comics from the 1970s and later, while increasing in value, rarely reach anywhere near the same value as 1960s issues, primarily because in the 1970s, the general public began to look at comics as a potentially valuable collectible. People took better care of them, and in many cases hoarded multiple copies.

What about 1980s favorites like *The Dark Knight Returns and Watchmen*? Here the demand is high, but the supply is really high. These series were heavily hyped at the time and were done by well-known creators, so copies were socked away in great quantities. We've come across more than one dealer who has 20-30 mint copies of every single 1980s comic socked away in a warehouse, waiting for the day when they're worth selling.

I should mention one surprise hit of the last couple of years. When Image Comics published *The Walking Dead #1* in 2003, it had a low print run and made no particular splash in the comics world. Once AMC made it into a television series, however, it was a whole different story. High-grade copies of #1 have been fetching $1,000 and up lately.

If you've bought comics at an auction house or on eBay, you might have seen some in CGC holders. Certified Guaranty Co., or CGC, is a third-party grading service that grades a comic book on a scale from 0.5 to 10. These numbers correspond with traditional descriptive grades of good, very fine, near mint and mint, with the higher numbers indicating a better grade. Once graded, CGC encapsulates the comic book in plastic. The grade remains valid as long as the plastic holder is not broken open. CGC has been a boon to the hobby, allowing people to buy comics with more confidence and with the subjectivity of grading taken out of the equation. Unless extremely rare, it's usually only high-grade comics that are worth certifying.

One aspect of collecting that has absolutely exploded in the last 20 years has been original comic art, and not just art for the vintage stuff. In fact, the most expensive piece Heritage Auctions has ever sold was from 1990: Todd McFarlane's cover art for *Amazing Spider-Man #328*, which sold for more than $650,000. It's not unusual for a page that was bought for $20 in the 1980s to be worth $5,000 now.

If you want to get into collecting original comic art, McFarlane would not be the place to start unless you've got a really fat wallet. I suggest picking a current comic artist you like who isn't yet a major "name." Chances are his originals will be a lot more affordable. Another idea is to collect the original art for comic strips. You can find originals for as little as $20, as long as you're not expecting a Peanuts or a Prince Valiant. Heritage Auctions (HA.com) maintains a free online archive of every piece of art they've sold and it is an excellent research tool.

Mister Miracle #1 (DC, 1971) CGC NM/MT 9.8, first appearances of Mister Miracle and Oberon. Death of Thaddeus Brown. Jack Kirby story, cover and art. Vince Colletta art.
.... **$2,748**

Courtesy Heritage Auctions, ha.com

As expensive as both comic books and comic art can be at the high-end of the spectrum, in many ways this is a buyer's market. In the old days you might search for years to find a given issue of a comic; now you can often search eBay and see 10 different copies for sale. Also, comic conventions seem to be thriving in almost every major city – and while the people in crazy costumes get all the publicity, you can also find plenty of vintage comic dealers at these shows. From that point of view, it's a great time to be a comic collector.

— Barry Sandoval

Barry Sandoval is Director of Operations for Comics and Comic Art, Heritage Auctions. In addition to managing Heritage's Comics division, Sandoval is a noted comic book evaluator and serves as an advisor to the *Overstreet Comic Book Price Guide*.

Crimes by Women #6 (Fox Features Syndicate, 1949). **$310**

Courtesy Heritage Auctions, ha.com

Superman #9 (DC, 1941) CGC VG 4.0 Off-white pages. Fred Ray cover, Joe Shuster art. CGC notes: "Cover detached." **$567**

Courtesy Heritage Auctions, ha.com

Showcase #9 Superman's Girlfriend Lois Lane (DC, 1957) CGC FN/VF 7.0. Off-white to white pages. One of the toughest Showcase issues to find in high grade. Lois Lane was the first Showcase character to get her own book, in a time when such honors were rare.. .... **$1,792**

Courtesy Heritage Auctions, ha.com

Wonder Woman #4 (DC, 1943), CGC Apparent VF+ 8.5, H. G. Peter cover and art. **$3,107**

Courtesy Heritage Auctions, ha.com

Green Lantern #88 (DC, 1972) CGC NM+ 9.6. White pages. Neal Adams cover. Carmine Infantino art. Backup feature is a previously unpublished Golden Age Green Lantern story. **$747**

Richie Rich Diamonds #1 (Harvey, 1972) CGC NM/MT 9.8. White pages. Giant-size issue. Little Dot, Little Lotta, and Cadbury backup stories. .. **$956**

Friendly Ghost Casper #179, File Copy Long Box Group (Harvey, 1975), VF. This full long box lot is filled with file copies of issues #179, which celebrates the 65th anniversary of the Cub Scouts. There are several bundles of the comics that are still bound in the original wrapping string. **$657**

Scooby Doo File Copies Group (Gold Key, 1970-74). Condition: Average FN/VF. Group includes 75 issues of Gold Key Scooby Doo. Represented are issues #5, 6, 7, 8, 15, 16, 17, 18, 19, 20, 21, and 25. Multiple copies of every issue except #5 and 7. From the Random House Archives. **$805**

Blue Ribbon Comics #1 Mile High Pedigree (MLJ, 1939) CGC NM+ 9.6. White pages. The single highest-graded copy of the very first MLJ (later known as Archie Publications) comic book is this Mile High copy. The issue features the first appearances of Dan Hastings, Richy the Amazing Boy and Rang-A-Tang the Wonder Dog, who also stars on the stylized cover attributed to Norman Danberg. Golden Age great Jack Cole contributed interior art... **$3,200**

Courtesy Heritage Auctions, ha.com

House of Secrets #92 (DC, 1971) CGC VF 8.0. Off-white to white pages. Origin and first appearance of the Swamp Thing. Grey tone cover and art by Bernie Wrightson............................ **$717**

Courtesy Heritage Auctions, ha.com

Tales to Astonish #40 (Marvel, 1963) CGC NM+ 9.6. White pages. Early Ant-Man adventure. Cover art Jack Kirby; interior art by Kirby and Steve Ditko. **$4,182**

Courtesy Heritage Auctions, ha.com

The Amazing Spider-Man #8 (Marvel, 1964) CGC NM+ 9.6. Off-white to white pages. In addition to the usual superior work from Stan Lee and Steve Ditko, this issue contains a Fantastic Four/Spider-Man backup story. **$7,187**

Courtesy Heritage Auctions, ha.com

Metal Men #1 (DC Comics, 1963) CGC 9.4 NM, Robert Kanigher story, Ross Andru and Mike Esposito cover and art, off-white pages, classic Silver Age comic... **$3,162**

Courtesy of Hakes Americana & Collectibles, hakes.com

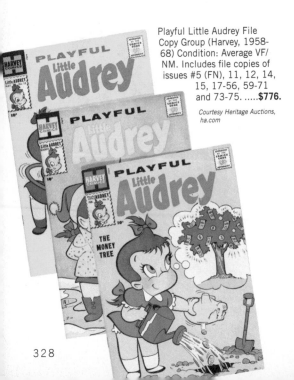

Playful Little Audrey File Copy Group (Harvey, 1958-68) Condition: Average VF/NM. Includes file copies of issues #5 (FN), 11, 12, 14, 15, 17-56, 59-71 and 73-75. .....**$776.**

Courtesy Heritage Auctions, ha.com

Donald Duck (Whitman, 1938). Condition: Apparent VG/FN. The first Donald Duck and Walt Disney comic book. Moderate professional restoration includes pieces added, spine reinforced, and color touch on cover. **$334**

Courtesy Heritage Auctions, ha.com

top lot!

Batman Debut Brings Super Price

When Detective Comics #27 hit the newsstand in 1939, Superman was the only superhero of note, save for some little-known characters destined for comic book obscurity. That all changed, however, with the introduction of "The Bat-Man."

Just how significant was Batman's debut? Detective Comics #27 is now one of the most desirable comic books on the market. A CGC-certified 5.0 copy of the issue sold for $710,000 in June 2017 at Metropolis Collectibles, Inc., New York. It was the highest price ever paid for a copy in that condition. Several years ago, a copy graded at 8.0, the highest known graded copy to exist, sold for $1,075,500.

"The demand for Golden Age keys is virtually unlimited as prices are rising beyond even our wildest estimations," Metropolis Collectibles COO Vincent Zurzolo said. "There's no one who doesn't know the Batman character, and many of the new buyers entering this market want the best of the best, making this one of the most-requested key issues."

Batman appeared in a six-page story in the May 1939 issue that also introduced the character of Commissioner Gordon. The second-to-last panel revealed that this mysterious Dark Knight was in fact millionaire Bruce Wayne, introduced earlier in the story. Created by artist Bob Kane, the issue cover is one of the most famous in the history of comics.

Kane and writer Bill Finger (generally credited as a co-creator of the Batman character) produced a hero to rival Superman without imitating the earlier character. Batman has been in continuous publication since 1939, a distinction only Superman – introduced in Actions Comics #1, June 1938 – shares among comic book characters.

Daredevil #4 Signature Series (Marvel, 1964)
CGC NM+ 9.6. Origin and first appearance of the
Purple Man. Jack Kirby cover. Joe Orlando and
Vince Colletta art. CGC notes, "Signed by Stan
Lee on 2/2/13." **$2,629**

Courtesy of Heritage Auctions, ha.com

Secrets Behind The Comics #1 Stan Lee File Copy
(Famous Enterprises Inc., 1947) Condition: VF.
Copy is one of the most important pieces from the
historically significant private collection of Stan
Lee. It is signed on the cover by Stan Lee, and
"From my personal collection - Stan Lee," on the
first inside page. **$488**

Funny Pages #10 (Centaur, 1937) Condition: FN.
White pages. **$358**

Shadow Comics V3 #11 (Street & Smith, 1944)
CGC FN 6.0 Off-white to white pages. Striking
grey tone-like cover art! CGC notes, "4 extra
staples, not from manufacturing. Original staple
removed." **$388**

10 Things You Didn't Know About LeRoy Robert Ripley (aka Robert L. Ripley)

1 LeRoy Robert Ripley (1890-1949), grew up in Santa Rosa, California, and played semi-pro baseball in his teens. He traveled to New York City in 1913 at the urging of his friend, writer Jack London. He tried out with the New York Giants, but after breaking his arm in a training game, effectively ending his chances at a big league baseball career, Ripley became a full-time cartoonist. It was at the suggestion of one of his editors that he dropped "LeRoy" and became "Robert L. Ripley" (the editor believed "LeRoy" didn't sound masculine enough).

2 In 1908, Ripley was paid $8 for his first commercial cartoon. Life magazine purchased Ripley's illustrated pun of a young woman pushing laundry through a wringer with the caption "The Village Bell Was Slowly Ringing." [belle]/[wringing]

3 Although he never completed high school (he was forced to drop out and work to help support his family after his father's death), in the midst of the Great Depression, in 1934, NBC was paying Ripley $3,000 per half-hour radio show; the cartoonist's King Features Syndicate contract was worth $7,000 per week; Ripley charged $1,000 per night to appear as a lecturer. When added to his other lucrative earnings, Ripley's income totaled more than a half-million dollars per year. (For comparison, $500,000 in 1934 translates to nearly $9 million in 2016.) He was well on his way to becoming the first cartoonist to earn $1 million per year – including Walt Disney.

4 After a two-year run at the Chicago World's Fair, which drew more than 2 million visitors and earned $1 million, in 1933 Ripley opened his first permanent "Odditorium" in Times Square, New York City. Ripley's attraction

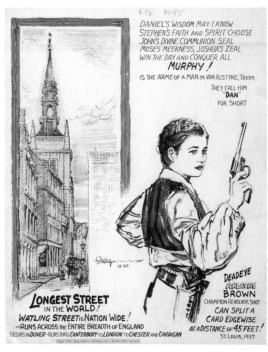

Robert L. Ripley Ripley's Believe It Or Not! daily comic strip original art dated 12-20-37 (King Features Syndicate, 1937), ink and grease pencil over graphite on textured Bristol board with an image area of 11 by 13 1/2 inches; excellent condition, ...**$717**

Courtesy of Heritage Auctions, www.ha.com

Robert Ripley Signed Envelope. 6.5" x 3.75". With a postal cancellation dated September 1, 1937. Signed "Ripley / 'Believe It or Not" under affixed cut-outportrait. Some soiling and light toning, handling wear, minor tear on left edge....... **$81**

Heritage Auctions, www.ha.com

Ripley Cartoon 4302.jpg
Robert Ripley Ripley's Believe It or Not!
Sunday Comic Strip Original Art dated 3-17-
35 (King Features Syndicate, 1935. This very
large page is created in ink and Conte crayon
over graphite on Coquille paper that measures
19.5" x 25.5". **$4,302**

Courtesy of Heritage Auctions, www.ha.com

portfolio has grown to more than 95 attractions in 10 countries. Attractions include 32 Ripley's Believe It or Not! Odditoriums, five Guinness World Records Museums and four Louis Tussaud's Wax Works - many of which hold items from Ripley's own personal collections. The Niagara Falls, Ontario, Odditorium reopened in May 2016 after a six-month, top-to-bottom makeover. "Ripley's has been entertaining Niagara Falls visitors for more than 50 years," said Tim Parker, Ripley's Niagara Falls general manager. "We're now proud to offer our biggest and best experience yet." Here, visitors can also see a rickshaw carved from jade, and an actual segment from the Berlin Wall.

5 Robert Ripley was quite charming and popular with women. Among others, Ripley found companionship in Hungarian antiques dealer Ruth Ross (nicknamed "Oakie"). She helped organize and display Ripley's eclectic collections of antiques and artwork, turning his private island, BION, into a private showcase that Ripley loved to show off to members of his social circle. When he entertained, he often did so dressed in Chinese garb because the culture fascinated him.

6 Ripley's first book, "Ripley's Believe It or Not!" was published by Simon & Schuster in 1929. The first edition, originally selling for $2.50, sold more than 500,000 copies. Thanks to the prolific print runs, first editions can be found today for less than $50. Simon & Schuster is still publishing Ripley books filled with amazing facts; there are dozens of titles listed at http://www.ripleys.com/publishing/.

7 A Believe It or Not! cartoon revealed "The Star-Spangled Banner" wasn't the official national anthem, sparking public outrage. Within a year, as a result of the publicity generated by Ripley, Herbert Hoover signed the bill on March 3, 1931, officially making the song the United States' national anthem.

8 While living at the New York Athletic Club, Ripley played in dozens of handball tournaments. He even won the NYAC singles handball championship in 1925.

9 Holly Palance, who hosted four episodes of the television show "Ripley's Believe It or Not!" from 1982 to 1984, played the part of Damien Thorn's ever-protective Nanny in The Omen (Twentieth Century Fox, 1976).

10 In 1949, while filming the 13th episode of his television show, Robert Ripley collapsed; he suffered a heart attack and died two or three days later. The subject of his final show: The story behind the military funeral song "Taps."

– Compiled by Karen Knapstein

"A Curious Man - The Strange and Brilliant Life of Robert "Believe It or Not" Ripley" by Neal Thompson, Crown Archetype, 2013, hardcover, 432 pages, $26 (available on Amazon.com for $19.84); http://www.nealthompson.com [bit.ly/RipleyLife] www.vanityfair.com; www.ripleys.com; www.huffingtonpost.com; www.biography.com/; www.legacy.com; www.pbs.org

COOKIE JARS

COOKIE JARS EVOLVED from the elegant British biscuit jars found on Victorian-era tables. These 19th century containers featured bail handles and were often made of sterling silver and cut crystal.

As the biscuit jar was adapted for use in America, it migrated from the dining table to the kitchen and, by the late 1920s, it was common to find a green-glass jar (or pink or clear), often with an applied label and a screw-top lid, on kitchen counters in the typical American home.

During the Great Depression – when stoneware was still popular but before the arrival of widespread electric refrigeration – cookie jars in round and barrel shapes arrived. These heavy-bodied jars could be hand-painted after firing. These decorations were easily worn away by eager hands reaching for Mom's baked goodies. The lids of many stoneware jars typically had small tapering finials or knobs that also contributed to cracks and chips.

The golden age of cookie jars began in the 1940s and lasted for less than three decades, but the examples that survive represent an exuberance and style that have captivated collectors.

It wasn't until the 1970s that many collectors decided – instead of hiding their money in cookie jars – to invest their money in cookie jars. It was also at this time that cookie jars ceased to be simply storage vessels for bakery and evolved into a contemporary art form.

The Brush Pottery Co. of Zanesville, Ohio, produced one of the first ceramic cookie jars in about 1929, and Red Wing's spongeware line from the late 1920s also included a ridged, barrel-shaped jar. Many established potteries began adding a selection of cookie jars in the 1930s.

The 1940s saw the arrival of two of the most famous cookie jars: Shawnee's Smiley and Winnie, two portly, bashful little pigs who stand with eyes closed and heads cocked, he in overalls and bandana, she in flowered hat and long coat. A host of Disney characters also made their way into American kitchens.

In the 1950s, the first television-influenced jars appeared, including images of Davy Crockett and Popeye. This decade also saw the end of several prominent American potteries, including Roseville, and the continued rise of imported ceramics.

A new collection of cartoon-inspired jars was popular in the 1960s, featuring characters drawn from the Flintstones, Yogi Bear, Woody Woodpecker, and Casper the Friendly Ghost. Jars reflecting the race for space included examples from McCoy and American Bisque. This decade also marked the peak production era for a host of West Coast manufacturers, led by twin brothers Don and Ross Winton.

Pearl China Co. "Cooky" & "Mammy" cookie jars. **$232**

Courtesy of Strawser Auctions, www.strawserauctions.com

For more information, see *Warman's Cookie Jars Identification and Price Guide* by Mark F. Moran.

Weller Mammy cookie jar. **$348**

Courtesy of Strawser Auctions, www.strawserauctions.com

Regal Puss N Boots cookie jar. **$58**

Courtesy of Strawser Auctions, www.strawserauctions.com

William Brownfield and Sons advertising cookie jar, c.1875, modeled as a turquoise glazed sack tied with an orange ribbon being gnawed by a white mouse, a second white mouse disappearing into a hole on the other side, the lid modeled as a pile of 'Peak Frean' biscuits, a brand of popular Victorian biscuits, 8". **$584**

Courtesy of Strawser Auctions, www.strawserauctions.com

Little Red Riding Hood Cookie Jar, excellent to Near Mint conditon, 13-1/4" tall........................ **$92**

Courtesy of Morphy Auctions, morphyauctions.com

Roseville art pottery Zephyr Lily cookie jar, green and brown, two open handles, original cover. Raised "Roseville / U.S.A / 5-8" on base. Roseville Pottery, Zanesville, Ohio, circa 1946, 10-1/2" h. **$196**

Courtesy of Jeffrey S. Evans & Associates, www.jeffreysevans.com

Hand-decorated art glass cookie jar, 9" h **$60**

Courtesy of Langston Auction Gallery, www.langstonantiques.com

Shawnee Pottery Mugsy cookie jar. **$20**

Courtesy of Mark Mattox Real Estate & Auctioneer, www.mattoxrealestate.com

Shawnee Winnie cookie jar. **$197**

Courtesy of Strawser Auctions, www.strawserauctions.com

Vintage cookie jar, hen with bonnet, ceramic, 8-3/4" x 6" x 7"..**$25**

Courtesy of Matthew Bullock Auctioneers, www.bullockauctioneers.com

Wood-tone ceramic cookie jar, Disneyland, 1970s, Country Bear Jamboree featuring "Big Al," 8-1/2C x 7" x 12" h.. **$225**

Courtesy of Van Eaton Galleries, vegalleries.com

Autumn Leaf cookie jar, Hall's, 9-1/2" h x 7-1/2" w.................. **$20**

Courtesy of Martin Auction Co., martinauctionco.com

Waterford "Holiday Heirlooms" painted porcelain "Georgian Santa Claus" cookie jar, 15" h, 13" w.. **$175**

Courtesy of DuMouchelles, www.dumouchelle.com

COPPER COLLECTIBLES

FEW PEOPLE REALIZE how important copper is to the various arts and antiques movements during the past 500 years. Copper has been used from the 8,000 BC. pre-Columbian era, whene soft, pure copper was mined into effigy figures, to the copper canvases.

It was also the first medium to be used by master painters such as El Greco, Brueghel, Reni, Wtewael, Chardin and Rembrandt, among others. Contrary to popular belief, most masterpieces were not painted on canvas or panels, but on copper metal. Renaissance era artists were extremely creative and tapped into their own mind, creativity, and resources with copper reigning high on the list.

In fact, according to the book, Copper as Canvas: Two Centuries of Masterpiece Painting on Copper, 1575-1775, from an exhibition and catalogue produced by the Phoenix Art Museum, suppliers of artists' materials are often forgotten when studying art works. However, evidence of their labor and trade materialized from personal marks occasionally found on the reverse of painting supports.

Pure copper is a pure chemical element with a reddish-orange color. Now used as the No. 1 conductor of heat and electricity, the metal is also used as a base of various metal alloys, such as sterling silver usedin jewelry, cupronickel used to make marine hardware and coins, and constantan used in strain gauges and thermocouples for temperature measurement.

Weathervane, American, circa 1900, gilt copper, in the form of an eagle, 26" l. x 15-1/2" h. x 33" w.
....**$2,250**

Heritage Auctions, HA.com

VISIT WWW.ANTIQUETRADER.COM

WWW.FACEBOOK.COM/ANTIQUETRADER

COPPER IN ART

Copper was the first metal to be smelted from its ore, c. 5000 BC, the first metal to be cast into a shape in a mold, c. 4000 BC and the first metal to be purposefully alloyed with another metal, tin, to create bronze, c. 3500 BC. But first it was used for art and utensils now considered valuable antiques.

Take the copper weathervane. The gold standard of New England antiques, the weather vane is one of the most collected items from the region. Figural in nature and often imaginative the values of these vanes have recently set new highs.

Hampden, Massachusetts', Stanton Auctions sold a spectacular, rare and important seahorse weathervane in late 2016 that handily beat its $20,000 pre-auction estimate to sell for $57,950. The 41-inch vane was a wonderful mixture of verdigris and tarnish that accented its indulgent design off perfectly. And in early 2017, Thomaston Place Auction Galleries offered a 19th century American Fire Engine Steam Pumper weathervane for $57,000. The pumper is drawn by two horses and having two cast firemen, in bronze, copper and zinc, on a later steel stand. The monumental piece is 88-1/2" wide by 56" tall on its stand.

COPPER UTENSILS

The price points and market for foreign collectible copper items as old as 100-years or older are both relatively affordable. A perfect example is the auction prices for Russian copper items. A 19th century hand-hammered copper creamer and sugar set, with brass accented handles, can be had for as little as $20. Oval copper plates from the Chinese Yuan dynasty (1271-1386) go unsold and early Tibetan inkwells gain at bid or two at $50.

The weak results are in stark contrast to early American copper items. A circa 1850 Early Blackfoot Hudson Bay beaver back dag knife (so named because the blade resembles a beaver's tail) measuring 12" long recently sold for $9,000. And a 5-3/4" x 2-1/2" Hudson Bay American Indian copper fish effigy beaded necklace can bring $300 or more in today's market.

Country Americana collectors still clamor for examples of early copper pots and pans and the distinct look years of use and storage can bring. But here is one area collectors should be warned. A new company is restoring these aged pieces to new functionality in a way that hasn't been seen since the 19th century or earlier. East Coast Tinning in East Greenwich, Rhode Island, is accepting pieces from across the United States for retinning. Owner Jim Hamann operates in a former textile mill building which is more than a century old. He has trained a few employees to aid in the restoration process, passing on the craft.

"Retinning is a periodic relining of the cooking surface," Hamann says in describing a technical definition of one of the main aspects of his restoration efforts. "It allows you to use a piece of cookware which might be 100 to 150-years-old. Having that cookware on your stove and that history in the pan, you wonder what was cooked in it before."

Hamann removes the old tin lining of a particular piece and joins in a new one with flux before buffing and polishing all surfaces, including the rich copper exterior sections.

The old character underneath stays, he says.

Rhinocéros mécanique, Francois Xavier LaLanne (French, 1927-2008), 1980, patinated copper 9-1/2 x 21-3/4 x 6-1/2 inches, Ed. 2/2, stamped inside hinged head panel: 2/2 FXL 80. ......**$203,000**

Heritage Auctions, www.ha.com

Molds, jelly or cream, Benham & Froud, circa 1860-1875, two molds in the forms of a lobster and a leaping fish, tin-lined, marks: orb and cross mark above the number "584", 2-7/8" h. x 6-1/4" l. **$4,012**

Northeast Auctions, www.northeastauctions.com

Kettles, set of three in similar form in graduating sizes, heights to handles: 2-7/8" h. to 4-1/8" h. **$767**

Northeast Auctions, www.northeastauctions.com

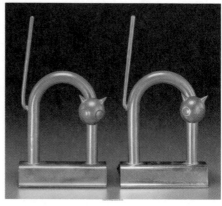

Incense burner, Japanese, Taisho Period (1912-1926), in ovoid form with tripod base and circular foot, domed cover with kirin finial, body decorated with relief bird and flower design, 12-1/4" h. ... **$325**

Eldred's Auctioneers & Appraisers, www.eldreds.com

Doorstops, pair, circa 1932, in the form of two hunch-backed cats, Chase Copper, artist Walter Von Nessen, Marks: CHASE, U.S.A., (logotype), 8-1/2" h. **$450**

Heritage Auctions, www.HA.com

COPPER COLLECTIBLES

Tea kettle, first half 20th century, W.A.S. Benson, maker, marks: initials separated by hammers, full name, patent No. and New Bond St., address. 14" h. .... **$100-$150**

The Canterbury Auction Galleries, www.thecanterburyauctiongalleries.com

Kettle, with stand, unmarked, 24" h. **$400**

Schneider Auctioneers, www.schneiderauctioneers.com

Bowl, painted copper in faux tortoise shell motif, raised on brass scroll feet and affixed with bail handles, 17" l. **$240**

Northeast Auctions, www.northeastauctions.com

Jewelry box, rare, Karl Kipp, hammered copper with German silver applied squares and central jade stone, suede lined, fine original patina, 5-1/2" d. x 2" h, an extremely well executed piece in exceptional condition, signed KK, excellent condition. **$40,000**

Treadway Gallery, www.treadwaygallery.com

Weathervane, American, 20th century., molded copper in the figural form of a grasshopper insect, 24" l. **$472**

Northeast Auctions, www.northeastauctions.com

Dish, circa 1614, flat dish with a slightly concave border and flared rim. Decorated to the center with the Wittelsbach coat of arms, surrounded by four cartouches with Old Testament and mythological decor, decorated to the spandrels with grotesque mascarons and figures amid tendrils, bordered by a chain ornament, rare as no other objects of this kind are known to exist from the early 17th c. **$10,000**

Lemperz, www.lempertz.com

▲ Weathervane, American late 19th century, copper molded figural form of a running horse, 15" h. x 22-1/2" l. **$708**

Northeast Auctions, www.northeastauctions.com

◄ Tobacco boxes, Dutch, 19th century, copper and brass, extensively engraved and inscribed on cover and base commemorating various military events, 5-7/8" l. and 6-1/8" l. **$826**

Northeast Auctions, www.northeastauctions.com

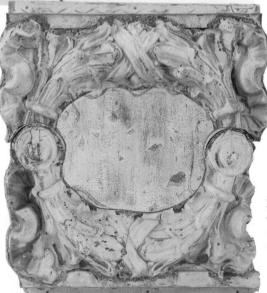

Architectural element, wreath form now fitted with mirror, copper with mint-green vere-de-gris surface, 36-1/4"h. x 35" l. **$720**

Northeast Auctions, www.northeastauctions.com

COUNTRY STORE

FEW CATEGORIES OF COLLECTIBLES are as fun and colorful as country store memorabilia. The staple of quality antiques shows and shops nationwide, the phrase often refers to such an expansive field of items that it's difficult to decide where "country store collectibles" begin and "advertising collectibles" end. However, that's one of the very reasons why the category remains so popular and one of the two reasons why this market is growing in value and appeal.

Country store collectibles are associated with items in use in general or frontier retail establishments dating from the mid-1800s and well into the 1940s. The country store was a natural evolution of the pioneer trading post as the more affordable source of day-to-day living items, baking and cooking supplies, or goods for general household and home garden use. Country store furniture is rare, but larger pieces usually include retail countertops and dry goods bins.

The appeal of country store memorabilia has never really waned during the last 40 years, however, the emergence of online trading in the late 1990s redefined items dealers once described as rare. Much like how mid-20th century rock and roll and entertainment memorabilia is used to decorate Applebee's Bar and Grill restaurants, so have country store collectibles been used to line the walls of Cracker Barrel Restaurant and Old Country Store establishments to evoke big appetites for comfort food.

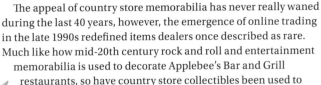

Country Store Meat Market sign, 30"h x 22". **$400**

Courtesy of Bright Star Antiques Co., www.brightstarantiques.com

Among items in high demand are original and complete store displays in top condition. These displays were originally intended to hold the product sold to customers and were not generally available for private ownership. Those that survive are highly sought after by collectors for their graphic appeal and their rarity. Until recently, restoration of these items would negatively impact auction prices. However, recent auction results show strong prices for these items if they are rare and retain most of the original graphics.

A great deal of time, talent, and production value was invested in these store displays. Think of them as the Super Bowl commercials of their day. With limited counter space and a captive audience, marketers used every technique and theme available to catch customers' eyes. And here is where the appeal of country store collectibles crosses over so many different categories of collectibles. A fine paper poster advertising DeLaval Cream Separators may appeal to those who collect farming items, cows and country maidens in addition to country store items. The same principle applies to store displays. Are they collected as country store items or as well-preserved examples of vintage advertising, or both?

This category was extremely popular between the late 1970s and the mid-1990s. It appears the hobby is reaching a point at which longtime collectors are ready to begin a new phase of their lives – one that requires fewer items and less space – and are offering these collections for the first time in decades. So if the old adage, "The best time to buy an antique is when you see it" is true, the country store collectibles category stands to grow as these large collections come to market and the crossover appeal catches the attention of a wide variety of collectors.

Counter cannisters, strong wear and oxidation with paint loss, Good-Very Good, each 12" l.................$30

Courtesy of Morphy Auctions, www.morphyauctions.com

Coffee bin, great graphics showing Uncle Sam smiling on the front, moderate soiling, dents, areas of paint loss and heavy rubs throughout, made by Norton Bros, Chicago, Good, 21" x 20-1/4" x 12-1/2".....$330

Courtesy of Morphy Auctions, www.morphyauctions.com

Coffee grinder, Enterprise Mfg. Co., painted cast iron, No. 7, vibrant painted surface, eagle finial, patriotic decals, 24" h. $500

Courtesy of Pook & Pook, pookandpook.com

Animal food bin, Wilbur Seed Meal Co.,
Milwaukee, advertising on top and four sides,
original label from Griep Bros., Syracuse, N.Y.,
16-1/4" x 36-1/4' x 19". **$3,000**

Courtesy of Showtime Auction Services, www.showtimeauctions.com

Blanke coffee bin, C.F. Blanke & Co., St. Louis,
excellent original condition, 21-1/2" x 33-1/2" x
16".. **$1,320**

Courtesy of Showtime Auction Services, www.showtimeauctions.com

Twelve-drawer pine cabinet, Maine, early 19th
century, with original barn red casein paint,
molded overhanging top, plank base, beveled-
edge drawers with half-spherical pocket interiors,
and possibly original stained pulls, very good
condition, 21" x 20-1/2" x 6-1/2". **$443**

Courtesy of Thomaston Place Auction Galleries, www.thomastonauction.com

Tin allspice store bin, Coburn & Co., New Haven,
Connecticut, circa 1890, 6-1/2" x 9-1/2"........ **$570**

Courtesy of Showtime Auction Services, www.showtimeauctions.com

George Washington cast iron string holder/dispenser, original paint, good condition. **$270**

Storage bin with three lift-top glass doors, 19th century, bootjack cutout base, old paint, 64" x 16" x 26" h................................**$1,560**

Oak post office made to sit atop store counter, circa 1910, with center postmaster's window with turned wooden bars and writing surface for customers, letter mail slot below, sliding paneled door above that was closed when post office was not open, case with cove-molded crown molding, flanked by glass windows with 24 individual mail addresses/cubbyholes for customers' mail with oak plates where name could be attached, all in original old varnish finish, 48" x 10" x 44" h.. .... **$605**

Figural Yankee Cigar countertop store advertisement, circa 1940, with red, white, and blue dancing majorette on wood base that reads "Waitt and Bond / Yankee Cigar – 5¢," signed Margit Nilsen, New York, craquelure, back end of baton missing, 16" h. **$615**

Curved glass and golden oak showcase, likely from F. E. Conrad's store at Fort Griffin, Texas, no accompanying documentation, excellent condition, 4' l x 2-1/2' h x 2' w. **$3,250**

Courtesy of Heritage Auctions, ha.com

Rare Borden's Ice Cream Elsie the Cow moving sculpture, circa 1936-1940s, original mercantile grocery store countertop advertising display, electrified, working, cow's mouth opens and closes, only moving kinetic sculpture known to exist, rubber outer layer with wear and cracking, 24-1/2" h x 16" d x 20" w. Elsie was the cartoon mascot for Borden Dairy Co.............................**$446**

Courtesy of North American Auction Co., www.northamericanauctioncompany.com

New York merchant's salt-glazed stoneware product jar, probably used to hold oysters or snuff, circa 1870-1880, approximately half-pint capacity, cylindrical form with slight shoulder and rounded mouth, Albany slip-glazed interior, lightly stamped "TODE BROS / 272 BOWERY / NEW YORK," stamped "TB" within circle under base, undamaged, some remnants of gold overpaint, 4-1/4" h, 2-7/8" dia. rim. **$192**

Courtesy of Jeffrey S. Evans & Associates, www.jeffreysevans.com

Softwood store pie cabinet with interior glass shelves, late 19th century, good condition with old surface, minor wear and losses, 30-1/2" h x 17" w x 17-3/4" d..**$206**

Courtesy of Conestoga Auction Co., www.contestogaauction.com

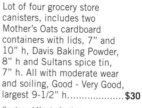

Lot of four grocery store canisters, includes two Mother's Oats cardboard containers with lids, 7" and 10" h, Davis Baking Powder, 8" h and Sultans spice tin, 7" h. All with moderate wear and soiling, Good - Very Good, largest 9-1/2" h.....................$30

Courtesy of Morphy Auctions, www.morphyauctions.com

Libby's cardboard country store play set, includes a large group of original store stock, housed in a custom Lucite case, 13-1/2" h, 17-1/2" w. $325

Courtesy of Pook & Pook, pookandpook.com

Advertising cash register on stand, 55-1/2" h, 21-1/4" x 18-3/4"..............................$250

Courtesy of Bright Star Antiques Co., www.brightstarantiques.com

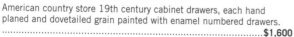

American country store 19th century cabinet drawers, each hand planed and dovetailed grain painted with enamel numbered drawers. $1,600

Courtesy of Bill Hood & Sons Art & Antique, hoodauction.com

Putnam Dyes wooden display cabinet, hinged front lid with a colorful cardboard insert of George Washington on horseback, inside lid and back are similar paper advertising signs, inside of the cabinet is divided into 24 compartments with the original labels, 21"w x 10"h x 8-1/2"d. $90

Courtesy of Rockabilly Auction Company, www.rockabillyauction.com

DISNEY

COLLECTIBLES FEATURING MICKEY Mouse, Donald Duck and other famous characters of cartoon icon Walt Disney are everywhere. They can be found with little effort at flea markets, garage sales, local antiques and toys shows, and online as well as through auction houses and specialty catalogs.

Of Disney toys, comics, posters and other items produced from the 1930s through the 1960s, look for the prewar Disney material which is by far the most desirable.

Good Housekeeping original painting of a scene in *Mickey's Magic Lamp* (Walt Disney, 1940). This unusual piece shows the story changes that could still occur up until a film's final release, as very little from this spread actually made it into the final film; the genie never even makes an appearance, and certainly never gets a bath. The entire title of the film was eventually changed to *Pluto's Dream House* and bears little resemblance to the spread in Good Housekeeping. (The magazine commissioned Disney to offer a monthly full-page preview of many of his upcoming shorts.) Featuring Mickey, Pluto, and the Genie, the painting appeared in the July 1940 issue. Framed and matted with glass front, 9" x 7". **$776**

Courtesy of Heritage Auctions, www.ha.com

Walt Disney Dopey tin litho walking wind-up toy, Marx, includes scarce original box marked "1938 Walt Disney Enterprises," toy itself has bright, clean litho, moving eyes, marked "Dopey" on hat, 8" h. **$325**

Courtesy of Dan Morphy Auctions, www.morphyauctions.com

Walt Disney tin litho Donald Duck duet toy, Marx, original figures' arms and drumsticks, ears on Goofy appear to be replacements, nice lithographed characters on base of duet, marked "Copyright 1946 Walt Disney Productions," 10-1/4" h. **$275**

Courtesy of Dan Morphy Auctions, www.morphyauctions.com

Tin Pluto wind-up, Marx, 1939, Walt Disney Productions, 8".. **$70**

Courtesy of American Antique Auctions, www.americanantiqueauctions.net

Marx tin lithograph wind-up Walt Disney's Donald Duck Duet with original box, 10" h, together with a Linemar tin lithograph wind-up Pluto trumpeter, 6-1/4" h. **$550**

Courtesy of Pook & Pook, www.pookandpook.com

Tin litho Ferdinand the Bull windup, Japanese, includes scarce original box marked "Walt Disney Productions" and "Linemar," toy has original flower and rubber horns and tail, difficult to find intact, marked "Walt Disney Productions," 5-1/4" x 3-1/2". **$200**

Courtesy of Dan Morphy Auctions, www.morphyauctions.com

► Walt Disney Mickey Mouse bobblehead, 1960. ....**$10**

Courtesy of Pioneer Auction Gallery, www.pioneerantiqueauction.com

Walt Disney Productions lollypop jar with Donald Duck, Mickey Mouse, and Ludwig Von Drake, 1961, says, "Lolly Pops for Good Little Boys and Girls," 7-3/4" h. **$60**

Courtesy of Mark Mattox Real Estate & Auctioneer, www.mattoxrealestate.com

Lot of two Fisher-Price paper-on-wood toys: Walt Disney Donald Duck Walker, marked "Walt Disney Productions," No. 765; and Pinky Pig, No. 695. Both made of wood and plastic with some general creasing and wear, largest is 8" h. **$25**

Courtesy of Dan Morphy Auctions, www.morphyauctions.com

Walt Disney talking tourist bus with original box, Japan, friction bus with battery-operated talking mechanism, original box, 13". **$350**

Courtesy of Milestone Auctions, www.milestoneauctions.com

Mickey Mouse children's toy ceramic tea set, Japan, circa 1935, 20 pieces comprising one teapot, one pitcher, five cups, six saucers, six plates, one covered sugar, polychrome designs of Mickey Mouse and Minnie with lustre, teapot marked "[MICKEY MOUSE] / COPR. BY / WALT E. DISNEY / MADE IN JAPAN" and other pieces marked "MADE IN / JAPAN," teapot 3-1/2" h. **$225**

Courtesy of Jeffrey S. Evans & Associates, www.jeffreyevans.com

Disney *Fantasia* fairy bowl, Vernon Kilns, 1940, console bowl #122 with fairy and flowers motif, well-marked on base, 2-1/4" h x 12-1/4". ... **$100**

Courtesy of Burchard Galleries Inc., www.burchardgalleries.com

▶ Lot of two: Seven Dwarfs soap set and Three Little Pigs ashtray. Walt Disney Seven Dwarfs snap-apart soap by Ben Rickert, new in box; ashtray marked "Walt Disney, Made in Japan," circa 1950s, 3-3/4" l... **$25**

Courtesy of Dan Morphy Auctions, www.morphyauctions.com

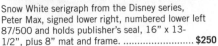

Snow White serigraph from the Disney series, Peter Max, signed lower right, numbered lower left 87/500 and holds publisher's seal, 16" x 13-1/2", plus 8" mat and frame. **$250**

Courtesy of Antiques & Modern Auction Gallery, www.antiquesmodern.com

Lady and the Tramp cartoon cel featuring the Siamese cats Si and Am, 1960s, matted in Walt Disney Classics cardboard frame with the Walt Disney Classics Disneyland label on back, 12" x 14", cel is 7-1/2" x 9-1/2"............................. **$350**

Courtesy of Burchard Galleries Inc., www.burchardgalleries.com

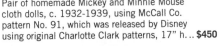

Pair of homemade Mickey and Minnie Mouse cloth dolls, c. 1932-1939, using McCall Co. pattern No. 91, which was released by Disney using original Charlotte Clark patterns, 17" h... **$450**

Courtesy of Pook & Pook, www.pookandpook.com

Disney Production drawing, "Donald's Golf Game," 1938. Preliminary pencil art for cartoon released in 1938, showing Donald addressing the ball, unknown animation artist on animation sheet, not removed from frame, graphite cartoon concept, framed to 18" x 15-1/4"................... **$275**

Courtesy of Phoebus Auction Gallery, www.phoebusauction.com

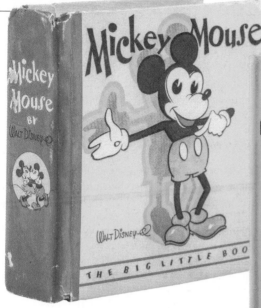

Walt Disney first edition Mickey Mouse, Whitman Publishing Co., Racine, WI, 1933; 316, [2] pp, nearly every other page illustrated, original pictorial boards, skinny Mickey on front, facsimile Disney signature, 10-1/2" x 8-1/2". **$350**

Courtesy of PBA Galleries, www.pbagalleries.com

Walt Disney first edition Donald Duck, Grosset & Dunlap, New York, 1936. First hardcover Donald Duck book, scarce in jacket, illustrations in color and black and white throughout by the staff of the Walt Disney Studios, original pictorial boards, pictorial dust jacket. **$425**

Courtesy of PBA Galleries, www.pbagalleries.com

Disney Studios The 'Pop-Up' Minnie Mouse, Blue Ribbon Books, New York, 1933, illustrated with three full-color, double-page pop-ups (two of which are on the endpapers) plus other illustrations by the staff of the Walt Disney Studios, original color pictorial boards, all complete and functioning, 9-1/2" x 7-1/4"..**$325**

Courtesy of PBA Galleries, www.pbagalleries.com

DOORSTOPS

DOORSTOPS

DOORSTOPS HAVE BEEN around as long as there have been doors. They were originally improvised from garden stones, wedges of wood, pieces of furniture, or any other objects heavy enough to prop doors open to ensure air circulation. Early decorative ones, which date from the late 1700s, were generally round and made of sand-cast brass or metal with flat, hollow backs.

By the early 19th century, scores of French and English households boasted fashionable three-dimensional iron doorstops in the shape of animals, flowers, and figurines. Some, called door porters, incorporated convenient long handles that were used to lift and place them easily.

Homes with French double doors often featured matching pairs, like matching eagles or horse hooves, Punch and Judy, or lions opposing unicorns. Today these sets range from $400-$900 each, depending on condition and themes.

Doorstops migrated to American shores after the Civil War, where due to Yankee frugality, they became smaller and lighter than European models.

During the height of their popularity – the 1920s through the mid-1940s – American homemakers could purchase doorstops, or coordinated sets that included doorknockers and bookends, for pennies in gift stores and through mail-order catalogs.

Fashionable Art Deco, circus, and nursery rhyme themes, along with figures like organ grinders, dapper gentlemen, Southern belles and flappers, reflected the times.

Cheery flower and flower-basket doorstops featuring bouquets of tulips, zinnias, pansies, black-eyed Susans or sunflowers, for example, celebrated the arrival of spring. Although some currently start at around $100 apiece, those that have survived with original paint in prime condition may fetch many times that amount.

Hubley's dog breed doorstops, which portray lifelike, highly detailed Doberman pinschers, German shepherds, cocker spaniels, French bulldogs, beagles and various types of terriers, and more, were also extremely popular. So were arched, curled, springing, or sleeping cats.

John and Nancy Smith, avid collectors and leading doorstop and figural cast iron authorities, as well as authors of *The Doorstop Book: An Encyclopedia of Doorstop Collecting*, find that beginners generally concentrate on certain themes like flowers, animals, people, or wildlife. Some seek doorstops produced by a particular foundry, including Albany, National, Eastern Specialty, Judd, Wilton, Litto, Virginia Metalcrafters, Waverly, or Spencer.

As their collections grow, however, many explore other themes as well. Nautical enthusiasts may collect clipper ship, sailor, lighthouse, and anchor doorstops. Sports fans may seek skiers, golfers, caddies, or football players. Animal lovers may populate menageries with Hubley honey bears and horses or Bradley & Hubbard parrots.

Cast iron Humpty Dumpty, numbered "661," from popular children's nursery rhyme, depicts Humpty Dumpty sitting on stonewall, 4-1/2" h......................................**$854**

Courtesy of Morphy Auctions, www.morphyauctions.com

VISIT WWW.ANTIQUETRADER.COM

WWW.FACEBOOK.COM/ANTIQUETRADER

Some prefer pets portrayed in character, like rabbits in evening dress, Peter Rabbits chomping on carrots, and strutting ducks in tophats. These fancies currently sell from $300-$2,000.

Other collectors search for bright, sassy, desirable and pricey Anne Fish Art Deco pieces like bathing beauties, Charleston dancers, and parrot, or Taylor Cook's brightly colored elephant on barrels, koalas, or fawns.

"In addition to their beauty," observes Lewis Keister, proprietor of East Meets West Antiques based in Los Angeles, "the historical value of many of these doorstops can be significant. One highly desirable doorstop, the yellow-slickered Old Salt fisherman, for example, is very appealing to both antique collectors and folk art collectors." So are the nostalgic, mellow-hued stagecoach, Conestoga wagon, Aunt Jemima, Victorian lady, fruit basket, horns of plenty, and cozy, rose-covered cottage doorstops. Even when doorstops outnumber doors, home decorators, charmed by their appeal, often display them as colorful accent pieces, bookends, or works of art lined up in custom-built shelving, antique cupboards, or along staircases.

Cast iron elephant, c. 1920, 8" h. $420

Courtesy of Copake Auction, Inc., www.copakeauction.com

Doorstops that feature outstanding sculptural quality, form and character are the most desirable of all. If they also bear identifying stamps, signatures, copyrights, studio names or production numbers (which often appear on their backs), their values rise even further.

In addition to desirability, rarity – possibly due to high production costs, short foundry existence, or even bad design – raises the value of vintage doorstops. Condition, however, determines their ultimate worth. Collectors should certainly buy doorstops that they like within a price range that they find comfortable. But they should be in the very best condition that they can afford. According to experts, only these will retain or increase in value over time. And some may increase considerably.

Today, for example, a rare, unusual, desirable doorstop that is also in mint condition – perhaps a vintage Uncle Sam, Halloween Girl, or Whistling Jim, may command as much as $10,000.

Because doorstops are cast objects, however, caution the Smiths, they lend themselves to reproduction. In addition to reuse of old molds, new designs are continually in production. "Older doorstops usually have smoother, more refined castings than reproductions, which are rougher or pebbly. Seams, if any, are usually tighter. Originals feature slotted screws or rivets, while reproductions, if cast in two or more pieces, are usually assembled with Philips-head screws. Moreover, artists generally painstakingly smoothed mold marks of vintage castings with hand files. Reproductions, however, are finished in minutes with power tools and tumblers. These leave coarser grinding marks."

Collectors should also look carefully at the wear patterns on possible buys. Most old doorstops were used for their original purpose – holding doors open. So potential buyers are advised to look for wear in the logical places: on their tops, where they were handled, and around their bases, where they were scuffed along the floor. Reproductions rarely resemble the real thing.

By studying as many collections as possible – by actually handling as many doorstops as possible, beginners can learn to differentiate between vintage pieces and reproductions.

Doorstops are readily found at antique shows, shops, and auctions. It is recommended, however, to purchase them from reputable dealers who not only specialize in cast iron items, but also guarantee their authenticity.

– Melody Amsel-Arieli

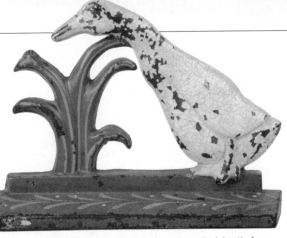

Cast iron duck and beetle doorstop, duck ready to pluck beetle from reeds, 10-1/2" l. **$125**

Courtesy of Morphy Auctions, morphyauctions.com

Hubley cast iron owl on a stump, flat backed, nickel plated, 5-1/4" x 10-1/4"..... **$264**

Courtesy of Showtime Auction Services, www.showtimeauctions.com

Cast iron peacock, Albany Foundry Co., 6-1/2" h. **$188**

Courtesy of Morphy Auctions, morphyauctions.com

Vintage Hubley painted iron three-geese doorstop, 8" h. **$211**

Courtesy of William J. Jenack Estate Appraisers & Auctioneers, www.jenack.com

Cast iron turkey, made by Davison, large casting well detailed with ruffled feathers and tail fanned outward, concave back, 12-1/2" h................ **$1,107**

Courtesy of Morphy Auctions, www.morphyauctions.com

top lot !

A Salem Witch doorstop was the top lot of doorstops sold during a November 2016 mixed-item auction at Bertoia Auctions. The doorstop, 1692 © Sarah W. Symonds, portrays a woman sweeping with a black cat at her feet, great casting effects and bold colors, and is 9-3/4" h. In excellent to pristine condition, the doorstop is very desirable and rare. Estimated at between $1,200 to $1,800, it sold at auction for $5,866.

COURTESY OF BERTOIA AUCTIONS, WWW.BERTOIAAUCTIONS.COM

Cast iron cat, c. 1920, 8-1/2" h. **$210**

Courtesy of Copake Auction, Inc., www.copakeauction.com

Cast iron black cat licking paw, marked: Copyright 1926 Waverly Studio Wilmette, Ill., 7-5/8" h. .. **$413**

Courtesy of Vero Beach Auction, www.verobeachauction.com

Cast iron crying pup dog, numbered "662," sad pup crying with paw up and patch over right eye, 7-1/2" h. **$438**

Courtesy of Morphy Auctions, www.morphyauctions.com

Cast iron Japanese Spaniel, C.J.O. Judd Mfg. Co. New Britain, Conn., flat backed, most original paint intact, 5" x 9-1/8". **$330**

Courtesy of Showtime Auction Services, www.showtimeauctions.com

Figural rabbit in sweater eating cabbage, cast iron, flat back, original paint, Albany Foundry Co., Albany, NY, second quarter 20th century, 8" h, 4-3/4" w. **$459**

Courtesy of Jeffrey S. Evans & Associates, www.jeffreysevans.com

Cast iron penguin, signed, "No 1, © 1930, Taylor Cook," 9-1/2" h. **$281**

Courtesy of Morphy Auctions, morphyauctions.com

Cast iron police boy, depicts boy wearing police hat and diapers with pacifier in mouth, companion dog sitting at his side, 10-3/4" h. **$1,230**

Courtesy of Morphy Auctions, www.morphyauctions.com

Casting of lobster half emerged from base, colored red overall, great cashing effects, very desirable, 12-1/2" h. **$3,088**

Courtesy of Bertoia Auctions, www.bertoiaauctions.com

Hubley cast iron poppies in clay pot, flat backed, most original paint intact, 6" x 7". **$60**

Courtesy of Showtime Auction Services, www.showtimeauctions.com

Cast iron black man "Chicken Snatcher," whimsical depiction of black man sneaking away with chicken under his coat, great cross collectible of black Americana and black memorabilia, extremely rare, 7-1/4" h. **$984**

Courtesy of Morphy Auctions, www.morphyauctions.com

Cast iron Little Red Riding Hood, Albany Foundry Co. **$219**

Courtesy of Morphy Auctions, www.morphyauctions.com

Cast iron pilgrim boy, made by Judd Co., double-sided doorstop, painted in realistic colors, 8-1/2" h. **$123**

Courtesy of Morphy Auctions, www.morphyauctions.com

Cast iron figural warrior, flat back, marked "B & H / 7795" to reverse, original paint, Bradley & Hubbard Manufacturing Co., Meridan, CT, first half 20th century, 12-3/4" h, 7" w. **$459**

Courtesy of Jeffrey S. Evans & Associates, www.jeffreysevans.com

Cast iron Capt. Erie standing in boat, rare variation with short oar, early repaint, 6-1/2" h. **$122**

Courtesy of Morphy Auctions, www.morphyauctions.com

Cast iron tulips, signed "Tulips (logo) Copr. 1929," Connecticut Foundry mark, "C" in triangle in circle, 6-3/4" h..$156

Courtesy of Morphy Auctions, morphyauctions.com

Cast iron yellow finch with rose trellis, Judd Company, numbered "1259," variation with bird, more difficult to find, 6-1/2" h........................$250

Courtesy of Morphy Auctions, morphyauctions.com

Cast iron Mammy, Hubley Foundry, Lancaster, Pennsylvania, 9" h. $330

Courtesy of Copake Auction, Inc., www.copakeauction.com

ENTERTAINMENT

THE SECRET IS OUT. Entertainment and movie props are big business in Hollywood.

Studios are doing a better job at controlling their props from big-budget films. Props are now being sold by the studio itself or through small companies owned by the studio. It has turned the entertainment collecting world on its head as quality material gets more difficult to find for traditional brick and mortar dealers and auctioneers.

By cutting out the middleman, studios can make a healthy profit on expenses they write off to produce a feature or a program. This trend shows the market for entertainment and movie props is stronger than ever and will continue to grow in the future.

According to Julien's Auctions, one of the world's largest auctioneers of entertainment and film props, the market has been growing steadily for the last three decades. "In the past 35 years, the Entertainment Memorabilia auction market has gradually emerged to become an important and unequivocal collecting category," according to the company.

Collectors can pinpoint the exact year entertainment prop collecting became a mainstream collecting category. The seminal MGM Studios auction in 1970 was a watershed moment for film scholars and the auction business, which essentiality created a new market for an area of collecting that previously only existed among a few film enthusiasts. The studio's objective was to simply consolidate space on an already overcrowded lot by creating a three-day film memorabilia auction to clear seven soundstages. A vast assortment of costumes, film props and related property from the studios beginnings dating from the 1920s were cataloged, tagged and placed on the auction block.

Highlights recall the full size sailing ship from *Mutiny on the Bounty* (1935), Elizabeth Taylor's wedding gown worn in *Father of the Bride* (1950), Clark Gable's trench coat worn in several films, a group of swimsuits worn by Esther Williams and Johnny Weissmuller's loin cloth worn in *Tarzan* films of the 1940s. However, the most coveted pieces sold were from *The Wizard of Oz* (1939) which included a pair of ruby red slippers worn by Judy Garland that hammered on the auction block for $15,000 ($94,252 in today's dollars).

"With the auction's blockbuster success, film enthusiasts and collectors soon recognized film memorabilia as a fertile and profitable area of collecting. In the following years, small boutique shops, specialty companies and private brokering businesses began to crop up and thrive selling recognized film props and screen-seen objects," according to Julien.

Since then, studios have recognized and embraced this booming market on their own.

HARRY POTTER

Despite the unabated demand for all things relating to Harry Potter, there exist very little Harry Potter film props available to the public, making that material that is available all the more valuable. The challenge with collecting Harry Potter prop items is that Warner Brothers have only ever officially released a very limited amount of them from the production. Those that have been release are mainly paper – but that paper is very valuable, indeed.

Every single prop and item used in the making of the films was numbered, checked in and checked out. When filming was completed, all of the props were carefully packed into 104 containers full of props and set dressings which are still being carefully archived and accounted for, says properties master Barry Wilkinson told The Los Angeles Times.

Wilkinson was the properties master, overseeing a team of dozens of staffers, who either searched for or manufactured every item used in the film. From the spoons used in The Great Hall in Hogwarts Castle to each magical cup, bottles, keys and even the books in Dumbledore's sanctum, the properties team is responsible for keeping track of each item.

BREAKING BAD AUCTION

Another good example of obtaining entertainment props is through a company called ScreenBid. This company assists studios with liquidating props, costumes and even iconic vehicles relating to various productions. An auction held to sell off props from the Emmy-winning AMC television show *Breaking Bad*, ScreenBid launched a publicity campaign around key pieces from the show's storyline.

Main character Walter White (played by Brian Cranston) single pair of underwear sold for $9,900 and a simple whiskey glass used by Cranston sold for an eye-popping $2,900. Similar auctions have been held for *Mad Men*, *Justified*, *True Blood* and *Sons of Anarchy*.

Like the MGM auction, the *Breaking Bad* sale changed the market for entertainment memorabilia. Now auctions are held for television productions still being produced and a digital storefront has opened where fans can spend no less than $500 to own a screen-used item from their favorite show.

The development has opened a world of wonderful and positive sources to the collector. Obtaining the props directly from the studios gives pieces strong provenance and allows the buyer to pay according to their budget, rather than compete with other collectors in a high-stakes auction.

One thing is for certain, the market for mid-range and high-value entertainment memorabilia and props will continue to grow as movie production studios and smaller producers, such as Netflix and Amazon, continue creating captivating content.

Television prop, CBS Television, *I Love Lucy*, 1951-1957, made of Styrofoam and fiberglass, painted gray to simulate concrete, with text reading "John Wayne" used in the first and second episodes of Season 5 - titled "Lucy Visits Grauman's" and "Lucy & John Wayne," original air dates October 3 and 10, 1955 - when Lucy steals the Duke's footprints from Grauman's Chinese Theatre, 24" x 36"........**$22,500**

top lot

Stallone's Jacket Is A Knockout

Long before Sylvester Stallone hit it big as Rocky Balboa he was just a regular with a dream – and a pretty cool leather jacket.

"I remember when I bought this jacket in Philadelphia. It was obviously quite a few years before I ever even thought about *Rocky*, before *Rocky* was even an idea," Stallone said of his now famous jacket. "This is what I would wear in my everyday life. And when the time came to do the movie, we didn't have a budget where we could afford an original wardrobe so I thought, Why don't I just wear the things that I think Rocky would wear, clothes from my real life?"

The jacket, which Stallone wore throughout *Rocky*, the surprise movie hit from 1976 that launched a movie franchise and Stallone's superstar career, sold at auction for **$149,000**. The leather jacket and other movie memorabilia from Stallone's career earned more than $3 million during a three-day sale in Los Angeles by Heritage Auctions. The auction featured 600 one-of-a-kind costumes, movie props, scripts, documents and other items from the actor-director's storied career.

IMAGES COURTESY HERITAGE AUCTIONS, WWW.HA.COM

His whole life was a million-to-one shot.

ROCKY

ROBERT CHARTOFF · IRWIN WINKLER · JOHN G. AVILDSEN · SYLVESTER STALLONE "ROCKY"
ALSO STARRING TALIA SHIRE · BURT YOUNG · CARL WEATHERS AND BURGESS MEREDITH · WRITTEN BY SYLVESTER STALLONE
PRODUCED BY IRWIN WINKLER AND ROBERT CHARTOFF · DIRECTED BY JOHN G. AVILDSEN · EXECUTIVE PRODUCER GENE KIRKWOOD · MUSIC BY BILL CONTI

United Artists
A Transamerica Company

Movie Prop, *Deadpool*, Sony Pictures, 2016, from the hit film Deadpool, actor Ryan Reynolds' screen-used sword, seen in the opening sequences of the movie, made of silver foam, 38" l. **$1,400**

PremiereProps, www.premiereprops.com

Movie costume, *Immortals*, Relativity Media, 2011, bloody-appearing costume with silver plastic chest plate with leather ties and samurai shoulders worn by actor Henry Cavill. .... **$1,500-$2,000**

PremiereProps, www.premiereprops.com

Television prop, Filmation, 1969, props from the original *Star Trek* series episode titled "The Trouble With Tribbles" featuring the character Cyrano Jones. **$956**

Heritage Auctions, www.HA.com

Movie costume, *Capote*, United Artists, 2005, screen-worn, charcoal grey Brooks Brothers cable-knit cardigan wool sweater and scarf worn by Philip Seymour Hoffman in the film. **$150**

PremiereProps, www.premiereprops.com

Maquette, *Freddy vs. Jason*, New Line Cinema, 2003, paint test marquette (pre-production model) created by the legendary make-up artist Dave Miller prior to the film, 21" h. x 16-1/2" w. **$700**

PremiereProps, www.premiereprops.com

365

Movie prop,
Endoskeleton Arm,
TriStar Pictures, 1991,
from *Terminator 2: Judgement Day*, steel and chrome appendage
is almost fully articulated and
highly detailed, accompanied by an
LOA from special effects expert Len E.
Burge II, who worked on the design and
construction of props for the movie.
.... **$10,755**

Heritage Auctions, www.ha.com

Movie costume, *Alpha Dog*, 2006,
SS Sage Hawaiian print button-
front shirt and pants worn by
singer-actor Justin Timberlake as
"Frankie" in the film.
.............................**$800-$1,200**

PremiereProps, www.premiereprops.com

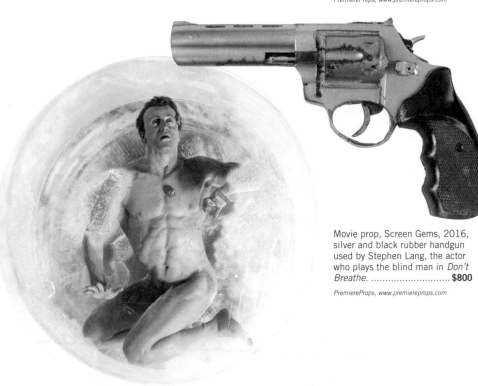

Movie prop, Screen Gems, 2016,
silver and black rubber handgun
used by Stephen Lang, the actor
who plays the blind man in *Don't Breathe*. **$800**

PremiereProps, www.premiereprops.com

Movie Prop, *Demolition Man*, Warner Bros., 1993, round acrylic chamber with mirror base and acrylic
lid that has been etched and painted to simulate frozen liquid; together with a prop figure of the movie
character John Spartan (played by Sylvester Stallone) who is put into suspended animation in the opening
sequence of the film, 55 1/2" dia. x 21" from the personal collection of Sylvester Stallone. **$9,010**

Heritage Auctions, www.hacom

Maquette, *Gremlins 2: The New Batch*, Amblin Entertainment, 1990, by make-up effects artist Rick Baker, pre-production model used for the film, 9" w x 10 1/2" t. **$250**

PremiereProps, www.premiereprops.com

Movie costume, signature evil queen dresses worn by Julia Roberts as the *Evil Queen*, designed by the late Oscar-winning costume designer Eiko Ishioka. **$10,500**

PremiereProps, www.premiereprops.com

Movie costume, Funny Girl, Columbia Pictures, 1968, screen-worn pink and silver detailed jacket from the 1968 movie starring Barbra Streisand. .... **$1,000-$1,500**

PremiereProps, www.premiereprops.com

Movie prop, The Specialist, Warner Bros., 1994, seven sticks, all red, each stamped "Dynamite" on the sides, bound together with black duct tape, prop "Evidence" label taped to front; used in the film with Sylvester Stallone as Ray Quick and Sharon Stone as May Munro, 9" l. **$1,500**

Heritage Auctions, www.HA.com

Movie prop, *Underworld: Rise of the Lycans*, Screen Gems, 2009, screen-used brown wood werewolf crossbow with three bows and three arrows, 26 ½ inches long. **$350**

PremiereProps, www.premiereprops.com

Photograph, *The Ten Commandments*, Paramount Pictures, 1956, original test exposure proof photograph from the 1955 hit movie, showing Yul Brenner and Anne Baxter, ...**$200**

PremiereProps, www.premiereprops.com

Movie Prop, *Rocky* and *Rocky II*, United Artists, 1976 and 1979, black rubber handball side stamped with blue text reading "Official / Seamless / 555;" kept by Stallone as "Rocky Balboa" in his pocket in many memorable scenes throughout both films. From the personal collection of Sylvester Stallone, ...**$32,500**

FARM COLLECTIBLES

THE HOBBY OF collecting farm tools and other farming items continues to remain bright, with prices still solid.

"Farm tools are definitely hot," according to Richard Backus, editor in chief of Farm Collector, a monthly magazine spanning small engines, tractors, and hand tools. One of the magazine's most popular articles is "Ten Agricultural Inventions that Changed the Face of Farming in America." It mirrors some of the most popularly collected tools and drives home the relevance of the hobby – without farm tools the United States would not be the prosperous country we know and love today (warts and all).

Rich Penn, CEO of Rich Penn Auctions, echoes that sentiment for farming collectibles in general. In spring 2016, the auction house held a three-day auction in Iowa of items in the late Fred Schwartz collection, which included hundreds of farming-related collectibles that saw sizzling sales.

"I don't think we've ever had an auction with this many ag-related items. I guess being in Iowa it was a natural, but bidders came from far beyond Iowa. Farming collectables are very hot today," Penn told Antiques & Auction News.

Included in the auctions were several hundred signs in porcelain, metal and wood. The top lot was an 80-inch high two-piece porcelain globe sign of the J. I. Case Eagle. In excellent condition, the sign soared to a winning bid of $10,500, according to Antiques & Auction News.

Weathervanes and other signs were also among the highlights at the auction. The top vane featured a standing mule and sold for $6,000; a zinc cow standing on an arrow sold for $4,750, even with bullet holes and damage to the arrow; other vanes with sheep and horse figures sold for more than $3,000; a 96-inch high die-cut metal sign of an ear of corn advertising Pioneer corn had a winning bid of $2,900; and two wooden bins for Wilbur's Seed Meal, in original mustard paint and great stenciling, brought $2,500 and $2,400.

Perhaps because of the recent farm-to-table food movement and a growing interest in early Americana, harvest items have become popular with collectors. John Lynch, owner of Rusty Gold Antiques and Flea Market in Conway, Ark., said he's noticed an uptick in demand for harvest tools and canning jars. "Anything vintage kitchen or farmhouse style is popular," said Lynch. "We sell butter molds, churns, apple peelers, and cider presses. As far as I know, nobody is actually using them—it's more for décor."

Prices range from $15 to $35 for the smaller tools, while larger items like cider presses can sell for $100 or more, depending on condition and rarity.

"A lot of tool collectors like the mechanical aspect of the fruit peelers and presses," Lynch said. "We also get lots of old round-rung barn ladders, which are very popular, and sell for about $5 a rung." Primitive hayforks and rakes also sell well for Lynch at around $25 to $30 each.

Farm equipment sign, J. I. Case Eagle on Globe, multi-colored diecut porcelain, 80" h x 33" w. **$10,500**

Courtesy of Rich Penn Auctions, www.richpennauctions.com

VISIT WWW.ANTIQUETRADER.COM

WWW.FACEBOOK.COM/ANTIQUETRADER

Three stoneware fruit jars with paper labels, Lutz & Schram Co. Apple Butter, Standard Quality Blackberry Jelly, and Heinz Peach Butter, 8-1/4" h. **$300**

Courtesy of Rich Penn Auctions, www.richpennauctions.com

Oak Meadow Brook cart, split seat, rear entry, tool box, whip holder, dash board, 50" wheels **$450**

Courtesy of A-OK Auction Company, www.aokauctioncompany.com

Child's wheelbarrow, made by the S.A. Smith Mfg. Co.-Brattleboro, VT, USA stamped on bottom, ash with original surface and stenciling, wood spoke wheels, 13" h x 39" l x 12" w. **$300**

Courtesy of Rich Penn Auctions, www.richpennauctions.com

Harness maker's trade sign, Johnson Halter horse head, painted papier-mâché with raised advertising on both sides, 22" h x 8" w x 21" d............................ **$700**

Courtesy of Rich Penn Auctions, www.richpennauctions.com

Vintage farming plow, wood and metal.................................. **$30**

Courtesy of Auctions by Adkins, LLC, auctionsbyadkins.com

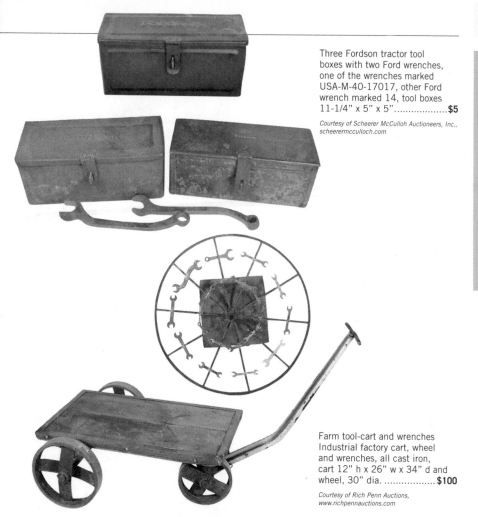

Three Fordson tractor tool boxes with two Ford wrenches, one of the wrenches marked USA-M-40-17017, other Ford wrench marked 14, tool boxes 11-1/4" x 5" x 5"..................**$5**

Courtesy of Scheerer McCulloh Auctioneers, Inc., scheerermcculloch.com

Farm tool-cart and wrenches Industrial factory cart, wheel and wrenches, all cast iron, cart 12" h x 26" w x 34" d and wheel, 30" dia. **$100**

Courtesy of Rich Penn Auctions, www.richpennauctions.com

Blue Mason jars are in high demand at the moment. "They're as hot as anything right now, and I can hardly keep them in stock," Lynch said. "We try to price them reasonably. I sell the pints and quarts for $7 and the bigger ones for $14, but other dealers sell them for more like $20 each." Like the harvest tools, Lynch believes collectors are using the jars for decorative purposes rather than canning. "I have one dealer who buys them in bulk," he said. "I think they're often used at weddings."

Backus compares the tool-making farmers of the 18th and 19th centuries to the fast-moving tech moguls behind the 1990s dot com boom and today's digital apps. Like today's iPhone app developer, a 19th century farmer who might be handy with a forge labored to invent a time-saving tool for himself and one that could possibly be marketed and make his family wealthy. Farm toolmakers were, in a sense, the original hackers. "They were very much the same," Backus said. "These tools revolutionized life and a farmer could double or quadruple his productivity. He could set up an engine to take care of a chore and run off and do something else."

American farm tool production occurred primarily on a small scale until the Industrial Revolution. Literally thousands of different manufacturers came and went until the late 1920s, Backus said, all of them vying for a slice of the growing and lucrative agricultural machinery market.

Burl domestic tool, 1797,
dated and initialed, likely used
for laundering, 30-3/4" l. **$338**

Courtesy of Skinner, Inc., skinnerinc.com

Antique Davis swing butter churn, pat 1879,
original paint and stenciling, made by the
Vermont Farm Machine Co in Belows Falls,
Vermont, last patent date is September 1879,
47" x 42"...**$140**

Courtesy of Milestone Auctions, www.milestoneauctions.com

COUPLE HAS BOUNTY OF TOOLS, HARVEST ITEMS

Editor's note: This is an excerpt from the cover story, "A Bountiful Gathering," by
Jessica Leigh Brown from *Antique Trader Magazine*.

Jim and Phyllis Moffet of Modesto, Ill., have one of the largest collections of farm
tools in the country. Tools related to corn harvesting and processing are their main
focus—Jim has published a book on corn shellers—but they also have a wide range
of fruit-related harvest items. "We have apple pickers, orchard ladders, and baskets,"
says Phyllis. "We have some antique baskets that were actually designed to create
store displays. You laid the apples you were going to show on the top into this tray,
filled it with apples over what you'd laid out, and then turned the basket over and you
have your basket with a nice looking pattern of fruit on top."

Jim describes the antique fruit pickers as having long handles so they could be used
from the ground level. "You could stand on the ground and reach up and pull off the
apples, oranges, or whatever fruit you were after," he says. "Some had sacks attached,
and the apples would roll down into the sack."

The Moffets have a range of fruit processing equipment in their collection, including
between 70 and 80 types of apple peelers. "We have apple peelers that will also chop the
fruit up into little chunks to help it dry quickly," says Jim. "The point of the early tools
was to reduce the apple down to where it will dry."

They also have a large collection of canning jars, including early stoneware. "You
couldn't see what was inside of them, and they were sealed with wax, predating
the later zinc lids," says Jim. "They had a tin lid that you poured the paraffin

Hog oiler, football style, cast iron, 18" h x 23" w x 14-1/2" d. $150

Courtesy of Rich Penn Auctions, www.richpennauctions.com

Unusual wooden butter churn, 19th century, 39" h, 25" w, 8-1/2" d. $180

Courtesy of Turkey Creek Auctions, www.antiqueauctionsfl.com

Antique John Deere corn husker, original paint remnants in green and yellow. $125

Courtesy of California Auctioneers, www.californiaauctioneers.com

wax over and then used a letter stamp to label the jar."

The Moffets appreciate the ease of searching online auction sites for specific items, but also stress their love of a good auction. "Visit an auction where they're selling out an estate, and it could be your best bet for obtaining some of these items," Jim says. "Also, we belong to several organizations related to collecting, including KOOKS (Kollectors of Old Kitchen Stuff) and the Mid-West Tool Collectors Association," adds Phyllis. "At their meetings, they usually have swapping or room sales where you can buy what someone else has bought for resale or gotten tired of. Collectors always dream of finding that one item they've been wanting for a low price, and sometimes it happens." said. "Farms had all these different implements and each one required special tools. And possibilities existed to create an accessory for it to make it work differently or even make it better than its original purpose. Without hesitation, there are a lot of one-of-a-kind items to be collected."

Most of these inventions were agricultural hand tools, and this is the category that dominates the antique farm tool hobby today. As small-town garages or commercial shops pushed for new ways to make more with less, countless tools were developed with ingenious uses. One of the most popular features in Backus' magazine is its "Mystery Farm Tools" column, in which subscribers submit photos of attic finds and barn thingamajigs hoping someone out there can explain its original use.

Farming collectors can easily spend their entire lives finding unique discoveries on a regular basis.

Resources: Farm Collector is a monthly magazine dedicated to the preservation of antique farm equipment. To subscribe, visit FarmCollector.com or call 866-624-9388.

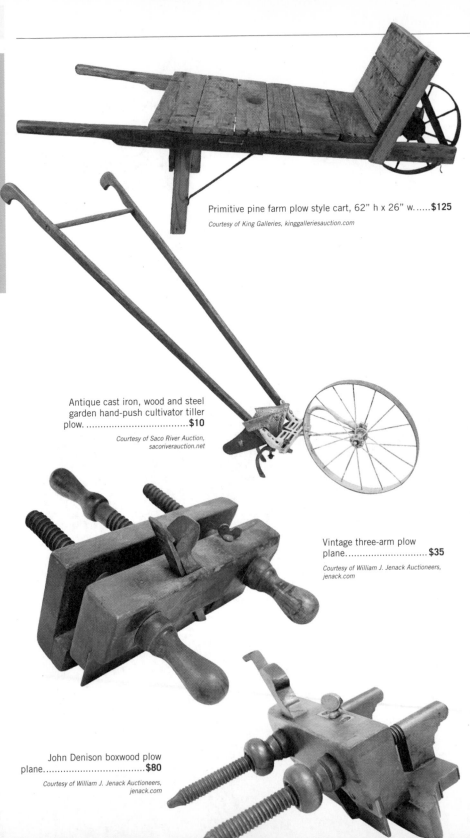

Primitive pine farm plow style cart, 62" h x 26" w......**$125**

Courtesy of King Galleries, kinggalleriesauction.com

Antique cast iron, wood and steel garden hand-push cultivator tiller plow. **$10**

Courtesy of Saco River Auction, sacoriverauction.net

Vintage three-arm plow plane.............................**$35**

Courtesy of William J. Jenack Auctioneers, jenack.com

John Denison boxwood plow plane......................................**$80**

Courtesy of William J. Jenack Auctioneers, jenack.com

FINE ART

ACCORDING TO THE 2016 TEFAF ART MARKET REPORT by Art Economics, sales of art globally were down 7 percent to $63.8 billion in 2015, compared to $68.2 billion in 2014. The amount of art transactions also decreased to 38.1 million, a 2 percent contraction. This will come as little surprise to anyone who has been watching headlines in recent months—in the art press, the pervading narrative has been one of a slowdown in the art market. But experts say collectors should take pause because cyclical contractions are natural, even healthy, for both the global economy and the art market alike.

Besides, the U.S. market bucked the trend, growing by 4 percent and establishing an even more dominant position on the global market. Some $27.3 billion worth of art was sold in the U.S. last year, a 4 percent increase over 2014. That is a smaller increase than the 10 percent year-over-year growth that was recorded from 2013 to 2014, but amid a landscape in which sales in every other major market center declined, the U.S. market is arguably at its most dominant global position in history.

Rich Americans are pouring new profits into modern and post-war and contemporary art with absolutely no end in sight, according to the annual TEFAF Art Market Report.

Online sales are also a leading driver of fine art sale, which may surprise some, but collectors and dealers are comfortable making purchases with only a website between them. This segment is expected to grow a whopping 25 percent per year and is estimated to reach $10 billion in five years.

Although multi-million dollar auction records tend to capture the most headlines, the market is seeing more art in general sold and at faster rates, and the market is currently growing by six percent a year, according to Arts Economics' annual report.

Duchess Olga Alexandrovna (1882-1960), "The Most Ground, Spring," oil on board, signed lower right, 16" x 20"; framed: 20-1/2" x 24-1/2".. **$1,500**

Courtesy of A.H. Wilkens Auctions & Appraisals, ahwilkens.com

These customers are much more selective about what they buy. So as condition sets the market for collectibles, the best examples of an artist's work influences prices. An artist's key works continue to bring the best prices as collectors remain mindful of both aesthetics and resale.

Collectors are looking for established names such as Andy Warhol, Roy Lichtenstein, Jasper

Johns, Robert Rauschenberg and Frank Stella. American artists like Jeff Koons, Jean Michel Basquiat, Christopher Wool and Richard Prince top the charts. U.K. artists Peter Droig and Damien Hirst are also at the top of the list along with German artist Martin Kippenberg and Chinese artists Zeng Fanzhi, Luo Zhongli, Chen Yifei and Zhang Xioagang.

Louis Bosworth Hurt (British, 1881-1929), "A Misty Morning, Scotch Cattle," oil on canvas, signed lower right: Louis B. Hurt, signed, titled, and inscribed on a label on stretcher: "A Misty Morning / Scotch Cattle / Louis B. Hurt / Stonebrook / Darley Dale / Matlock / England," 48" x 34"..**$1,375**

Courtesy of Heritage Auctions, ha.com

Ohara Koson (1877-1945), "Swallow Over Waves," 1910s, Japanese woodblock print, finely printed with applied gofun (ground oyster shell) to simulate ocean spray, 7-1/2" x 14-1/2". **$340**

Courtesy of Jasper52, www.jasper52.com

American School, mid-20th century, "Untitled (Man with Chisel)," oil on canvas, figural painting depicting a man with chisel in hand, apparently unsigned, framed approximately 26-1/4" x 24-1/2"; unframed approximately 22" x 20". **$200**

Courtesy of Ahlers & Ogletree Auction Gallery, www.aandoauctions.com

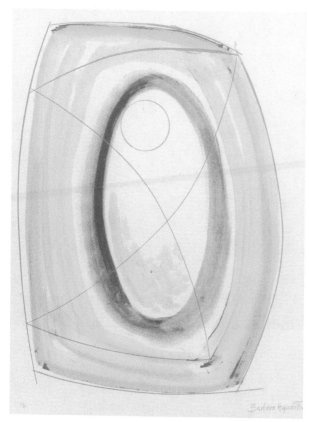

Barbara Hepworth (1903-1975), "November Green," lithograph printed in colors, signed in pencil, numbered 43/60 (total edition includes 10 artist's proofs), from Opposing Forms, on wove paper, published by Marlborough Fine Art, London, framed, 1970; image: 26-1/2" x 19-3/4", sheet: 30-3/8" x 22-7/8". **$2,500**

Courtesy of Sotheby's, sothebys.com

▼ Robert Allen Nelson (American, b. 1945), "Giant Pig," 1966, mixed media on paper (including lithography and collage) depicting a large pig with internal organs represented by gears and other inanimate mechanisms and objects, inscribed to lower right "Nelson Robt. A. Fall 1966 Grand Forks, North Dakota." Framed, approximately 33-1/2" x 41-1/4". **$500**

Courtesy of Ahlers & Ogletree Auction Gallery, www.aandoauctions.com

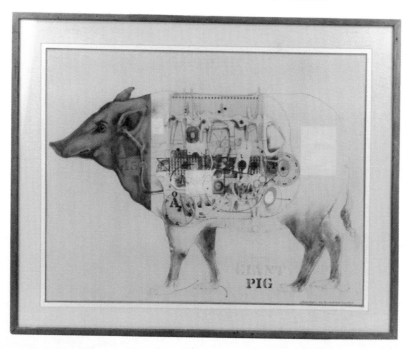

English School (late 18th/early 19th century), oil on canvas, a portrait of a young girl seated in a landscape with her pet dog, thought to be the Honorable Mary Legge, afterwards wife of John, 2nd Lord Sherborne, 30-1/2" x 25".................................. **$1,875**

Courtesy of Heritage Auctions, ha.com

▼ Yao Song (1648-1721), "Landscape After Wang Meng," with one seal of the artist ink on paper, album leaf, 9" x 7-5/8".......................... **$1,000**

Courtesy of Sotheby's, sothebys.com

▶ Shamanic raven mask, articulated jaw, carved wood, beads, 21" x 9" x 10"..........................**$1,100**

Courtesy of Material Culture, materialculture.com

▲ Larkin Goldsmith Mead (1835-1910), "Venezia," white marble, signed Larkin G. Mead (on reverse), 24" h. **$3,500**

Courtesy of Sotheby's, sothebys.com

▲ Central Asia, India, ca. early 20th century, cast bronze Shiva Nataraja, the Hindu deity regarded as both creator and destroyer of the universe, 10-1/4" w x 11-1/2" h. **$250**

Fine art-stone cricket China, Hongshan, 3500 to 2200 BCE, tutelary spirit figure depicting a cricket, expertly carved from a single piece of translucent, amber-hued stone, openwork under front legs and wings for suspension, 2-1/2" l x 1-3/4" h..........................**$300**

Courtesy of Artemis Gallery, www.artemisgallery.com

▶ After Marcel Debut (French, 1865-1933), Centaur and Maid, bronze with brown patina, inscribed along the base: Debut, 19" h.............**$625**

Courtesy of Heritage Auctions, ha.com

▲ A cast iron garden armillary sphere, mid-20th century, 39" h x 20" w x 20" d.......................**$400**

Courtesy of Heritage Auctions, ha.com

▶ Lucien Charles Edouard Alliot (French, 1877-1977), Edelweiss, bronzed spelter with polychrome, inscribed on base: LAlliot, 12" h on a 1/2" h marble base. **$250**

Courtesy of Heritage Auctions, ha.com

FINE ART REGIONALISM

LIKE JAZZ AND BLUEGRASS, Regionalism is a truly unique American form of art. The American realist modern art movement included paintings, murals, lithographs, and illustrations depicting realistic scenes of rural and small-town America primarily in the Midwest and Deep South. The artworks keep tight to the country's early agrarian roots and the hard-scrabble life many experienced during the Great Depression. Think "The Grapes of Wrath" immortalized in oil and pencils.

The movement arose in the 1930s – surprisingly during the strongest years of the sleek and streamlined Art Deco movement. It ended in the 1940s due to the end of World War II. Critics look back and now point to the five year span between 1930 and 1935 as the peak of the movement, although some artists created their greatest works well into the early 1950s, basing their influence and education by the movement's three most influential artists: Grant Wood, Thomas Hart Benton and John Steuart Curry. Despite major differences between the three (and their students) Regionalist art is often conservative and traditional, directly opposite of the rather flamboyant Continental art being produced, say, in France at the time.

During the mid-1970s Regionalist paintings were out of favor in the art world. Collectors often sold their paintings very cheaply or quality examples could be found very favorably at auction or even directly from the artists themselves. Critics derided the genre's stark, plain imagery in the age of Andy Warhol's modern take on Campbell's Soup Cans.

Perhaps the most famous American Regional painting is Grant Wood's American Gothic, which is annually ranked as American's favorite painting. Artists of the era built entire careers on murals painted during the Depression and the early 1940s. These works went on to influence artists whose most important work kept Regionalism alive after World War II and the rise of Modernism and Modernist artists.

The market for American Regional art is strong and growing stronger every year. Large-size, important works easily top seven figures and murals and mural studies command a half-million dollars. Price points for even lesser quality works span five figures and lithographs from the greats are attainable between $500 and $2,000 depending on the artist and the subject.

An ideal example is Merritt Mauzey's *Uncle Fud and Aunt Boo*. Painted in the 1930s, the oil on masonite depicts two figures exhausted from working their fields. Ironically, Uncle Fud, and Aunt Boo were well-known comedic radio characters created in the early 1930s by radio personality Bob Burns. They

Flood Disaster, 1951, Thomas Hart Benton (1889-1975), oil and tempera on canvas mounted on plywood (original), 25-1/2 x 36-½", signed Benton and dated 51.. **$1,874,500**

Sotheby's

were happy-go-lucky, barefoot, tobacco chewing, dirt-poor sharecroppers. Merritt Mauzey places these normally happy and carefree characters in the firm and horrible grip of the Dust Bowl. Instead of the light-hearted comic characters Americans were used to, Mauzey presents them toiling against the awful forces of the drought. The sky is not blue, but gray, brown, and orange – filled with blowing topsoil. Mauzey replaces the romantic images of Thomas Hart Benton's regionalism with his own regionalism of stark truth and the plight of the sharecropping farmer.

Mauzey's accurate, however dispiriting and bleak assessment of the farmer's plight held a place of pride in his heart. Mauzey kept Uncle Fud and Aunt Boo in his personal collection until his very last days, always declining to sell them. He finally sold both to pay for medical care. He sold the prized paintings to a long-time cotton broker, knowing at that point in time (the mid-1970s) only someone in the cotton industry would appreciate them. Uncle Fud and Aunt Boo were Mauzey's prize possessions until very near his death.

Brick Cleaners, circa, 1930, Jessie Davis (American, 1887-1969), oil on canvas, 26 x 22 inches, signed lower right..........................$30,000

Heritage Auctions, www.HA.com

Uncle Fud and Aunt Boo, circa 1930s, Merritt Mauzey, (1897-1973), oil on Masonite, 30 x 24 inches, signed lower right..........................$77,675

Services to be Held at 7:30 pm, Beaumont, Texas, 1952, Richard Gordon Stout (American, b. 1934), oil on board, 24 x 32 inches. **$9,375**

Heritage Auctions, www.HA.com

Lively Gathering in Town Square, Ethel Spears (American, 1903-1974), oil on canvas 29-7/8 x 40-1/4 inches, signed lower right.
.... **$3,250**

Heritage Auctions, www.HA.com

E Live Oak Pass, 1941, William Lewis Lester (American, 1910-1991), lithograph, 10 x 13-3/4 inches, Ed. 25, signature, date, title, and number lower center.
.... **$1,250**

Heritage Auctions, www.HA.com

▼ *Lonesome Road*, 1938, Thomas Hart Benton (American, 1889-1975), lithograph, 9-5/8 x 12-1/2 inches, Ed. 250, signed in pencil lower right, published by Associated American Artists, New York. **$812**

Heritage Auctions, www.HA.com

◄ *Swamp Girl*, 1953, Don Brown (1898-1958), oil on canvas, 32. x 24 inches, signed and dated lower right. **$9,858**

383

top lot

Southern Comfort

Born in Canton, Mississippi, and raised in the South, John McCrady (1911-1968) emerged as one of the best-known 20th century southern artists. The son of an Episcopal minister, McCrady studied at the Arts and Crafts Club of New Orleans, the Art Students League of New York and the University of Pennsylvania. While in New Orleans, McCrady painted *Portrait of a Negro* (at right), a groundbreaking work that earned him a one-year scholarship in New York and launched his career. In New York he was exposed to the teaching of Thomas Hart Benton and the art of the American regionalists. Returning to Louisiana, the influence of his teachers would shape his direction and career.

In 1946 when McCrady painted this extraordinary mural *Steamboat 'Round the Bend*, a nostalgic depiction of teenage boys frolicking along the banks of the Mississippi River, he was already being lauded as the "first-rate" painter from the South, "a star risen from the bayous." The work, an oil-on-canvas mural measuring 78" x 168", was commissioned in 1945 by Marie LaFanca, owner of Delmonico's, an upscale restaurant in New Orleans. McCrady was said to have been paid with dinners, drinks and an unknown fee for the work, which took him a year to complete. When done, the painting hung behind the restaurant bar.

Illustrating the appreciation and demand for Regionalism, the mural *Steamboat 'Round the Bend* sold at auction for $542,500.

Steamboat 'Round the Bend

Vermont Hills, William Stone Beeken (American, 1897-1952), oil on canvas, 25" x 30" signed and dated lower left. $275

Eldred's Auctioneers & Appraisers, www.eldreds.com

◄ *Campers in the Blue Ridge Mountains*, Thomas Worthington Whittredge (American, 1820-1910), oil on canvas, signed to lower right, framed approximately 34 x 44-3/4 inches. $40,000

Ahlers & Ogletree, www.aandoauctions.com

▼ *Brulatour Courtyard, French Quarter*, Knute Heldner (Swedish/New Orleans, 1877-1952), oil on canvas board, signed lower right, 12 x 9 inches. $500

Crescent City Auction Gallery, www.crescentcityauctiongallery.com

Country Hillside, Peter Lanz Hohnstedt (American, 1872-1957), oil on canvas, 24 x 29 inches, signed lower right: *P.L. Hohnstedt.* $1,792

Heritage Auctions, www.HA.com

Wisconsin Landscape, John Steuart Curry (American 1897-1946), oil on canvas, 18.5in. x 24.5 inches, signed lower right. Along with Thomas Hart Benton and Grant Wood, John Steuart Curry was one of the top artists of the regionalist movement. Provenance: Kennedy Galleries, New York. **$17,925**

Heritage Auctions, www.HA.com

▶ *Fertility*, 1939, Grant Wood (American 1891-1942), lithograph, 9 x 11-7/8 inches, Ed. 250 AAA, pub., signed lower right in pencil: *Grant Wood*; inscribed lower right *P-53*; and with Bess Heard stamp on the reverse. **$4,780**

Heritage Auctions, www.HA.com

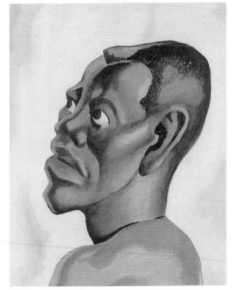

Our Good Earth, 1942, John Steuart Curry (American, 1897-1946), lithograph, 12-3/4 x 10-1/8 inches, signed in pencil in lower margin, pulished by Associated American Artists, New York.. **$1,875**

Heritage Auctions, www.HA.com

Negro Head, circa 1924, Thomas Hart Benton (American, 1889-1975), watercolor on paper, 20 x 16-1/4 inches, signed lower right: *Benton*. **$47,500**

Heritage Auctions, www.HA.com

FOLK ART/AMERICANA

FOR A NATION that takes deep pride in calling itself a nation of immigrants, American folk art and Americana acts like the ribbon tying our collective heritage together. Rich with evidence of German woodworking, Scottish ship-carving, or perhaps African tribal motifs, each work is one-of-a-kind and stands on its own, backed by good ol' American individuality. The fact that most works were completed by self-taught artists who had little to no formal training enhances the appeal to the collectors of American folk art and Americana. In one sense, the vernacular charm symbolizes the country's reputation for ambition, ingenuity, and imagination. There's little wonder why American folk art and Americana is more popular than ever.

The last few years saw several large folk art and Americana collections come to market with spectacular results. It also saw preservationists and scholars take major steps to ensure folk art remains an important art form in our national heritage.

Sotheby's presentation of the Ralph Esmerian collection of American folk art in early 2014 generated the highest proceeds for an American folk art collection. The 228-lot selection from the former chairman emeritus of the American Folk Art Museum was as noteworthy as its owner was notorious. Esmerian is serving a six-year federal sentence for fraud associated with the sale of jewelry and collectibles worth millions. The collection was ordered to be sold to provide restitution to victims and generated more than $10.5 million.

The collection held true American treasures. The top lot was a carved figure of Santa Claus by master carver Samuel Robb, the last figure he ever carved, in fact. Famous for his cigar store American Indian figures, Robb completed the 38" Santa in 1923 as a Christmas present to his daughter, Elizabeth. The figure more than doubled its pre-auction estimate to hammer for $875,000.

The sale meant that two Samuel Robb-carved figures achieved world records within just months of each other. The Maryland-based auction firm of Guyette, Schmidt and Deeter sold a rare Robb cigar store American Indian princess, circa 1880, in late 2013 for a record $747,000.

Another sign of this category's growing interest with collectors and the general public is the popularity of the only museum dedicated to the scholarly study and exhibition of the country's self-taught artisans, the American Folk Art Museum (www.folkartmuseum.org), New York City. The museum's more than 5,000 items were collected almost entirely through gifts. Collectors cheered in December 2013 when the museum digitized and gave away free 118 issues of *Folk Art* magazine (formerly *The Clarion*), originally published between winter 1971 and fall 2008. The trove may be accessed online at issuu.com/american_folk_art_museum.

Softwood side lid candle box, 19th century, decorative folk art painted decoration added at a later time, 3" h x 16" l x 4" d. **$303**

Courtesy of Contestoga Auction Co., www.conestogaauction.com

Weathervane, 20th century, on black-painted pole and rectangular metal base, the stylized stag depicted running with tail extended, antlers, 38-1/2" x 30", 80" overall. **$704**

Courtesy of Brunk Auctions,
www.brunkauctions.com

Wooden folk art barber shop pole made to resemble an American flag. **$461**

Courtesy of Morphy Auctions, morphyauctions.com

Wood-carved chicken that was done to sit on top of a pole, rustic folk art look, possibly carved as a trade sign, comes with custom base, chicken is 35" x 15".......................... **$600**

Courtesy of Milestone Auctions,
www.milestoneauctions.com

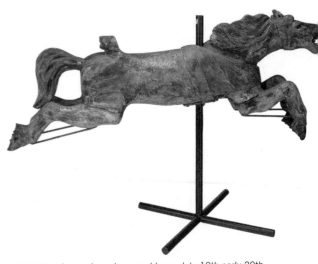

American Verdigris bonze weathervane, early 20th century, surmounted by a detailed windmill above a man leaning on fence with dog-form directional, base of a later vintage, 73" h. **$1,063**

Courtesy of Heritage Auctions, ha.com

Painted and carved wood carousel horse, late 19th-early 20th century, 23" h x 62" w. **$550**

Courtesy of Heritage Auctions, ha.com

▶ Pennsylvania folk art carved cane, attributed to Al Rader, decorated with spread-wing eagle, male lion, horse, stag, butterfly and floral motif, 35-1/2" l..$514

Courtesy of Contestoga Auction Co., www.conest ogaauction.com

Folk art wood and rubber doll's head sculpture, 20th century, 10-1/2" h....................................$49

Courtesy of Skinner Auctioneers and Appraisers, Inc., www.skinnerinc.com

Wood-carved song bird, signed "Joseph Moyer 1889" (Berks County, PA, 1883-1962), 3-1/2" h
....$303

Courtesy of Contestoga Auction Co., www.conestogaauction.com

Pair of American painted wood figures, 20th century, carved as man and woman praying in flames, 8-1/4" h, 4" w, 3-1/4" d....................$576

Courtesy of Neal Auction Co., www.nealauction.com

Primitive folk art horse, carved and painted wood, 17" x 25" x 5"....................................$125

Courtesy of Material Culture, www.materialculture.com

Wooden folk art marble game, early 1900s, comes with original stenciling, 28" l......$123

Courtesy of Morphy Auctions, morphyauctions.com

top lot

Rare oil on canvas board folk art painting of a black American baseball game, probably c. 1930. 17" h, 21-1/2" w.
....$3,690

Hand with ball sculpture, carved wood, gessoed with gilt and black paint, 25-3/4"h... **$484**

Folk art wooden polychrome painted salmon, c. 1910-20, directional from a N.H. boathouse, on custom stand, 40" l, 13" h, 18" h with stand.. **$450**

Northern European folk art cabinet, early 19th century, with faux grain and floral decoration, 71" h x 41" w x 18" d... **$861**

Courtesy of Kaminski Auctions, www.kaminskiauctions.com

Diminutive Tramp Art chest of drawers, early 20th century, 30-1/4" h x 17-1/4" w x 8-1/2" d....... **$138**

Courtesy of Heritage Auctions, ha.com

Folk art table with single drawer and marbles in "cages," 17" x 13" x 18" h............................ **$150**

Courtesy of Copake Auction, Inc., www.copakeauction.com

Hand-carved wooden coin box table with numerous images, 4" x 7- 1/2"........................ **$215**

Courtesy of Morphy Auctions, morphyauctions.com

Early Canadian folk art root chair with plank seat, old white paint, 30" h.................................... **$240**

Courtesy of Copake Auction, Inc., www.copakeauction.com

American Tramp Art jewelry box, c. 1910, constructed of cigar box wood and other scrap wood, in unique stepped geometric form, 10" h x 11-1/2" w... **$55**

Courtesy of Heritage Auctions, ha.com

American, likely Southern, school folk art trompe l'oeil painting, oil on board, a charming depiction of a rabbit with carrot, mounted behind chicken wire in a yellow pine frame, additional straw added at bottom edge for effect, signed indistinctly lower left (obscured by straw), late 19th/early 20th century, 7-1/2" x 8-7/8", 10" x 11-1/4" overall... **$747**

Courtesy of Jeffrey S. Evans & Associates, www.jeffreysevans.com

American Folk Art School "General Napoleon Bonaparte (1769-1821)," fabric, engraving, watercolor and mixed media on board, unsigned, late 19th/20th century, framed, 8-1/2" x 7"..... **$228**

Courtesy of Neal Auction Co., www.nealauction.com

▶ Folk art carved mirror, mixed woods, late 19th/ early 20th century, pierced surround with applied oak leaves, birds, flowers, acorns, deer, centered by an oval mirror with tooled border, 53-3/4" h, 34-1/2" w. **$3,321**

Courtesy of Skinner Auctioneers and Appraisers, Inc., www.skinnerinc.com

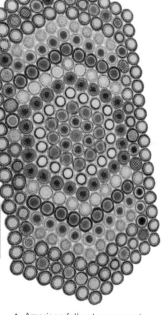

Folk art wall hanging by Kate "Granny" Donaldson, 1864-1960, Brasstown, North Carolina, crocheted figures, barnyard animals, flower basket and tree hand applied to handwoven wool panel, hemmed edges, top hanging slip for rod, 35-1/2" x 35". **$756**

Courtesy of Brunk Auctions, www.brunkauctions.com

▲ American folk art penny rug/ table mat, elongated hexagonal form with scalloped edges, pattern of multicolor wool cut-outs applied to cotton feed sack backing, first half 20th century, 29-3/4" x 60-3/4". **$311**

Courtesy of Jeffrey S. Evans & Associates, www.jeffreysevans.com

◀ American folk art pictorial hooked rug, design featuring two African-American hunters, one on horse, with dogs in a stylized landscape, all within a scalloped-edge oblong reserve, floral corner devices, black border, professionally mounted for display, mid-20th century, 32-1/2" x 58-1/2". **$405**

Courtesy of Jeffrey S. Evans & Associates, www.jeffreysevans.com

◀ Charles Wysocki, (California/ Michigan, 1928-2002), "Stony Farm – Vermont," oil on canvas, original wood frame, signed lower right "Charles Wysocki," 16" x 20". **$3,584**

Courtesy of Brunk Auctions, www.brunkauctions.com

FURNITURE STYLES
american

PILGRIM CENTURY 1620–1700

MAJOR WOOD(S): Oak

GENERAL CHARACTERISTICS:

- **Case pieces:** Rectilinear low-relief carved panels; blocky and bulbous turnings; splint-spindle trim

- **Seating pieces:** Shallow carved panels; spindle turnings

WILLIAM AND MARY 1685–1720

MAJOR WOOD(S): Maple and walnut

GENERAL CHARACTERISTICS:

- **Case pieces:** Paint-decorated chests on ball feet; chests on frames; chests with two-part construction; trumpet-turned legs; slant-front desks

- **Seating pieces:** Molded, carved crest rails; banister backs; cane, rush (leather) seats; baluster, ball and block turnings; ball and Spanish feet

QUEEN ANNE 1720-1750

MAJOR WOOD(S): Walnut

GENERAL CHARACTERISTICS:

- **Case pieces:**
  Mathematical proportions
  of elements; use of the
  cyma or S-curve broken-
  arch pediments; arched
  panels, shell carving, star
  inlay; blocked fronts;
  cabriole legs and pad feet

- **Seating pieces:** Molded
  yoke-shaped crest
  rails; solid vase-shaped
  splats; rush or upholstered seats; cabriole legs; baluster, ring, ball and block-turned
  stretchers; pad and slipper feet

CHIPPENDALE 1750-1785

MAJOR WOOD(S): Mahogany and walnut

GENERAL CHARACTERISTICS:

- **Case pieces:** Relief-carved broken-arch pediments; foliate, scroll, shell, fretwork
  carving; straight, bow or serpentine fronts; carved cabriole legs; claw and ball,
  bracket or ogee feet

- **Seating pieces:** Carved, shaped crest rails with out-turned ears; pierced,
  shaped splats; ladder (ribbon) backs; upholstered seats; scrolled arms;
  carved cabriole legs or straight (Marlboro) legs; claw and ball feet

FEDERAL (HEPPLEWHITE) 1785–1800

MAJOR WOOD(S): Mahogany and light inlays

GENERAL CHARACTERISTICS:

- **Case pieces:** More delicate rectilinear forms; inlay with eagle and classical motifs; bow, serpentine or tambour fronts; reeded quarter columns at sides; flared bracket feet

- **Seating pieces:** Shield backs; upholstered seats; tapered square legs

FEDERAL (SHERATON) 1800–1820

MAJOR WOOD(S): Mahogany, mahogany veneer, and maple

GENERAL CHARACTERISTICS:

- **Case pieces:** Architectural pediments; acanthus carving; outset (cookie or ovolu) corners and reeded columns; paneled sides; tapered, turned, reeded or spiral-turned legs; bow or tambour fronts; mirrors on dressing tables

- **Seating pieces:** Rectangular or square backs; slender carved banisters; tapered, turned or reeded legs

CLASSICAL (AMERICAN EMPIRE) 1815–1850

MAJOR WOOD(S): Mahogany, mahogany veneer, and rosewood

GENERAL CHARACTERISTICS:

- **Case pieces:** Increasingly heavy proportions; pillar and scroll construction; lyre, eagle, Greco-Roman and Egyptian motifs; marble tops; projecting top drawer; large ball feet, tapered fluted feet or hairy paw feet; brass, ormolu decoration

- **Seating pieces:** High-relief carving; curved backs; out-scrolled arms; ring turnings; sabre legs, curule (scrolled-S) legs; brass-capped feet, casters

VICTORIAN – EARLY VICTORIAN 1840–1850

MAJOR WOOD(S): Mahogany veneer, black walnut, and rosewood

GENERAL CHARACTERISTICS:

- **Case pieces:** Pieces tend to carry over the Classical style with the beginnings of the Rococo substyle, especially in seating pieces.

VICTORIAN – GOTHIC REVIVAL 1840–1890

MAJOR WOOD(S): Black walnut, mahogany, and rosewood

GENERAL CHARACTERISTICS:

- **Case pieces:** Architectural motifs; triangular arched pediments; arched panels; marble tops; paneled or molded drawer fronts; cluster columns; bracket feet, block feet or plinth bases

- **Seating pieces:** Tall backs; pierced arabesque backs with trefoils or quatrefoils; spool turning; drop pendants

VICTORIAN – ROCOCO (LOUIS XV) 1845–1870

MAJOR WOOD(S): Black walnut, mahogany, and rosewood

GENERAL CHARACTERISTICS:

- **Case pieces:** Arched carved pediments; high-relief carving, S- and C-scrolls, floral, fruit motifs, busts and cartouches; mirror panels; carved slender cabriole legs; scroll feet; bedroom suites (bed, dresser, commode)

- **Seating pieces:** High-relief carved crest rails; balloon-shaped backs; urn-shaped splats; upholstery (tufting); demi-cabriole legs; laminated, pierced and carved construction (Belter and Meeks); parlor suites (sets of chairs, love seats, sofas)

VICTORIAN – RENAISSANCE REVIVAL 1860–1885

MAJOR WOOD(S): Black walnut, burl veneer, painted and grained pine

GENERAL CHARACTERISTICS:

- **Case pieces:** Rectilinear arched pediments; arched panels; burl veneer; applied moldings; bracket feet, block feet, plinth bases; medium and high-relief carving, floral and fruit, cartouches, masks and animal heads; cyma-curve brackets; Wooton patent desks

- **Seating pieces:** Oval or rectangular backs with floral or figural cresting; upholstery outlined with brass tacks; padded armrests; tapered turned front legs, flared square rear legs

VICTORIAN – LOUIS XVI 1865–1875

MAJOR WOOD(S): Black walnut and ebonized maple

GENERAL CHARACTERISTICS:

- **Case pieces:** Gilt decoration, marquetry, inlay; egg and dart carving; tapered turned legs, fluted

- **Seating pieces:** Molded, slightly arched crest rails; keystone-shaped backs; circular seats; fluted tapered legs

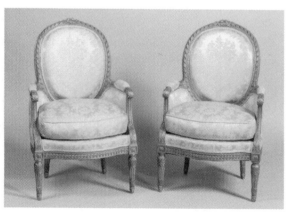

VICTORIAN – EASTLAKE 1870-1895

MAJOR WOOD(S): Black walnut, burl veneer, cherry, and oak

GENERAL CHARACTERISTICS:

- **Case pieces:** Flat cornices; stile and rail construction; burl veneer panels; low-relief geometric and floral machine carving; incised horizontal lines

- **Seating pieces:** Rectilinear; spindles; tapered, turned legs, trumpet-shaped legs

VICTORIAN JACOBEAN AND TURKISH REVIVAL 1870-1890

MAJOR WOOD(S): Black walnut and maple

GENERAL CHARACTERISTICS:

- **Case pieces:** A revival of some heavy 17th century forms, most commonly in dining room pieces

- **Seating pieces:** Turkish Revival style features: oversized, low forms; overstuffed upholstery; padded arms; short baluster, vase-turned legs; ottomans, circular sofas

- **Jacobean Revival style features:** heavy bold carving; spool and spiral turnings

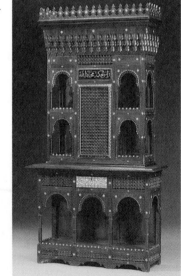

VICTORIAN – AESTHETIC MOVEMENT 1880–1900

MAJOR WOOD(S): Painted hardwoods, black walnut, ebonized finishes

GENERAL CHARACTERISTICS:

- **Case pieces:** Rectilinear forms; bamboo turnings, spaced ball turnings; incised stylized geometric and floral designs, sometimes highlighted with gilt

- **Seating pieces:** Bamboo turning; rectangular backs; patented folding chairs

ART NOUVEAU 1895–1918

MAJOR WOOD(S): Ebonized hardwoods, fruitwoods

GENERAL CHARACTERISTICS:

- **Case pieces:** Curvilinear shapes; floral marquetry; whiplash curves

- **Seating pieces:** Elongated forms; relief-carved floral decoration; spindle backs, pierced floral backs; cabriole legs

TURN-OF-THE-CENTURY (EARLY 20TH CENTURY) 1895–1910

MAJOR WOOD(S): Golden (quarter-sawn) oak, mahogany, hardwood stained to resemble mahogany

GENERAL CHARACTERISTICS:

- **Case pieces:** Rectilinear and bulky forms; applied scroll carving or machine-pressed designs; some Colonial and Classical Revival detailing

- **Seating pieces:** Heavy framing or high spindle-trimmed backs; applied carved or machine-pressed back designs; heavy scrolled or slender turned legs; Colonial Revival or Classical Revival detailing such as claw and ball feet

MISSION (ARTS & CRAFTS MOVEMENT) 1900–1915

MAJOR WOOD(S): Oak

GENERAL CHARACTERISTICS:

- **Case pieces:** Rectilinear through-tenon construction; copper decoration, hand-hammered hardware; square legs

- **Seating pieces:** Rectangular splats; medial and side stretchers; exposed pegs; corbel supports

COLONIAL REVIVAL 1890–1930

MAJOR WOOD(S): Oak, walnut and walnut veneer, mahogany veneer

GENERAL CHARACTERISTICS:

- **Case pieces:** Forms generally following designs of the 17th, 18th, and early 19th centuries; details for the styles such as William and Mary, Federal, Queen Anne, Chippendale, or early Classical were used but often in a simplified or stylized form; mass-production in the early 20th century flooded the market with pieces that often mixed and matched design details and used a great deal of thin veneering to dress up designs; dining room and bedroom suites were especially popular.

- **Seating pieces:** Designs again generally followed early period designs with some mixing of design elements.

ART DECO 1925–1940

MAJOR WOOD(S): Bleached woods, exotic woods, steel, and chrome

GENERAL CHARACTERISTICS:

- **Case pieces:** Heavy geometric forms
- **Seating pieces:** Streamlined, attenuated geometric forms; overstuffed upholstery

MODERNIST OR MID-CENTURY 1945–1970

MAJOR WOOD(S): Plywood, hardwood, or metal frames

GENERAL CHARACTERISTICS: Modernistic designers such as the Eames, Vladimir Kagan, George Nelson, and Isamu Noguchi led the way in post-war design. Carrying on the tradition of Modernist designers of the 1920s and 1930s, they focused on designs for the machine age that could be mass-produced for the popular market. By the late 1950s many of their pieces were used in commercial office spaces and schools as well as in private homes.

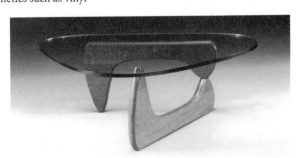

- **Case pieces:** Streamlined or curvilinear abstract designs with simple detailing; plain round or flattened legs and arms; mixed materials including wood, plywood, metal, glass, and molded plastics

- **Seating pieces:** Streamlined or abstract curvilinear designs generally using newer materials such as plywood or simple hardwood framing; fabric and synthetics such as vinyl used for upholstery with finer fabrics and real leather featured on more expensive pieces; seating made of molded plastic shells on metal frames and legs used on many mass-produced designs

DANISH MODERN 1950–1970

MAJOR WOOD(S): Teak

GENERAL CHARACTERISTICS:

- **Case and seating pieces:** This variation of Modernistic post-war design originated in Scandinavia, hence the name; designs were simple and restrained with case pieces often having simple boxy forms with short rounded tapering legs; seating pieces have a simple teak framework with lines coordinating with case pieces; vinyl or natural fabric were most often used for upholstery; in the United States dining room suites were the most popular use for this style although some bedroom suites and general seating pieces were available.

FURNITURE STYLES

english

JACOBEAN MID-17TH CENTURY

MAJOR WOOD(S): Oak, walnut

GENERAL CHARACTERISTICS:

- **Case pieces:** Low-relief carving; geometrics and florals; panel, rail and stile construction; applied split balusters

- **Seating pieces:** Rectangular backs; carved and pierced crests; spiral turnings ball feet

WILLIAM AND MARY 1689–1702

MAJOR WOOD(S): Walnut, burl walnut veneer

GENERAL CHARACTERISTICS:

- **Case pieces:** Marquetry, veneering; shaped aprons; 6-8 trumpet-form legs; curved flat stretchers

- **Seating pieces:** Carved, pierced crests; tall caned backs and seats; trumpet-form legs; Spanish feet

QUEEN ANNE 1702–1714

MAJOR WOOD(S): Walnut, mahogany, veneer

GENERAL CHARACTERISTICS:

- **Case pieces:** Cyma curves; broken arch pediments and finials; bracket feet

- **Seating pieces:** Carved crest rails; high, rounded backs; solid vase-shaped splats; cabriole legs; pad feet

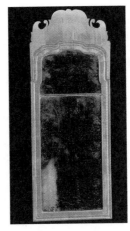 

GEORGE I 1714–1727

MAJOR WOOD(S): Walnut, mahogany, veneer, and yew wood

GENERAL CHARACTERISTICS:

- **Case pieces:** Broken arch pediments; gilt decoration, japanning; bracket feet

- **Seating pieces:** Curvilinear forms; yoke-shaped crests; shaped solid splats; shell carving; upholstered seats; carved cabriole legs; claw and ball feet, pad feet

GEORGE II 1727–1760

MAJOR WOOD(S): Mahogany

GENERAL CHARACTERISTICS:

- **Case pieces:** Broken arch pediments; relief-carved foliate, scroll and shell carving; carved cabriole legs; claw and ball feet, bracket feet, ogee bracket feet

- **Seating pieces:** Carved, shaped crest rails, out-turned ears; pierced shaped splats; ladder (ribbon) backs; upholstered seats; scrolled arms; carved cabriole legs or straight (Marlboro) legs; claw and ball feet

GEORGE III 1760–1820

MAJOR WOOD(S): Mahogany, veneer, satinwood

GENERAL CHARACTERISTICS:

- **Case pieces:** Rectilinear forms; parcel gilt decoration; inlaid ovals, circles, banding or marquetry; carved columns, urns; tambour fronts or bow fronts; plinth bases

- **Seating pieces:** Shield backs; upholstered seats; tapered square legs, square legs

REGENCY 1811–1820

MAJOR WOOD(S): Mahogany, mahogany veneer, satinwood and rosewood

GENERAL CHARACTERISTICS:

- **Case pieces:** Greco-Roman and Egyptian motifs; inlay, ormolu mounts; marble tops; round columns, pilasters; mirrored backs; scroll feet

- **Seating pieces:** Straight backs; latticework; caned seats; sabre legs, tapered turned legs, flared turned legs; parcel gilt, ebonizing

GEORGE IV 1820–1830

MAJOR WOOD(S): Mahogany, mahogany veneer and rosewood

GENERAL CHARACTERISTICS: Continuation of Regency designs

WILLIAM IV 1830-1837

MAJOR WOOD(S): Mahogany, mahogany veneer

GENERAL CHARACTERISTICS:

- **Case pieces:** Rectilinear; brass mounts, grillwork; carved moldings; plinth bases

- **Seating pieces:** Rectangular backs; carved straight crest rails; acanthus, animal carving; carved cabriole legs; paw feet

VICTORIAN 1837-1901

MAJOR WOOD(S): Black walnut, mahogany, veneers and rosewood

GENERAL CHARACTERISTICS:

- **Case pieces:** Applied floral carving; surmounting mirrors, drawers, candle shelves; marble tops

- **Seating pieces:** High-relief carved crest rails; floral and fruit carving; balloon backs, oval backs; upholstered seats, backs; spool, spiral turnings; cabriole legs, fluted tapered legs; scrolled feet

EDWARDIAN 1901-1910

MAJOR WOOD(S): Mahogany, mahogany veneer and satinwood

GENERAL CHARACTERISTICS: Neo-Classical motifs and revivals of earlier 18th century and early 19th century styles

FURNITURE

antique

FURNITURE HAS BEEN a major part of the collecting world for more than 100 years. It is interesting to note how this market has evolved.

In past decades, 18th century and early 19th century furniture was the mainstay of the American furniture market, but now the market is dominated by Modern and Mid-Century tastes, ranging from Art Deco through quality designer furniture of the 1950s and beyond (see "Modern Furniture" later in this section).

Today more furniture is showing up on Internet sites, and sometimes good buys can be made. However, it is important to deal with honest, well-informed sellers and have a good knowledge of what you want to purchase.

As in the past, it makes sense to purchase the best pieces you can find, whatever the style or era of production. Condition is still very important if you want your example to continue

BOOKCASES

Gustav Stickley two-door bookcase with tenon and key construction, signed with early Eastwood label, original finish, top refinished, 56" h x 51" w x 13" d...**$4,750**

Courtesy of California Historical Design, www.acstickley.com

An Edwardian gilt-brass mounted mahogany dwarf bookcase, early 20th century, three adjustable shelves, 37-1/2" h, 20-1/4" w, 9-1/4" d............................**$844**

Courtesy of Sotheby's, www.sothebys.com

◀ Early L&JG Stickley Onondaga period three-door bookcase with tenon and key construction and original chamfered board back, c1902-1904, unsigned, original finish, 70" w x 56" h x 12" d. **$8,500**

Courtesy of California Historical Design, www.acstickley.com

to appreciate in value in the coming years. For 18th century and early 19th century pieces, the original finish and hardware are especially important as it is with good furniture of the early 20th century Arts & Crafts era. These features are not quite as important for most manufactured furniture of the Victorian era and furniture from the 1920s and later. However, it is good to be aware that a good finish and original hardware will mean a stronger market when the pieces are resold. Of course, whatever style of furniture you buy, you are better off with examples that have not had major repair or replacements. On really early furniture, repairs and replacements will definitely have an impact on the sale value, but they will also be a factor on newer designs from the 20th century.

As with all types of antiques and collectibles, there is often a regional preference for certain furniture types. Although the American market is much more homogenous than it was in past decades, there still tends to be a preference for 18th century and early 19th century furniture along the Eastern Seaboard, whereas Victorian designs tend to have a larger market in the Midwest and South. In the West, country furniture and "western" designs definitely have the edge except in major cities along the West Coast.

Whatever your favorite furniture style, there are still fine examples to be found. Just study the history of your favorites and the important points of their construction before you invest heavily. A wise shopper will be a happy shopper and have a collection certain to continue to appreciate as time marches along.

▲ George III glazed mahogany desk/bookcase, England, late 18th century, the upper section with pierced fretwork and a shelved interior, over a lower section with fitted interior over four graduated long drawers and bracket feet, 83" h, 37-1/4" w, 20" d. **$554**

Courtesy of Skinner Auctioneers, www.skinnerinc.com

CHAIRS & SEATING

Suite of Edwardian furniture, circa 1900, includes a pair of armchairs, painted satinwood, 36" h x 23" w x 19" d; settee, painted satinwood, 36" h x 41" w x 19" d. **$1,107**

Courtesy of Kaminski Auctions, www.kaminskiauctions.com

Pair of American Rococo laminated rosewood slipper chairs, c. 1860, New York, keyhole backs with pierced scrolling foliage, cabriole legs.... **$1,280**

Courtesy of Neal Auction Co., www.nealauction.com

Pair of Chippendale chairs, Charleston, South Carolina, or British for the Charleston market, 1760-1775, each with pierced splat, upholstered slip seat and square legs with stretchers, each stamped on back rail "HN", seat braces and blocking are beech by sight, 37-1/2".............. **$3,328**

Courtesy of Brunk Auctions, www.brunk.com

Arthur Mathews Furniture Shops rocker, oak, original brown wash, shaped crest above a single incised back slat and rising on tapered legs terminating on outswept rocker rails, 39-1/2" h x 21" w x 18-1/2" d. **$756**

Courtesy of Clars Auction Gallery, www.clarsauctions.com

Stickley Arts & Crafts oak slat back arm chair, green seat cushion, "Quaint Furniture, Stickley Bros. Co Grand Rapids, Mich" label on underside, 34" h, 27-1/2" w. **$750**

Courtesy of DuMouchelles, www.dumouchelle.com

ench carved armchair, 19th c., upholstered in smooth crewel-look fabric and brass upholstery ck, skirt with center shell medallion and shell iees on the cabriole legs, 29" w x 29" d x 43" **$285**

urtesy of Charleston Estate Auctions, www.charlestonestateauctions.com

American classical mahogany armchair, early 19th c., Boston, tablet crest, conforming slat, scrolled arms, slip seat, turned legs............................ **$900**

Courtesy of Neal Auction Company, www.nealauctioncompany.com

CABINETS/STORAGE

Hepplewhite inlaid and banded flame mahogany sideboard, 19th c, one long silverware drawer flanked by two doors on six legs, fruitwood banded top and inlaid drawer and doors, original hardware, one door with single cellarette drawer, probably English, 72" l x 23" d x 36" h. **$410**

Courtesy of Charleston Estate Auctions, www.charlestonestateauctions.com

Early Connecticut Pilgrim chest, 17th c., applied walnut split column turned decoration flanking the recessed molded panels, raised on bun feet at front, blocks at back, the interior retaining the original covered till, 30-1/2" x 43" x 21-1/4".**$3,200**

Courtesy of Thomaston Place Auction Galleries, www.thomastonauction.com

Arts & Crafts cedar-lined Betty Joel chest, with label inside, "Token" handmade furniture, designed by Betty Joel, made by J. Emery at Token Works 1928, 25-1/2" h x 40" w x 22-1/2" d... **$123**

Courtesy of Kaminski Auctions, www.kaminskiauctions.com

American Aesthetic carved and inlaid mahogany cabinet, c. 1880, attributed to Associated Artists, New York, stepped pedimented top with reticulated brass gallery, frieze with bands of scrolled bellflowers, the whole with arched niches, turned supports with shelves, blocked base, 52-3/4" h, 54-3/4" w, 14-1/2" d. **$800**

Courtesy of Neal Auction Co., www.nealauction.com

Three-part china cabinet with convex center door flanked by concave side doors, late 19th/early 20th c., oak and glass, 67" x 49-1/2" x 19".... **$576**

Courtesy of Rago Arts and Auctions, www.ragoarts.com

American Classical mahogany washstand, mid-19th c., attributed to purveyor Prudent Mallard, New Orleans, metamorphic top with interior mirror and marble backsplash, four graduated drawers, molded base, 38" h, 35-3/8" w, 19-3/4" d. **$640**

Courtesy of Neal Auction Co., www.nealauction.com

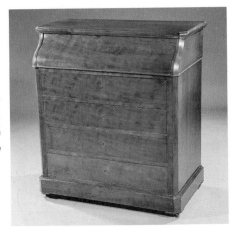

TABLES

Italian black walnut Rococo carved and pierced marble top console table, 19th c., heavily carved skirt and legs, with the carved and pierced skirt with central carved shell, cabriole legs with carved leaf and scroll, top is heavy black and white marble. **$1,300**

Courtesy of Charleston Estate Auctions, www.charlestonestateauctions.com

George III oak cricket table, English, late 18th/ early 19th century, circular top patina over a triangular frieze and three legs joining a lower shelf, 29" x 29" x 29"..................................... **$260**

Courtesy of Charleston Estate Auctions, www.charlestonestateauctions.com

Bellflower and urn inlaid mahogany pembroke table, attributed to Charleston, South Carolina, circa 1800, line-inlaid oval top with drop leaves, single line inlaid bow-front drawer flanked by urn and floral patera and set on finely tapered legs with line and descending bellflower chain inlay, set on brass casters, white pine, red cedar and cherry secondary, 28-3/4" x 30-1/4" x 41-3/4" open, 20-3/4" closed..............................**$20,480**

Courtesy of Brunk Auctions, www.brunk.com

American Chippendale carved mahogany tilt-top tea table, c. 1760-75, pie crust top, birdcage above fluted tapered stem, arched acanthus carved legs, padded claw feet, 30-1/2" h, 31-1/4" dia... **$500**

Courtesy of Neal Auction Company, www.nealauctioncompany.com

FURNITURE

FURNITURE

modern

MODERN DESIGN IS everywhere, evergreen and increasingly popular. Modernism has never gone out of style. Its reach into the present day is as deep as its roots in the past. Just as it can be seen and felt ubiquitously in the mass media of today – on film, television, in magazines, and department stores – it can be traced to the mid-1800s post-Empire non-conformity of the Biedermeier Movement, the turn of the 20th century anti-Victorianism of the Vienna Secessionists, the radical reductionism of Frank Lloyd Wright and the revolutionary post-Depression thinking of Walter Gropius and the Bauhaus school in Germany.

"The Modernists really changed the way the world looked," said John Sollo, a partner in Sollo Rago Auction of Lambertville, New Jersey. Sollo's partner in business, and one of the most recognizable names in the field, David Rago, takes Sollo's idea a little further by saying that Modernism is actually more about the names behind the design than the design itself, at least as far as buying goes.

No discussion of Modern can be complete, however, without examining its genesis and enduring influence. Modernism is everywhere in today's pop culture. Austere Scandinavian furniture dominates the television commercials that hawk hotels and mutual funds. Post-war American design ranges across sitcom set dressings to movie sets patterned after Frank Lloyd Wright houses and Hollywood Modernist classics set high in the hills.

You have to look at the dorm rooms of college students and the apartments of young people whose living spaces are packed with the undeniably Modern mass-produced products of IKEA, Target, Design Within Reach, and the like.

There can be no denying that the post-World War II manufacturing techniques and subsequent boom led to the widespread acceptance of plastic and bent plywood chairs along with low-sitting coffee tables, couches and recliners.

Norman Cherner red upholstered pretzel plywood chair, Plycraft, mid-20th century, 31" h x 26" w x 21-1/2" d. **$298**

Courtesy of North American Auction Co.,
www.northamericanauctioncompany.com

"The modern aesthetic grew out of a perfect storm of post-war optimism, innovative materials, and an incredible crop of designers," said Lisanne Dickson, director of 1950s/Modern Design at Treadway-Toomey.

"I think that the people who designed the furniture were maybe ahead of society's ability to accept and understand what they were doing," Sollo said. "It's taken people another 30 to 40 years to catch up to it."

There are hundreds of great Modern designers, many who worked across categories – furniture, architecture, fine art, etc. – and many contributed to the work of other big names without ever seeking that glory for themselves.

For more information on Modernism, see *Warman's Modernism Furniture & Accessories Identification and Price Guide* by Noah Fleisher.

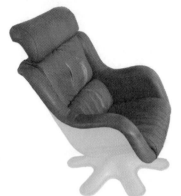

Yrjö Kukkapuro for Haimi Oy Finland classic mid-century modern adjustable leather chair and ottoman, 1964, rare and exceptional chair that's highly collectible, chair is 36" h x 27" d x 28" w with a 13-1/2" seat height, ottoman is 21-1/2" w x 21-1/2" d with a 14" seat height. **$1,200**

Courtesy of Le Shoppe Too, www.leshoppetoo.com

▶ Selig leather and bent wood lounge reading chair, circa 1960s, designed in a Danish Modern style much like the infamous James Eames/Herman Miller lounge chairs, features wider dimensions and a sturdier construction, includes original ottoman, chair is 39-1/2" h x 32" d x 31-1/2" w, ottoman is 15-3/4" h x 21-1/4" w x 17-1/2" d. **$500**

North American Auction Company, northamericanauctioncompany.com

Chrome and vinyl bar stools, round stools with yellow vinyl cushions on chrome base, 32" h, 16" dia. **$20**

Courtesy of Leonard Auction, Inc., www.leonardauction.com

▼ Pair of stools with blue vinyl upholstery, 15-3/4" h, 15-1/4" dia. **$80**

Courtesy of Leonard Auction, Inc., www.leonardauction.com

◀ Two mid-century living room chairs, unknown maker, one is 33" x 28" x 31", other chair is 32" x 27" x 34"................**$275**

North American Auction Company, northamericanauctioncompany.com

FURNITURE

Richard Schultz convertible sofa bed, designed in 1958, model no. 704 BC, Knoll Associates, retains manufacturer's label, 28" x 81" x 32"................................. **$5,760**

Courtesy of Los Angeles Modern Auctions, www.lamodernauctions.com

Large modern sofa with teak and stone insert in the manner of Kagan, maker unknown, 22" x 132" x 46".......................**$1,700**

Courtesy of Regency Auction House, regencyauctionllc.com

Orange over-upholstered sofa with wooden frame and pedestal base, by Tech Furniture, Inc., 29" x 85" x 37". **$100**

Courtesy of Cordier Auctions & Appraisals, www.cordierauction.com

Modern two-part credenza, maker unknown, 73" x 83-1/2" x 17-1/2". **$850**

Courtesy of Regency Auction House, regencyauctionllc.com

Set of two Sieling Furniture Co. bedside cabinets, original decal on inside right top drawers, each cabinet has two drawers, circa 1950s, 25-1/4" x 24" x 17".**$123**

Courtesy of Kaminski Auctions, www.kaminskiauctions.com

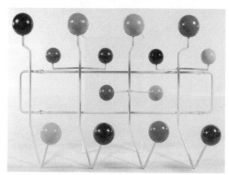

Mid-Century Modern "Hang-It-All" coat rack by Eames for Herman Miller , lacquered wood, enameled steel, attached sticker labels, 13" h, 19-3/4" w, 7" d. **$190**

Courtesy of Leonard Auction, Inc., www.leonardauction.com

◀ Maple Planner Group #1560 single pedestal desk, design by Paul McCobb (1917-1969) for Winchendon Furniture Company, rectangular top over two drawers at one side, all raised on turned tapered supports, 29" h, 48" w, 24" d.
.... **$475**

Courtesy of Austin Auction Gallery, www.austinauction.com

▶ Milo Baughman desk, designed c. 1954, Murray Furniture, 28-3/4" x 62" x 24-1/4". **$3,200**

Courtesy of Los Angeles Modern Auctions, www.lamodernauctions.com

Milling Road six-drawer bow-front chest and matching nightstand, North Carolina, 1950s, teak, chrome-plated brass, manufacturer labels, chest is 44-1/2" x 36" x 20-1/2", night stand is 32" x 24" x 20. .... **$544**

Courtesy of Rago Arts and Auctions, www.ragoarts.com

Mid-Century Danish modern sideboard with floating top, Denmark, 1966, 6 side drawers, sliding doors on cabinet base, sliding glass door top, Danish Furniture Control metal tag, Siebast metal label, 62" x 72" x 19-1/2". **$1,600**

Courtesy of A-1 Auction, a1auctiongallery.com

Falster Danish sideboard and hutch, book-matched Brazilian rosewood, 1969, sideboard is 30" h, 60" w, 18-1 /2" d, hutch is 28" h, 60" w, 13" d. **$1,476**

Courtesy of Richard Opfer Auctioneering, Inc., www.opferauction.com

Vanity by Arne Wahl Iversen for Vinde Mobelfabrik, Denmark, three sections, central vanity having a lift-up top with mirror and a divided interior, left section with drawer over two doors opening to shelved interior on one side and four pull-out trays on other side, right section with four drawers, marked with "Danish Furniture Makers Control," marked on back "Made in Denmark" and with "VM" logo, 104" w, 17-3/4" d, 29-3/4" h. **$200**

Courtesy of Ivy Auctions, Inc., ivyauctions.com

"Jacks" coffee table by Adrian Pearsall, oval glass top, teak base, 15-3/4" h, 59" l, 20"w. **$450**

Courtesy of Leonard Auction, Inc., www.leonardauction.com

Paul Frankl Johnson coffee table, True Grand Rapids metal label and stenciled model number 5005 #256, 48" x 36" x 14-1/2"................ **$6,000**

Courtesy of Vero Beach Auction, verobeachauction.com

Mid-Century Modern chrome and plate glass library steps, second half 20th century, possibly by the Pace Furniture Collection, New York City, three stair treads with 5/8" plate glass inserts, handrail along the right side and top, 52" h, 18" w, 31" d. **$650**

Courtesy of New Orleans Auction Galleries, www.neworleansauction.com

Charles and Ray Eames coffee table, designed in 1958, model no. 691, Herman Miller, 16-1/2" h x 36" dia. **$1,280**

Courtesy of Los Angeles Modern Auctions, www.lamodernauctions.com

GLASS

american brilliant cut glass

CUT GLASS IS made by grinding decorations into glass by means of abrasive-carrying metal or stone wheels. An ancient craft, it was revived in 1600 by the Bohemians and spread through Europe to Great Britain and America.

American cut glass came of age at the Centennial Exposition in 1876 and the World Columbian Exposition in 1893. America's most significant output of high-quality glass occurred from 1880 to 1917, a period now known as the Brilliant Period. Glass from this period is the most eagerly sought by collectors.

Punch bowl, Hobstar and Cane pattern, saw-toothed edge and deep scalloped rim, heavy bowl and stand, chip and surface scratches on the underside of the bowl where it meets the base, a one-quarter inch chip on the outside rim of the bowl, with surface scratches and fleabite chips on the top rim of the base, with two chips on the rim of the base, 13" h. x 14-1/2" d......**$390**

Courtesy of Wickliff &Associates Auctioneers, www.wickliffauctioneers.com

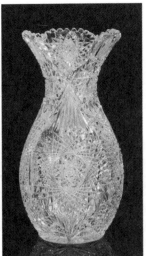

◄ Well-cut example of a bowling pin form vase, all-over cutting design on an extra-large vase, 14-1/2" x 7-1/2"........**$619**

Courtesy of Dirk Soulis Auctions, www.dirksoulisauctions.com

▶ Antique crystal vase, optic cut glass, chipped teeth on rim, 10-1/8" x 4-3/16"......................**$74**

Courtesy of Vidi Vici Gallery, www.vidivicigallery.com

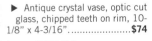

VISIT WWW.ANTIQUETRADER.COM

WWW.FACEBOOK.COM/ANTIQUETRADER

Known for its exquisite cut glass, the Libbey Glass Co. became synonymous with the Brilliant Period. Punch bowls are considered some of Libbey's most cherished pieces and include the Grand Prize pattern from the 1904 St. Louis World's Fair and the Stars and Stripes pattern presented to President William McKinley. Libbey was, as Edward Atlee Barber described in his 1900 publication *American Glassware*, "world-famous for the depth and richness of their cut designs, their simplicity and complexity of pattern, purity of color and prismatic brilliancy."

Fine vase, fans diamond and prism pattern design, tapering at base with mostly prism design, 8-1/2" d. at top x 10" h. **$94**

Courtesy of Clements, www.clementsantiquestn.com

Humidor with great cuts and Hobstar pattern foot, silver-plated flip top lid and an inside lid holder for adding material to maintain moisture within the tobacco, a few small flakes to the body with the silver plate in great condition. **$383**

Courtesy of Dirk Soulis Auctions, www.dirksoulisauctions.com

Fan-shaped vase, Hobstar pattern, crosscut diamond, step cut, prism and zipper motif, clear blank, 8" x 9-3/4" **$210**

Courtesy of Woody Auction, www.woodyauction.com

▶ Sugar shaker, Crosscut Diamond and Fan motif, sharp cutting, 4" d. **$150**

Courtesy of Woody Auction, www.woodyauction.com

Lamp, American made, early 20th century, 17-1/2" h. x 12" d. **$1,875**

Courtesy of Quinn Auction Galleries, www.quinnsauction.com

Squat vase, thick-cut Hobstar and Fan pattern, 19th century, notched rim with faceted neck, base well developed star, some small rim chips to edge, 6" h. x 11" d. **$160**

Courtesy of Leland Little Auctions, www.lelandlittle.com

Epergne, colorless, trumpet-form vase applied to a shallow bowl, with Hobstar, Buzzsaw, Fan and Strawberry Diamond motifs, late 19th/early 20th century, 12" h, 9" d. (bowl)........................... **$343**

Courtesy of Jeffrey S. Evans & Associates, www.jeffreysevans.com

Cookie jar, Hobstar and Sunburst motif, lapidary finial, one chip on the side, 8-1/2" h. with lid. **$265**

Courtesy of Dirk Soulis Auctions, www.dirksoulis.com

Group of three sterling and cut glass table articles, two pitchers and one vase, circa 1897, tall pitcher includes a sterling spout and collar decorated with vines and grapes over a notched Prism or Zipper patter; medium-sized pitcher – with sterling spout and collar monogrammed "S" with C-scroll and floral design over a notched Miters or Zipper and Punties pattern; vase also features a sterling scalloped mouth engraved with "1873" and "1898" centered with monogrammed letter "S" over a notched Miters or Zipper pattern; all sterling mounts hallmarked for Gorham, with "STERLING" and the trident date code for 1897. Tall pitcher is also numbered "S2986", medium pitcher numbered "S3031" and the vase "S2981", further stamped for retailer "CHARLES W CRANKSHAW", all pieces with scattered minor fleabites observed under a loop, minor pitting to mounted sterling, a couple small chips to edge of vase, small ding/split at spout rim of tall pitcher, tall pitcher 11-1/4" h, medium pitcher 9" h. (both bottom of spout), vase 6-1/3" h. **$868**

Lot of two pitchers, first by J. Hoare & Co., features Hobstar and Fan pattern cut design, with an applied notched handle and star cut base, signed; other a Flower and Button pattern with applied notched handle and star-cut base, unmarked, both 19th century, rim chips near spout of J. Hoare pitcher, about 10-1/2" h. **$123**

Courtesy of Leland Little Auctions, www.lelandlittle.com

▼ Vase, with a flared mouth over a baluster form body, decorated with Pineapple and Hobstar motifs, late 19th/early 20th century, scattered minor scratches commensurate with age, 14" h. x 6" d. **$375**

Courtesy of John Moran Auctioneers, www.johnmoran.com

10 Things You Didn't Know About Gabriel Argy-Rousseau

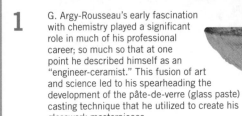

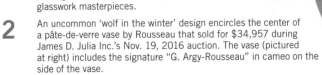

1 G. Argy-Rousseau's early fascination with chemistry played a significant role in much of his professional career; so much so that at one point he described himself as an "engineer-ceramist." This fusion of art and science led to his spearheading the development of the pâte-de-verre (glass paste) casting technique that he utilized to create his glasswork masterpieces.

2 An uncommon 'wolf in the winter' design encircles the center of a pâte-de-verre vase by Rousseau that sold for $34,957 during James D. Julia Inc.'s Nov. 19, 2016 auction. The vase (pictured at right) includes the signature "G. Argy-Rousseau" in cameo on the side of the vase.

3 His professional name is a combination of his birth name (Joseph-Gabriel Rousseau) and his wife's maiden name (Marianne Argyriades). The two were married in 1913. He was born in France (1885) and she in Greece.

4 Among his first 'large scale' showings was at the 1914 Exposition du Salon des Artistes Français (Salon of French artists), an annual art exhibition dating back to 1881, and held in Paris.

5 Characteristics of Art Nouveau and Art Deco styles of design are prevalent in his work, with elements of nature (flowers, animals), feminine figures and aspects of early mythology appearing most often.

6 During James D. Julia Inc.'s Fall 2016 Lamps, Glass & Fine Jewelry Auction, a footed pâte-de-verre bowl (pictured above), boasting a rich design of blackberries encircling both the interior and exterior against a frosted background, realized $1,185. Signed "G. Argy Rousseau" on the side, the bowl's design further includes blackberry leaves and vines.

7 To help spread the word about the unique pieces being created at Société Anonyme des Pâtes de Verre d'Argy-Rousseau — the company he formed with gallery and glass works owner Gustave Moser-Millot — Argy-Rousseau took out advertisements in magazines both within Europe and America. He also invested time and effort in creating leaflets that spoke about the intricate technique used to create the unconventional and illustrious glassworks.

8 With the spirit of invention very much alive in him, Argy-Rousseau filed several patents during WWI for possible use by the military. In addition, as a time and cost-savings measure, he developed processes that also resulted in production that was more assembly efficient. However, as the world suffered financial despair in 1929 the market for this high-profile glass shrunk.

9 Pieces by Argy-Rousseau that sold during James D. Julia's Nov. 19, 2016 auction ranged in price from $1,185 to nearly $35,000. There are a few examples of Argy-Rousseau's elegant glasswork from this auction that did not sell. (This includes the cendrier ashtray pictured at the top of the page, as part of the 10 Things You Didn't Know logo). The items will only be open to offers for a short period of time, visit www.jamesdjulia.com for more information.

10 Despite attempting to form his own studio — following the closure of his partnered company — the shift in interest from Argy-Rousseau's style of art glass to opalescent glass produced by Lalique and Daum, and the impact World War II had on access to raw material left Argy-Rousseau somewhat in the same place he began. Before his death in 1953, he finished his career working at a factory producing commercial porcelain, much like the one where he began his career. Today his glassworks attract attention at auctions and museums, and his techniques appeal to a new generation of glass artists.

– Compiled by Antoinette Rahn

Sources: http://www.macklowegallery.com; https://www.youtube.com/user/corningmuseumofglass; http://www.artnet.com; http://www.britishmuseum.com; http://www.jamesdjulia.com

GLASS

baccarat

BACCARAT GLASS HAS been made by Cristalleries de Baccarat, France, since 1765. The firm has produced various glassware of excellent quality as well as paperweights. Baccarat's Rose Tiente is often referred to as Baccarat's Amberina.

French gilt bronze and cut crystal candelabras and gilt bronze obelisk, circa 1900, 21" (obelisk).
.... **$1,045**

Courtesy of Cottone Auctions, www.cottoneauctions.com

Decanter and four tumblers set, markers' mark on all pieces, 10-1/4" h. (decanter), 4 ¼" h. (tumbler). **$444**

Courtesy of The Popular Auction, www.thepopularauction.com

Centerpiece bowl, crystal and bronze, glass carved and etched with an Art Nouveau seascape scene, with a partridge themed bronze base, impressed with the Baccarat mark, 14" x 6" x 7". **$6,250**

Courtesy of Concept Art Gallery, www.conceptgallery.com

Silver-plated, chrome and glass hurricane globes with acid-etched floral and geometric design, petal-form bases and aluminum candle nozzles, 20th century, unmarked, 16-1/4" h................. **$512**

Courtesy of Brunk Auctions, www.brunkauctions.com

Pair of Tallyrand ice buckets/wine coolers, French, 20th century, gold-tone detachable loop handle and top band over cut glass palm-form panels, cut base with Baccarat mark, 6" h. **$640**

Courtesy of Brunk Auctions, www.brunkauctions.com

Pair of three-light candelabras, gilt and enameled glass with suspended lusters throughout, unmarked, one candelabra is missing a lustre from the bottom central position, very good condition, 20-½" h. x 12-1/2" w.................. **$1,792**

Courtesy of Susanin's Auctions, www.susanins.com

Twelve-light glass chandelier, baluster-form standard cut in diamond patterns, with issuing tiered molded glass arms with reeded bobeches, hung with glass swags and faceted prisms, 26" h. x 22-12/" w. **$812**

Courtesy of New Orleans Auction Galleries, www.neworleansauction.com

Pair of glass and gilt silver candlesticks, short in stature with a circular foot on each, supporting a glass hurricane shade with serrated rim, gilt bands and a double row of incised fleur d' lye appear, each underside marked Gorham Sterling and hallmarked, shades acid etched Baccarat, 20th century, 15-3/4" h. **$406**

Courtesy of Auction Gallery of the Palm Beaches, Inc., agopb.com

Group of nine ruby cut to clear crystal aperitif glasses in two sizes, 19th century, excellent condition, very small chip to the rim of one of the taller glasses, seven glasses 4-3/4" h. x 2" d., two glasses 3-3/4" h. x 1-3/4" d. **$187**

Courtesy of MG Neely Auction, www.neelyauction.com

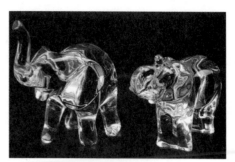

Two elephant figurines, signed Baccarat, good condition, 4-1/2" h and 3-1/2" h. **$155**

Courtesy of Kodner Galleries, www.kodner.com

Hanging lantern, cylindrical glass shade of electric blue glass featuring Russian genre scenes of Cossacks, a Troika etc. embossed blue glass on frosted blue background, with brass fittings, signed Baccarat, late 19th century, no electrification, 26" h. overall, 9" h. x 7-1/2" d. glass portion. **$2,124**

Pair of Art Nouveau Rock Crystal vases, circa 1870, asymmetrical bodies cut with leaves, with the Baccarat circular cipher impressed on the underside of each, 12-3/4" h. x 6" w. **$4,867**

Courtesy of Auction Gallery of the Palm Beaches, Inc., agopb.com

Pressed oval paneled frames cologne bottle, brilliant deep cobalt blue with elaborate gilt decoration, hexagonal form with panel-cut neck, factory-polished mouth, table ring, and pontil mark, original lily-form stopper numbered, circa 1845-1870, 6-5/8" h. overall, 3-3/4" h. bottle, 2-3/8" d. base.. **$280**

Courtesy of Jeffrey S. Evans & Associates, www.jeffreysevans.com

Five-piece amber stain dresser set with two cologne bottles with stopper, ring dish, lidded trinket jar and under tray, 10-3/4" w. x 8-1/2" d. (tray), 5-3/4" h. x 3-1/4" w. (decanters). **$413**

Courtesy of Dirk Soulis Auctions, www.dirksoulisauctions.com

Pair of crystal figurines in the form of seated bears with extended paws, both contain acid-etched Baccarat France mark to underside and original paper labels present, 3-3/4" h............... **$94**

Courtesy of Auction Gallery of the Palm Beaches, Inc., agopb.com

GLASS

bride's baskets

THESE BERRY OR FRUIT BOWLS were popular late Victorian wedding gifts, hence the name bride's basket was adopted. They were produced in a variety of quality art glass wares and sometimes were fitted in ornate silver-plate holders.

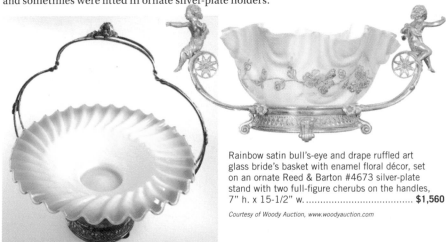

Rainbow satin bull's-eye and drape ruffled art glass bride's basket with enamel floral décor, set on an ornate Reed & Barton #4673 silver-plate stand with two full-figure cherubs on the handles, 7" h. x 15-1/2" w. **$1,560**

Courtesy of Woody Auction, www.woodyauction.com

Green and white bride's basket on floral silver-plated stand with handle, significant tarnish to silver, otherwise very good original condition, 13" w. x 11-1/2" h. **$142**

Courtesy of Dirk Soulis Auctions, www.dirksoulisauctions.com

Salesman sample bride's basket, enameled cased glass with ribbon edge, on a metal basket, excellent condition, 7" h. **$102**

Courtesy of Matthew Bullock Auctioneers, www.bullockauctioneers.com

Cream satin ruffled bride's basket with Coralene floral décor, on Monarch #556 silver-plate frame, bowl has some marks from silver-plate, 11" h. x 13-1/2" w. **$270**

Courtesy of Woody Auction, www.woodyauction.com

Circular peachblow bride's bowl with scalloped and folded rim decorated in floral enamels inside and out, polish pontil beneath the base, on a silver-plated stand with horizontal openwork handles on a waisted stem adjoining a hammered dome base with applied figural flowers and raised on four feet, very good condition, 10" h. x 12-1/2" w. **$590**

Courtesy of Dirk Soulis Auctions, www.dirksoulisauctions.com

Blue Coinspot pattern bride's basket with enamel bird, blossom and branch décor, set on Meriden #01509 silver-plate frame with ornate floral scroll, 8-1/2" h. x 11" w. **$240**

Courtesy of Woody Auction, www.woodyauction.com

Blown crimped and flared-rim iridescent bride's basket in pink and blue, Victorian era, on a white metal frame, 12-1/2" h. **$75**

Courtesy of Auction Gallery of Boca Raton, www.agobr.com

Double bride's basket with ruffled glass bowls and a silver-plated Pairpoint frame, circa 1900, missing flake to the interior of one bowl, broken-off foliage element to the putti – piece is present, supports of one bowl needs resoldering, Pairpoint MFG. Co., New Bedford, Mass, Quadruple plate, 2202, EC148, 16-3/4" h. x 21-1/2" w. x 9-1/2" d. **$500**

Courtesy of Heritage Auctions, www.ha.com

Cranberry and white opalescent square bride's basket with enamel décor, on silver-plate frame, 10" h. x 12" w. **$295**

Courtesy of Woody Auction, www.woodyauction.com

Scalloped clear pattern bride's basket with Cane and Diamond motif, on original Meriden #241 silver-plate stand featuring ornate embossed bird and floral design, 7" t. x 14-1/2" w. **$210**

Courtesy of Woody Auction, www.woodyauction.com

Scarce blue and white mottled cased satin "Peg" bride's bowl with Enamel Leaf and Nut décor, on Wilcox #764 silver-plate frame with original removable silver "Peg Cap" insert, 13" t. x 12" w. **$360**

Courtesy of Woody Auction, www.woodyauction.com

Ruffled edge Cobalt bride's bowl with gold hand-painted flowers and a white interior, on Rogers & Bros triple-plate stand marked on bottom, 12" h. x 10-1/2" w. x 9" d.. **$406**

Courtesy of Don Presley Auction, www.donpresley.com

▶ Ruffled bride's basket with pink and yellow exterior and white interior with enamel floral décor on the interior and exterior, set on a Webster #189 figural silver-plate stand featuring a full-figure cherub, 14" h. x 12" w. **$480**

Courtesy of Woody Auction, www.woodyauction.com

Three-arm bride's basket, pink cased ruffled bowl set on center stand with three hanging silver-plate sweetmeat baskets and a spoon, 12-1/2" t. x 14" w.. **$1,652**

Courtesy of Woody Auction, www.woodyauction.com

Unusual square cranberry, Vaseline and opal ware bride's basket with enamel décor, on Barbour #249 silver-plate frame featuring a female figure in motion, 16-1/2" h. x 10-1/2" w. **$600**

Courtesy of Woody Auction, www.woodyauction.com

GLASS

carnival

CARNIVAL GLASS IS what is fondly called mass-produced iridescent glassware. The term "carnival glass" has evolved through the years as glass collectors have responded to the idea that much of this beautiful glassware was made as give-away glass at local carnivals and fairs. However, more of it was made and sold through the same channels as pattern glass and Depression glass. Some patterns were indeed giveaways, and others were used as advertising premiums, souvenirs, etc. Whatever the origin, the term "carnival glass" today encompasses glassware that is usually pattern molded and treated with metallic salts, creating that unique coloration that is so desirable to collectors.

Early names for iridescent glassware, which early 20th century consumers believed to have all come from foreign manufacturers, include Pompeian Iridescent, Venetian Art, and Mexican Aurora. Another popular early name was "Nancy Glass," as some patterns were believed to have come from the Daum, Nancy, glassmaking area in France. This was at a time when the artistic cameo glass was enjoying great success. While the iridescent glassware being made by such European glassmakers as Loetz influenced the American market place, it was Louis Tiffany's Favrile glass that really caught the eye of glass consumers of the early 1900s. It seems an easy leap to transform Tiffany's shimmering glassware to something that could be mass produced, allowing what we call carnival glass today to become "poor man's Tiffany."

Grape and cable stippled glass plate, blue with a pie-crust edge, Northwood Co., first quarter 20th century, 9" d... **$373**

Courtesy of Jeffrey S. Evans & Associates, www.jeffreyevans.com

Carnival glass is iridized glassware that is created by pressing hot molten glass into molds, just as pattern glass had evolved. Some forms are hand finished, while others are completely formed by molds. To achieve the marvelous iridescent colors that carnival glass collectors seek, a process was developed where a liquid solution of metallic salts was put onto the still hot glass form after it was unmolded. As the liquid evaporated, a fine metallic surface was left which refracts light into wonderful colors. The name given to the iridescent spray by early glassmakers was "dope."

Many of the forms created by carnival glass manufacturers were accessories to the china American housewives so loved. By the early 1900s, consumers could find carnival glassware at such popular stores as F. W. Woolworth and McCrory's. To capitalize on the popular fancy for these colored wares, some other industries bought large quantities of carnival glass and turned them into "packers." This term reflects the practice where baking powder, mustard, or other household products were packed into a special piece of glass that could take on another life after the original product was used. Lee Manufacturing Co. used iridized carnival glass as premiums for its baking powder and other products, causing some early carnival glass to be known by the generic term "Baking Powder Glass."

Classic carnival glass production began in the early 1900s and continued about twenty years, but no one really documented or researched production until the first collecting wave struck in 1960

It is important to remember that carnival glasswares were sold in department stores as well as mass merchants rather than through the general store often associated with a young America. Glassware by this time was mass-produced and sold in large quantities by such enterprising companies as Butler Brothers. When the economics of the country soured in the 1920s, those interested in purchasing iridized glassware were not spared. Many of the leftover inventories of glasshouses that hoped to sell this mass-produced glassware found their way to wholesalers who in turn sold the wares to those who offered the glittering glass as prizes at carnivals, fairs, circuses, etc. Possibly because this was the last venue people associated the iridized glassware with, it became known as "carnival glass."

For more information on carnival glass, see Warman's Carnival Glass Identification and Price Guide, 2nd edition, by Ellen T. Schroy.

CARNIVAL GLASS COMPANIES

Much of vintage American carnival glassware was created in the Ohio valley, in the glasshouse-rich areas of Pennsylvania, Ohio, and West Virginia. The abundance of natural materials, good transportation, and skilled craftsmen that created the early American

Acorn Burrs pattern four-piece tablet set, amethyst: covered butter dish, sugar bowl, creamer and spooner, each N-in-circle trademark, H. Northwood Co., circa 1908, 4-1/8" h. to 6-3/8" h. $311

Courtesy of Jeffrey S. Evans & Associates, www.jeffreysevans.com

Grouping of eight items including four juice glasses with sunflower relief motif, two petal-like dishes with similar motif, handled pitcher with foliate motif, and a Northwood columnar vase marked to bottom with underline N., 13" h. x 4-1/2" w. x 4-1/2" d. for vase. $277

Courtesy of Peachtree & Bennett, peachtreebennett.com

pattern glass manufacturing companies allowed many of them to add carnival glass to their production lines. Brief company histories of the major carnival glass manufacturers follow:

CAMBRIDGE GLASS CO. (CAMBRIDGE)

Cambridge Glass was a rather minor player in the carnival glass marketplace. Founded in 1901 as a new factory in Cambridge, Ohio, it focused on producing fine crystal tablewares. What carnival glass it did produce was imitation cut-glass patterns.

Colors used by Cambridge include marigold, as well as few others. Forms found in carnival glass by Cambridge include tablewares and vases, some with its trademark "Near-Cut."

DIAMOND GLASS CO. (DIAMOND)

This company was started as the Dugan brothers (see Dugan Glass Co.) departed the carnival glass-making scene in 1913. However, Alfred Dugan returned and became general manager until his death in 1928. After a disastrous fire in June of 1931, the factory closed.

DUGAN GLASS CO. (DUGAN)

The history of the Dugan Glass Co. is closely related to Harry Northwood (see Northwood Glass Co.), whose cousin, Thomas Dugan, became plant manager at the Northwood Glass Co. in Indiana, Pennsylvania, in 1895. By 1904, Dugan and his partner W. G. Minnemayer bought the former Northwood factory from the now defunct National Glass conglomerate and opened as the Dugan Glass Co. Dugan's brother, Alfred, joined the company and stayed until it became the Diamond Glass Co. in 1913. At this time, Thomas Dugan moved to the Cambridge Glass Co., later Duncan and Miller and finally Hocking, Lancaster. Alfred left Diamond Glass, too, but later returned.

Understanding how the Northwood and Dugan families were connected helps collectors understand the linkage of these three companies. Their productions were similar; molds were swapped, retooled, etc.

Colors attributed to Dugan and Diamond include amethyst, marigold, peach opalescent, and white. The company developed deep amethyst shades, some almost black.

Forms made by both Dugan and Diamond mirrored what other glass companies were producing. The significant contribution by Dugan and later Diamond were feet – either ball or spatula shapes. They are also known for deeply crimped edges.

FENTON ART GLASS CO. (FENTON)

Frank Leslie Fenton and his brothers, John W. Fenton and Charles H. Fenton, founded this truly American glassmaker in 1905 in Martins Ferry, Ohio. Early production was of blanks, which the brothers soon learned to decorate themselves. They moved to a larger factory in Williamstown, West Virginia.

By 1907, Fenton was experimenting with iridescent glass, developing patterns and the metallic salt formulas that it became so famous for. Production of carnival glass continued at Fenton until the early 1930s. In 1970, Fenton began to reissue carnival glass, creating new colors and forms as well as using traditional patterns.

Colors developed by Fenton are numerous. The company developed red and Celeste blue in the 1920s; a translucent pale blue, known as Persian blue, is also one of its more distinctive colors, as is a light yellow-green color known as vaseline. Fenton also produced delicate opalescent colors including amethyst opalescent and red opalescent. Because the Fenton brothers learned how to decorate their own blanks, they also promoted the addition of enamel decoration to some of their carnival glass patterns.

Forms made by Fenton are also numerous. What distinguishes Fenton from other glassmakers is its attention to detail and hand finishing processes. Edges are found scalloped, fluted, tightly crimped, frilled, or pinched into a candy ribbon edge, also referred to as 3-in-1 edge.

IMPERIAL GLASS CO. (IMPERIAL)

Edward Muhleman and a syndicate founded the Imperial Glass Co. at Bellaire, Ohio, in 1901, with production beginning in 1904. It started with pressed glass tableware patterns as well as lighting fixtures. The company's marketing strategy included selling to important retailers of its day, such as F. W. Woolworth and McCrory and Kresge, to get glassware into the hands of American housewives. Imperial also became a major exporter of glassware, including its brilliant carnival patterns. During the Depression, it filed for bankruptcy in 1931, but was able to continue on. By 1962, it was again producing carnival glass patterns. By April 1985, the factory was closed and the molds sold.

Colors made by Imperial include typical carnival colors such as marigold. It added interesting shades of green, known as helios, a pale ginger ale shade known as clambroth, and a brownish smoke shade.

Dragon Lotus pattern bowl, 1920s, Fenton, blue iridescent ruffled edge bowl, 8-1/2" **$59**

Courtesy of Vero Beach Auction, www.verobeachauction.com

Bowl with Millersburg "Nesting Swan", circa 1920, 2-1/2" h. x 9" d. **$86**

Courtesy of EstateofMind, www.estateofmind.biz

Forms created by Imperial tend to be functional, such as berry sets and table sets. Patterns vary from wonderful imitation cut glass patterns to detailed florals and naturalistic designs.

MILLERSBURG GLASS CO. (MILLERSBURG)

John W. Fenton started the Millersburg Glass Co. in September 1908. Perhaps it was the factory's more obscure location or the lack of business experience by John Fenton, but the company failed by 1911.

The factory was bought by Samuel Fair and John Fenton, and renamed the Radium Glass Co., but it lasted only a year.

Colors produced by Millersburg are amethyst, green, and marigold. Shades such as blue and vaseline were added on rare occasions. The company is well known for its bright radium finishes.

Forms produced at Millersburg are mostly bowls and vases. Pattern designers at Millersburg often took one theme and developed several patterns from it. Millersburg often used one pattern for the interior and a different pattern for the exterior.

NORTHWOOD GLASS CO. (NORTHWOOD)

Englishman Harry Northwood founded the Northwood Glass Co. He developed his glass formulas for carnival glass, naming it "Golden Iris" in 1908. Northwood was one of the pioneers of the glass manufacturers who marked his wares. Marks range from a full script signature to a simple underscored capital N in a circle. However, not all Northwood glassware is marked.

Colors that Northwood created were many. Collectors prefer its pastels, such as ice blue, ice green, and white. It is also known for several stunning blue shades. The one color that Northwood did not develop was red.

Forms of Northwood patterns range from typical table sets, bowls, and water sets to whimsical novelties, such as a pattern known as Corn, which realistically depicts an ear of corn.

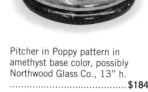

Pitcher in Poppy pattern in amethyst base color, possibly Northwood Glass Co., 13" h.
.... **$184**

Courtesy of Hartzell's Auction Gallery, www.hartzellsauction.com

UNITED STATES GLASS CO. (U.S. GLASS)

In 1891, a consortium of 15 American glass manufacturers joined together as the United States Glass Co. This company was successful in continuing pattern glass production, as well as developing new glass lines. By 1911, it had begun limited production of carnival glass lines, often using existing pattern glass tableware molds. By the time a tornado destroyed the last of its glass factories in Glassport in 1963, it was no longer producing glassware.

Colors associated with US Glass are marigold, white, and a rich honey amber.

Forms tend to be table sets and functional forms.

WESTMORELAND GLASS CO. (WESTMORELAND)

Started as the Westmoreland Specialty Co., Grapeville, Pennsylvania, in 1889, this company originally made novelties and glass packing containers, such as candy containers. Researchers have identified its patterns being advertised by Butler Brothers as early as 1908. Carnival glass production continued into the 1920s. In the 1970s, Westmoreland, too, begin to reissue carnival glass patterns and novelties. However, this ceased in February of 1996 when the factory burned.

Colors originally used by Westmoreland were typical carnival colors, such as blue

GLASS

Dugan "Farmyard" amethyst bowl with six ruffles and beaded rim, jeweled heart exterior pattern, Dugan Glass Co., 10-7/8" d. x 3-1/4" h. **$2,583**

Courtesy of William Bunch Auctions & Appraisals, www.bunchauctions.com

Pair of vintage marigold Jack in the Pulpit vases, hand blown, 8-3/4" h...**$31**

Courtesy of Auction Gallery of Boca Raton, www.agobr.com

Ten-piece cobalt, grape and cable punch bowl set, bowl with original Fenton paper label, 10-3/4" d. (punch bowl), 2-1/2" d. (cups). **$153**

Courtesy of Cordier Auctions & Appraisals, www.cordierauction.com

Water pitcher and six tumblers, Soda Gold pattern in smoke coloring, 7-1/2" h. **$108**

Courtesy of Woody Auction, www.woodyauction.com

Punch bowl, cups and compote in green with metallic glaze, 20th century, surface scratches and wear, good condition, 5" h. x 12" h...................**$74**

Courtesy of Leland Little Auctions, www.lelandlittle.com

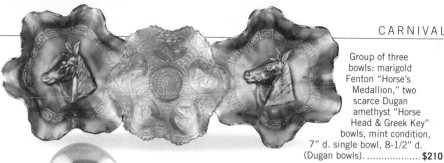

Group of three bowls: marigold Fenton "Horse's Medallion," two scarce Dugan amethyst "Horse Head & Greek Key" bowls, mint condition, 7" d. single bowl, 8-1/2" d. (Dugan bowls). **$210**

Courtesy of A-1 Auction, www.a1auctiongallery.com

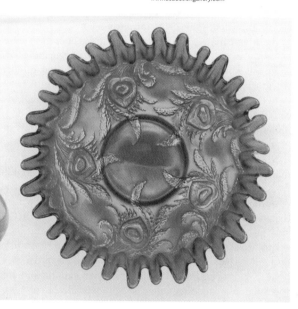

Bell from paperweight with interior decoration, good condition, 6-1/2" h. x 3-1/2" d...**$35**

Courtesy of Kennedy Auction Service, www.kennedysauction.com

Ruffled edge bowl in the Heart and Vine pattern, circa 1910, amethyst with shades of teal, purple and copper, straw marks and bubbles typical of antique glass, 3-1/4" h. x 8" d.........................**$80**

Courtesy of Antique 2 Modern, www.arnoldauction.com

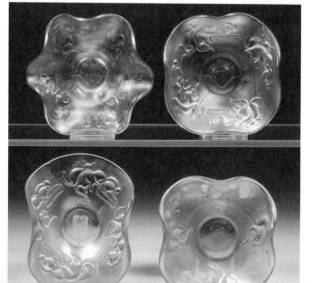

Lot of four Kittens pattern carnival glass articles: banana dish, six-ruffle bowl, and two four-ruffle bowls, marigold iridescent, Fenton Art Glass Co., first quarter 20th century, 1-1/4" to 1-1/2" h., 4-1/4" to 4-5/8" h. d. **$124**

Courtesy of Jeffrey S. Evans & Associates, www.jeffreysevans.com

GLASS

custard

"CUSTARD GLASS," AS collectors call it today, came on the American scene in the 1890s, more than a decade after similar colors were made in Europe and England. The Sowerby firm of Gateshead-on-Tyne, England had marketed its patented "Queen's Ivory Ware" quite successfully in the late 1870s and early 1880s.

There were many glass tableware factories operating in Pennsylvania and Ohio in the 1890s and early 1900s, and the competition among them was keen. Each company sought to capture the public's favor with distinctive colors and, often, hand-painted decoration. That is when "custard glass" appeared on the American scene.

The opaque yellow color of this glass varies from a rich, vivid yellow to a lustrous light yellow. Regardless of intensity, the hue was originally called "ivory" by several glass manufacturers who also used superlative sounding terms such as "Ivorina Verde" and "Carnelian." Most custard glass contains uranium, so it will "glow" under a black light.

The most important producer of custard glass was certainly Harry Northwood, who first made it at his plants in Indiana, Pennsylvania, in the late 1890s and, later, in his Wheeling, West Virginia, factory. Northwood marked some of his most famous patterns, but much early custard is unmarked. Other key manufacturers include the Heisey Glass Co., Newark, Ohio; the Jefferson Glass Co., Steubenville, Ohio; the Tarentum Glass Co., Tarentum, Pennsylvania; and the Fenton Art Glass Co., Williamstown, West Virginia.

Custard glass fanciers are particular about condition and generally insist on pristine quality decorations free from fading or wear. Souvenir custard pieces with events, places, and dates on them usually bring the best prices in the areas commemorated on them rather than from the specialist collector. Also, collectors who specialize in pieces such as cruets, syrups, or salt and pepper shakers will often pay higher prices for these pieces than would a custard collector.

Key reference sources include William Heacock's *Custard Glass from A to Z*, published in 1976 but not out of print, and the book *Harry Northwood: The Early Years*, available from Glass Press. Heisey's custard glass is discussed in Shirley Dunbar's *Heisey Glass: The Early Years* (Krause Publications, 2000), and Coudersport's production is well-documented in Tulla Majot's book, *Coudersport's Glass 1900-1904* (Glass Press, 1999). The Custard Glass Society holds a yearly convention and maintains a web site: www.homestead.com/custardsociety.

— James Measell

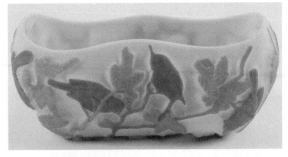

Planter with leaf and tree motif with cardinals on branches, 4" h. x 11" w.
.... **$99**

Courtesy of Chandler's International Auction,
www.chandlersauction.com

Burmese ruffled edge pitcher, 6" h. **$30**

Courtesy of Matthew Bullock Auctioneers, www.bullockauctioneers.com

Five-piece table set, Georgia Gem pattern with gilt decoration; covered butter dish and sugar, creamer, spooner, and celery vase, Tarentum Glass Co., circa 1900, 4" to 6" h. **$98**

Courtesy of Jeffrey S. Evans & Associates, www.jeffreysevans.com

Swirl bowl with enameled design of spring flowers, 4" h. x 14" d. **$154**

Courtesy of Echoes Antiques & Auction Gallery, www.echoesauctions.net

Seven-piece table set, Everglade pattern, Northwood; two butter dishes, two spooners, creamer, covered sugar, cruet bottle. **$413**

Courtesy of Woody Auction, www.woodyauction.com

Beaded circle spooner with gilt and polychrome-enamel decoration, circa 1904, H. Northwood Co., 4-1/4" h. **$37**

Courtesy of Jeffrey S. Evans & Associates, www.jeffreysevans.com

Covered butter dish, opaque blue with blue stain and gilt decoration, Chrysanthemum Sprig/Pagoda pattern, embossed "Northwood" script under base, circa 1899, 6" h. x 7-5/8" d. **$277**

Courtesy of Jeffrey S. Evans & Associates, www.jeffreysevans.com

Cracker jar, circa 1890-1895, shaded Burmese ground, enameled apple/cherry blossoms motif, marked on bottom "2594", quadruple-plate rim, bail handle, underside of lid marked MW/4404/a, Mt. Washington Glass Co., 6" h. plus bail handle. ...**$77**

Courtesy of Stony Ridge Auction, www.stonyridgeauction.com

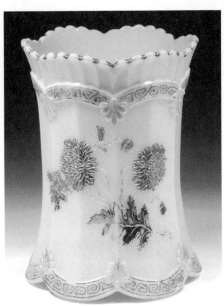

Celery vase, Chrysanthemum Spring, Pagoda pattern, green and pink staining and gilt decorations, with script "Northwood" trademark, 6-3/4" h. **$98**

Courtesy of Jeffrey S. Evans & Associates, www.jeffreysevans.com

Water pitcher, polychrome-enamel decoration, ball-form body with triangular rim and flying birds motif, applied blue handle, polished pontil mark, Harrach Glassworks, late 19th/early 20th century, 9-7/8" h. overall. **$149**

Courtesy of Jeffrey S. Evans & Associates, www.jeffreysevans.com

Salt and pepper shaker, enamel decorated, barrel form with foliate decoration, period two-part lids, fitted in a Pelton Bros. & Co. quadruple-plate stand, numbered "517", possibly Mt. Washington Glass Co., fourth quarter 19th century, 6-1/2" h. (stand) x 3-3/4" h. (shakers). **$61**

Courtesy of Jeffrey S. Evans & Associates, www.jeffreysevans.com

Toothpick holder, Wild Bouquet pattern with stained and gilt decoration, Northwood Glass Co., 2-1/2" h. overall. **$184**

Courtesy of Jeffrey S. Evans & Associates, www.jeffreysevans.com

Group of six holders; one Winged Scroll pattern match holder, Vermont pattern, Winged Scroll with rose décor pattern, Shell and Scales pattern, and rose décor toothpick holders. **$83**

Courtesy of Woody Auction, www.woodyauction.com

Four-piece table set, Louis XV pattern, gilt decoration, comprising covered butter dish and sugar bowl, creamer and spooner, circa 1898, 4-1/2" h. to 6-1/2" h. ... **$98**

Courtesy of Jeffrey S. Evans & Associates, www.jeffreysevans.com

Inverted Fan and Feathers eight-piece berry set, with pink stain and gilt decoration: master berry bowl, seven individual sauces/berry bowls, circa 1899; master 5-1/4" h. x 10" d., individual bowls 2-1/2" h. **$86**

Courtesy of Jeffrey S. Evans & Associates, www.jeffreysevans.com

GLASS

cut

CUT GLASS IS made by grinding decorations into glass by means of abrasive-carrying metal or stone wheels. An ancient craft, it was revived in 1600 by Bohemians and spread through Europe to Great Britain and America.

American cut glass came of age at the Centennial Exposition in 1876 and the World Columbian Exposition in 1893. America's most significant output of high-quality glass occurred from 1880 to 1917, a period now known as the Brilliant Period. Glass from this period is the most eagerly sought glass by collectors.

Cut cocktail accessories, cocktail shaker, with a diamond pattern body with a silverplate shaker cap, cordial glasses, each having a Hobstar motif around the bowl, surmounting ringed stem, resting on a circular foot, 3-1/4" h. x 1-1/2" d. **$246**

Courtesy of Austin Auction Gallery, www.austinauction.com

Banquet lamp, 20th century, Daisy and Button pattern, with orb shade over the woven wick and font, above baluster form standard, rising on circular foot, 30-1/2 h. x 9" d., 13-1/2 lbs. **$369**

Courtesy of Austin Auction Gallery, www.austinauction.com

Shaped vase, wheel cut and etched with stylized borders, with Champleve enamel frame, early 20th century, with the whole supported by three cherubs, mounted on an agate enamel circular base, some wear to glass, 15-1/4" h. x 8-1/4" d. **$3,125**

Courtesy of Roland New York, www.rolandantiques.com

▶ Glass decanter and stopper, probably Irish, 18th/19th century, with diamond cut body and canted square base, 1' x 1-1/2" h.... **$400**

Courtesy of Hannam's Auctioneers, www.hannamsauctioneers.com

Blue to clear cut vase, upper portion depicting two deer frolicking in a meadow, good condition overall, 13-1/2" h. x 6-3/4" d. **$156**

Courtesy of Roland New York, www.rolandantiques.com

French Tantalus holder with three cut decanter, some wear, one stopper has been repaired, 13-1/2" d. (centerpiece), 8-1/2" h. decanters... **$500**

Courtesy of Roland New York, www.rolandantiques.com

Cut glass decanter and carafe with grape form
handles, largest is 5" x 11-1/2".................... **$250**

Courtesy of Echoes Antiques & Auction Gallery, www.echoesauctions.net

White cut to cranberry glass chalice, gilt
decoration, some wear to gold, 8" h. x 5-5/8" d.
.... **$221**

Courtesy of William Bunch Auctions, https://www.bunchauctions.com

Victorian-era cruet or condiment set, fabulous
ornate holder crafted out of sterling Victorian era
cruet or condiment set, eight cut glass bottles
some with silver tops, bears English hallmarks for
1865, missing one stopper, some chips to glass,
good condition, 963 grams, 12-3/4" h. x 11" d.
.... **$750**

Courtesy of Hill Auction Gallery, www.hillauctiongallery.com

English Regency period George III cruet set,
crafted of sterling silver with eight different
cut crystal containers with silver tops, bears an
AHK monogram on most objects, wonderful rare
examples of craftsmanship, bears TH hallmarks
for 1815 London, spoon is a later replacement by
George William Adams, good condition. **$469**

Courtesy of Hill Auction Gallery, www.hillauctiongallery.com

Liquor decanter, 19th century, stopper might not be original, 11" h. without stopper, 14-5/8" h. overall. **$94**

Courtesy of Vidi Vici Gallery, www.vidivicigallery.com

▲ Continental vase, cut with Hobstars, Buzzstars, and panels of Russian, signed "Guver", 33" h. x 9" d. **$687**

Courtesy of New Orleans Auction Gallery, www.neworleansauction.com

◄ Art Deco cobalt blue hand cut to clear Bohemian Czech glass bowl, geometric design, 5 lbs, 4oz., 9-1/4" h. x 9-1/4" w. x 6" d..............**$130**

Courtesy of Charleston Estate Auction, www.charlestonestateauctions.com

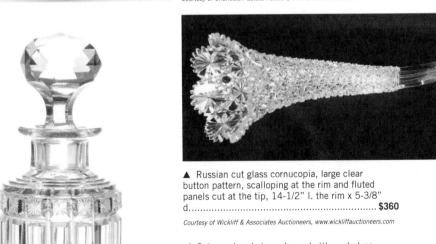

▲ Russian cut glass cornucopia, large clear button pattern, scalloping at the rim and fluted panels cut at the tip, 14-1/2" l. the rim x 5-3/8" d..**$360**

Courtesy of Wickliff & Associates Auctioneers, www.wickliffauctioneers.com

◄ Cut panel and star cologne bottle, colorless, cylindrical form with four-step shoulder, panel-cut neck, factory-polished top of mouth, ray cut base, original facet-cut stopped numbered to match the bottle, Boston & Sandwich Glass Co., 81/4" h. x 6" h. bottle, 3" d. base................................**$124**

Courtesy of Jeffrey S. Evans & Associates, www.jeffreysevans.com

GLASS

daum nancy

DAUM NANCY FINE GLASS, much of it cameo, was made by Auguste and Antonin Daum, who founded the factory in 1875 in Nancy, France. Most of their cameo and enameled glass was made from the 1890s into the early 20th century.

Cameo glass is made by carving into multiple layers of colored glass to create a design in relief. It is at least as old as the Romans.

Footed bowl with cameo decoration of blackberries, vines and leaves against a mottled background, signed Daum Nancy with the Croix de Lorraine on the side in cameo, 5-1/4" h. x 7-1/2" d... **$1,363**

Courtesy James D. Julia, Inc., Fairfield, ME, www.jamesdjulia.com

Cameo and enameled bowl with thistle flower design in shades of purple and red, with stems in shades of gray enamel with gilded highlights, against a background of green shading to mottled pink to frosted, signed Daum Nancy on the bottom with the Croix de Lorraine, 6" d. **$1,777**

Courtesy James D. Julia, Inc., Fairfield, ME, www.jamesdjulia.com

Art deco bowl, acid-etched pale amethyst, circa 1930, marked DAUM with Croix de Lorraine, Nancy, France, wear to underside, 3-3/4" h. x 6-3/4" d. **$875**

Courtesy Woody Auction, www.woodyauction.com

Vase, featuring enameled Dutch shore scene with windmill, buildings and trees near a lake with sailboats, set against an opalescent acid-textured background, signed Daum Nancy with the Croix de Lorraine in gold on the bottom, 2-3/4" h.......... **$711**

Courtesy James D. Julia, Inc., Fairfield, ME, www.jamesdjulia.com

VISIT WWW.ANTIQUETRADER.COM

WWW.FACEBOOK.COM/ANTIQUETRADER

Vitrified cameo maple leaf vase, with bright green and orange against a mottled yellow, purple and clear acid-textured background, engraved Daum Nancy with the Croix de Lorraine, internal crack not visible on the exterior, 20" t.
.... **$770**

Courtesy James D. Julia, Inc., Fairfield, ME, www.jamesdjulia.com

Yellow floral vase with cameo leaves and blossoms set against an acid-textured background, decorated with gilded highlights on the leaves and flowers as well as around the foot and upper rim, signed Daum Nancy with the Croix de Lorraine on bottom, 3" h. **$326**

Courtesy James D. Julia, Inc., Fairfield, ME, www.jamesdjulia.com

Pedestal foot vase, featuring black cameo sailing vessels in a harbor against a background of bright yellow, green and orange mottled grass, signed Daum Nancy with the Croix de Lorraine in cameo on side, 6-1/2" t. **$948**

Courtesy James D. Julia, Inc., Fairfield, ME, www.jamesdjulia.com

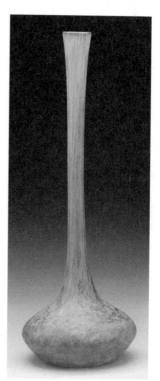

◀ Sunset vase, green cameo decoration of pine trees surrounding edge of a pond, boasting green ripple highlights against subtle orange water with rolling hills in the background, all against frosted cream colored sky with orange reflection on the pond to create view of a sunset, signed in cameo Daum Nancy with Croix de Lorraine on the side, 13-1/4" h. **$889**

Courtesy James D. Julia, Inc., Fairfield, ME, www.jamesdjulia.com

▶ Vase, internally decorated with mottled orange, yellow and cream with random mottled cream finish to exterior, bulbous body and slender neck, large engraved signature Daum Nancy with Croix de Lorraine on side, factory grind mark to edge of lip, 15-1/4" h.
.... **$592**

Courtesy James D. Julia, Inc., Fairfield, ME, www.jamesdjulia.com

GLASS

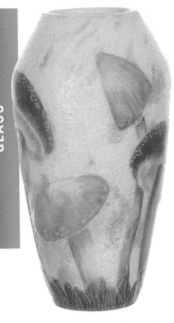

French cameo vase, yellow and orange mottled background features carved mushroom décor with highlights, signed Daum Nancy, 4-3/4" h. ... **$1,560**

Courtesy Woody Auction, www.woodyauction.com

Green acid cut vase, 40 fleur-de-lis emblems with gold stencil highlights, signed Daum Nancy, France, 7-1/4" h. x 3 ¼" d. **$720**

Courtesy Woody Auction, www.woodyauction.com

Vase, ice blue and white mottled body with brown mottled rim, signed Daum Nancy, 11-3/4" h. **$330**

Courtesy Woody Auction, www.woodyauction.com

Pillow vase with vitrified glass band on lower third, decorated with cameo flowers, stems and leaves, cameo stems are enameled in shades of brown, leaves in shades of green with white enameled flowers and red stamen, signed Daum Nancy with Croix de Lorraine on side, 3" h. **$1,540**

Courtesy James D. Julia, Inc., Fairfield, ME, www.jamesdjulia.com

Art deco vase, stylized floral design, green against an acid textured background, etched Daum Nancy France with the Croix de Lorraine on the foot, 11-1/4" h. **$1,185**

Courtesy James D. Julia, Inc., Fairfield, ME, www.jamesdjulia.com

Art deco amethyst bowl, marked Daum with Croix of Lorraine, Nancy, France, circa 1925, scuffing and museum wax residue to underside, 8-1/8" h. x 9-1/4" d. **$75**

Courtesy Heritage Auctions, www.ha.com

GLASS

depression glass

DEPRESSION GLASS IS the name of colorful glassware collectors generally associated with mass-produced glassware found in pink, yellow, crystal, or green in the years surrounding the Great Depression in America.

The homemakers of the Depression-era were able to enjoy the wonderful colors offered in this new inexpensive glass dinnerware because they received pieces of their favorite patterns packed in boxes of soap, or as premiums given at "dish night" at the local movie theater. Merchandisers, such as Sears & Roebuck and F. W. Woolworth, enticed young brides with the colorful wares that they could afford even when economic times were harsh.

Because of advancements in glassware technology, Depression-era patterns were mass-produced and could be purchased for a fraction of what cut glass or lead crystal cost. As one manufacturer found a pattern that was pleasing to the buying public, other companies soon followed with their adaptation of a similar design. Patterns included several design motifs, such as florals, geometrics, and even patterns that looked back to Early American patterns like Sandwich glass.

As America emerged from the Great Depression and life became more leisure-oriented again, new glassware patterns were created to reflect the new tastes of this generation. More elegant shapes and forms were designed, leading to what is sometimes called "Elegant Glass." Today's collectors often include these more elegant patterns when they talk about Depression-era glassware.

Depression-era glassware is one of the best-researched collecting areas available to the American marketplace. This is due in large part to the careful research of several people, including Hazel Marie Weatherman, Gene Florence, Barbara Mauzy, Carl F. Luckey, and Kent Washburn. Their books are held in high regard by researchers and collectors today.

Regarding values for Depression glass, rarity does not always equate to a high dollar amount. Some more readily found items command lofty prices because of high demand or other factors, not because they are necessarily rare. As collectors' tastes range from the simple patterns to the more elaborate patterns, so does the ability of their budget to invest in inexpensive patterns to multi-hundreds of dollars per form patterns.

For more information on Depression glass, see *Warman's Depression Glass Identification and Price Guide*, 6th Edition, or *Warman's Depression Glass Handbook*, both by Ellen T. Schroy.

PATTERN SILHOUETTE **Identification Guide**

Depression-era glassware can be confusing. Many times a manufacturer came up with a neat new design, and as soon as it was successful, other companies started to make patterns that were similar. To help you figure out what pattern you might be trying to research, here's a quick identification guide. The patterns are broken down into several different classifications by design elements.

ART DECO

Ovide

BASKETS

Lorain

BEADED EDGES

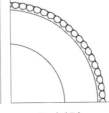

Beaded Edge

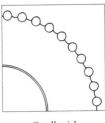

Candlewick

BIRDS

Delilah

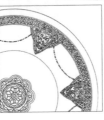

Georgian

Parrot

Peacock & Wild Rose

BLOCKS

Beaded Block

Colonial Block

BOWS

Bowknot

COINS

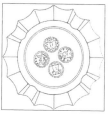

Coin

CUBES

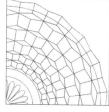

American

Cube

DIAMONDS

Cape Cod

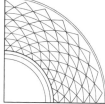

Diamond Quilted

English Hobnail

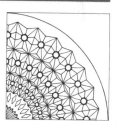

Holiday

Laced Edge

Miss America

Peanut Butter

Waterford

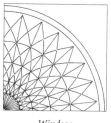

Windsor

ELLIPSES (FANS)

Crow's Foot

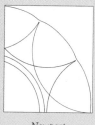

Newport

Romanesque

FIGURES

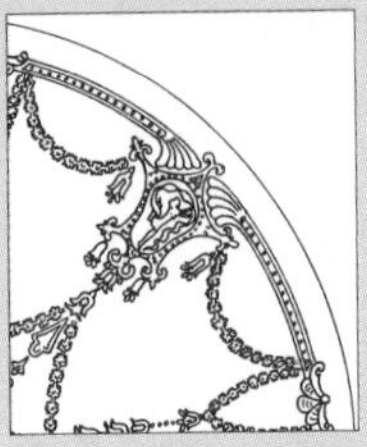

Cameo

Cupid

FLORALS

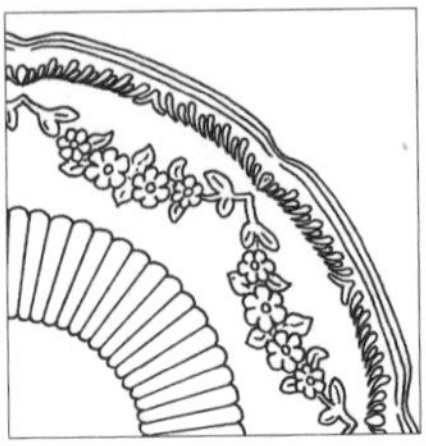

Alice

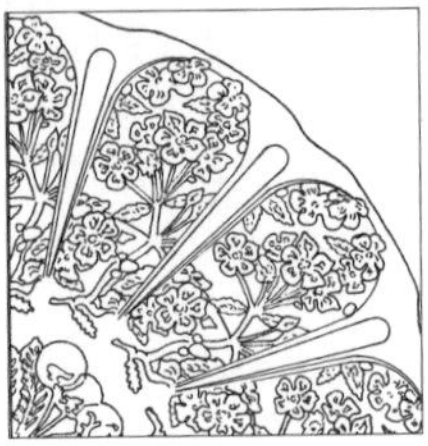

Cherry Blossom

Cloverleaf

Daisy

Dogwood

Doric

Doric & Pansy

Floragold

Floral

Floral and Diamond Band

Flower Garden with Butterflies

Indiana Custard

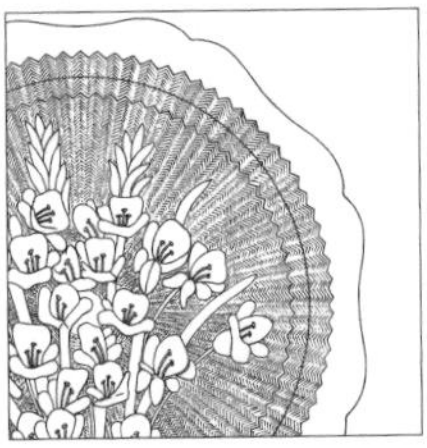

Iris

Jubilee

FLORALS *continued*

Mayfair (Federal)

Mayfair (Open Rose)

Normandie

Orange Blossom

Pineapple & Floral

Primrose

Rosemary •

Rose Cameo

Royal Lace

Seville

Sharon

Sunflower

Thistle

Tulip

Vitrock

Wild Rose

FRUITS

Avocado

Cherryberry

Della Robbia

Fruits

Paneled Grape

Strawberry

GEOMETIC & LINE DESIGNS

Cracked Ice

Cape Cod

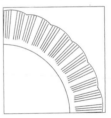

Cremax

Early American Prescut

Park Avenue

Pioneer

Sierra

Star

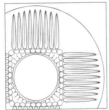

Starlight

Tea Room

HONEYCOMB

Aunt Polly

Hex Optic

HORSESHOE

Horseshoe

LEAVES

Laurel Leaf

Sunburst

LACY DESIGNS

Harp

Heritage

S-Pattern

Sandwich (Duncan Miller)

Sandwich (Hocking)

Sandwich (Indiana)

LOOPS

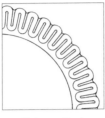

Christmas Candy

Crocheted Crystal

Pretzel

PETALS

Aurora

Block Optic

Circle

Colonial

National

New Century

Old Café

Ribbon

Roulette

Round Robin

Victory

PETALS/RIDGES WITH DIAMOND ACCENTS

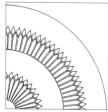

Anniversary

Coronation

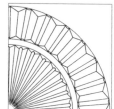

Fortune

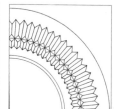

Lincoln Inn

Petalware

Queen Mary

PLAIN

Charm

Mt. Pleasant

PYRAMIDS

Pyramid

RAISED BAND

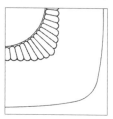

Charm

Forest Green

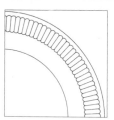

Jane Ray

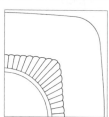

Royal Ruby

RAISED CIRCLES

American Pioneer

Bubble

Columbia

Dewdrop

Hobnail

Moonstone

Oyster & Pearl

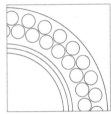

Raindrops

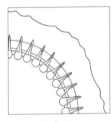

Radiance

Ships

Teardrop

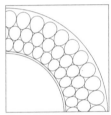

Thumbprint

RIBS

Homespun

RINGS (CIRCLES)

Manhattan

Moderntone

Moondrops

Moroccan Amethyst

Old English

Ring

SCENES

Chinex Classic

Lake Como

SCROLLING DESIGNS

Adam

American Sweetheart

Florentine No. 1

Florentine No. 2

Madrid

Patrick

Philbe

Primo

Princess

Rock Crystal

Roxana

Vernon

GLASS

SWIRLS

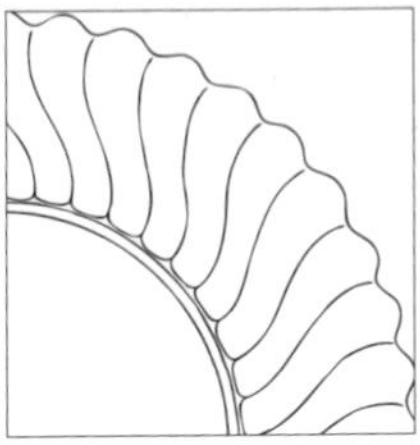

Colony

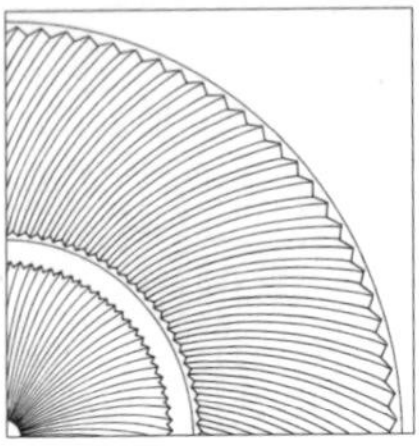

Diana

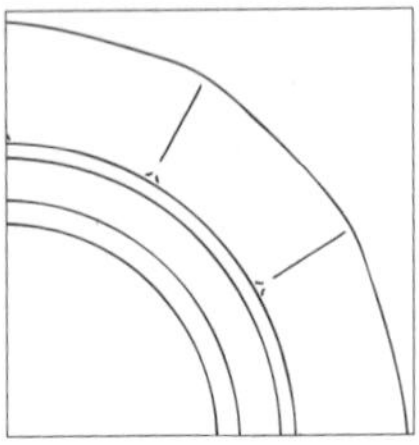

Fairfax

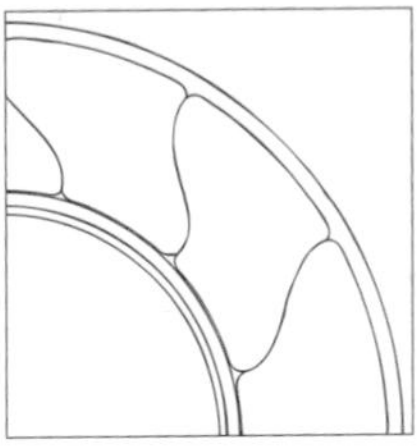

Jamestown

Spiral

Swirl

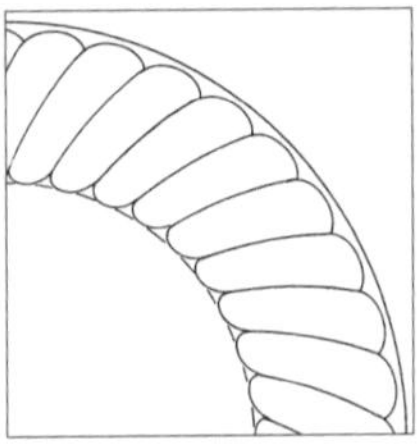

Swirl (Fire King)

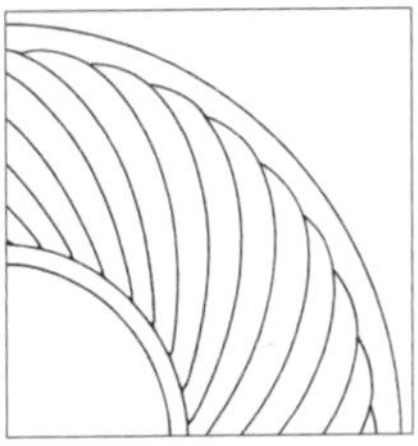

Twisted Optic

TEXTURED

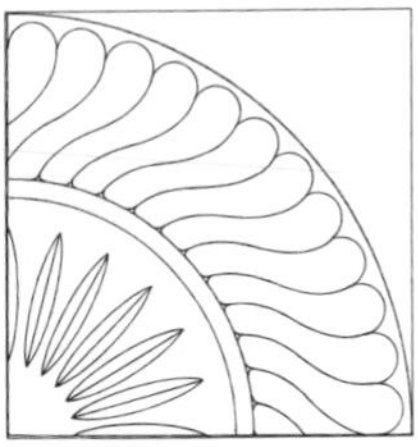

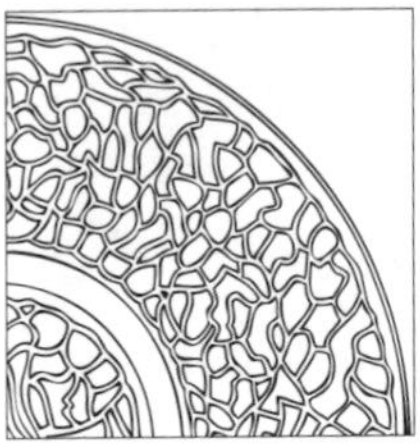

Cobalt Royal Lace pattern cookie jar and two berry dishes. **$58**

Courtesy of Strawser Auctions,
www.strawserauctions.com

Blue Mayfair pattern butter dish, sweet pea vase, and 8 1/2" plate.
....**$174**

Courtesy of Strawser Auctions,
www.strawserauctions.com

Grouping of cobalt blue glass, Royal Lace pattern, Hazel Atlas Glass Co., four plates 8" d., three plates 6" d., five saucers, three cups, two creamers and sugars, 10-1/4" d. bowl, six juice glasses 3-1/2" **$157**

Courtesy of Hartzell's Auction Gallery, Inc.
www.hartzellsauction.com

Six green tumblers, Fruits pattern, 4-1/4" t. **$24**

Courtesy of Hartzell's Auction Gallery, Inc.
www.hartzellsauction.com

Pink Miss America pattern set of 8 5-3/8" goblets (one shown).
.... **$128**

Courtesy of Strawser Auctions, www.strawserauctions.com

Pink Cubist pattern water pitcher. **$87**

Courtesy of Strawser Auctions, www.strawserauctions.com

Cobalt blue lidded butter dish, Royal Lace pattern, 6-1/2" d. x 3-1/2" h **$261**

Courtesy of Strawser Auction Group, www.strawserauctions.com

Pink Mayfair pattern pair 7 1/4" goblets, rare... **$197**

Courtesy of Strawser Auctions, www.strawserauctions.com

Saucer, green with lowered cup ring, Cameo pattern, Hocking Glass Co., circa 1930-1934, 6 1/4" d.
.... **$24**

Courtesy of Jeffrey S. Evans & Associates, www.jeffreysevans.com

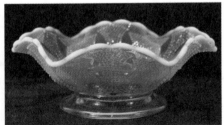

Glass bowl with Star of David, used as a charity bowl in synagogues during the 1920s, 2 3/4" h. x 8" d.
.... **$62**

Courtesy of Westport Auction, www.westportauction.com

Green lidded dish with beaded edges, 6-1/2" h. x 6" d. **$25**

Courtesy of Chandler's International Auctions & Estate Sales, www.chandlersauction.com

Eight tumblers, green, yellow and colorless examples, rib-optic body on circular foot with bust of George Washington appearing above "1732-1932", with a band of stars full around, circa 1932, irregularities as made, 4-1/2" h. **$73**

Courtesy of Jeffrey S. Evans & Associates, www.jeffreysevans.com

Pitcher, cobalt blue, Royal Lace pattern, Hazel Atlas Glass Co., 4" h. **$36**

Courtesy of Hartzell's Auction Gallery, Inc. www.hartzellsauction.com

Milk pitcher, green, Cameo pattern, Hocking Glass Co., circa 1930-1934, 6" h. **$192**

Courtesy of Jeffrey S. Evans & Associates, www.jeffreysevans.com

Yellow biscuit counter jar with lid, 6" d. x 7-1/2" h. **$36**

Courtesy of Vidi Vici Gallery

GLASS

durand

FINE DECORATIVE GLASS similar to that made by Tiffany and other outstanding glasshouses of its day was made by Vineland Flint Glass Works Co. in Vineland, New Jersey, first headed by Victor Durand Sr. and subsequently by his son, Victor Durand Jr., in the 1920s.

Shoulder form jar, iridescent blue with matching lid featuring an applied amber finial, signed "Durand 1964-6", lid cracked at finial, 7-1/4" t. **$227**

Courtesy Early Auction Company, www.earlyauctionco.com

Gold iridescent vase, pulled feather decoration and gold liner, with three applied gold feet, snapped and ground pontil, Durand, 4-1/2" d. x 2-1/2" t. ... **$307**

Courtesy of Forsythes' Auctions, www.forsythesauctions.com

Solid lavender vase, signed Durand, 5-3/4" t. x 6" d.
.... **$300**

Courtesy of Woody Auction, www.woodyauction.com

Silver blue lustre bulbous vase, opal Heart and Vine pattern, shape 1990, signed "Durand/V/1990/8", Vineland Flint Glass Works, 1924-1931, 7-3/4" t. x 4" d. rim **$498**

Courtesy of Jeffrey S. Evans & Assoc., www.jeffreyevans.com

Vase, pulled feather style Gold Luster iridescent glass, early 20th century, Durand, excellent condition, 6-1/2".................**$106**

Courtesy of Richard Hatch & Associates, www.richardhatchauctions.com

Butterscotch colored vase with green pulled swirl design, Durand, 7" t. **$420**

Courtesy of Woody Auction, www.woodyauction.com

Iridescent blue and silver threaded vase, Victor Durand, signed on bottom and numbered 1722-8, 8" t. **$312**

Courtesy Auction Gallery of Boca Raton, www.agobr.com

Iridescent green and blue vase in King Tut pattern, 8" t. x 5-1/4" w. **$630**

Courtesy of Bruce Kodner Galleries, www.brucekodner.com

Vase, opal ground with blue pulled decoration, urn form with a slightly flared rim, pulled feather design, gold iridescent trim, spider-webbing, polished pontil mark, signed "DURAND/V/1812-6", Vineland Flint Glass Works, circa 1930, 6-5/8 t. x 3-1/2" d. rim, 2-3/8" d. base. **$342**

Courtesy of Jeffrey S. Evans & Associates, www.jeffreysevans.com

Opal ground with gold and blue hearts, bulged cylindrical form, gold iridescent spider-webbing throughout, Heart and Vine pattern, Durand, factory-polished rim, signed "Durand", Vineland Flint Glass Works, circa 1930, 5" t. **$124**

Courtesy of Jeffrey S. Evans & Assoc., www.jeffreysevans.com

Blue iridescent vase forms mounted as lamps, Durand glass, threading in good condition, few minor losses, 6-1/4" t. glass form, with shade 15" t
.... **$375**

Courtesy of Alderfer Auction, www.alderferauction.com

Trio of swirled lustre glass and metal table lamps, circa 1910, Durand, 27" t., high glazed surface to the narrowest example, all in good condition, with slight wear and rubbing to the metal components
.... **$687**

Courtesy of Heritage Auctions, www.ha.com

Blue iridescent Beehive form vase, six horizontal ribs across the body, polished pontil mark, signed "Durand/20177, Vineland Flint Glass Works, circa 1930, 6-1/2" t. x 3" d. rim x 3" d. base.......... **$373**

Courtesy of Jeffrey S. Evans & Associates, www.jeffreysevans.com

Vase with Heart & Vine pattern, against a transparent yellow background with light gold iridescence, very good with some minor scratches to the side, 12-1/4" t. **$415**

Courtesy James D. Julia, Inc., Fairfield, Maine, www.jamesdjulia.com

GLASS

fenton

THE FENTON ART GLASS CO. was founded in 1905 by Frank L. Fenton and his brother, John W., in Martins Ferry, Ohio. They initially sold hand-painted glass made by other manufacturers, but it wasn't long before they decided to produce their own glass. The new Fenton factory in Williamstown, West Virginia, opened on Jan. 2, 1907. From that point on, the company expanded by developing unusual colors and continued to decorate glassware in innovative ways.

Two more brothers, James and Robert, joined the firm. But despite the company's initial success, John W. left to establish the Millersburg Glass Co. of Millersburg, Ohio, in 1909. The first months of the new operation were devoted to the production of crystal glass only. Later iridized glass was called "Radium Glass." After only two years, Millersburg filed for bankruptcy.

Fenton's iridescent glass had a metallic luster over a colored, pressed pattern and was sold in dime stores. It was only after the sales of this glass decreased and it was sold in bulk as carnival prizes that it came to be known as carnival glass.

Fenton became the top producer of carnival glass, with more than 150 patterns. The quality of the glass and its popularity with the public enabled the new company to be profitable through the late 1920s. As interest in carnival glass subsided, Fenton moved on to stretch glass and opalescent patterns. A line of colorful blown glass (called "off-hand" by Fenton) was also produced in the mid-1920s.

During the Great Depression, Fenton survived by producing functional colored glass tableware and other household items, including water sets, table sets, bowls, mugs, plates, perfume bottles and vases. Restrictions on European imports during World War II ushered in the arrival of Fenton's opaque colored glass, and the lines of "Crest" pieces soon followed. In the 1950s, production continued to diversify with a focus on milk glass, particularly in hobnail patterns. In the third quarter of Fenton's history, the company returned to themes that had proved popular to preceding generations and began adding special lines such as the Bicentennial series.

Innovations included the line of Colonial colors that debuted in 1963, including amber, blue, green, orange, and ruby. Based on a special order for an Ohio museum, Fenton in 1969 revisited its early success with "Original Formula Carnival Glass." Fenton also started marking its glass in molds for the first time.

The star of the 1970s was the yellow and blushing pink creation known as Burmese. This was followed closely by a menagerie of animals, birds, and children. In 1975, Robert Barber was hired by Fenton to begin an artist-in-residence program, producing a limited line of art glass vases in a return to the off-hand, blown-glass creations of the mid-1920s. Shopping at home via television was a phenomenon in the late 1980s when the "Birthstone Bears" became the first Fenton product to appear on QVC. In August 2007, Fenton discontinued all but a few of its more popular lines, and the company ceased production altogether in 2011.

For more information on Fenton Art Glass, see *Warman's Fenton Glass Identification and Price Guide*, 2nd edition, by Mark F. Moran.

Two Fenton celeste blue baskets, Family Signature Series, Coralene basket #412 and 90th Anniversary basket, 9-3/4" t. and 7" t., respectively.............**$71**

Courtesy of Vince Cassaro/Cordier Auction

Three pieces Mulberry glass with three items from the Honor Collection, ranging from 6-1/4" t. to 9" t.
.... **$165**

Courtesy of Vince Cassaro/Cordier Auction

Pink opalescent hobnail epergne with three flutes, 12" t. **$59**

Courtesy of Vince Cassaro/Cordier Auction

Single flute epergnes, including Vaseline with paper label and amethyst, 8-1/2" t. to 10" t **$165**

Courtesy of Vince Cassaro/Cordier Auction

Five-piece Frank Fenton Founder's red carnival water set #50 with paper label, pitcher 7-5/8" t., tumblers 4-1/4" t. **$106**

Courtesy of Vince Cassaro/Cordier Auction

Favrene Feathers vase with paper label and certificate of authenticity, #944 of 1250, 8-1/2" t. **$130**

Courtesy of Vince Cassaro/Cordier Auction

Ten-piece cobalt glass grape and cable punch bowl set, with paper label on bowl, bowl 10-3/4" d., cups 2-1/2" d. **$153**

Courtesy of Vince Cassaro/Cordier Auction

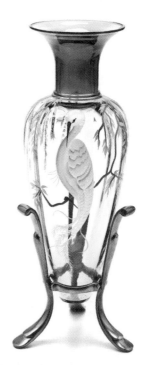

Mosaic vase #77 of 750, 13-1/4" t **$177**

Courtesy of Vince Cassaro/Cordier Auction

100 Year anniversary vase with brass base and paper label #22, 13" t. without base, 14-1/2" with base **$130**

Courtesy of Vince Cassaro/Cordier Auction

Mulberry vase with image of a heron #935/1250 situated on a brass stand, 12-1/2" t. **$265**

Courtesy of Vince Cassaro/Cordier Auction

GLASS

Three baskets with a cranberry form with the image of a woman playing golf, a ruby "Feeding Time" version, and a ruby version depicting the scene of a scarecrow in a field, 8-1/2" t. to 10" t. **$106**

Courtesy of Vince Cassaro/Cordier Auction

Grouping of three mulberry glass examples, including Gold Treasures Collection 2004 vase with paper label, vase #164/1750 with paper label, Connoisseur Collection 2000 Plum Blossoms basket #338/1950 with paper label, 7-1/4" t. to 10-1/2" t. **$165**

Courtesy of Vince Cassaro/Cordier Auction

Three-piece purple glass grouping, covered candy dish #108 with paper label, another candy dish, and vase with paper label, #108 candy dish 6-1/4" d., other dish 9" d., vase 6-1/4" t.......................... **$59**

Courtesy of Vince Cassaro/Cordier Auction

Five-piece cranberry glass selection, including four vases from various collections and a pitcher, 4-1/2" t. to 8-1/2" t..**$165**

Courtesy of Vince Cassaro/Cordier Auction

Three opalescent baskets, including a pink opalescent basket with strawberries and paper label, aqua basket with paper label, and turquoise basket, 6-1/2" to 10" w. **$83**

Courtesy of Vince Cassaro/Cordier Auction

Black marigold animal vases, from the 2005 Platinum Collection "Elephant Walk" and 2006 Connoisseur Collection "Mother's Love" giraffe vase, 6-1/4" t. to 8-1/4" t. **$265**

Courtesy of Vince Cassaro/Cordier Auction

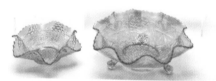

Five-piece marigold set with rose creamer, rose covered sugar, covered butter, leaf chain bowl, water lily footed bowl, 5" d. to 9-7/8" d. **$142**

Courtesy of Vince Cassaro/Cordier Auction

Moon and Star decanter set, with decanter and cups, all with paper labels, 12" decanter and 4-1/2" cups **$189**

Courtesy of Vince Cassaro/Cordier Auction

Dave Fetty blue hanging hearts pitcher #264/1250 with paper label and cobalt base, 8-3/4" t. without base **$106**

Courtesy of Vince Cassaro/Cordier Auction

GLASS

fostoria

THE FOSTORIA GLASS CO., founded in 1887, produced numerous types of fine glassware over the years. Its factory in Moundsville, West Virginia, closed in 1986.

Scarce crystal coin glass 1-1/2 gallon serving set; punch bowl, 12 cups and a glass ladle, punch bowl 14".. **$156**

Courtesy of Little Bull Auction & Sales Co., www.littlebullauction.com

Fostoria New Garland Topaz & Crystal Center Bowl, 5.5" h. X 12" d. Good condition. **$47**

Courtesy of Kenndy's Auction Service, www.kennedysauction.com

Straight side flower vase, June pattern in pink, Fostoria Glass Co., 8" t. **$185**

Courtesy of Strawser Auction Group, www.strawserauctions.com

◀ Topaz lemon glass tray with cream and sugar, June pattern, Fostoria, sugar 2-5/8" t., cream 2-3/4" t. **$46**

Courtesy of Strawser Auction Group, www.strawserauctions.com

VISIT WWW.ANTIQUETRADER.COM

WWW.FACEBOOK.COM/ANTIQUETRADER

American round cake salver, Fostoria #063, 20th century, 7-1/2" t. x 9-1/2 d. **$136**

Courtesy of Specialists of the South, Inc., www.specialistsofthesouth.com

Whisky glass of the Office of the Vice President of the United States, Hubert Humphrey, circa 1966, etched HHH, official original glassware, one glass has two fleabites to the rim, the other is mint, approx. 3-5/8" t x 3-1116" d **$44**

Courtesy of Vidi Vici Gallery, www.vidivicigallery.com

Lot of eight table articles, Atlanta/Square Lion pattern, colorless; six individual sauce/berry bowls, covered butter dish with engraved decoration, and creamer, circa 1895, 1-1/2" t. to 5" t. **$122**

Courtesy of Jeffrey S. Evans & Associates, www.jeffreyevans.com

Nativity scene comprising "The Magi," "The Shepherd," and "The Holy Family", 1688/3000, 7-3/4" t. **$156**

Courtesy of Nye & Company, www.nyandcompany.com

Covered butter dish, St. Bernard pattern, No. 450, colorless and frosted, circa 1894, 4-3/4" t. x 8" d. **$98**

Courtesy of Jeffrey S. Evans & Associates, www.jeffreyevans.com

▶ Covered compote, Frosted Artichoke pattern, No. 205, colorless with frosted high standard, Fostoria Glass Co., Fostoria, OH, circa 1891, 13" t. x 8" d. rim...**$245**

Courtesy of Jeffrey S. Evans & Associates, www.jeffreyevans.com

GLASS

Open compote and celery vase, Frosted Artichoke pattern, No. 205, colorless, circa 1891, compote 8" t. x 7-1/4" d., celery vase 5-1/2" t. **$135**

Courtesy of Jeffrey S. Evans & Associates, www.jeffreysevans.com

Vase in Rogene etched poppy pattern, Fostoria Glass Company, excellent condition, 9-1/2" t. **$124**

Courtesy of EstateOfMind, www.estateofmind.biz

Two Block pattern ruby-stained cruets, colorless, each with an appropriate stopper and souvenir decoration, first half 20th century, 5-3/4" t. **$49**

Courtesy of Jeffrey S. Evans & Associates, www.jeffreysevans.com

GLASS

galle

GALLÉ GLASS WAS made in Nancy, France, by Emile Gallé, founder of the Nancy School and leader in the Art Nouveau movement in France. Much of his glass, both enameled and cameo, is decorated with naturalistic motifs. The finest pieces were made in the last two decades of the 19th century and the opening years of the 20th.

Pieces marked with a star preceding the name were made between 1904, the year of Gallé's death, and 1914.

Cameo vase with mold-blown crocus flowers of white and purple, with green stems and leaves ascending from the foot, against a frosted citrine background, signed Galle on side near foot, top rim of vase has been reduced and one tiny fleabite appears near foot, 8" h. **$948**

Courtesy of James D. Julia, Inc., Fairfield, Maine, www.jamesdjulia.com

Early enameled vase, vertically ribbed amber glass body with flattened front and back, decorated with pink and white enameled flowers with green leaves and gilt stems that cover the front and back of the vase, front also boasts a blue cross with enameled flowers within, signed "Emile Galle Cristallerie de Depose" on underside in cameo signature, very good to excellent condition, 13" h. **$1,185**

Courtesy of James D. Julia, Inc., Fairfield, Maine, www.jamesdjulia.com

Floral vase with green and brown cameo decoration set against a frosted background, signed Galle in cameo on side of the vase, upper rim has been reduced and ground, 5-1/4" h. **$207**

Courtesy of James D. Julia, Inc., Fairfield, Maine, www.jamesdjulia.com

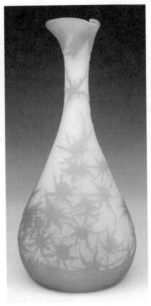

Vase with green cameo thistle decoration surrounding the bulbous body of the vase along the neck, set against a cream color that shades to a pink frosted background that tapers at the next and flares at the tri-corn top, signed Galle on side in cameo, 14-5/8" h. **$592**

Courtesy of James D. Julia, Inc., Fairfield, Maine, www.jamesdjulia.com

Vase, decoration of blue cameo iris flower with tall spiked leaves encircles the body, iris flowers set against a frosted yellow background, signed Galle in cameo on back, very good to excellent condition, 10" h. **$1,540**

Courtesy of James D. Julia, Inc., Fairfield, Maine, www.jamesdjulia.com

Jar, multicolored glass, acid embossed decoration of lilies, circa 1906-1914, signed "Galle", 6" h. **$302**

Courtesy of Marques Dos Santos, Lda., www.mdsleiloes.com

Silver-mounted circular bowl, green glass enameled with daisies and leaves in relief, silver on the rim and base, early 20th century, Galle Nancy cameo signature, 8-1/2" d. **$1,780**

Courtesy of John Nicholson Auctioneers, www.johnnicholsons.com

Acid etched cameo vase, plant and foliate decoration, marked Galle, first-quarter 20th century, 13" h. **$1,375**

Courtesy Alex Cooper Auctioneers, www.alexcooper.com

Seldom-seen vase with a white and dark lavender carved design of bats in flight – silhouetted by the scene of a moon over a village, signed and includes original Galle paper label on the base, 5-1/4" h. x 4" d. **$9,600**

Courtesy of Woody Auction, www.woodyauction.com

Cameo glass lamp base, frosted white background with lavender shading to green carved blossom and geometric overlay, signed, 15-1/2" h. **$480**

Courtesy of Woody Auction, www.woodyauction.com

Landscape bowl, amber overall against yellow frosted ground, consistent body color, marked "Galle", 6" d. **$512**

Courtesy of Neal Auction Company, www.nealauction.com

Faience jardinière, Egyptian revival style, impressed décor depose and impressed tablet mark with hieroglyphics, late 19th century, signed E. Galle a' Nancy on underside, 5" x 14-1/2" x 5" **$1,037**

Courtesy Royal Crest Auction, www.liveauctioneers.com/royal-crest-auctioneers

Cameo bowl, white background with orange carved blossom overlay, fire polished, signed Galle, 2-1/2" x 4-1/2" **$300**

Courtesy Woody Auction, www.woodyauction.com

Bearded Iris vase, fire polished, marked Galle, circa 1900, Nancy, France, 7-1/2" h.................... **$1,250**

Courtesy Heritage Auctions, www.ha.com

GLASS

GLASS

heisey

NUMEROUS TYPES OF fine glass were made by A.H. Heisey & Co., Newark, Ohio, from 1895. The company's trademark, an H enclosed within a diamond, has become known to most glass collectors. The company's name and molds were acquired by Imperial Glass Co., Bellaire, Ohio, in 1958, and some pieces have been reissued.

Sandwich plate, Orchid pattern, 14-1/4" d. **$130**

Courtesy of Dirk Soulis Auctions, www.dirksoulisauctions.com

Pitcher, Orchid pattern, holds 64 ounces, 9-1/2" h x 6" w. **$142**

Courtesy of Dirk Soulis Auctions, www.dirksoulisauctions.com

Three-piece crystal cocktail shaker, etched Orchid pattern with rooster head figural stopper, drop-in pouring spout, mid-20th century, tapering body with needle-point etching, 9-1/4". **$165**

Courtesy of Dirk Soulis Auctions, www.dirksoulisauctions.com

Seven Orchid pattern finger bowls, A.H. Heisey & Co., 2-1/2" h x 4-1/2" d. **$94**

Courtesy of Dirk Soulis Auctions, www.dirksoulisauctions.com

Pair of fish vases, Maiden's Blush pattern blush stained, colorless, signed with the H-in Diamond trademark, factory-polished bases, second quarter 20th century, 9" h x 3-3/4" d x 8-1/2" w. **$342**

Courtesy of Jeffrey S. Evans & Associates, www.jeffreysevans.com

Judaica-related No. 118 ruby stained tumbler, colorless with engraved foliate decoration, souvenir lettering in Hebrew and date "1897," A.H. Heisey & Co., late 19th century, 3-3/4" h. **$996**

Courtesy of Jeffrey S. Evans & Associates, www.jeffreysevans.com

Butter dish, Queen Anne pattern ruby stained, colorless with gilt decoration, signed with H-in-diamond trademark, pattern was introduced in 1907, 5-5/8" d. **$162**

Courtesy of Jeffrey S. Evans & Associates, www.jeffreysevans.com

Bead Panel and Sunburst pattern ruby stained water pitcher, No. 1235, colorless with applied handle, isolated area of wear to the staining, 9-1/2" h. **$200**

Courtesy of Jeffrey S. Evans & Associates, www.jeffreysevans.com

Locket on Chain pattern cruet, No. 160, colorless with pressed-facet stopper, minor band of interior residue, near the neck, 5-3/4" h. **$75**

Courtesy of Jeffrey S. Evans & Associates, www.jeffreysevans.com

Two Bead Panel and Sunburst pattern, covered sugar bowls, colorless, comprising ruby-stained and amber-stained examples, amber-stained chip to rim interior and a flake to rim exterior with wear throughout, 6-1/2" h. **$162**

Courtesy of Jeffrey S. Evans & Associates, www.jeffreysevans.com

Prince of Wales pattern ruby stained syrup pitcher, No. 335, period lid, cut-and-shut mark to the base, A.H. Heisey & Co., circa 1902, 6-3/4" h. **$280**

Courtesy of Jeffrey S. Evans & Associates, www.jeffreysevans.com

Ruby stained gas shade, No. 10, colorless, A.H. Heisey & Co., fourth quarter 19th century, 4" h x 7-3/4" d rim, 3-7/8" d fitter. **$112**

Courtesy of Jeffrey S. Evans & Associates, www.jeffreysevans.com

Bead Panel and Sunburst pattern, Maiden's blush-stained water pitcher, applied handle, 9-3/4" h. **$25**

Courtesy of Jeffrey S. Evans & Associates, www.jeffreysevans.com

Fancy Loop vases, lot of two, No. 1205, factory polished bases, A.H. Heisey & Co, circa 1896, 8-1/4" h. **$61**

Courtesy of Jeffrey S. Evans & Associates, www.jeffreysevans.com

Art Deco candlestick holder set of two, A.H. Heisey & Co., 6" x 3-1/16" x 7-7/8" h. **$25**

Courtesy of Vidi Vici Gallery, www.vidivicigallery.com

GLASS

imperial

FROM 1902 UNTIL 1984, Imperial Glass Co. of Bellaire, Ohio, produced hand-made glass. Early pressed glass production often imitated cut glass and may bear the raised "NUCUT" mark in the interior center. In the second decade of the 1900s, Imperial was one of the dominant manufacturers of iridescent or carnival glass. When glass collecting gained popularity in the 1970s, Imperial again produced carnival glass and a line of multicolored slag glass. Imperial purchased molds from closing glasshouses and continued many lines popularized by others including Central, Heisey, and Cambridge. These reissues may cause confusion but they were often marked.

Three-piece No. 403 ruby stained water set, comprising a water pitcher and two tumblers, one tumbler with a purple tint, each tumbler bears a few scattered minute bruises, 9-3/4" t. (pitcher), 4" t. tumbler.......................................**$124**

Courtesy of Jeffrey S. Evans & Associates, www.jeffreysevans.com

Three-in-one ruby stained glass/electric shade, colorless, circa 1902-1915, typical roughness to the fitter, as made, Imperial Glass Co., 4-1/8" t. x 4-1/4" d. rim, 2-1/8" d. fitter **$137**

Courtesy of Jeffrey S. Evans & Associates, www.jeffreysevans.com

Lead-lustre vase, blue iridescent with a glossy finish, cut and folded out tri-part rim, polished pontil mark, Imperial Glass Co., heavy interior residue not affecting the exterior, 6-1/2" t. **$62**

Courtesy of Jeffrey S. Evans & Associates, www.jeffreysevans.com

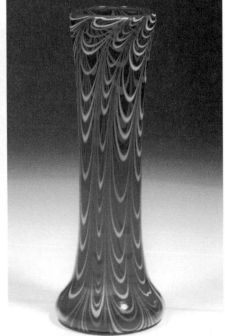

Decorated free hand vase, orange with flowing blue, shape 622, polished pontil mark, Imperial Glass Co., circa 1925, 8-1/2" t. x 2-1/4" d. rim, 3-1/4" d **$112**

Courtesy of Jeffrey S. Evans & Associates, www.jeffreysevans.com

Lead lustre vase in blue with seven groups of opal loopings, Imperial Glass Co., circa 1925, a few scratches near the rim of the vase, 9-1/8" t. x 2-1/2" d. rim x 3-1/4" d. base **$187**

Courtesy of Jeffrey S. Evans & Associates, www.jeffreysevans.com

Two table articles in ruby-stained Lace Band pattern, with blue enamel and gilt decoration, comprising a covered butter dish and covered sugar bowl, circa 1902, 6" t. and 6-1/2" t. **$149**

Courtesy of Jeffrey S. Evans & Associates, www.jeffreysevans.com

Four-piece table set, Jeweled Moon and Star pattern, colorless with blue and amber staining, comprising a covered butter dish, sugar bowl, creamer and spooner, each with applied red beads, pattern introduced 1896, 5" t. to 7-5/8" t. **$196**

Courtesy of Jeffrey S. Evans & Associates, www.jeffreysevans.com

Three-in-one ruby-stained basket, with colorless plume handle, engraved "Ohio State Fair/1931", Imperial Glass Co., early 20th century, 12-1/4" t. x 4-1/2" w. x 7-3/4" d. **$87**

Courtesy of Jeffrey S. Evans & Associates, www.jeffreysevans.com

Figural lion ruby-stained covered dish, underside of the cover embossed "PAT Aug-6-1889", base with a slight purple tint, 20th century, Imperial Glass Co., 6-3/4" t. x 6" w. x 7-1/4" d. **$249**

Courtesy of Jeffrey S. Evans & Associates, www.jeffreysevans.com

◀ E Cruet, No. 160 ruby stained, 4 ounces bulbous form body, star cut base, appropriate stopper, circa 1920, 5-1/8" t. **$174**

Courtesy of Jeffrey S. Evans & Associates, www.jeffreysevans.com

GLASS

Three-in-one ruby-stained jelly compotes, colorless, circa 1902-1905, 4-7/8" t. x 4-3/4" d. rims, 3-1/8" d. feet **$163**

Courtesy of Jeffrey S. Evans & Associates, www.jeffreysevans.com

Children's glass toy table set, lamp theme, comprising a covered butter dish, sugar bowl, creamer and spooner, Imperial Glass Co., circa 1910, 2-1/5" t. to 4-1/4" t. **$162**

Courtesy of Jeffrey S. Evans & Associates, www.jeffreysevans.com

▶ Seven-piece Tiger Lily pattern water set, marigold, No. 484, comprising a water pitcher and six tumblers, first quarter 20th century, 4-3/8" t. to 8-3/4" t. **$108**

Courtesy of Jeffrey S. Evans & Associates, www.jeffreysevans.com

Lead lustre vase, blue iridescent, polished pontil mark, circa 1925, 11-1/2" t. x 3-1/4" d. rim ... **$149**

Courtesy of Jeffrey S. Evans & Associates, www.jeffreysevans.com

Lead lustre vase in yellow with four groups of opal loopings, orange iridescent interior, polished pontil mark, circa 1925, Imperial Glass Co., 8-3/8" t. x 2-1/2" d. rim, 3-1/8" d. base **$100**

Courtesy of Jeffrey S. Evans & Associates, www.jeffreysevans.com

GLASS

lalique

RENÉ JULES LALIQUE was born on April 6,1860, in the village of Ay, in the Champagne region of France. In 1862, his family moved to the suburbs of Paris.

In 1872, Lalique began attending College Turgot where he began studying drawing with Justin-Marie Lequien. After the death of his father in 1876, Lalique began working as an apprentice to Louis Aucoc, who was a prominent jeweler and goldsmith in Paris.

Lalique moved to London in 1878 to continue his studies. He spent two years attending Sydenham College, developing his graphic design skills. He returned to Paris in 1880 and worked as an illustrator of jewelry, creating designs for Cartier, among others. In 1884, Lalique's drawings were displayed at the National Exhibition of Industrial Arts, organized at the Louvre.

At the end of 1885, Lalique took over Jules Destapes' jewelry workshop. Lalique's design began to incorporate translucent enamels, semiprecious stones, ivory, and hard stones. In 1889, at the Universal Exhibition in Paris, the jewelry firms of Vever and Boucheron included collaborative works by Lalique in their displays.

In the early 1890s, Lalique began to incorporate glass into his jewelry, and in 1893 he took part in a competition organized by the Union Centrale des Arts Decoratifs to design a drinking vessel. He won second prize.

Lalique opened his first Paris retail shop in 1905, near the perfume business of François Coty. Coty commissioned Lalique to design his perfume labels in 1907, and he also created his first perfume bottles for Coty.

In the first decade of the 20th century, Lalique continued to experiment with glass manufacturing techniques, and mounted his first show devoted entirely to glass in 1911.

During World War I, Lalique's first factory was forced to close, but the construction of a new factory was soon begun in Wingen-sur-Moder, in the Alsace region. It was completed in 1921, and still produces Lalique crystal today.

In 1925, Lalique designed the first "car mascot" (hood ornament) for Citroën, the French automobile company. For the next six years, Lalique would design 29 models for companies such as Bentley, Bugatti, Delage, Hispano-Suiza, Rolls Royce, and Voisin.

Lalique's second boutique opened in 1931, and this location continues to serve as the main Lalique showroom today.

René Lalique died on May 5, 1945, at the age of 85. His son, Marc, took over the business at that time, and when Marc died in 1977, his daughter, Marie-Claude Lalique Dedouvre, assumed control of the company. She sold her interest in the firm and retired in 1994.

For more information on Lalique, see *Warman's Lalique Identification and Price Guide* by Mark F. Moran.

Editor's Note: In some of the descriptions of Lalique pieces you will find notations like "M

Amber ormeaux vase molded with overlapping leaf design extending from the foot to neck, leading to a flared rim, signed on the underside in etched script "R. Lalique France No. 984", very good to excellent condition, 6-1/2" t. **$1,540**

Courtesy of James D. Julia, Inc., Fairfield, Maine, www.jamesdjulia.com

p. 478, No. 1100" or "Marcilhac 952, pg. 428." This refers to the page and serial numbers found in *René Lalique, maître-verrier, 1860-1945: Analyse de L'oeuvre et Catalogue Raisonné*, by Félix Marcilhac, published in 1989 and revised in 1994. Printed entirely in French, this book of more than 1,000 pages is the definitive guide to Lalique's work. Listings from auction catalogs typically cite the Marcilhac guide as a reference.

Bagatelle sparrow vase, signed Lalique France in script to base, 6-3/4" t. **$406**

Courtesy of Auction Gallery of Boca Raton, www.agbr.com

Lalique crystal jar decorated with nude figural design, 4-3/4" t.. **$156**

Courtesy of Kaminski Auctions, www.kaminski.com

Wheel carved Cire Perdue Frise Sapin et Branches vase, circa 1920, engraved 14-3-20, a commentary piece about Rene Lalique's appreciation for trees, 6-3/8" t.. **$45,000**

Courtesy of Heritage Auctions, www.ha.com

Vase, Versailles pattern, signed with etched signature, 13-3/4" t. x 9-1/2" d................... **$2,356**

Pair of "Le Messager" opaline candlesticks featuring a wreath of flowers with two sparrows in the center – on a hexagonal base, marked "R. Lalique, France" on base, 6-1/2" t. x 5-1/4" d. base. **$229**

Courtesy of Michaan, www.michaans.com

Two frosted Puffer Fish figures, detailed with tail to one side, signed "Lalique France" under base, 1-7/8" d. **$236**

Courtesy of Dirk Soulis Auctions, www.dirksoulisauctions.com

◀ Tête de Coq" car mascot in clear and frosted glass, 20th century, etched Lalique, scratches and scuffs throughout, multiple chips and flecks to the comb and large chip with long grinding mark to right side of face, and tip and lower right hand side of beak broken off, 6-1/2" t. x 6-1/2" d. x 3" w. .. **$130**

Courtesy of Rago Auctions, www.ragoarts.com

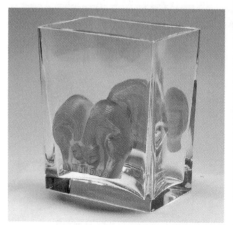

Vase decorated with amber animal heads on the handles, signed "Lalique France" on reverse, base, 7" **$375**

Courtesy of IEGOR Auctions, www.iegor.net

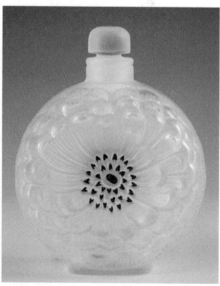

Frosted crystal perfume bottle, Dahlia pattern, rotund shape and motif of a Dahlia flower embellished with embossed leaves and ebonized dotted details along the center, marked "Lalique, France", 20th century, 5-1/4" t. x 4-1/8" l. x 2" w **$98**

Courtesy of Akiba Antiques, www.akibaantiques.com

▶ Pair "Messanges" art glass candlesticks with clear glass bobeche insert of hexagonal shape, frosted candle holder showing two birds sitting in floral wreath, 7" t. x 5"d ., 6-1/4 lbs **$461**

Courtesy of Austin Auction Gallery, www.austinauction.com

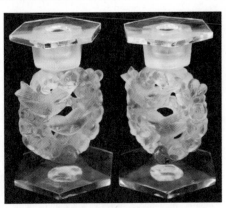

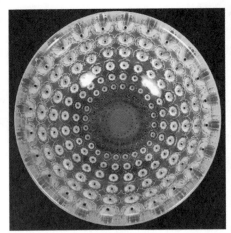

Frosted glass bowl, impressed blooms to exterior side, 20th century, signed on base, good condition, 10" d. **$406**

Courtesy of Auction Gallery of the Palm Beaches, www.agopb.com

Crystal dish with a frosted relief of a lion's head and mane, signed, Lalique France, good condition, 5-3/4" t. x 1-1/2" d. **$94**

Courtesy of Hill Auction Gallery, www.hillauctiongallery.com

Crystal "Luxembourg" figural group featuring three draped putti figures, signed on the reverse Lalique, small chip to base, 8" t., 5-3/4 lbs **$123**

Courtesy of Austin Auction Gallery, www.austinauction.com

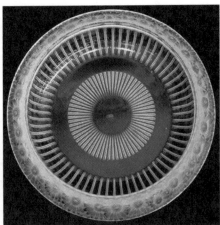

"Marguerite" crystal center bowl, sunflower border enclosing stylized stalks in a radial design to well, marked Lalique, 13-1/2" d., 7 lbs. **$492**

Courtesy of Austin Auction Gallery, www.austinauction.com

GLASS

libbey

IN 1878, WILLIAM L. LIBBEY obtained a lease on the New England Glass Co. of Cambridge, Massachusetts, changing the name to the New England Glass Works, W.L. Libbey and Son, Proprietors. After his death in 1883, his son, Edward D. Libbey, continued to operate the company at Cambridge until 1888, when the factory was closed. Edward Libbey moved to Toledo, Ohio, and set up the company subsequently known as Libbey Glass Co. During the 1880s, the firm's master technician, Joseph Locke, developed the now much desired colored art glass lines of Agata, Amberina, Peach Blow, and Pomona. Renowned for its cut glass of the Brilliant Period, the company continues in operation today as Libbey Glassware, a division of Owens-Illinois, Inc.

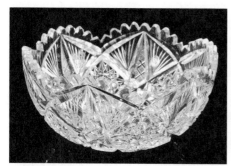

Bowl in Leota pattern, signed Libbey, 3-3/4" t. x 8" d. **$47**

Courtesy of Dirk Soulis Auctions, www.dirksoulisauctions.com

Deeply cut American Brilliant period cut glass bowl, Glenda pattern, signed Libbey, 4" t. x 8" d. **$189**

Courtesy of Dirk Soulis Auctions, www.dirksoulisauctions.com

Seven-piece pitcher and tumbler water set, features rose engraving on each, signed Libbey on base of pitcher and tumblers, 8" t. pitcher, 3-3/4" t. x 3" d. tumblers **$118**

Courtesy of Dirk Soulis Auctions, www.dirksoulisauctions.com

Cut glass bowl, signed inside the bowl "Libbey" with Libbey Glass Company's etched star in a circle trademark, 3-3/4" t. x 9" d **$385**

Courtesy of Dirk Soulis Auctions, www.dirksoulisauctions.com

Cut glass pitcher, cutting of hobstars and V shape downward cuts, signed Libbey, 8-1/2" t. x 7" d. **$83**

Courtesy of Dirk Soulis Auctions, www.dirksoulisauctions.com

Cut glass bowl, signed in center of bowl, Libbey, 2" t. x 9" d. **$106**

Courtesy of Dirk Soulis Auctions, www.dirksoulisauctions.com

Vase, Harvard pattern, Libbey, late 19th century, 12-1/4" t. x 4-1/2" d. **$165**

Courtesy of Dirk Soulis Auctions, www.dirksoulisauctions.com

◀ Square-shaped glass fernery, four footed, signed Libbey, 4" t. x 6" w. x 6" d. **$142**

Courtesy of Dirk Soulis Auctions, www.dirksoulisauctions.com

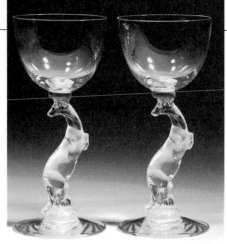

Pair of silhouette cocktail glasses with moonstone Kangaroo stems, factory polished bases with "Libbey" signature, second quarter 20th century, 6" t. **$162**

Courtesy of Jeffrey S. Evans & Associates, www.jeffreysevans.com

Cut glass compote/Taza, colorless, has a shallow bowl with floral and foliate decoration, set on a twist stem and circular base with foliate spray decoration, signed "Libbey" within circle trademark, first half 20th century, 5-5/8" t. x 7-1/4" d. **$162**

Courtesy of Jeffrey S. Evans & Associates, www.jeffreysevans.com

Amberina Jack-in-the-Pulpit vase, circa 1920s, Libbey acid stamp, some minor dirt to interior, 16-3/4" t. x 5-1/2" d. **$256**

Courtesy of Rago Auctions, www.ragoarts.com

Plate, colorless, central quatrefoil surrounded by flowers and flashed leaves, signed in center "Libbey" with saber mark, late 19th/early 20th century, 1" t. x 7" d. **$50**

Courtesy of Jeffrey S. Evans & Associates, www.jeffreysevans.com

▶ Cranberry cut to clear footed decanter, Nash Series, signed Libbey, includes pattern cut stopper, 12-1/4" t. **$767**

Courtesy of Woody Auction, www.woodyauction.com

Celery vase on pedestal cut in flashed hobstars and decorative nailhead vessicas – with a sawtooth scalloped rim and notched fluted stem, signed "Libbey" with sabre beneath, 9-3/8" t............................. **$454**

Courtesy of Humler & Nolan, www.humlernolan.com

GLASS

milk glass

THOUGH INVENTED IN Venice in the 1500s, the opaque glass commonly known as milk glass was most popular at the end of the 19th century. American manufacturers such as Westmoreland, Fenton, Imperial, Indiana, and Anchor Hocking produced it as an economical substitute for pricey European glass and china.

After World War I, the popularity of milk glass waned but production continued. Milk glass made during the 1930s and 1940s is often considered of lower quality than other periods because of the economic Depression and wartime manufacturing difficulties.

"Milk glass" is a general term for opaque colored glass. Though the name would lead you to believe it, white wasn't the only color produced.

"Colored milk glasses, such as opaque black, green, or pink, usually command higher prices," according to *Warman's Depression Glass* author and expert Ellen Schroy. "Beware of reproductions in green and pink. Always question a milk glass pattern found in cobalt blue. Swirled colors are a whole other topic and very desirable."

The number of patterns, forms, and objects made is only limited by the imagination. Commonly found milk glass items include dishes (especially the ever-popular animals on "nests"), vases, dresser sets, figurines, lanterns, boxes, and perfume bottles.

"The milk glass made by Westmoreland, Kemple, Fenton, etc., was designed to be used as dinnerware," Schroy said. "Much of the milk glass we see at flea markets and antique shows and in shops now is coming out of homes and estates where 1940-1950s-era brides are disposing of their settings.

"Care should be taken when purchasing, transporting, and using this era of milk glass as it is very intolerant of temperature changes," Schroy said. "Don't buy a piece at a flea market unless you can protect it well for its trip to your home. And when you get it home, let it sit for several hours so its temperature evens out to what your normal home temperature is. It's almost a given if you take a piece of cold glass and submerge it into a nice warm bath, it's going to crack. And never, ever expose it to the high temps of a modern dishwasher."

Soda fountain malt powder jar, with original metal lid, Carnation brand, jar in excellent condition, some denting to the lid, 9" t. x 6-1/4" d. **$108**

Courtesy Rich Penn Auctions, www.richpennauctions.com

So how do you tell the old from the new? Schroy said getting your hands on it is often the only way to tell. "Milk glass should have a wonderful silky texture. Any piece that is grainy is probably new," she said. "The best test is to look for the 'ring of fire,' which will be easy to see in the sunlight: Hold the piece of milk glass up to a good light source (I prefer natural light) and see if there is a halo of iridescent colors right around the edge, look for reds, blues, and golds. This ring was caused by the addition of iridized salts into the milk glass formula. If this ring is present, it's probably an old piece." However, 1950s-era milk glass does not have this telltale ring, she said.

Old milk glass should also carry appropriate marks and signs, like the "ring of fire"; appropriate patterns for specific makers are also something to watch for, such as Fenton's Hobnail pattern. Collectors should always check for condition issues such as damage and discoloration. According to Schroy, there is no remedy for discolored glass, and cracked and chipped pieces should be avoided, as they are prone to further damage.

— Karen Knapstein

Barber shop lamp, advertising Dandro Solvent dandruff hair tonic, early 20th century, back bar light with brass bass and milk glass stem with "Insist on Dandro Solvent" repeated four times around body, brass base has old patina and one crack, 34" t. x 9" w. **$3,900**

Courtesy Rich Penn Auctions, www.richpennauctions.com

Group of 10 Hopalong Cassidy cups and tumblers, all milk glass with black, green or blue graphics, all in excellent condition, up to 5" t. **$96**

Courtesy Rich Penn Auctions, www.richpennauctions.com

Profile portrait roundel of Peter Cooper (1791-1883), founder of the Cooper Union for the Advancement of Science and Art in New York City, after the original marble work by Charles Calverley, very good condition, 11" d. **$102**

Courtesy of Thomaston Place Auction Galleries, www.thomastonauction.com

Aladdin Nu-Type Model B milk glass kerosene table lamp and matching shade, Lincoln Drape pattern, fitted with a nickel-plated burner, matching shade and a colorless chimney, 10" t. **$125**

Courtesy of Alex Cooper Auctions, www.alexcooper.com

Pair of vases with blue rims, melon-ribbed body leading to a long, thin wasted neck, wide mouth which opens to a hand pulled, crimped ruffle with applied blue glass band, possibly Westmoreland, 9" t. x 7" w. **$61**

Courtesy of Rare-Era, www.rare-era.com

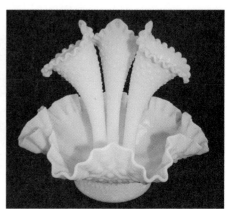

Epergne three horn hobnail in ruffled edge vase bowl, 9-1/2" t. **$31**

Courtesy of Auction Gallery of Boca Raton, www.agobr.com

British hollow rolling pin with transfer decoration of ships, captions "A Sailor's Farewell" with a sentimental poem, images of animals and blossoms, some loss to appliques, 29-1/2" x 3-1/4" d. **$240**

Courtesy of Thomaston Place Auction Galleries, www.thomastonauction.com

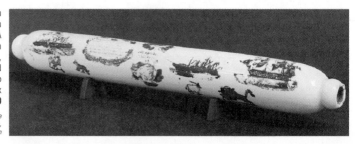

Handblown and shaped vases, satin finish, floral decoration, cylindrical shape, rough pontils on the undersides, air bubbles in the glass, early 19th century, 1lb. 4 oz., 8" t. x 3-1/8" d........ **$74**

Courtesy of Antiques and Art by IMEON

▲ Embossed owl miniature kerosene lamp, green painted highlights, red eyes, 8" t. **$720**

Courtesy of Woody Auction, www.woodyauction.com

Mid-century modern Fire King glass bowl, 8" d. x 2" t. **$7**

Courtesy of Pioneer Auction Gallery, www.pioneerantiqueauction.com

Rectangular prismatic milk glass box with gilt metal mounts and foliate frieze bands, some losses to gilding on central metal band, 3-1/4" t. x 5-1/4" w. x 3-1/2" d. **$125**

Courtesy of Auctions at Showplace, www.nyshowplace.com

Pair electrified lamps, milk glass shade and body molded in relief with lion masks, some roughness and chips to the upper and lower rims of both shade, some tarnishing to both metal bases, 15 lbs., 25" t. x 11" d. **$215**

Courtesy of Austin Auction Gallery, www.austinauction.com

McKee Dog covered dish, signed "McKee", McKee & Brothers, late 19th/early 20th century, 4-1/8" t. x 5-1/4" d. **$137**

Courtesy of Jeffrey S. Evans & Associates, www.jeffreysevans.com

GLASS

GLASS

moser

LUDWIG MOSER (1833-1916) founded his polishing and engraving workshop in 1857 in Karlsbad, Austria. Today this Czech Republic city is known as Karlovy Vary. He employed many famous glass designers, e.g., Johann Hoffman, Josef Urban and Rudolf Miller. In 1900, Moser and his sons, Rudolf and Gustav, incorporated Ludwig Moser & Sons.

Moser art glass included clear pieces with inserted blobs of colored glass, cut colored glass with classical scenes, cameo glass and intaglio cut. Many inexpensive enameled pieces were also made. Moser was one of the few Czechoslovakian glassmakers to sign their pieces. The slogan "King of Glass, Glass of Kings" is associated with the company because of its famous clientele who, in addition to Edward VII and the Austrian Imperial Court, include Pope Pius XI, the Turkish sultan Abdul Hamid II, King Luís I of Portugal and his wife, Maria Pia of Savoy

In 1922, Leo and Richard Moser brought Meyr's Neffe, their biggest Bohemian rival in art glass. Moser executed many pieces for the Wiener Workstatte in the 1920s.

Signed Moser Karlsbad cased art glass vase, 8-1/2" t., lavender shading to yellow with enamel trim highlights..........................**$420**

Courtesy of Woody Auction,
www.woodyauction.com

A Moser enameled glass and gilt bronze-mounted centerpiece, late 19th century, bronze trim to lip loose, some rubbing to gilding, gilt bronze mounts likely a later addition and lower mounts exhibit adhesive residue, 9 h x 12-3/4 w x 9-1/4 d inches **$937**

Courtesy of Heritage Auctions, www.ha.com

Unmarked Moser art glass vase, 8" t., rectangular, solid amber glass, figural lion-head feet, enameled blossom and butterfly décor. **$300**

Courtesy of Woody Auction,
www.woodyauction.com

Moser art glass vase , signed, with hexagonal rim and enamel and gilt floral decoration 11 1/4"
.... **$162**

Courtesy of Berman's Auction Gallery, www.bermansauctiongallery.com

Moser clear to green enameled pitcher with oak leaves, acorns, gilded edging, late 19th century. 5" x 5". **$562**

Courtesy of Quinn's Auction Galleries, www.quinns.com

Unmarked Moser art glass diamond shaped vase, 8-1/2", finely engraved dandelion décor with gold stencil highlights, good condition. **$360**

Courtesy of Woody Auction, www.woodyauction.com

Moser cut crystal wine glasses, "Birds of the Wild", in various colors, showing etched design of birds in different views, each with acid mark underfoot, each approximately 7 1/4 h. **$246**

Courtesy of Austin Auction Gallery, www.austinauction.com

▶ Moser glass gilded chalices, each having thick walls, pedestal foot beneath paneled trim, heavily gilded bodies showing figures in a pastoral landscape: (2) signed W. Berndt (Wolfgang Berndt) in amber; (1) pink glass, signed Walter; each approx 6" h, ... **$307**

Courtesy of Austin Auction Gallery, www.austinauction.com

GLASS

Pair of antique covered vases in a Mettalch style, turn of the century, depicting a man and a woman in biblical garb, 6-1/2" to top of lid, excellent condition.
.... **$937**

Courtesy of Auction Gallery of Boca Raton, www.agobr.com

Enameled ruby glass decanter with ring neck, decorated throughout with enamel flowers and gilding; with tall stopper, 23" h. overall.
.... **$812**

Courtesy of Alex Cooper Auctions, www.alexcooper.com

Moser fish scale decanter with stopper, chip to tip of stopper has been restored, 13-1/2" with stopper, 5" d. bottom **$184**

Courtesy of California Auctioneers, www.californiaauctioneers.com

Unmarked Moser cranberry art glass, 5-1/2" x 5-1/2", floral décor, clear ribbed applied glass feet, good condition. **$240**

Courtesy of Woody Auction, www.woodyauction.com

Pair of Art Deco Moser bud vases, ca. 1925, green art glass, enamel, gold, 7" x 2-1/4". **$330**

Courtesy of Jasper52, www.jasper52.com

GLASS

mt. washington

A WIDE DIVERSITY of glass was made by the Mt. Washington Glass Co. of New Bedford, Massachusetts, between 1869 and 1900. It was succeeded in 1900 by the Pairpoint Manufacturing Co. Throughout its history, the Mt. Washington Glass Co. made different types of glass including pressed, blown, art, lava, Napoli, cameo, cut, Albertine, Peachblow, Burmese, Crown Milano, Royal Flemish, and Verona.

GLASS

◀ Royal Flemish bulbous body vase decorated with multi-colored pansies, gilded sunburst medallions with a gold floral lace pattern against a satin background, further decorated with two applied leaf handles and gilded foot and top rim, very good to excellent, 5-1/2" h. **$592**

Courtesy of James D. Julia, Inc., Fairfield, Maine, www.jamesdjulia.com

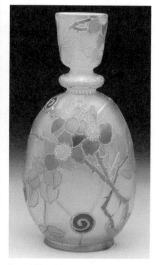

Peach Blow gourd-shaped vase decorated with enameled yellow rose blossom with green stems and leaves highlighted by gold gilding on a satin background, shading from blue to pink, unsigned but retains original "Mt. W.G.Co. Peach Blow" paper label on underside, very good to excellent, 8-1/4" h. **$1,066**

Courtesy of James D. Julia, Inc., Fairfield, Maine, www.jamesdjulia.com

Mt. Washington Royal Flemish 1546 coat-of-arms pitcher decorated with a stylized coat-of-arms in green and gold, having shield with helmet, crown and lion holding a 1546 banner, reverse features a gold shield with two black fleur-de-lis, set against a cream, rose and burgundy background panel with gilded trim, 10" h. **$177**

Courtesy of James D. Julia, Inc., Fairfield, Maine, www.jamesdjulia.com

Royal Flemish vase decorated with the Hedge Rose and Bulls-Eye pattern, with multi-colored roses, green leaves and thorny stems with gilded trim against a clear satin background, flared cup-style mouth and gilded rim, 9" h. **$888**

Courtesy of James D. Julia, Inc., Fairfield, Maine, www.jamesdjulia.com

Burmese creamer with applied wishbone feet, Mt. Washington Glass Co., fourth quarter 19th century, 3-3/4" h. **$280**

Courtesy of Jeffrey S. Evans & Associates, www.jeffreysevans.com

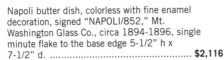

Napoli butter dish, colorless with fine enamel decoration, signed "NAPOLI/852," Mt. Washington Glass Co., circa 1894-1896, single minute flake to the base edge 5-1/2" h x 7-1/2" d. **$2,116**

Courtesy of Jeffrey S. Evans & Associates, www.jeffreysevans.com

Pair of egg-shaped salt and pepper shakers, opal with pale rose ground and plush/satin finish, embossed with gilt highlighted "Columbian 1893 Exhibition, Mt. Washington Glass Co./Smith Brothers," circa 1893, 1-3/4" h x 2-5/8" l. **$122**

Courtesy of Jeffrey S. Evans & Associates, www.jeffreysevans.com

▲ Burmese ribbed cruet with a glossy finish, applied opaque handle, matching pattern stopper with a lightly polish tip, Mt. Washington, fourth quarter 19th century, 6-1/2" h. **$186**

Courtesy of Jeffrey S. Evans & Associates, www.jeffreysevans.com

▲ Colonial ware water jug, ovoid form, shaded light green with gilt daisies and scroll work, satin finish, applied prunt to top and short spout, raised on a domed foot with rough-ground pontil mark and "0122" inscribed in red, Mt. Washington Glass Co., circa 1895, 11-1/2" h. **$467**

Courtesy of Jeffrey S. Evans & Associates, www.jeffreysevans.com

Grouping of three Mt. Washington light blue diamond quilted satin glass vases, colors fade from light to dark, 19th century, largest measures 10" h, others 8" h. **$154**

Courtesy of Bruneau & Co. Auctioneers, www.bruneauandco.com

Mt. Washington condiment set, white porcelain salt and pepper shakers with dandelion décor, on Pairpoint #722 silver-plate frame, 7-1/4" h. ... **$120**

Courtesy of Woody Auction, www.woodyauction.com

Lot of three individual open salts, two with shaded ground, various enameled floral decorations and satin finish, each melon form with beaded rim, one with gilt rim, Mt. Washington Glass Co., fourth quarter 19th century, 1-1/4" h x 1-5/8" d rim.. **$140**

Courtesy of Jeffrey S. Evans & Associates, www.jeffreysevans.com

◄ Crown Milano biscuit jar, cream and white mottled background with colorful floral décor and gold enamel trim highlights, ornate silver-plate lid and bail, 6" h. **$480**

Courtesy of Woody Auction, www.woodyauction.com

Rare Burmese vase finished with enamel decoration, polished pontil, Mt. Washington, very good condition, 12" h x 6-1/2" w. **$1,180**

Courtesy of Dirk Soulis Auctions, www.dirksoulisauctions.com

◄ Mt. Washington Crown Milano barrel form toothpick container with a molded amber collar and foot decorated with blue berries and fall leaves, good condition, 2-1/2" h. **$423**

Courtesy of Jaremos, www.jaremos.com

GLASS

murano

IN THE 1950S, the American home came alive with vibrant-colored decorative items, abstract art, and futuristic-designed furniture. The colorless geometry of the 1930s was out.

Over the last decade, mid-century design has once again gained favor with interior decorators, magazines, shows, and stores dedicated solely to this period. The bold colors and free-form shapes of mid-century modern Italian glass are emblematic of 1950s design. This distinctive glass has become a sought-after collectible.

Prices realized at auction for 1950s glass have seen a resurgence. However, there are still many items readily available and not always at a premium.

Italian glass can be found in many American homes. In fact, it is likely that some of the familiar glass items you grew up with were produced in Italy – the candy dish on the coffee table with the bright colors, the ashtray with the gold flecks inside. Modern glass objects from Italy were among the most widely distributed examples of 1950s design.

As with any decorative art form, there are varying levels of achievement in the design and execution of glass from this period. While you should always buy what you love, as there is never a guarantee return on investment, buying the best representation of an item is wise. In considering modern Italian glass, several points make one piece stand above another.

Italy has a centuries-old tradition of glassmaking, an industry whose center is the group of islands known as Murano in the lagoon of Venice. The most recognized and desirable Italian glass comes from three companies: Seguso, Venini and Barovier & Toso.

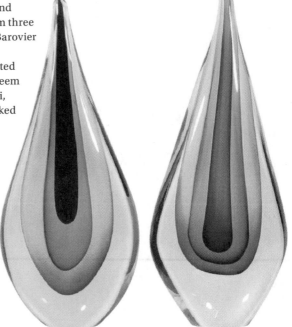

Italy offers a vast array of talented glass artists. Top end collectors seem to favor Carlo Scarpa from Venini, Napoleone Martinuzzi (who worked at Venini from 1925-1932), and Dino Martens of Aureliano Toso. You can expect to pay several thousand dollars for a fine piece by one of these artists.

Pair of mid-century modern sculptures, teardrop form, Sommerso technique with pink, green and blue, 11" t. **$137**

Courtesy of Antiques & Modern Auction Gallery, www.antiquesmodern.com

For slimmer collecting budgets, good quality examples by other artists are available and more affordable. Alfredo Barbini and Fulvio Biaconi (for Venini) are two of them. While some of their work does command top dollar, many of their pieces are priced for the novice collector.

A few mid-century designs can still be found that could prove to be sleepers in the near future. Look for Inciso vases by Venini, Aborigeni pieces by Barovier & Toso, and Soffiati examples by Giacomo Cappellin. Each of these designs is totally different from the other, yet all are reasonably priced in today's market.

Collectors should be aware that the most popular glass form is the vase, with glass sculpture following next in line. Popular sculptural forms include male or female nude figurals and pasta glass animals by Fulvio Biaconi.

Reproductions of the most famous forms of Italian glass are rampant. Some are marketed as such, while others are made to fool unsuspecting buyers. Also, and perhaps more confusing, many Italian glass designs are being produced to this day. The most common example of this is the Handkerchief vase. Originally produced by Piero Chiesa in 1937 for Fontana Arte, it was called the Paper Bag vase due to its crumpled shape. In the 1950s, Bianconi designed his own version for Venini. Since that time, generic manufacturers throughout Murano have produced countless unsigned imitations for the tourist trade. Almost all Venini handkerchief vases were signed, except for a few very valuable examples by Dino Martens.

Whether from the original manufacturer or another firm, Murano glass now being reproduced includes Sommerso designs, Barbini glass aquariums and bowls along with Oriente designs. Venini lamps have also been reproduced. No doubt there will be more reproductions to come.

Hand-blown green to light teal art glass polar bear sculpture on gold flecks pedestal, Sommerso technique, attributed to Alfredo Barbini, 5-1/4" l. x 3-3/4" h. **$93**

Courtesy of Jasper52, www.jasper52.com

"Pennellate" vase, Carlo Scarpa, mid-20th century, signed "Venini Murano", 6-3/8" t. x 6-5/8" d. **$1,875**

Courtesy of Kaminski Auctions, www.kaminskiauctions.com

◀ Blown incalmo decanter, signed and dated, Murano, Italy, 1986, original sticker label, good condition 14" t. x 3-1/4" d. **$1,560**

Courtesy of Rago Auction, www.ragoarts.com

▶ Corroso glass figure, mid-late 20th century, etched signature "L. de Roi," Murano, Italy, good condition, 40" t. **$260**

Courtesy of Rago Auction, www.ragoarts.com

Blown glass mushroom table lamp with swirl pattern, original Vetri Murano decal, mid-20th century, good condition, 14-1/2" t. x 12" d. **$162**

Courtesy of Rago Auction, www.ragoarts.com

Hand-blown, pink and white Zanrifico ribbons decorative bowl, features three different ribbon patterns, signed "Venini Murano Italia," 6-3/4" l. x 6-3/4" w. .**$88**

Courtesy of Jasper52, www.jasper52.com

Blown glass vase, circa 1930s, overall very good to excellent, several short scratches to shoulder, several small bubbles as made, 14-1/4" t. x 6" d. **$910**

Courtesy of Rago Auction, www.ragoarts.com

▶ Sommerso glass heart bowl, red set to colorless, minor scratches and fritting around rim, Murano, Italy, 3" t. x 6-1/4" d. **$24**

Courtesy of Auctions at Showplace, www.nyshowplace.com

Red cased glass pendant shades, mid 20th century, good condition, require wiring, 13" t. x 10" d.
.... **$130**

Courtesy of Rago Auction, www.ragoarts.com

▲ Murrine vase, good condition, 10-1/2" t. x 6" d.
.... **$975**

▶ Blown glass Murrine table lamp, with wood base and a single socket, two broken handles that were re-glued, circa 1950s, 10" t. x 7" d. **$390**

Courtesy of Rago Auction, www.ragoarts.com

Green and silver fleck bowl, Tutti Frutti pattern, studded with millefiori glass, circa 1950s, fragmentary paper label in blue and white to the back, 5-1/4" w. diagonally. **$60**

Courtesy of Jasper52, www.jasper52.com

GLASS

GLASS

northwood

NORTHWOOD GLASS CO. was founded by Harry Northwood, son of prominent English glassmaker John Northwood, who was famous for his expertise in cameo glass. Harry migrated to America in 1881 and, after working at various glass manufacturers, formed the Northwood Glass Co. in 1896 in Indiana, Pennsylvania. In 1902 he created H. Northwood and Co. in Wheeling, West Virginia. After Northwood died in 1919, H. Northwood and Co. began to falter and eventually closed in 1925.

Northwood produced a wide variety of opalescent, decorated, and special effect glasses, and colors like iridescent blue and green, which were not widely seen at the time.

Plate, Good Luck pattern, Marigold color, Northwood Glass Co., 9" d. **$99**

Courtesy of Woody Auction, www.woodyauction.com

Four-piece table set, amethyst with gilt and enamel scrolling and floral decoration, comprising a covered butter dish, sugar bowl, and a creamer and spooner, Northwood Glass CO., circa 1902, butter cover has a crack to rim, and minute flake to finial, minor wear to decoration, 4-3/8" t. x 6-7/8" d. to 7-3/4" t. **$98**

Courtesy of Jeffrey S. Evans & Associates, www.jeffreysevans.com

Water pitcher, Royal Ivy pattern, glossy finish, applied colorless handle, Northwood Glass Company, No. 287, 8" t. **$50**

Courtesy of Jeffrey S. Evans & Associates, www.jeffreysevans.com

Spanish Lace pattern cracker jar, Vaseline opalescent, silver-plated collar, cover and handle, Northwood Glass Co., minute denting to the color, 10-1/2" t. 5-3/4" t. to top of collar, 4-3/4" d... **$591**

Courtesy of Jeffrey S. Evans & Associates, www.jeffreysevans.com

Pink and white swirl design vase, with ribbed molding and square ruffled top, 8-3/4". **$150**

Courtesy of Woody Auction, www.woodyauction.com

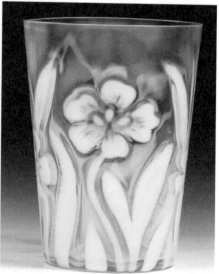

Blue opalescent tumbler, Daffodil pattern, factory-polished rim, circa 1903, 3-7/8" t. **$187**

Courtesy of Jeffrey S. Evans & Associates, www.jeffreysevans.com

Opaline Brocade/Spanish Lace pattern creamer, Vaseline opalescent with an applied reeded handle and factory-polished rim, minute roughness to the rim, as made, 4-1/2" t. **$236**

Courtesy of Jeffrey S. Evans & Associates, www.jeffreysevans.com

Sugar shaker, Leaf Mold pattern, No. 33, royal silver and case opal with cranberry spatter and mica flecks, period lid, late 19th century pattern introduced, 3-5/8" t. **$199**

Courtesy of Jeffrey S. Evans & Associates, www.jeffreysevans.com

Ribbed opal rings tumbler, colorless opalescent, factory-polished rim, circa 1888, a few minute nicks to rim interior, 3-7/8" t. **$162**

Courtesy of Jeffrey S. Evans & Associates, www.jeffreysevans.com

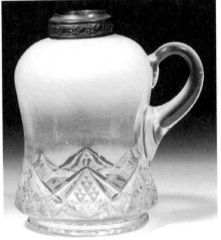

Finger lamp, Diamond Spearhead pattern, Vaseline opalescent, applied Vaseline handle, Northwood Glass Co., circa 1902, minor overall wear, collar with a split, 5-1/2" t. x 3-3/8" d. **$685**

Courtesy of Jeffrey S. Evans & Associates, www.jeffreysevans.com

Three-tier tankard water pitcher, blue opalescent, Coin Spot pattern, applied handle, late 19th/early 20th century, a few scattered minute potstones, 11-1/8" t. x 6-1/4" d. **$173**

Courtesy of Jeffrey S. Evans & Associates, www.jeffreysevans.com

Northwood No. 567 hobnail figural pump pitcher and log-form trough, Vaseline opalescent, late 19th/early 20th century, 6-3/4" t. (pump), 2-3/4" t. x 5" w. (trough). **$62**

Courtesy of Jeffrey S. Evans & Associates, www.jeffreysevans.com

Rose Du Barry/cased pink water pitcher, Leaf Umbrella pattern, No. 263, with applied colorless handle, early 20th century, minor inclusion under upper handle terminal as made, 8-1/2" t. **$373**

Courtesy of Jeffrey S. Evans & Associates, www.jeffreysevans.com

Threaded water carafe, Rubina swirl pattern, fourth quarter 19th century, Northwood Glass Co., 7-3/4" t. **$75**

Courtesy of Jeffrey S. Evans & Associates, www.jeffreysevans.com

Cranberry opalescent jar, Chrysanthemum Swirl pattern, circa late 19th century, minor flake and a manufacturing flaw to rim, 10-3/4" t. **$405**

Courtesy of Jeffrey S. Evans & Associates, www.jeffreysevans.com

GLASS

opalescent

OPALESCENT GLASS IS one of the most popular areas of glass collecting. The opalescent effect was attained by adding bone ash chemicals to areas of an item while still hot and refiring the object at tremendous heat. Both pressed and mold-blown patterns are available to collectors. Opalescent Glass from A to Z by the late William Heacock is the definitive reference book for collectors.

Opaline Brocade/Spanish Lace pattern tumblers, straight-sided forms, each with a factory-polished rim, Northwood Glass Co., 3-1/2" t.
.... **$373**

Courtesy of Jeffrey S.Evans & Associates, www.jeffreysevans.com

Rubina verde petal form trumpet vase, 19th century, cranberry opalescent upper portion blends into a verde green glass stem joined to a blown circular foot, the top cut, crimped and formed into folded petals, 11-1/4" t. x 5-1/2" d.
....**$106**

Courtesy of Dirk Soulis Auctions, www.dirksoulisauctions.com

Scarce Vaseline opalescent and oxblood berry set includes master berry bowl and six companion bowls, deep oxblood red glass blending Vaseline, internally decorated with flower heads and leafy branches, embossed petals at the pontil of the master bowl, partially polished pontil on each small berry bowl, master bowl 2-3/4" t. x 10-1/2" d. **$324**

Courtesy of Dirk Soulis Auctions, www.dirksoulisauctions.com

VISIT WWW.ANTIQUETRADER.COM

WWW.FACEBOOK.COM/ANTIQUETRADER

Lot of seven Irish with Meader pattern tumblers, Vaseline, Jefferson Glass Co., early 20th century, one tumbler with a sizeable chip to the base, another with sizeable chipping to the base, one example has heavy glass haziness, 3-3/4" t. **$87**

Courtesy of Jeffrey S.Evans & Associates, www.jeffreysevans.com

Actinia plate with opalescent Actinia coupe, France, circa 1933, opalescence is very light, some surface scratches, marked R. Lalique, France, 1-3/4" t. x 10-1/8" **$225**

Courtesy of Heritage Auctions, www.ha.com

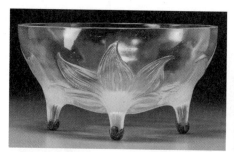

Lys bowl with silver-plated sabots, circa 1924, marked R. Lalique, France, minor area of mineral deposits to interior bowl, sabots not original to bowl, wear commensurate with age and use, 5" t. x 9-1/4". **$575**

Courtesy of Heritage Auctions, www.ha.com

Coquilles coupe, Wingen-sur-Moder, France, circa 1924, marked R. Lalique, light fleabiting and very small flake missing to rim, 3-1/2" t. to 9-3/8" t. **$212**

Courtesy of Heritage Auctions, www.ha.com

Victorian opalescent bride's bowl with bands of color glass radiating from the center to the intricately crimped and folded outer rim shaded in pink cased in clear glass, largely polished pontil, 4" t. x 10" d. **$53**

Courtesy of Dirk Soulis Auctions, www.dirksoulisauctions.com

Water pitcher, Vaseline, Beatty swirl, A.J. Beatty & Sons, 7-3/4" t. **$112**

Courtesy of Jeffrey S. Evans & Associates, www.jeffreysevans.com

Cranberry opalescent glass lemonade set in Daisy and Fern pattern; a pitcher with five glasses or tumblers, Fenton for LG Wright, circa 1952-1954, 9-1/4" t. (pitcher), 3-1/2 (tumblers). **$186**

Courtesy of Ahlers & Ogletree, www.aando.com

Set of three glass vanity items, Sabino Les Ondines pattern, Paris, France, post-1935, marks Sabino, Paris, inclusion to the interior rim of the lid to the smallest box, good condition, 6" d. (largest). ... **$237**

Courtesy of Heritage Auctions, www.ha.com

Vaseline opalescent ruffled four-trumpet lily epergne, mounted on beveled mirror base, good condition, 14-1/4" t. x 8" d. **$240**

Courtesy of Woody Auction, www.woodyauction.com

Manila/wreath and shell toothpick holder, Vaseline, polychrome-enamel decoration, Model Flint Glass Co., early 20th century, 2-1/2" t. **$100**

Courtesy of Jeffrey S.Evans & Associates, www.jeffreysevans.com

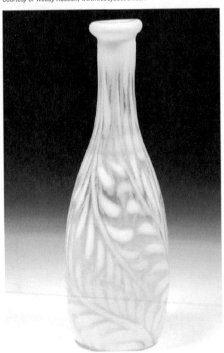

Fern bitters bottle, colorless opalescent, square form, polished pontil mark, West Virginia Glass Co., circa late 19th century, 8-1/4" t. x 2-1/2" square. ... **$174**

Courtesy of Jeffrey S. Evans & Assoc., www.jeffreysevans.com

GLASS

pairpoint

ORIGINALLY ORGANIZED IN New Bedford, Massachusetts, in 1880 as the Pairpoint Manufacturing Co. on land adjacent to the famed Mount Washington Glass Co., Pairpoint first manufactured silver and plated wares. In 1894, the two famous factories merged as the Pairpoint Corp. and enjoyed great success for more than 40 years.

The company was sold in 1939 to a group of local businessmen and eventually bought out by one of the group, who turned the management over to Robert M. Gundersen. Subsequently, it operated as the Gundersen Glass Works until 1952 when, after Gundersen's death, the name was changed to Gundersen-Pairpoint. The factory closed in 1956.

Subsequently, Robert Bryden took charge of this glassworks, at first producing glass for Pairpoint abroad and eventually, in 1970, beginning glass production in Sagamore, Massachusetts. Today the Pairpoint Crystal Glass Co. is owned by Robert and June Bancroft. They continue to manufacture fine quality blown and pressed glass.

Examples of Pairpoint glass designs are displayed in museums across the country, including New York's Metropolitan Museum of Art and Boston's Museum of Fine Arts. "Puffy" lamps with ornate polychrome glass shades are probably the most recognized Pairpoint items, selling for thousands of dollars at auction.

For more Pairpoint lamps, please see the "Lamps & Lighting" section.

Jewelry box, signature on the base, wreath-shape handle on lid has a break, 6" t. x 5" d. **$81**

Courtesy of Dirk Soulis Auctions, www.dirksoulisauctions.com

▼ Hand-painted dresser box, metal mounts, old satin lining, numbered 3213/144 under the base, 4" t. 10" w. x 6" d. **$162**

Courtesy of Dirk Soulis Auctions, www.dirksoulisauctions.com

Lot of four table articles, colorless, a pair of No. 364 shape comports with Barrington pattern to bowl and foot, pair of champagne glasses with Tassel pattern and panel-cut stems, first half of 20th century, comports 5-1/2" t. x 6" d., champagnes 4-1/4" t. **$100**

Courtesy of Jeffrey S. Evans & Associates, www.jeffreysevans.com

Lot of three engraved open compotes, one brown/amber with a deep bowl, an orange/amber with a shallow bowl, a cobalt blue with a shallow bowl, each with vintage decoration and polished pontil mark, first quarter 20th century, Pairpoint Corporation, 4" to 6-5/8" t. **$174**

Courtesy of Jeffrey S. Evans & Associates, www.jeffreysevans.com

Pair of compotes, cut glass in cobalt color, 6-1/2" t. x 8" w. **$27**

Courtesy of Kaminski Auctions, www.kaminskiauctions.com

Pair of amethyst vases with etched floral design and controlled bubble ball spacers, 12" t. **$265**

Courtesy of Sandwich Auction House, www.sandwichauction.com

Bulbous form jar, deep rose, decorated with enameled flowers, produced for Art Glass Society 1994 Texas Convention, marked MWAGS 1994 Texs', 8t. **$48**

Courtesy of Jaremos, www.jaremos.com

Liquor bottle with etched grapevine and leaf decoration, silver capped stopper with silver-plated tag, late 19th century, engraved "Spirits", plaster holding silver top deteriorated, wear from use, 8" t. **$125**

Courtesy of Alex Cooper Auctioneers, www.alexcooper.com

Tavern glass, colorless, shape D-1507 with hand-painted polychrome, floral decoration, second quarter 20th century, 6" t. **$62**

Courtesy of Jeffrey S. Evans & Associates, www.jeffreysevans.com

Pairpoint Corporation No. 1010 shape bowl in Daisy pattern, with band of diagonal fluting to the base edge full round and rayed base; and a No. A-262 shape comport with Daisy pattern decoration and rayed base, 5-3/4" t. x 7-1/2" d (comport), 3-7/8" t. x 11-3/4" d. (bowl). **$62**

Courtesy of Jeffrey S. Evans & Associates, www.jeffreysevans.com

Lot of two cut glass decanters, colorless, comprising an Adelaide pattern example with original stopper, late 19th century/first quarter 20th century, 9-1/2" t. and 11-1/4" t. **$187**

Courtesy of Jeffrey S. Evans & Associates, www.jeffreysevans.com

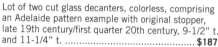

Cranberry glass cut to clear, footed centerpiece bowl with etched grape and leaf decoration, 4" t. x 14" d. **$270**

Courtesy of Duane Merrill & Co., www.merrillsauction.com

Decorated bowl, colorless lead glass, flared-rim bowl raised on a paperweight base, mid-20th century, 6" t. x 10" d.. **$24**

Courtesy of Jeffrey S. Evans & Associates, www.jeffreysevans.com

Centerpiece bowl, amethyst, #A-1065, grape engraved design, polished pontil, first half 20th century, moderate to heavy interior wear, Pairpoint Manufacturing Co., 5-1/2" t. x 12" d. rim. **$124**

Courtesy of Jeffrey S. Evans & Associates, www.jeffreysevans.com

Vase featuring basket décor with floral edge, 9" t. and 6-3/4" t. **$200**

Courtesy of Richard D. Hatch & Associates, www.richarddhatch.com

GLASS

pattern

THOUGH IT HAS NEVER been ascertained whether glass was first pressed in the United States or abroad, the development of the glass-pressing machine revolutionized the glass industry in the United States, and this country receives the credit for improving the method to make this process feasible. The first wares pressed were probably small flat plates of the type now referred to as "lacy," the intricacy of the design concealing flaws.

In 1827, both the New England Glass Co., Cambridge, Massachusetts, and Bakewell & Co., Pittsburgh, took out patents for pressing glass furniture knobs; soon other pieces followed. This early pressed glass contained red lead, which made it clear and resonant when tapped (flint). Made primarily in clear, it is rarer in blue, amethyst, olive green, and yellow.

By the 1840s, early simple patterns such as Ashburton, Argus and Excelsior appeared. Ribbed Bellflower seems to have been one of the earliest patterns to have had complete sets. By the 1860s, a wide range of patterns was available.

In 1864, William Leighton of Hobbs, Brockunier & Co., Wheeling, West Virginia, developed a formula for "soda lime" glass that did not require the expensive red lead for clarity. Although "soda lime" glass did not have the brilliance of the earlier flint glass, the formula came into widespread use because glass could be produced cheaply.

Free blown trumpet vases in an unusual deep swirling smoky amethyst, each with an inward folded rim, and joined by a wafer to a short baluster-form stem and applied circular foot with polished pontil mark, circa 1840-1860, Boston & Sandwich Glass Co., 12-3/4" t. x 4" d., 13" t. x 4-1/8" d. **$2,340**

Courtesy of Jeffrey S. Evans & Associates, www.jeffreysevans.com

Dragon salver/cake stand, colorless, M'Kee & Brothers, fourth quarter 19th century, minor surface scratching, compote bowl manipulated into a plate, attached by a wafer to a facetted knop stem and circular foot, 4-1/2" t. x 11" d. **$1,755**

Courtesy of Jeffrey S. Evans & Associates, www.jeffreysevans.com

Three-face Duncan No. 400 Elliptical pattern covered compote, with pie-crust rim and 44 oval beads, colorless, Geo. Duncan & Sons, Pittsburgh, Pa., late 19th century, 13" t. x 8-1/2" d. **$2,457**

Courtesy of Jeffrey S. Evans & Associates, www.jeffreysevans.com

Pressed glass hollow glass model of Independence Hall, Philadelphia, presumably a candy container and coin slot for use as bank with slide-on tin bottom closure, designed by William R. Kirchner probably for the 1876 exhibition, 5-1/5 t. x 3-1/2 d. **$442**

Courtesy of Dirk Soulis Auctions, www.dirksoulisauctions.com

Store countertop embossed glass Planters Peanuts jar, 20th century, pressed glass ornately decorated, lidded, some chips, good condition overall, 12" t. **$135**

Courtesy of Leland Little Auctions, www.lelandlittle.com

Eagle and shield pressed open salt, deep brilliant amber, raised on four feet, Boston & Sandwich Glass Co., 2-1/8" t. x 2" w. x 3-1/4" d. **$4,850**

Courtesy of Jeffrey S. Evans & Associates, www.jeffreysevans.com

Oval pressed open salt, deep amethyst, shaped rim, variant with collared foot, likely France, mid-19th century, loss of central scroll tips on one side and corresponding moderate chip/bruise to interior, some other losses/mold roughness to rim, foot with area of moderate chipping, roughness to edge, 1-3/4" t. x 2-1/2" w. x 3-1/2" d. **$236**

Courtesy of Jeffrey S. Evans & Associates, www.jeffreysevans.com

Irish pressed turn-over rim compote on foot, colorless lead glass, deep oval shape with medial honeycomb band, rim with rows of stars and prisms, raised on triple-knop stem and oval lobed "rose" foot with polished table ring, early 19th century, excellent condition, 9" t. x 13-1/2" x 9" d. **$500**

Courtesy of Jeffrey S. Evans & Associates, www.jeffreysevans.com

Pressed moon and stars fluid hand lamp, colorless, bell-form foot with molded handle and cut-and-shut mark under base, No. 1 fine-line collar, Boston & Sandwich Glass Co., 1850-1870, 4-3/8" t. to top of collar, 3-3/8" d. **$75**

Courtesy of Jeffrey S. Evans & Associates, www.jeffreysevans.com

Rectangular box of peacock blue glass, pressed in a Strawberry and Diaper pattern, with Ministry of Finance mark and date 1904 pressed in the base, polished metal mount with lock and initials J-A-G stamped on the lower mount behind the lock, 4" t. x 4-7/8" w. x 3-5/8" d. **$110**

Courtesy of Jasper52, www.jasper52.com

American pressed glass covered wagon dish in locomotive form, 19th century. **$83**

Courtesy of Dirk Soulis Auctions, www.dirksoulisauctions.com

Stained pressed glass shade, bead and tassel motif, late 19th/first quarter 20th century, excellent condition with a moderate check to the fitter, probably as made, 5-1/4" t. **$124**

Courtesy of Jeffrey S. Evans & Associates, www.jeffreysevans.com

Pressed muzzled bear jar, opaque black, embossed, "F.B. Strouse/N.Y." under base, Boston & Sandwich Glass Co., excellent condition, light flaking/mold roughness to base and cover rims, shallow chip to tip of one foot, moderate chip to reverse of one ear, 3-3/4" t. x 1-5/8" d. **$137**

Courtesy of Jeffrey S. Evans & Associates, www.jeffreysevans.com

Pressed block salver, Vaseline, F. H. Lovell & Co, fourth quarter 19th century, excellent condition overall with a few scattered pattern flakes to the underside of the plateau, 6-1/2" t. x 10" D. **$87**

Courtesy of Jeffrey S. Evans & Associates, www.jeffreysevans.com

Water pitcher, Hexagon block pattern, amber stained Hobbs No. 335, squat form, applied handle with pressed-feather design to upper terminal, etched floral decoration, Hobbs Brockunier & Co., late 19th century, 8-5/8" t. **$87**

Courtesy of Jeffrey S. Evans & Associates, www.jeffreysevans.com

GLASS

GLASS

peach blow

SEVERAL TYPES OF glass lumped together by collectors as Peach Blow were produced by half a dozen glasshouses. Hobbs, Brockunier & Co., Wheeling, West Virginia, made Peach Blow as a plated ware that shaded from red at the top to yellow at the bottom and is referred to as Wheeling Peach Blow. Mt. Washington Glass Works produced a homogeneous Peach Blow shading from rose at the top to pale blue in the lower portion. The New England Glass Works' Peach Blow, called Wild Rose, shaded from rose at the top to white. Gundersen-Pairpoint Co. also reproduced some of the Mt. Washington Peach Blow in the early 1950s, and some glass of a somewhat similar type was made by Steuben Glass Works, Thomas Webb & Sons, and Stevens & Williams of England. New England Peach Blow is one-layered glass and the English is two-layered.

Another single-layered shaded art glass was produced early in the 20th century by New Martinsville Glass Mfg. Co. Originally called "Muranese," collectors today refer to it as New Martinsville Peach Blow.

Blown satin glass Peach Blow vase, bulbous form with a flared rim, done in graduated shades of pink rose to cream colored Satin Glass with hand-laid Coralene enamel decoration, cased glass interior in white color, 7-3/4 t. **$324**

Courtesy of Auction Gallery of Boca Raton, www.agbr.com

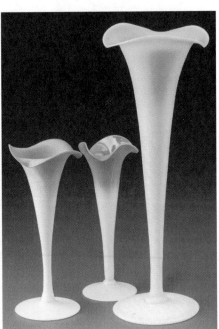

Three American lily vases, satin and gloss finishes, Peach Blow and rose color schemes, early 20th century, 14-3/8" t. (tallest)............................**$250**

Courtesy of Heritage Auctions, www.ha.com

Hobbs Wheeling Coral No. 22 Moran vase and stand, glossy finish, polished pontil mark, original amber five-griffin stand, Hobbs, Brockunier & Co., circa 1886, vase with professional restoration to the rim, 9-7/8". **$871**

Courtesy of Jeffrey S. Evans & Assoc., www.jeffreysevans.com

Decanter, deep rose to pink with plush finish, original stopper, applied circular foot, polish pontil mark, Gunderson Glass Works, 11-1/2" t. 3-3/4" d. **$37**

Courtesy of Jeffrey S. Evans & Assoc., www.jeffreysevans.com

Pair decorated Peach Blow vases with enamel, 19th century, decorated with fronds and flowers, black enamel numbering on each base, 4-3/4" t. x 3" d. **$106**

Courtesy of Dirk Soulis Auctions, www.dirksoulisauctions.com

Sugar and creamer bowl, minor wear to both, excellent condition, 2-3/4'" t. **$187**

Courtesy of Morphy Auctions, www.morphyauctions.com

Six-piece group of Victorian Peach Blow art glass, comprising a miniature lamp with associated cased glass shade, a barber's bottle, a shoe-form bud vase, sating vase with pinched rim, a glossy Burmese vase and an enameled toothpick with quilted diamond embossed pattern, largest example is 9-1/4" t. **$2,176**

Courtesy of Jackson's, wwww.jacksonauctions.com

Jack-in-the-pulpit vase, opaque white with unusually light pink to the plume, applied circular foot, Gunderson Glass Works, mid-20th century, 9-1/4" t. x 4" d. (Plume) 3-1/8" d. foot. **$100**

Courtesy of Jeffrey S. Evans & Assoc., www.jeffreysevans.com

Bottle vase, 19th century, with gold enamels and high relief decoration of hanging prunus embellished by a bird in flight, exceptional detail within the enamel, base is polished, 9" t. x 3-3/4" d. **$189**

Courtesy of Dirk Soulis Auctions, www.dirksoulisauctions.com

GLASS

phoenix

THE PHOENIX GLASS CO. of Beaver, Pennsylvania, was established in 1880. Known primarily for commercial glassware, the firm also produced a molded, sculptured, cameo-type line from the 1930s until the 1950s.

Clear red glass with pressed floral motif, circa 1930s, 10-1/4" t. x 4-1/4" d. **$219**

Courtesy of John Moran Auctioneers,
www.johnmoran.com

Art Deco grasshopper vase, early 20th century, mold formed with purple painted decoration, 8-1/4" t. **$154**

Courtesy of Leland Little Auctions,
www.lelandlittle.com

Blackberry pattern vase, Martello line, raised molded glass honey-colored finish vase, with all-over blackberry vine and cricket motif, 18-1/4" t. x 9-1/4" d. **$281**

Courtesy of John Moran Auctioneers,
www.johnmoran.com

Four-piece water set, cranberry with opal spatter, comprising a water pitcher with a duckbill spout, and three tumblers, Phoenix Glass Co., 9" t. .... **$137.**

Courtesy of Jeffrey S. Evans & Assoc., www.jeffreysevans.com

Honeycomb-Optic pattern tumbler, bronze opalescent, factory-polished rim, excellent condition overall with a flake to the rim, as made, 3-5/8" t. **$173**

Courtesy of Jeffrey S. Evans & Assoc., www.jeffreysevans.com

Honeycomb-Optic pattern cheese dish, ruby cased over opal glass, applied amber finial, matching underplate, Phoenix Glass Co., 7" t. x 11" d. .. **$280**

Courtesy of Jeffrey S. Evans & Assoc., www.jeffreysevans.com

Spatter water pitcher, colorless with opal and apricot flakes, Spot-Optic pattern, shouldered form with crimped top, duckbill spout, applied colorless reeded handle, and polished pontil mark, fourth quarter 19th century, 8-1/4" t. **$112**

Courtesy of Jeffrey S. Evans & Assoc., www.jeffreysevans.com

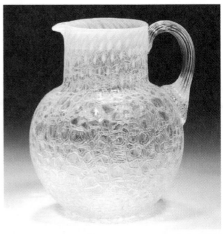

▶ Pitcher, Spot-Optic Craquelle pattern, colorless opalescent, with light opalescent at the rim, with a mostly plain body, applied reeded handle, polished pontil mark, 7-5/8" t. **$112**

Courtesy of Jeffrey S. Evans & Assoc., www.jeffreysevans.com

Blue and tan long vase, Love Birds pattern, 6" t. x 5" w. x 8-1/2" d. **$100**

Courtesy of Jeffrey S. Evans & Assoc., www.jeffreysevans.com

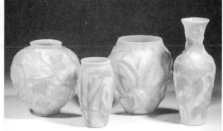

Lot of four vases, including a pine cone, fern and floral example, each opaque white with satin finish and staining in green, brown, blue or pink, and a custard Dragonfly example with state blue staining, first half 20th century, 6" t. to 9-1/4" t. **$187**

Courtesy of Jeffrey S. Evans & Assoc., www.jeffreysevans.com

Water pitcher, Diamond Quilt pattern, air-trap Mother of Pearl, cased shaded rose, duckbill spout, ruffled rim, applied frosted reeded handle, painted floral and foliate decoration, polished pontil mark, fourth quarter 19th century, some minor wear, 8-1/2" t.
.... **$187**

Courtesy of Jeffrey S. Evans & Assoc., www.jeffreysevans.com

Wild geese oval vase, opaque white with blue stain, factory-polished rim, Phoenix Glass Co. and Consolidated Lamp & Glass Co., second quarter 20th century, 9-1/4" t. x 3-1/4" w. x 6-3/4" d. **$50**

Courtesy of Jeffrey S. Evans & Assoc., www.jeffreysevans.com

Mother-of-Pearl satin water pitcher, Raindrop/ Windows air trap pattern, blue die-away to crystal, polychrome-enamel decoration, duckbill rim, applied frosted reeded handle, polished pontil mark, Phoenix Glass Co., fourth quarter 19th century, 7-1/2" t.
.... **$276**

Courtesy of Jeffrey S. Evans & Assoc., www.jeffreysevans.com

GLASS

pressed

PRESSED GLASS IS one of the largest collecting categories in all of antiques, and the number of pieces sold at auction each year easily surpasses more than 3,500 examples in today's market.

Pressed glass was originally produced to imitate expensive cut glass owned mainly by the wealthy. It is made by pressing molten glass either mechanically or manually into textured molds. Unless removed by hand, each piece will retain mold lines, even on pieces with extensive detailing.

In recent years, three lots stunned the collecting community and refocused attention on a category many had not thought about in years. Each gives in inside look at how the hobby is changing as longtime collections are finally offered after years in private hands.

A bidding war broke out over a 2-1/4" high x 3-1/8" wide pressed glass rectangular salt made by the Providence Flint Glass Works of Providence, Rhode Island. The diminutive blue salt is signed "Providence" on the base and its auctioneers, the Hess Auction Group, dated the piece sometime between 1831 and 1833. A conservative absentee bid of $200 opened the lot and then things got interesting. Floor bidders used $100 increments to push the salt to $2,500 before Internet bidders advanced the pace to $3,750. But it was a paddle on the floor that claimed it at $4,720, fully 10 times its low estimate of $400.

The lovely salt was from the private collection of renowned glass and china specialist Corinne Machmer, a familiar face at many Pennsylvania shows and shops. Machmer's lifelong collection also turned out a unique dark purple salt in the form of a boat, which sold to a phone bidder for $7,316. One of a group offered in the auction, the 1-1/2" high x 3-3/4" wide boat salt is signed on the stern "Pittsburgh" and was produced by the Sturbridge Flint Glass Works of Pittsburgh, Pennsylvania, between 1828 and 1835.

Pressed Roman Rosette nappie on foot, colorless, shallow pressed nappie with a petal rim, raised on a free-blown baluster-form stem and broad circular foot with rough pontil mark, attributed to the Fort Pitt Glass Works, Pittsburgh, Pa., circa 1830-1840, 3-7/8" t. x 6-1/8" d. **$137**

Courtesy of Jeffrey S. Evans & Associates, www.jeffreysevans.com

Centerpiece bowl, Vaseline, circa 1920, McKee Glass Co., 5-3/4" t. x 11-3/4" d. **$62**

Courtesy of Jeffrey S. Evans & Associates, www.jeffreysevans.com

A few months later, Skinner, Inc. auctioned a rare pair of marbleized blue pressed glass tulip vases from the Boston & Sandwich Glass Co. of Sandwich, Massachusetts, for $23,370. The 9-7/8" tall pair was estimated to bring between $2,000 and $3,000, but the sale marked the first time the circa 1845-1865 vases were offered at auction in nearly 50 years. The set was last purchased at an auction held by noted early American glass auctioneer Richard A. Bourne in November 1967.

"The American glass market overall began to stabilize in 2015 and we are seeing that trend continue in 2016," said Jeffrey S. Evans, the nation's leading specialist early American pressed glass auctioneer. "Certain categories like 19th century free-blown wares and bottles/flasks continue to draw strong demand and are performing well."

Evans's firm made headlines after a pair of brilliant peacock green pressed loop/leaf vases sold for $11,400. The pair was fashioned in a seven-loop bowl and raised on a seven-loop circular foot, likely by the Boston & Sandwich Glass Co. between 1845 and 1860. It is only one of two pairs Evans has ever offered, the other being from the 50-year collection of the late Lois Hirschmann of Marion, Massachusetts (sold to benefit the Sandwich Glass Museum's Endowment Fund).

However, examples of early American pressed glass commanding four and five figures at

Apothecary jar, Mascotte pattern, colorless, tall cylindrical form with band of pattern at top of jar, ground stopper with band of thumbprints at top, which is repeated on the stem, first quarter 20th century, 15" t. x 2-3/4" d. **$124**

Courtesy of Jeffrey S. Evans & Associates, www.jeffreysevans.com

auction are only 2% of the overall market (according to historical sale data available on LiveAuctioneers, BidSquare, and Invaluable). Extremely rare examples continue to take top lot honors when they appear, but auctioneers like Evans are busy these days, overseeing the sale of thousands of pieces of glass each year. Collectors such as Machmer and Hirschmann are revealing their treasures after decades of enjoyment at a time when most examples of pressed glass sell for less than $100 and exemplary pieces can be had for between $100 and $5,000.

"Pressed glass and Victorian glass has seen increased interest," Evans said, "but demand is still having a hard time keeping up with the large volume of material coming onto the market."

Rather than lament over the generally lower prices for mid-range examples in less than mint condition, we see the pressed glass hobby as an ideal time to begin collecting and learning about America's diverse history of glass making. On every front, the hobby is welcoming new students: Once expensive reference books are now affordable; online auction hosting sites make it easy to buy functional and historical American glassware made during the late 1700s and 1800s for less than $75; and newcomers to the hobby can still learn a great deal from a generation that researched glassmaking and founded glass museums more than any other.

"There are numerous active glass pages on Facebook," Evans said, "including several established glass clubs that are contributing to market growth and drawing new collectors. This bodes well for the future of the glass market."

Octagon oblong open salt, deep amethyst, rim serrated on top and edge, rare proof, possibly Boston & Sandwich Glass Co., 1-1/4" t. x 2-1/4" w. x 3-1/8" d. $311

Courtesy of Jeffrey S. Evans & Associates, www.jeffreysevans.com

Lot of five assorted candlesticks, canary yellow, three hexagon shaped and one Loop and Leaf pattern, Boston & Sandwich Glass Co., circa 1840-1860, minor to moderate imperfections, 6-3/4" t. x 7-1/8" d. $62

Courtesy of Jeffrey S. Evans & Associates, www.jeffreysevans.com

Etling "Etaleune" glass vase, Edmond-Laurent, gray glass globular shape vase with stylized floral and leaf decoration marks, "Etaleune" "Paris, France", overall good original condition with minor pitting to the body, 10-1/8" t. x 8" d. $122

Courtesy of Simpson Galleries, www.simpsongalleries.com

Flint glass ale glass, colorless and frosted lead glass, with two frosted reserves, one featuring a maiden while the other shows a cat, S. Reich & Co., fourth 19th century, 6" t. $236

Courtesy of Jeffrey S. Evans & Associates, www.jeffreysevans.com

Novelty stove covered dish, Vaseline, King, Son & Co., circa 1889, very good condition overall with scattered chipping to the rim, a chip to one foot and a chip to the finial, 5" t. x 4-1/4" w. x 5-3/4" d. $112

Courtesy of Jeffrey S. Evans & Associates, www.jeffreysevans.com

Open salt, Cornucopia and Scroll pattern, violet blue, serrated large-scallop rim, minor inner-rim flake and a hint of mold roughness to top rim, scattered minor flakes to table ring, 1-3/8" t. x 2-3/8" w. x 3-3/8" d. $405

Courtesy of Jeffrey S. Evans & Associates, www.jeffreysevans.com

Blue salt, Providence Flint Glass Works, Providence, Rhode Island, circa 1831-1833, signed "Providence" on base, unique, 2-1/4" h. x 3-1/8" w. **$4,720**

Courtesy of Hess Auction Group, www.hessauctiongroup.com

Amethyst vertical rib blown glass cruet, applied loop handle with foliate terminal and original stopper, 7-1/4" h. **$8,260**

Courtesy of Hess Auction Group, www.hessauctiongroup.com

Open salt, Beaded Scroll and Basket of Flowers pattern, opal opaque, raised on four scrolled feet, rayed star base, thick heavy pressing, Boston & Sandwich Glass Co., 1-7/8" t. x 2" w. x 3-1/8" d. **$137**

Courtesy of Jeffrey S. Evans & Associates, www.jeffreysevans.com

Round open sale, colorless, plain rope rim, scarce, Boston & Sandwich Co., light flake to rope rim, 1-1/4" t. x 3-1/8" d. **$467**

Courtesy of Jeffrey S. Evans & Associates, www.jeffreysevans.com

Pair of etched glass whale oil lamps, Grape pattern on blow glass front, pressed glass bases and double wick burners, 10" t. **$201**

Courtesy of Dirk Soulis Auctions, www.dirksoulisauctions.com

Carnival glass bowl, ribbon-edge iridescent leaf and grape design, 7-1/2" dia. **$50**

Courtesy of Specialists of the South, Inc., www.specialistsofthesouth.com

Two casters, colorless, fourth quarter 19th/early 20th century, molded swirl and Zipper panel examples, each fitted in signed and numbered quadruple-plate stand, makers unverified, 6-3/4" and 10"..............................$70

Courtesy of Jeffrey S. Evans & Associates, Inc., www.jeffreysevans.com

Tumbler, colorless non-lead glass, mid-19th century, eight-panel form embossed with "LOUIS N. BONAPARTE PRESIDENT" arched above profile bust, reverse with "R. F. / 1848" within cartouche with flags and battle axes, polished table ring, 3-1/2" h., 2-3/4" dia. rim.....................$40

Courtesy of Jeffrey S. Evans & Associates, Inc., www.jeffreysevans.com

Esther pattern amber-stained seven-piece water set, Riverside Glass Works, 1896, colorless with polychrome-enamel decoration, pitcher with applied colorless handle with pressed feather design to upper terminal, six tumblers with factory polished bases, 3-3/4" to 10-1/8" h. $150

Courtesy of Jeffrey S. Evans & Associates, Inc., www.jeffreysevans.com

Ale set, five-piece colorless hobnail with cranberry and yellow staining, fourth quarter 19th century, pitcher with applied handle and applied prunt to lower terminal, four ale glasses with factory polished bases, probably European, 7" to 10-3/4" h. $120

Courtesy of Jeffrey S. Evans & Associates, Inc., www.jeffreysevans.com

◄ Monkey-decorated amber-stained colorless water pitcher, possibly Valley Glass Co., Beaver Falls, Pennsylvania, circa 1890, rayed base, rare as only recorded stained water pitcher, 8-1/2" h.
.... $950

Courtesy of Jeffrey S. Evans & Associates, Inc., www.jeffreysevans.com

Bowl and platter commemorating Queen Victoria's Diamond Jubilee, 1897, bowl 9-1/2" dia., 1-1/2" h., oval platter 9" l. x 7-3/4" w. **$15**

Courtesy of Heritage Auctions, ha.com

Pitcher, spatter, colorless with cranberry and opal flakes, Northwood Glass Co., fourth quarter 19th century, circular-form crimped rim, applied colorless handle with pressed-fan design to upper terminal, 8-1/2". **$50**

Courtesy of Jeffrey S. Evans & Associates, Inc., www.jeffreysevans.com

Opalescent figural boat inkstand with pewter hinged lid, New England Glass Co., circa 1870-1890, lightly embossed "PAT'D AUG. 9. 1870", 2-3/8" h. x 5-1/2" l. **$150**

Courtesy of Jeffrey S. Evans & Associates, Inc., www.jeffreysevans.com

Compote, vaseline art glass, optic-patterned bowl with factory polished rim, possibly Czech, first half 20th century, Vaseline (black lighted) circular twisted stem with applied ruby crimped decoration, figural vaseline and ruby decorative flower, ruby foot with pressed fan design, 8" h., 6-1/2" dia. bowl rim. **$475**

Courtesy of Jeffrey S. Evans & Associates, Inc., www.jeffreysevans.com

Last Supper tray, amber, Indiana Glass Co., 11" l. x 7" w................**$5**

Courtesy of Main Street Mining Co. Auctions, www.mainstreetmining.com

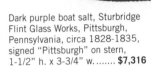

Dark purple boat salt, Sturbridge Flint Glass Works, Pittsburgh, Pennsylvania, circa 1828-1835, signed "Pittsburgh" on stern, 1-1/2" h. x 3-3/4" w. **$7,316**

Courtesy of Hess Auction Group, www.hessauctiongroup.com

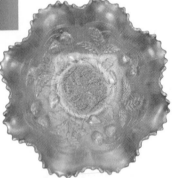

Carnival glass ruffled bowl, Stippled Strawberry pattern, ice blue, with basket weave back, possibly unique, 9" w......**$18,000**

Courtesy of Seeck Auctions, www.seeckauction.com

Vases, circa 1845-1860, Boston & Sandwich Glass Co., deep peacock green, each deep seven-loop bowl with conforming rim, raised on seven-loop circular foot, wafer construction, 9-1/2" h., 4-7/8" dia. rim, 3-3/4" dia. foot. **$9,500**

Courtesy of Jeffrey S. Evans & Associates, Inc., www.jeffreysevans.com

Candlesticks, Dolphin Double-Step pattern, rare set of four, likely Boston & Sandwich Glass Co., circa 1845-1870, electric/copper blue, each six-petal socket with lower extension, medium dolphin-form standard and square base, wafer construction, 9-7/8" h., 3-5/8" sq. base. **$4,000**

Courtesy of Jeffrey S. Evans & Associates, Inc., www.jeffreysevans.com

Dish and tray, circa 1845-1855, Boston & Sandwich Glass Co., horn of plenty/comet (OMN) rectangular covered honey dish or casket with undertray, colorless lead glass, domed cover with pattern on interior and octagonal finial, dish with even-scallop rim, smooth base edge, and inverted diamond-point pattern in base, tray with same even-scallop rim and base pattern, Horn of Plenty pattern modified to fit on shoulder, rare and important, dish 5-1/2" h. x 4" x 6-1/2", tray 4-5/8" x 7". **$4,750**

Courtesy of Courtesy of Jeffrey S. Evans & Associates, Inc., www.jeffreysevans.com

Sugar bowl, cobalt blue octagonal form, probably made by New England Glass Co. or possibly by Curling, Robertson & Sons of Pittsburgh, California, circa 1850-1870, two different alternating scroll and acanthus leaf designs in panels, circular foot with pattern underneath, lacking cover, 3-7/8" h., 4-7/8" dia. rim, 3" dia. foot. **$50**

Courtesy of Jeffrey S. Evans & Associates, Inc., www.jeffreysevans.com

Novelty smoke set, Vaseline (uranium), fourth quarter 19th century, single piece, match holder with threaded design, cigarette holder with alternating textured panels, 3-7/8" h. **$70**

Courtesy of Jeffrey S. Evans & Associates, Inc., www.jeffreysevans.com

Vase, medium honey amber, Boston & Sandwich Glass Co., circa 1840-1860, small-size version, hexagonal bowl with flared six-scallop rim, no reinforcement ridge to scallops, five lines through each upper loop, hexagonal foot with factory polished lower mold lines and table ring, single-piece construction, 4-3/4" h., 3-1/4" dia. rim, 2-5/8" dia. foot. **$850**

Courtesy of Jeffrey S. Evans & Associates, Inc., www.jeffreysevans.com

Rare and important basket, deep fiery opalescent, Boston & Sandwich Glass Co., circa 1840-1855, bowl with 32-point rim above 16 vertical staves, 34-point star under slumped conical base, hexagonal knop and flared base, wafer construction, 8" h., 8-1/4" dia. rim, 5-1/4" dia. foot. **$7,000**

Courtesy of Jeffrey S. Evans & Associates, Inc., www.jeffreysevans.com

Waisted loop cologne bottle, probably Boston & Sandwich Glass Co., circa 1840-1870, medium green with original gilt decoration, medium-size hexagonal bottle with panel-cut neck, factory polished lip and pontil mark, original flower-form stopper with gilt decoration, each unit numbered 28, 5-5/8" h. overall, bottle 3-5/8" h., 3-1/8" dia. base.
.... **$250**

Courtesy of Jeffrey S. Evans & Associates, Inc., www.jeffreysevans.com

GLASS

GLASS

quezal

IN 1901, MARTIN BACH and Thomas Johnson, who had worked for Louis Tiffany, opened a competing glassworks in Brooklyn, New York, called the Quezal Art Glass and Decorating Co. Named for the quetzal, a bird with brilliantly colored features, Quezal produced wares closely resembling those of Tiffany until the plant closed in 1925. In general, Quezal pieces are more defined than Tiffany glass, and the decorations are brighter and more visible.

Opal shade decorated with bi-color leaves, body tightly caressed in golden threads, nice marigold interior, engraved "Quezal", crimped ruffling at the bottom edge, 2-1/2" t. fitter. **$121**

Courtesy of Humler & Nolan, www.humlernolan.com

Ruffled shade with complicated double design of "Zipper & Drizzle" in gold reflecting magenta highlights over opal, gold interior, engraved "Quezal", excellent condition, bright gold interior, 5-1/2" t. x 5-1/2" d. **$363**

Courtesy of Humler & Nolan, www.humlernolan.com

Bullet form hall shade, Roberts #1 featuring green feathers with bright golden tips over opal, gold interior, signed "Quezal", tiny open bubbles, 8-1/4" t. x 5" d. **$514**

Courtesy of Humler & Nolan, www.humlernolan.com

Favrile bud vase with swirl relief, bearing original Quezel label, 4" t. **$156**

Courtesy of Roland New York, www.rolandauctions.com

Pair of shades, one base marked Bach's in the casting, each signed "Quezal", circa 1920, very good original condition, 6-1/4" t. x 4" d. **$472**

Courtesy of Dirk Soulis Auctions, www.dirksoulisauctions.com

VISIT WWW.ANTIQUETRADER.COM

WWW.FACEBOOK.COM/ANTIQUETRADER

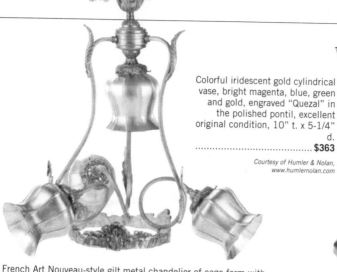

Colorful iridescent gold cylindrical vase, bright magenta, blue, green and gold, engraved "Quezal" in the polished pontil, excellent original condition, 10" t. x 5-1/4" d.
.... **$363**

Courtesy of Humler & Nolan,
www.humlernolan.com

French Art Nouveau-style gilt metal chandelier of cage form with central floriform pieced candle cup at top, the three scrolling leafy rods terminating in a floriform pierced candle cup, gold aurene bell shaped, ribbed glass shades, early 20th century, base circulet decorated with leafy foliage, 19" t.. x 13" d.............................. **$620**

Courtesy of Ahlers & Ogletree Auction Gallery, www.aandoauctions.com

Lot of six gold Quezal art glass shades, bulbous body form with slightly flaring lip and bright gold iridescence showing flashes of green and pink, one pair of the shades present a rich gold iridescence with red highlights, while a single shade with a vertically ribbed body features gold iridescence with red and green highlights, each is signed in the fitter "Quezal", 5-1/4" t. to 6" t. **$652**

Courtesy of James D. Julia, Inc. , Fairfield, Main, www.jamesdjulia.com

Floriform pulled feather art glass vase gold iridescent interior with green pulled feather motif, signed on bottom with form number, excellent condition, 5-1/2" t. x 5-1/2" d.
.... **$387**

Courtesy of MBA Seattle Auction,
www.mbaauction.com

▶ Pulled decoration vase, opal ground with deep green and iridescent decoration, urn form, golden iridescent interior, polish pontil mark, signed "Quezal", first quarter 20th century, 6" t.
....**$1,183**

Courtesy of Jeffrey S. Evans & Associates, www.jeffreysevans.com

Vase, bright gold iridescent hooked feather design extending upward from the foot against a white background, with a gold iridescent neck leading to a green pulled feather design descending to just above the hooked feathers at foot, finished with a bright gold iridescent Zig-Zag pattern over the top of the green pulled feathers, interior of the mouth is also finished with a bright gold iridescence, signed on the pontil "Quezal 487" with the artist initial "P", 4-1/2" t. **$1,303**

Courtesy of James D. Julia, Inc., Fairfield, Main, www.jamesdjulia.com

Shoulder form vase, opal glass decorated with a gold feather chain pattern, signed "Quezal", good condition, 6" t. ...**$847**

Courtesy of Jaremos, www.jaremos.com

Vase, white background with green and gold pulled feather design, iridescent gold interior, signed "Quezal", 10-3/4" t. **$1,020**

Courtesy of Woody Auction, www.woodyauction.com

Vase with Blue Heart and Vine pattern, against a gold lustre background with a gold lustre interior, circa 1925, excellent condition, 7-1/4" t. **$762**

Courtesy of Dan Morphy Auctions, www.danmorphyauctions.com

Vase from the Innovation Line, base glass executed in variegated laminated layers imitating Agate, circa 1905, fine iridescent finish on the exterior and a highly iridescent interior with highlights of green and gold, 5" t..................... **$603**

Courtesy of Dan Morphy Auctions, www.danmorphyauctions.com

Scarce vase in Form #1700, executed in an Orange and Blue Coil pattern, against a creamy white opal background with an orange gold lustre interior, circa 1925, old Quezal form, 6-3/4" t. **$1,206**

Courtesy of Dan Morphy Auctions, www.danmorphyauctions.com

Open salt, gold iridescent, low form molded with 16 ribs, signed "Quezal" within the polished pontil mark, first quarter 20th century, 1" t. x 2-3/4" d **$236**

Courtesy of Jeffrey S. Evans & Associates, www.jeffreysevans.com

GLASS

steuben

FREDERICK CARDER, AN Englishman, and Thomas G. Hawkes of Corning, New York, established Steuben Glass Works in 1903 in Steuben County, New York. In 1918, the Corning Glass Co. purchased the Steuben company. Carder remained with the firm and designed many of the pieces bearing the Steuben mark. Probably the most widely recognized wares are Aurene, Verre De Soie and Rosaline, but many other types were produced. The firm operated until 2011.

Seven various iridescent art glass shades: four bear remnants of silver fleur-de-lis marks and Steuben marking, two are unmarked, two bell-shaped shades are similar but vary in color and brightness, three bulbous shades are similar in shape, but also vary in color and brightness, three bulbous shades have chips to the fitter, a bell-shaped shade has a single chip to the fitter, and the squat round shade also has a chip to the fitter, shades range in size from 4-1/4" h to 5-1/4" h. **$592**

Courtesy of James D. Julia, Inc., Fairfield, Maine, www.jamesdjulia.com

Crystal sculpture, "Castle of Dreams", features frosted castle and rock walls sculpted against a clear diamond-shaped base, designed by D. Dowler, signed "Steuben" on the underside, good condition, 6" h x 9-3/4" w. **$1,066**

Courtesy of James D. Julia, Inc., Fairfield, Maine, www.jamesdjulia.com

Art glass with flared rim
and swirled body on plain
round base, signed "Steuben
Aurene," 9-3/4" h. **$750**

*Courtesy of Nadeau's Auction Gallery,
www.nadeauauctions.com*

Gold Aurene iridescent
lampshade, flared form with
ribbed design, 5-1/8" h. **$125**

*Courtesy of Auction Gallery of Boca Raton,
www.agobr.com*

Vase, Aurene blue and gold
iridescent, possesses a ground
and polished pontil, early
20th century, signed "Steuben
Aurene 6998" along the edge
of the foot, 8-7/8" h. **$344**

*Courtesy of Bruneau & Co. Auctioneers,
www.bruneauandco.com*

Threaded plate, probably early Steuben, good condition, 10" d. .. **$219**

Courtesy of Auction Gallery of Boca Raton, www.agobr.com

White Cluthra vase, opaque
with bubble interior, a baluster
form with a high neck, rolled
rim and applied handles on the
sides, excellent condition, 10-
1/2" h x 7-1/2" w x 7" d.. **$1,168**

*Courtesy of Fontaine's Auction Gallery,
www.fontainesauction.com*

Six Gold Aurene shades, early 20th century,
5-1/2" d., fitter rim 2-1/4" d. **$676**

Courtesy of Cottone Auctions, www.cottoneauctions.com

Aurene vase, iridescent shades of blue and pink,
marked "Aurene" and numbered "221,"
4-1/2" h. **$500**

Courtesy of Concept Art Gallery, ww.conceptgallery.com

Blue Aurene perfume bottle, strong blue rich
iridescent, signed Steuben and numbered,
excellent condition with dauber shape, 7" h. ... **$324**

Courtesy of Richard D. Hatch & Associates, www.richardhatchauctions.com

Jadite pitcher, alabaster handle, excellent condition,
9-1/2" h. **$531**

Courtesy of Richard D. Hatch & Associates, www.richardhatchauctions.com

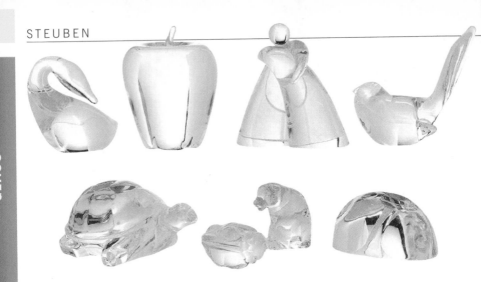

Clear crystal table figures, 20th century, preening gander, apple, embracing figures, songbird, turtle, seated bear, frog and ladybug form, range in height 2-1/4" h to 5-1/2" h. **$512**

Courtesy of Brunk Auctions, www.brunk auctions.com

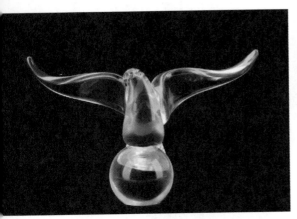

Streamlined crystal sculpture depicting an eagle resting on a round orb, signed by James Houston, catalog number 8130, underside incised "Steuben," minor scattered surface scratches, largely contained to underside of base and commensurate with shelf contact, 7" h overall x 11-1/4" w x 3-3/4" d. **$434**

Courtesy of Ahlers & Ogletree Auction Gallery, www.aandoauctions.com

Cabinet vase decorated with brick red iridescent hooked feather design, descending from lip against a creamy white background, finished on interior rich purple iridescence with blue highlights, exterior iridescent decoration has flashes of gold, green and pink, signed on underside "Aurene 651" with remnants of original Steuben Glass Works paper label, 2-1/2" h. .. **$1,185**

Courtesy of James D. Julia, Inc., Fairfield, Maine, www.jamesdjulia.com

Bowl with green jade acid cut back design of Oriental trees and flowers all against acid textured calcite background, very good to excellent condition, 8" d. **$711**

Courtesy of James D. Julia, Inc., Fairfield, Maine, www.jamesdjulia.com

GLASS

tiffany glass

TIFFANY & CO. was founded by Charles Lewis Tiffany (1812-1902) and Teddy Young in New York City in 1837. Originally called Tiffany, Young and Ellis, the name was shortened to Tiffany & Co. in 1853 when Charles Tiffany took control and shifted the firm's focus to jewelry.

By the 1860s, Tiffany & Co. had established itself as America's most prestigious and reputable firm, first by importing the best of European goods and then by manufacturing its own wares of the highest quality. From 1867 until the end of the century, Tiffany exhibited and won medals at international expositions in Paris and the United States.

Charles' son, Louis Comfort Tiffany (1848-1933), was an American artist and designer who worked in the decorative arts and is best known for his work in stained glass. This outstanding American glass designer established Tiffany Glass Co. in 1885, and in 1902, it became known as Tiffany Studios, producing glass until the early 1930s.

Tiffany revived early techniques and devised many new ones. His work in large part defined both the Art Nouveau and Aesthetic movements. In the world of antiques and collectibles, his name is ubiquitous – even those who do not collect Tiffany Studios items know who he is and what his work looks like.

Because Tiffany Studios' glass is so widely loved and collected, there is a significant market in fakes, especially at the higher end of the spectrum, most specifically in lamps. This makes verification the most important thing to look for when it comes to Tiffany Studios.

For more Tiffany lamps, please see the "Lamps & Lighting" section.

Gold Favrile bowl with ribbed sides and a gold iridescent finish with strong pink and blue highlights, signed "L.C.T. Favrile" on the underside, 9-3/4" h. **$592**

Courtesy of James D. Julia, Inc., Fairfield, Maine, www.jamesdjulia.com

Gold Favrile vase with subtle vertical feather design surrounding the body, finished in bright gold iridescence with strong green, purple and pink highlights, rests on a round inverted saucer foot, signed "L.C. Tiffany-Inc. Favrile 1559" on the underside, accompanied by the original Tiffany Favrile paper label, very good to excellent condition, 8-1/4" h. **$1,066**

Courtesy of James D. Julia, Inc., Fairfield, Maine, www.jamesdjulia.com

Gold Favrile cup, green iridescent pulled design encircles the body, with creamy white zig-zag pattern extending over top of the other decoration, set against a gold iridescent background, finished with gold iridescent reeded handle, interior shows strong pink and blue highlights, signed on underside "L.C. Tiffany-Favrile V69," very good to excellent with some minor wear to iridescence on handle, 2" h. **$414**

Courtesy of James D. Julia, Inc., Fairfield, Maine, www.jamesdjulia.com

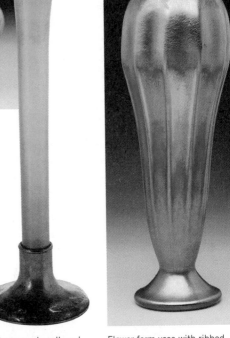

Gold cylindrical vase, flaring slightly at top to a hexagonal scalloped rim, set into a removal foot enameled in shades of blue, green and peach, New York, 1920s, vase is engraved "L.C.T. Favrile" on bottom and base is marked "LOUIS C. TIFFANY FURNANCES INC." along with a round maker's symbol and "LCT 152 M," 16-1/4" h. **$704**

Courtesy of Brunk Auctions, www.brunkauctions.com

Flower-form vase with ribbed body and bright iridescence finish with shading from platinum at foot to purple at middle and gold at top, vase is signed "L.C. Tiffany-Favrile Exhibition Piece 1571L" on underside, good to excellent, 11-1/2" h. **$1,777**

Courtesy of James D. Julia, Inc., Fairfield, Maine, www.jamesdjulia.com

Gold iridescent bowl, signed "L.C. Tiffany-Favrile #1883" on underside, 2-1/4" h x 8" d. **$330**

Courtesy of Woody Auction, www.woodyauction.com

Iridescent gold bowl with open pontil base, signed "1575 L.C. Tiffany Favrile" on underside, good condition, 5" h x 9-1/4" d. **$1,736**

Courtesy of Kodner Galleries, Inc., www.kodner.com

Favrile iridescent vase, blue on base fading to green across the body and finishing to a rose color at the top, "L.C.T. Favrile c-1641" etched on underside, 6-3/4" h. **$605**

*Courtesy of Sarasota Estate Auction,
www.sarasotaestateauction.com*

Favrile bud vase set in acid-washed partial silvered bronze base, New York, early 20th century, glass marked "LCT," base marked "Tiffany Studios New York 711," vase in overall good condition, 13-1/2" h x 3-1/2" d. **$975**

*Courtesy of Rago Arts and Auction Center,
www.ragoarts.com*

Gold iridescent bud vase mounted in a blue and gold enamel base, marked Tiffany Furnaces #150, 13" h. **$780**

*Courtesy of Woody Auction,
www.woodyauction.com*

Four Favrile wine glasses with slightly flared rims, New York, early 20th century, two glasses have LCT paper labels, light wear to undersides otherwise in good condition, signed, 6" h x 3" d. **$780**

Courtesy of Rago Arts and Auction Gallery, www.ragoarts.com

Slag glass and bronze letter holder and square inkwell brush, with beading and ball feet on the divided holder, Tiffany Studios, good condition on both, 5-1/4" h (letter holder) 2-3/4" h (inkwell brush). **$406**

Courtesy of Auction Gallery of the Palm Beaches, www.agopb.com

Favrile glass bowl with twisted rib and scalloped rim, silvery blue iridized finish and gold highlights, early 20th century, base is inscribed "1284-L.C.T.," 8-1/4" d. **$448**

Courtesy of Jackson's Auction, www.jacksonsauction.com

Grouping of a pastel green and white opalescent plate and pedestal sherbet cup, marked "LCT-Favrile", 8-3/4" d (plate), 2-1/4" h x 5" h (cup). **$300**

Courtesy of Woody Auction, www.woodyauction.com

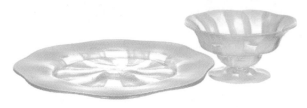

Favrile plate in blue pastel with white lightly opalescent flaring bands radiating from center of the plate against clear glass background leading to light pastel blue rim, very good to excellent condition, 8-7/8" d. **$474**

Courtesy of James D. Julia, Inc., Fairfield, Maine, www.jamesdjulia.com

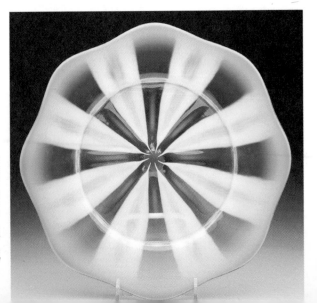

GLASS

wave crest

NOW MUCH SOUGHT after, Wave Crest was produced by the C.F. Monroe Co., Meriden, Connecticut, in the late 19th and early 20th centuries. It was made from opaque white glass blown into molds, then hand-decorated in enamels, and metal trim was often added. Boudoir accessories such as jewel boxes, hair receivers, etc., predominated.

Opal jewel tray in Helmschmied Swirl bank pattern, blue with hand-colored pink flowers, no lining, signed with a pink ink stamp under the base, very good condition overall, 2-1/4" h x 6-1/2" d. **$35**

Courtesy of Dirk Soulis Auctions, www.dirksoulisauctions.com

Two vases decorated with floral design, each with gold plated trimmings, each marked "Wave Crest" on underside, large footed vase with raised rococo design, 8-1/2" h x 4" d, small vase with ornate handled rim, 5-3/4" h x 3-3/4" d. **$162**

Courtesy of Alderfer Auction, www.alderferauction.com

Square blown out pale pink glass footed dresser or necklace box, with a lid featuring a hand-painted floral spray within scroll rococo-style borders, mounted with ornate ormolu banded lid that bears a fleur-de-lis clasp, marked on bottom in pink "Wave Crest The C.F.M. Co Trade Mark," 6" h x 5" w x 5" d. **$310**

Courtesy of Auction Gallery of Boca Raton, www.agobr.com

Wall plaque, hand painted with cast metal frame, late 19th century/early 20th century, C.F. Monroe Wave Crest, glass is in very good condition, small losses to the frame, total weight is just under two pounds, 11-1/4" d. **$1,599**

Courtesy of Nest Egg Auctions, www.nesteggauctions.com

VISIT WWW.ANTIQUETRADER.COM

WWW.FACEBOOK.COM/ANTIQUETRADER

Hand-decorated, multi-colored cigar humidor with daisy motif, slight green blush tone on opal ware, blown-out shell pattern lid, 7-1/2" h x 6" d. **$184**

Courtesy of Auction Gallery of Boca Raton, www.agobr.com

Vanity box in Egg Crate form, satin lined interior, enameled sides of jeweled flower heads and vinery on a red ground, raised on brass masked legs, marked with the red Wave Crest decal, 5" h x 7" w x 3-1/2" d. **$442**

Courtesy of Dirk Soulis Auctions, www.dirksoulisauctions.com

Puffy or Egg-Crate glass hand-painted ferner/ planter, C.F. Monroe Wave Crest, very good condition with tarnished brass insert, 3-1/2" h x 9" w, 2-1/2 pounds. **$123**

Courtesy of Nest Egg Auctions, www.nesteggauctions.com

Glass box with floral décor and gilt patterns, late 19th to early 20th century, very good condition, total weight is 10-1/2 ounces, 3" h x 4-1/4" d. ... **$61**

Courtesy of Nest Egg Auctions, www.nesteggauctions.com

Medium opal box in the blown out Shell pattern with hand-decorated pink flowers, hinged gold mount, no lining, signed under the base, 2-3/4" h x 4" d. .. **$47**

Courtesy of Dirk Soulis Auctions, www.dirksoulisauctions.com

Group of five hand-painted boxes, early 20th century; four circular examples, two with swirl decoration, one with blown-out decoration, each with hand-painted foliate decoration, having gilt metal mounts, one having a silk lined interior, two with "Wave Crest Trade Mark" red mark on base, one impressed "Wave Crest," one apparently unmarked, large-footed egg crate box, with bright gilt metal mounts and raised on scroll cast feet – with a silk lined interior and the "Wave Crest Trade Mark" red mark to base, accompanied by the book, "Wave Crest the Glass of C.F. Monroe" by Wilfred R. Cohen, largest item 6-1/2" h x 6-1/2" w x 6-1/2" d. **$1,480**

Courtesy of Morton Auctioneers, www.mortonhouston.com

An opal footed vase with beaded rim with hand-decorated pink flowers, signed with a pink ink stamp under the base, very good, 9-1/2" h. **$53**

Courtesy of Dirk Soulis Auctions, www.dirksoulisauctions.com

Hinged dresser box, marked "Collar and Cuffs," circa 1903 by C.F. Monroe Co., hand-painted opal glass decorated with shades of green and white snowball hydrangeas, with brass trim and brass wreath clasp, includes rose-colored lining, marked '2304' on bottom, measures 6" h x 8" d. **$383**

Courtesy of Dirk Soulis Auctions, www.dirksoulisauctions.com

Decorated opal ware, egg carton glass Wave Crest "Collars and Cuffs" box, marked in red "Wave Crest" on underside, 6" h x 7"w x 7"d. **$159**

Courtesy of Alderfer Auction, www.alderferauction.com

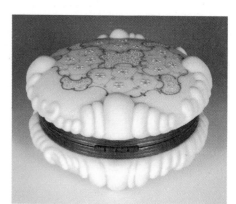

Large opal box in the blown out Baroque Shell blank, nicely decorated, hinged gold mount, no lining, signed under the base, small area of oxidation on the metal mount, no lining, very good overall, 4" h x 7-1/2" d. **$94**

Courtesy of Dirk Soulis Auctions, www.dirksoulisauctions.com

HARRY POTTER COLLECTIBLES

AFTER MAKING HIS DEBUT in the June 1997 book, *Harry Potter and the Philosopher's Stone*, by J.K. Rowling, Harry Potter has become the favorite wizard of millions of Muggles around the world.

Twenty years on, Harry Potter has also become one of the most successful franchises in the world and continues to expand with new films, books, plays, amusement parks, and more on the horizon. Whenever there's fan frenzy about a new book, movie or any other development, it boosts the franchise across the board and one of the areas that continues to rapidly grow is the collectibles market of items associated with the books and movies.

Some of these items often have no trouble auctioning for hundreds of thousands of dollars, such as Rowling's writing chair that sold for almost $400,000 - or even millions, like a handwritten copy of *The Tales of Beedle the Bard* that Amazon paid $4 million for. Many movie props like wands and quidditch brooms, and books, particularly first editions, also sell for five figures or more.

Values for early *Harry Potter* first edition books continue to climb. As if written in the stars, the first edition, first printing is the rarest and most valuable of all editions. Securing an original copy is extremely difficult and even former library copies fly through auction houses like a seeker during a quiddich match.

Just seven years ago, a first edition, first printing copy (signed and inscribed by Rowling) with solid provenance to her early years as a writer sold for $23,900. Now standard copies from the late 1990s routinely sell between $10,000 and $16,000 on up. Condition makes all the difference: A copy "virtually as new" sold for an astounding $43,750 at auction. The former owner knew the book had value and wrapped it inside a first edition, later printing dust jacket.

With the books a near instant hit with children and later adults, it was only natural for them to be adapted into motion pictures. Assorted collectibles produced in 2001 in conjunction with the first eight *Harry Potter* movies are deep and diverse and among the most valuable and rare items, including limited edition original movie posters, baseball caps, movie props, LEGO sets, lamps, holiday ornaments, first edition book sets, and even period bronze sculptures that are increasing in value on the secondary market.

Demand is so strong that items with even peripheral ties to the films and books are seeing an up-tick in interest and values. The market for "mystical-looking" flags made 70 years ago and other antique, vintage, and retro round eye glasses similar to those worn by Harry, yet produced decades before the original book series, are now sought after by adult cosplayers. These fans are seeking more collectibles and new ideas for more elaborate costumes and collections. Movie props continue to soar in value and successful replica companies have opened to meet demand for movie prop weapons and wands and even these items have begun increasing between collectors ... but there is no replacement for the real thing.

"The world of Harry Potter is one that reaches all ages," said John Lohmann, owner at Harry Potter prop seller Animation Ink Archives, which has been selling animation art and movie prop for 25 years. "They were not just books for kids, but for everyone. With the movies,

Rowling chair
The April 2016 purchase of the chair used by J.K.
Rowling while writing the first two *Harry Potter* books
for $394,000 by Jeff Bezos, founder and CEO of
Amazon, raised the ceiling on such collectibles and
refocused collector attention on the wide world of
unique items relating to the books and movies.

when they could actually see the world of Harry Potter,
everyone wants a piece of it - not a toy or a theme park replica,
but the real thing. Something when watching the movies, they
can point to and say, 'Hey, that's mine!'

"To some collectors, having a robe worn by Daniel Radcliffe in the films is almost like
having Darth Vader's black cape from the *Star Wars* films."

Despite this demand, there exists very little Harry Potter film props available to the public,
making the material that is available all the more valuable. The challenge with collecting
prop items is that Warner Brothers has only ever officially released a limited amount of them
from the productions.

"Hero wands, robes, and broom sticks are highly collectible and sought-after," Lohmann
said. He should know. His company once sold a single wand for $16,000.

Take the gray linen overcoat worn by Gary Oldman (Sirius Black) in *Harry Potter and the
Prisoner of Azkaban*. The famous coat was expected to sell for around $5,000, but ultimately
fetched a staggering $30,082 by the auction's end.

For the earlier films, some items were rented to the production or given away for
marketing purposes and they can be legally owned and sold. This is the case with Hagrid's
crossbow from *Harry Potter and the Sorcerer's Stone*. It was acquired from Bapty Armory in

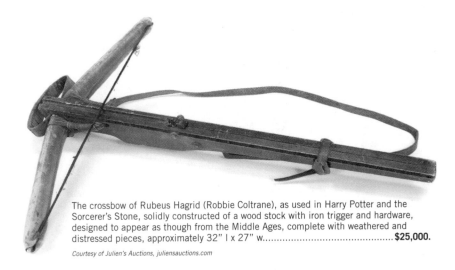

The crossbow of Rubeus Hagrid (Robbie Coltrane), as used in Harry Potter and the Sorcerer's Stone, solidly constructed of a wood stock with iron trigger and hardware, designed to appear as though from the Middle Ages, complete with weathered and distressed pieces, approximately 32" l x 27" w..**$25,000.**

Courtesy of Julien's Auctions, juliensauctions.com

England, which rented the piece to production for filming. It was sold in a Hollywood prop auction for $25,000.

The most obvious prop from the films might be Harry's own eyeglasses, a pair of which, from the collection of Simon Murray, spectacle maker, were sold at auction. The iconic glasses were first described by author J.K. Rowling and became an integral part of Harry's signature look and persona.

"Props from the first film are generally most desired," said Lohmann. "It's such a joy to see people's faces when we can offer them a piece of film and animation history."

Movie posters can be bought for much more obtainable prices because of their size. Framing and displaying a poster of gigantic proportions is expensive and requires custom frames. Without framing, the posters risk being damaged every time the owner unrolls them to enjoy the artwork. You could say that big posters are like Godric Gryffindor's Sword – double edged. Many can be bought for under $50 and upward to $150+. One of the rarest and most valuable posters is a lenticular one sheet prototype for *Harry Potter and the Prisoner of Azkaban* (Warner Brothers, 2004) that was never issued by Warner Brothers. It depicts Harry Potter's long suffering Uncle Sirius Black (Gary Oldman) and in a brilliant marketing ploy, Warner's created this poster to mimic the "Wanted" posters used in the movie itself. They are valued between $3,800 and $4,000.

For more information on Harry Potter collectibles, see *Harry Potter: The Unofficial Guide to the Collectibles of Our Favorite Wizard* by Eric Bradley.

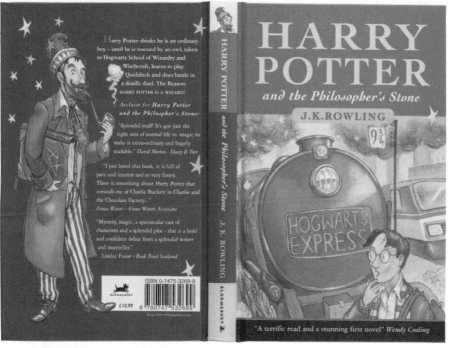

A first edition, first printing of Harry Potter and the Philosopher's Stone, 1997, in like new condition, has surpassed the ranks of first edition James Bond titles and first edition copies of Lord of the Rings by J. R. R. Tolkien in terms of collector worth. .... **$43,750.**

Courtesy of Bonhams, Bonhams.com

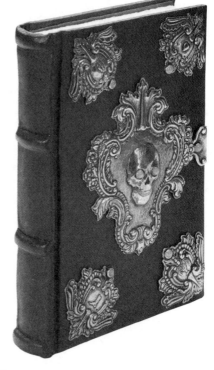

A rare copy of J.K. Rowling's hand-written and illustrated The Tales of Beedle the Bard edition was given to the publisher who launched her career. Rowling gave the edition to mark the publication of the final book in the Harry Potter series......**$467,000**

Courtesy of Sotheby's, sothebys.com

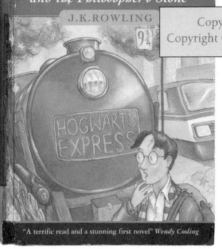

First edition, first printing, one of 500 copies of the first and rarest of the Harry Potter books, and one of approximately 300 copies sent to British libraries. Featuring "Copyright © Text Joanne Rowling 1997" (rather than "J. K. Rowling"), and "Taylor1997" (rather than "Taylor 1997") on the copyright page. This particular copy was once the property of the West Sussex Libraries, evidenced by the library stamp. **$15,535**

Courtesy of Heritage Auctions, HA.com

For the astute fans of the Harry Potter series, a complete set of seven large octavo volumes of the first American editions of the series can be worth thousands. This set, including The Sorcerer's Stone, Chamber of Secrets, Prisoner of Azkaban, Goblet of Fire, Order of the Phoenix, Half Blood Prince, and Deathly Hallows, was published in New York by Arthur A. Levine / Scholastic Press, 1998-2007... **$2,987.**

Courtesy of Heritage Auctions, HA.com

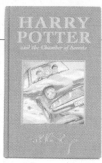

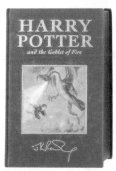

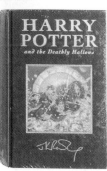

A complete set of the Bloomsbury deluxe limited editions, first printings. Comprises: Harry Potter and the Philosopher's Stone, Deluxe First Printing [1999]; Harry Potter and the Chamber of Secrets, Deluxe First Printing [1999]; Harry Potter and the Prisoner of Azkaban, Deluxe First Printing [1999]; Harry Potter and the Goblet of Fire, Deluxe First Printing [2000]; Harry Potter and the Order of the Phoenix, Deluxe First Printing [2003]; Harry Potter and the Half-Blood Prince, Deluxe First Printing [2005]; Harry Potter and the Deathly Hallows, Deluxe First Printing [2007]. Seven octavo volumes, all in the original cloth, final three titles still in publisher's shrinkwrap. .... **$2,700.**

Courtesy of PBA Galleries, PBAGalleries.com

Signed twice by J. K. Rowling and 15 members of the film, Harry Potter and the Deathly Hallows, a first American, first printing copy features a rare collection of principal cast members such as Ralph Fiennes (Lord Voldemort), Richard Griffith (Vernon Dursley), Tom Fenton (Draco Malfoy), Helena Bonham Carter (Bellatrix Lestrange), Rupert Grint (Ron Weasley), Daniel Radcliffe (Harry Potter), Bonnie Wright (Ginny Weasley), Fiona Shaw (Petunia Dursley), Michael Gambon (Albus Dumbledore), Emma Watson (Hermione Granger), Alan Rickman (Severus Snape), Evana Lynch (Luna Lovegood), and six others............**$3,500**

Courtesy of Heritage Auctions, HA.com

A pair of silver metal wire frame glasses with round clear lenses, worn by Daniel Radcliffe in his role as Harry Potter in Harry Potter and the Sorcerer's Stone is one of several pairs of glasses made for the film.....................**$20,000.**

Courtesy of Julien's Auctions, juliensauctions.com

This English-made wool-nylon blend sweater was worn by an actor in one of the later Harry Potter movies. It is gray with scarlet-and-gold piping of the Gryffindor house on the hem and cuffs, and bears a "Property of Hogwarts" tag sewn inside the collar. The sweaters in the first two films in the series were of a lighter gray color, with additional piping around the collar..........**$286.**

Courtesy of Heritage Auctions, ha.com

This antique Welsh dragon flag from the 1920s is an example of "Potter-like" items used for Harry Potter décor. ....**$150.**

Harry Potter and the Goblet of Fire (Warner Brothers, 2005), one sheet DS Advance movie poster, has never been used or displayed, rolled, Mint, 27" x 40". .... **$131.**

Courtesy of Heritage Auctions, ha.com

Harry Potter and the Order of the Phoenix (Warner Brothers, 2007), one sheet DS Advance movie poster with Voldemort image, rolled, Very Fine-, 27" x 40". .... **$26.**

Courtesy of Heritage Auctions, ha.com

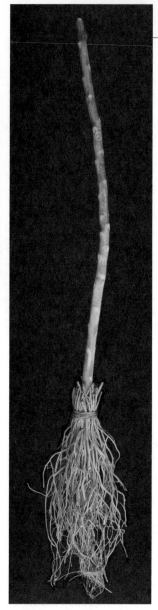

A detailed prop production-used broomstick, constructed of fiberglass GRP material, purchased from a crew member before the release of the first movie. .... **$2,860.**

Courtesy of Eubanks Auctions,
ewbankauctions.co.uk

Harry Potter's long suffering Uncle Sirius Black (Gary Oldman) is depicted on this amazing one sheet prototype for Harry Potter and the Prisoner of Azkaban (Warner Bros., 2004) that was never issued by Warner Bros. In a brilliant marketing ploy, Warner created this poster to mimic the "Wanted" posters used in the movie and tried to duplicate a motion effect. As you move back and forth before the poster, the image of Black begins to disappear. After creating six of these full-size prototypes, Warner decided that it was too expensive to put them into full production and so the project was dropped. This is probably the most rare of all the lenticular posters produced, near mint/mint, 25-3/4" x 40"..**$3,800-$4,000.**

Courtesy of Heritage Auctions, ha.com

HISTORICAL AMERICANA

HISTORICAL AMERICANA WALKS a fine line between so many collecting genres. Folk art, manuscripts, political pinbacks and ceramics can all easily fall within their own collecting category. Historical Americana collectors seek to document America's political and cultural heritage, from its birth as a republic to the present. So although it may appear to be a 'catch-all' category on its surface, historical Americana is a thriving collecting category for that very reason. And auction records continue to fall year after year.

For instance, an outstandingly preserved hand-painted, double-sided jugate banner from the 1844 Presidential campaign of James K. Polk sold for $185,000 in 2015 and claimed the world record as the most valuable piece of historical political Americana ever sold at public auction.

"Simply, this is the finest political banner known to exist and fully deserving of a new world record," said Tom Slater, Director of Americana Auctions at Heritage Auctions, the world's leading historical Americana auctioneer, which managed the sale. "Not only is this banner historically important to early American political campaigns, it is true work of art unique in the world of Americana memorabilia and American folk art."

When it appeared at auction, it represented just the second time the banner has been seen publically in more than 30 years. This seems to be the trend in historical Americana at the dawn of the 21st century – longtime collectors have reached the age when it is time to sell and old collections are appearing on the market for the first time.

These collections do not always have to set price records to be of historical importance to our country. Some items show America at its best – a U.S. flag arranged in the "Great Star" pattern of 33 stars, depicting America's struggle during Antebellum, or the very light bulbs developed by Thomas A. Edison in his New Jersey laboratory, a shining example of American ingenuity. Some show the country at its worst.

Take Charles Guiteau, the radical who assassinated President James A. Garfield. An important private collection of artifacts and documents relating to the Presidential assassin, including a newly discovered manifesto in which he "justifies" shooting President Garfield, made its auction debut in mid-2017. Most of the items were saved by the warden of the jail in which Guiteau was being held and passed down through his family. Recently discovered pages from Guiteau's 1882 book, written from jail while awaiting his execution, titled The Truth and The Removal are among the only pages of Guiteau's manuscript known to exist in private hands. The collection sold for just shy of $10,000 but to the country, the archive was an invaluable look at the inside of a man who changed U.S. history.

"Presidential assassins are well known, but few archives give a look inside the thinking behind their thoughts and actions like this one offers historians," said Tom Slater, director of Americana at Heritage Auctions. "From photographs to hair samples and even the bullets fired into his prison cell in an attempted assassination of Guiteau himself, no other archive comes close in complexity and completeness."

Among the most evocative pieces from the private collection included pieces of the ropes used to bind and hang Guiteau; a group of items including bullets fired through his window cell in an assassination attempt; a cribbage board hand-carved from wood from the assassin's coffin and even two glass vials containing a substantial sample of the assassin's hair and, the other, containing poison, sent to him by his sister, presumably in the hope that he would choose to take it and cheat the hangman.

It might be a macabre example, but it shows just how diverse historical Americana is and how valuable these artifacts are to the story of our nation, as dark and as hopeful as it may sometimes seem.

Banner, 1844, James K. Polk and George M. Dallas, double-sided jugate, rare candidates, ex. Berman Collection, 76-1/2" w. x 75" l................... **$185,000**

Heritage Auctions, www.HA.com

Banner, 1844, Henry Clay and James K. Polk, important and comical banner, art depicts Clay giving Polk a drubbing, but Polk would prevail at the ballot box, text reads: "Thus Polk the scoundrel tries; Our tariff low to lay; While to its rescue flies; The gallant Henry Clay.", hand-painted muslin, mounted on linen, 35" x 42-1/2". **$31,250**

Pitcher, 1840, William Henry Harrison campaign item, four portrait panels with log cabins above each and patriotic eagles below, "The Ohio Farmer" above the portrait and his name below, manufactured by the American Pottery Company of Jersey City, New Jersey, 11-3/4" t. **$37,500**

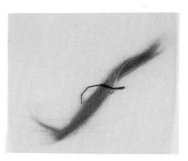

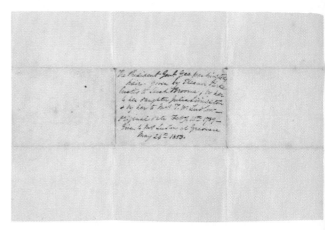

Hair, 1789, George Washington, substantial lock, held together with blue thread, light reddish-brown, accompanied by three pieces of period documentation or provenance, 3-1/2" l. **$32,500**

Parka, 1926, Admiral Richard E. Byrd's personal seal-fur parka with hood. Byrd first rose to national prominence in 1926 when he claimed to have flown over the North Pole, the first man to do so, for which he received the Congressional Medal of Honor and broad acclaim, 44" l. **$7,500**

Vase, circa 1940s, ceramic with glazed finish, Franklin Delano Roosevelt caricature, logo of mfg. Lee T. Wheeler Designs, 6-1/4" h. **$89**

Pinback, circa 1910s, Theodore Roosevelt, color Equality Pin button titled "Equality" showing President Theodore Roosevelt and Booker T. Washington sharing a shot of whiskey at a White House dinner, 1-1/4" dia., ... **$3,750**

Dress and sash, circa 1910s, woman's Suffrage parade dress and sash, beige linen, with a diagonal sash in classic Suffrage movement colors, sash is double-sided. **$6,875**

Flag, circa February 14, 1859 to January 29, 1861, "Antebellum Flag," hand-stitched cotton flag with 33 stars in the canton, arranged in the "Great Star" pattern, 46" w. x 32" t. **$18,125**

Pinback, 1908, Taft and Sherman Miss Liberty jugate, depicting the Republican candidates beneath the outstretched arms of Lady Liberty, Whitehead & Hoag back paper, 1-1/4" d.
.... **$275**

Paperweight, circa 1889-1892, Electrification of New York City cable cross-section paperweight, glass and silver-plated presented to Samuel Insull (1859-1938), containing a cross-section of lubricated copper coil used in the electrification of New York City when that city converted from gas to electric, 4" w. x 1" t. **$1,000**

▲ Light bulbs, 1894, Thomas A. Edison Patent Infringement Case Court Exhibits, collection of five light bulbs and one socket many of which, if not all, were used in patent infringement lawsuits filed by the Edison Electric Light Company in the late 19th century, sizes vary from 2-1/2" to 5-1/5" l.. **$30,000**

Button, 1908, petroliana, early automobile novelty, button showing an early open-air car, inscribed: "Automobile Carnival New York Apr. 6-11 '08.", a pot-metal omnibus-style car hangs from a ribbon, rare, 1-1/4" **$150**

Badges, circa mid-20th century, pop culture assortment of 31 novelty badges relating to classic radio, film and television shows and serials, including Buck Rogers, Captain Kangaroo, Dragnet, Davy Crockett, Dick Tracy, the Lone Ranger and others, various sizes. **$325**

Weathervane, circa 1920-1930, figural vane in form of Native American Indian holding a tomahawk in a war-like stance, as well as a bow in the other hand, with arrows in his quiver. **$625**

Ambrotype, 1860, important, Abraham Lincoln, George Clark 1860 campaign ambrotype, features the "Cooper Union" portrait by Mathew Brady, 2-1/8" w. x 2-1/2" l. **$20,000**

Cigarette holder, circa 1940s, Franklin D. Roosevelt's personally-owned, hand-carved, floral design encircling the middle section and overall nicotine stains, 4-3/4". **$875**

Ash tray, 1898, "Uncle Sam vs. Spain", hand-painted ceramic ash tray that depicts Uncle Sam and a bullfighter grappling over a large cigar labeled "Cuba", from the Scott W. Dolson Collection, 7-1/2" l. x 3-1/2" w. **$812**

ILLUSTRATION ART

EXPOSURE PLAYS AN important role in collector demand and values for illustration art, which has proven itself over the last decade as one of the most popular and dynamic art genres in the country.

Take for instance "Hello Everybody!," a calendar illustration originally produced for Brown & Bigelow in the late 1920s. Artist Rolf Armstrong created the carefree pastel on board of a young lady with a bright smile at the nexus of the Roaring '20s and the Great Depression. Popular reaction was enthusiastic. The artwork appeared as a calendar illustration, on playing cards, puzzles, a die-cut advertising sign for Orange Kist soda pop, and as the cover for the March 1929 edition of *College Humor* magazine. According to Janet Dobson's *Pin Up*

Marc Tauss, Vanished New York, cover art for Jay McInerney's novel Bright Lights, Big City (1984), photography, dyes, color pencil, airbrush and glaze chromogenic print paper, 6 1/2" x 6 3/4".......... **$11,250**

Courtesy of Swann Galleries, swanngalleries.com

Dreams: The Glamour Art of Rolf Armstrong, early works such as "Hello Everybody!" defined the vision of feminine beauty for the next 40 years and earned Armstrong the title of "Father of the Pin-Up Artists." The exposure and reputation of the artist generated strong demand when the original work finally came up for auction when its sale price was pushed to $30,000.

"Hello Everybody!" represents the type of subject matter that is attracting mainstream attention.

"It's really what we think of as classic images in all genres that speak directly and powerfully to a specific time period – whether it's a 1940s *Saturday Evening Post* cover, 1950s science-fiction paperback cover, or 1960s Gil Elvgren calendar pin-up," said Todd Hignite, vice president at Heritage Auctions, the world's largest auctioneer of illustration art and related works.

Interestingly, as the market for illustration art matures, auctioneers are reclassifying works as American fine art and offering works by artists with household names along with other artists such as Grandma Moses, Leroy Neiman, or by the Wyeths. Norman Rockwell's works now routinely bring in excess of $2 million at auction, but his early illustration art, steeped in sentimentality and strong national pride, may be found for less than $100,000.

"Well-known artists such as Rockwell did indeed work in advertising – many illustrators did – and it's certainly less expensive than a magazine cover by the same artist," Hignite said.

Although industry watchers are excited to see many illustration artists make the leap from illustration art to American fine art, there are dozens, perhaps thousands, of artists whose identity is still lost but whose art lives on. Currently these works are anonymously attributed simply as "American artist," but that doesn't mean research has stopped looking into the identity of these artists. Scholars have been given a boost in recent years thanks to collectors who remain fascinated by various styles.

"The scholarship and research in the field is very active and between exhibitions, publications, and more dealers handling the work, is increasing all the time, but there's still a lot of work to be done in terms of identifying art," Hignite said. "Oftentimes artists didn't sign their paintings, and if their style isn't immediately identifiable, there's a good deal of digging to do. Much of the best research actually comes from devoted fans and collectors, who doggedly put together extensive checklists and track down publication histories, check stubs from publishers, biographies, etc., to try and enhance our understanding of the history."

This confluence of awareness, appreciation, and a growing nostalgia for mid-century works have more than doubled values for pieces offered just a few short years ago. Hignite credits the increase to a matter of supply and demand. "I think simply the opportunity to see a steady supply of great art by Elvgren has increased the demand," he said. "If you see one of his paintings in person, there's no question of his painting talent, and collector confidence increases as we see such a steady growth and consistent sales results."

George Petty (American, 1894-1975), ... so take my advice and just bet your shirt! Early variant of July 1941 Esquire Magazine centerfold, watercolor and gouache on Whatman Water Color Board with overlays and cut-outs, 13-1/2" x 22", signed lower right, verso contains Campbell-Ewald stamp with manuscript description, title and magazine date in pencil.................. **$7,500**

Courtesy of Swann Galleries, swanngalleries.com

top lot

Frazetta's Fantastical Masterpiece

At The Earth's Core, a 1974 masterpiece by fantasy and science fiction artist Frank Frazetta, sold for **$1,075,500** at Heritage Auctions. The sale established a world-auction record for the work of this hugely popular artist.

The 21" x 29" oil on canvas hung in the Frazetta Museum for years. His paintings appeared on book covers every year from 1963 through 1996, however, *At The Earth's Core* stands out as an enduring classic image of Frazetta's work.

The legendary writer Edgar Rice Burroughs used the illustration for the cover of the first Pellucidar paperback novel. Frazetta's meticulous attention to detail in both the foreground and the background tell an entire story in one image—a talent that established Frazetta as the master of modern fantasy art.

"If you are a collector of Mr. Frazetta's vision and talent, this is the painting to have," Todd Hignite, Vice President of Heritage Auctions, said of one of Frazetta's most important works. "It represents everything he did so well, from painting the female form to depicting realistic monsters and cliffhanger scenarios."

Born in Brooklyn, New York, in 1928, and widely regarded as the godfather of fantastical illustration, Frazetta influenced a generation of artists and filmmakers with dramatic images of muscled male warriors defending curvaceous maidens from creatures seemingly spawned in hell. He also painted powerful, sensual women not to be trifled with. Some of the more notable collectors and fans of his work include Steven Spielberg, George Lucas, Peter Jackson, Clint Eastwood and Sylvester Stallone. Frazetta died in 2010. He was 82.

Frazetta was inducted into the comic book industry's Will Eisner Comic Book Hall of Fame in 1995 and the Jack Kirby Hall of Fame in 1999. His art was also used to illustrate movie posters and rock album covers for such bands as Molly Hatchet and Nazareth.

W.W. Denslow, illustration from The Wonderful Wizard of Oz (1900), pen and ink and pencil on paper, 13 1/4" x 12 1/4 inches, Scarecrow and two Munchkins shown. A classic illustration from a great American fairy tale. The majority of the original Denslow drawings from the book are preserved in the Print Department of The New York Public Library. .... **$30,720.**

Courtesy of Swann Galleries, swanngalleries.com

Diana Thorne, Dogs & More Dogs, double-page spread from Nothing But Dogs by Earl Marvin Rush. New York: Grosset & Dunlap, 1947. Mixed media with ink, chalk, and wash on board, 5 1/2" x 14 1/2", unsigned. Registration marks and printer's notes in margins...**$1,125**

Courtesy of Swann Galleries, swanngalleries.com

Sam Cherry, Untitled, c. 1959, oil on canvas board, 22" x 18", signed lower left, original illustration for a Western romance story................ **$3,585**

Courtesy of Heritage Auctions, ha.com

Coby Whitmore (American 1913-1988), Schlitz Beer, ad illustration, gouache on board, 22.75" x 16.5", signed lower right. **$2,630**

Courtesy of Heritage Auctions, ha.com

Al Buell (American, 1910-1996). Pin-Up with a Pitchfork, oil on board 21" x 17", signed center left. Painting reproduced in The Great American Pin-Up by Charles G. Martignette and Louis K. Meisel, Taschen, 1996................................ **$4,481**

Courtesy of Heritage Auctions, ha.com

Elmer Simms Campbell (American, 1906-1971), I used to know her – four checkbooks ago, watercolor, gouache, and pencil on board, 15" x 9 3/4", signed in image, lower right, dated September 1936 on verso. **$2,375**

Courtesy of Swann Galleries, swanngalleries.com

Olivia de Berardinis (American, b. 1948), Sophia Loren, 1984, charcoal and pencil on paper; 28" x 19 1/2", signed lower left. **$2,250**

Courtesy of Heritage Auctions, ha.com

Zoe Mozert (American, 1904-1993), Reading the Times, pastel on board, 15 1/2" x 11", signed lower right, from the estate of Charles Martignette. **$3,585**

Courtesy of Heritage Auctions, ha.com

Knute O. Munson (American 20th Century), Top Service is Delivered, c. 1949, pastel on illustration board, 32" x 24", signed center-left (on the package)... **$2,125**

Courtesy of Heritage Auctions, ha.com

Billy DeVorrs, As Good As It Gets, circa 1950, pastel on board, 23" x 18.5", signed lower right, appeared in The Great American Pin-Up by Charles G. Martignette and Louis K. Meisel, Taschen, 1996. ....**$13,125**

Courtesy of Heritage Auctions, ha.com

Rudy Nappi, Reefer Girl, paperback cover, 1953, oil on board, 17.5"x 13.5", signed lower right. This iconic illustration appeared in a slightly different form as the cover to Jane Manning's novel, Reefer Girl, Cameo Books #330, 1953, described as: "The frank, biting story of a young girl of the slums, and how she was caught in the toils of evil." From the estate of Charles Martignette. **$26,290**

Courtesy of Heritage Auctions, ha.com

Gil Elvgren (American 1914 - 1980). A Good Catch, illustration used for NAPA Auto advertisement, oil on canvas, 30" x 27", signed lower right..**$15,000**

Courtesy of Heritage Auctions, ha.com

Malcolm Smith (1912-1966), original Pin-up/ Glamour Art (1942), most likely published as a magazine cover, or calendar print, oil on canvas, approximately 34" x 24", signed and dated (42) lower right... **$3,910**

Courtesy of Heritage Auctions, ha.com

David Levine (American, 1926-2009), Donald Trump, pen and ink on paper, 14" x 11", published in *The New York Review of Books*, May 22, 1988. Signed and dated in ink, lower right and titled in pencil on verso along with Levine archivist David Leopold's catalog number for the image penned in upper left. From the artist's estate. **$1,875**

Courtesy of Swann Galleries, swanngalleries.com

Bart Forbes (American, b. 1939), Joe DiMaggio, 1999, oil on canvas, 21" x 16", signed lower right. **$2,750**

Courtesy of Heritage Auctions, ha.com

Robert A Heindel (American, 1938-2005). Olympics, TV Guide cover illustration (unpublished), circa mid 1970s, oil, watercolor and gesso on Masonite, 24" x 19 3/4", unsigned. **$200**

Courtesy of Heritage Auctions, ha.com

John J. Lomasney (Irish, 1899-1989). In the Heat of the Night, 1967, gouache on artboard, mixed media; 44" x 28". The Lomasney Collection consists of over 800 hand-painted film posters originally displayed in The Royal Hawaiian Theater in Honolulu from 1930s to 1980s. Spanning 50 years of cinematic history, the posters were called a "treasure trove of art" by the New York Post. The Lomasney Collection was acquired by tennis legend John McEnroe and displayed in his Soho, NYC gallery. McEnroe donated the collection to Lifebeat, Music Fights HIV/AIDS to support their HIV prevention efforts. **$260**

Courtesy of Heritage Auctions, ha.com

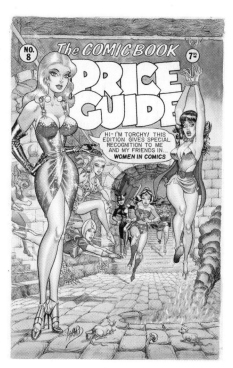

Bill Ward, Overstreet Comic Book Price Guide #8 Cover Painting Original Art, 1978, watercolor over graphite on illustration board, 12 1/2" x 20"; showcases his creation, Torchy, along with other classic female characters: Hawkgirl, Bullet Girl, Sheena (Queen of the Jungle), Miss Fury, Wonder Woman, Lady Luck and Phantom Lady for an edition that had a focus on "Women in Comics." **$17,925**

Courtesy of Heritage Auctions, ha.com

JEWELRY

JEWELRY HAS HELD a special place for humankind since prehistoric times, both as an emblem of personal status and as a decorative adornment. This tradition continues today. We should keep in mind, however, that it was only with the growth of the Industrial Revolution that jewelry first became cheap enough so that even a person of modest means could wear a piece or two.

Only since around the mid-19th century did certain forms of jewelry, especially pins and brooches, begin to appear on the general market as a mass-produced commodity and the Victorians took to it immediately. Major production centers for the finest pieces of jewelry remained in Europe, especially Italy and England, but less expensive pieces were also exported to the booming American market and soon some American manufacturers also joined in the trade. Especially during the Civil War era, when silver and gold supplies grew tremendously in the U.S., did jewelry in silver or with silver, brass or gold-filled (i.e. gold-plated or goldplate) mounts begin to flood the market here. By the turn of the 20th century all the major mail-order companies and small town jewelry shops could offer a huge variety of inexpensive jewelry pieces aimed at not only the feminine buyer but also her male counterpart.

Inexpensive jewelry of the late 19th and early 20th century is still widely available and often at modest prices. Even more in demand today is costume jewelry, well-designed jewelry produced of inexpensive materials and meant to carefully accent a woman's ensemble. Today costume jewelry of the 20th century has become one of the most active areas in the field of collecting and some of the finest pieces, signed by noted designers and manufacturers, can reach price levels nearly equal to much earlier and scarcer examples.

Jewelry prices, as in every other major collecting field, are influenced by a number of factors including local demand, quality, condition and rarity. As market prices have risen in recent years it has become even more important for the collector to shop and buy with care. Learn as much as you can about your favorite area of jewelry and keep abreast of market trends and stay alert to warnings about alterations, repairs or reproductions that can be found on the market.

For more information on jewelry, see *Warman's Jewelry Identification and Price Guide*, 5th edition, by Christie Romero or *Warman's Costume Jewelry Identification and Price Guide* by Pamela Y. Wiggins.

Jewelry Styles

Jewelry has been a part of every culture throughout time, reflecting the times as well as social and aesthetic movements. Jewelry is usually divided into periods and styles. Each period may have several styles, with some of the same styles and types of jewelry being made in both precious and non-precious materials. Elements of one period may also overlap into others.

Georgian, 1760-1837. Fine jewelry from this period is quite desirable, but few good-quality pieces have found their way to auction in recent years. Sadly, much jewelry from this period has been lost.

Victorian, 1837-1901. Queen Victoria of England ascended the throne in 1837 and remained queen until her death in 1901. The Victorian period is a long and prolific one, abundant with many styles of jewelry. It warrants being divided into three sub-periods: Early or Romantic period dating from 1837-1860; Mid or Grand period dating from 1860-1880; and Late or Aesthetic period dating from 1880-1901.

Sentiment and romance were significant factors in Victorian jewelry. Often, jewelry and clothing represented love and affection, with symbolic motifs such as hearts, crosses, hands, flowers, anchors, doves, crowns, knots, stars, thistles, wheat, garlands, horseshoes and moons. The materials of the time were also abundant and varied. They included silver, gold, diamonds, onyx, glass, cameo, paste, carnelian, agate, coral, amber, garnet, emeralds, opals, pearls, peridot, rubies, sapphires, marcasites, cut steel, enameling, tortoiseshell, topaz, turquoise, bog oak, ivory, jet, hair, gutta percha and vulcanite.

Sentiments of love were often expressed in miniatures. Sometimes they were representative of deceased loved ones, but often the miniatures were of the living. Occasionally, the miniatures depicted landscapes, cherubs or religious themes.

Hair jewelry was a popular expression of love and sentiment. The hair of a loved one was placed in a special compartment in a brooch or a locket, or used to form a picture under a glass compartment. Later in the mid-19th century, pieces of jewelry were made completely of woven hair. Individual strands of hair would be woven together to create necklaces, watch chains, brooches, earrings and rings.

In 1861, Queen Victoria's husband, Prince Albert, died. The queen went into mourning for the rest of her life, and Victoria required that the royal court wear black. This atmosphere spread to the populace and created a demand for mourning jewelry, which is typically black. When it first came into fashion, it was made from jet, fossilized wood. By 1850, there were dozens of English workshops making jet brooches, lockets, bracelets and necklaces. As the supply of jet dwindled, other materials were used such as vulcanite, gutta percha, bog oak and French jet.

By the 1880s, somber mourning jewelry was losing popularity. Fashions had changed and the clothing was simpler and had an air of delicacy. The Industrial Revolution, which had begun in the early part of the century, was now in full swing and machine-manufactured jewelry was affordable to the working class.

Edwardian, 1890-1920. The Edwardian period takes its name England's King Edward VII. Though he ascended the throne in 1901, he and his wife, Alexandria of Denmark, exerted influence over the period before and after his

Georgian emerald and diamond ring, central pear-shaped emerald weighing approx. 4 ct, with diamond accented laurel wreath form surround, atop a single diamond weighing approx. 0.25 ct., silver and gold mounted, circa 1800, total approx. weight 4.3 dwt, size 5. .... **$4,200**

Courtesy of Clarke Auction Gallery, clarkeny.com

Victorian 10k yellow gold earrings, circa 1900, large pear-shaped tiger eye center stones. **$350**

Courtesy of Pawn Zone, pawnzone.com

Edwardian gold and amethyst three-piece set, includes two cushion-shaped amethyst brooches, one in lozenge shaped 18k filigree in the Persian style, the other in conforming 14k frame with strung seed pearls, and a 14k yellow gold long chain with faceted amethyst stations. Largest amethyst is 22.7 x 19.77 x 11.4 mm, longest brooch 1-1/2", chain 54"................................ **$1,600**

*Courtesy of Rago Arts and Auction Center,
ragoarts.com*

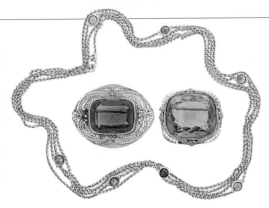

Arts & Crafts sterling silver and hardstone brooch, with openwork design, 2-1/8" w **$74**

Courtesy of Skinner Inc., skinnerinc.com

Art Nouveau pin, sterling silver, depicting profile of a woman's face, marked 925, approx. total weight 14 grams, 2-1/8" h, 1-3/4" w, 1/4" d................. **$250**

*Courtesy of Sterling Associates,
www.sterlingauctionservices.com*

ascension. The 1890s was known as La Belle Epoque. This was a time known for ostentation and extravagance. As the years passed, jewelry became simpler and smaller. Instead of wearing one large brooch, women were often found wearing several small lapel pins.

In the early 1900s, platinum, diamonds and pearls were prevalent in the jewelry of the wealthy, while paste was being used by the masses to imitate the real thing. The styles were reminiscent of the neo-classical and rococo motifs. The jewelry was lacy and ornate, feminine and delicate.

Arts & Crafts, 1890-1920. The Arts & Crafts movement was focused on artisans and craftsmanship. There was a simplification of form where the material was secondary to the design. Guilds of artisans banded together. Some jewelry was mass-produced, but the most highly prized examples of this period are handmade and signed by their makers. The pieces were simple and at times abstract. They could be hammered, patinated and acid etched. Common materials were brass, bronze, copper, silver, blister pearls, freshwater pearls, turquoise, agate, opals, moonstones, coral, horn, ivory, base metals, amber, cabochon-cut garnets and amethysts.

Art Nouveau, 1895-1910. In 1895, Samuel Bing opened a shop called "Maison de l'Art Nouveau" at 22 Rue de Provence in Paris. Art Nouveau designs in the jewelry were characterized by a sensuality that took on the forms of the female figure, butterflies, dragonflies, peacocks, snakes, wasps, swans, bats, orchids, irises and other exotic flowers. The lines used whiplash curves to create a feeling of lushness and opulence.

1920s-1930s. Costume jewelry began its steady ascent to popularity in the 1920s. Since it was relatively inexpensive to produce, it was mass-produced. The sizes and designs of the jewelry varied. Often, it was worn a few times, disposed of and then replaced with a new piece. It was thought of as expendable, a cheap throwaway to dress up an outfit. Costume jewelry became so popular that it was sold in both upscale and "five and dime" stores.

During the 1920s, fashions were often accompanied by jewelry that drew on the Art Deco movement, which got its beginning in Paris at the "Exposition Internationale des Arts Décoratifs et Industriels Modernes" held in 1925. The idea behind this movement was that form follows function. The style was characterized by simple, straight, clean lines, stylized motifs, and geometric shapes. Favored materials included chrome, rhodium, pot metal, glass, rhinestones, Bakelite, and celluloid.

One designer who played an important role was Coco Chanel. Though previously reserved for evening wear, the jewelry was worn by Chanel during the day, making it fashionable for millions of other women to do so, too.

With the 1930s came the Depression and the advent of World War II. Perhaps in response to the gloom, designers began using enameling and brightly colored rhinestones to create whimsical birds, flowers, circus animals, bows, dogs and just about every other figural form imaginable.

Retro Modern, 1939-1950. Other jewelry designs of the 1940s were big and bold. Retro Modern had a more substantial feel to it and designers began using larger stones to enhance the dramatic pieces. The jewelry was stylized and exaggerated. Common motifs included flowing scrolls, bows, ribbons, birds, animals, snakes, flowers, and knots.

Sterling silver now became the metal of choice, often dipped in a gold wash known as vermeil.

Designers often incorporated patriotic themes of American flags, the V-sign, Uncle Sam's hat, airplanes, anchors, and eagles.

Postwar Modern, 1945-1965. A movement that emphasized the artistic approach to jewelry making. It is also referred to as Mid-Century Modern. This approach was occurring at a time when the Beat Generation was prevalent. These avant-garde designers created jewelry that was handcrafted to illustrate the artist's own concepts and ideas. The materials often used were sterling, gold, copper, brass, enamel, cabochons, wood, quartz, and amber.

1950s-1960s. The 1950s saw the rise of jewelry that was made purely of rhinestones: necklaces, bracelets, earrings and pins. The focus of the early 1960s was on clean lines: Pillbox hats and A-line dresses with short jackets were a mainstay for the conservative woman. The large, bold rhinestone pieces were no longer the must-have accessory. They were now replaced with smaller, more delicate gold-tone metal and faux pearls with only a hint of rhinestones.

At the other end of the spectrum were psychedelic-colored clothing, Nehru jackets, thigh-high miniskirts and go-go boots. Beads, large metal pendants and occasionally big, bold rhinestones accessorized the look. By the late 1960s, tthe hippie look was born and the rhinestone had, for the most part, been left behind.

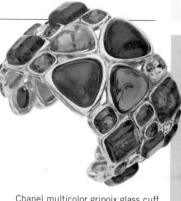

Chanel multicolor gripoix glass cuff bracelet, in gold tone hardware, blue, purple, green, red, orange, yellow and amber gripoix glass inlays, classic example of Chanel's exquisite taste in costume jewelry, 2" w x 6" l...................... **$2,125**

Courtesy of Heritage Auctions, ha.com

Diamond, synthetic sapphire, platinum bracelet, circa 1940, full-cut diamonds weighing a total of approximately 4.40 carats, enhanced by Swiss-cut synthetic sapphires, set in platinum, gross weight 21.60 grams, 7" x 1/2". **$3,500**

Courtesy of Heritage Auctions, ha.com

A Nanna Ditzel silver oyster brooch for Georg Jensen, designed 1956, stamped: GEORG JENSEN, 925 S, DENMARK, 328, NJ, 2-1/8" l. **$200**

Courtesy of Heritage Auctions, ha.com

Vintage designer costume jewelry necklace by Trifari, open work style with scrolled links accented throughout with white-colored rhinestones, marked "Trifari," 15-1/2" l..**$125**

Courtesy of Auction Gallery of Boca Raton, LLC, www.liveauctioneers.com/auction-gallery-of-boca-raton-llc

BRACELETS SETS

Edwardian enamel, platinum-topped gold bracelet, blue and black enamel applied on platinum atop 14k gold, 7" x 5/8". **$375**

Courtesy of Heritage Auctions, ha.com

Art Nouveau gold bracelet, Riker Bros., 14k gold bangle weighs 18.90 grams, marked for Riker Bros., marked 14K RB, inscribed: "Clara H. Grover," 7-1/2" x 1/2"....................**$750**

Courtesy of Heritage Auctions, ha.com

Art Nouveau diamond, plique-à-jour enamel, gold bracelet, French, European-cut diamonds weighing approximately 0.45 carat, set in 18k gold with French hallmarks, 16.20 grams, 7-1/4" l. **$2,750**

Courtesy of Heritage Auctions, ha.com

Kalo Shop silver and green chrysoprase bracelet, Chicago, circa 1910, marks: HAND WROUGHT STERLING, KALO, 7-1/8" circumference, 1.36 troy ounces. **$1,188**

Courtesy of Heritage Auctions, ha.com

Antonio Pineda silver and tiger's eye bracelet, Taxco, Mexico, circa 1953, heavy gauge silver with stepped links, each centered by carved tiger's eye medallions with Aztec warriors, chain and box clasp, marks: ANTONIO, TAXCO (within crown), SILVER 970, HECHO EN MEXICO, ZZ747, (eagle-17), 7-3/4" l, 4.28 troy oz. **$1,063**

Courtesy of Heritage Auctions, ha.com

BROOCHES & PINS

Sapphire and diamond brooch, Chaumet, designed as an insect with single cut diamond eyes and mesh gold wings with round cut sapphire accents, signed with French assay marks, accompanied by box, gross weight: 3.83 dwt, 1" l. **$1,586**

Courtesy of Morphy Auctions, www.morphyauctions.com

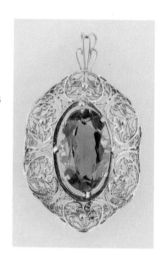

Victorian enamel brooch, navette form with detailed 14k gold with blue and white enamel accents, gross weight 14.51 dwt., 2" w.... **$793**

Courtesy of Morphy Auctions, www.morphyauctions.com

Gold metal and brown topaz brooch, 14k yellow gold surrounding the 6+-carat brown topaz done in filigree technique, brooch can also be worn as pendant, stamps on the verso side illegible, 2" l................**$123**

Courtesy of Morphy Auctions, www.morphyauctions.com

Watermelon tourmaline
pendant, 18k, 14 dwts........**$732**

*Courtesy of Morphy Auctions,
www.morphyauctions.com*

Retro ruby, diamond and gold
double-clip brooch, 14k yellow
gold ribbon double clip brooch,
set with 18 full-cut diamonds and
circular-cut rubies, some rubies
are synthetic, 31.7 gms gross wt,
3-1/8" x 1-3/8"...................**$813**

*Courtesy of John Moran Auctioneers,
www.johnmoranauctioneers.com*

Aquamarine and white gold bar pin, 14k white gold bar brooch
centering a rectangular aquamarine measuring 13.7 x 12.1 x 6.9
mm, weighing approximately 8.15 cts., 2-3/4" l..........................**$406**

Courtesy of John Moran Auctioneers, www.johnmoranauctioneers.com

Bakelite banana brooch.......**$110**

*Courtesy of Strawser Auctions,
www.strawserauctions.com*

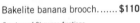

Limoges porcelain brooch of corting couple with sterling rim, 2-1/2".
....**$23**

Bakelite heart brooch...........**$116**

*Courtesy of Strawser Auctions,
www.strawserauctions.com*

*Courtesy of Strawser Auctions,
www.strawserauctions.com*

Victorian diamond, platinum, gold brooch, very good condition, European-cut diamond weighs approximately 0.45 carat, set in 14k gold, and single-cut diamonds weigh a total of approximately 0.15 carat, set in platinum, gross weight 4.70 grams, 2-3/8" x 5/8". $275

Courtesy of Heritage Auctions, ha.com

Art Nouveau gold, enamel, pearl and diamond watch pin, 14k gold, circa 1910, measuring 34 mm across, set with iridescent gold and violet enameled leaves, half pearls and a central diamond, pin stem and catch, 5.1 gram wt. **$275**

Courtesy of Heritage Auctions, ha.com

Victorian woven hair, mother-of-pearl, seed pearl, gold mourning brooch, seed pearls and locks of hair set against mother-of-pearl, encased in 14k gold having a woven hair frame, gross weight 6.90 grams, 1-3/8" x 1-1/8". **$200**

Courtesy of Heritage Auctions, ha.com

Lapis lazuli, diamond, gold hummingbird brooch, 10.60 x 8.85 x 4.80 mm, diamonds weigh a total of approximately 0.35 carat, set in 14k gold having rhodium finished accents, 10.60 grams, 1-3/8" x 1-1/8". **$688**

Courtesy of Heritage Auctions, ha.com

EARRINGS

Vintage 18k yellow gold and jade fish-shaped Oriental earrings. ... **$106**

Courtesy of Omega Auction Corp., www.omegaauctioncorp.com

Vintage 14k jade earrings, carved foliate design, 14k gold prong set, clip-ons, 3" l. **$230**

Courtesy of Vero Beach Auction, www.verobeachauction.com

Vintage dangle earrings, 14k gold, 14k yellow gold 4.9 gr., threaded posts, double dangle design, 1-3/4" l...**$330**

Courtesy of Main Street Mining Co. Auctions, www.mainstreetmining.com

Vintage 14k yellow gold synthetic color change corundum earrings, screw backs, stones approximately 15mm x 10mm. **$115**

Courtesy of Vero Beach Auction, www.verobeachauction.com

NECKLACE & PENDANTS

◄ Art Nouveau tourmaline, cultured pearl, and gold pendant, tourmaline measures 13.90 - 13.95 x 7.75 mm and weighs approximately 12.70 carats, set in 14k gold, 4.80 grams, 2" x 13/16". **$325**

Courtesy of Heritage Auctions, ha.com

Vintage lady's gold and pearl necklace, marked, 18k heart-form pendant with conforming mabe pearl surrounded by 16 round melee diamonds, 20th century, chain marked 14k, total weight 11.6 dwt., 16" l..**$436**

Courtesy of Jeffrey S. Evans & Associates, www.jeffreysevans.com

Margot de Taxco enameled silver pendant brooch necklace, Taxco, Mexico, circa 1955-1978, brown, black and yellow champlevé enamel, bellflower-form links connecting to detachable diamond-form pendant with pin clasp to verso, box clasp, marks: MARGOT DE TAXCO, STERLING, HECHO EN MEXICO (eagle-16), 5604, 1.91 troy oz, 15-5/8" l with chain..............................**$475**

Courtesy of Heritage Auctions, ha.com

Vintage natural butterscotch amber bead necklace, graduated oval beads, smallest is 10mm wide, largest is 20mm wide, double knotted, 65 grams, 40" l. .**$1,320**

Courtesy of Main Street Mining Co. Auctions, www.mainstreetmining.com

Victorian diamond, turquoise, gold locket-pendant-brooch, 14k gold "C" catch and bail and base metal pinstem, one diamond has a surface reaching inclusion, one turquoise cabochon is missing, glass case on the reverse is cracked, diamonds 1.70 x 1.30 mm and 1.40 x 1 mm, and turquoise 1 x 0.70 mm to 3.25 x 2.80 mm, 18 grams, 3-3/16" x 1-3/8".**$475**

Courtesy of Heritage Auctions, ha.com

Vintage gold and pearl double-strand necklace, uniform 7mm beads, ornate gold clasp set with diamond chips, mid-20th century, "800" and illegible hallmarks, 23" l. **$420**

Courtesy of Jeffrey S. Evans & Associates, www.jeffreysevans.com

RINGS

▲ Vintage 14k yellow gold ring with large onyx accented with pearl, size 4-3/4. ....**$196**

Courtesy of Vero Beach Auction, www.verobeachauction.com

Vintage lady's 14k gold, diamond and ruby ring, marked, filigree dome setting with central round melee diamond surrounded by six round rubies, 20th century, total weight: 4.4 dwt, size 5-1/2..................................**$160**

Courtesy of Jeffrey S. Evans & Associates, www.jeffreysevans.com

Vintage lady's 14k gold and jade ring, marked, modern textured setting with oval jade and single melee diamond on table, 20th century, total weight 8.3 dwt., size 8. .... **$405**

Courtesy of Jeffrey S. Evans & Associates, www.jeffreysevans.com

Vintage c1940s men's 14k yellow gold and diamond Masonic ring with secret compartment, secret compartment lifts to reveal information and/or important dates from Brothers' journey, weighs 5.9 grams, size 9-1/2.. **$288**

Courtesy of Vero Beach Auction, www.verobeachauction.com

Vintage 1940s 14k yellow gold 3+-carat moonstone ring, size 3-1/2................................. **$207**

Courtesy of Vero Beach Auction, www.verobeachauction.com

Edwardian pearl, diamond, platinum-topped gold ring, center diamond weighs approximately 0.20 carat, accent diamonds weigh a total of approximately 0.40 carat, with pearl, set in platinum-topped 14k gold, gross weight 4.90 grams, size 3-1/2 (sizeable). **$575**

Courtesy of Heritage Auctions, ha.com

Vintage handmade 18k yellow gold and amethyst ring, amethyst approximately 25mm, weighs 7 grams, size 5-1/4... **$184**

Courtesy of Vero Beach Auction, www.verobeachauction.com

Two-piece Georg Jensen silver and labradorite jewelry suite, Copenhagen, Denmark, circa 1933-1945, necklace and double-strand bracelet each with leaf and seed design composed of alternating links of cast petals and seeds with bezel set cabochon labradorite, marks to necklace: GEORG JENSEN, STERLING, DENMARK, 1, necklace is 15" l. **$5,000**

Courtesy of Heritage Auctions, ha.com

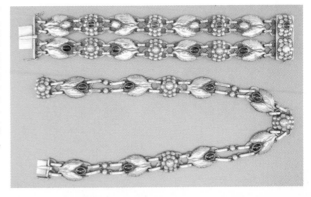

COSTUME JEWELRY

Ciner rhinestone earrings, oval cut faceted topaz-colored foilbacked rhinestones set in yellow metal bezels, marked Ciner on clip band, 1-1/4" x 3/4". **$18**

Courtesy of Main Street Mining Co. Auctions, www.mainstreetmining.com

Vintage Hattie Carnegie triple-strand glass and molded bead necklace, gold-tone hardware, marked Hattie Carnegie...................................... **$48**

Courtesy of Main Street Mining Co. Auctions, www.mainstreetmining.com

Coro thistle brooch, marked Coro, 2-1/2". **$132**

Courtesy of Main Street Mining Co. Auctions, www.mainstreetmining.com

Coro enamel and rhinestone peacock costume jewelry brooch................. **$75**

Courtesy of Strawser Auctions, www.strawserauctions.com

Coro pink flower brooch, marked Coro, approx. 2" x 2-1/2". **$30**

Courtesy of Main Street Mining Co. Auctions, www.mainstreetmining.com

Vintage Coro flower brooch, marked Coro, 2" w, 2-1/2" h. **$30**

Courtesy of Main Street Mining Co. Auctions, www.mainstreetmining.com

JEWELRY

Coro iris trembler brooch, enamelwork yellow metal with 5 red rhinestones set in the trembler, back marked Coro, 3-1/4" x 2".........................**$60**

Courtesy of Main Street Mining Co. Auctions, www.mainstreetmining.com

Sterling Craft by Coro floral brooch, enamel painted leaves and petals, marked Sterling Craft by Coro, Des. Pat. Pend., 21.4 grams, 4-1/4". **$54**

Courtesy of Main Street Mining Co. Auctions, www.mainstreetmining.com

Eisenberg Christmas tree brooch.................................**$17**

Courtesy of Strawser Auctions, www.strawserauctions.com

Eisenberg dress clip............**$186**

Courtesy of Strawser Auctions, www.strawserauctions.com

▶ Vintage Miriam Haskell faux pearl necklace, silver tone, floral theme with multi-color faux pearls and beads, marked Miriam Haskell, 24" l. **$132**

Courtesy of Main Street Mining Co. Auctions, www.mainstreetmining.com

▶ Vintage Hobé blue floral necklace, marked Hobé, 16-1/4"...............**$54**

Courtesy of Main Street Mining Co. Auctions, www.mainstreetmining.com

Choker necklace by Kenneth Jay Lane, set with polished "coral" stones surrounded by faceted "jeweled" mesh bands, inscribed "K.J.L.," 14-1/4" l. $94

Courtesy of Roland Auctioneers & Valuers New York, www.rolandauctions.com

Kenneth Jay Lane necklace, marked KJL for Avon, 18-3/4" l. $18

Courtesy of Main Street Mining Co. Auctions, www.mainstreetmining.com

Vintage Lisner necklace, marked Lisner, 16" l. $36

Courtesy of Main Street Mining Co. Auctions, www.mainstreetmining.com

SchiaparelliNecklace
Vintage Schiaparelli necklace, marked Schiaparelli, 17".
....$84

Courtesy of Main Street Mining Co. Auctions, www.mainstreetmining.com

Vintage Regency rhinestone necklace, marked Regency, approx. 16-1/2". $30

Courtesy of Main Street Mining Co. Auctions, www.mainstreetmining.com

Vintage signed Monet bracelet and earrings, both pieces signed MONET.....$41

Courtesy of Omega Auction Corp., www.omegaauctioncorp.com

Vintage Schreiner of New York brooch, gold tone with faux pearl center, pink cabochon, rhinestones, marked, 2-3/8" l. **$60**

Courtesy of Main Street Mining Co. Auctions, www.mainstreetmining.com

Floral brooch, prong-set rhinestones, marked Stanley Hagler N.Y.C., 3-1/2" l. **$120**

Courtesy of Main Street Mining Co. Auctions, www.mainstreetmining.com

Stanley Hagler NYC earrings, clip-on style, marked Stanley Hagler NYC, approx. 1-1/4" dia. **$72**

Courtesy of Main Street Mining Co. Auctions, www.mainstreetmining.com

Stanley Hagler NYC blue rhinestone earrings, marked Stanley Hagler NYC, 1-1/2". **$96**

Courtesy of Main Street Mining Co. Auctions, www.mainstreetmining.com

▼ Trifari sterling silver frog brooch. **$139**

Courtesy of Strawser Auctions, www.strawserauctions.com

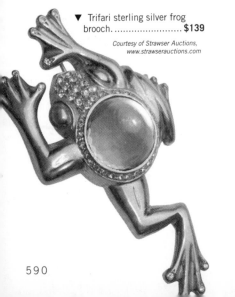

Albert Weiss brooch and earring set, prong-set rhinestones, clip-on earrings, original box, marked Weiss, brooch 2-1/2", earrings 1". **$30**

Courtesy of Main Street Mining Co. Auctions, www.mainstreetmining.com

KITCHENWARE

EVERYONE KNOWS THAT the kitchen is the hub of the home. So when the wildly successful "Downton Abbey" series started streaming across television screens, the show's Edwardian kitchen became a visual primer on class and comfort in our increasingly uncertain times.

That vision not only riveted viewers to each "Downton Abbey" installment, but the show's anti-snobbery theme created a new market niche for antique kitchen collectibles.

When stoic butler Mr. Carson chides housekeeper Mrs. Hughes about a new-fangled electric toaster, antique dealers nationwide said vintage toasters flew off the shelves.

"We simply could not believe how much interest 'Downton Abbey' has sparked in antique kitchen utensils," said Rege Woodley, a retired antique dealer in Washington, Pennsylvania. "I sold one of my antique rolling pins to my neighbor for $100 because it looked like the one used by Mrs. Patmore, the cook in 'Downton Abbey.'"

Pat Greene, owner of Nothing New Antiques, said she is excited about all the "Downton Abbey" fuss and hopes her antique kitchenwares fetch some lasting prices, too. "My rolling pins usually go for $5 to $10, but I'm seeing a big rush on my cookie cutters," said Greene of Pittsburgh.

Mary Kirk of New Alexandria, Pennsylvania, collects old antique cookbooks and was especially interested in trying to prepare some of the food served in the "Downton Abbey" show. "I am extremely interested in trying to prepare the eggs poached with spinach – a dish that poor young kitchen maid Daisy had to prepare during one show scene," said Kirk, a retired librarian. Because of the show's lengthy shooting schedule, producers have reported that most of the food served during production consists of light salads.

Jimmy Roark of Nashville, Tennessee, said he has not seen as large a rush for his kitchen collectibles as a result of the show. "What I see is a more gradual demand for these items," said Roark, who operates a small antique collectibles shop in his garage. "I sell a lot of my cookie cutters, antique wooden bowls, and vintage mixer beaters during the holidays."

Still, the "Downton Abbey" magic continues to seed interest in a broad swath of antique kitchen utensils and artifacts from Bennington mixing bowls to turn-of-the-century tiger wood rolling pins.

Chriss Swaney antique wooden three-piece kitchenware set, includes wooden tree garlic press, flat butter mold, and hand layout rolling pin. **$70**

Courtesy of Connoisseur Auctions, new.liveauctioneers.com/auctioneer/1910/connoisseur-auctions

Stephen White of White & White Antiques & Interiors of Skaneateles, New York, said interest in vintage antique kitchenware remains steady. He was quick to feature his rare whale ivory-crested Nantucket rolling pin valued at $425. "I have unusual kitchen antiques from hand food choppers to copper pots," he said.

"When you think of Pittsburgh, you can't escape the long history that the H.J. Heinz Co. has here," said Toni Bahnak of Candlewood Antiques in Ardara, Pennsylvania. "We have rare old vinegar bottles and ketchup bottles that denote an era when the Heinz Co. made its own glass," Bahnak said.

Industry experts say ketchup and pickle collectibles rose in value because of the business deal that saw the H.J. Heinz Co. purchased by Warren Buffett's Berkshire Hathaway and 3G Capital, which was co-founded by Jorge Lemann, one of Brazil's richest men. Even before the blockbuster deal was announced, some Heinz memorabilia collectors reported that their antique bottles and jars were fetching higher prices than normal.

"I had one of my antique vinegar bottles sell for about $225 and I think I could have gotten more for it," said Ruth Oslet, an antiques collector from Waynesburg, Pennsylvania. She sold it to a marketing executive who collects business memorabilia.

Tom Purdue, a long-time collector of food company antiques, said history and nostalgia play an important role in what people remember and want to save for their modern kitchens. "I can remember the distinct smell of my grandmother's old pickle jars and Heinz horseradish in her musty old kitchen where she used a hand pump to wash dishes," said Purdue, an 89-year-old former blacksmith from Wheeling, West Virginia.

The ever-expanding business reaches back to 1869 when Henry John Heinz and neighbor L. Clarence Noble began selling grated horseradish, bottled in clear glass to showcase its purity. It wasn't until 1876 that the company introduced its flagship product, marketing the country's first commercial ketchup.

Not all history, though, is tied to corporate America. Family memories still stoke the embers of home cooking although many young people today find fast food the fuel of the future.

"I still have my family's old cornbread recipe and I use it all the time," said Elizabeth Schwan, gallery director for Aspire Auctions in Pittsburgh.

Schwan, who scans the country for antiques, admits she has a soft spot for old kitchen utensils. "Flower-sifters, antique copper mixing bowls, and rolling pins were all part of my heritage because my family grew up on a Kentucky farm," Schwan said. "I can still smell the homemade bread and jams."

And like most farm families, the kitchen served as a meeting place and refuge from a long day's work. "Between verbal debates about what to plant on the south flats, we would help our parents churn butter and chop wood for the old country stove," said Myrtle Bench, 91, of Washington, Pennsylvania.

But as a young America turned from the agricultural frontier in the late 1890s and began to embrace a manufacturing economy, automation replaced han dcrafts, and the kitchen became a new testing ground for a variety of modern gizmos like the automatic dishwasher.

The automatic dishwasher was a toy for the rich when an electric model was introduced on 1913 by Willard and Forrest Walker, two Syracuse, New York brothers who ran a hardware store when they were not tinkering with kitchen machines. The new dishwasher sold for $120 (the equivalent of $1,429 in today's dollars), a hefty premium over the $20 the Walkers charged for their popular hand-cranked model and also more expensive than a gasoline-powered washer the brothers put on the market in 1911.

"You can still find some of the old hand-crank washers, but I like to spend my time finding kitchen utensils that reflect how people prepared their food," said Dirk Hayes, a freelance cook from Uniontown, Pennsylvania. "I love watching 'Downton Abbey' because the kitchen scenes really give you a flavor of how the food was prepared. I never had that kind of staff, but it's fun to dream," said Hayes, who collects rolling pins and antique carving knives.

A collection of 19th/early 20th century wooden kitchen utensils, thirteen pieces comprising a large rolling pin, a pastry pin, butter molds with carved rosettes and carved pineapple butter paddles and cookie boards-one with a large figure on each side, longest is 29" l. $300

Courtesy of Jackson's International Auctioneers and Appraisers, jacksonauction.com

Lot of three boxes: two storage and one salt box, 19th century, biggest is 6" h, 10" d. $175

Courtesy of Turner Auctions + Appraisals, turnerauctionsonline.com

▶ A group of 11 American brass, copper, and iron items, 19th century, comprising a copper and wood bed warmer together with a tear-shaped pan, two round pans, five ladles, a small spatula, and a spoon.

....$425

Courtesy of Jackson's International Auctioneers and Appraisers, jacksonauction.com

Antique copper kitchenware including a tray, coffee pot, sugar/creamer, pot on stand, ewers, hanging vessel. Tray is 21" x 15". $50

Courtesy of Litchfield County Auctions, litchfieldcountryauctions.com

◄ Lot of copper kitchenware including two pans, funnel, ewer, two vessels with handle, oversized kettle, and two miscellaneous lids. Largest is approximately 25" d. $125

Courtesy of San Rafael Auction Gallery, sanrafaelauction.com

▼ Koninklijke Goedewaagen Blauw Delft Porcelain, collection of 17 pieces, includes three candlesticks, lidded urns, plates vase, dishes and bowls, maker's mark on bottom reads: Koninklijke Goedewaagen Blauw Delft Holland Handwerk. Height of double gourd-shaped vase: 9" and width of large double handled bowls (including handles) is 13-1/2"..$50

Courtesy of Sterling Auction & Realty Services, sterlingauctionservices.com

Lot of vintage Pyrex kitchenware in primary colors, including five mixing bowls and casserole dishes with glass lids. $50

Courtesy of Invited Sales, invitedsales.com

Vintage 1950-60s Guardian Service 13-piece hammered aluminum kitchenware set, includes three-stack pot roaster trio set with glass lids, turkey/chicken roaster with a platter which can be doubled as a lid (13" l, 10" w, 4" d), handled large stock canning pot with lid (11" w, 5" d), three cooking pots with glass lids (one is 9" w, 4-3/4" deep; one is 9" w, 4" d; and one is 6" w, 2-1/2" d), another cooking/roasting pot with lid 12" across, serving platter 15-1/2", octagon griddle/platter/serving tray with handles about 16-1/2", trivet 12" round. Lot also comes with one extra Guardian triangle pot lid and a Club vintage aqua turquoise aluminum roasting pot that's 10" w, 4" d. **$110**

Courtesy of Premier Auction Galleries, premierauctiongalleries.com

Iron case copper scale, English, circa 1900, made by Saltier, 12" h... **$650**

Courtesy of Tiroche Auction House, tiroche.com.il

▲ Lot of 18 vintage green glass kitchenware items including bowls, salts, vase, mugs. **$40**

Courtesy of Robert Slawinski Auctioneers, Inc., slawinski.com

◄ Villeroy and Boch French Garden Charm Collection three-piece ceramic canister set with decorative lids, tallest measures 11" h. **$60**

Courtesy of The Benefit Shop Foundation, thebenefitshop.org

Lot of two Hall China Company of Ohio teapots with bright red glazes, 20th century, "HALL'S / SUPERIOR / QUALITY / KITCHENWARE / MADE IN / U.S.A." on base; one numbered 1400, and one with a gilt "1" below mark, 6" to 6-1/4" h.
....$100

Courtesy of Jeffrey S. Evans & Associates, jeffreyevans.com

Goodell Bonanza apple peeler and corer, cast iron, excellent working condition, 5" h x 23" w x 6-1/2" d..$275

Courtesy of Rich Penn Auctions, richpennauctions.com

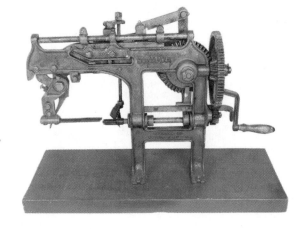

Lot of 1970s frog glass and ceramic serving ware and accessories, including eight ceramic mugs, one lily pad-shaped ceramic dish, pair of ceramic salt and pepper shakers, ceramic cookie jar (9" h), two ceramic creamers, three lidded bowls, three hand-painted glasses (6-1/4" h), six hand-painted glasses (5-3/4" h)..................$60

Courtesy of Sterling Auction & Realty Services, sterlingauctionservices.com

LAMPS & LIGHTING

LIGHTING DEVICES HAVE been around for thousands of years, and antique examples range from old lanterns used on the farm to high-end Tiffany lamps. The earliest known type of lamp was the oil lamp, which was patented by Aimé Argand in 1784 and mass-produced starting in the 19th century. Around 1850 kerosene became a popular lamp-burning fluid, replacing whale oil and other fluids.

In 1879 Thomas A. Edison invented the electric light, causing fluid lamps to lose favor and creating a new field for lamp manufacturers. Decorative table and floor lamps with ornate glass lampshades reached their height of popularity from 1900-1920, due to the success of Tiffany and other Arts & Crafts lamp makers such as Handel.

Bronze Hanukah lamp, Polish or German, late-18th/early-19th century, with baluster stem and scroll and bud branches, pricket sconces linked by a brass plate, 33-1/2" l. **$3,250**

Courtesy of Sotheby's, www.sothebys.com

VISIT WWW.ANTIQUETRADER.COM

WWW.FACEBOOK.COM/ANTIQUETRADER

Tiffany Studios Grapevine table lamp, bronze, art glass, New York, early 20th century, Grapevine pattern shade reveals blown in green glass from inside the shade, fitted over a single socket within harp on circular ribbed base, all in verdigris patina, numbered Tiffany Studios New York, 419, 13-1/2" h, aperture 2-1/8"..................**$2,829**

Courtesy of Skinner Auctioneers and Appraisers, www.skinnerinc.com

Tiffany Studios bronze harp floor lamp base, circa 1910, stamped TIFFANY STUDIOS, NEW YORK, 123; 55" h... **$1,250**

Courtesy of Heritage Auctions, www.ha.com

Twelve-light Lily table lamp, bronze, art glass, made for Quezal, New York, 1901-25, twelve sockets with gold iridescent lily-form shades signed Quezal, the stems joined to lily pad base with veined leaves, unmarked, 20-3/8" h, base dia. 11-3/4", shade aperture dia. 1-1/8".......... **$4,920**

Courtesy of Skinner Auctioneers and Appraisers, www.skinnerinc.com

Fairy phonolamp tabletop lamp and phonograph, bronze-type metal with floral painting decoration, original 25" dia shade, newer power cord, 39" h.
.... **$738**

Courtesy of Morphy Auctions, www.morphyauctions.com

A bronze and marble figural canine desk lamp, 20th century, 22" h x 14-1/2" w x 8" d........... **$688**

Courtesy of Heritage Auctions, www.ha.com

Wilkinson table lamp, leaded shade on a painted Wilkinson table base, shade unmarked, base marked 523, 20-1/2" h. **$2,214**

Courtesy of Morphy Auctions, www.morphyauctions.com

Handel scarlet macaw table lamp, reverse-painted glass, patinated metal, painted by Henry Bedigie, Meriden, Connecticut, c. 1921, domical shade reverse-painted with two scarlet macaw within a tropical foliate and floral surround, fitted with a three-socket cluster on a bronzed metal base with branch detail, tree trunk, and roots on circular foot, signed HB on shade, marked Handel lamps on shade ring, and with felt tag on base........ **$4,920**

Courtesy of Skinner Auctioneers and Appraisers, www.skinnerinc.com

A cloisonné enamel pricket candlestick, Qing Dynasty, Qianlong Period, of square section with a tall domed base rising to an archaistic zun-form middle section below a wide drip pan, supporting the tall columnar neck and upper drip pan, brightly enameled with lotus lappets, prunus blooms, taotie masks and confronted kuilong, partly reserved on a leiwen-imitation ground and all reserved on a turquoise-blue enamel ground, horizontally divided by cast lotus lappets and keyfret borders, and vertically segmented by three registers of flanges, later fitted for electricity and converted into a lamp, height of candlestick 16-3/4". **$7,500**

Courtesy of Sotheby's, www.sothebys.com

A Rococo-style giltwood floor lamp, early 20th century, 78" h. **$937.50**

Courtesy of Heritage Auctions, www.ha.com

Pierre Guariche "Cerf Volant" floor lamp, model No. G30, lacquered metal, brass, circa 1952, produced by Pierre Disderot, Cachan, 57-7/8" **$15,604**

Courtesy of Sotheby's, www.sothebys.com

A stylish Art Deco figural shop display mannequin lamp, circa 1935, the head and hands in wood, she holds a fan which conceals a lamp fitment, on stepped base with mirror flex panels, 17-1/2" h x 21-1/2" w. **$1,535**

Courtesy of Bonhams, www.bonhams.com

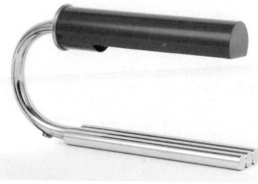

Gilbert Rohde table lamp, chromium-plated and enameled brass, circa 1933, produced by Mutual-Sunset Lamp Manufacturing Company, Brooklyn, NY., 7" x 14" x 2-1/2". **$1,375**

Courtesy of Sotheby's, www.sothebys.com

M. LeVerrier (1891-1973) Art Deco monkey lamp, cast metal and stone, in the form of a monkey holding a lantern, looking, listening and whispering-the antithesis of the three wise monkeys (see no evil, hear, no evil, speak no evil), green patina, signed M. LeVerrier, raised on a green marble plinth, wired with a 6-volt voltage converter with 12 -volt bulb, 6-1/2" h. **$1,230**

Courtesy of Skinner Auctioneers and Appraisers, www.skinnerinc.com

A French Art Nouveau polychrome pottery figural floor lamp with Loetz feather-pulled iridescent glass shade, Klostermuhle, Austria, circa 1905, marks: F. ROY, 45-1/2" h..............**$3,000**

Courtesy of Heritage Auctions, www.ha.com

L

LAMPS & LIGHTING

Vintage Danish pendant lamp, likely by Fog and Morup, made of copper, teak and pespex roundels, 12" dia. **$60**

Courtesy of Dickins Auctioneers, www.dickinsauctioneers.com

Poul Henningsen pendant lamp, shade PH 4/4, impressed pat-appl copper, patinated bronze, circa 1928, 29-1/2" drop as shown, 15-3/4" dia. **$9,375**

Courtesy of Sotheby's, www.sothebys.com

Paavo Tynell adjustable ceiling light, model No. A1957, with original counterweight mechanism and ceiling canopy, patinated and lacquered perforated brass, circa 1955, produced by Taito Oy, Helsinki, Finland, shade is 14-1/2" h, 7-1/2" dia....................... **$7,500**

Courtesy of Sotheby's, www.sothebys.com

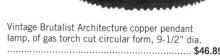

Vintage Brutalist Architecture copper pendant lamp, of gas torch cut circular form, 9-1/2" dia.
.... **$46.89**

Courtesy of Dickins Auctioneers, www.dickinsauctioneers.com

An Empire-style enameled composite and gilt bronze lamp base, early 20th century, 29" h. **$300**

Courtesy of Heritage Auctions, www.ha.com

A pair of Louis XVI-style gilt metal three-light wall sconces, late 19th century, 31" h x 16" w x 7-1/2" d. ....**$1,625.**

Courtesy of Heritage Auctions, www.ha.com

MAPS & GLOBES

MAP COLLECTING IS growing in visibility thanks to discoveries and sales of historically important maps. It remains a surprisingly affordable hobby when one considers most maps made in the early 19th century are hand-colored and represent the cutting edge of scientific knowledge at the time. Most examples from the last 400 years are available for less than $500, and engravings depicting America or its states may be owned for less than $150. Larger maps are usually worth more to collectors.

Globes, or terrestrial globes, have been around for centuries, taking back to the 1400s, when owning a globe was a rarity and reserved for only those with titles or riches. As time passed, globes became more widely available. Today antique globes offer collectors a unique view of the world as it existed in history.

GLOBES COMMANDING MORE AT AUCTION

"The globe market is very strong," says Kyle Lambalzer, who writes on his blog Collecting Antique and Vintage Globes [antiqueglobes.blogspot.com]. "Those in the best condition are very strong, globes like many antiques I think are very strong at the high end of the market, quality and condition will always bring a high price. The past two years have been generally stable to up for globes. Auction prices recently have been very good for the best examples."

Lambalzer says the most popularly collected globes today are those with a mid-century look - black ocean globes in particular. Smaller globes, eight inches or less in diameter, are also hot. "Vintage Tellurion models are on fire right now," he says.

New Orleans' Neal Auction Company offered a strong selection of antique and vintage globes in early 2017 to much collector interest. A circa 1866, fine American table globe, the cartouche reading "Loring's Nine and half Inch Terrestrial Globe, Boston, Josia Loring, Drawn and Engraved by W.H. Annin" sold within estimate for $2,562. Collectors zeroed in on the odd and unusual, such as a circa 1927 American 6" puzzle globe made by the Geographical Educator Company, New York, which sold for $1,708. The quizzical globe sphere is divided into seven sections, and then sub-divided with jigsaw maps of the continents. Another oddity also brought significant bidding as a 19th century German miniature novelty globe, attributed to Carl Bauer of Nuremburg, sold for $1,098. The unusual 1-3/4" diameter globe is tipped into a box and is actually an accordion strip showing 28 nationalities, labeled in French, English, and German.

Perhaps the most surprising sale was that of a late 19th century Laing's Planetarium, on a finely-turned wooden frame with a 3-inch globe of the earth on an elaborate pulley system showing the movements of Venus and the sun, which sold for $2,806, against a $1,000 pre-auction estimate.

The best advice for new collectors? From Lambalzer's perspective, newbie collectors should buy what they like: "But buy the best examples they can afford," he said. "Modern globes (those after WWII) are collectible to a point. But after 1960 there are few globes that are desirable generally speaking.

"Globes pre-1930 and especially from before 1900 are harder to find but good examples still come up for sale on a regular basis. New collectors usually start collecting maps and globes because they like history, or they are interested in a certain region of the world. For example a person very interested in WWII might want a globe from before, during, and after the conflict."

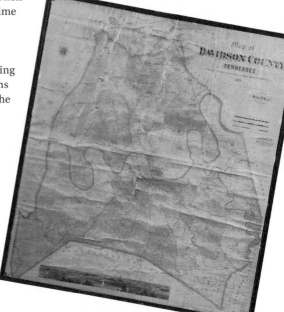

Map, 1779, Early English Engraved Map of Charleston, South Carolina, titled "An Exact Prospect of Charlestown, the Metropolis of the Province of South Carolina", after the painting by Bishop Roberts. Engraved by William Henry Toms for London Magazine and published in 1779, 2nd edition, unframed, 8-1/4" h. x 21-3/4" w., ...$4,012

Case Antiques Auctions & Appraisals, www.caseantiques.com

Lambalzer said globe collectors are connected online much more than one might think. "I use social media in the form of my blog, Pinterest, and I link posts on Facebook occasionally," he said. "The collector market for globes is surprisingly larger than I thought when I started blogging. I've met collectors on four continents via the web."

MAPS HOLDING STEADY

Values for antique maps hinge on a variety of factors. Unlike globes, the market for maps is highly fragmented based on interest for particular areas, periods, colors, size and budget. Once these factors are addressed, the collector has a very good idea of exactly what to focus on at auction or from other collectors, according to the longtime map seller Geographicus.

The ideal place for the beginning collector to purchase maps is commonly used auction sites such as eBay and Etsy.com. The challenging facing newbie collectors are the rampant reproductions of vintage and antique maps. Even maps from the 1940s are being reproduced at a rapid rate, let alone maps from the mid- to late-19th century. It's a "buyer beware" world out there in the map category. Experienced collectors can turn to online websites such as fleaglass.com, which brings together the world's top sellers of antique scientific instruments, including maps and globes. Prices are higher at specialty sites but the sellers are vetted and what is represented is authentic.

One of the top resources to learn about antique and vintage maps is the David Rumsey Collection, a historical map collection of more than 76,000 maps and images online. The collection includes rare 16th through 21st century maps of America, North America, South America, Europe, Asia, Africa, Pacific and the World. Rumsey has donated his entire physical map collection to Stanford University where it is housed at the David Rumsey Map Center in the Stanford Library.

Map, 1871, Foster Map of Davidson County, Large, early and scarce map of Davidson County – "NASHVILLE, TENNESSEE, FROM ACTUAL SURVEYS MADE BY ORDER OF THE COUNTY COURT OF DAVIDSON COUNTY, 1871" surveyed and mapped by Wilbur F. Foster, Civil and Topographical Engineer; Engraved, printed and manufactured by G.W. and C. B. Colton of New York, 54" x 49" sight................................. $8,260

Case Antiques Auctions & Appraisals, www.caseantiques.com

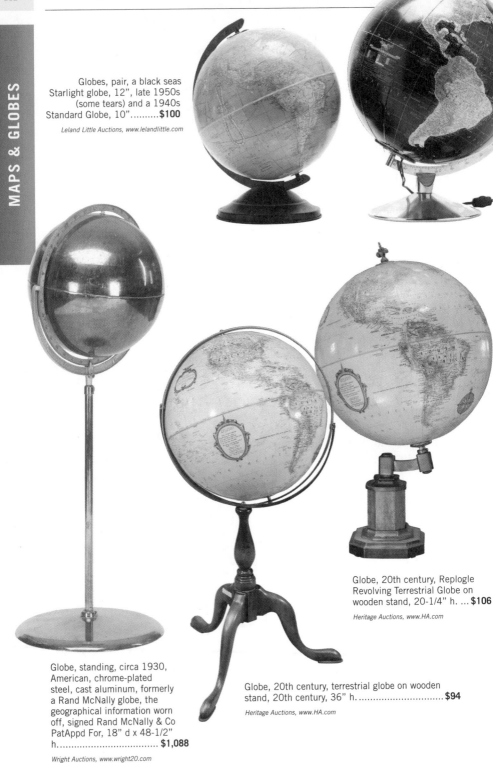

Globes, pair, a black seas
Starlight globe, 12", late 1950s
(some tears) and a 1940s
Standard Globe, 10"..........**$100**

Leland Little Auctions, www.lelandlittle.com

Globe, standing, circa 1930,
American, chrome-plated
steel, cast aluminum, formerly
a Rand McNally globe, the
geographical information worn
off, signed Rand McNally & Co
PatAppd For, 18" d x 48-1/2"
h.................................... **$1,088**

Wright Auctions, www.wright20.com

Globe, 20th century, Replogle
Revolving Terrestrial Globe on
wooden stand, 20-1/4" h. ... **$106**

Heritage Auctions, www.HA.com

Globe, 20th century, terrestrial globe on wooden
stand, 20th century, 36" h. **$94**

Heritage Auctions, www.HA.com

◀▲ Globe, mid-19th century, Holbrook's Apparatus Mfg. Co. Hinged Terrestrial Pocket Globe, Wethersfield, Connecticut, marks: HOLBROOK'S APPARATUS Mfg. Co., WETHERSFIELD, CT, 2-7/8" d. **$1,625**

Heritage Auctions, HA.com

▼ Lithograph, color, World Map After Gerardus Mercator, framed, 20-1/2" x 29"........ **$550**

Heritage Auctions, www.HA.com

Globe, circa 1920, Hughes & Son Mahogany Cased Star Globe, 8" h. **$2,031**

Heritage Auctions, www.HA.com

Globe, 20th century, inlaid with precious stones to denote continents, with stand, 15" x 13", globe measures 8" d.. **$80**

Don Presley Auction, www.donpresley.com

Map, 1853, Daniel Burgess, configuration of the West prior to the inclusion of Colorado, Idaho, Wyoming, Montana, Nevada and Arizona; New Mexico Territory is shown with the pre-Gadsden Purchase border plus the northern extension into today's Colorado; Oregon and Washington extend to the Continental Divide and a huge Nebraska Territory occupies the area to the east with a small area northeast of Utah labeled Kansas, states/territories are labeled with their population; locates numerous Indian tribes and military forts, from an 1857 Smith's Atlas of Modern and Ancient Geography, 8-1/4" x 10-1/4", ... **$120**

Jasper52, jasper52.com

Map, 1814, copperplate engraved map of Greece by Robert Wilkinson, full original hand coloring, 8-1/2" x 10", ... **$30**

Jasper52, jasper52.com

Map, Engraving with Hand Coloring of a World Map after Abraham Ortelius, framed, 12-1/4" x 17-1/4", ..**$350**

Heritage Auctions, HA.com

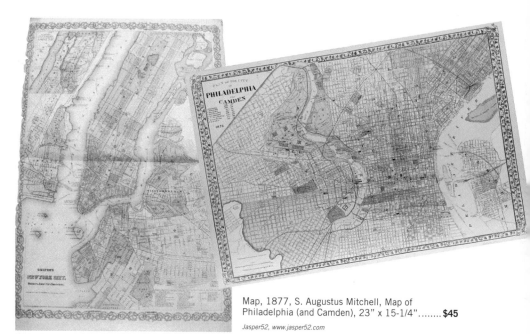

Map, 1877, S. Augustus Mitchell, Map of Philadelphia (and Camden), 23" x 15-1/4"........**$45**

Jasper52, www.jasper52.com

Map, 1865, C. B. Colton, New York City Map, showing New York City Brooklyn, Jersey City, Hoboken, shows ward districts, parks, streets, wards, buildings, rail lines, wharfs and many other features, inset shows Upper NYC and part of Westchester County, a large format map from a Civil War edition of "Colton's General Atlas," colored. 24" x 17" **$160**

Jasper52, www.jasper52.com

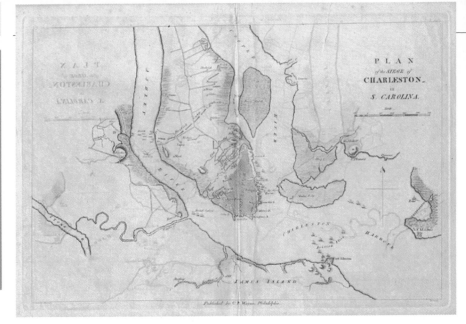

Map, 1807, "Plan of the Siege of Charleston in S. Carolina", published C.P. Wayne, Philadelphia, withdrawn from book, showing the location of downtown Charleston, Fort Sullivan (later named Fort Moultrie), Sullivan's Island, James Island, Fort Johnson, Ashley River, Cooper River and Stono River in 1780. The Siege of Charleston was a major engagement fought between March 29 and May 12, 1780 during the American Revolutionary War. The British, following the collapse of their northern strategy and their withdrawal from Philadelphia, shifted their focus to the American Southern Colonies, 18" x 11," $170

Raynors' Historical Collectible Auctions, hcaauctions.com

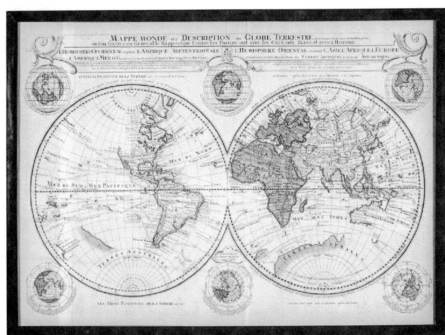

Map, 1750s, French, world map with explorers' routes and dates, hand-colored in double hemisphere, titled "Mappe Monde ou Description du Globe Terrestre," by Hendrik de Leth, map presents the World as Two Globes, no continent is shown in the southern regions, and the shape of Australia, which is shown connected to New Guinea and New Zealand, was uncertain, 26-1/2" w x 18.3/4" t. $1,200

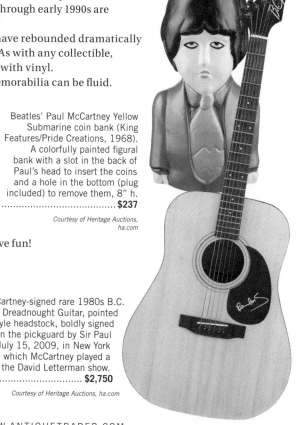

MUSIC MEMORABILIA

THE STATE OF the hobby for those who collect music and related memorabilia is healthy. Before the economy went south in 2008, multiple buyers might be in the market for a pricey item, such as a fully signed photo of The Beatles. The resulting bidding battle could drive the price up to $10,000. Today, pristine and rare examples of coveted items can bring hundreds of thousands of dollars. (See Beatles Collectibles earlier in the book to view record values for items from The Fab Four) Quality items from recongizable and popular performers are always in demand. The Beatles and Elvis remain the most popular but other artists are emerging as well.

Artists from the late 1970s and 1980s, especially hard rock, heavy metal and pop acts, are poised to be the next generation of headlining acts for collectors. Bruce Springsteen, Nirvana and Punk memorabilia is growing in value. Memorabilia from recently deceased stars such as Prince and David Bowie is commanding top dollar.

And just as the desired artists are changing, so too are some of the items that are being collected. Concert posters are practically nonexistent today because there isn't much of a need for them anymore. Also on the endangered species list: ticket stubs, printed magazines, handbills and promotional materials. These items from the 1950s through early 1990s are collected with great enthusiasm today.

Vinyl records, once thought dead, have rebounded dramatically for listening pleasure and collecting. As with any collectible, demand, rarity and condition are key with vinyl.

Other than major players, music memorabilia can be fluid. Always collect what you like.

Investing in music memorabilia can be a risky proposition for newbies. Build a collection around your passion, be it punk, disco, concert posters, or all things Neil Diamond.

Strive to acquire items that are in the best condition possible and keep them that way. Always put a priority on provenance while weighing quantity and rarity. And most of all: have fun!

Beatles' Paul McCartney Yellow Submarine coin bank (King Features/Pride Creations, 1968). A colorfully painted figural bank with a slot in the back of Paul's head to insert the coins and a hole in the bottom (plug included) to remove them, 8" h.
.... **$237**

Courtesy of Heritage Auctions, ha.com

Paul McCartney-signed rare 1980s B.C. Rich Acoustic Dreadnought Guitar, pointed "Warlock"-style headstock, boldly signed in silver ink on the pickguard by Sir Paul McCartney on July 15, 2009, in New York City, the day on which McCartney played a rooftop concert for the David Letterman show.
.... **$2,750**

Courtesy of Heritage Auctions, ha.com

VISIT WWW.ANTIQUETRADER.COM

WWW.FACEBOOK.COM/ANTIQUETRADER

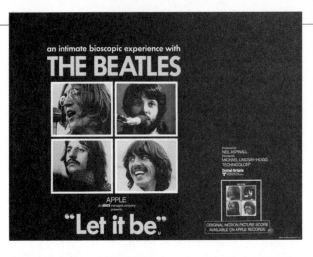

The Beatles – "Let It Be" (United Artists, 1970) British quad poster, mounted on linen, Very Fine+, 30" x 40"........................ **$1,314**

Courtesy of Heritage Auctions, ha.com

The Beatles "Yellow Submarine" (United Artists, 1968) British Pressbook, 10 pages, displaying much of the publicity and posters used to promote the film, includes a merchandising sheet showing product meant to be promoted with the film, design by Heinz Edelmann, Very Fine+, 14-1/4" x 9-3/4"..

$167

Courtesy of Heritage Auctions, ha.com

▼ Ringo Starr-signed color photo, circa 1968, autographed "Ringo Starr" by Beatles drummer in black ink, 8" x 11-1/4"........**$325**

Courtesy of Heritage Auctions, ha.com

▼ *Help!* (United Artists, 1965) lobby cards starring The Beatles, Very Fine, 11" x 14"...**$335**

Courtesy of Heritage Auctions, ha.com

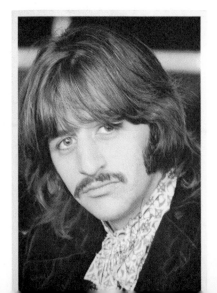

The Who, *The Kids Are Alright* (New World, 1979) movie photos, starring Roger Daltrey, John Entwistle, Keith Moon, Peter Townsend and Ringo Starr, Near Mint, 8" x 10"...............................**$65**

Courtesy of Heritage Auctions, ha.com

Steely Dan concert poster for an appearance at the Robertson Gym at the University of California, Santa Barbara, in 1974, Very Fine, 14-1/2" x 22-1/2"...**$79**

Courtesy of Heritage Auctions, ha.com

Roy Orbison-signed concert contract, dated March 30, 1973, for two consecutive shows on April 14 and 15, 1973, at the Swing Auditorium in San Bernardino, California. Included in this lot are two typed letters, to and from Acuff Rose Artists Corp. concerning the contract and payment for the shows, and one 8-1/2" x 11" black-and-white photo of the rock 'n' roll legend. **$575**

Courtesy of Heritage Auctions, ha.com

A pastel-on-paper portrait of Frank Zappa, from the estate of Frank and Gail Zappa, 18-1/2" x 15-1/4".. **$576**

Courtesy of Julien's Auctions, juliensauctions.com

Dr. Dre-signed "The Aftermath" poster, promotional poster for Dr. Dre's 1996 compilation, signed by the acclaimed rapper, producer, and mogul "Dr. Dre/ 96" in gold paint pen, Very Good+, approximately 18" x 24"....... **$500**

Courtesy of Heritage Auctions, ha.com

Atlanta Rhythm Section-signed "A Rock and Roll Alternative" RIAA Gold Record Sales Award (Polydor PD-1-6080, 1976) for their biggest hit single, "So Into You," signed in gold on the glass by "Ronnie Hammond," "Dean Daughtry," and "Barry Bailey." Plaque reads "Presented to Tim Riley to Commemorate the Sale of More Than 500,000 Copies of the Polydor Records Long-Playing Record Album 'A Rock & Roll Alternative'." framed, 17" x 21"..................... **$425**

Courtesy of Heritage Auctions

A group of three Prince guitar picks: the first is from the Welcome 2 America Tour, white "marble" plastic with "W2A" printed in purple on one side and "Prince" printed in script on the other; second has the Love symbol in gold metallic foil imprinted on both sides of a plastic hologram pick; third is a transparent blue plastic pick that also has the Love symbol in gold metallic foil imprinted on both sides.................................. **$896**

Courtesy of Julien's Auctions, juliensauctions.com

PETROLIANA

GASOLINE- AND OIL-RELATED collectibles are called petroliana. The category is dominated by signs, but it also includes posters, cans, premiums, lights, and service station items. Pieces are collected for display and a premium is placed on eye appeal and condition.

As with all advertising items, factors such as brand name, intricacy of design, color, age, condition, and rarity drastically affect value. Signs enjoying the hottest demand are those measuring 30 to 42 inches, in near mint condition, and with interesting graphics and bright colors.

Reproductions, fantasy pieces, and fakes have plagued petroliana collectors for decades. The relatively recent boon in the category has ushered in a new and diverse tidal wave of merchandise designed for fast profit, particularly porcelain signs. Brands such as Sinclair, Indian, Oilzum, and Mobilgas are actively sold on websites and at flea markets across the nation. These mass-produced signs are getting increasingly more difficult to distinguish from authentic, vintage survivors of the early 20th century.

The only way to avoid reproductions is experience: making mistakes and learning from them; talking with other collectors and dealers; finding reputable resources (including books and websites), and learning to invest wisely, buying the best examples one can afford.

Marks can be deceiving, paper labels and tags are often missing, and those that remain may be spurious. Adding to the confusion are "fantasy" pieces, globes that have no vintage counterpart, and that are often made more for visual impact than deception. There is another important factor to consider. A contemporary maker may create a "reproduction" sign or gas globe in tribute of the original, and sell it for what it is: a legitimate copy. Many of these are dated and signed by the artist or manufacturer, and these legitimate copies are highly collectible today. Such items are not intended to be frauds.

But a contemporary piece may pass through many hands between the time it leaves the maker and wind up in a collection. When profit is the only motive of a reseller, details about origin, ownership, and age can become a slippery slope of guesses, attribution, and – unfortunately – fabrication.

Beacon Security Gasoline "A Caminol Product" Lighthouse die-cut sign, 48" x 30", likely the finest example know to exist. **$55,000**

A few tips to keep in mind when purchasing petroliana signs:

1. No two porcelain signs are ever truly identical. The original process used to make them was imperfect to begin with – each color layer of enamel was added and baked on in a special

kiln at temperatures specific to each color. It's entirely natural that imperfections would occur, and authenticators now rely on these variations in much the same way as the FBI uses fingerprints.

2. Original signs are made of steel, not aluminum. A magnet will be attracted to an authentic sign.

3. Most circular signs are 28, 30, 42, or 48 inches in diameter. Look for telltale signs of use: scratches and deep chips around hang holes, even scratches around the perimeter from frames, rust on exposed steel in place of missing enamel.

For more information about petroliana, consult *Warman's Gas Station Collectibles* by Mark Moran. For more advice on how to intelligently buy petroliana signs, check out *Picker's Pocket Guide – Signs: How to Pick Antiques Like a Pro.*

Used Cars "Safety Tested" Oldsmobile sign, 42" d. **$4,250**

Atlantic Motorboat Oil "Brand New Power" counter-top display with round quart metal can.......**$525**

FINDING A FAKE

AUTHENTICATING A SIGN IS BEST LEFT TO PROFESSIONALS, BUT HERE ARE A FEW TIPS THAT CAN HELP:

- Be leery of rust spots that have not darkened with age.
- Enamel chips that expose gleaming steel is a bad sign.
- Watch out for uneven application of the porcelain.
- Missing mounting holes or grommets that appear unused are red flags
- Missing or smudged maker's marks are concerns.
- Authentic signs often, but not always, feature some type of stamp or markings on the back, either a maker's initials or a number denoting the enamel colors used on the front.
- Different enamel colors were layered on top of one another in the making of the sign, beginning with a white base coat. If you can feel the transition between one color and another then chances are the sign is original.

Greyhound with graphics sign, 24" x 40"...........................$450

▼ Mileage Gasoline with tire in motion logo sign, 14" x 20". $400

◄ Harbor Petroleum Products double-sided porcelain die-cut sign with sea plane graphics. $8,250

▼ Oliver Farm Implements "Plowmakers For The World" sign with logo, 14" x 48". $2,200

Golden West Oil Company sign, with Baby Blue Mountains graphics. **$2,700**

BMW convex sign with classic logo, rare prewar piece, 24" d. **$2,250**

Ford (mid-size) oval sign, 23" x 33". **$950**

Certified Garages Of America Association & Authorized Member By Invitation metal sign................................ **$3,700**

New old stock (NOS) John Deere two-legged Deer embossed self-framed sign, 42" x 38". **$375**

North Dakota Route 28
Highway sign, 15" x 15".....**$375**

▼ Oldsmobile Service
porcelain flange sign, 16" x
22"...................................**$900**

Vespa Service scooter sign with
logo, 31" d. **$1,500**

Shell (shark-tooth shape) sign,
48" x 48". **$1,750**

Speedwell Motor Oil porcelain flange sign with "Running Made Easy" logo...........**$600**

▲ Hard-to-find Studebaker Rockne Authorized Service Genuine Parts sign with logos. **$3,500**

◄ Five-pound metal can for Packard Cup Grease by Wolverine Lubricants........... **$375**

Original and hard-to-find Porsche Stuttgart sign with classic crest, dating to the 1960s. **$4,500**

Reliable Premium Regular 13-1/2" lenses in the original Capco globe body............. **$7,700**

PINBACKS

CONSIDERED THE DEAN of the pinback button, Ted Hake, namesake of Hake's Americana & Collectibles, says at least 2 million buttons have crossed his palms since 1960. It was in his junior year of high school when he discovered the little metal disks with interesting sayings or promotional images. Since then, he has gone to manage the sale of some of the largest and most important collections of pinback buttons to ever come to market – and he says that market remains strong and vibrant.

"After some 57 years and 2 million buttons, almost every day I still come upon buttons I'm seeing for the first time," he said. "Now is an ideal time to get into the hobby of collecting pinback buttons in the two broad categories of both political and non-political buttons."

The pinback button has been used in the United States since the first presidential inauguration in 1789, as George Washington supporters produced a slogan button which was designed to be sewn to the lapel of a coat or worn as a pendant. It wasn't until modern times that the pinback as we know it came to be. Benjamin S. Whitehead patented the first innovation to the design in 1893 by inserting a sheet of transparent film made ofcelluloidover a photograph mounted on abadgeto protect the image from scratches and abrasion. The innovation opened the door to his company (eventually renamed Whitehead & Hoag) to produce any manner of political or promotional button imagination would allow.

"My first large collection, about 50,000 buttonscame in the mid-1970s from the estate of Joe Stone in Toledo, Ohio, who started his collection as a boy in 1921 when he picked up a button from the street while on an errand for his mother," Hake recalls. "His collection became the basis for my book *Collectible Pin-Back Buttons 1896-1986."* By far my largest collection, around a million pieces in all categories, came from the estate of Greenwich Village collector Marshall Levin. From the 1960s through 1999, Marshall was the consummate button collector of the modern era. He established relationships with most of the New York City area button manufacturers and attended every protest rally and industry trade show he possibly could."

POLITICAL PINBACKS

Following World War II a handful of presidential campaign button collectors somehow found each other, joined forces and established the American Political Items Collectors (www.apic.us). The club had its first real growth spurt in the mid-1960s. There was very little documentation of the material at that point and what existed focused on the pre-button era items (mostly campaign tokens) prior to 1896.

Hake was the first to begin to document presidential campaign items with his 1974 book on the subject

Pinback, 1904, Alton B. Parker, diecut celluloid, crowing rooster with portrait of candidate at bottom, rooster and portrait are one piece of cello, and are affixed to thin metal back w/five tabs, 1-1/8" w x 1-7/8" t. **$1,740**

Hake's Americana & Collectibles, www.hakes.com

▲ Collection of Vintage NASA Pinback Buttons, 121 Pieces, Alan Shepard's Mercury flight in 1961 to the Space Shuttle missions in the 1980s, with Gemini, Apollo and Skylab in between, various sizes. **$1,000**

Heritage Auctions, www.HA.com

▶ Pinback, 1908, William Jennings Bryan, Western Buttons And Badges Denver Colo. back paper, fixed bar pin on reverse, portrait of Bryan set atop a map of the United States w/text at top "W. J. Bryan Our Next President." Additional slogans include: "Money Of The Constitution"; "Silver And Gold At 16 To 1"; "No Imperialism"; "No Trusts" and "The Home Of The Free And The Brave." Rare, 1-1/5", ...**$2,457**

Hake's Americana & Collectibles, www.hakes.com

▶ Pinback, 1900, William Jennings Bryan, filled metal back imprinted "Balto Badge & Nov Co.", fixed stick pin, portrait of a left facing Bryan is flanked by American flags and goddess figures, one holding a staff and the other a laurel wreath crown. Latin slogans around border translate as "The Hope Of The People Is The Supremacy Of The Law", "Where Liberty Dwells, There Is My Country" and "I Care About The Future," high-grade example, rare. **$1,900**

Hake's Americana & Collectibles, www.hakes.com

The Encyclopedia of Political Buttons 1896-1972. He followed up in 1977 with Political Buttons Book II 1920-1976 and Political Buttons Book III 1789-1916. All three books catalog some 15,000 buttons and other types of presidential campaign artifacts. Between these books and later books on particular types of items (ribbons, textiles, china, inaugural medals, etc.) collectors today have many resources for learning which items are common and which are scarce to rare. This is enhanced even more by internet sites such as eBay, Worthpoint and prices realized records for the past auctions of many different auction houses.

"The easy availability of historical pricing information, I feel, is the key factor contributing to the significant prices being paid for select and seldom offered presidential campaign items," Hake said.

For politicals, there are two reasons this is a great time to collect. For the collector on a budget, between eBay and auction houses, there is much historic but "common" material steadily available at very collector friendly prices. From 1896, the first year buttons were used, "common" McKinley or Bryan presidential campaign buttons can be bought in the $10-$25 range for beautiful, undamaged, pieces over 120 years old.

Pinbacks collection, complete set of King Features buttons (only missing one) that includes Popeye, Olive Oyl, Wimpy, Jeep, Flash Gordon, Dale Arden, and Little Annie Rooney, five different Superman pins, three Supermen of America pins, four Captain Marvel buttons, with a Spy Smasher, four different Dick Tracy, a Sergeant Preston pin, Shield G-Man Club pin, Flash Gordon button, Buck Rogers, Phantom Club, Tim Tyler's Luck Ivory Patrol Club, American Eagle Defenders, a "Some Swell Sweater" Little Orphan Annie Pin, Popeye and Wimpy on Saturday Chicago Americanpins, Lone Ranger, Joe Palooka, Steve Canyon, and Prince Valiant. The Flash and Wonder Woman, cloisonné pin for the Captain America Sentinels of Liberty, a Mandrake Magicians Club pin, and a Little Orphan Annie Secret Society pin, three small pins that feature Krazy Kat, Mutt and Jeff, Spirit pin that is the only modern age item included, various sizes. ... **$4,541**

Heritage Auctions, www.HA.com

Pinback, maker Parisian, Chicago, News Junior League Center Field, concave metal back and fixed horizontal bar pin, 1-1/4". **$140**

Hake's Americana & Collectibles, www.hakes.com

Pinback, 1896, Boss Peanut Roasters, Whitehead & Hoag back paper used only in 1896, wagon's side reads "Fresh Roasted", rare, 7/8". **$289**

Hake's Americana & Collectibles, www.hakes.com

Pinback, circa 1896-98, Whitehead & Hoag back paper, considered first Hershey's Chocolate button, pictured is well dressed young boy at table with china serving pieces for cocoa, tiny caption below reads "Bitter Sweet." Scene flanked at sides by "Trade Mark," only known example to exist, 7/8"............ **$118**

Hake's Americana & Collectibles, www.hakes.com

Pinback, Steve Allen's rare and personally owned Rat Pack pin, in the shape of a rat, with stone red eyes, engraved "Steve Allen" on the front, 1" x 1/2",......... **$500**

Premiere Props, www.premiereprops.com

Pinback, c. 1904, the black baker instructs "Ask Your Grocer" as he displays handsome bread loaf made from Duluth Imperial Flour, 1-3/4". **$157**

Hake's Americana & Collectibles, www.hakes.com

NON-POLITICAL PINBACKS

Non-political pinbacks, for the most part, have always been affordable, Hake says. Some of the most popular categories are Santa Claus, colorful early 19thcentury product advertising especially farm machinery, gun powder and cars, World's Fairs (1901-1964), sports, in particular baseball, and entertainment focused buttons for comic characters, movie cowboys, famous movies and early television.

"If your budget can handle rarities, this is also a great time to collect as many of the collections formed in the early collecting era of the 1960s, which are now coming to market," Hake said. "Many of these collections hold rarities of which few examples are known. These gems will briefly be available on the market and then re-enter collections where they will be held for years to come."

Pinback, circa 1900-1912, superb color showing Arabian chieftain on his black stallion, , rare, 1-1/2" **$118**

Hake's Americana & Collectibles, www.hakes.com

Pinback, circa 1900-1912, back paper used only during these years, scarce, 1-1/4".. **$150**

Hake's Americana & Collectibles, www.hakes.com

Pinback, circa 1907-1920, with Bastian back paper only used these years, disheveled man with bottle, open collar and vest captioned below "Feel Like Hell!" stands next to dapper man perfectly groomed captioned below "Blue Jay Fixed Me", 1-1/4". **$118**

Hake's Americana & Collectibles, www.hakes.com

Pinback, circa 1907-1920, with Bastian back paper only used these years, color depiction of assumed brothers with younger holding product package and admonishing with pointed finger his frowning older brother who is pouring a dose into a spoon, rare, 1-1/4" **$118**

Hake's Americana & Collectibles, www.hakes.com

Pinback, circa 1910, without maker name or back paper, for tuberculosis sanatorium which opened outside Montreal near the town of Ninette, "Tag Day" (charity fundraiser where contributor's are given a tag as a thank you), button was likely issued a month later for the official opening ceremony, rare, 1-1/4". **$118**

Hake's Americana & Collectibles, www.hakes.com

Pinback, 1912, Theodore Roosevelt large metal, "Hat in the Ring" Badge.Rough Rider hat hangs loosely in center of the ring with relief letters: "My hat is in the ring. Teddy." from the Scott W. Dolson Collection, 2" dia., ... **$500**

Heritage Auctions, www.HA.com

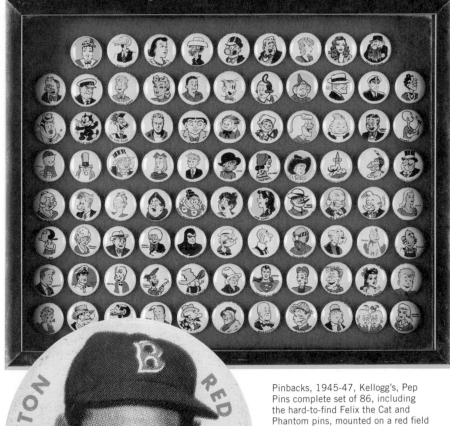

Pinbacks, 1945-47, Kellogg's, Pep Pins complete set of 86, including the hard-to-find Felix the Cat and Phantom pins, mounted on a red field and framed in a shadow box measuring approximately 11" x 9". **$956**

Heritage Auctions, www.HA.com

▲ Pinback, Ted Williams, one of the rarest buttons in the set of 60 different, 1-1/8"........**$115**

Hake's Americana & Collectibles, www.hakes.com

▶ Pinback, circa 1900, without back paper or maker name issued, only a few known, rare, 1-2/5"............**$160**

Hake's Americana & Collectibles, www.hakes.com

POSTERS

THE MARKET FOR collectible movie posters as well as vintage posters of all types is seeing a welcomed resurgence following a few soft years during the Great Recession. Record prices are returning to this hobby and more and more rarities are coming out of collector's closets and otherwise being brought to market. In most cases, the hobby's greatest surprises are those that surprised the owner in the first place.

New discoveries are literally coming out of the woodwork and defunct theaters and homes are being renovated and posters are found as insulation behind walls, under floors and stuffed in window sills. In late 2015, a trove of a 17 rare movie posters discovered under a linoleum floor in southern Pennsylvania sold for more than $200,000 at Heritage Auctions, the world's largest auctioneer of vintage posters. The find held lost pieces of Hollywood history – including five, never-before-seen posters such as Clark Gable's first starring role and the Style D one sheet for Tarzan The Ape Man, which sold for $83,650. The stash was discovered last summer by Bob and Dylan Basta while renovating a back room of a $40,000

The Good, the Bad and the Ugly (PEA, 1966), Italian premiere displays, set of 3, starring Clint Eastwood, Lee Van Cleef and Eli Wallach in the feature roles, 39" x 110". **$31,070**

VISIT WWW.ANTIQUETRADER.COM

WWW.FACEBOOK.COM/ANTIQUETRADER

home their father purchased at auction. When Bob and Dylan removed a dated linoleum floor they discovered layers of newspapers from the 1940s and 14 movie posters from obscure films they had never heard of well as the well-known Tarzan.

"When you work on homes like this all your life you always dream of that day when you actually find something rare and it seldom comes," said Robert Basta, a contractor. "I'm excited for my boys, now they have a story and a memory that will last their lifetimes."

Robert said many people would place paper, especially newspapers, under linoleum to help cushion the floor and eliminate wear. But once his sons started researching the movie titles online they quickly learned the posters under the floor were not your average discovery. The collection held the only known surviving movie posters for *Congorilla* (Fox, 1932), an early 1932 documentary filmed in Africa ($2,390); *Sporting Blood* (MGM, 1931) Clark Gable's first starring role; *Tess of the Storm Country* (Fox, 1932), an Academy Award nominated film starring Janet Gaynor and Charles Farrell ($776) and *Any Old Port*, an MGM short starring the comedy duo Laurel and Hardy ($8,962).

"It took a day or so to sink in until we realized these weren't going to a local auction," Basta said. It helped that the home the family was renovating was located just a few blocks away from a defunct movie theater.

In recent years, several important posters were found in this manner. Grey Smith, director of vintage posters at Heritage Auctions, says there are three things that influence the demand for a movie poster.

THE FILM
Collectors that love a film would like to have an original release poster. Values for Academy Award-wining posters are generally higher than those of non-award winners. The universal appeal adds to the boost in demand in the long run.

THE TALENT
For a collector who wants to complete a run of all of the films done by Clark Gable, they will buy a poster just for that reason alone. A one sheet poster for *Red Headed Woman* (MGM, 1932) starring the lovely Jean Harlow is worth roughly $70,000-$80,000 because of the demand for the colorful poster. Harlow's face glows out of the red background in astoundingly vivid stone litho color making her appear to be demonic, which her character lives up to.

THE GRAPHICS
A number of films that are not were not terribly successful films but have posters with truly outstanding graphics see significant demand in today's market. For instance, the obscure exploitation film *Marihuana* or *Assassin of Youth* is valued at about $12,000 was a 1937 film on the dangers of smoking cannabis. The graphics are so much fun, Smith says, they are so over the top that it really draws in collectors .

The same goes for 1950s B-movies that were never huge commercial successes, such as *Attack of the 50 Foot Woman*, which went down in history for its movie poster rather than the film itself.

RECENT RECORDS
When only-known posters reach the market they can set new price ceilings for the hobby. The only known copy of the U.S. release one sheet from the 1927 lost cinema classic London After Midnight (MGM, 1927) sold recently for $478,000, breaking the record for the most valuable movie poster ever sold at public auction. "This is one of the most sought-after posters of the 20th century and the only example known to exist," said Smith. "This was the only copy of the rare U.S. one sheet known to exist."

The Maltese Falcon (Warner Brothers, 1941), half sheet, thriller, style B, starring Humphry Bogart, Mary Astor, Peter Lorre, Elisha Cook Jr., and Sydney Greenstreet, 22" x 28". **$13,145**

The Raily's Cycling Act (Affiches Marci Bruxelles, 1890) advertising poster, Belgian, advertises a traveling Western-themed show that included a cowboy doing tricks not on a horse, but a bicycle instead, 32-1/4" x 45". **$776**

Heritage Auctions, www.HA.com

The Astounding She Monster (American International, 1958), one sheet, science fiction, starring Shirley Kilpatrick, Robert Clarke, Kenne Duncan, Marilyn Harvey, Jeanne Tatum, Ewing Miles Brown, Scott Douglas and Al Avalon. Directed by Ronald V. Ashcroft, artwork by Albert Kalli, 27" x 41". **$575**

Weiss Auctions, www.weissauctions.com

Concert Poster, Janis Joplin, June 26, 1968, New York Aerodrome Concert, Schenectady NY, "Live In Concert, 2 Shows," art by Gary Butts, artist's proof copy, signed in pencil by artist, 1 of approx. 35 pulled from the screen, 14" x 22," mint. **$12,000**

Weiss Auctions, www.weissauctions.com

World War II Propaganda poster set: "More Production" (War Production Board No. A-11, 1942) printed by the U.S. Government Printing Office, depicting Hirohito, Mussolini, and Hitler victoriously pursued down a slope by the giant snowball of increasing U.S. war production, 28-1/2» x 40»; "Pour It On!" (War Production Board No. A-14, 1942) printed by the U.S. Government Printing Office, depicting the powerful forging of U.S. aircraft, ships and submarines for the war effort, 28-1/2" x 40". **$358**

Heritage Auctions, www.HA.com

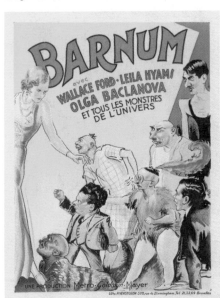

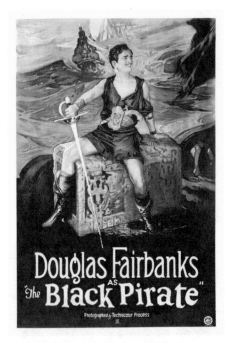

Freaks (MGM, 1932), Belgian, *Freaks* was MGM's answer to Universal Studio's monsters, by introducing people to the garish world of the circus sideshow, replete with bearded lady, vain acrobats, pinheads, a armless and legless man, dwarves and a hermaphrodite, rare, 24" x 31", ...**$28,680.**

Heritage Auctions, www.HA.com

The Black Pirate (United Artists, 1926), adventure, one sheet, starring Douglas Fairbanks, 27" x 41", ... **$6,672**

Heritage Auctions, www.HA.com

Motivational Poster (Facebook.com, 2010s) "Don't Mistake Motion for Progress", screen print, designed by Ben Barry, and produced with Everett Katigbak in Facebook.com's Analog Research Lab, 1/100, 18" X 24".. **$454**

Heritage Auctions, HA.com

Motivational Poster Set (Facebook.com, 2010s) "Move Fast and Break Things" and "What Would You Do if You Weren't Afraid", screen print, designed by Ben Barry, and produced with Everett Katigbak in Facebook.com's Analog Research Lab, 1/100, 18" x 24".. **$836**

Heritage Auctions, www.HA.com

Silver Bullet (Screencraft, R-1930s) Western, three sheet, starring Tom Tyler, Jayne Regan, Lafe McKee, and Charles King. Directed by Bernard B. Ray. Poster is in three sections, as originally printed, 41" x 78".. **$61**

Heritage Auctions, www.HA.com

The Barn Dance (Columbia, 1929), animation, stock one sheet, starring Mickey Mouse, posters from Mickey's early days before Disney made the switch from Columbia to United Artists are extremely rare, such as this stock one sheet the famous mouse's fourth animated short, rare, 29" x 42".. **$14,937**

Heritage Auctions, www.HA.com

The Bride of Frankenstein (Universal, 1935), title lobby card, starring Boris Karloff, Colin Clive and Brigitte Helm, the follow-up to the 1931 horror classic Frankenstein proved that sequels were not necessarily lesser quality vehicles than the original. 11" x 14". **$51,385**

Heritage Auctions, HA.com

Motivational Poster (Facebook.com, 2010s) "Slow Down and Fix Your Shit", screen print, designed by Ben Barry, and produced with Everett Katigbak in Facebook.com's Analog Research Lab, 1/100, 18" x 24". **$1,135**

Heritage Auctions, HA.com

The Perils of Pauline, 1914, Pathe - Eclectic, adventure, six sheet, Episode 18 - *The Tragic Plunge*, starring Pearl White, only remaining copy of this stone litho six sheet, 79-1/2" x 81-1/2". **$14,937**

Heritage Auctions, www.HA.com

The Wizard of Oz (MGM, 1939), half sheet, style A, starring Judy Garland, 22" x 28". **$71,700**

Heritage Auctions, www.HA.com

POSTWAR DESIGN

POSTWAR DESIGN, OR MID-CENTURY MODERN, describes mid-20th century developments in modern design, architecture and urban development. It is a style that is now recognized by scholars and museums worldwide as a significant design movement. It is also the lone segment of the furniture market that is still seeing significant price increases and volume movement among dealers and auction houses in today's market. However, demand is not limited to furniture.

The period collectors now seek spans 1945 through 1979. This includes posters, objets d'art, lamps, and even electronics. Naturally, a 34-year period will see a tremendous amount of change in taste and style but it is just this very reason why the period appeals to so many people – particularly Millenials and other young buyers.

The period distinguishes itself from Modernism, which lasted from 1920 to 1945. After this period, mass-produced wares brought high-design into the home at an affordable cost. Made from cast aluminum to chrome to brightly colored plastics, the period embraced new technologies to create an array of consumer goods that are now in high demand on the secondary market.

According to Noel Riley in her book *The Elements of Design*, the 1940s and 1950s were a period of transition between the austerity of the Second World War and its aftermath of rationing and shortages, and the youthful, exuberant design revolution of the 1960s. Impelled by the Modernist principles of functionalism, the contemporary aesthetic was defined by new materials and the development of technologies to use the effectively, as well as a spirit of optimism and confidence. It was a vigorous period in design, with bold shapes, bright colors, and practical solutions to the needs of daily life.

PLASTICS

A perfect example of these bold colors, new technologies and practical design are popularly collected bowls made of melamine plastic, popular among American home makers through the 1940s, 50s, 60s and 70s.

During the 1940s, new technologies made the production of plastic dinnerware possible and it subsequently became extremely popular in homes across America. According to JustCollecting.com, Melamine, a thermo set plastic material, was used in many factories and in much dinnerware production by the late 1940's. American Cyanamid was one of the leading manufacturers and distributors of melamine powder to various plastics molders. They name-branded their version "Melmac". Melamine, and more specifically "Melmac", was marketed by American Cyanamid as a wonder plastic. These bowls, now collected under the term Texas ware, sell for as much as $50 each on auction sites such as eBay and commerce sites such as Etsy.com.

Chair, Don Shoemaker (American, 20th century), Sling Chair (set of two), circa 1950, oiled rosewood, leather, 28" l x 23-1/4" w x 29" d. **$2,375**

Heritage Auctions, www.HA.com

CERAMICS

Post-war ceramics enjoyed the same explosion of color and style as artists tossed conventions out and ushered in a new era of elegant shapes and progressive patterns. The hourglass form was favored in the 1950s and this form is an excellent method to date ceramics from this period.

Although genre busting, the ceramics of the Postwar era strictly adhered to functionality, combining organic shapes with ease of use. This period saw the emergence of Danish studio potters who took influence from Japan and organic forms from nature to create distinctive and innovative soft shapes.

Artist Berndt Friberg's hand-thrown haresfur vases (now valued at $600 and up) exemplify this approach, as do bell-form tall mid century vintage lamps, dating from the 60s. These familiar lamps feature a smooth and textured ceramic body with drip glazed decoration in vivid hues. The stem and base are often wood.

TEXTILES

A bolt of circa 1949-50 Salvador Dali surreal art fabric recently sold for $3,750 at auction. Schiffer Prints commissioned an assortment of Modernist artists, architects, and industrial designers to create a Modern textile range. Designers included: Salvador Dali, Ray Eames, George Nelson, Bernard Rudofsky, Abel Sorenson, George Nelson, Irving Harper, Paul McCobb and Edward J. Wormley.

Schiffer didn't alter or modify the patterns and did not impose a theme or color palette. The results were dramatic. "Unquestionably it is the most brilliant single collection of all modern prints introduced since the war," declared the New York Times on June 22, 1949, when Schiffer Prints introduced their Stimulus line at the Architectural League of New York.

Dali designed three Surrealist prints chosen by Schiffer for production in 1949: Seste Elenique, Afternoon Stones, and Sonata d'Ete. Later that year Schiffer issued a second collection incorporating Dali's final two prints for them, Leaf Hands and Spring Rain.

The results set the tone for Post-war draperies, dresses, shirts, pants, and nearly every other form of textile worn or seen through the period.

Coffee table, A.H. Stock Model 1500 Boomerang grand coffee (or cocktail) table, with a design that was featured at the 1962 World's Fair. .... **$300-$500.**

John McInnis Auctions, www.mcinnisauctions.com

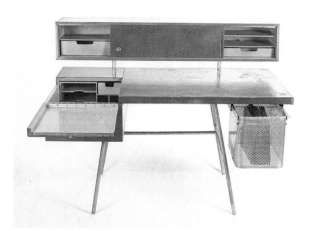

Sconces, pair, France, 1950s, stitched saddle leather, gilt metal, paper shades, two sockets each, unmarked, 20-1/2" t x 17-1/2" w x 6-1/2" t. **$5,625**

Rago Arts and Auction Center, www.ragoarts.com

Desk, George Nelson, mahogany veneer desk made for Herman Miller, with leather writing surface, a lid and top cabinet that both open to reveal shelves. .... **$300-$500.**

John McInnis Auctions, mcinnisauctions.com

Slagelse_Mobelvaerk.jpg Loveseat, Slagelse Mobelvaerk designer, Denmark, 1950s, Stained wood, brass, lambswool, leather, unmarked, 31 1/2" t x 62" w x 33" d. **$2,625**

Rago Arts and Auction Center, ragoarts.com

top lot

Vladimir Kagan Sofa and Table

Born in Germany, the son of a Russian cabinetmaker, Vladimir Kagan (1927-2016) created streamlined furniture that celebrated form yet never sacrificed function. Kagan, who was inducted in the Interior Design Hall of Fame in 2009, worked in the heart of the progressive establishment, creating furniture for the United Nations in New York, for Disney, General Electric and GM. His celebrity clients included Marilyn Monroe and Gary Cooper. Kagan used wood as a sculptural element, with seductive curves and twists, without ever losing sight of the craft and skill needed to construct them.

This sofa and sofa table, which sold at a Rago Arts Auction for $26,250, is a w
example of his work. Commissioned in 1969, the vibrant curved sofa is 96 inche
curved table was designed specifically so that it cannot be seen when looking a
of the sofa. Kagan used Lucite and zebrawood veneer. The sofa was reupholste
with fabric personally selected by Kagan, who supervised the work in his shop.

Chair, Finn Juhl (1912 - 1989), Niels Vodder, NV-45 lounge chair, Denmark, 1950s, sculpted teak, leather piping, cloth upholstery, branded, 33" x 27" x 31". **$9,375**

Rago Arts and Auction Center, www.ragoarts.com

Cabinets, pair, DF-2000 cabinets, Raymond Loewy (1893-1986), Compagnie D'Esthetique Industrielle, France, 1970s, enameled steel, acrylic, laminate, manufacturer label to one, 30" x 61" x 21-1/2" and 29 1/2" x 41" x 21". **$3,750**

Rago Arts and Auction Center, www.ragoarts.com

Armchairs, Pierre Jeanneret (1896-1967), 10 V-leg armchairs from the Chandigarh administrative buildings, France/India, 1950s, teak, upholstery, cane, unmarked, 31" x 19-3/4" x 20"................. **$31,250**

Rago Arts and Auction Center, www.ragoarts.com

Server, Jean Cocteau design (French, 1889-1963), Tri-Level Server, circa 1950, painted melamine, 11" h. x 8" dia. **$2,000**

Heritage Auctions, www.HA.com

◄ Chair, Hans Wegner and Johannes Hansen, Bear Chair, Denmark, 1960s, Oak, upholstery, unmarked, rare, 37" x 36" x 37"....**$21,250**

Rago Arts and Auction Center, www.agoarts.com

► Rocking chair (no. 175F), New York, 1970s, Vladimir Kagan Designs Inc., sculpted walnut, wool, leather, unmarked, 39" x 32" x 43" **$11,875**

Rago Arts and Auction Center, www.ragoarts.com

▲ Sofa, three-seat sofa, Phil Powell (1919-2008), New Hope, PA, 1960s, Sculpted walnut, upholstery, Unmarked, 28" x 78-1/2" x 32". **$20,000**

Rago Arts and Auction Center, www.ragoarts.com

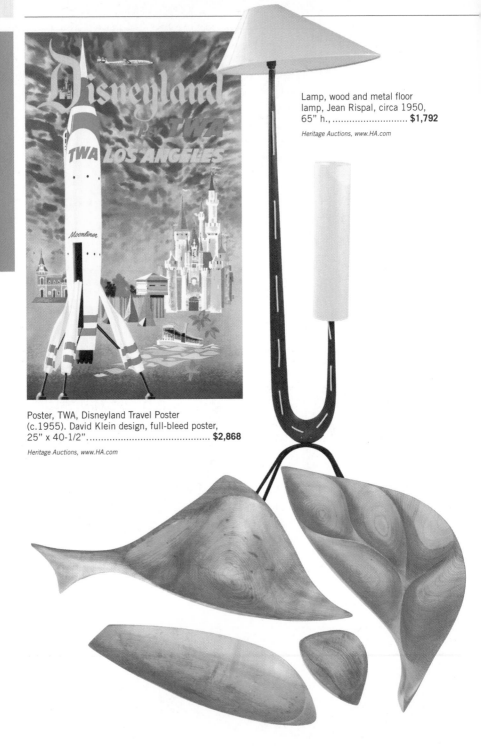

Lamp, wood and metal floor
lamp, Jean Rispal, circa 1950,
65" h., ... **$1,792**

Heritage Auctions, www.HA.com

Poster, TWA, Disneyland Travel Poster
(c.1955). David Klein design, full-bleed poster,
25" x 40-1/2".. **$2,868**

Heritage Auctions, www.HA.com

Bowls and trays, Emil Milan, circa 1973-1976, carved English oak, birch and maple, each with incised
signature and material to underside, 3-3/4" x 27-1/4" x 12-1/2"...**$325**

Heritage Auctions, www.HA.com

QUILTS

EACH GENERATION MADE quilts, comforters, and coverlets, all intended to be used. Many were used into oblivion and rest in quilt heaven, but for myriad reasons, some have survived. Many of them remain because they were not used but stored, often forgotten, in trunks and linen cabinets.

A quilt is made up of three layers: the top, which can be a solid piece of fabric, appliquéd, pieced, or a combination; the back, which can be another solid piece of fabric or pieced; and the batting, the center layer, which can be cotton, wool, polyester, a blend of poly and cotton, or even silk. Many vintage quilts are batted with an old blanket or even another old, worn quilt.

The fabrics are usually cotton or wool or fine fancy fabrics like silk, velvet, satin, and taffeta. The layers of a true quilt are held together by the stitching – or quilting – that goes through all three layers and is usually worked in a design or pattern that enhances the piece overall.

Quilts made from a seemingly single solid piece of fabric are known as wholecloth quilts, or if they are white, as whitework quilts. Usually such quilts are constructed from two or more pieces of the same fabric joined to make up the necessary width. They are often quilted quite elaborately, and the seams virtually disappear within the decorative stitching. Most wholecloth quilts are solid-colored, but prints were also used. Whitework quilts were often made as bridal quilts and many were kept for "best," which means that they have survived in reasonable numbers.

Wholecloth quilts were among the earliest type of quilted bedcovers made in Britain, and the colonists brought examples with them according to inventory lists that exist from colonial times. American quiltmakers used the patterns early in the nation's history, and some were carried with settlers moving west across the Appalachians.

Appliqué quilts are made from shapes cut from fabric and applied, or appliquéd, to a background, usually solid-colored on vintage quilts, to make a design. Early appliqué quilts dating back to the 18th century were often worked in a technique called broderie perse, or Persian embroidery, in which printed motifs were cut from a piece of fabric, such as costly chintz, and applied to a plain, less-expensive background cloth.

Appliqué was popular in the 1800s, and there are thousands of examples, from exquisite, brightly colored Baltimore Album quilts made in and around Baltimore between circa 1840 and 1860, to elegant four-block quilts made later in the century. Many appliqué quilts are pictorial with floral designs the predominant motif. In the 20th century, appliqué again enjoyed an upswing, especially during the Colonial Revival period, and thousands were made from patterns or appliqué kits that were marketed and sold from 1900 through the 1950s.

Pieced or patchwork quilts are made by cutting fabric into shapes and sewing them together to make a larger piece of cloth. Patchwork became popular in the United States in the early 1800s. The patterns are usually geometric, and their effectiveness depends heavily on the contrast of not just the colors themselves, but of color value as well.

Colonial clothing was almost always made using cloth cut into squares or rectangles, but after the Revolutionary War, when fabric became more widely available, shaped garments were made, and these garments left scraps. Frugal housewives, especially among the westward-bound pioneers, began to use these cutoffs to put together blocks that could then be made into quilts. Patchwork quilts are by far the most numerous of all vintage-quilt categories, and the diversity of style, construction, and effect that can be found is a study all its own.

Dating a quilt is a tricky business unless the maker included the date on the finished item, and unfortunately for historians and collectors, few did. The value of a particular example is affected by its age, of course, and educating yourself about dating methods is invaluable. There are several aspects that can offer guidelines for establishing a date. These include fabrics, patterns, technique, borders, binding, batting, backing, quilting method, and colors and dyes.

In recent years many significant quilt collections have appeared in the halls of museums around the world, enticing both quilters and practitioners of art appreciation. One of the most noted collections to become a national exhibition in 2014 was the Pilgrim/Roy Collection. The selection of quilts included in the "Quilts and Color" exhibition, presented by the Museum of Fine Arts in Boston, was a mix of materials and designs, represented in nearly 60 distinct 19th and 20th century quilts.

For more information on quilts, see *Warman's Vintage Quilts Identification and Price Guide* by Maggi McCormick Gordon.

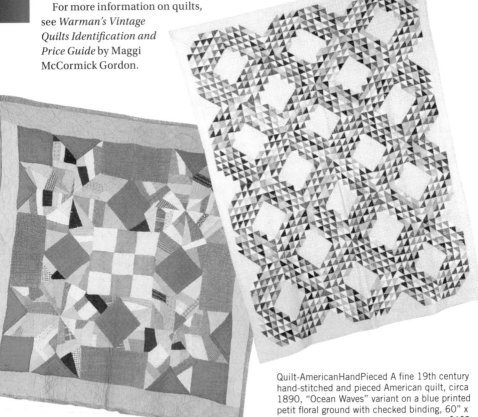

Quilt-AmericanHandPieced A fine 19th century hand-stitched and pieced American quilt, circa 1890, "Ocean Waves" variant on a blue printed petit floral ground with checked binding, 60" x 78". $120

Courtesy of Jackson's International Auctioneers and Appraisers, jacksonauction.com

Mennonite crib quilt, circa 1900, with a hand stitched and pieced crazy sample design with nine blocks, stars and squares on a blue ground with blue backing and blue stitched quilted designs of diagonal stripes, endless loops and floral baskets, 38" x 39". $200

Courtesy of Jackson's International Auctioneers and Appraisers, jacksonauction.com

Applique quilt with floral, bird and pineapple
design, 75" x 86".. **$1,500**

Courtesy of Alderfer Auction, alderferauction.com

Lone Star variation pieced
quilt, colorful design, 72" x
75"................................... **$450**

Courtesy of Alderfer Auction, alderferauction.com

Quilt with diamonds/squares, 19th
century, 81" x 104". **$90**

*Courtesy of EstateOfMind Auctions,
liveauctioneers.com/estate-of-mind*

Antique quilt with "Lemon Peel" pattern, 20th
century, 64" x 76". **$500**

Courtesy of EstateOfMind Auctions, liveauctioneers.com/estate-of-mind

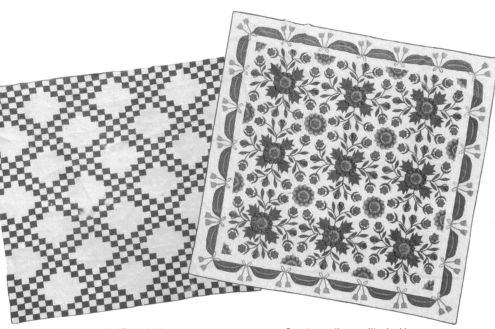

Star of Bethlehem quilt, c. 1915, Pennsylvania Mennonite, maroon, orange, tan, and pale yellow with triple border, hand-pieced and hand-quilted, basted Velcro mount at top and bottom corners, Excellent condition, 76-1/2" square. **$180**

Courtesy of Farmer Auctions, farmer-auctions.com

Amish Shoofly variation cotton quilt, c. 1925, piecing in shades of blue, green and purple, wide purple border with green binding, decorative hand-quilting throughout, basted Velcro mount at top, 44-1/2" l x 34-1/2" w. **$160**

Courtesy of Farmer Auctions, farmer-auctions.com

Antique quilt, "Triple Irish Chain" heart trapunto, 19th century, 70" x 77". **$60**

Courtesy of EstateOfMind Auctions, liveauctioneers.com/estate-of-mind

Country applique quilt, cheddar whig rose/tassel, drape border, 19th century, 84" x 84"...... **$800**

Courtesy of EstateOfMind Auctions, liveauctioneers.com/estate-of-mind

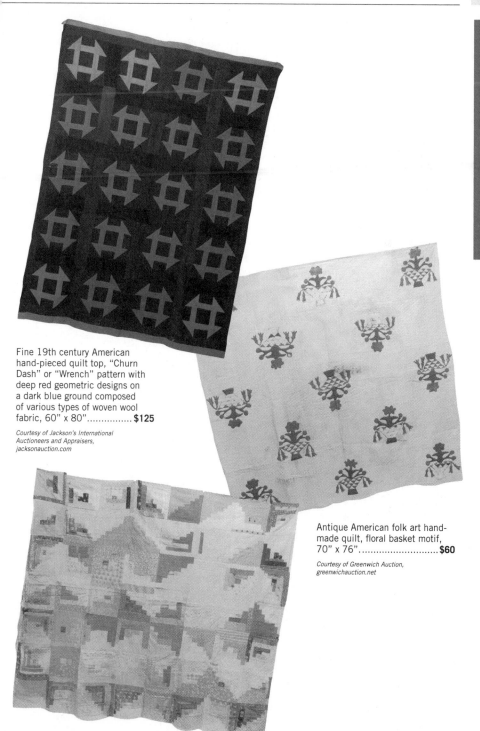

Fine 19th century American hand-pieced quilt top, "Churn Dash" or "Wrench" pattern with deep red geometric designs on a dark blue ground composed of various types of woven wool fabric, 60" x 80"................ **$125**

Courtesy of Jackson's International Auctioneers and Appraisers, jacksonauction.com

Antique American folk art hand-made quilt, floral basket motif, 70" x 76".............................**$60**

Courtesy of Greenwich Auction, greenwichauction.net

Antique American folk art hand-made quilt with log cabin pattern/patch work style, approximately 70" x 60".. **$60**

Courtesy of Greenwich Auction, greenwichauction.net

Early Canadian quilt, 48" x
64"...................................**$225**

Courtesy of Copake Auction Inc.,
copakeauction.com

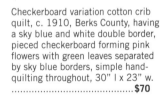

Checkerboard variation cotton crib
quilt, c. 1910, Berks County, having
a sky blue and white double border,
pieced checkerboard forming pink
flowers with green leaves separated
by sky blue borders, simple hand-
quilting throughout, 30" l x 23" w.
....**$70**

Courtesy of Farmer Auctions, farmer-auctions.com

Crazy quilt, 19th century, 66" x 69".
....**$575**

Courtesy of Copake Auction Inc., copakeauction.com

10 Things You Didn't Know About Quilts

1 Coverlets (woven bedcovers) came into popularity in the early 19th century in the U.S., and were more common than quilts during this time period.

2 These woven items were often made of cotton and wool, and in many instances people would bring their request for a coverlet to a local weaver to be constructed.

3 In the early 1800s, French inventor Joseph Marie Jacquard designed an attachment that would fit on a loom, allowing for more intricate designs to be incorporated in a coverlet. The attachment reportedly saved time and money, and utilized a punch card process.

4 In January 2011, Pook and Pook, Inc. sold an uncommon red and white jacquard coverlet, with an eagle border, constructed by Garret William Van Doren in 1836. The coverlet commanded $2,430 (with buyer's premium).

5 In the early-to-mid 19th century, a jacquard coverlet could be purchased for anywhere from $2 to $15 (depending on size and design).

6 The National Museum of the American Coverlet is located in Bedford, Pennsylvania. The museum's holdings include an extensive collection of coverlets, along with a display of weaving devices. The Museum regularly offers classes in textile making. (www.coverletmuseum.org)

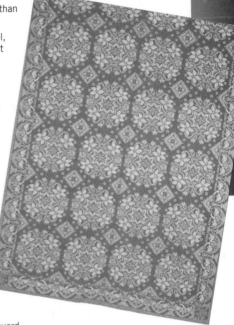

7 In America, the practice of making coverlets using jacquard looms and similar devices began to fade during the fourth quarter of the 19th century. The import of cheaper materials into the U.S. became a difficult hurdle for weavers to overcome.

Red and white jacquard coverlet, boasting a detailed eagle image border, circa 1836, sold for $2,430.

Photo courtesy Pook & Pook, Inc.

8 Some of the factors that impact the value of antique coverlets sold on the secondary market today include condition, family provenance or origin of the maker, intricacy of details and pattern.

9 Very few jacquard looms still exist today, but at the Shelburne Museum in Shelburne, Vermont, there is a scarce 1890s jacquard loom featured in an exhibition of barn-frame looms. (www.shelburnemuseum.org)

10 A four-color, two-part jacquard coverlet, with a floral center and geometric border, made in Lancaster County, Pennsylvania, and signed "J. Brosey, (Manheim) E. Danner 1848," realized $2,178 in November 2015, when it was brought to auction by Conestoga Auction Company — a division of Hess Auction Group.

– Compiled by Antoinette Rahn

A two-part jacquard coverlet that sold for $2,178. See #10 for more information.

Photo courtesy Conestoga Auction Company

Sources: www.colonialsense.com; www.drloriv.com; www.liveauctioneers.com; www.shelburnemuseum.org; www.coverletmuseum.org

RECORDS

BEFORE YOU CAN determine a record's worth, you need to grade it. When visually grading records, use a direct light, such as a 100-watt desk lamp, to clearly show all defects. If you're dealing with a record that looks worse than it sounds, play grade it. You also need to assess the condition of each sleeve, cover, label, and insert. Think like the buyer as you set your grades. Records and covers always seem to look better when you're grading them to sell to someone else than when you're on the other side of the table, inspecting a record for purchase. If in doubt, go with the lower grade. And, if you have a still sealed record, subject it to as many of these same grading standards as you can without breaking the seal.

Goldmine Grading

MINT (M): Absolutely perfect. Mint never should be used as a grade unless more than one person agrees the item meets the criteria; few dealers or collectors use this term. There is no rule for calculating mint value; that is best negotiated between buyer and seller.
- Overall Appearance: Looks as if it just came off the manufacturing line.
- Record: Glossy, unmarred surface.
- Labels: Perfectly placed and free of writing, stickers, and spindle marks.
- Cover/Sleeve: Perfectly crisp and clean. Free of stains, discoloration, stickers, ring wear, dinged corners, sleeve splits, or writing.

NEAR MINT (NM) OR MINT MINUS (M-): Most dealers and collectors use NM/M- as their highest grade, implying that no record or sleeve is ever truly perfect. It's estimated that no more than 2% to 4% of all records remaining from the 1950s and 1960s truly meet near-mint standards.
- Overall Appearance: Looks as if it were opened for the first time. Includes all original pieces, including inner sleeve, lyric sheets, inserts, cover, and record.
- Record: Shiny surface is free of visible defects and surface noise at playback. Records can retain NM condition after many plays provided the record has been stored, used, and handled carefully.
- Labels: Properly pressed and centered on the record. Free of markings.
- Cover/Sleeve: Free of creases, ring wear, cutout markings, and seam splits. Picture sleeves look as if no record was ever housed inside. Hint: If you remove a 45 from its picture sleeve and store it separately, you will reduce the potential for damage to the sleeve.

VERY GOOD PLUS (VG+) OR EXCELLENT (EX+): Minor condition issues keep these records from a NM grade. Most collectors who want to play their records will be happy with VG+ records.
- Overall Appearance: Shows slight signs of wear.
- Record: May have slight warping, scuffs or scratches, but none that affects the sound. Expect minor signs of handling, such as marks around the center hole, light ring wear, or discoloration.
- Labels: Free of writing, stickers, or major blemishes.
- Cover/Sleeve: Outer cover may have a cutout mark. Both covers and picture sleeves may have slight creasing, minor seam wear or a split less than 1" long along the bottom.

The Beatles, *Yesterday And Today* (Capitol T-2553) 1966 mono original unpeeled (second state) "Butcher" cover LP, unopened, East Coast example (factory number "3" on back cover). Yellow inner sleeve is visible at opening. One small breathe hole in front cover shrink wrap. Front slick has been applied over catalog number in top right corner of cover. Right corners of cover slightly "pushed" **$4,500**

Rockaway Records

VERY GOOD (VG): VG records have more obvious flaws than records in better condition, but still offer a fine listening experience for the price.
- Overall Appearance: Shows signs of wear and handling, including visible groove wear, audible scratches and surface noise, ring wear, and seam splits.
- Record: Record lacks its original glossy finish and may show groove wear and scratches deep enough to feel with a fingernail. Expect some surface noise and audible scratches (especially during a song's introduction and ending), but not enough to overpower the music.
- Labels: May have minor writing, tape, or a sticker.
- Cover/Sleeve: Shows obvious signs of handling and wear, including dull or discolored images; ring wear; seam splits on one or more sides; writing or a price tag; bent corners; stains; or other problems. If the record has more than two of these problems, reduce its grade.

VERY GOOD MINUS (VG–), GOOD PLUS (G+) OR GOOD (G): A true G to VG- record still plays through without skipping, so it can serve as filler until something better comes along; you can always upgrade later. At most, these records sell for 10% to 15% of the near mint value.
- Overall Appearance: Shows considerable signs of handling, including visible groove wear, ring wear, seam splits, and damaged labels or covers.
- Record: The record plays through without skipping, but the surface sheen is almost gone, and the groove wear and surface noise is significant.
- Labels: Worn. Expect stains, heavy writing, and/or obvious damage from attempts to remove tape or stickers.
- Cover/Sleeve: Ring wear to the point of distraction; dinged and dog-eared edges; obvious seam splits; and heavy writing (such as radio station call letters or an owner's name).

FAIR (F) OR POOR (P): Only outrageously rare items ever sell for more than a few cents in this condition, if they sell at all. More likely, F or P records and covers will end up in the trash or be used to create clocks, journals, purses, jewelry, bowls, coasters or other art.
- Overall Appearance: Beat, trashed, and dull. Records may lack sleeves or covers.
- Record: Vinyl may be cracked, scratched, and/or warped to the point it skips.
- Labels: Expect stains, tears, soiling, marks, and damage, if the label is even there.
- Cover/Sleeve: Heavily damaged or absent.

The Beatles (Apple/EMI, 1978), sealed Limited-Edition Records (2) Red & Blue Vinyl. Featuring two sealed limited edition 2 disc vinyl records for *The Beatles: 1962-1966* (also known as "The Red Album") and *The Beatles: 1967-1970* ("The Blue Album"). Mint. **$109**

Heritage Auctions

The Beatles (Capitol Records, R-1970s). Original Factory Sealed Vinyl Record SWBO. A very lightly used, unrestored vinyl record, still in its original factory packaging. Near Mint. **$149**

Heritage Auctions

Jefferson Airplane, *Takes Off* (RCA, R-1973), autographed album cover by Marty Balin, Grace Slick, Spencer Dryden, Jack Casady, Paul Kantner, and Jorma Kaukonen. No letter of authenticity . **$197**

Heritage Auctions, ha.com

The Beatles, *Souvenir Of Their Visit to America*, V.J. Records, V.JEP 1- 903, vinyl Near Mint, album cover shows wear. **$80**

Carden Family Auction Service

Michael Jackson Signed *Bad* LP (Epic, 1987). A vinyl record of Jackson's 1987 smash hit album, autographed by the King of Pop in silver paint marker on the record itself. Matted, displayed and framed to an overall 26" x 17.5". In Excellent condition. **$1,500**

Heritage Auctions, ha.com

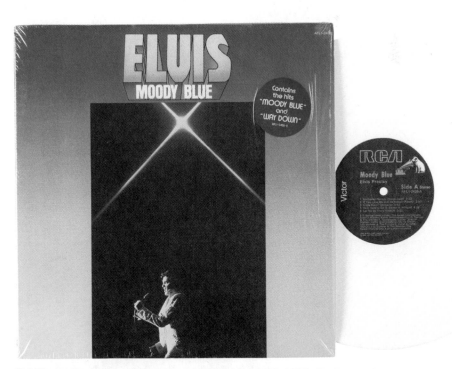

Elvis Presley *Moody Blue* white vinyl stereo LP (RCA AFL1-2428, 1977). The final studio album released before Elvis' death. Any colored vinyl version aside from the black or blue was produced in incredibly limited numbers, and were intended for RCA Records in-house use only. Condition: NM 8 (sleeve)/ EX 7 (disc)..**$937**

Heritage Auctions, ha.com

Elvis Presley, *Elvis Presley*, RCA EPB 1254, Double EP, with the silver line RCA labels. 7-inch 45s. First edition, 1957. Light ringwear on front and back cover. Cover grade VG+ vinyl VG+. **$50**

Elvis Presley, *Elvis Christmas Album*, RCA LOC 1035, mono LP, red vinyl, 1957. ....**$20,000**

The Rolling Stones, *England's Newest Hit Makers*, 1964, LP, London Records (LL3375 Mono), Fair condition **$30**

Desert West

Peter Frampton, *Frampton Comes Alive!*, A&M, SP-3703, 1976, double album considered one of the best live rock recordings of all time.............. **$12**

It's a Small World book and record (Disneyland, 1964) Disneyland record featuring songs from the "It's a Small World" attraction with an accompanying full-color illustrated book, 12-1/2" x 12-1/2", 11 pages. **$125**

Van Eaton Galleries

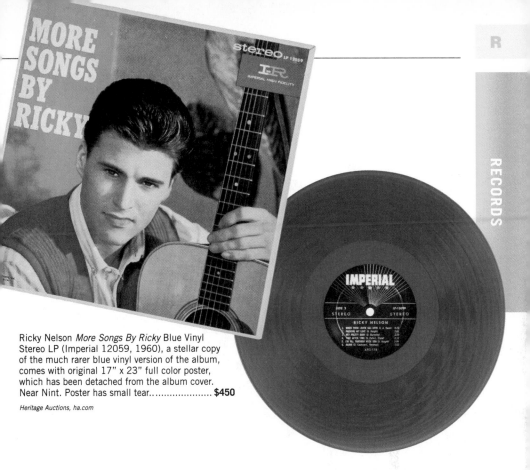

Ricky Nelson *More Songs By Ricky* Blue Vinyl
Stereo LP (Imperial 12059, 1960), a stellar copy
of the much rarer blue vinyl version of the album,
comes with original 17" x 23" full color poster,
which has been detached from the album cover.
Near Nint. Poster has small tear...................... **$450**

Heritage Auctions, ha.com

The Replacements, *Stink*, 12" vinyl, 45 RPM, EP,
Twin/Tone Records (TTR 8228), 1982, sealed.... **$40**

PashCo Posters

The Kinks, *Greatest Hits*, 1966, Reprise (R-
6217). **$25**

Bremo Auctions

Neil Young, *Harvest*,
1972, Reprise Records
(MS 2032).
.... **$10**

Bremo Auctions

▲ Alice Cooper, *Billion Dollar
Babies,* album, 1973, Warner Bros.
(BS2685), factory sealed, embossed
gatefold cove, includes set of cards
perforated on inside of gatefold.
Comes with a billion dollar banknote
foldout and a printed inner sleeve
with lyrics. **$324**

▶ The Colt 45's, *I Know I Love You/
Northern Soul*, 7-inch, 45 RPM, Good
condition. **$647**

Led Zeppelin, *Houses of The Holy*, LP, 1973, Atlantic (SD 7255) **$30**

Denise Ryan Auctions

◄ Metallica, *And Justice For All,* 1988, double album, Elektra Records, factory sealed **$269**

► Nirvana, *Nevermind*, album, US release, DGC (24425), 1991, VG+, Inner sleeve, NM. **$350**

SALESMAN SAMPLES

SALESMAN SAMPLES ARE not as rare as one might think but they are valuable and the market for them remains strong and robust. In general salesman samples can come in all shapes and sizes.

The days of the traveling salesman carrying a sample of his company's wares rarely darkened the doorstep of the average home. That task was reserved for the Sears & Roebuck Catalog, that annual doorstop that advertised itself as the "cheapest supply store on Earth."

Records show that the collecting term "salesman sample" is relatively recent term. During the 1970s, The Antique Trader Price Guide to Antiques included the items under its "Miniatures" category. Prices have increased 10 fold during that time and the collectibles have blossomed into a standalone category. Sometimes salesman samples also would have been classified under categories of the items, such as Furniture or Clocks.

Some defy classification. A salesman sample grain or corn silo was once produced, circa 1900, made of individual tongue and groove wood boards that are banded around the circumference. The model stands about 16" tall with its two-piece metal roof. The value of such an unusual salesman's sample can surpass $1,000 or more.

Salesman samples were almost always used in pitches to dry goods stores across the country during the mid-19th and early 20th century. In fact, salesman samples became pretty rare at the first quarter of the 20th century after the arrival of a more reliable postal system and a cheaper means of sending catalogs from suppliers directly to companies. Prior to those innovations, manufacturers depended on men who were willing to travel with a miniature sample and expound upon the benefits of the item.

That's part of the appeal of salesman's sample: They were not available to the general public and only the salesman and the shopkeeper were the only ones who really interacted with the object.

In rare cases, examples were placed on display for consumers to examine. This was especially the case with farm salesman samples.

Salesman's sample, Holy Bible, circa 1880, Globe Bible Publishing Co., Philadelphia, embossed and gilded leather covers, includes samples of different covers, spines, color lithograph prints, etc., blank pages at back to record subscribers, 12 1/2" x 10"....**$80**

Jeffrey S. Evans & Associates, www.jeffreysevans.com

DIFFERENT FROM TOYS

Some auctions houses do not know the difference between a salesman sample and toys from the same era. A miniature stove, highly detailed and complete with working accoutrements, can easily confuse both seller and buyer alike.

"The term salesman sample is often misused," according to Larry and Carole Meeker, antiques dealers and brokers in antique salesman samples. "Many sellers assume their toy stove, washer, sewing machine or other object is a salesman sample when in fact it is just a toy, and then proceed to grossly overvalue /overprice their mass produced toy."

VISIT WWW.ANTIQUETRADER.COM

WWW.FACEBOOK.COM/ANTIQUETRADER

Salesman sample, Kellogg Select-O-Phone Demonstration Kit with original carry case, features include secret conference feature, "lookout", and "busy" to assure a private line, party line ringing, no delay calling etc., demonstration kit folds together so the top fits over and latches to the base, ... **$400**

Rockabilly Auction Company, rockabillyauction.com

This same dilemma also arises with early steam toys. It is oftentimes hard to differentiate Model Steam Engine between what are obviously toys by such outfits as Jensen, Weyden, Plank, Marklin and others, and what are obviously shop built machinist made models of steam engines. These toys are often found in shops with tags mistakenly identifying them as salesman samples, or claiming toys from the 1980's are antiques from the 1880's. The Germans made some very detailed and exacting toy steam engines that look just like full size steam engines, but they are still toys. Then there are the detailed models of actual steam engines that have been made ever since the engines were made.

"Many people argue that in order for an object to be properly called a salesman sample it must have a case or box that it would be carried in that the door-to-door salesman would utilize," the Meekers say. "This is not always true. It might be an indication, or be useful as a negotiation ploy if what you have is in one, but the fact is many salesman samples never had a box and were not intended to."

You can still see salesman samples in use today. The next time you visit a department store, take a trip down the camping aisle. There you will likely see examples of small pup tents that are exact replicas of the tents on sale on the shelves below.

The same is true with toys. Toy aisles are now filled with interactive salesman samples that show off all the lights and movements a toy can perform. These are really no different than the salesman samples of yore.

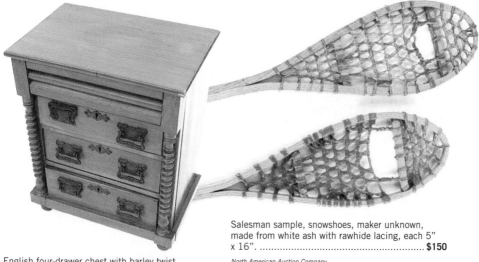

Salesman sample, snowshoes, maker unknown, made from white ash with rawhide lacing, each 5" x 16". **$150**

North American Auction Company,
www.northamericanauctioncompany.com

English four-drawer chest with barley twist columns, 14 1/2" x 9 3/4" x 17 1/2". **$24**

Roland Auctioneers & Valuers New York, www.rolandsantiques.com

Salesman sample, circa 19th century, workbench, walnut, 5" h. x 16" w. **$800**

EstateofMind Auctions, www.estateofmind.biz

Salesman sample, metal oven, maker unknown, accurate copy with burners, handles, pans, and more,. 17" x 14",... **$500**

Milestone Auctions, milestoneauctions.com

Salesman sample, stove, maker unknown, with original carrying trunk, tan marblized enamel finish with black enameled trim, black-splash with warming shelf, four burner cooking surface and hot water tank on right side, marked on oven door "Bake-Well," 15" w. x 9-1/4" d x 17" h., ... **$800**

Forsythes' Auctions, LLC, forsythesauctions.com

Salesman's sample, seeder 9" h. x 17" l. x 10-1/4" w. **$325**

Bright Star Antiques, www.brightstarantiques.com

Salesman sample, printing press, model of a Goss Cox-O-Type "flat bed" press, commonly used from 1910-1968, in its original leather case, with fabric belts, a steel base plate, and a painted iron press, 12 1/4" w. **$800**

Pook & Pook, Inc., www.pookandpook.com

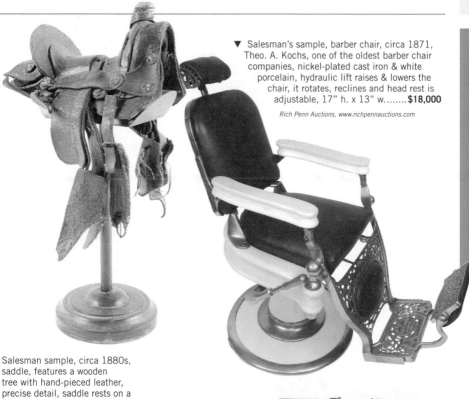

▼ Salesman's sample, barber chair, circa 1871, Theo. A. Kochs, one of the oldest barber chair companies, nickel-plated cast iron & white porcelain, hydraulic lift raises & lowers the chair, it rotates, reclines and head rest is adjustable, 17" h. x 13" w........**$18,000**

Rich Penn Auctions, www.richpennauctions.com

Salesman sample, circa 1880s, saddle, features a wooden tree with hand-pieced leather, precise detail, saddle rests on a wooden stand, 3-1/2" w x 5" t x 6" l.................................. **$325**

North American Auction Company, www.northamericanauctioncompany.com

Salesman sample, safe, marked "Manganese Steel Bank Safe," original felt lined wooden carrying case, rare, 17" l.**$13,000**

Morphy Auctions, www.morphyauctions.com

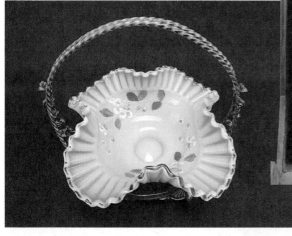

Salesman Sample, Bride's Basket, maker unknown, enameled cased glass with ribbon edge, rare, 7" l. x 6 1/2" w. x 2-1/2" t. **$85**

Matthew Bullock Auctioneers, bullockauctioneers.com

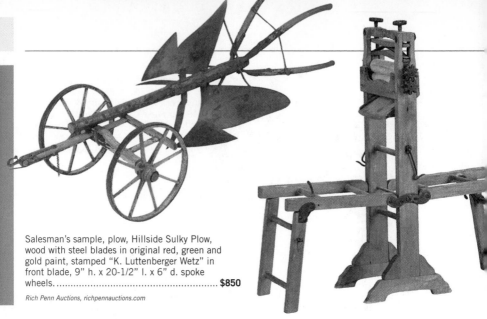

Salesman's sample, plow, Hillside Sulky Plow, wood with steel blades in original red, green and gold paint, stamped "K. Luttenberger Wetz" in front blade, 9" h. x 20-1/2" l. x 6" d. spoke wheels. **$850**

Rich Penn Auctions, richpennauctions.com

Salesman sample, wringer, marked "American Wringer Co. New York," wood with cast metal pieces, 5" w. x 15" l. x 16" t........................... **$225**

Morphy Auctions, www.morphyauctions.com

Salesman sample, grain cleaner, New Superior Salesman Sample Grain Cleaner, retains original stenciling and paint, 26" t. **$1,100**

Morphy Auctions, www.morphyauctions.com

Salesman sample, windmill, marked "Beard Mfg Co. Model M Angola Ind." early, original paint, 19" t.. **$6,000**

Morphy Auctions, www.morphyauctions.com

◄ Salesman sample, casket, marked "Aurora® Casket Co. Inc. / Because you care. / 32 ounce copper accoseal", sheet copper and aluminum, 21-1/2" t. x 29" w. x 14" d............................. **$75**

Morphy Auctions, www.morphyauctions.com

SPORTS

PEOPLE HAVE BEEN saving sports-related equipment since the inception of sports. Some of it was passed down from generation to generation for reuse; the rest was stored in closets, attics, and basements.

Two key trends brought attention to sports collectibles. First, decorators began using old sports items, particularly in restaurants. Second, collectors began to discover the thrill of owning the "real" thing.

There are collectible items representing nearly every sport, but baseball memorabilia is

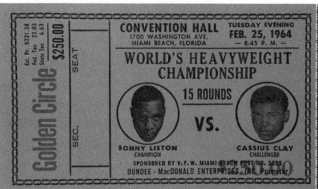

1964 Cassius Clay vs. Sonny Liston full golden circle proof ticket, 6" x 2-1/2", originated from the collection of promoter Freddie Lewis. All four corners are touched, but the ticket is crease free **$2,629**

Courtesy of Heritage Auctions, HA.com

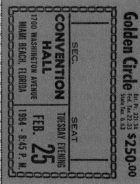

◀ 1972 Munich Olympics individual floor exercise gold medal from The Olga Korbut Collection, designed by Gerhard Marcks and produced at the Bavarian Mint, medal is crafted from 175 grams of gilt silver, and measures 66 millimeters in diameter. Letter of provenance from Olga Korbut ....**$52,800.**

Courtesy of Heritage Auctions, HA.com

▶ Vince Lombardi's 1956 New York Giants world champions 10k gold ring from the Lombardi Collection, a 20-point real diamond sits atop a dark blue stone with "N.Y. GIANTS WORLD CHAMPIONS N.Y. 47 CHI. 7" surrounds the perimeter, the right shank has a raised "NFL 56" and the left shank depicts the Giants logo over the New York skyline and "19" at the bottom, "V.T. Lombardi is engraved inside in script lettering, the ring is size 12..**$50,131**

Courtesy SCP Auctions, www.scpauctions.com

probably the most well-known segment. The "national pastime" has millions of fans, with enthusiastic collectors seeking out items associated with players such as Babe Ruth, Lou Gehrig, and others who became legends in their own lifetimes. Although baseball cards, issued as advertising premiums for bubble gum and other products, seem to dominate the field, there are numerous other items available.

Sports collectibles are more accessible than ever before because of online auctions and several auction houses that dedicate themselves to that segment of the hobby. Provenance is extremely important when investing in high-ticket sports collectibles. Being able to know the history of the object may greatly enhance the value, with a premium paid for items secured from the player or directly from their estate.

1947 Stan Musial Hillerich & Bradsby advertising 15" x 24" sign, original easel back is present and complete **$406**

Courtesy of Heritage Auctions, HA.com

Circa 1908 St. Louis Browns fold-out novelty 5-1/2" x 3-1/2" postcard produced by the H. E. Smith company of St. Louis, Missouri, the front of the postcard features a photo of a game in progress, above which is a flap that reads "Official American League Ball"................................ **$2,700**

Courtesy of Robert Edwards Auctions, www.robertedwardsauctions.com

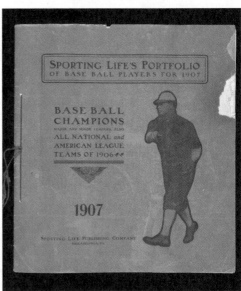

Complete set of 1907 W601 Sporting Life team composites housed in its original portfolio, printed on heavy enamel paper, numerous Hall of Fame players are featured, including Christy Mathewson, Ed Walsh, Jack Chesbro, Willie Keeler, Nap Lajoie.. **$5,100**

Courtesy of Robert Edwards Auctions, www.robertedwardsauctions.com

1948 Leaf Baseball Premium Felt Pennants Collection featuring eight different pennants, includes Boston Braves, Chicago White Sox, Cincinnati Reds, Detroit Tigers, New York Giants, Philadelphia Athletics, St. Louis Browns and Washington Nationals
....**$520**

Courtesy Goldin Auctions, goldinauctions.com

▼ Tony Gwynn's 1995 National League Silver Slugger Award from the Gwynn Collection, features full sized 34" silver-plated bat attached to a wooden home plate, trophy is 35" tall.... **$7,075**

Courtesy SCP Auctions, www.scpauctions.com

T213 Coupon Cigarettes Johnny Evers card, graded GOOD PSA 2........................**$90**

Mile High Card Company, www.milehighcardco.com

▶ Christian Laettner's 1992 Naismith College Player of the Year trophy, from the Laettner Collection, trophy is just under 20" tall with a 7-1/2" x 7-1/2" x 5" wooden base, "NAISMITH" in shiny gold-colored lettering adorns each upper side of the base, a brown plaque on the base's front side reads "NAISMITH COLLEGE PLAYER OF THE YEAR – 1992 – Christian Laettner – Duke University"
....**$15,034**

Courtesy SCP Auctions, www.scpauctions.com

top lot

Air Converse?
Jordan's Shoes Fly High at Auction

It may be difficult to imagine today but before there was a Nike Air Jordan there was simply Michael Jordan. And that Michael wore Converse basketball shoes.

The last pair of Converse worn by Jordan, arguably the greatest basketball player to lace up a pair of sneakers, set the sports memorabilia world abuzz when they sold for $190,372 during an SCP Auctions event. Jordan wore the classic Converse while scoring a game-high 20 points as the United States defeated Spain 96-65 in the gold medal game of the 1984 Olympics in Los Angeles

Jordan gave the Converse, the last pair of shoes he wore in competition as an amateur, to an 11-year-old ball boy who got them signed in the locker room after the gold medal game. The ball boy turned out to be the son of former Los Angeles Lakers great Gail Goodrich, who oversaw game operations at The Forum in Los Angeles during the Olympic tournament.

The 1984 U.S. Men's Basketball team was USA's last amateur

IMAGE COURTESY GETTY IMAGES

squad to win an Olympic gold medal, and in many circles is considered the best amateur basketball team. In addition to Jordan, the team was led by future Hall of Famers Patrick Ewing and Chris Mullin, and coached by Bobby Knight. The team went undefeated in eight games in the Olympics, with an average margin of victory of more than 30 points per game.

After the 1984 Olympics, Jordan signed a shoe contract with Nike that would lead to the most famous brand of basketball shoes in the history of the sport, Air Jordan. The Jordan brand now sponsors more than 20 pro basketball players and various lines of clothing and casual wear.

The previous record for game-worn basketball shoes was $104,765 paid for Jordan's Nike shoes worn during the epic "Flu Game" in the 1997 NBA Finals. That game 5 of the finals against the Utah Jazz became part of NBA lore when Jordan scored 38 points while battling the affects of food poisoning or a flu virus.

These Michael Jordan-worn Converse basketball shoes sold for nearly $200,000 at auction.

IMAGE COURTESY SCP AUCTIONS

▶ Circa 1910 Piedmont Cigarettes oversized tri-fold advertising 61" x 40" sign, the imagery centers around a panoramic view of a Dead Ball Era game....... **$36,000**

Courtesy of Heritage Auctions, HA.com

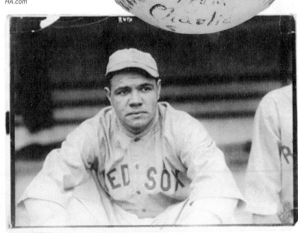

◀ 1911 World Series press pin (Philadelphia Athletics), just the fourth example ever to surface in a major sports auction, and the only one lacking even the smallest hint of wear or damage
....**$108,000**

Courtesy of Heritage Auctions, HA.com

▶ 1908 Chicago Cubs World Series championship last out baseball, handwriting upon the baseball is, "World Series, Tigers & Cubs, Oct. 14, 1908, From Charlie Schmidt" **$119,500**

Courtesy of Heritage Auctions, HA.com

1933 Goudey #106 Nap Lajoie, graded EX-MT PSA 6
....**$43,776**

Courtesy Memory Lane Inc., www.memorylaneinc.com

"Bain" Type I 1915 Babe Ruth rookie 5" x 7" Red Sox photo, full PSA Type I LOA, this PSA Type I original image was taken by none other than the iconic photographer George Grantham Bain, with his trademark "Bain News Service" stamp affixed to the verso....... **$41,226**

Courtesy Memory Lane Inc., www.memorylaneinc.com

New York Yankees original "Yankee Stadium" seat
.... **$310**

Courtesy of Heritage Auctions, HA.com

1960 Armour Coins Hank Aaron Milwaukee Braves, graded GEM MINT PSA 10 GEM MINT
.... **$137**

Mile High Card Company,
www.milehighcardco.com

▶ 2016 World Champion Chicago Cubs team signed unopened Methuselah (6 liters) bottle of Luc Belare Rose Champagne, the bottle stands around 22" tall, bottle has been signed by 26 members of the 2106 World Champion Chicago Cubs in silver sharpie including Kris Bryant, Ben Zobrist, Javier Baez, Jake Arietta, David Ross, Addison Russell and more
.... **$2,510**

Courtesy SCP Auctions, www.scpauctions.com

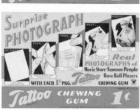

1933-34 Tattoo Orbit Gum advertising signs collection featuring six promoting cards and pin backs, display signs were used to promote the Tatto orbit products **$2,270**

Courtesy of Heritage Auctions, HA.com

TOYS

NO OTHER HOBBY touches collectors, and people in general, quite like toys. The people who collect vintage toys are simply revisiting their first collection. In some cases, they never left it. That's the thing about toy collecting: You can find amazing examples in abundant supply from any time period – especially your own.

Sales data shows you'll have lots of company in your toy collecting hobby, but also lots of competition for finer examples. The collectible toy business is one of the largest in both the retail market and the secondary market, and is also perhaps one of the first types of established collecting genres ever defined. It's interesting to note that FAO Schwarz, founded in 1862 as America's first toy store, launched its "Toy Bazaar" antique toy department in the early 1960s to meet collector demand. Toy collecting is an old and venerated hobby.

No figures are kept for the number of vintage collectible toys sold every year, but the number sold at auction is growing. At any given time, more than five million toys are for sale or taking bids on eBay. LiveAuctioneers, one of the world's largest auction-hosting websites, shows an estimated half-million toys were sold by brick and mortar auction houses at auction during the last 20 years. In many cases, these sales have set new records as collections finally come to market after decades in private hands.

Among these private collections, few reached the size, scope, and value of that owned by Donald Kaufman, whose family founded Kay Bee Toys in 1922, and who decided in 2009 to sell his collection. Kaufman felt collectors would care for the toys better than any museum ever could. It took four auctions to sell the great Kaufman collection of automotive toys for a record $12.1 million. The collection stands as the most valuable of its kind in history.

You don't need to spend $12 million on toys to have an amazing collection. But it certainly helps to bring a fraction of the passion Kaufman brought to his hobby. You probably have a few toys hanging around the house, and it's never been easier to find unusual examples. Adding to them can become addictive, especially when you find ones you had as a kid ... or the ones you always wanted.

Toy collecting allows for an infinite number of specialized collecting variations. Want cast iron cars made between 1930 and 1940? You could start with the Hubley Manufacturing Co. and collect by size. Only want dolls that were first introduced as paper dolls in the early 1950s? Betsy McCall is your gal. Have an affinity for pre-war metal squirt guns made in Michigan? Versions made by All Metal Products Co., better known as Wyandotte Toys, can be found for $20 on up, depending on condition. With toys, your collection can be as specialized

PICKER'S POCKET·GUIDE

TOYS

How to **Pick Antiques** like a Pro

CLOCKWORK TOYS + HOT WHEELS + TOY PREMIUMS
+ ACTION FIGURES + ROBOTS & SPACE TOYS + LEGO
+ DOLLS + TRAINS + VIDEO GAMES + AND MORE!

ERIC BRADLEY

or as general as you want it to be.

Toy values are chiefly influenced by demand, rarity and condition, but there are other factors as well: authenticity, exposure, provenance, quality and, most importantly, condition.

Authenticity is black or white. There are no gray areas with authenticity: Either the toy is right or it is wrong. It is either authentic or it is a fake.

Exposure influences demand for a work and brings prestige to its owner. When Steve Geppi, the president and CEO of Diamond Comic Distributors, paid $200,000 for the world's most valuable action figure – the first handcrafted prototype of the 1963 G.I. JOE action figure – the sale made international news and earned a Guinness World Record. Exposure is crucial for building collector demand around a single piece or an entire category.

Provenance explains an established history of ownership. Once a vintage toy has entered the secondary market it develops a provenance. A famous owner can add at most 15 percent or more on the value of a toy, but there are exceptions and this changes dramatically depending on who owned the toy in the past. When Leonardo DiCaprio sold part of his action figure collection at Morphy Auctions in 2006, values were stronger than expected, thanks to his famous name.

Quality may be a subjective criterion; however, a well-constructed toy is hard to find and fewer still survive for decades or even centuries. The more time you spend looking at quality toys, the easier it is to recognize good craftsmanship when you see it.

Condition is of the utmost importance in today's collector market. The most valuable items are in original condition with minimal restoration or alterations. This "best or nothing" approach to condition has probably been the most influential change in the hobby during the last decade. Values of toys in mid-range to low condition have fallen while values of rare toys in top condition often skyrocket beyond all expectations.

Tin car, circa 1950s, Japan, Yonezawa, "Tin Atom Racer," 16" l. **$1,300**

SeriousToyz, www.serioustoyz.com

Wagon, fire wagon with two horses, yellow paint and a fire patrol wagon with two horses and paint, 7-1/2" t. x 16" l...**$700**

Woody Auction, www.woodyauction.com

Pull toy, circa 1920, carved and painted wooden horse pull toy, England, cream-colored horse with black spots, and a horsehair mane and tail, leather bridle and harness, brown platform with four wheels, unmarked. Height to top of horse 18-1/5" h. **$225**

Eldred's Auctioneers & Appraisers, www.eldreds.com

Figure, mechanical Yellow Kid, circa 1890s, figure wears yellow nightshirt and has moving, mechanical arm action activated by wire lever on back that causes him to tip hat, body is wooden block with attached cast metal head, hands (attached to wires) and hat, rare, 6-3/4" t. **$863**

Hakes Americana & Collectibles, Hakes.com

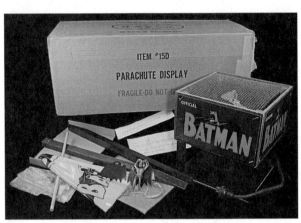

Parachute Toy, 1966, Rayline Batman, toy retail display, black pole is assembled to hang the toy (a hard plastic Batman figure with a thin vinyl parachute, meant to be thrown into the air to float down). When fan is activated, the parachute fills and Batman moves around, appearing to be constantly floating downward 27" x 11" x 10.5". **$4,066**

SeriousToyz, www.serioustoyz.com

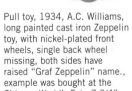

Pull toy, 1934, A.C. Williams, long painted cast iron Zeppelin toy, with nickel-plated front wheels, single back wheel missing, both sides have raised "Graf Zeppelin" name., example was bought at the Chicago World's Fair, 7-3/4". **$177**

Hakes Americana & Collectibles, www.Hakes.com

Truck, 2000, "Miniature Hess First Truck" Clear Body Variation, 2000, made in China, an ultra-rare version of the mini Hess truck sold in stations that year, created with a see-through body, exclusively for the family of John Hess, box is 7", truck is 4-1/2". $8,130

SeriousToyz, serioustoyz.com

Friction toy, circa 1956, Japan, Nomura, original cardboard box, illustrated lid contains long tin litho truck with rubber tires, the vehicle moves forward/backward, it simultaneously rotates a trio of three-dimensional tin litho riders, scarce. 8-1/4" **$260**

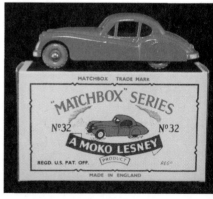

▲ Toy, 1966, Mattel, 3-1/2" x 5" Batman design and "Bat-Bomb" raised lettering, toy was designed to be thrown while holding tether, each time Bat-Bomb struck something, cap would fire, 9" x12" blister card **$240**

Balloon toy, 1931, A.C. Gilbert Co., set No. 1362, lid features images of balloons and children making/playing w/them, contents allowed user to "Make Balloons At Home" using process that required one to "Simply Dip The Form In Liquid Rubber And Dry," 10" x 18" x 2-1/2" deep cardboard box....................................... **$292**

Toy car, 1957, Moko-Lesney, England Matchbox "Jaguar XK 140" #32 in box; red body, gray plastic wheels. .... **$226.**

Figures, 1967, Wrather Corp., pair, each contains 3-3/4" Lone Ranger and Tonto figure and 4-3/4" long Silver and Scout horses, with accessories, scarce, 7 x 9" blister cards..........................**$145.38**

Figure, 1960, Japan, Nippon/Nomura, Frankenstein figure in original cardboard box, vinyl head/hands/feet, fabric outfit and tin litho base. Frankenstein produces a screeching noise as he moves his upper body and arms, his pants fall to expose his underwear and his face lights red as if embarrassed, 13.5" t. **$228**

Hakes Americana & Collectibles, www.Hakes.com

Playset, 1965, Ideal Toy Corp, MGM, deep textured vinyl-covered case contains set from *The Man From U.N.C.L.E.* including passport with lenticular front panel, wallet/billfold plastic cap firing gun "U.N.C.L.E." logo sticker, scarce, from the Tesco Vee Collection. 10-1/2" x 15" x 2-1/2" **$944**

Hakes Americana & Collectibles, www.Hakes.com

Wind-up, 1922, Germany, Fontaine Fox, tin litho wind-up with built-in key, toy includes die-cut tin figure of The Skipper, trolley is designed to stop and shake slightly as The Skipper turns the controller before it continues on its way, 2-1/2" x 5" x 6-3/4" **$325**

Hakes Americana & Collectibles, www.Hakes.com

Wind-up, 1923, Germany, Fontaine Fox, tall tin litho toy with built-in key, toy depicts Katrinka pushing a wheelbarrow that contains a separate tin figure of Jimmy, she pushes the wheelbarrow forward, stopping every so often to lift up the wheelbarrow before continuing, 3-1/2" x7-1/4" x 5-1/4" **$638**

Hakes Americana & Collectibles, www.Hakes.com

Wind-up, circa 1920s, Ferdinand Strauss Corp., illustrated cardboard box contains tin litho train car with four separate tin litho dimensional chickens attached to top, surrounding tin litho feed pan, built-in key, train car moves in wide circle as hens and chicks bob up and down as if pecking at food, 4-3/4" x 8-3/8" x 2-1/4" **$460**

Hakes Americana & Collectibles, www.Hakes.com

▲ Pull toy, 1929, Enland, Deans Rag Book Co. Ltd., metal tricycle with wire frame body and metal wheels has 12" tall seated doll attached at handlebars and pedals, stuffed cloth doll, this Sunshine doll was produced for one year, scarce, 5-1/4" w x 7-1/4" l,. **$230**

Hakes Americana & Collectibles, www.Hakes.com

◄ Push toy, circa 1950s, Metal Masters Co. of Philadelphia, PA., all wood with applied paper labels on wooden front/back panels and thick cardboard sides, scarce, 7-1/2" w 17-1/5" l x 9-5/8" t **$190**

Hakes Americana & Collectibles, www.Hakes.com

10 Things You Didn't Know About Bobbleheads

1 Figurines with moving heads have many names. Some of those names include: bobbleheads, nodders, nodding heads, wobblers, and moving heads. Nodding figurine examples are made of composition, papier mache, porcelain, plastic.

Lego bobblehead "Pig Pen" figure, original label on base. Height 5 1/2 inches. Minor paint loss $40 (excluding buyer's premium).

Courtesy of John McInnis Auctioneers, www.mcinnisauctions.com

2 German nodders were made of ceramic and began production in the late 1700s/ early 1800s. In the 20th century, commercialized bobble head dolls were made of paper mache and then switched to the more durable ceramic.

3 A Russian short story published in 1842, titled "The Overcoat" (or "The Cloak") by Nicolai Gogol, describes the main character as having a neck "like the necks of those plaster cats which wag their heads, and are carried about upon the heads of scores of image sellers." (The short story can be read online at bit.ly/1RGJbVY.)

Bobbleheads from left: Paul Bunyan, Canadian Mountie, Big Boy, Ben Casey and another Paul Bunyan. Very nice with only extremely minor wear here and there. Condition (Excellent Plus). Size Largest: 7-1/2" T. $225.

Courtesy of Dan Morphy Auctions, www.morphyauctions.com

4 In 1960, Major League Baseball imported paper mache bobbleheads for each team to give away. Additional bobbleheads of specific players were made to commemorate the World Series. The players were Roberto Clemente, Mickey Mantle, Roger Maris, and Willie Mays, although the "personalized" bobbleheads had the same faces as the generic team bobbleheads.

5 Bobbleheads reached the height of their popularity in the 1960s but interest waned by the end of the 1970s. However, a limited Willie Mays giveaway by the San Francisco Giants on May 9, 1999, commemorating the 40th anniversary of Candlestick Park, is credited with breathing new life into bobblehead collecting.

6 If you can think of a subject, it is highly likely there is a bobblehead available. If you can't find one, there are many companies that make custom and personalized bobbleheads from photos (for less than $75). Here are a few options: www.bobblemaker.com; www.allbobbleheads.com; www.bobblemaker.com; www.bobbleheads.com.

7 In 2012, the TBS talk show "Conan" (teamcoco.com) produced one of the largest bobblehead dolls documented. Made primarily from high-density foam, the Conan O'Brien Bobble Head stands 17 feet tall; O'Brien gifted the "bobble-statue" to the city of Chicago. After the Art Institute of Chicago rejected installation, the giant bobblehead found a home at Harold's Chicken Shack on Wabash Avenue. (View the "Conan" bobblehead installation video at https://youtu.be/l7UOV3sazQw.)

8 Antique Place, Hallandale, Florida, sold a German Shafer and Vater bisque figurine of two women with bobble heads having tea and reading a book for $600 (excluding buyer's premium) in December 2015. The circa 1920 porcelain figurine, stamped "Made in Germany" on the bottom measures 6 inches high.

9 Subscribers to the academic legal journal The Green Bag (http://www.greenbag.org) may receive bobbleheads of Supreme Court Justices, although the editors "make no promises about when we will make them or who will get them." All prototypes of the Supreme Court Justice bobbleheads (and samples of all the production versions) are archived at the Lillian Goldman Law Library at the Yale Law School.

10 The National Bobblehead Hall of Fame and Museum is in the works in Milwaukee, Wisconsin. You can follow its progress at www.bobbleheadhall.com.

– Compiled by Karen Knapstein

Sources: The Cardboard Connection (http://www.cardboardconnection.com); Bleacher Report (http://bleacherreport.com); www.bobbleheads.com; www.popculturespot.com; www.cbsnews.com; www.greenbag.org; Bobblehead Hall of Fame and Museum (http://www.bobbleheadhall.com).

VINTAGE ELECTRONICS

THERE'S PLENTY OF history to collect in the ever-growing and expanding category of vintage electronics. From the dawn of the Electrical Age (which spans 1600-1800) to the household innovations of today, the depth and variety of vintage electronics makes it one of the fastest-growing collectible segments in the hobby.

This is because of an influx of younger collectors (generally mid-20s to mid-40s) who happen to be the first generation to live with mobile, digital technology crucial to modern life. But don't think this category is regulated to "vintage" finds: It's quite amazing to realize that the very first book to combine the study of static electricity and the scientific method, *De Magnete* by Sir William Gilbert, was published in 1600 – the same year William Shakespeare oversaw the first production of *A Midsummer Night's Dream*.

Despite the innovation and constantly changing adaptations, the principals of electronics have remained unchanged for more than 100 years. Non-collectors might be surprised to learn that the same basic technology that made the original ViewMaster a commercial hit in 1938 is the basis of today's latest virtual reality technology. Presenting two photographs of the same object from slightly different angles is the basis of the Oculus Rift virtual reality device (which may itself be a hot collectible in the next 25 years).

Some of the most sought-after examples of vintage electronics in today's hobby include rare or mint condition video game consoles and games; calculators from the early 1970s; and personal computers from the very early years of the technology, such as the Hewlett Packard 9100A released in 1968 or the KENBAK – 1, which sold for $35,000 at auction in early 2015. By the time you read this chapter, the average cost of a laptop computer is about $600, while the resale value of its 40+ year-old-grandfather starts at about $1,200 and ends at more than $600,000 for one of the scant 63 surviving examples of the Apple 1 computer assembled by Steve Jobs and his friends in 1976.

Vintage electronics falls into the category I call a "usable collectible"; vintage electronics collectors put a premium on usability over decorative value. A good example is the growing popularity of collecting vintage

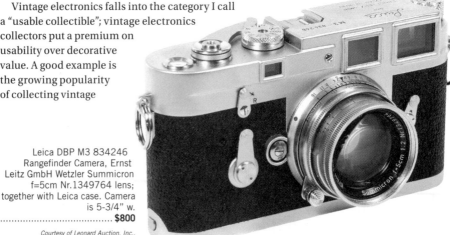

Leica DBP M3 834246 Rangefinder Camera, Ernst Leitz GmbH Wetzler Summicron f=5cm Nr.1349764 lens; together with Leica case. Camera is 5-3/4" w.
.... **$800**

Courtesy of Leonard Auction, Inc.,
leonardauction.com

electronics that surround music. Collectors fuel a robust hobby by hunting down obscure and obsolete EL34 tubes made in the early 1960s in West Germany by Telefunken (generally found at $75-$100). The tubes were used in amplifiers made by companies such as Marshall and Hi-Watt and are now prized by collectors and audiophiles who restore amps for the sole purpose of recreating the unique "British-tone" that made the music of The Beatles and Led Zeppelin. Was the music produced by the young Eric Clapton rooted in his imagination and creativity? Absolutely. Were the unique British amps and EL34 tubes crucial in enhancing his harmonic consistency? Without a doubt. So while it might be easy to find parts of a vintage Marshall amp from the days of The British Invasion for about $50 to $200, a near-mint/mint amp in perfect working order will likely cost between $1,500 and $5,500. American examples from the 1950s can command five figures.

One popular niche to appear in the last five years is the emergence of the collection and restoration of vintage boombox stereos, which were a commercial hit in the 1970s and 1980s. Collectors have formed clubs across the country, founded an active Facebook page (Boomboxery), and even an annual event, the First Annual Boomboxery International Blaster Summit in September 2016 in Las Vegas.

In the special case where an assortment of low-value vintage electronic parts are so badly damaged so as to have no collectible value, dealer/artisans like Ed Kautsch of Sanger, Texas, have embraced Steampunk to blend early technological nostalgia with a sculpture's flair. Under his business name of The Steampunk Ballroom (etsy.com/shop/steampunkballroom), his handmade lamps, sculptures, and clocks pay homage to captivating Victorian devices. Kautsch's creations are mostly purchased by young collectors. He sees it as a new and interesting way to introduce a love of collecting vintage objects to the Wi-Fi generation. One of his creations is a functional lamp sculpture titled "Time Machine Experiment No 51" and it retails for $165.

Resources: *Retro-Electro: Collecting Technology: From Atari to Walkman*, Pepe Tozzo, Universe Publishing.

Bang & Olufsen stereo equipment including a pair of Beovok 5700 stereo speakers made in Denmark, together with a Beogram 3000 turntable (shown), a Beomaster 2400 receiver and a box of cables, 45 records and pamphlets...................**$180**

Courtesy of Leonard Auction, Inc., leonardauction.com

Two-piece lot: PAT-4 transistor/diode-style preamplifier, manufactured from a Dyna-Kit, and a Stereo 120 all-silicon transistor amplifier. The Stereo 120 is a basic power amplifier for use with separate preamplifiers, pieces are in fair used condition and showing some external tarnishing and wear, both in working condition. **$55**

Courtesy of Worth Auctions, worthauctions.com

Page Boss Mine Paging Phone, was a state of the art communications tools for mine workers, manufactured by Pyott Boone Electronics, front door opens up to access battery and wiring, 6-1/2" w x 12" h....... **$15**

Courtesy of Haw River Junktion, LLC, hawriverjunktion.com

Vintage Lionel Electronic Phonograph with original box, No. 42110-21, aqua and white, needle component on arm missing, includes all paperwork...**$20**

Courtesy of Lemar Auctions and Estate Services, lemarauctions.com

Axe-Amp was the first marketed product by Lab.gruppen, a Swedish electronics company founded in 1979, Serial No. 831-006, 110V-120, made completely out of wood with a leather strap affixed to it, 19" x 8-1/2" x 18". Johnny Winter is pictured with this amp and one of the company's co-founders in a photo from 1981.............................**$500**

Courtesy of Guernsey's, guernseys.com

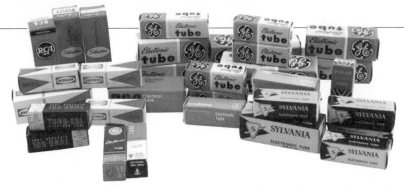

Various vintage electronic tubes, mixture of sizes and brands including GE, RCA, TS, Sylvania, and Traid Tube Corporation. **$30**

Courtesy of Affiliated Auctions, affiliatedauctions.com

Mamiya M645 medium format camera and winder, first series of 4.5cm X 6cm SLR made by Mamiya, features an electronic focal plane shutter. The M645 J (1979) Junior is like the original model with shutter speeds from 1s to 1/500 but with the mirror lockup feature removed, only made for export, includes a 80mm lens and 150mm lens with additional carrying case and a power winder, camera is 5-1/4" h and 6-3/4" l. **$60**

Courtesy of Bremo Auctions, bremoauctions.com

SAE Mark II B home stereo power amp, built between 1971 and 1978, features an all-aluminum black chassis and separate gain controls for each channel, 17" x 13-1/2" x 5-3/4"..................**$70**

Courtesy of Worth Auctions, worthauctions.com

Beatles rare "Electric Apple" prototype sound light box by "Magic Alex" Mardas (UK, 1967), as used for the Apple Boutique's grand opening. This yellow-painted, hand-fabricated wooden box is an exceedingly rare device, as there were approximately only four ever made as prototypes, and it never went to mass production. Worthy of the finest Beatle collections, it measures 15-1/4" x 9" x 4-1/4". **$1,000**

Courtesy of Heritage Auctions, ha.com

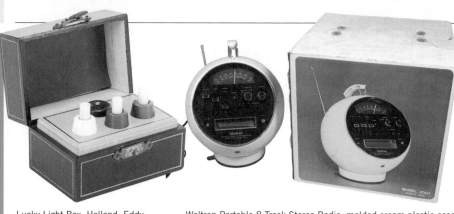

Lucky Light Box, Holland: Eddy Taytelbaum, 1960s, spectator is asked to guess which of the three switches will cause the light bulb to light up, but no matter how many guesses he is given, the spectator is always wrong, housed in a painted wooden carrying case.
.... **$225**

Courtesy of Potter & Potter Auctions, potterauctions.com

Weltron Portable 8 Track Stereo Radio, molded cream plastic case, original box, Model #2001, 13" h x 10" w x 10" d....**$100**

Courtesy of Uniques & Antiques, Inc., uniquesandantiques.com

Mignonphonic Vanitrola Portable Gramophone, suitcase style, reproducer marked on rear Mignonphonic Vanitrola, Walker Products Co. New York, and Swiss made, Thorens anchor appears on reproducer front, interior of case marked Vanitrola, hand-crank clockwork mechanism, miniature turntable with screw-on disc to hold records, plays 78 rpm records, leather covered case measures approximately 9" x 5-1/2" x 3-1/2".
.... **$140**

Courtesy of D.G.W. Auctioneers Inc., dgwauctioneers.com

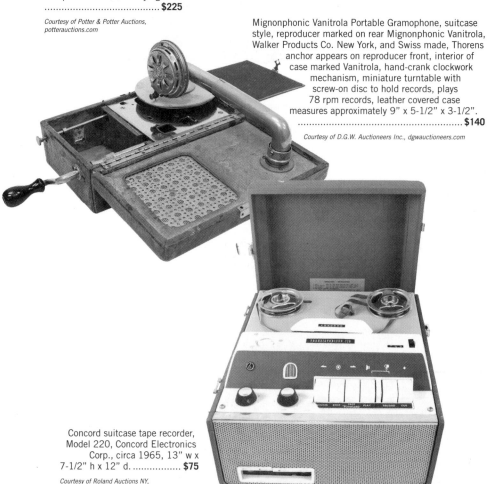

Concord suitcase tape recorder, Model 220, Concord Electronics Corp., circa 1965, 13" w x 7-1/2" h x 12" d. **$75**

Courtesy of Roland Auctions NY, rolandantiques.com

WATCHES

THE NEW AUDIENCE for vintage watches is global.

"The vintage watch market is in a very healthy state at the moment," Phillip's Auctions' Paul Maudsley, recently told the Business of Fashion (BOF). "Each year new collectors come on board and gain an understanding of the various specialist collected brands, and prices rise steadily."

Rolex and Patek Philippe Phillip's remain at the top of the vintage and antique watch market, which experts say is worth in the region of $2 billion annually. The market for watches priced below $10,000 is white hot at the moment even as early versions of emerging brands gain a young and affluent following.

It appears classic style never goes away – it just gets more expensive.

Interest, too, is increasing for watches that were once deemed too stuffy for a younger generation to wear. Brands such as Vacheron Constantin, Audemars Piguet and Breguet, to name a few are being seen through fresh eyes. All this despite the fact manufacturers pump dozens of new brands into the marketplace every year.

Pocket watch, Swiss rare and very fine Carillon minute repeating three-motion automaton with gold, enamel and diamond case, circa 1900.
....................................**$21,250**

Heritage Auctions, www.HA.com

"Most people think that watch sales start with price, but that's not the case," says Lloyd Amsdon, one of the founders of WatchFinder & Co, which sells pre-owned and vintage watches online and through a small network of UK retail outlets, in an interview with BOF. "The biggest single factor is choice. Retailers don't sell Rolexes made over the last 50 years; they sell the new ones. Vintage and pre-owned open up the market and give consumers more choice."

MARKET GROWTH

Vintage watch collecting has been a robust hobby since the 1960s. But sellers of vintage watches are now turning to social media outlets such as Instagram, subject exclusive blogs, and online storefronts to snag new watch fans and satisfy demand. The internet's most dependable vintage watch website, Hodinkee, opened an online store recently to help consumers locate dependable vintage watches at affordable prices.

Customers from the Middle East, London, China and Hong Kong are making up much of the vintage watch consumption market in the United States. It's easier to own a vintage watch and it's now seen as chic to sport a brand that is different than the newest label. Collecting vintage watches can be an addictive hobby thanks to the thousands of brands and styles available produced across the last 125 years.

Wristwatch, Chanel, ladies' model J12 watch, automatic movement, a ceramic case and bracelet, the bezel and bracelet set with diamonds (color G-H, clarity VS2), marked with manufacturer's mark to dial and case, "J12", "QUARTZ", and "SWISS MADE", 1" dia., length 6" l. **$3,750**

Ahlers & Ogletree, www.aandoauctions.com

NOT AN INVESTMENT

Like any collectible, experts will warn collectors not to rely too heavily on the value of vintage watches increasing in the future. Just as the vintage watch market is seeing an uptick, the modern watch market is seeing a downswing. The same could happen to vintage watches at a moment's notice, according to Maudsley. "Whether its modern or vintage watches, they should be looked upon for their aesthetics, technical function and so on, not purely as investments — we have the stock market for that," he told BOF. "But that said, if a watch purchase is driven by a passion for the pieces, an understanding of the quality and rarity, and the buyer has done their research, then they have proven to have risen in price."

It is important to note the market for general pocket watches (as dependable as they may seem) is not nearly as strong as the market for vintage wristwatches. Tastes and clothing change and no one seem to have the pocket space for a pocket watch next to their iPhone. A vintage wristwatch makes a completely different statement.

FUTURE POTENTIAL

Here is one example of the boon in value vintage watches have experienced during the last 40 years. The Horological Society of New York recently unearthed four wrist and pocket watches that had spent the last 40 years in a long forgotten vault. They were donated to the society at a time when the vintage watch market was in its infancy, said Heritage Auctions watch expert Michael Fossner.

The vault held two wristwatches: an Audemars Piguet 18K Gold Square Wristwatch Ref. 5128BA Signed Tiffany & Co. Circa 1960, which sold for $5,0000, and a Patek Philippe Ref. 3514 18k Gold Automatic Wristwatch, which hammered for $15,000. And two pocket watches: an Audemars Piguet 18K Gold Ultra-Thin Pocket Watch Signed Tiffany & Co. Circa 1959, which sold for $4,600 and a Piaget $20 Saint Gaudens Gold Coin Watch Signed Cartier, which ended at $4,000. The proceeds benefited the HSNY Endowment Fund.

"These great watches by Patek, Audemars Piguet, Piaget and others were of modest value when donated to the Society, where they were consigned to a vault and forgotten, oblivious to the skyrocketing market outside," he said.

As the HSNY auction shows, the vintage watch market is still very much a new and unexploited marketplace. As thousands of people worldwide begin to gain interest in vintage watches, can the vintage market keep pace before demand outstrips supply? Only time will tell.

Wristwatch, Hamilton Automatic 64028-4, case: gold plated, stainless steel back, asymmetrical, screw back, acrylic crystal, black dial, applied gold markers, luminous dots, date at 3.................... **$187**

Heritage Auctions, www.HA.com

Wristwatch, Longines 14k Gold, two-body case, enameled onyx and tiger's eye finish, applied gold markers, gold Dauphine hands, 17 jewels, manual wind................................. **$362**

Heritage Auctions, www.HA.com

Wristwatch, Longines vintage platinum, curved back, silver dial, diamond set indexes and Arabic numerals, white gold baton hands, manual wind... **$600**

Heritage Auctions, www.HA.com

Pocket watch, Illinois 21 Jewel Sangamo Special, circa 1916, white case, gold filled, 16 size, vertical stripes and crest on the back, dial: double sunk, full Montgomery numerals, blue spade hands....................... **$225**

Heritage Auctions, www.HA.com

Wristwatch, Rolex, ref. 6263, gold oyster superlative chronometer officially certified Cosmograph with rare sigma dial, circa 1980, case: No. 6018935, 18k yellow gold, signed Rolex. **$46,250**

Heritage Auctions, www.HA.com

Wristwatch, Gerald Genta, ref. G.3359-4, very fine platinum skeletonized perpetual calendar sith moon phases, case: platinum, two body, 35 mm, transparent case back, sapphire crystals, rounded and beaded crown, dial: transparent with tritium round hour indexes, auxiliary mother-of-pearl dial rings for the date, the days of the week, the months and the leap year cycle, aperture for the moon phases on a lapis-lazuli background, luminous baton hands, movement: skeletonized automatic, caliber 1058, fully engraved rhodium finished bridges and plates, 29 jewels, skeletonized rotor with the initials "GG", monometallic balance, shock absorber, signed: Gerald Genta. **$13,750**

Heritage Auctions, www.HA.com

Pocket Watch, Waltham rare premier Maximus 18K gold, circa 1909, heavy 18k yellow-gold case, double hinged back, plain on the back, outer edge and bezel are deeply engraved with flowers and scroll patterns, two-tone silver dial signed Premier Maximus, case is signed Waltham, Wadsworth Quality 18 Karat Gold. **$6,875**

Heritage Auctions, www.HA.com

Wristwatch, Pierre Kunz Grande Date Sport with retrograde seconds, steel case no. 461, sapphire crystal, red texalium dial, applied steel luminous markers and numerals, grande date aperture at 12, silvered retrograde 30 seconds sector at 6, black super luminova hands, automatic winding. Signed: Pierre Kunz. **$4,500**

Heritage Auctions, www.HA.com

Watch, Record Watch Co. Art Nouveau Sector, circa 1905, .800 fine silver case, fan form, hinged back and bezel with high relief repousse Art Nouveau floral motifs, cuvette engraved "Sector Watch", signed: Record Watch Co. S.A. Tramelan........................ **$3,500**

Heritage Auctions, www.HA.com

Wristwatch, Gruen "1500 Feet" steel automatic diver's watch, case: stainless steel, bi-directional rotating bezel, screw down case back and crown, recessed crystal with steel screw down retaining bezel, dial: orange, large applied steel markers, steel baton hands. . **$750**

Heritage Auctions, HA.com

Wristwatch, Perrelet unusual stainless steel large moonphase watch with diamonds and rubies, Ref. A1040/5, stainless steel case, no. A0006, automatic winding, original black crocodile strap, signed: Perrelet. **$3,125**

Heritage Auctions, www.HA.com

Wristwatch, Hamilton Everest Electric, case: 10k yellow gold filled, two body, asymmetric with extended top with hour markers and numeral 12, golden center dial, white border with applied gold dot markers and Arabic numerals, blued luminous hands.................. **$275**

Heritage Auctions, www.HA.com

Wristwatch, Breitling Ref. A 57035 Steel "Colt", case: matte stainless steel, three body, 38 mm, screw down back, rotating bezel with raised rider tabs, screw down crown with guard, dial: silver, luminous Arabic numerals, inner 24 hour numerals, date aperture at three, luminous baton hands, movement: quartz standardization, band: leather, steel buckle, signed: Breitling, with inner and outer boxes... **$781**

Heritage Auctions, www.HA.com

Watch, Tiffany & Co. enamel and gold pendant, applied platinum frame with small diamonds dial and movement signed Tiffany & Co......... **$1,000**

Heritage Auctions, www.HA.com

Wristwatch, Saro, Swiss center stop seconds, base metal case, two body, start/stop buttons on the left side, black dial, luminous Arabic numerals, luminous hour and minute hands. **$84**

Heritage Auctions, www.HA.com

Watch, Armand & Cie Geneva 18k gold mandolin form watch, circa 1890s, case: 18k gold, four body, gold cuvette, flip open rounded front cover, hinged back with dark blue and black enameled accents, engraved and chased, dial: white enamel, blue Roman numerals in gold circular frames, gold filigree hands, movement: nickel finish, 10 jewels, cylinder escapement, cuvette is signed Armand & Cie Geneva. **$1,150**

Heritage Auctions, www.HA.com

Wristwatch, Rolex Unused Ref. 6671/9, white gold and diamond, Cellini Cellissima, 18k white gold case, two body, pave diamond bezel, sapphire crystal, pink dial, white gold Roman chapters, white gold tapered baton hands, black crocodile strap and original 18k white gold deployant clasp, signed: Rolex Cellini. **$5,000**

Heritage Auctions, www.HA.com

WILDLIFE ART

AT COPLEY FINE ART AUCTIONS winter auction, pre-auction estimates flew the coop just as the selection of bird decoys would have if they were alive.

A finely-carved example of the a yellowlegs shorebird thought to have been carved by Bill Bowman or Charles Sumner Bunn a half century ago saw its $70,000 estimate fall when the gavel fell for $90,000 in early 2017. The example displayed the elegant features noted for these artists: an elegant inserted bill, eye grooves, glass eyes, a pronounced shoulder wing and perfectly painted surface in dry paint, Copley said.

Records fell for several other examples of wildlife art, which seems to be the norm in this increasingly popular genre for collectors and museum curators.

The decoy market is showing signs of a tremendous recovery after several years of lower-than-expected auction prices for even the most celebrated carvers. Investment-grade decoys are again brining close to six-figure sums and collectors are not afraid to bid aggressively to own key decoys that have had much exposure in either books on the topic or museum exhibitions.

"The most popular genre collected today seems to be animals from the farm, said Rod Zullo, a wildlife sculptor artist and fellow of the National Sculpture Society. "Horses and dogs continue to touch the personal needs of today's collectors."

Zullo says he personally continues to see an improvement of the market as the economy improves: "The better the economy, the more disposable income, hence better prices and more sales."

PAINTINGS

It appears 19th century oils are performing much better than they have in the recent past. The oil on canvas titled *Pointer and Quail*, 1892, by Edmund Henry Osthaus (born in Hildesheim, Germany, in 1858) seared its $30,000 pre-auction estimate to sell for $63,000. And a second Osthaus' oil on canvas hunting scene titled *On Point*, depicting two hunting dogs who have spotted their quarry, sold for $44,400 against a $25,000 pre-auction estimate.

Frederick Stone Batcheller's *Woodcock and Quail*, circa 1855 - a stunning still life of a day's bounty - blew its $5,000 estimate out of the water when it sold for $11,400. Of course these high-flying auction prices generally do not attract first-time wildlife art collectors. Many start at smaller price points.

Zullo suggests finding a resource you can trust. "The best advice I can give to

Painting, "Balancing Act, Great Horned Owl," 1991, Guy Joseph Coheleach, (American, b.1933), acrylic on board, 30" x 40", signed lower right: Guy Coheleach ©
....**$12,500**

Heritage Auctions, www.HA.com

a new collector is to find a dealer you can trust and that has a proven track record of advising collectors," he said. "The collector should head the advice from the dealer as to what subject matter, and genre is a solid investment, but they should also remember, art is about what you like, not what someone else likes."

CONTEMPORARY SCULPTURE

When the well-known Judson C. and Nancy Sue Ball collection hit the market a few years ago it released a number of contemproary wildlife sculptures to collecting acclaim. Jonathan Kenworthy's *Leaping Wildebeest*, 1991, a bronze with brown patina, hammered for $55,000 following interest from four bidders and Antoine-Louis Barye's *Bear Fleeing from Dogs*, a bronze with brown patina, sold for $10,625.

Two more lots exceeded estimates as Kenneth Rodney Bunn's *Vantage Point*, 1997, a wonderful depiction of a bear perched on a log, sold for $27,500, and Michael Coleman's *Moose*, 1998, a bronze with brown patina, ended at $23,125, beating out a renowned Albert Bierstadt *Pink Butterfly*, circa late 1800s, which sold for $18,875.

It appears collectors are seeking bold representations of wildlife scenes and portraits that capture the majesty of the wilderness and its big-game animals.

TODAY'S TALENT INCREASING SALES

Contemporary artists are increasingly taking advantage of social media as a way to promote their art and observations on the art world.

"Social media is today what websites where 15 years ago," Zullo said. "It's important to have a presence, but it can be overdone. You don't want the public to see so much of your work that they become overwhelmed.

"Sharing work, and ideas is good, but be careful not to be so common," Zullo advises. "People become bored with your work. Try to keep it as special as it truly is. Social media is a balance of enough but not too much. It does connect the artist with other like minds and that is a good thing."

Painting, "Jungle Cruiser," Jennifer Morgan, acrylic on canvas, 24" x 48". **$560**

Heritage Auctions, www.HA.com

Sculpture, "Bald Eagle Head Study for Into the Air" Bob Guelich (b. 1944), bronze, 7" x 9" x 6". **$400**

Vogt Galleries Texas, www.vogtauction.com

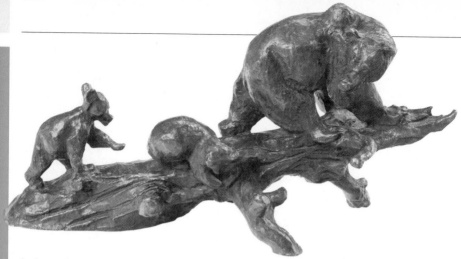

Sculpture, "Mountain Mother," 1919, Charles Marion Russell (American, 1864-1926), bronze with brown patina, 7-1/5" h., inscribed on base with artist symbol: CM Russell / 19. .... **$21,250**

Heritage Auctions, www.HA.com

Painting, "Jack Rabbit," Paul Gaisford (British, b. 1941), watercolor and gouache on board, 7-1/2" x 4-1/4", signed lower right: Paul / Gaisford. **$300**

Heritage Auctions, www.HA.com

Painting, "His Domain", circa 1916, Carl Clements Moritz Rungius (American, 1869-1959), oil on canvas, 30" x 40", signed lower right: C. Rungius. **$245,000**

Heritage Auctions, www.HA.com

Sculpture, "Recumbent Bison," Edward Kemeys (American, 1843-1907), bronze with brown patina, 2-3/4" h., inscribed along the base: Edward Kemeys Jr., stamped on the base: Roman Bronze Works Inc. N.Y. **$3,000**

Heritage Auctions, www.HA.com

Print, "Black-bellied Darter, Plotus Anhinga" (No 64, Plate CCCXVI), 1836, John James Audubon (American, 1785-1851), hand-colored engraving with aquatint and etching on J. Whatman dated 1836, 30" x 21-3/4," engraved, printed, and colored by R. Havell, London. $27,500

Heritage Auctions, www.HA.com

Sculpture, "Royal Elk," 1984, Clark Everice Bronson (American, b. 1939), bronze with brown patina, 15-3/4" h., inscribed on the base: 1984 / 56/75 / Clark Bronson / NAWA / "Royal Elk", inscribed along the base: Big Sky Casting. **$4,000**

Heritage Auctions, www.HA.com

Lithograph, "Rocky Mountain Sheep," John James Audubon (American, 1785-1851), hand-colored lithograph plate LXXIII from "The Viviparous Quadrupeds of North America," Printed and colored by J.T. Bowen, Philadelphia, 1845, 21-5/8" x 27"... **$937**

Heritage Auctions, www.HA.com

Painting, "Trout and Creel," Victor Higgins (American, 1884-1949), oil on canvas laid on panel, 19-5/8" x 15-5/8", signed and inscribed lower right: Victor Higgins / ...SK / J.H.R......**$32,500**

Heritage Auctions, www.HA.com

Painting, "First Snow," Manuel Garza (b. 1940), oil on canvas, 16" x 20". **$3,200**

Vogt Galleries Texas, www.vogtauction.com

Bowl, circa 1000 - 1400 AD, rectangular vessel with pie crust banding on the rim forms the body of a seated deer with the head extending from the rim, the legs in relief on the front, back, and underside, and a small tail exposed at the back. The example is an unusual one, with squared and block-like features. It would have served as a container for food offerings needed in the after-life., ... **$2,000**

Heritage Auctions, HA.com

Sculpture, "Pheasant" by Alexandre Ouline (French, 20th Century), circa 1930, partial gilt bronze, marble, 9-1/4" x 21" x 4", base signed "Ouline, figure stamped BRONZE................... **$437**

Heritage Auctions, www.HA.com

▲ Duck Decoy, F.M. Barteau carved and painted wood decoy duck, 20th century, engraved to underside: CARVED AND PAINTED ESPECIALLY FOR THE SOUTHLAND CORPORATION, BY F.M. BARTEAU OF CHURCH'S FRIEND CHICKEN INC., 5-3/4" h. x 14" l................................... **$162**

Heritage Auctions, www.HA.com

Sculpture, "Devil Fish," Continental School (20th Century), bronze with brown patina 18" h., inscribed on base: C. Renard. **$1,250**

Heritage Auctions, www.HA.com

Scarf, Loewe Silk Scarf in carved sood frame: Hunting Dogs and Pheasants, marks: LOEWE, 37-1/2" x 36"..**$57**

Heritage Auctions, www.HA.com

▼ Decoy, carved black duck decoy, stamped twice, "A.E. Crowell, maker, East Harwich, Mass" in rectangles, (ex. Channing Howe estate, Duxbury, MA), 6 1/2" h., 13 1/2" l. **$3,600**

Willis Henry Auctions Inc., www.willishenryauctions.com

WORLD WAR II COLLECTIBLES

DURING THE SEVEN decades since the end of World War II, veterans, collectors, and nostalgia-seekers have eagerly bought, sold and traded the "spoils of war." Souvenir collecting began as soon as troops set foot on foreign soil. Whether Tommies from Great Britain, Doughboys from the United States, or Fritzies from Germany, soldiers looked for trinkets and remembrances that would guarantee their place in the history. Helmets, medals, firearms, field gear, daggers and other pieces of war material filled parcels and duffel bags on the way back home.

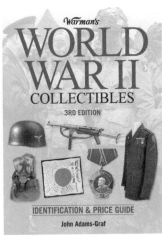

Warman's
WORLD WAR II
COLLECTIBLES
3RD EDITION

IDENTIFICATION & PRICE GUIDE
John Adams-Graf

For more pricing information, consult WWII Collectibles, 3rd Edition, by John Adams-Graf and available from KrauseBooks.com

As soon as hostilities ended in 1945, the populations of defeated Germany and Japan quickly realized they could make money selling souvenirs to the occupation forces. The flow of war material increased. Values became well established.

Over the years these values have remained proportionally consistent, and though values have increased dramatically, demand has not dropped off a bit. In fact, World War II collecting is the largest segment of the militaria hobby.

Surprisingly, the values of items had been a closely guarded secret. Unfortunately, the hobby relied on paying veterans and their families far less than a military relic's worth with the hope of selling later for a substantial profit. This attitude has given the hobby a bad reputation.

The advent of the Internet, though, significantly leveled the playing field for sellers and buyers. Online information gave the uninitiated an idea of value.

But a little information can be dangerous. The value of military items resides in variation. Whether it is a difference in manufacturing technique, material or markings, the nuances of an item will determine the true value. Don't expect 20 minutes on the Internet – or even glancing through this section – to teach you these nuances. Collectors are a devoted bunch. They have spent years and hundreds, if not thousands, of dollars to establish the knowledge base that enables them to navigate through the hobby.

Japanese WWII Naval Officer's Dirk
.... **$575**

www.AdvanceGuardMilitaria.com

VISIT WWW.ANTIQUETRADER.COM

WWW.FACEBOOK.COM/ANTIQUETRADER

▼ German SS Berghaus in Bayrischzell tea cup made by Bauscher / Weiden. **$145**

US Army Air Force M115 Aerial Bomb Tail Fuse. **$75**

Japanese WWII Chosen (Korea) Occupation Government Official Parade Sword. **$325**

USN/USMC M40 Flight helmet with volcano cups and AN6530 goggles.. **$695**

W

WORLD WAR II

◄ German NSKK chained officer's dagger, RZM M7/66 1952 (Carl Eickhorn). **$2,975**

www.AdvanceGuardMilitaria.com

◄ German 1st SS Panzer Division "Leibstandarte Adolf Hitler" BeVo Cuff title: Tunic Removed. **$795**

www.AdvanceGuardMilitaria.com

▲ German SS "Totenkopf" enlisted man's collar tab. **$475**

www.AdvanceGuardMilitaria.com

▲ US 1941-dated, first pattern mountain rucksack. **$95**

www.AdvanceGuardMilitaria.com

German Army enlisted man's / NCO belt buckle. **$60**

www.AdvanceGuardMilitaria.com

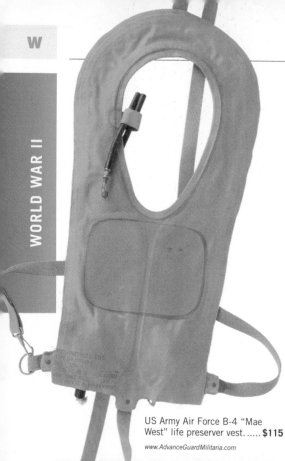

US C-Ration (B-unit), unopened with key. **$100**

John Adams-Graf

US Army Air Force B-4 "Mae West" life preserver vest. **$115**

www.AdvanceGuardMilitaria.com

German Kriegsmarine U-Boat Type 7 x 50 Binoculars. **$950**

The Ruptured Duck

U.S. Property-marked Colt 1908 semi-automatic hammerless pocket pistol attributed to Air Force Major General Robert W. Douglass Jr., WWII fighter commander and postwar USAF-Europe Chief of Staff, with box. **$7,475**

Rock Island Auction Company

▶ Golden Hitler Youth Leader's Sports Badge.. **$535**

The Ruptured Duck

▲ US M1923 Rifle Cartridge
Belt dated 1942................... **$50**

www.AdvanceGuardMilitaria.com

German Luftwaffe officer's
dagger, second pattern.
.... **$395**

www.AdvanceGuardMilitaria.com

US Navy M422a flight jacket.
.... **$625**

www.AdvanceGuardMilitaria.com

US Army Air Force officer's
British-style European Theater
Operation (ETO) jacket and
British-made "pink" trousers.....**$425**

www.AdvanceGuardMilitaria.com

German Army officer's dress
dagger with portepee and
hangers. **$495**

www.AdvanceGuardMilitaria.com

Russian WWII Cossack wool fur cap ("papacha")................ **$200**

Mohawk Arms Inc.

Waffen-SS Panzer M43 Cap......................... **$2,000**

Grenadier Militaria

▲ German Army Cavalry Officer's "Crusher Style" Visor Cap. **$900**

Grenadier Militaria

▶ German War Veterans visor cap. **$250**

Mohawk Arms Inc.

▶ German WWII N.S.D.A.P. standard bearer's gorget. **$700**

Mohawk Arms Inc.

Model 1938 Luftwaffe Paratrooper Helmet.... **$5,400**

The Ruptured Duck

US Paratrooper M1C Helmet with camouflage net.
.... **$2,450**

The Ruptured Duck

Italian Officer Overseas Cap. **$290**

The Ruptured Duck

▼ German RMBO Official's
Visor Cap. **$5,300**

Grenadier Militaria

◄ German Army Second
Pattern Tropical Sun Helmet.
.... **$325**

Grenadier Militaria

US "Ike" jacket with British-made 7th Army shoulder insignia. **$95**

John Adams-Graf

US Navy WAVES uniform..... **$165**

Mohawk Arms Inc.

▶ German WWII Kriegsmarine automobile fender pennant. **$395**

Mohawk Arms Inc.

◀ US Army China-Burma-India ("CBI") Field Jacket with "blood chit" flag on reverse. **$400**

Grenadier Militaria

▼ U.S. Purple Heart ("slot brooch" with no name on reverse or number on side). ...**$65**

John Adams-Graf

German WWII 1939 1st Class Iron Cross, screw-back.................. **$225**

Mohawk Arms Inc.

Italo-German Campaign Medal in Africa. **$115**

The Ruptured Duck

British 1939-1945 Star medal.
.... **$20**

John Adams-Graf

German WWII War Merit Cross
with Swords and issue envelop.
....$30

Mohawk Arms Inc.

Spanish Order of Isabella the Catholic,
Commander's Cross (6th Model, 1938-1975) with
case. $155

Hermann Historica

▲ Belgian WWII Cross of War
Leopold III. $20

Grenadier Militaria

German WWII Silver Wound Badge with case.... $130

Mohawk Arms Inc.

SPECIAL CONTRIBUTORS
AND ADVISORS

The following collectors, dealers, sellers and researchers have supported the *Antique Trader Antiques & Collectibles Price Guide* with their pricing and contacts over the years. Many continue to serve as a valuable resource to the entire collecting hobby, while others have passed away. We honor all contributors past and present as their hard work and passion lives on through this book.

John Adams-Graf

Andre Ammelounx

Mannie Banner

Tom Bartsch

Ellen Bercovici

Sandra Bondhus

James R. and Carol S.
   Boshears

Bobbie Zucker Bryson

Emmett Butler

Dana Cain

Linda D. Carannante

David Chartier

Les and Irene Cohen

Amphora Collectors
   International

Les and Irene Cohen

Marion Cohen

Neva Colbert

Marie Compton

Susan N. Cox

Caroline Torem-Craig

Leonard Davis

Bev Dieringer

Janice Dodson

Del E. Domke

Debby DuBay

Susan Eberman

Steve Evans

Joan M. George

Roselyn Gerson

William A. and Donna J. Gray

Pam Green

Linda Guffey

Carl Heck

Alma Hillman

K. Robert and Bonne L. Hohl

Ellen R. Hill

Joan Hull

Hull Pottery Association

Louise Irvine

Helen and Bob Jones

Mary Ann Johnston

Donald-Brian Johnson

Dorothy Kamm

Edwin E. Kellogg

Madeleine Kirsh

Vivian Kromer

Curt Leiser

Gene Loveland

Mary McCaslin

Pat Moore

Mark F. Moran

Reg G. Morris

Craig Nissen

Joan C. Oates

Ed Pascoe

Margaret Payne

Gail Peck

John Petzold

Dr. Leslie Piña

Michael Polak

Joseph Porcelli

Arlene Rabin

John Rader, Sr.

Betty June Wymer

LuAnn Riggs

Tim and Jamie Saloff

Federico Santi

Ellen Schroy

Arlyn Sieber

Mary Sieber

Peggy Sebek

Steve Stone

Michael Strawser

Phillip Sullivan

Chriss Swaney

Mark and Ellen Supnick

Tim Trapani

Jim Trautman

Bruce and Vicki Waasdorp

Elaine Westover

Kathryn Wiese

Laurie Williams

Nancy Wolfe

Mark Wollemann

PRICING, IDENTIFICATIONS, AND IMAGES PROVIDED BY:

LIVE AUCTION PROVIDERS

AuctionZip
113 West Pitt St., Suite C
Bedford, PA 15522
(814) 623-5059
www.auctionzip.com

Artfact, LLC
38 Everett St., Suite 101
Allston, MA 02134
(617) 746-9800
www.artfact.com

LiveAuctioneers, LLC
2nd Floor
220 12th Ave.
New York, NY 10001
www.liveauctioneers.com

AUCTION HOUSES

A-1 Auction
2042 N Rio Grande Ave., Suite E
Orlando, FL 32804
(407) 839-0004
http://www.a-1auction.net/

Allard Auctions, Inc.
P.O. Box 1030
St. Ignatius, MT 59865
(406) 745-0500
(800) 314-0343
www.allardauctions.com

American Bottle Auctions
2523 J St., Suite 203
Sacramento, CA 95816
(800) 806-7722
americanbottle.com

American Pottery Auction
Vicki and Bruce Waasdorp
P.O. Box 434
Clarence, NY 14031
(716) 759-2361
www.antiques-stoneware.com

Antique Helper Auction House
2764 East 55th Pl.
Indianapolis, IN 46220
(317) 251-5635
www.antiquehelper.com

Apple Tree Auction Center
1616 West Church St.
Newark, OH 43055-1540
(740) 344-4282
www.appletreeauction.com

Artingstall & Hind Auctioneers
9312 Civic Center Dr., #104
Beverly Hills, CA 90210
(310) 424-5288
www.artingstall.com

Arus Auctions
(617) 669-6170
www.arusauctions.com

ATM Antiques & Auctions, LLC
811 SE US Hwy. 19
Crystal River, FL 34429
(352) 795-2061
(800) 542-3877
www.charliefudge.com

Auction Team Breker
Otto-Hahn-Str. 10
50997 Köln (Godorf), Germany
02236 384340
www.breker.com

Backstage Auctions
448 West 19th St., Suite 163
Houston, TX 77008
(713) 862-1200
www.backstageauctions.com

Belhorn Auctions, LLC
2746 Wynnerock Ct.
Hilliard, OH 43026
(614) 921-9441
auctions@belhorn.com
www.belhorn.com
www.potterymarketplace.com

Bertoia Auctions
2141 DeMarco Dr.
Vineland, NJ 08360
(856) 692-1881
www.bertoiaauctions.com

Bonhams
7601 W. Sunset Blvd.
Los Angeles, CA 90046
(323) 850-7500
www.bonhams.com

Briggs Auction, Inc.
1347 Naamans Creek Rd.
Garnet Valley, PA 19060
(610) 566-3138 (Office)
(610) 485-0412 (Showroom)
www.briggsauction.com

Brunk Auctions
P.O. Box 2135
Asheville, NC 28802
(828) 254-6846
www.brunkauctions.com

Matthew Bullock Auctioneers
409 E. Stevenson Rd.
Ottawa, IL 61350
(815) 970-7077
www.bullockauctioneers.com

Bunte Auction Services and Appraisals
755 Church Rd.
Elgin, IL 60123
(847) 214-8423
www.bunteauction.com

Butterscotch Auction Gallery
608 Old Post Rd.
Bedford, NY 10506
(914) 764-4609
www.butterscotchauction.com

Capo Auction
3601 Queens Blvd.
Long Island City, NY 11101
(718) 433-3710
www.capoauctionnyc.com
Suite 6 Imperial Studios
3/11 Imperial Rd.
London, England
SW6 2AG
+44 (0) (207) 806-5530
www.charlesmillerltd.com

Charlton Hall Auctioneers
912 Gervais St.
Columbia, SC 29201
www.charltonhallauctions.com

Cherryland Postcard Auctions
Ronald & Alec Millard
P.O. Box 427
Frankfort, MI 49635
(231) 352-9758
CherrylandPostcards.com

Christie's New York
20 Rockefeller Plaza
New York, NY 10020
www.christies.com

Cincinnati Art Galleries
225 East Sixth St.
Cincinnati, OH 45202
www.cincinnatiartgalleries.com

Clars Auction Gallery
5644 Telegraph Ave.
Oakland, CA 94609
(510) 428-0100
www.clars.com

Clements
7022 Hwy 153
Hixson, TN 37343
(423) 842-5992
www.clementsantiques.com

The Coeur d'Alene Art Auction
8836 North Hess St., Suite B
Hayden, ID 83835
(208) 772-9009
www.cdaartauction.com

John W. Coker, Ltd.
1511 W. Hwy. 11E
New Market, TN 37820
(865) 475-5163
www.antiquesonline.com

Collect Auctions
(888) 463-3063
collectauctions.com

Conestoga Auction Co./ Division of Hess Auction Group
768 Graystone Rd.
Manheim, PA 17545
(717) 898-7284
www.conestogaauction.com

Constantine & Pletcher
1321 Freeport Rd.
Cheswick, PA 15024
(724) 275-7190
Fax: (724) 275-7191
www.cpauction.info

Copake Auction, Inc.
266 Route 7A
Copake, NY 12516
(518) 329-1142
www.copakeauction.com

Cowan's Auctions
6270 Este Ave.
Cincinnati, OH 45232
(513) 871-1670
www.cowanauctions.com

CRN Auctions, Inc.
57 Bay State Rd.
Cambridge, MA 02138
(617) 661-9582
www.crnauctions.com

Dargate Auction Galleries
326 Munson Ave.
McKees Rocks, PA 15136
(412) 771-8700
Fax: (412) 771-8779
www.dargate.com

Rachel Davis Fine Arts
1301 West 79th St.
Cleveland, OH 44102
(216) 939-1190
www.racheldavisfinearts.com

Decoys Unlimited, Inc.
P.O. Box 206
2320 Main St.
West Barnstable,
MA 02668-0206
(508) 362-2766
decoysunlimited.net

DGW Auctioneers & Appraisers
760 Kifer Rd.
Sunnyvale, CA 94086
www.dgwauctioneers.com

Dickins Auctioneers Ltd.
Calvert Rd.
Middle Claydon
Buckingham, England
MK18 2EZ
+44 (129) 671-4434
www.dickinsauctioneers.com

Dirk Soulis Auctions
529 W. Lone Jack Lees
Summit Road
Lone Jack, MO 64070
(816) 697-3830
www.dirksoulisauctions.com

Doyle New York
175 E. 87th St.
New York, NY 10128
(212) 427-2730
www.doylenewyork.com

**Dreweatts &
Bloomsbury Auctions**
24 Maddox St.
London, England W1S 1PP
+44 (207) 495-9494
www.dreweatts.com/

Dumouchelle Art Galleries
409 E. Jefferson Ave.
Detroit, MI 48226
(313) 963-6255
www.dumouchelle.com

Elite Decorative Arts
1034 Gateway Blvd., #108
Boynton Beach, FL 33426
(561) 200-0893
www.eliteauction.com

Fine Arts Auctions, LLC
324 S. Beverly Dr., #175
Beverly Hills, CA 90212
(310) 990-2150
www.fineartauctionllc.com

Fontaine's Auction Gallery
1485 W. Housatonic St.
Pittsfield, MA 01210
www.fontainesauction.net

Forsythes' Auctions, LLC
P.O. Box 188
Russellville, OH 45168
(937) 377-3700
www.forsythesauctions.com

Fox Auctions
P.O. Box 4069
Vallejo, CA 94590
(631) 553-3841
Fax: (707) 643-3000
www.foxauctionsonline.com

Frasher's Doll Auction
2323 S. Mecklin Sch. Rd.
Oak Grove, MO 64075
(816) 625-3786

J. Garrett Auctioneers, Ltd.
1411 Slocum St.
Dallas, TX 75207
(214) 683-6855
www.jgarrettauctioneers.com

Garth's Arts & Antiques
P.O. Box 369
Delaware, OH 43015
(740) 362-4771
www.garths.com

Glass Works Auctions
Box 180
East Greenville, PA 18041
(215) 679-5849
www.glswrk-auction.com

The Golf Auction
209 State St.
Oldsmar, FL 34677
(813) 340-6179
thegolfauction.com

**Gray's Auctioneers
& Appraisers**
10717 Detroit Ave.
Cleveland, OH 44102
(216) 226-3300
graysauctioneers.com

**Great Gatsby's Antiques
and Auctions**
5180 Peachtree Industrial Blvd.
Atlanta, GA 30341
(770) 457-1903
www.greatgatsbys.com

Grogan & Co.
22 Harris St.
Dedham, MA 02026
(781) 461-9500
www.groganco.com

Guyette & Deeter
24718 Beverly Rd.
St. Michaels, MD 21663
(410) 745-0485
Fax: (410) 745-0487
www.guyetteandschmidt.com

GWS Auctions, LLC
41841 Beacon Hill # E
Palm Desert, CA 92211
(760) 610-4175
www.gwsauctions.com

**Ken Farmer Auctions
and Appraisals**
105 Harrison St.
Radford, VA 24141
(540) 639-0939
www.kfauctions.com

**Hake's Americana
& Collectibles**
P.O. Box 12001
York, PA 17402
(717) 434-1600
www.hakes.com

**Hamilton's Antique &
Estate Auctions, Inc.**
505 Puyallup Ave.
Tacoma, WA 98421
(253) 534-4445
www.joe-frank.com

Norman Heckler & Co.
79 Bradford Corner Rd.
Woodstock Valley, CT 06282
www.hecklerauction.com

Heritage Auctions
3500 Maple Ave.
Dallas, TX 75219-3941
(800) 872-6467
www.ha.com

Hess Fine Auctions
1131 4th St. N.
St. Petersburg, FL 33701
(727) 896-0622
www.hessfineauctions.com

Hewlett's Antique Auctions
PO Box 87
13286 Jefferson St.
Le Grand, CA 95333
(209) 389-4542
Fax: (209) 389-0730
http://www.hewlettsauctions.com/

Holabird-Kagin Americana
3555 Airway Dr., #308
Reno, NV 89511
(775) 852-8822
www.holabirdamericana.com

Homestead Auctions
3200 Greenwich Rd.
Norton, OH 44203
(330) 807-1445
www.homesteadauction.net

**Bill Hood & Sons Art &
Antique Auctions**
2925 S. Federal Hwy.
Delray Beach, FL 33483
(561) 278-8996
www.hoodauction.com

Humler & Nolan
The Auctions at Rookwood
225 E. Sixth St., 4th Floor
Cincinnati, OH 45202
(513) 381-2041
Fax: (513) 381-2038
www.humlernolan.com

iGavel Auctions
229 E. 120th St.
New York, NY 10035
(212) 289-5588
www.igavelauctions.com

Ivy Auctions
22391 Hwy. 76 E.
Laurens, SC 29360
(864) 682-2750
www.ivyauctions.com

**Jackson's International
Auctioneers & Appraisers**
2229 Lincoln St.
Cedar Falls, IA 50613
jacksonsauction.com

James D. Julia, Inc.
P.O. Box 830
203 Skowhegan Rd.
Fairfield, ME 04937
(207) 453-7125
jamesdjulia.com

**Jeffrey S. Evans
& Associates**
2177 Green Valley Ln.
Mount Crawford, VA 22841
(540) 434-3939
www.jeffreysevans.com

John Moran Auctioneers
735 West Woodbury Rd.
Altadena, CA 91001
(626) 793-1833
www.johnmoran.com

Julien's Auctions
9665 Wilshire Blvd., Suite 150
Beverly Hills, CA 90210
(310) 836-1818
www.juliensauctions.com

Just Art Pottery
Greg and Lana Myroth
1184 Rentsch Drive
East Peoria, IL 61611
(309) 690-7966
www.justartpottery.com

Kaminski Auctions
564 Cabot St.
Beverly, MA 01915
(978) 927-2223
Fax: (978) 927-2228
www.kaminskiauctions.com/

Kennedy Auctions Service
160 West Court Ave.
Selmer, TN 38375
(731) 645-5001
www.kennedysauction.com

Lang's Sporting Collectibles
663 Pleasant Valley Rd.
Waterville, NY 13480
(315) 841-4623
www.langsauction.com

Legend Numismatics
P.O. Box 9
Lincroft, NJ 07738
(800) 743-2646
www.legendcoin.com

Legendary Auctions
17542 Chicago Ave.
Lansing, IL 60438
(708) 889-9380
www.legendaryauctions.com

**Los Angeles
Modern Auctions**
16145 Hart St.
Van Nuys, CA 91406
(323) 904-1950
www.lamodern.com

Leslie Hindman Auctioneers
1338 West Lake St.
Chicago, IL 60607
(312) 280-1212
www.lesliehindman.com

Louis J. Dianni, LLC
Antiques Auctions
May 1-Oct. 15:
982 Main St., Suite 175
Fishkill, NY 12524
Oct. 20-April 15:
1304 SW 160th Ave., Suite 228A
Sunrise, FL 33326
https://louisjdianni.com

Love of the Game Auctions
P.O. Box 157
Great Meadows, NJ 07838
loveofthegameauctions.com

Main Street Mining Co.
2311 East Loop 820 N.
Fort Worth, TX 76118
(817) 616-5001
https://mainstreetmining.com

Manifest Auctions
361 Woodruff Rd.
Greenville, SC 29607
(864) 520-2208
Fax: (864) 520-2210
manifestauctions.com

Manitou Auctions
205 Styer Dairy Rd.
Reidsville, NC 27320
(336) 349-6577
www.manitou-auctions.com

Manor Auctions
2415 N. Monroe St.
Tallahassee, FL 32303
(850) 523-3787
Fax: (850) 523-3786
www.manorauctions.com

Mark Mattox Auctioneer & Real Estate Broker, Inc.
3740 Maysville Rd.
Carlisle, KY 40311
(859) 289-5720
http://mattoxauctions.com/auctions/

Martin Auction Co.
100 Lick Creek Rd.
Anna, IL 62906
(618) 833-3589
www.martinauctionco.com
martinauctioncompany@gmail.com

Martin J. Donnelly Antique Tools
5523 County Rd. 8
Avoca, NY 14809
(607) 566-2617
www.mjdtools.com

Matt Maring Auction Co.
P.O. Box 37
Kenyon, MN 55946
(507) 789-5227
www.maringauction.com

Material Culture
4700 Wissahickon Ave.
Philadelphia, PA 19144
(215) 849-8030
www.materialculture.com

Matthews Auctions
111 South Oak St.
Nokomis, IL 62075-1337
(215) 563-8880
www.matthewsauctions.com

John McInnis Auctioneers & Appraisers
76 Main St.
Amesbury, MA 01913
(978) 388-0400
Fax: (978) 388-8863
www.mcinnisauctions.com

McLaren Auction Service
21507 Highway 99E
Aurora, OR 97002
(503) 678-2441
www.mclarenauction.com

McMasters-Harris Auction Co.
P.O. Box 755
Cambridge, OH 43725
www.mcmastersharris.com

Michaan's Auctions
2751 Todd St.
Alameda, CA 94501
(510) 740-0220
www.michaans.com

Midwest Auction Galleries
925 North Lapeer Rd.
Oxford, MI 48371
(877) 236-8181
or (248) 236-8100
Fax: (248) 236-8396
www.midwestauctioninc.com

Mile High Card Co.
7200 S. Alton Way, Suite A230
Centennial, CO 80112
(303) 840-2784
www.milehighcardco.com

Milestone Auctions
3860 Ben Hur Ave., Unit 8
Willoughby, OH 44094
(440) 527-8060
www.milestoneauctions.com

Dan Morphy Auctions
2000 N. Reading Rd.
Denver, PA 17517
(717) 335-3435
morphyauctions.com

Mohawk Arms, Inc.
P.O. Box 157
Bouckville, NY 13310
(315) 893-7888
www.militaryrelics.com

Mosby & Co. Auctions
5714-A Industry Ln.
Frederick, MD 21704
(240) 629-8139
www.mosbyauctions.com

Neal Auction Co.
4038 Magazine St.
New Orleans, LA 70115
(504) 899-5329
www.nealauction.com

Nest Egg Auctions
30 Research Pkwy.
Meriden, CT 06450
(203) 630-1400
www.nesteggauctions.com

New Orleans Auction Gallery
1330 St. Charles Ave.
New Orleans, LA 70130
www.neworleansauction.com

Nico Auctions
4023 Kennett Pike, Suite 248
Greenville, DE 19807
(888) 390-0201
www.nicoauctions.com

Noel Barrett Vintage Toys @ Auction
P.O. Box 300
Carversville, PA 18913
(215) 297 5109
www.noelbarrett.com

North American Auction Co.
78 Wildcat Way
Bozeman, MT 59718
(800) 686-4216
www.northamericanauctioncompany.com

Northeast Auctions
93 Pleasant St.
Portsmouth, NH 03801
(603) 433-8400
Fax: (603) 433-0415
www.northeastauctions.com

O'Gallerie: Fine Arts, Antiques and Estate Auctions
228 Northeast 7th Ave.
Portland, OR 97232-2909
(503) 238-0202
www.ogallerie.com

Omaha Auction Center
7531 Dodge St.
Omaha, NE 68114
(402) 397-9575
www.omahaauctioncenter.com

Omega Auction Corp.
1669 W. 39th Pl.
Hialeah, FL 33012
(786) 444-4997
www.omegaauctioncorp.com

Pacific Galleries Auction House and Antique Mall
241 South Lander St.
Seattle, WA 98134
(206) 441-9990
Fax: (206) 448-9677
www.pacgal.com

Past Tyme Pleasures
39 California Ave., Suite 105
Pleasanton, CA 94566
www.pasttyme1.com

PBA Galleries
133 Kearny St., 4th Floor
San Francisco, CA 94108
(415) 989-2665
www.pbagalleries.com

Phoebus Auction Gallery
18 East Mellen St.
Hampton, VA 23663
(757) 722-9210
www.phoebusauction.com

Pioneer Auction Gallery
14650 SE Arista Dr.
Portland, OR 97267
(503) 496-0303
www.pioneerantiqueauction.com

Pook & Pook, Inc.
463 East Lancaster Ave.
Downingtown, PA 19335
(610) 269-4040
www.pookandpook.com

Potter & Potter Auctions
3759 N. Ravenswood Ave., #121
Chicago, IL 60613
(773) 472-1442
www.potterauctions.com

Premier Auction Galleries
12587 Chillicothe Rd.
Chesterland, OH 44026
(440) 688-4203
Fax: (440) 688-4202
www.pag4u.com

Don Presley Auction
1319 West Katella Ave.
Orange County, CA 92867
(714) 633-2437
www.donpresley.com

Preston Hall Gallery
2201 Main St., Suite #820
Dallas, TX 75201
(214) 718-8624
www.prestonhallgallery.com

Profiles in History
26901 Agoura Rd., Suite 150
Calabasas Hills, CA 91301
(310) 859-7701
www.profilesinhistory.com

Purcell Auction Gallery
2156 Husband Rd.
Paducah, KY 42003
(270) 444-7599
www.purcellauction.com/

Quinn's Auction Galleries
360 S. Washington St.
Falls Church, VA 22046
(703) 532-5632
www.quinnsauction.com

Rago Arts & Auctions
333 N. Main St.
Lambertville, NJ 08530
(609) 397-9374
www.ragoarts.com

Red Baron's Antiques
8655 Roswell Rd.
Atlanta, GA 30350
(770) 640-4604
www.rbantiques.com

Richard Opfer Auctioneering, Inc.
1919 Greenspring Dr.
Lutherville-Timonium, MD 21093
(410) 252-5035
www.opferauction.com

Rich Penn Auctions
P.O. Box 1355
Waterloo, IA 50704
(319) 291-6688
www.richpennauctions.com

RM Auctions
One Classic Car Dr.
Blenheium, Ontario
N0P 1A0 Canada
+1 (519) 352-4575
www.rmauctions.com

Robert Edward Auctions
P.O. Box 7256
Watchung, NJ 07069
(908) 226-9900
www.robertedwardauctions.com

Rock Island Auction Co.
7819 42 St. West
Rock Island, IL 61201
(800) 238-8022
www.rockislandauction.com

Roland Auction NY
80 E 11th St.
New York, NY 10003
(212) 260-2000
www.rolandauctions.com

RR Auction
5 Route 101A, Suite 5
Amherst, NH 03031
(603) 732-4280
www.rrauction.com

Saco River Auction Co.
2 Main St.
Biddeford, ME 04005
(207) 602-1504
www.sacoriverauction.com

Scheerer McCulloch Auctioneers
515 E Paulding Rd.
Fort Wayne, IN 46816
(260) 441-8636
www.smauctioneers.com

SCP Auctions, Inc.
32451 Golden Lantern, Suite 308
Laguna Niguel, CA 92677
(949) 831-3700
www.SCPauctions.com

Seeck Auction Co.
Jim and Jan Seeck
P.O. Box 377
Mason City, IA 50402
www.seeckauction.com

SeriousToyz
1 Baltic Pl.
Croton on Hudson, NY 10520
(866) 653-8699
www.serioustoyz.com

Showtime Auction Services
22619 Monterey Dr.
Woodhaven, MI 48183-2269
(734) 676-9703
www.showtimeauctions.com

Skinner, Inc.
357 Main St.
Boston, MA 01740
(617) 350-5400
www.skinnerinc.com

Sloans & Kenyon Auctioneers and Appraisers
7034 Wisconsin Ave.
Chevy Chase, MD 20815
(301) 634-2330
www.sloansandkenyon.com

Sotheby's New York
1334 York Ave.
New York, NY 10021
(212) 606-7000
www.sothebys.com

Specialists of the South, Inc.
544 E. Sixth St.
Panama City, FL 32401
(850) 785-2577
www.specialistsofthesouth.com

Stanley Gibbons
399 Strand
London
WC2R 0LX
England
+44 (0)207 836 8444
www.stanleygibbons.com

Stanton Auctions
PO Box 326
106 E. Longmeadow Rd.
Hampden, MA 01036
(413) 566-3161
www.stantonauctions.com

Carl W. Stinson, Inc.
293 Haverhill St.
Reading, MA 01867
(617) 834-3819
www.stinsonauctions.com

Stefek's Auctioneers & Appraisers
18450 Mack Ave.
Grosse Pointe Farms, MI 48236
(313) 881-1800
www.stefeksltd.com

Stephenson's Auctioneers & Appraisers
1005 Industrial Blvd.
Southampton, PA 18966
(215) 322-6182
www.stephensonsauction.com

Stevens Auction Co.
301 North Meridian St.
Aberdeen, MS 39730-2613
(662) 369-2200
www.stevensauction.com

Strawser Auctions
P.O. Box 332
Wolcottville, IN 46795
www.strawserauctions.com
Sullivan & Son Auction, LLC
1995 E. County Rd. 650
Carthage, IL 62321
(217) 743-5200
www.sullivanandsonauction.com

Swann Auction Galleries
104 E 25th St., # 6
New York, NY 10010-2999
(212) 254-4710
www.swanngalleries.com

Teel Auction Services
619 FM 2330
Montabla, TX 75853
(903) 724-4079
www.teelauctionservices.com

Theriault's – The Doll Masters
P.O. Box 151
Annapolis, MD 21404
(800) 638-0422
www.theriaults.com

Thomaston Place Auction Galleries
51 Atlantic Hwy.
Thomaston, ME 04861
(207) 354-8141
www.thomastonauction.com

John Toomey Gallery
818 North Blvd.
Oak Park, IL 60301
(708) 383-5234
http://johntoomeygallery.com

Tory Hill Auction Co.
5301 Hillsborough St.
Raleigh, NC 27606
(919) 858-0327
www.toryhillauctions.com

Tradewinds Antiques & Auctions
24 Magnolia Ave.
Manchester-by-the-Sea,
MA 01944
(978) 526-4085
www.tradewindsantiques.com

Treadway Gallery, Inc.
2029 Madison Rd.
Cincinnati, OH 45208
www.treadwaygallery.com

Turkey Creek Auctions, Inc.
13939 N. Hwy. 441
Citra, FL 32113
(352) 622-4611
(800) 648-7523
www.antiqueauctionsfl.com

Turner Auctions + Appraisals
461 Littlefield Ave.
South San Francisco, CA 94080
(415) 964-5250
(310) 997-0400
(888) 498-4450
www.turnerauctionsonline.com

Vero Beach Auction
492 Old Dixie Hwy.
Vero Beach, FL 32962
(772) 978-5955
Fax: (772) 978-5954
www.verobeachauction.com

Victorian Casino Antiques Auction
4520 Arville St., #1
Las Vegas, NV 89103
(702) 382-2466
www.vcaauction.com

Wiederseim Associates, Inc.
PO Box 470
Chester Springs, PA 19425
(610) 827-1910
www.wiederseim.com

Philip Weiss Auctions
74 Merrick Rd.
Lynbrook, NY 11563
(516) 594-0731
www.weissauctions.com

William J. Jenack Estate Appraisers & Auctioneers
62 Kings Highway Bypass
Chester, NY 10918
(877) 282-8503
www.jenack.com

Witherell's Art & Antiques
300 20th St.
Sacramento, CA 95811
(916) 446-6490
witherells.com

Woodbury Auction, LLC
50 Main St. N.
Woodbury, CT 06798
(203) 266-0323
www.woodburyauction.com

Woody Auction
317 S. Forrest St.
Douglass, KS 67039
(316) 747-2694
www.woodyauction.com

Wright
1440 W. Hubbard St.
Chicago, IL 60642
(312) 563-0020
www.wright20.com

Zurko Promotions
115 E. Division St.
Shawano, WI 54166
www.zurkopromotions.com

INDEX